Revised Edition

Mastering
American
History

Philip L. Groisser, Ph.D.
High School Superintendent
New York City Board of Education
Formerly Social Studies Supervisor,
New York City

Sadlier-Oxford
A Division of William H. Sadlier, Inc.
New York
Chicago
Los Angeles

PREFACE

Every teacher of American History in secondary schools is keenly aware of the formidable bulk and complexity of the material included in the present-day course. Moreover, there is greater emphasis than ever before on *ideas,* and on correlation of past events with the momentous developments now taking place in the United States and throughout the world. Such *new* requirements call for a *new* type of supplementary text, realistically designed to help the hard-pressed students and to lighten the teacher's load. To meet these needs, the author of MASTERING AMERICAN HISTORY has sought to reach new standards in style of presentation, completeness, pedagogical aids, and level of scholarship.

MASTERING AMERICAN HISTORY is characterized by a wealth of relevant and highly organized detail. Yet, this material is developed in such a way that the average student can read it quickly, organize it meaningfully in his mind, and assimilate it for future reference. Using clear, precise language, the author has aimed to divide and subdivide the material into small thought units that are logically and pedagogically sound. All extraneous points have been excluded, yet the text covers every aspect of the American history course required by even the most exacting syllabi. Moreover, the use of tabular summaries and the reintroduction of important topics in different contexts help the student to gain a firm grasp of details and to organize them into meaningful patterns.

MASTERING AMERICAN HISTORY makes use of the most recent interpretations and findings in various fields of American history. A few examples are: the causes of the American Revolution, the background of the Civil War, the Progressive Era, and the New Deal. Also noteworthy is the careful and mature analysis of the basic forces and principles that have helped to shape our nation — nationalism, democracy, sectionalism, industrialism, urbanization, etc. Closely related to this is the development of concepts in other areas of the social studies, such as geography, economics, sociology, and anthropology.

One well-rounded unit of MASTERING AMERICAN HISTORY serves to focus attention on the principles and practices of our government, as it developed and as it actually functions today. The treatment is unusually complete, realistic, and rigorously up-to-date.

The section on problems of American democracy analyzes the most pressing problems of our society in such areas as urbanization, environmental protection, measures against poverty, and the status of blacks and other racial and ethnic groups. Here and throughout the text, there is full recognition of the role of minorities in building America.

The unit on foreign affairs makes highly effective use of the area-study approach to introduce an orderly pattern into this many-sided and ever shifting field.

iii

A "capstone" chapter on political developments since the Civil War restores the chronological sense that many teachers find sorely lacking in problem-oriented courses. Here, the student is given a "feel" for the various historical periods, as well as a firm grasp of the problem, developments, successes and failures of each post-Civil War administration.

In addition to serving as a resource text in American history, this book provides historical focus and essential background for recently developed courses in problems of American democracy, political science and various mini-courses in the social and behavioral sciences. It can also give direction and support to the student who may be engaged in independent study in any area of the social sciences.

MASTERING AMERICAN HISTORY offers more than 450 essay questions and 2500 objective questions, conveniently arranged after each chapter and each unit. They include a wide variety of question types, ranging in difficulty from recall-drill to challenging thought problems. On an overall basis, they provide an excellent means of preparing for Regents examinations, College Entrance tests, scholarship tests, and school examinations.

Complementing the text and questions are maps, cartoons, graphs, and other illustrations which convey essential information, express points of view, and help to arouse the student's interest.

The author would like to express his gratitude to Mr. Marvin Feldman of Lafayette High School for his many cogent suggestions and for his careful reading of the final manuscript.

P. L. G.

NOTE ON THE NEW EDITION

MASTERING AMERICAN HISTORY has been updated frequently throughout the years to keep pace with the rapidly shifting national and international scenes. The revision embodied in this New Edition is unusually comprehensive, involving not only a vast number of changes in specific details but also a modification of the overall point of view, more suitable for the last quarter of the 20th century. The governmental-political presentation now brings the story of our nation to the election of 1976 and the post-Watergate, bicentennial era. Social and economic processes and problems have been suitably redocumented and reinterpreted. The area-study survey of foreign affairs includes the key developments of the 1970s that have reshaped, and are reshaping, Africa, the Middle East, Asia, the Communist world and other key regions. To increase the usefulness of the revised text, the index has been completely refurbished.

CONTENTS

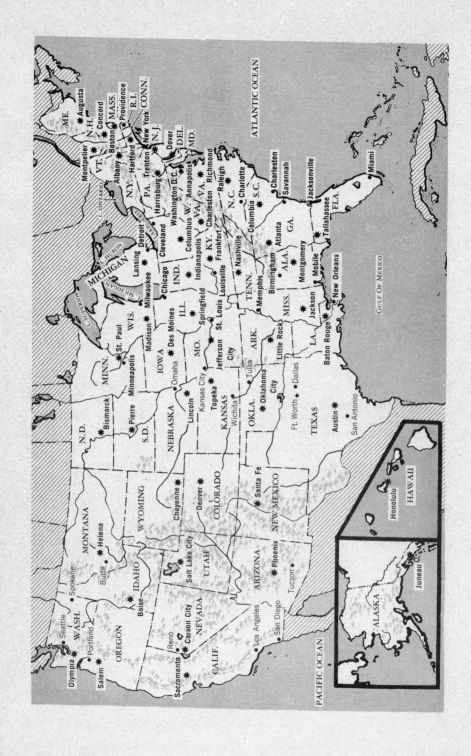

CHAPTER 1 ────────────────────────

Exploration and Colonization of the New World

The history of the United States begins in Europe. The discovery, exploration, and early settlement of America were all part of a series of social, economic, and political changes in Europe known as the *Commercial Revolution*. The Commercial Revolution opened distant parts of the globe to Europeans, resulted in a shift of the center of trade from the Mediterranean to the Atlantic, and led to new developments in commerce and industry.

Reasons for Discovery and Exploration. The early voyages of discovery that resulted in the exploration of the New World were closely related to the new ideas, interests, and activities that marked the change in Europe from medieval to modern times. There were several important forces that lay behind the expansion of Europe at this time.

1. *Search for New Routes to the East.* In the 15th century, the national states bordering on the Atlantic Ocean were eager to find a new route to the East that would break the monopoly of the Italian city-states on trade with the East, and that would also be safe from pirates. European trade with the East had been stimulated by the Crusades of the 12th and 13th centuries. During the Commercial Revolution, it developed even further.

2. *National Rivalries.* The heads of the rising national states were eager to promote the wealth and glory of their countries and themselves. They began to look upon exploration as a means of achieving these ends.

3. *"Gold, Glory, Gospel."* The great explorers were often spurred on by the hope of becoming rich, the desire to push into unknown lands, and the craving for individual glory. In addition, many pious Christians and missionaries hoped to convert the natives of foreign lands to Christianity. These motives for the exploration of the New World are summed up in the phrase, "Gold, Glory, Gospel" (the "Three G's").

4. *New Knowledge.* The growth of scientific and geographic knowledge during the Renaissance paved the way for overseas expansion. Equipped

1

with this new information, navigators and explorers traveled around the southern tip of Africa, sailed to America, and even went around the world. Thrilling accounts of the wonders of the Orient were brought back to Europe by travelers like the famous MARCO POLO. Inventions like the *magnetic compass* and the *astrolabe* were invaluable to sailors.

THE GREAT EXPLORATIONS OF THE NEW WORLD

COUNTRY EXPLORED FOR	EXPLORER	DATE	ACHIEVEMENT
Portugal	Diaz	1488	Sailed around Cape of Good Hope
	Da Gama	1498	Reached Calicut in India
	Cabral	1500	Discovered Brazil
	Vespucci	1501	Explored coast of South America
Spain	Columbus	1492	Discovered West Indies (America) and opened the New World
	Balboa	1513	Discovered the Pacific Ocean
	Ponce De Leon	1513-21	Explored the Florida coast
	Magellan	1519-22	Led the expedition which first circumnavigated the globe by sailing westward around the southern tip of South America. (Magellan died en route in the Philippines)
	Cortez	1519-21	Conquered the Aztecs of Mexico
	Pizarro	1531-36	Conquered the Incas of Peru
	De Soto	1539-42	Explored the Mississippi Valley
	Coronado	1540-42	Explored what is now the southwestern part of United States
England	Cabot	1497	Explored coast of North America in vicinity of Nova Scotia and Labrador
	Drake	1577-80	Led first expedition after Magellan to sail around the world
	Gilbert	1583	Unsuccessful colony established in Newfoundland
	Raleigh	1587	Unsuccessful colony established in Virginia
France	Verrazano	1524	Explored Atlantic coast
	Cartier	1534-35	Discovered and explored St. Lawrence River
	Champlain	1603-16	Founded Quebec
	Marquette and Joliet	1673	Explored the Mississippi Valley
	La Salle	1682	Traced Mississippi to its mouth
The Netherlands	Hudson	1609	Discovered the Hudson River and sailed up it to the site of Albany

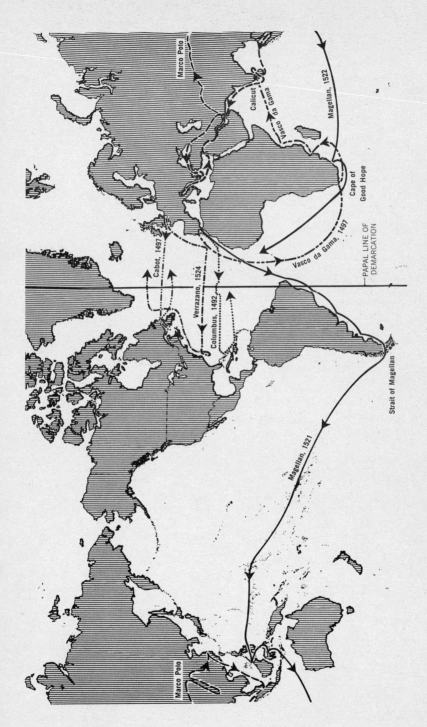

The main voyages of exploration that opened the new world beyond Europe.

Conflicting Claims. The many explorations of the New World led to conflicting territorial claims among the European nations. An interesting attempt to settle these claims occurred as early as 1494, when the Spanish rulers induced Pope Alexander VI to establish a *Papal Line of Demarcation*. This in effect divided the "heathen world" between Spain and Portugal. The placement of the line gave Spain virtually all of the Americas, except for an area roughly equivalent to modern Brazil, which went to Portugal. Other nations, of course, did not recognize the validity of this division.

Colonial Empires in the New World. The achievements of the European explorers and adventurers enabled the various nations of Europe to claim territories in the New World, and thus laid the basis for the establishment of colonial empires. These empires are described below.

The Spanish Empire. Starting in the West Indies (Cuba, Puerto Rico, Santo Domingo, Jamaica), Spain established colonies in most of South and Central America, and in what is now Mexico, New Mexico, Arizona, and California. More than a quarter of a century before the English set up their first successful colony, the Spanish had established over 200 cities and towns. *St. Augustine* (1565) and *Santa Fe* (1605), the two oldest cities in the United States, were Spanish settlements. At the height of their empire, 200,000 Spaniards ruled over five million Indians and Negroes. Although they governed harshly and obtained vast stores of gold and silver from the mines of Mexico and Peru, the Spanish transplanted their culture, laws, religion, and language to the New World. They established the first universities, cathedrals and printing presses in the Western Hemisphere.

The French Empire. Beginning with the settlement of Quebec in 1608, the French established a series of outposts and trading centers along the Great Lakes and the Mississippi and St. Lawrence Rivers from New Orleans on the Gulf of Mexico to Nova Scotia. They also took possession of several of the "sugar islands" of the West Indies (Guadeloupe, Martinique, Santo Domingo). By 1750 about 80,000 French colonists inhabited New France, as the vast area claimed by France was called.

The French settlers introduced French laws, language, and customs and developed a thriving fur trade with the Indians. The Indians were treated fairly, and Catholic missionaries worked actively among them. Despite these developments, New France remained weak, underdeveloped, and sparsely settled. Few Frenchmen came because of autocratic rule by French governors, religious restrictions, strict control by the government of trade and industry, and lack of good soil and climate for agriculture. Moreover, the French kings showed little interest in their American dominions.

The Portuguese, Swedish, and Dutch Empires. Portugal, Sweden, and Holland established less important empires in the New World.

1. *Portugal.* As a result of the Papal Demarcation Line of 1494, the Portuguese settled along the eastern coast of South America, and laid claim to the vast region now known as Brazil. Though it remained there for 300 years, Portugal made little effort to develop its colony. The most important Portuguese legacies to Brazil were the Portuguese language, which is still spoken there, and the Catholic religion.

2. *Sweden.* Sweden established a short-lived colony on the Delaware River from 1638 to 1655. *New Sweden,* as it was called, was conquered by the Dutch, who in turn surrendered it to the English.

3. *Holland.* After Henry Hudson explored the river that bears his name, the Dutch settled in the Hudson Valley, Delaware, and New Jersey. They also sponsored colonies in Guiana and the West Indies. Their short-lived empire in North America (called *New Netherland*) lasted less than half a century. In 1664, the city of *New Amsterdam,* on Manhattan Island, was surrendered to an English fleet and was renamed *New York.* Most of the Dutch migrants settled in the Hudson Valley, where they engaged in farming and the fur trade. The Dutch West India Company made large grants of land along the banks of the Hudson to individuals, called *patroons,* who were supposed to bring over their own settlers. The patroons attempted (unsuccessfully) to run these estates in a feudal manner.

The English Empire. Although England began to build an overseas empire later than the other European nations, she became the most successful colonizer of all.

1. *Reasons for English Colonization.* England set up colonies in the New World for a number of reasons. **(a)** A basic aim of English policy was to oppose and weaken Spain. One way of doing this was to set up a rival empire in the New World. **(b)** English merchants wished to make profits from trade with the New World. **(c)** The English ruling class regarded overseas colonies as an outlet for a growing population and as a place to settle dissatisfied groups. **(d)** The Tudor and Stuart monarchs wanted to increase England's prestige.

2. *Agencies of English Colonization.* English settlements in the New World were established in two ways.

(a) The kings granted colonization privileges to *chartered trading companies.* These were "joint stock companies," made up of stockholders who shared in both the profits and losses of the colonies, and who often emigrated themselves. Virginia, for example, was established by the London Company (1607).

(b) Frequently the kings made royal grants to one or more favorites, called *proprietors,* who then undertook to establish their own colonies. Maryland is an example of a *proprietorship,* established by Lord Baltimore (1634).

3. *Extent of the English Empire in America.* By the 18th century, English colonization had resulted in the organization of 13 colonies along the Atlantic seaboard of North America, and several more in the West Indies (*e.g.,* Barbados, Bahamas, Jamaica). By 1763 there were two million inhabitants in the English empire in America.

4. *Success of the English Colonies.* The English colonies differed from the Spanish and French in several important respects. **(a)** They were founded by private enterprise, rather than directly by the government. **(b)** Religious dissenters were allowed to settle in the colonies. **(c)** The English colonies were given a large measure of self-government.

REVIEW TEST (Chapter I)

Select the number preceding the word or expression that best completes each statement or answers each question.

1. All of the following are reasons for the great voyages of exploration and discovery that opened up the New World *except* (1) national rivalries (2) rise of feudalism (3) desire for adventure and personal gain (4) new knowledge

2. The countries directly affected by the Papal Demarcation Line of 1494 were (1) England and France (2) Portugal and Spain (3) Spain and Holland (4) France and Italy

3. The Mississippi River was explored by La Salle and by (1) Marquette (2) Cabot (3) Drake (4) Magellan

4. Which of the following was the first Spanish settlement in what is now the United States? (1) Santa Fe (2) San Diego (3) Los Angeles (4) St. Augustine

5. Which of the following was an achievement of the French empire in North America? (1) the introduction of the French language, law, and customs (2) a large and growing population in the French colonies (3) complete freedom of religion (4) colonial self-government

6. All were reasons for English colonization of the New World *except* (1) the desire for commercial supremacy (2) the need for a population outlet (3) the desire to obtain the wealth of the Mayan and Incan civilizations (4) the desire for national prestige

7. The patroon system was a characteristic of the New World settlements of (1) England (2) Sweden (3) France (4) Holland

8. Which of the following was *not* associated with English colonization? (1) chartered trading companies (2) proprietorships (3) intermarriage with the Indians (4) seizure of New York from the Dutch

9. The Swedish colonists who came to the New World around 1650 settled in (1) New York (2) Delaware (3) Virginia (4) Pennsylvania

10. English settlement of the 13 colonies took place in the (1) 14th and 15th centuries (2) 15th and 16th centuries (3) 16th and 17th centuries (4) 17th and 18th centuries

Select the item in each group which does NOT belong with the others.

1. Explored for Portugal: Cabral, Diaz, Da Gama, De Leon
2. Explored for Spain: Columbus, Balboa, Drake, De Soto
3. Explored for France: La Salle, Champlain, Verrazano, Pizarro
4. Explored for England: Vespucci, Cabot, Gilbert, Raleigh
5. Reasons for exploration: power, superstition, wealth, religion

Essay Questions

1. Discuss three reasons for the discovery and exploration of the New World.

2. Explain why Englishmen and their rulers were interested in establishing colonies in the New World.

3. Discuss two ways in which English settlements in the New World differed from those of Spain and France.

The Colonial Period
(1607-1776)

The period during which the 13 American colonies belonged to Britain is referred to as the *Colonial Period*. This period lasted nearly as long as the one in which we have been an independent nation. We study this period in some detail because it was during this time that many of our present ideas and institutions began to take shape.

Part 1 — ESTABLISHING AND GOVERNING THE COLONIES

Throughout its history the United States has been a refuge for the discontented and oppressed peoples of Europe. The steady stream of immigration that was to make America great began during the Colonial Period.

Causes of English Migration to America. The motives of the French and Spanish migrants to the New World are often summed up, as we have seen, in the phrase "Gold, Glory, Gospel." While some English settlers also had these goals in mind, most came primarily to create a better way of life for themselves. The first successful English colony on the North American seaboard was *Virginia* (1607); the last to be established was *Georgia* (1732).

1. *Political Causes.* Many Englishmen came to America to find political freedom or to escape the unsettled conditions which resulted from the struggles between the kings and Parliament.

2. *Religious Causes.* Migrants came to America to escape religious persecution and to establish communities where they could worship God in their own way. Religious discrimination in England in the 1600's forced many of those who did not agree with or fully accept the supremacy and doctrines of the Anglican Church to seek refuge in America. Included among these *dissenters* were *Puritans* (Anglicans who wished to "purify" the Anglican Church of Catholic doctrines), *Separatists* (Protestants who refused to conform to the established Church), and Roman Catholics (who refused to change their beliefs or their allegiance to the Pope as head of the Church). Between 1640 and 1660, when the Puritan-led Parliament controlled the government, many members of the Anglican Church who had supported the Stuarts had to flee. Also, William Penn led in founding a colony as a refuge for *Quakers*.

3. *Economic Causes.* The most important reasons for emigration to the American colonies were economic. People left England because the *enclosure laws* pushed many farmers off the lands they had formerly tilled, because *inflation* made prices too high, and because there was *widespread unemployment*. The emigrants wanted land, jobs, and better lives for themselves and their families. Also, to businessmen, overseas trading posts and colonies meant opportunities for *greater profits*. They supplied money and leadership to colonizing ventures, and often went along themselves to supervise these enterprises.

Non-English Immigration to the Colonies. Many groups besides the English came to England's American colonies during the colonial era. By the time of the American Revolution, fully one-third of the population of the 13 colonies was made up of people of non-English origin. This is summarized in the following chart.

IMMIGRATION TO THE AMERICAN COLONIES

NATIONALITY	MAJOR REASON FOR COMING	WHERE THEY SETTLED
English	To find religious and political freedom and a better way of life.	In all 13 colonies, along the Atlantic seaboard.
Scotch-Irish	To find religious freedom and economic improvement.	Settled mainly in Pennsylvania and the Southern colonies; by 1775 about 300,000 were in the colonies.
German	To escape religious and dynastic wars of 17th century (especially *Thirty Years War*, 1618-48)	About 200,000 settlers came in the 17th and 18th centuries. Most settled in Pennsylvania (the "Pennsylvania Dutch"); others, in Maryland, Virginia, the Carolinas and New York.
French, Swiss, Dutch, and others	To find religious freedom and economic improvement.	French Huguenots settled in South Carolina and several Northern colonies. Swiss came to Pennsylvania and North Carolina. Welsh, Irish-Catholics, and Scotch Presbyterians settled in Middle and Southern colonies. Jews settled in the cities of most colonies. Swedes and Dutch settled in New Sweden (Delaware) and New Netherland.

NOTE: The *Northern Colonies (New England)* included New Hampshire, Massachusetts, Rhode Island, Connecticut.

The *Middle Colonies* included New York, Pennsylvania, New Jersey, Delaware.

The *Southern Colonies* included Maryland, Virginia, North Carolina, South Carolina, Georgia.

How the Colonies Were Governed. The English colonies were allowed a relatively large measure of self-government. This was the result of the British tradition of liberty and also of conditions which made it difficult for the Crown to administer the colonies tightly during the 17th century.

1. *Types of Colonies.* Three types of colonies were organized. They differed mainly in the way the governor was selected. **(a)** In the *charter* or *self-governing colonies,* such as Connecticut and Rhode Island, the governor was chosen by the colonists. **(b)** In the *proprietary colonies,* such as Pennsylvania, Maryland, and Delaware, the governor and other high officials were selected by the proprietor. **(c)** In the *royal* or *crown colonies,* such as New York, Virginia, and Georgia, the governor and other officials were chosen by the King.

2. *Instruments of Colonial Government.* To a large extent each colony controlled its own internal affairs during most of the Colonial Period.

(a) Charter. Each colony had a grant of privileges from the King, known as a *charter.*

(b) Governor. The governor had the power to veto or approve colonial laws. The legislature of each colony, however, paid its governor's salary. This "power of the purse" was used frequently to withhold the governor's salary until he agreed to a piece of desired legislation.

(c) Council. Most colonies had a *Council* which advised the governor, shared in the lawmaking, and acted as the upper house of the legislature. Most Councils were appointed rather than elected. They had to approve laws passed by the colonial assemblies, and they also served as the highest courts.

(d) Assembly. Laws for the colony were made by an elected representative *Assembly,* with considerable powers, including the power to tax, spend money, and petition the Crown. All of this provided valuable training in self-government by stimulating the interest of the people in public affairs, developing a spirit of independence, and accustoming a body of citizens to the administration of government.

(e) Local Government. Local government was run entirely by the colonists themselves. In New England, where people lived comparatively close together, the *town* became the unit of self-government. In the Southern colonies, where the population was spread out because of the large plantations, local government was based on the *county.* In the Middle colonies, the system was mixed.

(f) Colonies and Parliament. In theory, the King and Parliament had the right to supervise colonial affairs and veto laws passed by the colonial legislatures. In practice, they rarely did so until the 1700's. Parliament for the most part regulated the external trade of the colonies through navigation laws. From time to time, the English government sent officials to the colonies to investigate conditions, and by 1763 each colony was represented in Parliament by a special agent. Benjamin Franklin of Pennsylvania was the most famous and influential of these special agents.

3. *Trend to Royal Colonies.* When a colony got into unusual difficulties or engaged in practices or actions considered dangerous to the Crown, its charter might be revoked. In this event, it became a *royal colony.* This trend began in the late 1600's. As a result, by 1775, the status of the colonies was as follows:

> Eight were *royal colonies* — Massachusetts, New Jersey, New York, New Hampshire, Virginia, North Carolina, South Carolina, Georgia.
>
> Three were *proprietary colonies* — Delaware, Pennsylvania, Maryland.
>
> Two were *self-governing colonies* — Connecticut, Rhode Island.

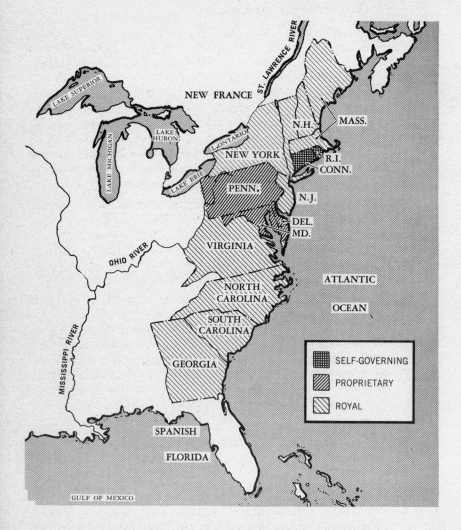

This map shows the status of the colonies as of 1775.

Efforts Toward Colonial Unity. For much of the Colonial Period, there was little cooperation among the 13 colonies. Each colony had its own separate ties to Britain and acted in many respects as a semi-independent country. In each colony there was much *local* patriotism. Lack of an adequate network of roads or other communications systems often made it easier for colonies to deal with the mother country than with each other. Colonies often engaged in bitter boundary disputes resulting from unclear and overlapping charter provisions. Despite these forces working against union, there were some attempts at cooperative action. In spite of their failure, these attempts may be considered the beginnings of what was later to become the United States of America.

1. *The New England Confederation (1643).* To provide joint protection against the Indians, French, and Dutch, four New England colonies (Massachusetts, Plymouth, Connecticut, and New Haven) formed the *New England Confederation* in 1643. Each colony sent two representatives to a common council. The Confederation lasted until 1684, and it helped the colonists wage a successful war against the Indians in 1675-76 (King Philip's War). The Confederation collapsed, however, because the smaller colonies resented the attempt of Massachusetts to dominate it. Despite its short life, the New England Confederation was a ground-breaking attempt at union, and it gave the colonists valuable experience in intercolonial action and in delegating authority to properly chosen representatives.

2. *The Albany Congress (1754).* The *Albany Congress* was a second noteworthy attempt at unity among the colonies. In 1754, just before the French and Indian War, seven Northern colonies sent representatives to Albany (New York) to try to work out a plan of union. The Congress was called by Britain to develop intercolonial cooperation in the face of growing French influence in the Ohio Valley and in lower Canada.

Benjamin Franklin drew up the *Albany Plan of Union.* It called for a president-general appointed by the King, and a council made up of delegates selected by colonial assemblies. The council was to have power to levy taxes for the common defense, subject to the veto of the president and the Crown. Though the Albany Congress approved this plan, it was rejected by the colonies and the British Parliament. The plan was important, however, because it proposed a federal plan of government, with specific powers given to the central authority. This foreshadowed the basic framework of United States government under the Constitution.

Early Resistance to Arbitrary Rule. The American colonists early developed a tradition of resistance to what they considered arbitrary or unjust rule. Such resistance was directed not only against British authority but even against colonial governments.

1. *Bacon's Rebellion.* In 1676, a Virginian frontier planter, NATHANIEL BACON, led a rebellion against the government of the colony because it had failed to consider the needs of the frontiersmen. Specifically, Bacon charged, the government had not provided protection against the Indians. Bacon's sudden death at the height of his success led to the collapse of the movement.

2. *End of the Dominion of New England.* In 1684, King James II made an effort to simplify the administration of the colonies, to bring them more directly under the Crown, and to punish the continued disregard by Massachusetts of royal edicts. The King's scheme was to unite the New England colonies, New York, and New Jersey into a so-called *Dominion of New England.* The governor of the new dominion, Sir EDMUND ANDROS, ruled harshly, restricting colonial liberties and levying heavy taxes. However, during the Glorious Revolution of 1688 in England, the colonists forced the hated Andros out of office and imprisoned him. The Dominion collapsed.

3. *Protests Against Writs of Assistance.* During the French and Indian War, the British government began to issue *writs of assistance.* These were blank search warrants, intended to help enforce the Act of Trade and prevent smuggling by colonists. The colonists objected vigorously to the use of such warrants. The opposition was led by JAMES OTIS, a Boston lawyer, who argued that the writs violated the rights of Englishmen, specifically the principle that "a man's home is his castle."

4. *Frontier vs. Seaboard.* No sooner did the colonization of America begin than some colonists pushed westward, settling near the mountains and in the fertile valleys between the ranges. On many occasions, the Western frontier farmers showed strong opposition to the policies of colonial legislatures. The frontiersmen complained that the legislatures were dominated by rich merchants and landowners living on the seaboard or eastern sections of the colonies. In North Carolina, South Carolina, Pennsylvania, New Jersey, Massachusetts, and elsewhere Westerners protested and sometimes took violent action against heavy taxes, inadequate political representation, failure to provide protection, land monopolies, and high court fees. It has been said that the Western farmers in the 13 colonies fought the American Revolution as much to overthrow domination by the conservative Eastern legislatures and governors as to win independence from Britain.

REVIEW TEST (Chapter 2 — Part I)

Select the number preceding the word or expression that best completes each statement or answers each question.

1. For what purpose did most Englishmen come to America in the Colonial Period? (1) for religious freedom (2) for economic opportunity (3) for social equality (4) for political asylum

2. What was the name of the government-supported Church of England for most of the 17th century? (1) Anglican (2) Catholic (3) Lutheran (4) Puritan

3. The colonists gained valuable experience in solving problems jointly through the (1) Glorious Revolution (2) Albany Congress (3) New England Confederation (4) Dominion of New England

4. All of the following were types of colonial organization *except* (1) royal (2) charter (3) dominion (4) proprietary

5. In most of the 13 colonies, the settlers gained experience in self-government by (1) choosing governors to administer colonial affairs (2) sending representatives to England to vote in Parliament (3) regulating trade with England (4) electing members of colonial assemblies

6. During the first half of the 18th century the colonial assemblies frequently used "the power of the purse" to (1) check the royal governors (2) encourage political union among the colonies (3) obtain money from England (4) extend suffrage in the frontier regions

7. During the Colonial Period political differences were most bitter between (1) residents of the Atlantic seaboard and those of the frontier (2) colonists in the North and colonists in the South (3) Federalists and Antifederalists (4) manufacturing interests and agricultural interests

8. Which type of colony predominated by the time of the American Revolution? (1) royal (2) proprietary (3) self-governing (4) commonwealth

9. What was, next to the English, the largest group to come to the colonies in the 17th and 18th centuries? (1) Germans (2) French (3) Scotch-Irish (4) Dutch

10. Originally, the "Pennsylvania Dutch" came from (1) Holland (2) Switzerland (3) Germany (4) Great Britain

Match each name in Column A with the item in Column B that is most clearly identified with it.

A	**B**
1. James Otis	*a.* Freedom of worship for Quakers
2. Nathaniel Bacon	*b.* Able Dutch governor of New York
3. William Penn	*c.* Protested failure of seaboard interests to protect interests of frontiersmen
4. Benjamin Franklin	
5. Edmund Andros	*d.* Hated by the colonists for harsh rule
	e. Protested against writs of assistance
	f. Sponsor of plan to unite the colonies

Essay Questions

1. Discuss three important reasons for migration to the English colonies in America.

2. Explain the difference between royal, proprietary, and self-governing colonies, and give two examples of each type.

3. Discuss the role of each of the following in the government of the English colonies during the Colonial Period: (a) the colonial charter (b) the Governor (c) the Council (d) the Assembly (e) local government (f) Parliament.

4. (a) Discuss two reasons for the failure of the 13 colonies to unite. (b) Describe two attempts at cooperative action by the colonies before 1760.

5. Explain why it has been said that the seeds of resistance to arbitrary rule were beginning to develop long before the American Revolution. Give two examples of such resistance.

Part II — GROWTH OF DEMOCRACY IN THE COLONIES

Although the English colonies could not be considered democratic in the modern sense of the word, the Colonial Period saw the beginning of many of the ideas and practices which have since made the United States one of the world's greatest democracies.

Reasons for the Growth of Democracy in Colonial Times. Several factors help explain the growth of democracy in colonial America.

1. *The English Heritage.* Settlers from Britain brought to America the "rights of Englishmen." These were the rights and principles established by custom (common law) or found in the great charters of English liberty, notably the Magna Carta, Petition of Right, and Bill of Rights. Colonial charters guaranteed these rights to settlers. They included *trial by jury, prohibition of search or arrest without a warrant, habeas corpus, protection of property,* and *freedom of speech and assembly.* Other principles growing out of the English experience which colonists brought to the New World were: the institution of *representative government,* the idea of a *two-house (bicameral) legislature,* and the concept of *control by the people's representatives of the expenditures of the government.*

2. *Nature of the Population.* Colonial America was a "melting pot" of different races and nationalities. (See chart on page 8.) This provided opportunities for the growth of tolerance and respect for differences, as well as for democratic cooperative living.

3. *Effects of Frontier Conditions.* Throughout most of the Colonial Period, the great majority of settlers lived along or close to the edge of the wilderness. The *frontier* affected the national character and development in significant ways. Life on the frontier promoted a sense of self-reliance, a spirit of independence, a faith in progress, and a belief in individual effort and equality.

Milestones in the Growth of Democracy. Many of the democratic aspects of American life and government can be traced back to developments in the 13 colonies.

1. *Representative Government.* The election of the *Virginia House of Burgesses* in 1619 marked the beginning of representative government in America and established the idea of popularly elected colonial assemblies. Each of the eleven "cities" or "hundreds" of Virginia elected two representatives *(burgesses)* to the assembly, for the most part landowners and merchants. The Virginia pattern of allowing the people to choose representatives for a lawmaking body spread to all the other colonies.

2. *Self-Government.* Before they landed at Plymouth, the Pilgrims signed the *Mayflower Compact* (1620), in which they agreed to establish a

14

government and obey all laws for the good of the colony. This was the first instance of self-government or self-determination in American history. It also contained the germ of the idea of *government by consent of the governed* in America.

3. *Written Constitutions.* In 1639, the representatives of the three Connecticut settlements of Hartford, Wethersfield, and Windsor drew up the first written constitution in America, the *Fundamental Orders of Connecticut.* It set up a strong government for the colony, based upon the principles of *majority rule, consent of the governed,* and *protection of minority rights.* The idea of written constitutions to protect the liberties of the people has become characteristic of American government. By the time of the Revolution, all the colonies had written constitutions.

4. *Town Meetings.* In New England, where the township was the unit of local government, all major decisions were made by a *town meeting.* Most heads of families could attend. Town meetings are still part of the New England way of life. This is considered an example of *direct democracy.*

5. *Freedom of the Press.* In 1735, the famous *Zenger Case* provided the basis for one of our most cherished traditions — freedom of the press. JOHN PETER ZENGER was a German printer who had emigrated to New York, where he became the publisher of the *New York Weekly Journal.* He was brought to trial for publishing articles that criticized the royal governor of

This old print shows the trial of Peter Zenger. The accused stands at the right, while his lawyer addresses the court.

New York and his party. Zenger's able defense lawyer, ANDREW HAMILTON, won his acquittal on the grounds that statements he had made in his paper did not constitute libel, and that free discussion of public questions was vital to democratic government.

6. *Religious Freedom.* Although many of the colonists had come to America to escape religious persecution in Europe, they were not always overly tolerant of other religions. Despite this fact, several cornerstones of religious freedom were established in America in colonial times.

> (a) ROGER WILLIAMS, who had been expelled from Massachusetts for his belief in religious liberty, founded a new colony in *Rhode Island.* Here, freedom of worship was extended to all.

> (b) The *Maryland Toleration Act* (1649) extended religious freedom to all Christians. (Maryland had been founded as a refuge for Catholics.)

> (c) Settlers of all Christian sects were also made welcome in *Pennsylvania,* where WILLIAM PENN had set up a refuge for Quakers (the Society of Friends).

By the 18th century, official religious persecution in the 13 colonies had largely ended, although all religions were still not fully equal under the law.

Limitations on Colonial Democracy. In the 13 colonies, the people in general took a more active part in government and politics than was true anywhere in Europe at that time. Yet, it must be emphasized that full political and personal rights, as we understand them today, did not exist anywhere in the colonies. **(1)** There were *religious and property qualifications* for voting and holding office. **(2)** *Women* could not vote or hold office and had limited property rights. **(3)** *Slavery* was legal and widespread. **(4)** There were *sharp class differences* between the aristocracy (officials, prosperous merchants, large landowners, professionals) and the rest of the population (small farmers, tradesmen, laborers, Negro slaves). **(5)** *Primogeniture,* the exclusive right of the first-born son to inherit his father's land, was common. In some areas, particularly in the South, this was accompanied by *entail,* which provided that the family that had originally acquired land was never allowed to sell it. This made for rigidity in property relationships and for fixed social classes.

REVIEW TEST (Chapter 2—Part II)

Select the number preceding the word or expression that best completes each statement or answers each question.

1. Representative government began in the English colonies with the (1) framing of the Mayflower Compact (2) meeting of the Virginia House of Burgesses (3) passage of the Maryland Toleration Act (4) town meetings of Massachusetts

2. The Mayflower Compact was an agreement to (1) allow only the Puritans to worship in the new colony (2) defend the New England colonies from the Indians (3) pass such rules and laws as the good of the colony demanded (4) purchase land from the Indians for the new settlement

3. The Mayflower Compact was an important step in the growth of democracy because it (1) was the first written constitution in the New World (2) indicated that the people were the source of political authority (3) laid down the principle of separation of powers (4) guaranteed religious freedom to all settlers

4. "Direct democracy" is best illustrated by the (1) United States Congress (2) New England town meeting (3) Virginia House of Burgesses (4) French Parliament

5. In colonial Virginia, the House of Burgesses represented chiefly the interests of the (1) English government and the clergy (2) plantation owners and the merchants (3) tenant farmers and the indentured servants (4) craftsmen and the unskilled laborers

6. A celebrated victory for the American ideal of freedom of the press was the (1) Dartmouth College case (2) Zenger case (3) Danbury Hatters' case (4) case of Gibbons against Ogden

7. Which of the following features of our heritage was derived from England? (1) "direct democracy" (2) written constitutions (3) representative government (4) federal system of government

8. Which of the following democratic principles had made the greatest advance by the end of the Colonial Period? (1) universal manhood suffrage (2) religious liberty (3) public education (4) emancipation of slaves

9. The House of Burgesses and the New England town meetings were similar in that both (1) originated in the New England states (2) were forms of self-government (3) were established by the Articles of Confederation (4) were free of vetoes by colonial governors

10. Which of the following pairs contributed most to the establishment of religious freedom in the 13 colonies? (1) Thomas Hooker — John Winthrop (2) William Penn — Roger Williams (3) Lord Baltimore — Cotton Mather (4) Anne Hutchinson — Samuel Adams

State whether each of the following statements is true or false. If the statement is false, replace the word or phrase in **boldface type** *with the one which will make it correct.*

1. The principle of written constitutions was begun in America with the drawing up of the **Petition of Right.**

2. The Zenger Case arose out of criticism of the actions of **Parliament.**

3. Freedoms arising out of custom and Parliamentary statutes that were brought to America by English settlers were known as the **Rights of Englishmen.**

4. For his religious convictions Roger Williams was expelled from the colony of **Massachusetts.**

5. At the end of the Colonial Period, slavery was **illegal** in most of the colonies.

Essay Questions

1. Colonial experience helped lay the foundation of our democratic heritage. Show how each of three developments during the Colonial Period influenced the growth of democracy in our country.

2. Show how each contributed to the struggle for human rights: William Penn, Roger Williams, Peter Zenger

3. Discuss the effects of frontier conditions on the growth of democracy in the 13 colonies.

Part III — HOW THE COLONISTS MADE A LIVING

The way in which the colonists made a living was influenced by their needs, their skills, and the geography of America.

The Geography of Colonial America. The geography of America was well suited for the development of a thriving civilization by an industrious people. **(1)** America was richly endowed with *natural resources.* The soil was rich, the forests thick with many varieties of trees and abounding in wildlife of all sorts, and the waters filled with all kinds of fish. **(2)** A *temperate climate* and *abundant rainfall* encouraged settlement, and made possible the exploitation of the natural resources of the continent. **(3)** The *topography* of the east coast region of the 13 colonies was advantageous to colonial development. The Appalachian Mountains served as a natural barrier between the English colonies and the French, but the mountain passes and gaps permitted pioneers and frontiersmen to move westward and trade with the Indians. Also, the region's many rivers, lakes, and good harbors facilitated commerce and transportation.

Land Ownership in the Colonies. Most settlers were attracted to the English colonies in the hope of securing land.

1. *New England.* In New England *small farms* rather than large estates became the general landowning pattern. Colonial legislatures granted land to townships or town groups, which in turn distributed smaller sections to settlers *(freeholders).* Certain lands (for example the pasture land) were held by each community for common use.

2. *Middle and Southern Colonies.* The landholding system in the Middle and Southern colonies was one of the *large estates* and *quitrents.* This resulted from the huge semi-feudal grants originally given to Crown favorites or proprietors. In addition to keeping large blocks of land for themselves, big landowners assigned smaller sections to *tenant farmers,* who paid *quitrents* for the use of the property. Attempts to avoid payment of quitrents were frequent, and there were many "rent wars" against rent collectors.

3. *Land Speculation.* Many shrewd landowners and businessmen bought up good land in the western portion of the colonies, beyond the fringes of settlement, and held it for a rise in value.

The Labor System. One of the more important concerns of colonial farmers and businessmen was the problem of obtaining laborers. This was made more difficult by the fact that ambitious workers soon made enough money to buy their own farms. *Indentured servants* and *slaves,* therefore, became a substantial part of the early labor force.

1. *Indentured Servants.* Indentured servants were Europeans who sold themselves into temporary bondage in return for passage to America. Their contracts required them to labor for their masters for three to seven years without pay. When they had served out their contracts, they were released and given some money, tools, seed, clothes, and possibly land.

2. *Negro Slavery.* By the late 17th century, Negro slaves had become an important element in the labor force of the colonies. Most of them were used on Southern rice and tobacco plantations. By 1775, slaves had replaced indentured servants as the main type of non-free labor. (NOTE: The first blacks brought from Africa beginning in 1619 were regarded as indentured servants. The institution of chattel slavery evolved in the 1640's and was well established by the 1660's.)

Agriculture, the Basic Occupation in the Colonies. Agriculture was the basic occupation in the colonies. About 90% of the colonists were farmers, planters, or agricultural laborers.

1. *Colonial Farming Methods.* Farming was difficult in the colonial era. Land often had to be cleared of trees and stones, and agricultural tools and methods were crude. On most of the small "family farms," the farmer and his family produced just enough for their own needs *(subsistence farming)*.

2. *Farming in New England.* The rocky, hilly soil and long New England winters made farming in that region less profitable than elsewhere. Most products were grown for food or feed, including corn, rye, oats, barley, sheep and cattle. Many farmers worked at lumbering and trapping in their spare time to earn cash to buy what they could not grow or make.

3. *Farming in the Middle Colonies.* The Middle colonies of New York, New Jersey, Pennsylvania, and Delaware were known as the "bread," "food," and "produce" colonies. Good soil and climate enabled the farmers of this region to grow great quantities of a variety of crops and livestock.

4. *Farming in the Southern Colonies.* The *plantation system* developed in the Southern colonies. Helped by fertile soil and a warm climate, large estates in the *tidewater* area (the coastal plain) were farmed by planters owning many slaves. Great quantities of *cash* (staple) *crops* were grown for sale and export; *tobacco* was the leading cash crop. Other leading staple crops included rice and indigo. Small farmers, who held few or no slaves and who actually outnumbered the large planters, farmed the area between the tidewater and the mountains (the *Piedmont*).

Other Colonial Industries. The colonists engaged in a number of pursuits in addition to agriculture. *Fishing* and *whaling* were important in most coastal areas, particularly New England. New Englanders also made profits by *distilling rum* and *building ships* for fishing, commerce, and the royal navy. *Lumbering* took place in New England and the Southern colonies. *Fur trading* with the Indians was important in nearly every colony. Since the average farmer was largely self-sufficient, *manufacturing* did not become a major industry. Nevertheless, by the 1700's, a large variety of small manufacturing establishments had developed to meet the needs of the growing population; for example, blacksmith shops, shoe shops, iron works, and grist mills.

Colonial Commerce. The colonists developed trade relations with foreign countries, especially in Europe and the West Indies. New York, Boston, Philadelphia, and Charleston became leading commercial centers.

1. *Trade with West Indies.* The grain, meat, fish, lumber, and manufactured goods of the New England and Middle colonies were traded for the sugar and molasses of the West Indies.

2. *Trade with England.* The tobacco, rice, indigo, and naval stores (tar, pitch, etc.) of the Southern colonies were exchanged for English manufactured goods.

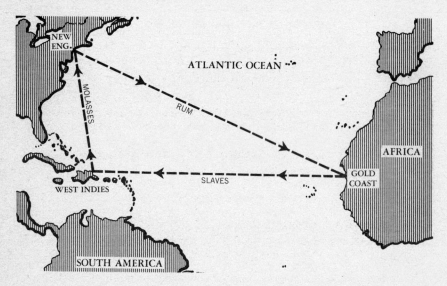

One of the popular routes of colonial triangular trade.

3. *Triangular Trade.* The need for cash and the fact that neither England nor the West Indies needed all their exports, forced the New England colonies to develop a system of three-legged trade routes, called *triangular trade.* Triangular trade brought gold and silver to the colonies, and good profits to merchants and shipowners. Three popular routes were:

(a) *New England* rum was exchanged for slaves in *Africa.* These slaves were exchanged for gold, sugar, and molasses in the *West Indies.* The gold, sugar, and molasses were brought back to *New England* and exchanged for rum.

(b) The grain, meat, fish, furs, and lumber of *New England* were shipped to *Europe* and traded for wine, fruit, and gold. These products were brought to *England* and exchanged for manufactured goods, which were shipped back to *New England.*

(c) Grain, meat, fish, and lumber were exchanged in the *West Indies* for sugar, fruit, and molasses. These were traded in *England* for manufactured goods, which were brought back to *New England*.

4. *The Scarcity of Money.* Colonial commerce was hampered by a scarcity of money. Since England sold more in the way of finished goods to the colonies than she bought from them in the way of foodstuffs and raw materials, the available gold and silver in the colonies was continually being shipped to the mother country to make up the difference in this *unfavorable balance of trade.* Southern planters especially were in constant debt to English merchants.

(a) To solve the problem of lack of currency with which to exchange goods and do business, colonists frequently resorted to *barter* arrangements (direct exchange of one type of goods for another). This was unsatisfactory because it was difficult and awkward to measure the value of one article in terms of another.

(b) Another frequent, but not completely satisfactory, arrangement was the issuance of *paper money* by colonial legislatures to pay government expenses. Overissuance of this unbacked currency lessened its value and led to rising prices and inflation. English merchants particularly did not like payment in "cheap" paper money.

The Regulation of Colonial Industry and Commerce by England. Like other nations with colonies in the 17th and 18th centuries, England attempted to regulate colonial trade and industry for her own benefit in accordance with the doctrine of *mercantilism*.

1. *Mercantilism.* Mercantilism was a theory of trade which held that a nation's wealth and power depended upon the amount of gold and silver it could amass. To do this the following policies were considered essential:

(a) A *favorable balance of trade* was to be achieved. This would be done by selling more to the colonies than was bought from them. The difference would be paid by the colonies in gold and silver.

(b) Colonies were to be used as sources of raw materials and as markets for the manufactured goods of the mother country.

2. *The Regulation of Trade and Manufacturing in the Colonies.* England applied the mercantile theory of trade to her colonies in the New World. Her methods of doing this are referred to as the "Old Colonial System."

(a) A series of *Navigation Acts* in the late 17th and early 18th centuries required that: **(1)** all goods exported to or from the colonies had to be shipped in English vessels; **(2)** certain specific or "enumerated commodities" (such as tobacco, sugar, cotton, and indigo) had to be sent only to England or English colonies; **(3)** imports from Europe had to be brought *first* to English ports for the payment of import duties, *before* being sent to America.

(b) *The Molasses Act of 1733* placed high duties on sugar and molasses imported from the non-British (French and Dutch) West Indies.

(c) In addition to restricting trade, Parliament attempted to limit colonial industry. The *Woolens Act* (1699) forbade the shipment of woolen goods, even to neighboring colonies. The *Hat Act* (1732) prohibited the sale of hats and felts outside of the colony in which they were made. The *Iron Act* (1750) forbade the manufacture of finished articles of iron.

3. *Effects of Manufacturing and Trade Restrictions on the Colonies.* British trade and manufacturing restrictions angered the American colonists. They resented being regulated for the benefit of the businessmen in the mother country. Therefore, they disregarded the restrictions on manufacturing, and practiced widespread smuggling to evade the Acts of Trade. As a result, early British restrictions did not really hinder colonial business very much.

4. *"Salutary Neglect."* In the 17th century England was involved in wars with Holland, France, and Spain, as well as with domestic crises, rebellions, and dissatisfaction with Stuart rule. As a result, Parliament and the Crown pursued a policy of *laissez-faire* (let alone) toward the colonies, a policy often called "salutary neglect," for under it the restrictions on colonial trade and industry were only loosely enforced, and the colonists were generally left free to develop their own way of life.

5. *Tightening of Regulation in the 18th Century.* In the 1700's England began to tighten up her regulation of the colonies. Customs collectors, judges, and naval officers, paid by Parliament, were sent to America, and were made directly responsible to the Crown. Parliament attempted to control colonial currency, and new Acts of Trade (*e.g.*, the *Molasses Act*) were passed. After 1763, Parliament took even more vigorous action to enforce the Acts of Trade. Colonial opposition to such measures brought on friction which helped set the stage for the American Revolution.

6. *Britain's Point of View.* Parliament was not actually trying to punish the colonies by regulating their economic life. English statesmen, naturally, believed that the mother country was more important than its colonies. They felt that colonial trade with other countries, especially colonial purchases elsewhere of goods that were also made in England, resulted in economic loss. Moreover, Britain did not consider the American colonies any more important than her empire in India, or her possessions in the West Indies.

7. *Some Benefits to Colonies.* The colonies were actually aided by some of Britain's policies. *Bounties* (special bonuses) were paid by Parliament for the production and sale of naval stores, tobacco, and indigo to England. The requirement that all colonial trade be carried on in English vessels brought tremendous gains to colonial shippers and shipbuilders. (The colonists were considered Englishmen.) Finally, the colonists were given British military and naval protection.

REVIEW TEST (Chapter 2—Part III)

Select the number preceding the word or expression that best completes each statement or answers each question.

1. All of the following were terms associated with landholding in the colonies *except* (1) freeholders (2) quitrents (3) primogeniture (4) salutary neglect

2. In what colony was the ownership of large estates the prevailing pattern? (1) Virginia (2) Massachusetts (3) Connecticut (4) Rhode Island

3. The colonial labor supply was characterized by (1) the use of Indians as farm laborers (2) a large number of indentured servants (3) an oversupply of craftsmen (4) a concentration of workers in urban centers

4. The leading staple crop of the Southern colonies in colonial times was (1) rice (2) corn (3) tobacco (4) livestock

5. In the Colonial Period the meat, fish, and manufactured articles of the New England colonies were traded for the sugar and molasses of (1) the West Indies (2) Canada (3) England (4) the Middle colonies

6. According to the mercantile theory, a nation with colonies should (1) import more than it exports (2) avoid placing limitations on the trade of its colonies (3) encourage exports to bring in money from abroad (4) export raw materials and import finished products

7. Which legislation of the British Parliament concerning the 13 colonies most clearly illustrates the principles of mercantilism? (1) Intolerable Acts (2) Navigation Acts (3) Stamp Act (4) Proclamation of 1763

8. As a result of Great Britain's mercantile policies, the colonists were forbidden to export (1) cotton (2) indigo (3) tar (4) wool

9. In some of the 13 colonies, England tried to discourage (1) the manufacture of ironware (2) the consumption of tea (3) shipbuilding (4) the production of tobacco and turpentine

10. To overcome the scarcity of gold and silver caused by England's trade policies the colonists did all of the following *except* (1) develop a system of triangular trade (2) issue paper money (3) make manufacturing the major industry (4) sell tobacco, naval stores, and ships to the mother country

Supply the word or expression that correctly completes each statement.

1. Whaling became an important industry in the . . ? . . colonies

2. The name given to such articles as tar and pitch needed in shipbuilding in colonial times was . . ? . . .

3. The type of farming which provides a farmer with just enough to feed his own family is . . ? . . farming.

4. By 1775 . . ? . . had replaced indentured servants as the major source of unpaid labor in the colonies.

5. In addition to New York, two important "bread" or "food" colonies were . . ? . . and . . ? . . .

Essay Questions

1. Show how each of the following contributed to the development of the American colonies in the Colonial Period: (a) resources (b) climate (c) topography.

2. What were the outstanding characteristics of colonial agriculture and landholding in (a) New England (b) the Middle colonies (c) the Southern colonies?

3. How did England both help and restrict the economic life of its American colonies?

Part IV — SOCIAL AND CULTURAL LIFE IN COLONIAL AMERICA

Although the Europeans who came to America brought Old-World customs and traditions with them, the new "American" society which they developed was markedly different from the old European one they had abandoned.

Colonial Society. Before the American Revolution the inhabitants of the English colonies lived for the most part along the Atlantic coast.

1. *Population.* Once the colonies were settled, population grew rapidly. It is estimated that the population of the 13 colonies increased from about 300,000 in 1700 to about 3,000,000 in 1775. By the time of the Revolution (1776), about two-thirds of the colonists were descendants of the original settlers.

2. *Areas of Settlement.* Most of the population lived on farms, spread out thinly along the Atlantic coast or close to it. However, from the beginning settlers had moved into the Appalachian highlands, and before the Revolution several settlements had been established in what are now Kentucky and Tennessee. This *moving frontier* and *westward movement* were to be among the most important and characteristic developments of American history until about 1890.

3. *Social Classes.* Distinct social classes developed in the colonies. They were based for the most part on wealth rather than birth. At the top of the "social ladder" were Southern planters, large landowners, wealthy merchants, and a few professionals. Beneath this group in social prestige were people who comprised the backbone of colonial America — the small farmers, craftsmen, shopkeepers, laborers, and most of the professionals. At the bottom of this class structure were the indentured servants and the slaves.

4. *Living Conditions.* In general, the family was the focal point of colonial life. The home became the center of education and religious observance, and the family cared for the sick and aged. From an early age children were kept busy with household chores, under a strict discipline. Usually, people married young.

> *(a)* The small farmers and townsmen dressed plainly, ate food which they ordinarily produced for themselves, and lived in simple, wooden homes which they built and furnished with homemade tools and utensils. The wealthier classes dressed in luxurious European fashion, built spacious, even elaborate, homes, and supplied them with handsome, often imported, furnishings.
>
> *(b)* Though the average colonist had little time for amusement, he liked to hunt, fish, and swim. Colonists also enjoyed log-rollings, harvesting and husking bees, and occasional fairs. In New England, the stern Puritan background of the colonists led to the banning of many forms of amusement.

Religion in the Colonies. Religion was an important part of colonial life. During the Colonial Period there was a significant growth of religious toleration.

1. *Religious Influences.* Most colonists were deeply religious, and this affected their conduct. The Puritans of New England insisted on regular church attendance and strict observance of the Sabbath. They banned dancing, card-playing, and theater-going. Prayer before meals and bedtime and frequent readings of the Bible were colonial customs. Though the colonists shared the common beliefs of Christianity, there were many religious denominations to be found throughout the colonies.

2. *Established Churches.* Most colonies had an "established" or "state" church, supported by taxes. Rhode Island, Pennsylvania, New Jersey, and Delaware, where there was no established church (*separation of church and state*), were exceptions.

3. *Development of Religious Toleration.* Although established churches continued to predominate, there was complete freedom of religion in Rhode Island. More limited freedom in Maryland and Pennsylvania was granted in the first half of the 17th century. By 1775 religious freedom had made more progress in America than anywhere else in the world.

Colonial Education. The beginnings of the American school system can be traced back to the Colonial Period. Although most colonists did not receive a formal school education, an increasing number of educational opportunities became available as time went on.

1. *Parish* or *church schools* were the first to be set up in many places, to teach the Bible and religion.

2. The first *public* (tax-supported) *schools* were set up under the famous *Massachusetts Act* of 1647 which required towns of 50 families or more to establish an elementary school, and towns of 100 families to establish a *Latin Grammar School* (college preparatory).

3. Other communities, especially in New England, took similar steps. Even in these public schools, where the "3R's" were taught, the main aim was religious training.

4. Later in the Colonial Period private *academies* made their appearance. These were forerunners of our modern high school.

5. By the time of the Revolution, nine *colleges* had been established. Although boys could train for such professions as law and medicine, most of these first institutions of higher learning were organized to train for the ministry. *Harvard* (1636), *William and Mary* (1693), and *Yale* (1701) were the first three colleges to be established.

6. By and large the quality of colonial education was poor. Schoolhouses were primitive; teachers were not well trained; books were few in number; and most schools did not admit girls. Communities often had to depend on the services of a traveling schoolmaster, who stayed only a short time.

In Adam's Fall
We finned all.

Thy Life to mend,
This Book attend.

The Cat doth play,
And after flay.

A Dog will bite
A Thief at Night.

An Eagle' flight
Is out of fight.

The idle Foot
Is whipt at SchooL

Praife to GOD for learning to Read.

T H E · Praifes of my Tongue
    I offer to the LORD,
That I was taught and learnt fo young
    To read his holy Word.

2 That I was brought to know
    The Danger I was in.
By Nature and by Practice too
    A wretched flave to Sin:

3 That I was led to fee
    I can do nothing well ;
And whether fhall a Sinner Hee
    To fave himfelf from Hell.

— U. S. Office of Education

Typical pages from the famous *New England Primer.* Note the emphasis
on religious themes.

7. Despite all its weaknesses, the educational system of the colonies produced a higher proportion of the population who could read and write than most other countries of the world could boast at the time.

Cultural Achievements. In the century and a half before the American Revolution, the colonists slowly began to develop a distinct culture of their own. In the 18th century a growing number of books were printed or imported. The number and size of private libraries increased, and several circulating libraries were established. Nearly every home had a Bible or Book of Common Prayer, an almanac, and a cookbook.

1. *Literature.* Perhaps the most significant cultural achievements of the colonial era lay in the field of literature.

> (a) Although most books continued to be written by Europeans, the Colonial Period saw the birth of an American literature. Noteworthy were the religious writings of ROGER WILLIAMS, COTTON MATHER, and JONATHAN EDWARDS; the poetry of MICHAEL WIGGLESWORTH and PHILIP FRENEAU; and the historical writings of JOHN SMITH, WILLIAM BRADFORD, JOHN WINTHROP, and THOMAS HUTCHINSON.

> (b) Starting with the *Boston News Letter* of 1704, over 60 newspapers were begun before the Revolution. Though they were small in size and usually printed weekly, they were passed on from hand to hand. Also, the development of a postal system in the late 17th and early 18th centuries promoted the interchange of ideas and information.

2. *The Arts.* Few outstanding contributions were made in the fine arts (painting, sculpture, music, drama, architecture). However, the design of colonial mansions showed a simple grace and good taste that has influenced building styles to the present day. In addition, a number of painters won wide recognition. These included JOHN SINGLETON COPLEY, BENJAMIN WEST, GILBERT STUART, and CHARLES WILSON PEALE. They specialized in portraits of famous men.

3. *Science.* As was also true in Europe at the time, colonial science was not well advanced. Colonists were superstitious and believed in demons, omens, and witchcraft. In the notorious "witchcraft epidemic of 1692," over 150 persons in Salem, Massachusetts, were imprisoned for witchcraft, and 20 were executed. Despite this situation, individual Americans made important contributions to science. These included: DR. BENJAMIN RUSH (medicine), DAVID RITTENHOUSE (astronomy and mathematics), JOHN BARTRAM (botany), and BENJAMIN FRANKLIN (natural history, electricity, and invention).

Benjamin Franklin, (1706-90). The person who best represented the achievements of colonial America was BENJAMIN FRANKLIN, often called "the first civilized American." Franklin was one of history's great many-sided men. He made important contributions in education, science, culture, and diplomacy.

> (*a*) Among his numerous achievements were: pioneer experiments in electricity; the invention of the bifocal lens, the lightning rod, and the Franklin stove; authorship of a famous autobiography; publication of *The Pennsylvania Gazette* and *Poor Richard's Almanac;* establishment of some of the first subscription circulating libraries; and the organization of the first learned society in America (the *American Philosophical Society*).

> (*b*) Before the Revolution, Franklin served as postmaster for the colonies and as colonial agent for Pennsylvania in London. He also drew up the Albany Plan of Union. During the Revolution he helped frame the Declaration of Independence and, as Minister to France, was instrumental in securing French assistance for the colonies. At the Constitutional Convention in 1787, Franklin's great ability as a compromiser helped bring forth the Constitution of the United States.

REVIEW TEST (Chapter 2 — Part IV)

Select the number preceding the word or expression that best completes each statement or answers each question.

1. What is a primary source of information on early days in colonial New England? (1) a novel about Shays' Rebellion (2) the writings of Washington Irving (3) an American history textbook (4) William Bradford's *History of Plymouth Plantation*

2. Early colonial interest in education was due primarily to a desire to encourage (1) democracy in government (2) an enlightened public opinion (3) the reading of the Bible (4) religious toleration

3. In the New England colonies, grammar schools were generally maintained by the (1) towns (2) English government (3) Anglican Church (4) colonial legislatures

4. Which person would most likely have had a college education during colonial times? (1) a teacher (2) a lawyer (3) a doctor (4) a clergyman

5. Which of the following was found in a majority of the 13 English colonies on the eve of the American Revolution? (1) established churches (2) feudal-type landholding (3) government-supported schools (4) universal manhood suffrage

6. Which colony had the greatest degree of religious tolerance? (1) Connecticut (2) Maryland (3) Massachusetts (4) South Carolina

7. The beginnings of the public school system can be traced to the colony of (1) New York (2) Massachusetts (3) Rhode Island (4) Virginia

8. By the end of the Colonial Period the colonists had made most progress in the field of (1) science (2) drama (3) medicine (4) journalism

9. The description, "He ranks with Leonardo Da Vinci, Michelangelo, and Thomas Jefferson, as one of history's great many-sided men," most appropriately applies to (1) John Smith (2) Benjamin West (3) Benjamin Franklin (4) George Washington

10. The "Salem Trials" were evidences of (1) democratic progress (2) cultural improvement (3) superstition and intolerance (4) England's violation of the right of self-government

Select the number of the item that correctly identifies the description in **boldface type.**

1. Colonial Painter: (1) John Bartram (2) Gilbert Stuart (3) John Smith (4) Roger Williams

2. Colonial Religious Leader: (1) Jonathan Edwards (2) Charles Peale (3) Thomas Hutchinson (4) Peter Minuit

3. Colonial Scientist: (1) John Bartram (2) William Bradford (3) John Copley (4) Cotton Mather

4. Colonial "Best Sellers": (1) Encyclopedias (2) Biographies (3) Plays (4) Almanacs

5. Colonial Medical Research: (1) David Rittenhouse (2) Benjamin Franklin (3) Benjamin Rush (4) Philip Freneau

Essay Questions

1. Describe the following characteristics of the Colonial Period: (a) rapid population growth (b) a moving frontier.

2. Compare the class structure of the colonies with present-day social classes in the United States.

3. Explain why you would or wouldn't have enjoyed living in colonial New England.

4. Describe a significant development or shortcoming in each of the following in the Colonial Period: (a) religion (b) education (c) art (d) science.

CHAPTER 3

Establishing an Independent Nation (1756-83)

The French and Indian War produced a chain of events which led eventually to the colonists' declaration of independence and a struggle to win freedom from British rule.

Part I — SIGNIFICANCE OF THE FRENCH AND INDIAN WAR

The *French and Indian War* (1756-63) was the last phase of a series of wars between England and France which lasted from 1689 to 1763. The wars resulted from rivalry for worldwide supremacy, and they were fought in Europe, Asia, and North America.

Anglo-French Rivalry in North America. In the 17th and 18th centuries, France expanded her influence in the Ohio and Mississippi Valleys by continued exploration and the establishment of missions, forts, and trading posts. This led to rivalry with England over fur trade, fisheries, and territory, the result of which was a series of conflicts in North America between England and France.

The French and Indian War. The French and Indian War was a struggle for control of the Ohio Valley. The French had established a series of forts in disputed territory along the Ohio and its tributaries—an area which certain Virginian and British landowners had hopes of settling themselves. These forts were part of a chain which connected France's territory of Louisiana with her Canadian possessions. War resulted when the British decided to end the French threat (the "Gallic Peril") by forcing them out of the disputed territory.

1. *Events.* Although war was not officially declared until 1756, actual fighting began in 1754 when George Washington and a company of Virginia militiamen under command of the British General Braddock were defeated in a skirmish with French troops in the vicinity of Fort Duquesne (Pittsburgh).

   (*a*) France's well-disciplined army, superior leadership, strategically located forts, and strong Indian allies won the opening phases of the war by defeating British expeditions sent to capture Montreal and Louisburg.

29

(b) When William Pitt became British Prime Minister, the tide turned. Under Pitt's effective leadership, the British took Fort Duquesne and Louisburg in 1758, Quebec in 1759, and Montreal in 1760. The military climax of the war was General Wolfe's defeat of General Montcalm, which resulted in the British capture of the French stronghold of Quebec.

(c) In defeating France in North America, England enjoyed the advantages of control of the seas and greater population and resources in its colonies. Also, leaders like William Johnson kept the powerful Iroquois Indians loyal to the English.

(d) Although the American colonists aided the British, they did not offer their wholehearted support. American militiamen resisted being sent outside their own colonies. Several colonies either refused to raise or evaded paying taxes for the support of the war. In addition, during the war colonists continued to trade illegally with Canada and the French West Indies.

2. *Results.* The *Peace of Paris* (1763), ending the French and Indian War, was part of an overall peace settlement which concluded the struggle between England and France in Europe and Asia, as well as in America. Great Britain secured more territory at one time, in one treaty, than any other nation has ever obtained. **(a)** *From France* she received the remainder of Canada, and all French possessions east of the Mississippi. **(b)** *From Spain,* France's ally, Britain received Florida. **(c)** Louisiana, including New Orleans, was ceded to Spain by France, to repay her for losses in the struggle. **(d)** All that remained in French hands in North America after the war were the small fishing islands of St. Pierre and Miquelon, off Newfoundland, and the sugar islands of Guadaloupe and Martinique in the West Indies.

3. *Importance of the French and Indian War.* The French and Indian War was important to the future emergence of the United States in several ways.

(a) It resulted in a more independent attitude of the colonists toward the mother country, since they no longer needed her for protection against the French.

(b) It gave the colonial assemblies and military leaders additional prestige and valuable experience, as they had been called upon to finance, equip, and participate in military expeditions against the French.

(c) Colonial militiamen gained a good deal of self-assurance. They felt that in the fighting they had proved themselves at least the equals of English troops.

(d) Finally, and perhaps most importantly, the war resulted in a changed attitude on Great Britain's part toward the colonies. Britain decided to tighten its control over the colonies.

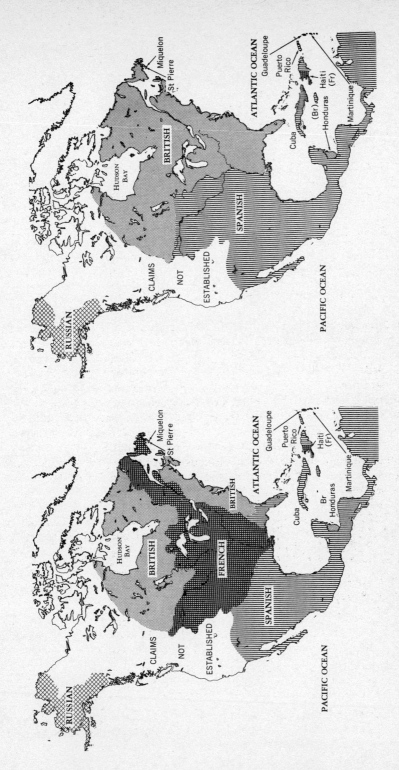

The map on the left shows North America before the French and Indian War; the map on the right shows North America after that conflict. Notice that France was entirely eliminated from the mainland.

REVIEW TEST (Chapter 3—Part I)

Select the number preceding the word or expression that best completes each statement or answers each question.

1. The French and Indian War was a part of   (1) the effort of Napoleon to establish world domination   (2) an attempt by colonial people to throw off imperialism   (3) the struggle between England and France for world supremacy   (4) the rivalry between England and Spain for colonies

2. The most important cause of the French and Indian War was   (1) the expansion of French influence in the Ohio and Mississippi Valleys   (2) the desire of the English colonists to annex Canada   (3) Indian raids on frontier settlements   (4) the Pontiac Conspiracy

3. In defeating France in North America, England's advantages included all of the following *except*   (1) friendship with the Iroquois Indians   (2) control of the seas   (3) a military alliance with Spain   (4) a larger population in its American colonies

4. The French and Indian War was fought in the period   (1) 1702–13   (2) 1742–48   (3) 1752–59   (4) 1756–63

5. Which of the French actions in disputed territory did most to anger the English? (1) the establishment of missions   (2) the building of forts   (3) the expansion of fur trapping   (4) the establishment of trading posts

6. Which military leader was not on the same side as the others in the French and Indian War? (1) Washington   (2) Braddock   (3) Montcalm   (4) Wolfe

7. The decisive victory in the French and Indian War was the capture of   (1) Quebec   (2) Louisburg   (3) Montreal   (4) Fort Duquesne

8. The Peace of Paris (1763) ended conflict between England and France in North America, Europe and   (1) South America   (2) Africa   (3) the Middle East   (4) Asia

9. The English statesman whose policies helped turn the tide for England was   (1) King George III   (2) Oliver Cromwell   (3) William Burke   (4) William Pitt

10. An important result of the French and Indian War was that it   (1) ended the Indian menace   (2) caused France to cede her claims west of the Mississippi to England   (3) encouraged a spirit of independence in the colonies   (4) lessened England's restrictions on the colonists

Indicate whether each of the following statements is **true** *or* **false**. *Give one fact or reason in support of each true statement, and reword correctly those statements which are false.*

1. The French threat to North America was known as the "Gallic Peril."

2. George Washington's military leadership was most important in bringing final defeat to the French forces in America.

3. The American colonists fought wholeheartedly for English victory in the French and Indian War.

4. As a result of the French and Indian War Britain received Florida from Spain.

5. All that remained in French hands in North America after the French and Indian War was Louisiana.

Essay Questions

1. Show how Anglo-French rivalry in North America brought about military conflict, ending in the French and Indian War.

2. Outline the immediate results of the French and Indian War.

Part II — CAUSES OF THE AMERICAN REVOLUTION

The *War for Independence,* or *American Revolution* as it is usually called, resulted from colonial resistance to England's attempt to tighten its control over its 13 American colonies. Underlying the revolt, which at first was for greater home rule rather than independence, was the failure of each side to understand the other's point of view.

The "New Colonial System." After the French and Indian War, England decided to tighten its control over the colonies. The new policy is referred to as the "New Colonial System," in contrast to the "Old Colonial System" of "salutary neglect" (see page 22). Four factors help account for the British decision to regulate colonial life more strictly.

1. The British felt that it was necessary to furnish increased protection against the Indians. With the end of French influence in the Ohio Valley, American colonists settled in increasing numbers west of the Appalachians. Angry at being cheated by fur traders, and furious over the loss of their hunting grounds, the Indians went on the warpath, captured British forts, and raided frontier settlements (*Conspiracy of Pontiac, 1763*).

2. The British needed additional revenue because the heavy expenses of the French and Indian War had drained the treasury. It was felt that the colonists should be made to pay their share of the costs of colonial administration and protection.

3. The British were convinced that continued violation of trade laws by the colonists had to be stopped. They were especially bitter over the sale by colonists of food and other supplies to the French in Canada, during the war.

4. Finally, the new king, George III, who ascended the throne in 1760, was determined to increase royal authority by stricter supervision of the colonies.

Elements of the New Colonial Policy. Britain attempted to exercise increased control in several ways—by restricting westward expansion, by enforcing existing laws more strictly, by levying new taxes, and by attempting to decrease the powers of colonial legislatures.

1. *Restrictions on Westward Expansion.* The Pontiac Rebellion convinced the British that they had to take immediate action on the problems brought about by colonial expansion west of the Appalachians. Therefore, a permanent standing army for the colonies was established, and by the *Royal Proclamation of 1763* colonists were ordered to remain east of the Allegheny Mountains. The territory between the Alleghenies and the Mississippi River was reserved for the Indians. Settlers already west of the Alleghenies were ordered to leave.

2. *Enforcement of Existing Laws.* At the urging of George Grenville, Finance Minister from 1763 to 1765, Parliament provided for stricter enforcement of existing laws. Customs inspectors were forced to be more diligent. *Writs of Assistance* were used more widely to search for smuggled goods, and the British navy was used to prevent smuggling. Persons accused of smuggling or otherwise violating the Acts of Trade were tried in British Admiralty Courts, where there was no trial by jury, instead of in colonial courts.

3. *New Taxes.* Under Grenville and his successor, Townshend, a series of new taxes and restrictions were enacted *(Grenville and Townshend Programs).*

(a) The *Sugar Act* (1764) lowered duties on foreign molasses, to reduce the temptation to smuggle; but it increased duties on refined sugar and imposed new duties on wines, silks, and other formerly duty-free articles.

(b) The *Currency Act* (1764) forbade the issuance of paper money by the colonies and ordered payment of debts in gold and silver.

(c) The *Quartering Act* (1765) forced the colonists to furnish food, supplies, and lodgings for British troops where there was insufficient barrack space.

(d) The *Stamp Act* (1765) required the purchase of stamps for all newspapers, licenses, pamphlets, and legal and commercial documents. (It was the first attempt to raise revenue *within* the colonies by a *direct tax.*)

(e) The *Townshend Acts* (1767) imposed import duties on tea, paper, glass, and paint, after the repeal of the Stamp Act in 1766.

4. *Restrictions on Colonial Governments.* In an effort to restrict the power of colonial governments, Parliament took steps to strengthen the hands of royal governors. **(a)** Ten thousand British troops were stationed in and around large cities like New York and Boston. **(b)** Cases involving violations of British laws were shifted from colonial to British courts. **(c)** Starting in 1767, under the Townshend Acts, governors and judges were paid by the Crown, rather than by the colonies. **(d)** From time to time colonial legislatures were suspended, for example, when the New York Legislature protested the quartering of troops in the colony in 1767.

American Resistance to the New Colonial Policy. Americans were at first angered, and then infuriated by the increased British controls, which began during a postwar depression.

1. *Antagonism to the New Program.* Almost all Americans were in one way or another adversely affected by the New Colonial Policy. **(a)** Planters, farmers, and frontiersmen were bitter over restrictions on westward expansion. **(b)** Lawyers, editors, printers, and businessmen, the most outspoken groups in the colonies, were vexed by the stamp tax. **(c)** Merchants and

Southern planters were especially irritated by the new taxes on imports. **(d)** Colonial legislators resented the attempts to increase the powers of the royal governors. **(e)** Householders were incensed over the possibility of the quartering of troops in their own homes. **(f)** Colonists everywhere were embittered over British attempts to meddle in internal colonial affairs.

2. *Measures Taken to Oppose the British Program.* The colonists resisted the new program at every step.

(a) They persisted in disobeying British laws. Smuggling and westward expansion continued.

(b) Protests against violations of American rights were sent to Parliament. The colonists argued that their rights as Englishmen were being infringed, and that there could be "no taxation without representation."

(c) A new spirit of intercolonial cooperation developed. Nine colonies sent representatives to the *Stamp Act Congress* (October, 1765) in New York. This Congress drew up a resolution protesting the Stamp Act, and organized a boycott of British goods. In 1768 the Massachusetts Legislature issued a *Circular Letter* calling on all colonies to join in protesting the Townshend Acts.

(d) Led by the merchants, colonists organized *boycotts* of British-made goods, to make their opposition concrete. Boycotts were organized after the Stamp Act and Townshend Acts. The Stamp Act boycott was so effective that Parliament repealed that much disliked Act in 1766. (However, at the same time, Parliament passed the *Declaratory Act* (1766), restating the right of the Crown and Parliament to tax and govern the colonies.) So harmful to British interests was the boycott against the Townshend Acts of 1767, that Parliament repealed all taxes except the tax on tea.

(e) Colonial opposition also resulted in occasional violence. The *Sons of Liberty* and other patriot groups led riots against the hated stamp tax, burned stamps, damaged homes of customs officials, and tarred and feathered merchants who continued to trade with Britain. In 1770, the first clash between Americans and British troops occurred, the so-called *Boston Massacre.* British troops stationed in Boston were so angered by a jeering mob of Bostonians that they lost their heads and fired into the crowd, killing five Americans.

Steps Leading to the Outbreak of Revolution. The passage of a new *Tea Act* in 1773 started a series of events which led directly to the American Revolution.

1. *A Period of Calm, 1770-73.* After the repeal of the Townshend Acts in 1770, the boycott of British goods (except on tea) was called off, and feeling between the colonists and mother country grew less tense. Nevertheless, friction did break out from time to time; for example, the *Gaspée,* a British revenue cutter engaged in tracking down smugglers, was burned off Rhode Island in 1772.

2. *The Radicals Organize.* Most colonists, like Benjamin Franklin, were *"moderates"* who were willing to forgive Britain for her past mistakes and resume normal relations. Others, led by Samuel Adams of Massachusetts and Patrick Henry of Virginia, urged continued resistance, emphasized defense of colonial rights, and laid plans for future action. These *"radicals"* formed *Committees of Correspondence* (first organized by Samuel Adams in Massachusetts in 1772) to keep in touch with one another. The *Sons of Liberty* and *Daughters of Liberty* met frequently and continued to organize the boycott on tea.

3. *The Boston Tea Party (1773).* At the urging of the new Prime Minister, Lord North, and his followers, Parliament tried to help the British East India Company sell its surplus tea in America by exempting it from the usual export tax and giving it a monopoly on the transport and sale of tea to America. All tea brought into the colonies was to be subject to a small import duty (*Tea Act* of 1773). Although this law made it possible for the Company to sell tea at a lower price than tea smuggled into the colonies from Holland and France, the colonists resented the duty and reacted violently. In Boston and New York, ships carrying tea were not allowed to enter the harbors. In other places, the colonists prevented the sale of British tea. In December, 1773, following a mass protest meeting, a group of men disguised as Indians climbed aboard a vessel of the East India Company in Boston harbor and dumped its tea into the water. This incident is known as the *Boston Tea Party.*

Courtesy of Culver Pictures, Inc.

An old print depicting the Boston Massacre — it is believed that the first man killed was a Negro, Crispus Attucks.

4. *The Intolerable Acts (1774).* As a result of the Boston Tea Party, the British government decided to punish not only Boston but all of Massachusetts as an example to the other colonies. To this end, it passed a series of laws which became known as the *Intolerable Acts* or *Coercive Acts.*

(*a*) The port of Boston was closed to shipping until the colony paid for the destroyed tea.

(*b*) The privileges of self-government which Massachusetts had enjoyed were greatly limited. Town meetings were to be called only with the consent of the royal governor.

(*c*) British officials who might be accused of serious crimes in Massachusetts were to be tried in England, or in other colonies.

(*d*) Under a new *Quartering Act,* the colonists of Massachusetts were ordered to furnish lodging, food, and other supplies to British troops at 24-hours notice.

(*e*) The *Quebec Act* of 1774, passed at the same time as the Intolerable Acts, was not intended directly as a punitive measure, but it had the same effect. It extended the boundaries of the province of Quebec southward to the Ohio River and westward to the Mississippi. This antagonized Massachusetts and other colonies which had land claims in this western region.

5. *Unified Action by the Colonies.* The colonies took a major step toward an open break with Britain when they called the *First Continental Congress* in 1774, as a result of the Intolerable Acts. (See below.)

The First Continental Congress (1774). The angry reaction to the Intolerable Acts by all groups of colonists, moderates as well as radicals, united the colonies in opposition to British actions as never before. This new feeling of unity led to the calling of the *First Continental Congress.*

1. The Intolerable Acts convinced most colonists that the mother country was intent on destroying their political and economic liberty, and on limiting their future expansion. Even moderates, who had been willing to see England's point of view, felt that Britain had gone too far.

2. In September, 1774, fifty representatives from twelve colonies met in Philadelphia to protest the Intolerable Acts. Although the radicals dominated the Congress, they toned down their demands in order not to alienate the more moderate members.

3. The Congress took the following steps: **(a)** It denounced British treatment of Massachusetts. **(b)** It approved the *Suffolk Resolves,* which declared the Intolerable Acts void. **(c)** It advised the colonies to raise and train militias. **(d)** It drew up a *Declaration of Rights and Grievances,* demanding a return to the colonial status of 1763. **(e)** It drew up a plan (known as *The Association*) for a boycott of export and import trade with Britain. **(f)** The delegates also agreed to meet in 1775, as the *Second Continental Congress.*

The Fighting Begins. After the First Continental Congress both sides took measures which helped pave the way for the outbreak of actual fighting.

1. *The Build-up.* The positions of both parties hardened to the point where conflict became almost inevitable. **(a)** The *Association* was vigorously enforced by the radicals. **(b)** Patriotic *"Minutemen"* and other volunteer groups in each colony began to store arms and train for possible hostilities. **(c)** The King and Parliament took the attitude that the colonists were in a state of rebellion and must be subdued. They imposed additional restraints on colonial commerce. **(d)** The unyielding position of Parliament caused many Americans who had been neutral to join the ranks of the patriots.

2. *The First Battle.* The first battle of the Revolution occurred at a time when feeling was running high on both sides. General GAGE, the British military governor of Massachusetts, sent English troops to seize military supplies that were being collected by the colonists in Concord. Also, the "rebel leaders" JOHN HANCOCK and SAMUEL ADAMS were to be arrested. Warned of the British move by PAUL REVERE, WILLIAM DAWES, and others, colonial Minutemen attempted to stop the British at *Lexington* and at *Concord* (April 19, 1775). Several Americans were killed in the fighting. Although the British destroyed some military stores at Concord, they were attacked by the reinforced colonists while returning to Boston, and suffered heavy losses. Thus began the American Revolution.

Underlying Causes of the American Revolution. The complexity of historical developments is shown by the fact that historians give different answers to the question, "Which were the *most* important causes of the American Revolution?" Students must therefore examine a number of causes that have been suggested in order to interpret properly the events leading to the outbreak of the Revolution.

1. *Political Causes.* An increasing number of historians today believe that political and constitutional issues were the basic causes of the Revolution.

> (a) Britains and Americans differed over the way in which they viewed the Empire. The British felt that self-government was a favor, granted by the mother country, and one that could be taken away or restricted if necessary. The colonists, on the other hand, felt that self-government rested on "consent of the governed," and not upon royal favor. They believed that Britain could not curtail their "American Rights" (or what in their opinion were actually the Rights of Englishmen).

> (b) The British believed that Parliament had the right to pass legislation for all parts of the Empire. The colonists drew a distinction between legislation and taxation. They argued that Parliament could *legislate* for them, but could not *tax* them, since it did not represent them.

(c) The British believed in the theory of *virtual representation;* that is, each member of Parliament represented all Englishmen, no matter where they lived. The Americans believed in the theory of *actual representation.* They claimed that they were not represented in the British government because there was no member of Parliament selected from the 13 colonies to present their views there. The colonists insisted that the colonies were bound to England by personal union with the Crown, rather than by legislative union through Parliament. These differences explain why the colonists argued that there could be no taxation except through their own colonial legislatures.

2. *Economic Causes.* Other historians believe that economic factors must also be considered underlying causes of the Revolution. They argue that British restraints on colonial trade and manufacturing, particularly after the French and Indian War, aroused a growing dissatisfaction on the part of colonial merchants and planters and caused these groups to play a leading role in the events that led to the Revolution, particularly in the early stages of trouble.

3. *Social Causes.* Social factors also contributed to the discontent which made the social climate ripe for revolution.

(a) The non-propertied and poorer groups in the colonies were unhappy over the political, social, and economic privileges and opportunities of the wealthier classes. To them, revolution and independence meant the end of privileged classes, more land, and greater political and social equality.

(b) In addition, and given increasing consideration in recent years, is the fact that over the years, the colonies had developed an independent point of view, or national consciousness, all their own. Though content to remain part of the Empire, with personal loyalty to the Crown, American colonists saw less and less reason for being governed by a mother country over 3000 miles away, which, in their opinion, knew and cared little about the special problems of living in the New World. John Adams, second President of the United States, had this in mind when he later said, "The Revolution was effected before the war commenced . . . The Revolution was in the hearts and minds of the people."

4. *Unwillingness to Compromise.* A number of historians have pointed to psychological factors that in their opinion were most important in bringing on the Revolution. They argue that the colonists and the mother country drifted into hostilities between 1763 and 1775 because they misunderstood each other's point of view, and because they would not compromise.

(a) Most Americans did not realize, or were not willing to understand, that the *Grenville Program* and the *Townshend Acts* were basically attempts to make the colonies share the costs of their own government and protection, rather than attempts to punish or discriminate against them.

(b) The King and most members of Parliament did not understand that the majority of colonists, even as late as 1775, were loyal subjects who insisted only on what they had come to believe were their established rights and principles.

(c) The desire of the more radical leaders and groups among the colonists to resist British measures with force and violence together with their anti-British "propaganda" made it difficult for their English friends, like Burke and Pitt, to get Parliament to adopt a conciliatory attitude.

(d) The mistaken belief of King George III and his supporters that the colonists were in open rebellion after the Boston Tea Party led to punitive measures (*e.g.,* the Intolerable Acts) which only served to unite the colonists in firmer resistance.

(e) Throughout the period, Britain insisted upon the *duties* of colonists; while the colonists insisted upon their *rights* as Englishmen. Misunderstandings such as these caused leaders on both sides to act out of injured pride and resentment, rather than with a reasonable desire to compromise.

REVIEW TEST (Chapter 3 — Part II)

Select the number preceding the word or expression that best completes each statement or answers each question.

1. One reason for England's abandonment of the policy of "salutary neglect" was (1) a desire to encourage American colonial manufacturing (2) a need to strengthen the British navy (3) the demonstrated ability of the colonies to look after themselves (4) the necessity of correcting defects in her system of colonial control

2. The colonists' main objection to the Proclamation of 1763 was that it (1) prohibited the issuance of paper money (2) discouraged settlement on the Western lands (3) increased the tax on sugar imported from the French West Indies (4) required the colonial authorities to provide housing for British troops stationed in America

3. At the time of the American Revolution, the King of England was (1) an absolute monarch (2) a limited monarch (3) a benevolent despot (4) a figurehead

4. The colonists' main objection to the Stamp Act was that it (1) discouraged trade with the French West Indies (2) hindered colonial manufacturing (3) infringed upon their rights as Englishmen (4) favored lawyers and editors at the expense of farmers

5. Which of the following punished the colonists of a single colony only? (1) Stamp Act (2) Molasses Act (3) Quebec Act (4) Intolerable Acts

6. The colonists opposed British taxation policies most effectively by (1) entering into nonimportation agreements (2) negotiating commercial agreements with France (3) using writs of assistance (4) demanding the recall of colonial governors

7. British retaliation to colonial resistance is best illustrated by the (1) Boston Tea Party (2) Intolerable Acts (3) Navigation Acts (4) Stamp Act

8. In which of the following pairs is the first event or development a cause of the second? (1) Boston Tea Party — passage of the Intolerable Acts (2) meeting of First Continental Congress — outbreak of the French and Indian War (3) Battle of Saratoga — adoption of the Declaration of Independence (4) Stamp Act Congress — enactment of the Navigation Acts

9. The chief factor that makes for sound interpretation of history is the (1) author's patriotism (2) weight of the evidence (3) approval of the government (4) trend of public opinion

10. Which is the least satisfactory explanation for the American Revolution? (1) differences in points of view (2) taxation without representation (3) growing interference with American economic life (4) England's desire to curtail the "rights of Englishmen"

Indicate the chronological order in which the events in each group occurred, by writing the numbers 1, 2, 3, in the appropriate spaces.

A
........Proclamation of 1763
........End of French and Indian War
........Sugar Act

B
........Navigation Acts
........Grenville Program
........Townshend Acts

C
........Stamp Act
........Stamp Act Congress
........Declaratory Act

D
........Formation of Committees of Correspondence
........Boston Massacre
........Boston Tea Party

E
........Battles of Lexington and Concord
........First Continental Congress
........Intolerable Acts

Essay Questions

1. "Historical change may not necessarily bring improvement." Show to what extent this statement is true with reference to England's adoption of a "new colonial policy" for the 13 colonies after the French and Indian War.

2. Discuss two reasons why the colonies felt they were justified in declaring their independence from England.

3. Show one way in which each of the following leaders helped bring on the American Revolution: Samuel Adams, James Otis, Patrick Henry, George Grenville, George III.

4. Explain three ways in which in 1775 the average Englishman's point of view on the causes of the American Revolution would probably have differed from that of the average colonist.

With the issuance of the *Declaration of Independence* on July 4, 1776, the American Revolution became the "War for Independence." This famous document affected not only the course of the Revolution, but has influenced the development of democracy ever since.

The Second Continental Congress. When the *Second Continental Congress* met in Philadelphia in May, 1775, as had been planned the previous year, Boston was under siege by the New England militia, and Fort Ticonderoga had been captured by colonial forces led by Ethan Allen.

1. *First Actions.* The Congress took immediate measures to do something about the crisis, despite conservative opposition to any steps which might worsen relations between Britain and the colonies. **(a)** It assumed control of colonial affairs. **(b)** It sent the "Olive Branch" petition to the King, asking him to make attempts at reconciliation by curbing Parliament. **(c)** It declared the colonies' intention to fight and began to raise and equip an army. **(d)** It appointed GEORGE WASHINGTON Commander-in-Chief of the army. **(e)** It issued a *"Declaration of Causes for Taking Up Arms."* **(f)** On July 4, 1776, it adopted the *Declaration of Independence*.

2. *Importance.* The Second Continental Congress acted as the government for the colonies during the Revolution, from 1775 to 1781. It recruited and equipped an army, negotiated an alliance with France, borrowed money, and sent representatives abroad to secure foreign assistance. It also drafted the *Articles of Confederation,* which set up a new government for the colonies in 1781.

The Growth of a Desire for Independence. When hostilities began at Lexington and Concord, most colonists wanted no more than a settlement of their differences with England and an end to burdensome restrictions. Several factors, however, were at work which led to a growing desire for complete independence.

1. Continued fighting and bloodshed made relations between Britain and the colonies increasingly bitter and uncompromising. In this regard, the colonists were particularly angered by the use of *Hessian* (German) soldiers, and by British attempts to encourage Indian raids against frontier communities.

2. Americans were encouraged to further resistance by the British evacuation of Boston early in 1776.

3. Colonial leaders came to realize that in order to negotiate treaties for foreign trade and assistance with France and other countries, it was necessary for them to be considered independent.

4. The publication and widespread popularity of the pamphlet *Common Sense,* by THOMAS PAINE, helped pave the way for the final severing of ties with the mother country. *Common Sense* urged open revolt against the "Royal Brute of England," and argued that it was absurd for an island to rule a continent.

The Declaration of Independence. The Second Continental Congress adopted the Declaration of Independence on July 4, 1776, after approving a motion to that effect made a month earlier by Richard Henry Lee. The Declaration was largely the work of THOMAS JEFFERSON, with some minor assistance by BENJAMIN FRANKLIN. This world-famous document consists of a statement of principles, a listing of grievances, and a formal declaration of independence. In drawing it up Jefferson drew heavily on the thinking of John Locke and other 18th-century philosophers of the "Enlightenment."

1. *Principles of the Declaration of Independence.* In the opening paragraphs of the Declaration, the framers set down the principles of democracy and human rights which guided their thinking. These principles are listed below:

(a) *Equality.* All men are created with equal rights. ("All men are created equal.")

(b) *Unalienable Rights.* Men have certain God-given rights. ("They are endowed by their Creator with certain unalienable rights, that among these are Life, Liberty, and the Pursuit of Happiness.")

(c) *Purpose of Government.* Governments are set up to protect these unalienable rights ("to secure these rights governments are instituted among men").

(d) *Consent of the Governed.* Just governments are servants of the people. They rest on the "consent of the governed."

(e) *Right of Revolution.* When governments become unjust, the people have the right, for serious and long-standing grievances, to overthrow them, and set up other governments. ("Whenever any form of Government becomes destructive of these ends, it is the right of the people to alter or abolish it and to institute a new Government . . .".)

2. *Statement of Grievances.* The philosophical opening of the Declaration is followed by a long list of 27 grievances against the King, including such actions as the quartering of troops, the suspension of colonial legislatures, and the levying of taxes without colonial consent. This listing makes up the longest portion of the document.

3. *The Formal Declaration of Independence.* The Declaration of Independence concludes by stating that because it has become impossible to preserve peace with Britain, after every possible attempt at compromise, "these United Colonies are, and of Right ought to be Free and Independent States."

4. *Significance of the Declaration.* In the sense that it was issued to rally support for the war and consequently lays all of the blame for the difficulties on the shoulders of the King, the Declaration of Independence was revolutionary propaganda. Nevertheless, it had both immediate and long-range importance.

(a) *Immediate Results.* The Declaration changed the aims of the war. What had started as a struggle for the redress of grievances now became a struggle for independence. The Declaration caused the King to declare the colonies in open rebellion, thereby forcing colonists to take sides for or against the patriot cause. It also made it possible for foreign nations to recognize openly the independence of the colonies and to come to their assistance.

(b) *Long-Range Effects of the Declaration.* The Declaration of Independence is considered one of the most important documents in world history. It served as a model for the later French Declaration of the Rights of Man, and it inspired the revolutionists who helped the Spanish-American colonies break away from Spain in the early 19th century. It has continually guided the thinking of fighters for freedom, including nationalist leaders in Asia and Africa during the 20th century. Also it has become the cornerstone of American democratic tradition.

A historic moment — John Hancock signing the Declaration of Independence.

REVIEW TEST (Chapter 3 — Part III)

Select the number preceding the word or expression that best completes each statement or answers each question.

1. The significance of Thomas Paine's *Common Sense* was that it (1) suggested a plan of reconciliation with England (2) outlined a "common sense" approach to commonwealth status (3) argued that protests of the colonies should be made only to Parliament (4) pointed out how illogical it would be to continue loyalty to the king

2. All are quotations from the Declaration of Independence *except* (1) "nor shall any person . . . be deprived of life, liberty, or property without due process of law" (2) "Governments are instituted among men deriving their just powers from the consent of the governed" (3) ". . . that whenever any form of Government becomes destructive of these ends, it is the right of the people to alter or to abolish it. . . ." (4) "We hold these truths to be self evident, that all men are created equal . . ."

3. Which of the following is specifically mentioned in the Declaration of Independence as an unalienable right? (1) pursuit of happiness (2) private property (3) office-holding (4) suffrage

4. Which is *not* a part of the Declaration of Independence? (1) a statement of the rights of the individual (2) a listing of the grievances against the King (3) a framework of the type of government desired (4) an assertion of the freedom of the colonies

5. The chief significance of the Declaration of Independence is that it (1) expressed for the first time the right of the people to petition the government (2) attracted thousands of Loyalists to the colonial cause (3) enlisted the support of the French government for the American Revolution (4) furnished a body of ideals for future generations

All of the following headlines could have appeared in colonial newspapers in 1775–77. Number them in chronological order.

WASHINGTON APPOINTED COMMANDER-IN-CHIEF

SECOND CONTINENTAL CONGRESS CONVENES

ARTICLES OF CONFEDERATION DRAFTED

JEFFERSON HEADS COMMITTEE TO DRAFT DECLARATION OF INDEPENDENCE

ALLEN AND GREEN MOUNTAIN BOYS CAPTURE TICONDEROGA

Essay Questions

1. (a) State four principles of the Declaration of Independence. (b) For each of two of these principles give a recent example of an event in the United States that shows the principle is still alive today.

2. Giving specific illustrations, show how one foreign government today pursues policies contrary to the principles of the Declaration of Independence.

3. In what sense can the principles of the Declaration be described as part of America's debt to European thought?

4. Why is the Declaration of Independence considered one of the most important documents in world history?

Part IV — THE AMERICAN REVOLUTION

Because the American Revolution created a new nation, later to become the United States of America, it is important to understand its nature and results.

Military Highlights of the American Revolution. The American Revolution lasted from 1775 to 1781. Hostilities ended with American victory at Yorktown.

1. *Opening Events (1775).* Armed conflict began at Lexington and Concord in April, 1775. The colonists forced the British back to Boston and laid siege to that city. Early in this campaign the British drove the colonials off a hill overlooking the city. Although they lost this famous *Battle of Bunker Hill* (really Breed's Hill), the Americans gave a good account of themselves and found that they could stand up against regular British troops. In 1775, the Americans captured the fortresses of *Ticonderoga* and *Crown Point* along the Lake George-Lake Champlain frontier. Later in the same year American generals BENEDICT ARNOLD and RICHARD MONTGOMERY tried unsuccessfully to take Canada.

2. *Washington's Early Victories and Defeats (1776).* Several noteworthy military actions occurred during 1776. **(a)** Under pressure by George Washington and the American army, General William Howe and the British troops were forced to withdraw from Boston and to transfer their activities from New England to the Middle colonies. **(b)** After the Declaration of Independence, the British landed a large army of 30,000 men to reinforce their troops in America. **(c)** The British captured New York City after the *Battle of Long Island,* and forced Washington's army to retreat across the Hudson into New Jersey, and then into Pennsylvania. **(d)** Washington recrossed the Delaware during a snowstorm on Christmas night, caught the British by surprise, and defeated them at *Trenton* and at *Princeton.*

3. *The Battle of Saratoga — Turning Point of the War (1777).* The British planned a three-pronged attack designed to separate New England from the rest of the colonies and give Britain control of the Hudson River and New York State. The plan suffered from poor execution and bungling on the parts of General HOWE, General BURGOYNE, and Colonel ST. LEGER. Thus, in October, 1777, General Gates was able to defeat Burgoyne in the crucial *Battle of Saratoga.* This battle is considered the turning point of the Revolution because it raised American morale and resulted in the signing of a treaty with France against Britain. France, eager to revenge her defeat in the French and Indian War, provided invaluable assistance to the colonies in supplying men, ships, and matériel. Spain and Holland also declared war on Great Britain.

4. *Military Stalemate (1778-80).* Although each side won victories between 1778 and 1780, neither was able to obtain a decisive advantage.

(a) *Valley Forge.* After spending a bitter winter of suffering and hardship at *Valley Forge, Pennsylvania,* in 1777-78, Washington established his headquarters in New Jersey. For the next three years he fought no major engagements. Meanwhile, New York City remained in British hands.

(b) *The War in the West.* During 1778-79, GEORGE ROGERS CLARK led a small American detachment into the *Northwest Territory* (north of the Ohio River) and after an amazing march through swamps and wilderness drove the British out of the strongholds of Kaskaskia and Vincennes. His victories ended the Indian menace and British control of the region.

(c) *War on the Sea.* In the same period, Americans were encouraged by the successful actions of American sea captains, like JOHN PAUL JONES and JOHN BARRY, against British naval vessels. In addition, American *privateers,* operating out of American and French ports, inflicted much damage on British merchant (supply) ships. (A privateer is a privately-owned vessel granted permission to attack enemy commerce.)

(d) *War in the South.* During the last years of the Revolution, the fighting shifted to the South. The British evacuated Philadelphia in 1778 and turned their attention to the Southern colonies, where pro-British sentiment was strong. Despite successes in Georgia, the Carolinas, and Virginia, the British were not able to control much territory. They were often defeated by colonial guerrilla leaders such as MARION, SUMTER, and PICKENS, and they were fatigued by the skillful retreats of General GREENE.

5. *Final Victory at Yorktown (1781).* The defeat of British General CORNWALLIS and his army at *Yorktown, Virginia,* in 1781, ended the major military action of the War for Independence. In the fall of 1781, Cornwallis was trapped on the Yorktown Peninsula by American and French troops led by WASHINGTON, ROCHAMBEAU, and LAFAYETTE. When a French fleet under Admiral DE GRASSE landed additional troops and beat off an English naval force sent to land British reinforcements, Cornwallis was forced to surrender (October 19, 1781). Because France, Spain, and Holland continued to fight Britain abroad, the final *Treaty of Paris,* ending the war, was not signed until 1783.

Problems Faced by the Americans During the Revolution. In order to fight the Revolution, the colonists had to face many hardships and to find solutions to political, financial, and military problems.

1. *The Problem of the Tories or Loyalists.* It has been estimated that at the time of the Declaration of Independence, only about one-third of the colonists actively supported the war. They came mainly from among the small farmers, craftsmen, Southern planters, and frontiersmen. Another third, the Loyalists or Tories, who came mainly from among the larger Northern landowners, wealthy merchants, rich professionals, and members of the Anglican Church, believed that more was to be gained by remaining under British control than by breaking away. (The remaining third of the colonists, at least passively, accepted the idea of independence.)

(a) During the war many Tories plotted against the American forces and gave aid to the British. Other Tories tried to stay neutral.

(b) The Tories were considered traitors to the American cause and were dealt with harshly. Thousands fled to Canada or otherwise left the colonies, and Tory property was confiscated by many of the states. (It should be noted that after the Declaration of Independence the colonies became independent states.)

(c) Because of the struggle between Tories and Patriots, the American Revolution has been called a civil war as well as a war for independence.

2. *The Problem of Financing the Revolution.* Since the Second Continental Congress did not have the power to levy taxes, raising money to finance the Revolution was a major problem. Congress attempted to solve this problem in several ways. (a) It issued paper money (*Continental currency*), which depreciated rapidly in value because it was not backed by gold or silver. (b) It asked the states for money, but received very little. (c) It issued bonds. (d) It borrowed about eight million dollars from France, Spain, and Holland. (e) It received financial support and assistance from patriotic Americans like ROBERT MORRIS, who became Superintendent of Finance, and HAYM SALOMON, who contributed his fortune to the American cause.

3. *Maintaining an Army.* Raising and keeping an army in the field was a difficult task during the Revolution. The American forces consisted of a small *Continental Army* which seldom numbered more than 5000 men. This was reinforced from time to time by soldiers from the *state militias*. In the early years of the war especially, the army was inexperienced and lacked competent leaders. The soldiers were frequently short of food and supplies, and on occasions mutinied when Congress could not pay them. Militiamen were usually farmers, who went home after a few months of service. For these reasons Washington at no time had more than about 14,000 men under his command, and usually far fewer than that. Washington's efforts to get men and supplies were continually hampered by opposition both in and out of Congress.

Reasons for the American Victory. The Americans won the Revolution in spite of considerable British advantages.

1. *British Advantages.* Several factors favored the British in the struggle. (a) As we have seen, the colonists were divided in their support of independence. (b) Britain had far greater financial resources with which to obtain supplies and soldiers. (c) The British troops and officers were better

trained and disciplined than the American soldiers, particularly at the beginning of the war. **(d)** For most of the war Britain controlled the seas, and, at one time or another, most of the principal colonial ports.

2. *American Advantages.* The following factors helped bring victory to the colonists, in spite of Britain's superior strength.

> (*a*) Britain was unable to wage the war efficiently. **(1)** After 1778 she was fighting France, Holland, Spain, and the colonies all at the same time, and in different parts of the world. **(2)** Her distance from the scene of battle made it difficult to communicate with her commanders, and also to send supplies and reinforcements. **(3)** Inefficiency and corruption in the British government caused confusion and delays. **(4)** The war was not very popular with the British people, and many leaders in Parliament sympathized with the colonists. **(5)** The British were unable to crush colonial resistance because they were unable to control more than a few areas and key cities at any one time.

> (*b*) Since their homes and families were in danger, American soldiers fought with a patriotic spirit which the British soldiers lacked. Some British generals, like Sir William Howe, felt more friendly than hostile to the colonists. Also, Britain's hired soldiers were unwilling to endure the type of suffering faced by Washington and his men at Valley Forge.

> (*c*) As the war went on, the Americans developed able officers, like NATHANAEL GREENE and GEORGE ROGERS CLARK. In addition, foreign officers, like Marquis LAFAYETTE of France, Baron VON STEUBEN of Prussia, and THADDEUS KOSCIUSKO and CASIMIR PULASKI of Poland, brought considerable skill and experience to the colonial army.

> (*d*) George Washington became a powerful symbol of the colonies' determination to win. His devotion to duty earned him the respect of his soldiers, and he was always able to keep an army in the field despite enormous hardships. Also, he persevered in spite of plots against his leadership and traitorous acts among his officers (such as Benedict Arnold's attempt to turn West Point over to the British in 1779).

> (*e*) A major factor in the defeat of the British was the extensive aid in money, supplies, men, and naval support given by France to the colonies.

The Treaty of Paris (1783). The *Treaty of Paris* ended the war. It was skillfully negotiated for America by BENJAMIN FRANKLIN, JOHN ADAMS, and JOHN JAY, who were sent as peace commissioners. Under its terms:

1. American independence was recognized by Britain.

2. The United States was granted the territory bounded by the Great Lakes on the north, the Mississippi River on the west, and the 31st parallel on the south (the northern boundary of Florida, which Britain ceded back to Spain).

3. American rights to fish off the coast of Newfoundland were recognized.

4. Congress promised it would recommend that the states restore confiscated property to the Loyalists.

5. Congress agreed to permit Britain to recover debts owed by Americans to British creditors.

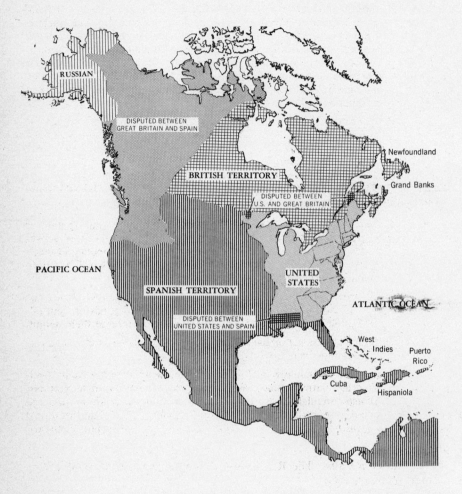

This map shows the United States in 1783 after the Treaty of Paris. As indicated, the young country had several territorial disputes. These were soon to involve the new government in serious foreign problems.

Results of the American Revolution. The American Revolution produced or speeded up such important changes in the political, economic, and social life of the colonies that it has been referred to as a *social movement* as well as a military struggle.

1. *Political Results.* The Revolution resulted in important changes in both state and national governments.

    (a) The 13 colonies became independent states.

    (b) *New state constitutions* were drawn up in most states. They contained noteworthy democratic features. **(1)** *Bills of rights* were included, protecting personal rights, such as trial by jury and freedom from unreasonable search and seizure. **(2)** The state governments were divided into separate executive, legislative, and judicial branches, as in colonial times. **(3)** The powers of the governors were limited. **(4)** Most states organized two-house (bicameral) legislatures, both chosen by popular vote. **(5)** Western communities were given increased representation in the assemblies.

    (c) A government for the new nation was established under a constitution called the *Articles of Confederation.* The Articles provided for a union of states with a central government of limited powers *(weak central government).*

2. *Economic Results.* Noteworthy changes occurred in the economic life of the country.

    (a) Due to the overissuance of unbacked paper currency during the war by both the states and the central government, *inflation* became rampant and caused much hardship. Prices soared and money declined sharply in value. (The common expression, "Not worth a Continental," resulted from this experience.)

    (b) American *industry and manufacturing were stimulated* during the war, because the supply of English manufactured goods was cut off. New industries developed, and existing ones increased their output.

    (c) With the removal of the British restraints, *American trade* with foreign nations *increased.*

    (d) The Revolution resulted in *more democratic distribution of land.* Tory and Crown estates were broken up and sold in smaller sections. Old semi-feudal forms of land inheritance such as *primogeniture* and *entail* were abolished. The *quitrent* system was ended, and *westward expansion* was resumed, enabling more farmers to obtain their own land.

3. *Social Results.* The Revolution also produced a number of democratic social changes.

    (a) Laws prescribing the death penalty for minor offenses were repealed, and penalties for non-payment of debts were made less harsh.

    (b) The further importation of slaves was ended in most states, and provisions for abolition or gradual emancipation of slaves were made in most Northern states, particularly during the early 19th century.

    (c) Religious toleration made further advances during and after the Revolution. Church and state were separated in most states, dissenting sects won religious freedom, and in many states religious qualifications for office-holding were ended.

(d) With the removal of British officials and Loyalist influence, class distinctions became less important and less noticeable.

4. *A Moderate Revolution.* Unlike other great revolutions, such as the French Revolution of 1789 and the Russian Revolution of 1917, the American Revolution was a moderate and even a conservative one. The existing political and economic system, though changed in some respects, was not overthrown. Aside from the mistreatment of many Tories, there was no attack upon the lives and property of the wealthier classes. Though there were numerous democratic advances, a number of undemocratic practices were allowed to continue, in many cases until much later. These included property qualifications for voting and office-holding, indentured servitude, and slavery.

5. *Effects of the Revolution Abroad.* The American Revolution established the first great republic of modern times based on the principles of *consent of the governed, personal liberty,* and *equality of opportunity.* It was the first successful revolt in modern times of a colony against its mother country, and it had important consequences abroad. In England it helped weaken the king's control over Parliament, and later it served as an example for a rebellion in Canada (1837) which resulted in the development of the *dominion system* of self-government within the British Empire. It served also as an example for the French Revolutionists of 1789, and for the rebellion of Spain's South American colonies in the 19th century.

REVIEW TEST (Chapter 3 — Part IV)

Select the number preceding the word or expression that best completes each statement or answers each question.

1. One reason why many Southern plantation owners favored the American Revolution was that they (1) disliked British control over the slave trade (2) hoped to escape payment of debts owed to British bankers (3) feared that the British would abolish slavery (4) opposed Britain's high tariff policies

2. One reason why France came to our aid during the Revolutionary War was that (1) the French government was devoted to democratic ideals (2) the Estates General forced the King to help (3) the French expected to regain Louisiana (4) the French wanted revenge on England

3. The names Steuben, Lafayette, and Kosciusko are associated with (1) leadership of Hessian troops quartered in the American colonies (2) 17th-century nationalistic movements in Western Europe (3) foreign support for the North in the Civil War (4) foreign aid to Americans during the Revolutionary War

4. John Adams, Robert Morris, and Haym Solomon were alike in that they all (1) were immigrants from England (2) performed valuable nonmilitary service during the American Revolution (3) served as delegates to the Constitutional Convention (4) signed the Declaration of Independence

5. Why did the paper money issued during the American Revolution depreciate so rapidly? (1) Parliament declared it counterfeit. (2) There was no security behind it. (3) Before the war only gold and silver coins had been in circulation. (4) Congress could borrow no money abroad.

6. George Washington was to the American Revolution what Sun Yat-sen was to the Revolution in (1) China (2) Indonesia (3) Japan (4) Korea

7. What proportion of the American colonists is estimated to have wanted a complete break with England before the Declaration of Independence was issued? (1) about 10% (2) about one-third (3) about 50% (4) about two-thirds •

8. During the Revolution the average American patriot looked upon the Tories as (1) helpful allies (2) hired mercenaries (3) sympathetic neutralists (4) undeserving traitors

9. At the close of the American Revolution, which did *not* become one of the boundaries of the United States? (1) Great Lakes (2) Gulf of Mexico (3) Mississippi River (4) St. Lawrence River

10. What revolution in Europe was influenced most directly by our American Revolution? (1) Industrial Revolution (2) French Revolution (3) Glorious Revolution (4) Puritan Revolution

Correctly match the name of each military episode or battle in Column A with the item in Column B that is most clearly identified with it.

A	**B**
1. Yorktown	*a.* Bitter winter of suffering
2. Saratoga	*b.* Capture of New York City by British
3. Bunker Hill	*c.* Early defeat for the Americans
4. Valley Forge	*d.* Ended Indian menace in the Northwest territory
5. Long Island	*e.* Brought about final victory
	f. Turning point of the Revolution

Essay Questions

1. Explain an important contribution of each to American success in the Revolution: (a) John Paul Jones (b) Lafayette (c) Admiral de Grasse (d) Robert Morris (e) Haym Solomon (f) Thomas Jefferson (g) Baron von Steuben (h) George Rogers Clark.

2. By the end of the American Revolution George Washington had become "first in the hearts of his countrymen." Explain why.

3. Mention three problems faced by the Americans during the Revolution and show how each was handled.

4. Explain three factors that made possible colonial victory in the Revolution.

5. List two territorial, two political, two economic, and two social results of the American Revolution.

6. Why has the American Revolution been called: (a) a Civil War and (b) a conservative revolution?

CHAPTER 4

The Nation Under the Articles of Confederation

Between 1781 and 1789 the new nation was governed under the *Articles of Confederation*. Despite some solid achievements in this era, much dissatisfaction resulted from the weaknesses of the new government, and from its inability to cope with the serious economic and diplomatic problems it faced.

The Articles of Confederation. The type of government established by the Articles of Confederation reflected the experience of the colonies under British rule and the resulting distrust of a strong centralized government. The Articles also showed the effects of earlier attempts at union such as the *New England Confederation* (1643), the *Albany Congress* (1754), and the *First and Second Continental Congresses* (1774–81). Though drafted in 1777, the Articles were not adopted until 1781 because of Maryland's insistence that states with land claims between the Appalachian Mountains and the Mississippi give up such claims.

1. *Nature of the Union.* Under the Articles the 13 former colonies were united in a league of *sovereign* (independent) *states,* called *The United States of America.*

2. *The National Government.* The national government consisted only of a *Congress,* established to make laws for the good of the country as a whole. In Congress, each state was given one vote, but was permitted to send between two and seven delegates to represent it.

3. *Powers of Congress.* Congress was given the power to declare war, make peace, regulate the currency, borrow money, establish a postal system, manage Indian affairs, and settle disputes between the states.

4. *Laws and Amendments.* Laws could be passed only by an affirmative ("yes") vote of *nine* states. Amendments to the Articles required the consent of *all* the states.

Weaknesses of the Articles of Confederation. The long existence of the states as separate colonies and the fear that centralized rule might become tyrannical led the framers of the Articles to set up a government which lacked certain vital powers. Indeed, the Articles set up a confederation or a league of states, rather than a nation, as we understand the term.

1. *Lack of Executive and Judicial Departments.* Because no separate executive or judicial departments were created, the central government had

to depend upon state governments to enforce its laws, and upon state courts to interpret them.

2. *Tax Difficulties.* Congress lacked the power to levy taxes. To obtain necessary funds it had to ask the states to make contributions. Between 1781 and 1789, the states gave Congress less than one-fifth of what it requested. Because Congress could not raise money to support an army through taxation, it had to rely on the militias of the states for defense.

3. *Lack of Control Over Trade.* Congress also lacked the power to regulate interstate and foreign trade. Although it could make commercial treaties, it could not enforce them. Nor could it levy tariffs on imports or exports.

4. *Difficulties in Lawmaking.* It proved extremely difficult to get the agreement of nine states, needed to enact laws. This was complicated by the fact that there were seldom more than nine or ten states present in Congress to vote.

Achievements Under the Articles. In spite of its many shortcomings, the Confederation must be credited with several important achievements.

1. *Peace.* The Confederation negotiated the final peace settlement which brought the Revolution to a successful conclusion.

2. *Unity.* It kept the country together until a stronger central government was established.

3. *Adjustment of Conflicting Land Claims.* The Confederation succeeded in having the states surrender their Western land claims to the national government, and it created a national territorial domain north and west of the Ohio River (the *Northwest Territory*).

4. *Land Policy.* The Confederation established a land policy for the West which served as a valuable model for the future admission of territory into the Union. This is described below.

Land Ordinances of 1784 and 1785. These Ordinances, proposed by Thomas Jefferson, provided for dividing the Northwest Territory into states. The land was to be surveyed into townships six miles square. Each township was subdivided into 36 sections of 640 acres each, and the land was then sold by the section, half section (320 acres), quarter section (160 acres), or smaller units, at a dollar an acre. The money from the sale of one section in each township was to be set aside for schools.

The Northwest Ordinance. This law, passed in 1787, is considered the most significant of all the achievements under the Articles. The Ordinance set a lasting pattern for the organization of new territorial government. It provided for gradual self-government, the admission of new states, and the guarantee of personal liberties.

1. *Division into States.* The Northwest Ordinance provided for the eventual division of the Northwest Territory into from three to five states.

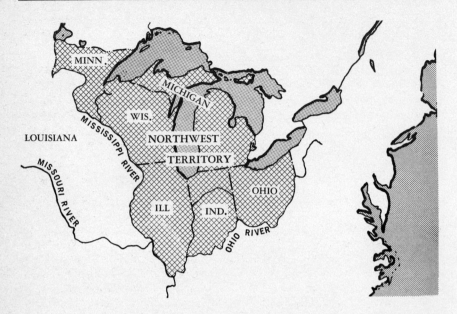

2. *Territorial Government.* When the Territory had 5000 free, adult, male inhabitants, it could establish a Territorial government consisting of an elected legislative house plus a legislative council, a governor, and judges, all appointed by Congress.

3. *Admission of New States.* As indicated, the Northwest Territory was to be divided into from three to five states. As soon as the population of one of these potential states reached 60,000, it could adopt a constitution, elect its own governing officials, and enter the Union on an equal footing with all other states. In this way, Ohio, Indiana, Illinois, Michigan, and Wisconsin entered the Union. (Note that part of what was later to become Minnesota was included in the Territory.)

4. *Democratic Guarantees.* The Ordinance also provided for other democratic practices, including the guarantee of freedom of speech and religion, trial by jury, the prohibition of slavery, and the encouragement of public education.

The Critical Period. The years 1781-87 have been referred to as the *Critical Period* of American history because the government was faced with such serious problems at home and abroad that many feared the Union would break up. These are discussed below.

NOTE: A number of historians nave recently argued that the *Critical Period* was not as "critical" as it is often painted. They feel that the problems faced by the young United States of America under the Articles were actually no more serious than those inevitably faced by any new or emerging nation, including the newly independent nations of Asia and Africa today.

Foreign Problems. The weaknesses of the national government resulted in a loss of prestige which led to serious disputes with foreign nations. (See map on page 50.)

1. *Trouble with Great Britain.* Ill-will between Britain and her former American colonies continued into the post-Revolutionary period. Britain refused to withdraw from the Northwest fur trading posts inside the American borders. She claimed that this was due to Congress's failure to get the states to repay debts owed to British merchants, and to halt confiscation of Loyalist property. Still resentful over the success of the Revolution, Britain also refused to send a minister to the United States, or to open her West Indian ports to American ships.

2. *Trouble with Spain.* Spain was anxious to prevent the future territorial and commercial expansion of the colonies, since this would threaten the Spanish empire in America. Taking advantage of her control of the island of New Orleans at the mouth of the Mississippi, Spain refused to allow Westerners the "right of deposit" — that is, the right to place their goods ashore at New Orleans or elsewhere, for transfer to ocean-going vessels, without payment of a duty. In addition, Spanish agents incited the Indians and encouraged plots against the United States. Western settlers were so angered at the failure of Congress to obtain the right of deposit that they threatened to secede from the Confederation, or to fight the Spanish themselves.

3. *Trouble with France.* During the Critical Period, the American government even lost the respect and good will of France. The French were angered by the inability of Congress to pay its debts, particularly since at that time the French government was on the verge of bankruptcy. French businessmen were unhappy over the fact that their sales in the American market were not increasing as much as had been expected.

4. *Trouble with the Barbary Pirates.* One of the clearest signs of the new nation's lack of prestige and military power was the seizure of American ships and the mistreatment of American sailors by the Barbary states of North Africa (Tunis, Tripoli, Morocco, and Algiers). Unable to secure funds either to pay tribute to the pirates or to build a navy to oppose them, Congress had to stand by helplessly while American shipping was driven from the Mediterranean.

Domestic Problems. American failures abroad were matched by difficulties at home, and Congress was equally helpless to solve these internal problems.

1. *Lack of Respect for the National Government.* The national government under the articles of Confederation failed to win respect from the states and from the people. Requests for funds were usually ignored by the states. Moreover, the powerless government was blamed for the economic hard times which followed the Revolution.

(a) *Businessmen* complained because Congress could not keep out British goods which were being "dumped" into American ports at low prices. Moreover, business in general was hampered by the fact that there was no standard currency. Congress did not mint coins of its own, and foreign coins were not uniform in weight or value. States issued unbacked paper money which usually dropped in value.

(b) *Shippers* were unhappy because Britain refused to allow the United States to trade with the West Indies, and because France and Spain closed several of their Western Hemisphere ports to American ships.

(c) *Bondholders and other creditors* lost faith in the government because it could not meet interest payments on the national debt, to say nothing of repaying the principal.

(d) *Lenders of money* were hurt by state laws which forced them to accept depreciated paper money in payment of debts.

2. *Quarrels Between the States.* State disputes and tariff wars made for much bitter feeling. Some states levied taxes on products "imported" from other states. For example, New York placed customs fees on garden produce from New Jersey. In return, New Jersey put a heavy tax on the Sandy Hook Lighthouse, owned by New York but within New Jersey's territorial limits.

3. *Shays' Rebellion (1786).* Dissatisfaction with the economic situation extended to debtors too. Most debtors at the time favored the issuance of cheap money, so that they could more easily pay their debts. When state legislatures controlled by property owners defeated bills for the issuance of paper money, angry debtors stormed courthouses and prevented judges from handing down judgments against persons who could not meet their financial obligations. In 1786, DANIEL SHAYS (an army officer during the Revolution) and a group of angry debtors forced several courts in Massachusetts to close. Though state troops put down *Shays' Rebellion,* as it was called, it demonstrated the bitter discontent of the times. Indeed, conservative groups in the country were so alarmed by this uprising and other similar incidents that they supported the movement for a strong central government which would be powerful enough to uphold the right of contract.

REVIEW TEST (Chapter 4)

Select the number preceding the word or expression that best completes each statement or answers each question.

1. Most state constitutions drafted after the Declaration of Independence contained provisions for (1) an elected legislature (2) universal manhood suffrage (3) the election of the upper house of the legislature by the lower house (4) gradual emancipation of slaves

2. A loose union of states by whose consent the central government operates is (1) a federal union (2) an autocracy (3) a confederation (4) a dictatorship

3. An important reason for the delay in the ratification of the Articles of Confederation was that (1) some states laid claim to Western lands (2) the Articles did not provide a Bill of Rights (3) there was no provision for an executive branch (4) each state delegation could cast only one vote

4. Under the Articles of Confederation the central government could do all of the following *except* (1) wage war (2) levy taxes (3) regulate currency (4) borrow money

5. Which of the following was true under the Articles of Confederation? (1) Amendments required a unanimous vote of the states. (2) Congress had the power to control interstate commerce. (3) The central government was supreme over the states. (4) The executive branch was stronger than the legislative.

6. An important accomplishment of the United States under the Articles of Confederation was (1) support of the principle of free education (2) free navigation of the Mississippi River (3) establishment of the domestic credit of the United States (4) recognition of the prestige of the United States by European governments

7. One reason why the Northwest Ordinance (1787) is important in United States history is that it established (1) a policy for the sale of public lands in small parcels (2) the pattern for national control of conservation (3) a democratic pattern for governing territories (4) the right of slave owners to take their slaves into any territories acquired in the future

8. Shays' Rebellion grew out of the inability of Congress under the Articles of Confederation to control (1) currency (2) foreign affairs (3) interstate commerce (4) disputes between the states

9. In 1786, which person would most likely have favored Shays' Rebellion? (1) a Boston merchant (2) a New England sea captain (3) a Massachusetts Senator (4) a Massachusetts farmer

10. During the Critical Period the issue of the "right of deposit" caused bad feelings between the United States and (1) France (2) Spain (3) the Barbary Pirates (4) Britain

State whether each of the following statements is true or false. If the statement is false, replace the word or phrase in **boldface type** *with one which will make it correct.*

1. Under the Articles each state was given **one** vote in Congress.

2. Under the Articles laws could not be passed unless **all** states gave their consent.

3. The **Northwest Ordinance** established a pattern for the survey and sale of Western lands.

4. During the Critical Period Americans were angered by the failure of **Britain** to withdraw from Northwest fur posts.

5. The Barbary Pirates preyed upon American commerce off the coast of **Mexico**.

Essay Questions

1. "The defects of the Articles of Confederation were in no way responsible for the hard times. It had not produced them, nor could the best government in the world have removed them."

(a) What defects of the government of the United States does the author of the above quotation have in mind?

(b) Giving evidence, explain why you agree or disagree with the point of view that is expressed.

2. Explain fully why the Northwest Ordinance is considered one of the most significant pieces of legislation ever enacted by the national government.

3. Describe briefly three achievements of the national government during the Critical Period, in addition to the passage of the Northwest Ordinance.

4. Give evidence to show that the national government lacked respect both at home and abroad during the Critical Period.

REVIEWING UNIT ONE

Select the number preceding the word or expression that best completes each statement or answers each question.

1. The Mayflower Compact was an important step in the growth of American democracy because it (1) guaranteed to the Puritans the right of trial by jury (2) provided a basis of self-government for the Plymouth colony (3) freed the indentured servants on the *Mayflower* (4) laid down the principle of separation of church and state

2. An important cultural achievement during the Colonial Period was the (1) development of a distinctive style of American music (2) printing of newspapers to influence public opinion (3) advance in medical science that eliminated superstition (4) establishment of apprenticeship schools for children of factory workers

3. As a result of the French and Indian War, Great Britain decided to (1) abolish her mercantile policy (2) allow the colonies representation in the English Parliament (3) encourage trade between her American colonies and the French West Indies (4) end her colonial policy of "salutary neglect"

4. The Proclamation Line of 1763 was intended primarily to (1) reduce friction between the Indian and the English colonists (2) punish the colonists for participating in the Boston Tea Party (3) permit the English Parliament to organize new colonies in the area west of the Appalachian Mountains (4) secure for the king a monopoly of the fur trade in the area west of the Proclamation Line

5. In dealing with the British during the period 1764–75, the American colonists were most effective when they used (1) "salutary neglect" (2) petitions (3) sabotage and violence (4) economic boycotts

6. All of the following ideas are expressed in the Declaration of Independence *except* (1) All men are created equal. (2) Government exists to protect man's rights to life, liberty, and the pursuit of happiness. (3) All people should have the right to vote. (4) Government rests upon the consent of the governed.

7. The principles of the Declaration of Independence can be described as (1) an extension of the thinking of John Locke (2) Hamilton's contribution to political philosophy (3) concepts of government inconsistent with accepted American ideals (4) a defense of our federal form of government

8. One reason for the importance of the Northwest Ordinance (1787) was that it provided for (1) the "right of deposit" (2) the sale of Western lands (3) free navigation of the Great Lakes (4) the eventual admission of new territories as equal states

9. Which best reflects the economic hardships of the "Critical Period"? (1) enforcement of the Navigation Acts (2) publication of *Common Sense* (3) adoption of the Northwest Ordinance (4) outbreak of Shays' Rebellion

10. Which is the most valid generalization that can be drawn from a study of the Colonial Period in United States history? (1) Domination by the Church of England was unacceptable to the 13 colonies. (2) Widespread unrest on the part of ordinary people is the secret of a successful revolution. (3) Economic boycott can be an effective means of protest. (4) Crushing taxation is very liable to bring about revolutionary discontent.

*On the time line, the letters **A** through **D** represent time intervals, as indicated. For each event listed below, give the letter of the time interval during which the event occurred.*

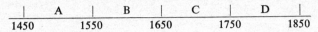

	A		B		C		D	
1450		1550		1650		1750		1850

1. Patroons begin to settle in the Hudson Valley.

2. Fundamental Orders of Connecticut drawn up.

3. Shays' Rebellion occurs.

4. Virginia established by London Company.

5. Townshend Acts repealed.

6. Verrazano explores Atlantic Coast.

7. England receives all French possessions in North America east of Mississippi River.

8. James Otis makes fiery protest against Writs of Assistance.

9. First public schools provided for in Massachusetts.

10. St. Augustine, oldest city in the United States, established by Spain.

Give a brief definition or explanation of each of the following historical terms:

Mercantilism	Chartered colony
Established church	Primogeniture
Unalienable rights	Home rule

Select the name listed below to which each of the following brief descriptions most closely applies.

SAMUEL ADAMS	NATHANIEL BACON
BENJAMIN FRANKLIN	CASIMIR PULASKI
WILLIAM PENN	GILBERT STUART
MARQUIS DE MONTCALM	BENEDICT ARNOLD
PATRICK HENRY	PAUL REVERE

FRANCIS MARION

1. I was a foreigner who helped the American cause during Revolutionary War.

2. During the Colonial Period I gained fame as a writer, diplomat, and scientist.

3. My portraits of George Washington and others brought me fame at home and abroad.

4. I was the radical leader who helped organize committees of correspondence.

5. I fought a successful guerrilla war against the British in the South during the Revolutionary War.

6. In the colony I founded for Quakers other religions were tolerated.

7. I led a rebellion against despotic government 100 years before the issuance of the Declaration of Independence.

8. I alerted the Minutemen to British troop movements against Concord.

9. The defeat of my army on the Plains of Abraham before Quebec was the turning point in the struggle between the French and English in America.

10. I was the able American general who defected to the English during the American Revolution.

Essay Questions

1. "The Spanish have long been criticized for their colonization of the New World. It is time to praise their achievements in addition to condemning their failures." Explain the meaning of this statement, and by giving supporting evidence indicate the extent to which you agree or disagree with the point of view expressed.

2. Show how the 13 colonies were all influenced by their English heritage with respect to each of three of the following: (1) law and court procedures (2) individual rights (3) structure of government (4) religious beliefs (5) architecture.

3. In the Colonial Period of United States history (1607–1776), both democratic and undemocratic practices existed side by side.

(a) Show how each of three of the following practices of this period contributed materially to the growth of democracy in the United States: (1) House of Burgesses (2) New England Town Meeting (3) founding of Rhode Island (4) the Zenger case (5) the Declaration of Independence.

(b) Describe three present-day practices or institutions that we have inherited from the Colonial Period.

4. Show one way in which each of three of the following contributed to the revolt of the American colonies against England: (1) geography (2) mercantilism (3) rights of Englishmen (4) Proclamation of 1763 (5) conflicts between royal governors and legislatures.

5. Discuss the significance of the American Revolution for (a) the United States and (b) the world.

6. In recent years some able historians have tried to prove that the Critical Period was not as critical as formerly thought. (a) Explain why the years 1781–87 are generally referred to as the Critical Period. (b) Explain the possible reasoning of those who argue that the Critical Period was not as critical as had been supposed.

7. Giving historical evidence, prove the truth of each of the following: (a) Radical leaders helped promote the outbreak of the American Revolution. (b) The Northwest Ordinance set up a procedure for territories to become states. (c) Foreign countries helped the 13 colonies win their independence.

CHAPTER 5

The Constitution
Is Drawn Up and Adopted

The *Constitution of the United States* was drawn up because of serious dissatisfaction with the Articles of Confederation. It was adopted mainly because of the efforts of a small group of determined men. It created a new form of government in which a strong central government shared powers with the states (a *federal union*).

The Calling of the Constitutional Convention. The weaknesses of the government of the Confederation, and the political, social, and economic difficulties of the time, led to the calling of a *Constitutional Convention* to amend the Articles.

1. *Dissatisfied Groups.* Throughout the 1780's different groups in the United States agitated for a stronger national government than the one provided under the Articles of Confederation. *Merchants* wanted a government that could regulate commerce and secure favorable treatment abroad; *manufacturers* hoped for a government that would erect tariff barriers against foreign goods; *land speculators* favored a government strong enough to keep the Indians in check and the frontier open for settlement; *holders of government bonds* wanted a government willing and able to pay its debts; *creditors* and *financiers* (money lenders) wanted a government that could establish a uniform, stable currency and curb the inflation caused by the paper money issued by the states.

2. *The Mount Vernon and Annapolis Conventions.* Attempts to secure more effective regulation of *interstate commerce* led to efforts to create a stronger form of government. Representatives from *Virginia, Maryland, Pennsylvania,* and *Delaware* met at Mount Vernon, Virginia, in 1785 to settle disputes over navigation on the Potomac River and Chesapeake Bay. At their recommendation, a second meeting of five states was held at Annapolis, Maryland, in 1786. At the *Annapolis Convention* Alexander Hamilton of New York urged that all the states meet in Philadelphia in May, 1787, to remedy the numerous defects of the Articles of Confederation.

The Constitutional Convention. The convention to revise the Articles of Confederation, popularly known as the *Constitutional Convention,* met in Philadelphia from May to September, 1787. Instead of revising the Articles, this assembly drew up the *Constitution of the United States of America.*

1. *The Delegates.* The 55 delegates to the Convention came from all the states except Rhode Island. They were chosen by their state legislatures.

> (a) Most of the delegates were men of distinction and talent, with long records of service to their states and country.

> (b) Most were conservative men of property, who wanted a stable society, and therefore a stronger government.

> (c) The leaders of the Convention included some of the most honored figures in American history. JAMES MADISON of Virginia has been called the "Father of the Constitution" because of the leadership he provided, and the detailed notes of the proceedings he took. GEORGE WASHINGTON of Virginia served as President of the Convention. BENJAMIN FRANKLIN, honored "elder statesman," gave wise and timely counsel which often made compromise possible when it seemed that the Convention might break up in disagreement. GOUVERNEUR MORRIS of Pennsylvania was largely responsible for the final wording of the Constitution. ALEXANDER HAMILTON of New York was a forceful advocate for setting up a strong central government. Later he was a leader in the fight for ratification.

> (d) Others who participated in the Convention with distinction included: EDMUND RANDOLPH and GEORGE MASON of Virginia, JAMES WILSON of Pennsylvania, LUTHER MARTIN of Maryland, WILLIAM PATERSON of New Jersey, and JOHN DICKINSON of Delaware.

2. *Absentees.* Some of the most noted men of the day were not present at the Constitutional Convention. THOMAS JEFFERSON, JOHN ADAMS, and JOHN JAY could not be there because of other public duties. SAMUEL ADAMS was not selected as a delegate. PATRICK HENRY was chosen as a delegate but refused to attend.

3. *Areas of Agreement of the Convention.* Although much time at the Convention was spent in ironing out differences, the members, as a group, agreed for the most part on the basic principles of what had to be done. **(a)** They agreed that the Articles of Confederation had to be scrapped rather than revised, and they decided to draw up a new basic law. **(b)** They believed that the new government should be *republican* in form, with a chief executive to be elected by the people or by their representatives. **(c)** They believed that the ultimate source of authority should be the people themselves *(popular sovereignty),* but they also wanted to be sure that property rights and minority rights would be protected. **(d)** They believed that the more conservative or stable elements in the nation should be in a position, through the government, to check possible "excesses of democracy." **(e)** The delegates wanted a *strong central government* that would have effective power to tax and to regulate interstate and foreign commerce. **(f)** They were in favor of a government in which powers would be divided among *executive, legislative,* and *judicial* branches in such a way that no single branch could become excessively strong.

The Compromises of the Constitution. While the members of the Constitutional Convention agreed on the general type of government they wanted, they often disagreed sharply on how best to achieve their purposes. Many of these differences of opinion had to be adjusted by compromise. For this reason, the Constitution has been called a *"bundle of compromises."* The following chart outlines three important compromises of the Constitution, dealing with problems of the nature of the national legislature, representation, the slave trade, commerce, and taxation. Other important compromises resulted in the electoral system of electing the President (see page 97), and the nature of the division of power between the national government and the states (see page 75).

CONSTITUTIONAL COMPROMISES

NAME OF COMPROMISE	OPPOSING POINTS OF VIEW	FINAL AGREEMENTS
Great Compromise (Connecticut Compromise)	The *large states* favored a bicameral (two-house) legislature, with representation according to population (*Virginia Plan*). The *small states* wanted a unicameral (single-house) legislature, in which all states would have equal representation. (*New Jersey Plan*)	The Great Compromise provided for a two-house legislature. (1) In the lower house (*House of Representatives*) representation was to be based on population. (2) In the upper house (*Senate*) representation was to be equal for all states. NOTE: This famous compromise, considered the most important one at the Convention, was drawn up after several weeks of bitter debate.
Three-Fifths Compromise	The *slave states* wanted Negro slaves to be counted for purposes of representation in Congress, but *not* for taxation by the Federal government. The *free states* wanted the slaves to be counted for purposes of taxation, but *not* for representation.	The Three-Fifths Compromise provided that for *both* representation and taxation, five Negroes were to be counted as three whites.

[*Continued on p. 66*]

Compromise on Commerce, Taxation, and Slave Trade

The *North* wanted the new government to have full power to regulate all interstate and foreign commerce.

The *South* feared being outvoted on matters of trade regulation by the more populous Northern states. Southerners opposed taxes on exports since they depended on the sale abroad of tobacco and other staples. They did not want interference with the slave trade.

The Compromise on Commerce, Taxation, and Slave Trade provided for the following:

To satisfy the South:

(1) A two-thirds vote of the Senate was required for the ratification of treaties.

(2) No export taxes could be imposed by Congress.

(3) There was to be no interference with the slave trade for 20 years; duties on slaves brought into the country could be no more than $10 a head.

(4) Free states were to return fugitive (runaway) slaves to the slave states.

To satisfy the North:

It was agreed that Congress could regulate interstate commerce by a simple majority vote in Congress.

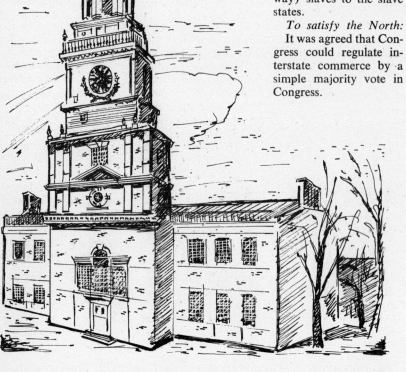

Constitution Hall in Philadelphia. Here the Constitutional Convention met from May to September, 1787, to draw up the Constitution of the United States of America.

ARTICLES OF CONFEDERATION AND CONSTITUTION COMPARED

As the following outline shows, the Constitution succeeded in remedying the major defects of the Articles and satisfied the great majority of the delegates at the Convention.

WEAKNESSES OF ARTICLES OF CONFEDERATION	HOW REMEDIED BY CONSTITUTION
There was no separate executive branch to carry out the laws of Congress.	A separate executive department was created, headed by the *President,* to enforce the Constitution and laws enacted under it, and to conduct foreign relations.
There was no national judiciary to handle offenses against national laws and disputes between states.	A judicial department was created, headed by a *Supreme Court,* to handle offenses against Federal laws, disputes between states, and cases involving foreign diplomats.
Congress did not have the power to levy taxes.	Congress was given the power to levy and collect taxes, thus freeing it from dependence upon financial contributions by the states.
Congress could not regulate interstate and foreign commerce.	Congress was given the power to regulate commerce between the states and with foreign nations, thus enabling it to make enforceable trade treaties with foreign nations.
The states, as well as Congress, had the power to coin money.	Only Congress was given the right to coin money and regulate its value, in order to provide a single national monetary standard.
Congress was in no position to support an army and navy, since it could not collect taxes. It had to depend on the support of state militias.	Congress's power to tax made it possible to create a national army and navy, thereby freeing the national government from dependence upon state militias in matters of security and defense. In addition, state militias were put under the control of Congress.
It was difficult to pass laws under the Articles, since an *affirmative vote of nine states was required.*	Under the Constitution the process of law-making was eased by the requirement that bills be passed by a *majority vote* of Congress in order to become laws.
The requirement of *unanimous consent* of all the states made amendment of the Articles almost impossible.	The Constitution provided for amendment by two-thirds of Congress and three-quarters of the states. This made change more possible.

The Struggle to Ratify the Constitution. The last article of the Constitution provided that it was to go into effect when ratified by conventions in *nine* states. Ratification was achieved in June, 1788, after a bitter struggle between the *Federalists,* who supported the Constitution, and the *Antifederalists,* who opposed it.

1. *Federalists vs. Antifederalists.* The struggle to ratify the Constitution took nearly a year.

> (a) The Federalists favored the Constitution. They felt that a strong central government would best serve the interests of the country without sacrificing the interests of the states. In general they came from the well-to-do and propertied classes. Among their leaders were ALEXANDER HAMILTON, JAMES MADISON, BENJAMIN FRANKLIN, and GEORGE WASHINGTON.

> (b) The Antifederalists opposed the Constitution. They feared that a strong central government might suppress the liberties of the people; they attacked the lack of a *Bill of Rights;* they argued that the Constitution favored the few rather than the many; they opposed the establishment of a sound currency as being against the interests of the majority of the people, who were farmers and usually debtors. In general, the Antifederalists were supported by the poorer classes, including debtors and small farmers. Antifederalist leaders included PATRICK HENRY, RICHARD HENRY LEE, SAMUEL ADAMS, and JOHN HANCOCK.

NOTE: One should not get the oversimplified impression that *all* wealthy people supported the proposed Constitution, and that *all* of the poorer people were against its adoption. For example, many workingmen in the cities supported the Constitution because they thought that it would lead to improved economic conditions and therefore to better employment opportunities and higher wages. On the other hand, a significant number of wealthy landowners in New York State and elsewhere opposed the new basic law because they feared it would lead to heavy taxes on their property. It should be noted, too, that many patriots supported the new Constitution because they considered it necessary for the survival of the nation, without regard to its effects on their own immediate economic interests.

2. *Advantages of the Federalists.* Although the Federalists were probably outnumbered by the Antifederalists, several factors gave the former the advantage in the battle for ratification.

> (a) The Federalists were better organized and more skilled in political affairs. In some states they promised to add a bill of rights after the Constitution was adopted.

> (b) As supporters of the Constitution, they were offering a *positive* program for the future — not merely defending the status quo.

> (c) The Federalists were better represented in state legislatures and state conventions. Many poorer citizens could not vote, and the newly settled backwoods regions were, in general, underrepresented.

(*d*) Federalist leaders such as Washington and Franklin commanded the respect of nearly all the people.

(*e*) The Federalists presented their views in a series of 85 essays, first printed in a New York newspaper and later collected in book form as *The Federalist*. These essays, written by Hamilton, Madison, and Jay, clearly explained the organization of the new government under the Constitution and forcefully presented its advantages. The effect was to convince many people that ratification would be best for the country as a whole. To this day, *The Federalist* is considered a brilliant political document and one of the best commentaries on the Constitution.

3. *Ratification.* Although the vote was close in such key states as Massachusetts, New York, and Virginia, the Constitution was ratified in June, 1788, when the convention of the ninth state voted for it. By July, 1788, eleven states had given their approval. North Carolina did not ratify until a Bill of Rights was added in 1789 (page 123). Rhode Island gave its consent in 1790, when it became clear that it would be treated as a foreign nation unless it came into the Union.

The New Government. The first elections under the Constitution were held in February, 1789. George Washington was elected President and John Adams, Vice President. Although the first Congress met on March 4, 1789, the new government did not actually get under way until Washington's inauguration on April 30.

REVIEW TEST (Chapter 5)

Select the number preceding the word or expression that best completes each statement or answers each question.

1. The Philadelphia Convention (1787) was called for the purpose of (1) choosing a President for the new republic (2) revising the Articles of Confederation (3) planning a campaign to suppress Shays' rebellion (4) drafting a new Constitution

2. Which occurred first? (1) Annapolis Convention (2) calling of the Constitutional Convention (3) adoption of the Articles of Confederation (4) publication of *The Federalist*

3. Which of the following pairs a state with the constitutional position it advocated in the Constitutional Convention? (1) New Jersey—states should be represented in the federal government on the basis of population (2) South Carolina—states must accept the supremacy of national action on every issue (3) Virginia—every state should be equally represented in a federal legislature (4) Connecticut—Congress should consist of two houses, one in which representation is based on population and one in which states are equally represented

4. At the Constitutional Convention, the Great Compromise was agreed upon to settle the controversy between the (1) slave states and free states (2) Southern states and Northern states (3) farm states and industrial states (4) large states and small states

5. Which of the following compromises made at the Constitutional Convention was later changed by a constitutional amendment? (1) the Great Compromise (2) the tariff compromise (3) the three-fifths compromise (4) the compromise on separation of powers

6. The delegates to the Constitutional Convention (1787) were strongly influenced in their decisions by their (1) faith in direct democracy (2) distrust of the states (3) fear of unchecked majorities (4) belief in compulsory education

7. The framers of the Constitution agreed on the need for (1) a weak central government (2) Congressional control of interstate commerce (3) amendments by three-quarters of Congress (4) state control of currency

8. The Constitution differed most from the Articles of Confederation in that the Constitution (1) gave greater power to the state governments (2) made the amendment process more difficult (3) gave greater power to the Federal government (4) changed the method of admitting new states into the Union

9. Most of the opposition to the federal Constitution in 1788 came from (1) bankers (2) farmers (3) lawyers (4) merchants

10. In some states, the supporters of the federal Constitution won the approval for the ratification of the Constitution by promising that after adoption (1) the vote would be extended to all free males (2) slavery would be abolished (3) a "bill of rights" would be added (4) the President would be elected directly by the voters

Select the name or item in each group that does **NOT** *belong with the others.*

1. Leaders at the Constitutional Convention: Benjamin Franklin, George Washington, Thomas Jefferson, Roger Sherman

2. Not present at the Constitutional Convention: John Adams, John Jay, Alexander Hamilton, Patrick Henry

3. Favored ratification of the Constitution: James Madison, Edmund Randolph, Gouverneur Morris, Samuel Adams

4. Antifederalist leaders: Patrick Henry, William Paterson, Samuel Adams, Richard Henry Lee

5. Wrote the Federalist Papers in defense of the Constitution: George Washington, Alexander Hamilton, James Madison, John Jay

Essay Questions

1. State briefly the role of each of the following at the Constitutional Convention: George Washington, Benjamin Franklin, James Madison, Alexander Hamilton, Gouverneur Morris.

2. Explain three important compromises at the Constitutional Convention.

3. "Though they compromised differences, most delegates to the Convention were in agreement on basic principles." Explain and give evidence of the truth of this statement.

4. Discuss two reasons for opposition to the proposed constitution and show how opposition to its ratification was overcome.

5. Show how the framers of the Constitution tried to overcome five weaknesses of the Articles.

The Government of the United States Under the Constitution

Governments are organized to promote justice, order, and liberty. The *Constitution of the United States* provides for a system of government that has served our country well for almost two hundred years. Under the Constitution the United States has grown and prospered in freedom. Since its adoption, the Constitution has served as a model for the basic laws of many new nations. Today it has become the oldest written constitution of any major nation.

Part I — THE ORIGINS AND PRINCIPLES OF THE CONSTITUTION

In order to understand the government of the United States one must begin by studying the basic ideas and principles of the Constitution.

Sources of the Constitution. In drawing up the Constitution the framers were guided by the experience and wisdom of the past.

1. *Colonial Experiences.* The Constitution shows the influence of colonial charters and colonial governments. It shows a preference for a republican form of government, rather than a monarchy. (A *republic* is a form of government in which the head of the government is an elected or nominated president, not an hereditary ruler.)

2. *State Constitutions.* Many parts of the Constitution can be traced back to provisions of the new state constitutions written during the American Revolution. For example, the Preamble resembles the introduction to the Massachusetts Constitution.

3. *Experiences under the Articles of Confederation.* The dissatisfaction with the weak central government provided by the Articles of Confederation caused the delegates at the Constitutional Convention to make provision for a strong central government. At the same time, the delegates selected from the Articles certain provisions which they found satisfactory, and included these in the Constitution. For example, in the Constitution, as in the Articles, there is a provision against accepting titles of nobility; also, Congress was given the power to fix standards of weights and measures.

4. *British Customs and Traditions.* The delegates to the Convention were also influenced by British customs and traditions, including *common law* (law based on custom and precedent), the *jury system,* and the great *charters of English liberty* — the *Magna Carta* (1215), the *Petition of Right* (1628), and the *Bill of Rights* (1689).

5. *Political Philosophers.* Finally, the Constitution shows the influence of the thinking of outstanding 17th- and 18th-century English and French philosophers. The founding fathers were in agreement with the theory of *natural rights* and the idea of *representative government,* as advocated by LOCKE. They accepted the idea of *separation of government* into executive, legislative, and judicial branches, as outlined by MONTESQUIEU. They were in accord with the idea of *popular sovereignty,* as championed by ROUSSEAU.

Underlying Principles of United States Government. Government in the United States rests upon certain basic principles expressed in the Constitution, and reinforced by practice.

1. *Popular Sovereignty.* Sovereignty in government means supreme power or authority. Under the Articles of Confederation sovereignty was placed in the hands of the states. Under the Constitution it is put into the hands of the people. The principle of popular sovereignty is set forth clearly in the Preamble, or introduction to the Constitution, as follows:

> "We, the people of the United States . . . do ordain and establish this Constitution for the United States of America."

NOTE: Since the adoption of the Constitution, disputes have arisen from time to time between supporters of the doctrine of *nationalism,* who hold that the people of the *nation as a whole* are sovereign, and the advocates of the doctrine of *states' rights,* who believe that the people are sovereign *within each state.* (Other aspects of these doctrines will be explored later.)

2. *Limited Government.* In order to prevent tyranny and abuse of the liberties of the people, the makers of the Constitution limited as well as defined the powers of the national and state governments. **(a)** The organization of the national government, as well as the powers given and denied to the state and national governments, are set forth in written form (the Constitution is a *written* constitution.) **(b)** The three branches of government are separated *(separation of powers),* and each is given power to prevent the others from becoming too powerful *(checks and balances).* **(c)** Individual liberties and personal rights are safeguarded against encroachment by federal and state governments by a *written* "Bill of Rights."

3. *Representative Government.* The Constitution established a *representative democracy,* in which the government is run by representatives chosen by the people directly or indirectly.

4. *Federalism.* In order to retain the states as important parts of the government, and at the same time unite the nation into a powerful union, the framers of the Constitution built a *federal union.* Under the principle of *federalism,* the states have the powers necessary to take care of local problems, while the national or Federal government has the powers necessary to deal with problems of the nation as a whole. This is also called *division of powers.*

5. *Supremacy of Civilian over Military Authority.* Because they believed that military power and despotism (tyranny) were closely related, the framers of the Constitution provided for civilian control of the military establishment. Under this principle of *civilian supremacy*: **(a)** Only Congress can declare war *(Article I).* **(b)** Military appropriations cannot be made for more than two years *(Article I).* **(c)** Troops may not be quartered in any home without consent of the owner *(Third Amendment).* **(d)** The national government may not deprive people of the right to keep and bear arms *(Sixth Amendment).*

6. *National Supremacy.* To avoid difficulties that might arise if Federal and state laws conflicted, the Constitution established the principle of *national supremacy,* according to which the Federal Constitution, acts of Congress, and treaties are superior to state constitutions and laws *(Article VI).*

7. *Supremacy of the Constitution.* To protect the form of government established from being overthrown by any single branch of government, or by the states, the framers included the stipulation that the Constitution is the "supreme law of the land." All laws of Congress, treaties, state constitutions, and state and local laws rank below it in authority. Under the principle of *judicial review,* set forth by Supreme Court Justice John Marshall at the beginning of the 19th century, the Supreme Court has the right to declare laws of Congress unconstitutional. (Marshall based his opinion on *Article VI, Section 2,* and *Article III, Section 2.*)

8. *Flexibility.* By outlining a procedure for keeping the Constitution up to date through amendments and through expansion of the powers of Congress, the founding fathers made it an adaptable and flexible instrument of government. So successful were they that the document is as usable today as it was in 1789.

REVIEW TEST (Chapter 6 — Part I)

Select the number preceding the word or expression that best completes each statement or answers each question.

1. Essential characteristics of a democratic form of government are (1) isolation and neutrality (2) efficiency and uniformity (3) freedom and tolerance (4) class distinction and exclusion of inferior races

2. The ultimate source of all political power in the United States lies in the (1) people of the United States (2) laws made by Congress (3) state constitutions (4) United States Constitution

3. An essential of a republic is (1) a two-party system (2) a government of elected officers (3) a bicameral legislature (4) universal suffrage

4. A practice of the United States derived from English sources is (1) the system of amending the Constitution (2) a cabinet responsible to the President (3) trial by jury (4) the method of electing a chief executive

5. The United States is considered a federal type of government because the Constitution provides that (1) powers be divided among legislative, judicial, and executive branches (2) powers be divided among state and national governments (3) the states be guaranteed a republican form of government (4) individuals be granted civil rights

6. In adopting the principle of separation of powers, the thinking of the framers of the United States Constitution was most influenced by the writings of (1) Locke (2) Rousseau (3) Voltaire (4) Montesquieu

7. The principle of checks and balances was introduced to prevent (1) federalism (2) national supremacy (3) judicial review (4) tyranny

8. What feature of our Federal government is derived from the British constitution? (1) method of choosing the chief executive (2) method of amending the Constitution (3) system of checks and balances (4) inclusion of a Bill of Rights

9. "This Constitution . . . shall be the supreme law of the land" is an original quotation from (1) a Supreme Court decision by Marshall (2) the Constitution of the United States (3) the Northwest Ordinance (4) the Articles of Confederation

10. The principle of national supremacy was made part of the Constitution in order to (1) avoid conflicts between Federal and state laws (2) protect the President from slander and vilification (3) guarantee the rights of states to govern themselves (4) insure the supremacy of civil authority over military authority

Match each principle of United States government in Column A with the item in Column B that most clearly identifies it.

A	**B**
1. Popular sovereignty	*a.* Only Congress can declare war
2. Limited government	*b.* National and state governments divide responsibilities
3. Civilian supremacy over the military	
4. Federalism	*c.* Treaties take precedence over state and local laws
5. Flexibility	*d.* "We, the people of the United States . . ."
	e. The amending process
	f. A written constitution

Essay Questions

1. William E. Gladstone, famous 19th-century British statesman, called the United States Constitution, "The most wonderful work ever struck off at one time by the brain and purpose of man." (a) Explain what was unusual about the Constitution as an 18th-century document. (b) To what extent was Gladstone correct in stating that the Constitution was "struck off at one time?" Explain.

2. List the principles of United States government that are found in the Declaration of Independence.

3. Show how the Constitution reflects each of the following: (a) colonial experiences (b) new state constitutions after the Revolution (c) experiences under the Articles of Confederation (d) British traditions and customs.

Part II — THE DIVISION OF POWERS

Under the federal system, powers of government are divided between the national and state governments. Each is also limited in its authority.

The Division of Powers. The Tenth Amendment clearly sets forth the division of powers, as follows:

"The powers not delegated to the United States by the Constitution, nor prohibited by it to the States, are reserved to the States respectively, or to the people."

1. *Delegated Powers.* The powers granted to the national government are called *delegated, expressed,* or *enumerated* powers because they are specifically listed as powers of Congress in *Article I, Section 8* of the Constitution. Under this section the Federal government, through Congress, is given the power to:

Lay and collect taxes
Borrow money
Regulate interstate and foreign commerce
Establish uniform rules of naturalization and bankruptcy
Coin money and regulate its value
Punish counterfeiters
Establish post offices and post roads
Grant patents and copyrights
Create courts lower than the Supreme Court

Punish piracy and violations of international law
Declare war
Raise and support armies
Provide and maintain a navy
Regulate the conduct of the armed forces
Call out the state militias in emergencies
Regulate the establishment and training of state militias
Have jurisdiction over the area in which the national capital is established.

2. *Implied Powers.* Clause 18 of *Article I, Section 8* gives Congress *implied* powers in addition to the 17 delegated powers listed above. These are powers which are "necessary and proper" for Congress in order to carry out its delegated powers.

(a) *Article I, Section 8, Clause 18* states that Congress shall have the power "to make all laws which shall be necessary and proper for carrying into execution the foregoing powers, and all other powers vested by this Constitution in the government of the United States, or in any department or officer thereof."

(b) Because this clause enables Congress to increase or stretch the powers of the national government it is called the *elastic clause.*

(c) Examples of implied powers granted to Congress under the elastic clause are these: **(1)** Under its delegated power to regulate interstate and foreign commerce, Congress has the (implied) power to regulate the building of power dams across rivers, and to improve rivers and harbors. **(2)** Under its power to borrow money, Congress has the power to issue bonds. **(3)** On the "general welfare" clause of the Preamble, Congress bases its power to pass social security laws. (Note that implied powers are *not* explicitly enumerated in the Constitution.)

75

(d) Over the years the powers of the national government have been considerably increased by a *broad* or "loose" interpretation of the elastic clause; that is, by court acceptance of many acts of Congress as being necessary and proper in the exercise of its delegated powers. Those who oppose or who have opposed the extension of national power under the elastic clause are said to favor a *narrow* or "strict" interpretation of the Constitution. At times there have been bitter disputes between supporters of both points of view.

3. *Reserved Powers.* Under the Tenth Amendment, powers not granted to Congress nor denied to the states are *reserved* to the states or the people. Today, these are commonly called *states' rights.* These *reserved* or *residual* powers leave to the states the authority to do many things, including the right to:

Regulate marriage and divorce
Regulate the carrying of firearms
Charter corporations
Control education

Establish voting requirements
License doctors and dentists
Build roads
Provide for community health

4. *Concurrent Powers.* Under the Constitution, certain powers are granted to Congress (*Article I, Section 8*), but are *not* denied to the states (*Article I, Section 10*). Such powers, therefore, may be exercised by *both* state and Federal governments. These *concurrent powers* include the right to lay and collect taxes, borrow money, hold elections, and enact bankruptcy laws.

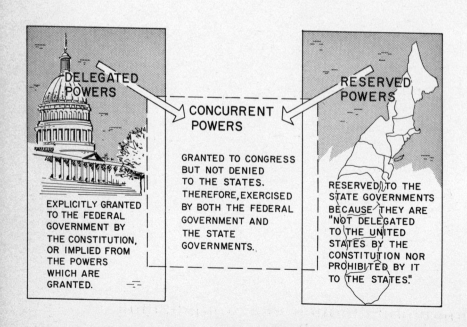

DELEGATED POWERS

EXPLICITLY GRANTED TO THE FEDERAL GOVERNMENT BY THE CONSTITUTION, OR IMPLIED FROM THE POWERS WHICH ARE GRANTED.

CONCURRENT POWERS

GRANTED TO CONGRESS BUT NOT DENIED TO THE STATES. THEREFORE, EXERCISED BY BOTH THE FEDERAL GOVERNMENT AND THE STATE GOVERNMENTS.

RESERVED POWERS

RESERVED TO THE STATE GOVERNMENTS BECAUSE THEY ARE "NOT DELEGATED TO THE UNITED STATES BY THE CONSTITUTION NOR PROHIBITED BY IT TO THE STATES."

Restrictions on State and National Governments. In order to make clearer the limits of governmental powers, and thus to prevent tyranny, the Constitution places *restrictions* on both the national and state governments. These restrictions are summarized below:

POWERS DENIED TO NATIONAL GOVERNMENT UNDER CONSTITUTION

(Article I, Section 9; Amendments 1-8)

1. Tax exports
2. Grant titles of nobility
3. Restrict freedom of religion
4. Give one state preference over another in matters of commerce
5. Impose direct taxes which are not proportionate to the population of states*
6. Change state boundaries without consent of the state involved
7. Abridge freedom of speech or press
8. Curtail the right of the people to assemble peaceably
9. Impose excessive bail or cruel and unusual punishments
10. Take private property for public use without just compensation
11. Deprive any person of life, liberty, or property without due process of law

POWERS DENIED TO STATES UNDER CONSTITUTION

(Article I, Section 10; Amendments 13-19)

1. Tax exports
2. Tax imports
3. Grant titles of nobility
4. Enter into treaties
5. Coin money
6. Keep troops or ships of war in time of peace
7. Deny persons equal protection of the laws
8. Prevent persons from voting because of race, color, or sex
9. Make a law impairing the obligation of contracts
10. Deprive any person of life, liberty, or property without due process of law

Obligations of National and State Governments. The Constitution also imposes certain *obligations* on the national and state governments.

1. *The National Government Must:*

    (a) *Guarantee each state a republican form of government.* All states must be governed by representatives of the people.

    (b) *Protect each state against invasion or domestic violence.* Under this provision the President, as Commander-in-Chief of the armed forces, can use Federal troops to put down riots or looting within state boundaries. Normally he does not do so unless the governor of the state requests such action. Federal assistance is also given to states under this provision when natural disasters strike in the form of floods, hurricanes, forest fires, earthquakes, etc. The President may also use the armed forces to carry out Federal court orders.

---

*This provision was modified by the Sixteenth Amendment, which empowers Congress to tax incomes directly.

(c) *Grant new states the same rights as all other states.* For example, Alaska and Hawaii, since their admission as states, have been entitled to the same privileges enjoyed by each of the older states.

2. Each State Government Must:

(a) *Give full faith and credit to the laws and proceedings of other states.* This means that each state must honor such things as contracts, birth certificates and court judgments made in other states. (*Exceptions:* States are *not* required to enforce the criminal laws of other states, or to honor divorces granted by courts of one state to citizens of another.)

(b) *Grant to citizens of other states all the "privileges and immunities" of its own citizens.* These include the right to live within its borders; the right to make contracts and buy or sell property; and the right to sue in its courts.

(c) *Return criminals to the state in which they committed their crimes (right of extradition).* In this matter the Supreme Court has ruled that although a governor can be *asked* to return a fugitive he may not be *compelled* to do so.

The Changing Nature of the Federal System. As the United States has grown from an infant nation to a world power, certain noteworthy trends have developed in Federal-state and interstate relations.

1. *Growing Authority of the National Government.* A broad or "loose" interpretation of the Constitution has made it possible for the Federal government to expand its activities in many areas of national and local life. For example, under its power to regulate interstate and foreign commerce, Congress has passed laws regulating rail, truck, bus, and air travel; business monopolies and labor unions; maximum hours and minimum wages; immigration, banks, and radio, telephone, and television communications.

2. *Increasing Federal-State Cooperation.* In recent years there has been a tendency for the Federal and state governments to work together to solve common problems. Several examples may be cited:

(a) The Federal Bureau of Investigation (FBI) has helped state and local governments solve crimes and capture criminals.

(b) The United States Department of Agriculture has worked closely with state agricultural colleges and agencies.

(c) Under the *grant-in-aid program,* the Federal government has for some years granted billions of dollars annually to states (and localities) for programs in such areas as housing, health, roads, training of veterans, and law enforcement. The state must "match" the Federal appropriations to receive the funds.

(d) More recently, under a *revenue-sharing program,* the Federal government has begun to turn back some of its tax revenues to the states (and localities) for programs which they themselves plan and administer.

3. *Interstate Relations.* In the past few decades states have cooperated to solve common problems. Today hundreds of *interstate compacts* are in force. These are compacts under which two or more states enter into agreements with one another. For example, the states of New York and New Jersey have created the *Port of New York Authority* to run their airports, tunnels, bridges, and bus terminals. Twenty-six states are cooperating in a *Compact to Conserve Oil and Gas.*

REVIEW TEST (Chapter 6—Part II)

Select the number preceding the word or expression that best completes each statement or answers each question.

1. The powers delegated to the national government by the Constitution are found in the (1) elastic clause (2) powers reserved to the states (3) enumerated powers of Congress (4) decisions of the Supreme Court

2. Which of the following is an example of the exercise of a delegated power of Congress? (1) purchase of the Louisiana Territory (2) ratification of the Twelfth Amendment (3) construction of the Cumberland Road (4) passage of the Naturalization Act of 1798

3. The "elastic clause" of the Constitution (Article I, Section 8) provides that Congress shall have the power to make all laws that shall be necessary and proper (1) to provide for the common defense (2) to provide for the general welfare (3) to regulate commerce between states (4) to carry into execution the other powers granted to it by the Constitution

4. An example of the use of an implied power by Congress would be (1) the enactment of a law regulating railroads (2) a declaration of war (3) the passage of an excise tax (4) the passage of a tariff bill

5. The residual (reserved) powers in the United States Constitution refer to those powers that are (1) given to Congress (2) denied to the states (3) given to both the states and the Federal government (4) left to the states or to the people

6. The reserved powers of our Constitution are illustrated by the fact that (1) no state may coin money (2) only Congress may establish post offices (3) voting qualifications differ from one state to another (4) senators from each state are now elected by the people

7. The Constitution of the United States guarantees to each state (1) an equal share of the taxes (2) Federal aid for flood control (3) a republican form of government (4) the power to grant patents to inventors

8. Which best illustrates the use of concurrent powers? (1) real estate taxes (2) gasoline taxes (3) taxes on imports (4) bridge tolls

9. The Constitution of the United States specifically denies to the states the power to (1) establish a Federal bank (2) amend the Constitution (3) levy taxes (4) make treaties

10. The Constitution prohibits both the national government and the state governments from (1) negotiating treaties (2) taxing imports (3) levying excise taxes (4) passing *ex post facto* legislation

11. Which of the following illustrates the fact that the United States has a federal system of government? (1) Congress passes laws, but the President enforces them. (2) The President appoints Cabinet members, but the Senate must approve them. (3) Congress enacts laws, but the Supreme Court has the power to declare laws of Congress unconstitutional. (4) The national government regulates interstate commerce, but state governments regulate commerce within the states.

12. Under our federal system of government a state may *not* on its own initiative (1) establish a bicameral legislature (2) lower the voting age to 18 (3) increase its number of representatives in Congress (4) establish a system of public schools

13. By means of grants-in-aid the Federal government has been able to (1) influence state programs in the area of highway building (2) increase the power of local schoolboards (3) safeguard the system of checks and balances (4) force states to establish minimum wage legislation

14. The legal process by which the governor of one state in the United States secures the return of a criminal from another state is known as (1) waiver (2) extradition (3) eminent domain (4) *ex post facto*

15. Which basic principle of the United States Constitution has been involved in the controversy between those who advocate states' rights and those who favor an increase in Federal power (1) separation of powers (2) division of powers (3) due process of law (4) concurrent powers

Indicate the kind of power illustrated by each of the following statements. Use the following symbols:

D, for a delegated power

I, for an implied power

R, for a reserved power

C, for a concurrent power

1. The power to charter National Banks
2. The power to grant patents
3. Issuing drivers' licenses
4. The power to tax incomes
5. The regulation of interstate commerce
6. Congress passes a Bankruptcy Act
7. The sale of U. S. Savings Bonds
8. A compulsory education law
9. The apprehending of criminals
10. Establishing a post office in a new surburban community

Essay Questions

1. Explain two ways in which the Constitution protects states' rights.

2. Explain why the makers of the Constitution established the principle of division of powers. Give one reason for or against this principle.

3. What does each of the following provide in regard to the division of powers under the Constitution? Article I, Section 8; Article I, Section 9; Article I, Section 10; Amendment 10.

4. List 5 powers of (a) the Federal government (b) the state governments.

5. (a) Why has the Federal government been able to greatly expand its activities under the Constitution? (b) Give one argument for and one argument against this growth of national authority.

Part III — THE SEPARATION OF POWERS IN THE NATIONAL GOVERNMENT

Under the Constitution, the Federal government is composed of three branches, each with its own separate powers. This principle of organization is called *separation of powers*.

Separation of Powers. The Constitution distributes powers among the *legislative, executive,* and *judicial* branches.

1. *Legislative Branch.* The legislative branch (Congress) has the power to make the laws *(Article I)*. In practice Congress is assisted by government agencies which are given the power to make rules and regulations for certain industries. Such *quasi-legislative* agencies and commissions include the *Interstate Commerce Commission (ICC)*, the *Security Exchange Commission (SEC)*, and the *Federal Trade Commission (FTC)*.

2. *Executive Branch.* The executive branch (the President) carries out and enforces the laws *(Article II)*. In practice the President is helped by many agencies, departments, and individuals.

3. *Judicial Branch.* The Supreme Court and lower courts created by Congress have the responsibility for exercising the judicial powers of government *(Article III)*. They interpret and apply the laws in cases which are brought before them.

Checks and Balances. One of the unique features of United States government is its *system of checks and balances.* In order to prevent the rise of tyranny and to maintain a balance of power, the Constitution gives each of the branches of the national government powers to check or restrain the other two. This is illustrated in the following chart.

LEGISLATIVE CHECKS AND BALANCES

Congress Can Check the President by	*Congress Can Check the Courts by*
1. Refusing to pass laws requested by the President	**1.** Initiating or approving amendments to the Constitution
2. Overriding a Presidential veto	**2.** Increasing or decreasing the size of the Supreme Court
3. Impeaching the President and removing him from office	**3.** Deciding which cases may be appealed to the higher courts
4. Refusing to ratify proposed treaties or confirm Presidential appointments	

EXECUTIVE CHECKS AND BALANCES

The President Can Check Congress by

1. Vetoing bills passed by Congress
2. Calling Congress into special session
3. Appealing to the public for support of his programs

The President Can Check Courts by

1. Appointing new or additional judges with consent of Senate
2. Refusing to carry out court orders. (However, this might be grounds for censure or impeachment.)

JUDICIAL CHECKS AND BALANCES

The Courts Can Check Congress by

Declaring acts of Congress unconstitutional

The Courts Can Check the President by

1. Declaring acts of the executive unconstitutional
2. Declaring unconstitutional, laws backed by the President

Advantages and Disadvantages of Separation of Powers and Checks and Balances. The principles of separation of powers and checks and balances have been both praised and criticized.

1. *Advantages.* Those who favor these principles argue that they have worked well for the most part. **(a)** It is maintained that they have compelled the three branches of government to work together and to compromise differences, in order to avoid stalemate. **(b)** They have prevented the rise of tyranny or dictatorship in the United States.

2. *Disadvantages.* Several basic criticisms have been made of the separation of powers and checks and balances.

(a) Each branch on occasion has been charged with usurping powers that belong to the other branches. Some Presidents have been criticized for attempting to dominate Congress through their popularity with the people, or through their power to dispense jobs *(patronage)*. Congress has been criticized for improper interference with executive powers through committee investigations affecting the executive branch. The courts have been charged with improperly assuming powers that belong to the President and Congress.

(b) A second criticism is that separation of powers sometimes leads to stalemate and lack of positive accomplishment. For example, it may be impossible to enact much-needed legislation if the President is of one political party and Congress is controlled by another.

REVIEW TEST (Chapter 6—Part III)

Select the number preceding the word or expression that best completes each statement or answers each question.

1. The system of checks and balances in our government was adopted to (1) prevent a strong executive from gaining too much power (2) prevent the formation of political parties (3) check states' rights (4) secure religious freedom

2. The terms "checks" and "balances" in the Constitution of the United States refer to (1) keeping the national budget in balance (2) maintaining the balance of power in Congress between slave states and free states (3) the establishment of a cabinet to check on the President (4) control exercised by one branch of the government on the action of other branches of the government

3. Which illustrates the system of checks and balances in our government? (1) The Federal and state governments levy taxes. (2) The President vetoes an act of Congress. (3) The President is summoned before a congressional investigating committee. (4) The House of Representatives removes from office a member of the President's Cabinet.

4. Article I of the Constitution outlines the powers of (1) the President (2) Congress (3) the Supreme Court (4) none of these

5. The President may do all of the following *except* (1) veto bills passed by Congress (2) call Congress into special session (3) increase the size of the Supreme Court (4) appeal to the public to support his program

Select the letter of item in each group which does **NOT** *belong with the others.*

1. Judicial checks on the President: (a) declaring unconstitutional laws passed at the President's request; (b) declaring acts of the President unconstitutional; (c) impeaching the President

2. Congressional checks on the President: (a) approving an amendment to limit the President's powers in treaty making; (b) overriding a Presidential veto; (c) calling a special session of Congress

3. Presidential checks on Congress: (a) discharging uncooperative Senators; (b) addressing the nation on television; (c) vetoing bills

4. Congressional checks on the Courts: (a) initiating an amendment to limit the Court's powers; (b) requesting that the Supreme Court reconsider a decision; (c) changing the number of Supreme Court justices

5. Quasi-legislative agencies: (a) are Congressional committees that prepare laws (b) make rules and regulations; (c) are illustrated by the Federal Trade Commission and the Interstate Commerce Commission

Essay Questions

1. The Constitution provides for a system of checks and balances among the three major branches of our national government; however, at times, one particular branch has taken leadership in national affairs. (a) Explain why the makers of the Constitution provided for a system of checks and balances, and give two specific illustrations of checks and balances as provided in the Constitution. (b) Select any two of the major branches of our national government: the Presidency, the Congress, the Supreme Court. For each of the two branches selected, show, by giving two specific examples, how that branch of government exercised leadership in national affairs during one period in our history.

2. Give a brief explanation of each of the following terms or phrases: separation of powers; checks and balances; patronage; judicial legislation

3. Discuss two criticisms of the separation of powers under the Constitution.

4. Give two arguments advanced by supporters of the checks and balances system.

Part IV — THE ORGANIZATION AND OPERATION OF THE LEGISLATIVE BRANCH

Under the Constitution Congress is the legislative or lawmaking branch of government *(Article I, Section 1)*. In this discussion we shall see how Congress carries out its important role in government.

How Congress Is Organized. Congress is a two-house or bicameral legislative body, consisting of the *House of Representatives* and the *Senate*.

1. *Length of Term.* Each term of Congress lasts two years. The first term began on March 4, 1789. The 96th Congress began on January 3, 1977.

2. *Length of Session.* Each term of Congress is made up of two sessions. The first session begins on January 3, following an election year; the second session begins the following January 3. Election years are even-numbered years. Although Congress tries to complete its business by the end of July, it has in recent years found this increasingly difficult to do. Indeed, the 88th Congress remained in session throughout all of 1963 in its first session.

3. *Special Sessions of Congress.* The Constitution gives the President the power to call special sessions of Congress, or of either house, whenever he thinks it necessary. For example, President Franklin D. Roosevelt called a special session of Congress when, World War II broke out in September, 1939.

Organization of the House of Representatives and Senate. The organization of the House of Representatives and Senate is indicated by the following chart.

THE ORGANIZATION OF CONGRESS

FEATURES	HOUSE OF REPRESENTATIVES	SENATE
Size	435 members. (Each state is represented according to population. Congress reapportions seats after each ten-year census.) At present each Representative represents about 470,000 people.	100 members. (Each state has two Senators.)
Qualifications of Members	A Representative must be at least 25 years of age, a citizen for at least 7 years, and a resident of the state from which he or she is elected.	A Senator must be at least 30 years of age, a citizen for at least 9 years, and a resident of the state from which he or she is elected.

FEATURES	HOUSE OF REPRESENTATIVES	SENATE
Election of Members	By the voters of each Congressional District within the state. The entire House is elected every two years.	By the voters of the entire state. One-third of the Senate is elected every two years.
Length of term	Two years.	Six years.
Salary	$57,500 plus allowances (*e.g.,* travel, office expenses).	$57,500 plus allowances.
Exclusive or Special Powers	1. To originate revenue (income-producing) bills. 2. To elect a President if no candidate receives a majority of the electoral votes. 3. To impeach civil (non-military) officials for misconduct in office.	1. To confirm (approve) Presidential appointments. 2. To approve treaties made by the President, by a two-thirds vote. 3. To elect a Vice President if no candidate receives a majority of electoral votes. 4. To try officials who have been impeached. (The Senate sits as a court.)
Presiding Officer	The *Speaker.* Elected by members of the House; same voting power as any other member; receives $75,000 and $10,000 expenses. The Speaker is the most important member of the House and usually exercises broad powers.	The *Vice President.* Called the "President of the Senate"; votes only in case of a tie vote; receives $75,000 plus $10,000 expenses. In his absence the Senate is presided over by a *President pro-tempore.* The Vice President and President *pro-tem* have little power in carrying on work of Senate.

The Senate and House Compared. Although the Senate and House of Representatives are given equal legislative powers and are alike in important respects, there are also many noteworthy differences between them.

1. *Similarities.* The Senate and House are alike in that:

(a) Each house must pass a bill before it can become a law.

(b) Each house determines its own operating procedures.

(c) Each house may expel members by a two-thirds vote.

(d) In each house a majority of the members must be present for business to be conducted. (The number of members who must be present in any organization for business to be conducted legally is called a *quorum.*)

(e) Members of both houses may not be arrested for minor offenses while on official Congressional business, or while going to or from Congress.

(f) Members cannot be sued for what they say in Congress or in any official printed document, such as the *Congressional Record*. (The Constitution requires the keeping of an official journal of proceedings of each house.)

(g) Members of both houses enjoy the privilege of free postage for official business (the *"franking"* privilege).

(h) Most members of both houses have generally had previous political experience in government.

(i) Most have been lawyers, businessmen, or professionals. They often give up higher paying jobs for the privilege of serving their country.

2. *Differences.* The House of Representatives and Senate differ from each other in certain important respects:

(a) Each house has certain powers which it alone may exercise. (See chart on previous page.)

(b) The average age of Representatives is usually several years lower than that of Senators.

(c) The average Senator enjoys more prestige than the average Representative. He serves a longer term, and is a member of a smaller body; therefore, he is usually considered more important as an individual. In addition, Senators are members of a continuing body, and, because of the way in which they are elected, at any given time at least two-thirds of them are experienced legislators.

(d) In debate on the floor, Senators may speak for an unlimited length of time; members of the House are ordinarily restricted to one hour.

Powers of Congress. The chief duty and responsibility of Congress is to make the laws of the land. Congress also has a number of non-legislative powers. It elects the President, the Vice President, or both, if the Electoral College is unable to do so; it undertakes investigations; it proposes amendments to the Constitution; and it has the power to impeach governmental officials for wrong-doing and to remove them from office. These additional powers, however, do not detract from the fact that Congress is, above all, a lawmaking body.

How Bills Are Introduced. An item of legislation presented to Congress for enactment is called a *bill.* When and if a bill is passed by Congress and approved by the President (or possibly passed by Congress over a Presidential veto), it is called a *law.*

In recent years, over 30,000 bills have been introduced into Congress each term. Fewer than 10% of them become law.

Bills may be introduced only by members of Congress. In the House of Representatives a bill is introduced by dropping it into a box (hopper) on the clerk's desk. In the upper house, Senators introduce bills by addressing the Presiding Officer. A bill may be introduced in either chamber, although in most cases they are introduced in both houses at the same time.

Who Writes Congressional Bills? Although Congressmen write some of the bills they introduce, most of these pieces of legislation today are written by other persons. Many bills are drafted by members of the executive branch; representatives of business, labor, education, and other "pressure groups;" private citizens; and other members of Congress.

Types of Bills. There are several different types of measures on which Congress may act.

1. A *public bill,* such as the Social Security Act, applies to many people, or to the nation as a whole.

2. A *private bill,* such as an individual pension law, relates to specific persons or places.

3. A *joint resolution* is an action by both houses which has the effect of law and must be submitted to the President for approval. It is used to make minor changes in existing laws, to extend them if they are about to expire, and to endorse agreements already made by the President. It may also be used to take the place of a formal treaty and thus to get around the two-thirds majority required in the Senate. For example, a joint resolution led to the annexation of Texas in 1845.

4. A *concurrent resolution* is an action taken by both houses which does not involve a legislative matter and therefore need not be approved by the President. Congress may use such a resolution to offer sympathy, to register a vote of censure, or to express its concern over some situation.

5. A *simple resolution* is passed by one house as a guide for its own use — for example, a resolution to establish a special committee.

6. A *rider* is a provision which has nothing to do with the main subject of the bill to which it is attached. In general, bills of whatever type deal with only one subject, but occasionally either house may attach a rider to an important bill. The bill in question is usually one which is essential and certain of passage, such as an appropriations bill. Thus, the rider may get through, although it would fall by the wayside if introduced as a separate bill. Usually, the purpose of this device is to avoid executive disapproval.

Procedure After a Bill Has Been Introduced. After a bill has been introduced, it must go through a rather lengthy process before it becomes a law. Very few of the bills introduced ever complete this process.

1. When a bill has been introduced, the clerk gives it an identifying number, prefixed by *H.R.* in the House and *S.* in the Senate. Thus, a bill may be known as *H.R.2125* or *S.1760.*

2. The clerk then reads the title of the bill to the chamber. This is called the "first reading."

3. The Speaker of the House or the President of the Senate then refers the bill to the appropriate *standing committee* of that chamber.

The Committee System of Congress. We have noted above that more than 30,000 bills are introduced in each session of Congress. It would be a practical impossibility for Congress as a whole to consider each of these bills. They are, therefore, submitted to small groups of Congressmen, known as *committees*. An understanding of the committee system is basic to an understanding of how a bill becomes law.

1. *Standing Committees.* There are 21 standing *committees* (that is, permanent committees) in the House and 18 in the Senate. The committees in each of the chambers are listed below. Note that in most cases they have parallel duties and responsibilities. Generally speaking, the name of a standing committee indicates quite clearly the area within which it has authority. There are, however, several cases in which this is not true. The *Rules Committee* of the House, considered the most powerful committee in Congress, decides *which bills* are to be brought to the floor of the House for discussion, *when* this discussion is to take place, and for *how long*. The *Ways and Means Committee,* also in the House, handles revenue bills (taxes, tariffs, appropriations). In practice, most committees are divided into smaller *subcommittees* in order to work more efficiently.

STANDING COMMITTEES OF SENATE

Aeronautical and Space Sciences
Agriculture and Forestry
Appropriations
Armed Services
Banking and Currency
Budget
Commerce
District of Columbia
Finance
Foreign Relations
Government Operations
Interior and Insular Affairs
Judiciary
Labor and Public Welfare
Post Office and Civil Service
Public Works
Rules and Administration
Veterans Affairs

STANDING COMMITTEES OF HOUSE

Science and Astronautics
Agriculture
Appropriations
Armed Services
Banking, Housing and Urban Affairs
Budget
Interstate and Foreign Commerce
District of Columbia
Ways and Means
Foreign Affairs
Government Operations
Interior and Insular Affairs
Judiciary
Education and Labor
Post Office and Civil Service
Public Works
Rules
Veterans Affairs
Merchant Marine and Fisheries
House Administration
Standards of Official Conduct

2. *Other Types of Committees.* There are other types of committees in Congress, in addition to the standing committees.

(a) The two houses may set up a *joint committee* to enable them to act as a single body on some special problem. Examples are the Joint Committee on Atomic Energy and the Joint Committee on Congressional Operations.

(b) Either house may set up a *select special committee* for a limited period of time to do a particular job. An example is the select Senate committee chaired by Senator Sam Ervin that investigated the Watergate affair in 1973.

(c) *Conference committees* representing both houses are frequently set up when the chambers have passed somewhat different versions of the same bill. The conference committee has the task of producing a single bill acceptable to both the Senate and the House.

(d) Congress may set up *joint committees,* composed of members of both chambers. The best known body of this type today is the Joint Committee on Atomic Energy.

3. *How a Standing Committee Works.* Suppose that a bill which deals with the problems of agriculture is introduced. This would be submitted to the Agriculture Committee (Agriculture and Forestry in the Senate). The first task of the committee is to decide whether to give the bill detailed study and consideration. About nine of ten bills submitted to each committee are "pigeon-holed," that is, put aside, usually permanently. A bill set aside in this way is rarely discharged for further action; it almost always "dies in committee."

When a committee wishes to consider a bill, the members may do individual research. Also, *public hearings* may be held to get additional information or opinions. At such hearings, qualified experts, as well as representatives of interested groups and of the general public, may be invited or allowed to give testimony. After such hearings have been held and the committee has completed its study and discussion, the members decide by majority vote whether or not to send the bill to the particular house of Congress with a favorable recommendation. Frequently, a bill is reported out or discharged in amended form — that is, with a change or changes in its provisions.

4. *Committee Organization and Membership.* Committees vary in size. Since the *Legislative Reorganization Act* of 1946, members of the House have usually been limited to serve on one committee, but Senators (because of their smaller number) may serve on two or even three committees. In both chambers, committee members are nominated by the respective party caucuses. (*Party caucuses* are closed meetings of party members called to decide policy.) The majority party in each house organizes the committees, but the minority party is always given representation on each committee according to a ratio agreed on by the party leaderships. This is usually more or less proportionate to the numerical strength of the two parties in that house. (It should be noted that all these rules for the functioning of committees are the result of custom — not of constitutional provisions or statutes.)

5. *Committee Chairpersons.* Each committee of Congress has its head or chairperson. Next to the presiding officers in each house, the heads of major committees are considered the most important members of Congress.

"Strong" committee chairmen have played an important role in the making of laws through their control of committee operations, and their influence in determining whether bills will be reported out favorably or unfavorably, or perhaps simply "tabled" so that no action will be taken on them.

Until 1975, committee chairmen were selected under the *rule of seniority*. This meant that each committee chairmanship went regularly to the member belonging to the majority party who had the longest continuous service in Congress. (Chairmanships of subcommittees were awarded on the same basis.) In 1975, however, Congress gave the majority "caucus" in each party the right to vote for committee chairmen. In effect, this ended the seniority system, although length of service continues to be an important factor (among others) in selecting chairpersons.

Putting a Bill on the Calendar. After a bill has been reported out by the standing committee, it is given a "second reading" and is then placed on a calendar of the House or Senate. The *calendar* indicates the order in which bills are to be taken up by the house in question. The House has several calendars for different types of bills.

Debating the Bill. Bills are debated and discussed on the floor of the House and Senate before a vote is taken.

1. Because of the large size of the House, debate there is sharply limited. Under one of its rules, no speaker can speak on any point for more than an hour without unanimous consent of the members present. The House usually discusses bills as a "Committee of the Whole." Under this procedure debate can be speeded up, because rules are simpler. When the committee finishes its work, the House goes back into formal session for the vote.

2. Because of its smaller size, the Senate has unlimited debate. Each Senator may speak as long as he wishes, subject only to the *cloture* rule.

Voting on Bills. Bills are voted upon after being discussed. Most often members vote by *voice vote,* that is, by shouting "Yea" or "Nay" in answer to the presiding officer's questions on whether or not they favor the bill. Another common type of vote is a *roll-call vote,* or record vote, in which each member's vote is recorded individually by the Clerk. Bills that are approved are sent by the House to the Senate, and vice versa.

Conference Committee. When the Senate or House passes bills which are not identical, or when one house does not accept the changes made by the other, a *conference* or *compromise committee* is appointed to iron out the differences. A conference committee consists of an equal number of Representatives and Senators. The bill agreed to by the conference committee is referred back to each house for approval.

Action by the President. The final step in the process of lawmaking is taken by the President.

1. A bill which has been passed by the House and the Senate goes to the President for his approval or veto.

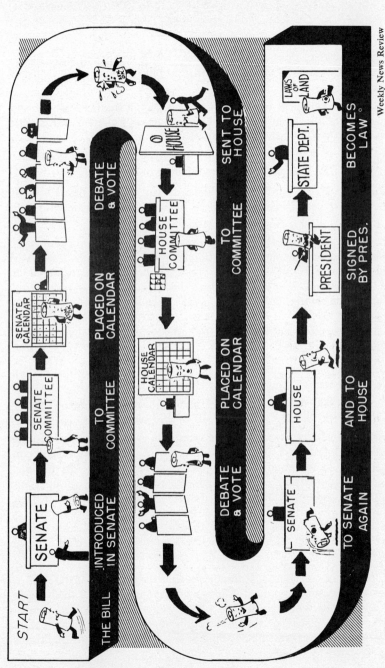

Typical life history of a bill that begins in the Senate.

2. A bill which is signed (approved) by the President goes to the Secretary of State, who affixes the Great Seal of the United States and declares that the bill is now the law of the land.

3. If the President does not sign or veto a bill within ten days of receiving it, and Congress is still in session, the bill becomes a law without his signature.

4. If Congress adjourns within ten days after a bill has been sent to the President, and the President has not taken any action on it, the bill is considered to be "killed." This procedure is called a *pocket veto.*

5. When the President vetoes a bill, he must send it back to the House in which it originated, together with a statement of his objections.

6. Congress can "override" a Presidential veto by a two-thirds vote in each house. It is usually very difficult to obtain such majorities.

Criticism of Our Lawmaking Procedures. A number of procedures associated with the enactment of legislation in the United States have been criticized as unwise or undemocratic. These criticisms have centered on *pressure groups and lobbyists, filibustering, seniority, gerrymandering, "pork-barrel" legislation, "log-rolling,"* and *unequal representation.*

Pressure Groups and Lobbyists. Many individuals and groups try to influence the making of laws.

1. *Pressure groups* try to influence public opinion for or against certain bills. They hope that as a result of their efforts, large numbers of voters will write to their Congressmen (or put pressure on them in other ways) to vote for or against bills in which they are interested.

2. *Lobbyists* are representatives of pressure groups who are sent to Washington to influence Congressmen directly. Nearly every sizable organized interest in the country has a lobby in Washington; this includes business, labor, agriculture, veterans, professionals, religious groups, and consumer organizations. Their lobbyists are usually highly skilled (and often highly paid) individuals who work for or against the bills favored or opposed by their sponsors. They try to exert influence by testifying at hearings, by providing information, by talking to Congressmen, and in other ways.

3. Lobbies are considered so important that they have been referred to as the "third house of Congress." Those who have investigated their operations most carefully feel that, in spite of occasional abuses, lobbies are an important and necessary part of our representative type of government, since they permit the expression of opinions by organized groups of citizens.

4. In an effort to eliminate some of the undesirable aspects of lobbying, such as secrecy, the *Legislative Reorganization Act* of 1946 required all lobbyists to register with Congress. This, however, has had only limited effect.

Filibustering. One of the most criticized of all Congressional procedures is *filibustering.* This practice, which may take place in the Senate (not in the House), is known as "talking a bill to death."

1. Filibusters occur when one or more Senators opposed to a bill try to stall further action on it by talking for periods of time on any subject, using the Senatorial privileges of unlimited debate. Their hope is that the rest of the Senate will agree to drop the bill, or change it in some acceptable fashion, in return for a suspension of the filibuster. (Note that while a filibuster is in progress, the business of the Senate is at a standstill.)

2. Under the *cloture (closure) rule,* adopted in 1917, the Senate may limit debate to one hour per Senator. Until 1975, cloture could take effect if approved by two-thirds of the Senate members present and voting. Since Senators hesitated to curb their colleagues' right of unlimited debate, cloture was seldom voted. In 1975, to make cloture less difficult to achieve, the requirement was changed to three-fifths (60 votes) of the total membership of the Senate. It remains to be seen whether this challenge will be significant in making it easier to invoke cloture.

Seniority Rule. According to a longstanding custom or unwritten rule, key posts in Congress, especially committee chairmanships, went until recently to members who had served longest. Critics charged that this rigid system ignored special abilities, discouraged younger members, and gave the most important jobs to those members who were repeatedly re-elected because they came from "safe" districts (especially in the South) where one party was dominant. As a result of reforms introduced in 1975, the majority caucus in each chamber may now vote on committee chairmen. Several long-time committee chairpersons have already been replaced.

Unequal Representation. For a number of years it had become increasingly clear that rural areas were continuing to send more than a proportionate number of representatives to the national and state legislatures, despite the fact that the nation was becoming increasingly urban. This resulted from election districts that had unequal numbers of voters. In a series of notable decisions the Supreme Court started a movement to end this undemocratic feature of government. In *Baker v. Carr* (1962) the Court ruled that if state lawmakers did not take steps to end unequal representation, the Federal Courts would intervene to force them to do so. In *Reynolds v. Sims* (1964) the Court followed through on this warning, ruling that both houses of state legislatures must be apportioned on the basis of population alone. In *Wesberry v. Sanders* (1964), it further declared that each U.S. Congressional district must have approximately the same population as every other. As a result of these *"one man, one vote" decisions,* most states have already taken steps to reapportion their state legislatures. Although this redistribution of political power was expected to give greater representation to *urban* areas, the results thus far have helped the *suburbs* more than the cities. Urban areas (the inner cities) continue to be in many cases under-represented.

Gerrymandering. *Gerrymandering* is the drawing of boundary lines of Congressional districts by state legislatures, so that the party in power gets as many seats as possible. Opportunities to gerrymander occur after each census, when the number of seats alloted to the various states in the House of Representatives may be readjusted in accordance with changes in population. For example, because of population changes during the 1960's, six states gained one or more seats in the House, and eleven lost seats. (California gained five; New York lost two.) There may also be gerrymandering of districts for state and local elections. Generally, it is considered an unfair tactic. (See the map below.)

Gerrymandering is sometimes done by lumping all the opposition strongholds into one large district, in order to make adjoining districts safe for the majority party. Sometimes the party in power carves out a peculiarly shaped legislative district to collect scattered votes into a district which that party has a good chance to win.

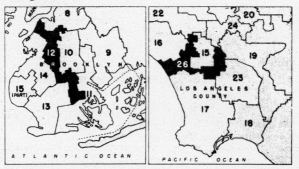

Here we see two gerrymandered districts as they appeared in the 1960's. The 12th Congressional District in Brooklyn, New York, was created under Democratic auspices; the 26th Congressional District in Los Angeles County, under Republican auspices. The purpose in both cases was much the same—to maximize the advantage of the dominant party. Both districts have since been modified.

"Pork-barrel" Legislation. Congressmen are eager to show their constituents ("the folks back home") that they are working actively for them. To do this, Congressmen often try to obtain passage of bills providing for construction projects in their own districts or states. Such "pork-barrel" projects, as they are popularly known, may include post office buildings, veterans' hospitals, highways, improvements of rivers and harbors, etc.

The term "pork barrel" certainly does not suggest that all Federal construction projects are unnecessary and wasteful. But it is true that in the past, some projects of doubtful utility have been undertaken, and that the location of some facilities has been determined largely by political pressure.

"Log-rolling." Closely linked to the "pork-barrel" is "log-rolling," or trading of votes. What this means in effect is that Congressman **A** will vote for a bill strongly favored by Congressman **B**, provided Congressman **B** agrees to vote for a bill strongly favored by Congressman **A**.

REVIEW TEST (Chapter 6—Part IV)

Select the number preceding the word or expression that best completes each statement or answers each question.

1. How many members of either house must be present to constitute a quorum, according to the United States Constitution? (1) one-half (2) a majority (3) two-thirds (4) three-fourths

2. What is the smallest number of members of Congress that a state, regardless of its population, may have? (1) 5 (2) 2 (3) 3 (4) 4

3. The constitutional reason for the census in the United States is to (1) apportion the states' memberships in the House of Representatives (2) determine the number of eligible voters (3) fix the geographic center of the population of the United States (4) find out the size of the labor force

4. It is expected that recent Supreme Court reapportionment decisions will bring about (1) a shift in political power from rural to urban areas (2) an increase in Republican strength in Congress (3) better representation of farm interests in Congress (4) an increased representation in Congress for states with growing populations

5. The importance of the Rules Committee of the House of Representatives stems largely from the Committee's (1) control over bills presented to the floor of the House for action (2) power to appoint committees (3) function of introducing appropriations bills (4) role as liaison between the House and the President

6. For which purpose are congressional investigating committees established? (1) to examine the qualifications of members of Congress (2) to collect evidence for the United States Attorney General (3) to hear appeals from individuals unjustly accused of crime (4) to gather information as a basis for remedial legislation

7. In the legislative process a conference committee is usually appointed (1) when Congress desires to investigate corrupt practices in government (2) when the President wishes to call Congress into special session (3) after the President has vetoed an act of Congress (4) after the Senate and the House have passed different versions of the same bill

8. According to Federal law all lobbyists must (1) confine their activities to the lobbies cf Congress (2) refrain from influencing the United States Senators (3) reside in Washington (4) register with the Secretary of State

9. Cloture has on rare occasions been invoked by the United States Senate in order to (1) end a filibuster (2) deprive the President of his right to send troops abroad (3) challenge the right of the House of Representatives to initiate money bills (4) reverse a decision of the Supreme Court on integration

10. Which action of the United States Senate requires a simple majority vote? (1) ratification of a treaty (2) approval of an appointment (3) passage of a bill vetoed by the President (4) conviction of an impeached official

11. Which of the following required a two-thirds vote of the United States Senate to be legally binding? (1) appointment of Warren Burger as Chief Justice of the United States Supreme Court (2) U.S. membership in NATO (3) declaration of war on Germany (4) negotiation of a reciprocal trade agreement with Canada by the U. S. Secretary of State

12. The United States Senate differs from the House of Representatives in that (1) the Senate introduces all revenue bills (2) membership in the Senate is based on population (3) the Senate approves Presidential appointments (4) Senators must be native born Americans

13. An example of a power belonging only to the United States House of Representatives was the (1) ratification of the North Atlantic Treaty in 1949 (2) introduction of the 1969 tax bill (3) confirmation of President Nixon's nomination of William Rogers as Secretary of State (4) introduction of the 1964 farm bill

14. The Congressional Record is published because (1) publication is required by Federal law (2) publication has become a practice that is part of the unwritten constitution (3) keeping such a record is required by the Constitution (4) the President traditionally requests a report of all action taken by Congress

15. No bill may become a law without the approval of (1) the United States Supreme Court (2) the President (3) a two-thirds vote of the Senate (4) both houses of Congress

Supply the word or statement that correctly completes each statement.

1. We shall next elect members of the House of Representatives in . . ? . . (month and year).

2. The minimum age for election to the Senate is . . ? . . .

3. A provision of a bill that is concerned with a matter not directly related to the bill itself is called a . . ? . . .

4. Permanent committees of the House or Senate are known as . .? . . committees.

5. When Congressmen call out "Yea" or "Nay" in voting on a bill, this is called a . . ? . . vote

6. A Congressman's constituents are the . . ? . . in his district.

7. Members of the House of Representatives may ordinarily speak for . . ? . . (length of time).

8. Approximately . . ? . . (number) Senators will be elected in the next national election.

9. The name of the present *president pro tem* of the Senate is . . ? . . .

10. The name of the present Speaker of the House is . . ? . . .

Essay Questions

1. Explain the role of each of the following in the political life of the United States: (a) the committee system in Congress (b) lobbying (c) gerrymandering.

2. Show how leadership in Congress is affected by the fact that some states elect the same individuals year after year.

3. Describe two ways in which members of Congress may make it difficult for a President's legislative program to be enacted.

4. Explain two ways in which the House of Representatives is like the Senate, and two ways in which it is different.

5. Explain how the two-party system affects the organization and work of Congress.

6. Discuss two reasons for agreeing or disagreeing with each of the following statements. (a) Filibustering is an undemocratic process. (b) Congressional hearings have accomplished very little. (c) A Senator enjoys greater prestige than a Representative. (d) The "one man, one vote" decision is necessary for the effective working of our democratic form of government.

Part V—THE EXECUTIVE BRANCH

The President of the United States is considered the world's most powerful elected head of state. As Chief Executive of the United States government he has tremendous authority and reponsibility in domestic and foreign affairs. He is the symbol of the American people at home and abroad, as well as a respected leader in world affairs. The Executive Branch of the government consists of the President, the Vice President, the heads of departments, and the Presidential advisors and assistants.

Constitutional Provisions for the Election of the President. Under the Constitution, elections for the Presidency occur every four years, in even-numbered years. The delegates to the Constitutional Convention provided for an *indirect* method of election by means of an *Electoral College (Article II)*. Although the procedure for electing a President was simple at first, it became more complex with the development of political parties. It has also become more democratic. The President is now truly the "people's choice."

1. *Electoral College.* The Constitution provides for the election of a President by a "college of electors." In this Electoral College each state has as many electors as its combined number of Senators and Representatives. Thus, New York State, with *2* Senators and *41* Representatives, has *43* electoral votes; California has *40* electoral votes (*2* Senators and *38* Representatives). Each state may select its electors as it sees fit. To be elected President or Vice President by the Electoral College, a candidate must receive a majority of the electoral votes. Today there are *538* votes in the Electoral College. (These include votes for the 100 Senators, the 435 Representatives, and 3 electoral votes for the District of Columbia, provided by the Twenty-third Amendment.)

2. *Weaknesses of Original Electoral Vote.* In the first four national elections (1789, 1792, 1796, 1800) each elector cast two ballots, each for a different person. The Constitution provided that the candidate who received most votes (but a majority was necessary) would be President; the runner-up would be Vice President. The weakness of this system became apparent in the election of 1796, when John Adams, a Federalist, was elected President, while his rival, Thomas Jefferson, a Democratic-Republican, was elected Vice President.

3. *Twelfth Amendment Changes.* In 1804, the Twelfth Amendment changed the original method of election by providing that each elector cast one ballot for President and a second separate ballot for Vice President. It was passed in order to prevent a recurrence of what happened in the election of 1800. In that election all the Republican electors had cast their ballots for both Thomas Jefferson and Aaron Burr. Although the majority intended that Jefferson be President and Burr Vice President, the tie vote in the Electoral College made it necessary for the House of Representatives to make the final decision. (Jefferson was chosen.)

97

Nominating Candidates for the Presidency. In the first three Presidential elections, before the rise of political parties, members of the Electoral College nominated as well as elected the President and Vice President, as had been intended by the framers of the Constitution. When political parties developed, this original method of nomination was changed. (1) From 1800 to 1828 a *caucus* of Congressional leaders from each party nominated its preferred candidate or candidates. (2) Beginning with the election of 1832, the caucus system was replaced by the *National Convention* as the method of selecting the candidates for President and Vice President. This procedure, explained in the following section, is still in use today.

The National Convention. In order to nominate candidates for the Presidency and Vice Presidency each party holds its own National Convention sometime in July or August of the election year. In addition to selecting Presidential and Vice Presidential candidates, the delegates to the national conventions adopt statements of party principles and policies, called *party platforms*.

The Presidential Campaign. The Presidential campaign involves the most vigorous and intense activity on the American political scene.

1. *Role of the Candidate.* After a brief rest following their nominations at the Convention, the candidates seek to make themselves and their views known to the electorate (the voters). They make major speeches in key cities, which are televised to the entire country, grant interviews to the mass communications media, and travel back and forth across the country making person contacts with local citizens and political leaders.

2. *Role of the Parties.* The Presidential candidates rely not only upon the work of their own separate campaign organizations, but also upon the regular party organizations throughout the country. All these groups hold political meetings, issue campaign literature, make speeches, sponsor broadcasts, and try in every possible way to induce voters to support the local and national party "ticket" (list of candidates). Frequently local party groups must be appealed to on the basis of purely local issues.

While each party is working to elect the President and Vice President, it also tries hard to elect Senators and Representatives to Congress. Often, the party that wins the Presidency also "captures" both houses of Congress. (That this is not *always* true, however, was shown in the elections of 1956, 1968, and 1972 in which Republicans Dwight D. Eisenhower and Richard Nixon were elected to the Presidency at the same time that the Democrats retained control of both houses of Congress.)

3. *Length and Financing of Campaigns.* At present, the Presidential campaign lasts for about ten weeks. Because these campaigns have become so expensive and such a physical and emotional strain for all involved, it has been suggested that they be shortened considerably. Also, there is strong support for more effective limitation and control of campaign spending, to eliminate concealed contributions and to cut down the advantage of the party with the biggest "campaign chest."

The National Election. The Presidential contest is decided on *election day*—the Tuesday after the first Monday in November of every fourth year.

1. *States Set Guidelines.* Elections are held in each state according to it own voting procedures.

2. *Parties Select Electors.* Each party presents a list of electors, equal in number to the combined number of its Senators and Representatives in Congress. Electors are ordinarily nominated by state party conventions, or by central party committees in each state.

3. *Voters Pick Electors.* On election day, qualified voters go to the polls to vote for electors, who in turn will choose the President and Vice-President. In a few states the names of the electors are printed on the ballot. In most states, however, only the names of the candidates for President and Vice President appear. Since the electors are pledged in advance to support the party's candidates, their individual identity is not important. The voter is really voting for a President and Vice President through the mechanism of the Electoral College.

4. *Winner Takes All.* Under a "winner-take-all" system, the party in each state that receives the largest number of votes elects its entire slate of electors and gets all the state's electoral votes.

5. *Election Results.* Since all the electors have promised to vote for their party's candidates in the Electoral College, the outcome of most elections can be determined as soon as the returns are in.

Selection of the President and Vice President by the Electoral College. Although the nation knows unofficially who will be its next President and Vice President as a result of the election-day returns, these officials are not *officially* chosen until January 6, following election day.

1. *Electoral College Meets and Votes.* In December, the electors assemble in their state capitals as the Electoral College, and cast their ballots for President and Vice President. The ballots are then sealed and sent to the President of the Senate in Washington. On January 6, the President of the Senate opens the ballots and counts them in the presence of both houses of Congress.

2. *President and Vice President Are Inaugurated.* The "President-elect" and "Vice President-elect" take their oath of office and begin their duties on January 20. This is called the *inauguration*. In his "inaugural oath," the President swears (or affirms) to preserve, protect, and defend the Constitution of the United States.

3. *When Neither Candidate Receives a Majority.* If neither candidate receives a majority of the electoral votes for President, the House of Representatives selects the President from among the three candidates receiving the highest number of votes in the Electoral College. In this election each state delegation casts one vote, and a majority (now 26 votes) is needed to select the President. This method of selection has occurred twice: in 1800 (Jefferson elected), and in 1824 (J. Q. Adams elected). Fears that it might occur again in the election of 1968 as a result of the third party candidacy of George Wallace revived opposition to the Electoral College system. (See below.)

If neither candidate for Vice President receives a majority of the votes in the Electoral College, the Senate decides between the two candidates who received the highest number of votes. All Senators vote as individuals, and a majority is needed to elect. This has taken place once, in 1837, when Richard Johnson was chosen Vice President by the Senate.

Criticism of the Electoral System.

1. *Arguments Against the Electoral System.* Several important arguments have been advanced against the electoral system.

(a) The most frequent criticism of the electoral system is that it *makes possible the election of "minority Presidents."* These are Presidents who receive a majority of the electoral votes, but less than a majority of the popular votes. This is made possible by the fact that the party that receives the most votes in any state receives all its electoral votes, no matter how close the election is. Candidates who carry the larger states, even by the slimmest margins, can win in the Electoral College, despite the fact that they may lose in the smaller states by tremendous margins. The following examples illustrate this point. (1) In 1876 Rutherford B. Hayes became President by the close margin of 185 to 184 votes in the Electoral College. At the same time he received 250,000 fewer popular votes than his rival, Samuel Tilden. (2) In 1888, Benjamin Harrison was elected President by an electoral vote of 233 to 168, although his rival, Grover Cleveland, received 95,000 more popular votes than he. (3) Abraham Lincoln (1860), Woodrow Wilson (1912), and Richard Nixon (1968) were elected when there were more than two strong candidates running for the Presidency. Each received a majority in the Electoral College, although each had far fewer popular votes than the combined total of his opponents.

(b) A second argument against the electoral system is that the electoral vote very *often gives an inaccurate picture of the popular vote.* In the election of 1968, for example, Richard Nixon (Republican) got 43.5% of the popular vote, defeating his Democratic opponent, Hubert Humphrey, by less than one-half of one per cent of the popular vote. In the Electoral College, however, Nixon received 56% of the electoral votes, and Humphrey 36%.

(c) A third major criticism of the Electoral College is that *in most states electors are not required to vote for the candidates of the party* in whose name they are chosen. In the elections of 1948, 1956, 1960, and 1968, individual electors refused to support the candidates of the party which carried their state. These defections did not change the results of the elections, but they point up a danger which still exists.

2. *Proposed Changes in the Electoral System.* In the past 150 years reformers have suggested over 500 constitutional amendments to change the present electoral system, which is admittedly unfair. Narrow margins of victory in recent elections have led to support for a drastic overhauling of the system. Nonetheless, powerful political interests continue to block change. The major obstacle to electoral change, Congressional leaders agree, is not outright opposition to the idea of reform but rather the difficulty in getting enough Congressmen to support a single plan. (A two-thirds vote of each house of Congress would be required.) Three proposals that have received strong support are outlined below:

> *(a)* *Direct Popular Election of the President.* Some advocate abolishing the Electoral College altogether, and choosing the President by a direct popular vote. Under an amendment proposed by Senator Birch Bayh, the candidate with the largest number of popular votes would become President if he got at least 40% of the total. If there were several candidates and none got 40%, the two leading contenders would have a second run-off election.

> *(b)* *District Vote.* Under a second proposal each state would be divided into electoral districts of equal population. The voters in each district would choose one elector, plus two "at large" on a statewide basis.

> *(c)* *Proportional Vote.* An increasingly popular proposal is to have each state's electoral vote divided among the various parties in proportion to their popular vote. This plan is opposed by labor, minority, and other groups in large pivotal states, who benefit under the present winner-take all system because it forces Presidential candidates to make positive efforts to gain their support.

Presidential Qualifications, Compensation, and Term.

1. *Qualifications.* The President must be a native-born citizen, at least 35 years of age. He must have lived in the United States at least 14 years.

2. *Compensation.* Congress fixes the President's salary. At present the President receives a salary of $200,000 a year, and a nontaxable allowance of $50,000 to help defray official expenses. In addition, up to $60,000 a year (also nontaxable) is allowed for official travel expenses and entertainment.

> *(a)* The President is also entitled to the use of the White House as a residence, other residential and travel facilities, a staff of assistants, medical and dental care, and other privileges of office.

> *(b)* Since 1958, former Presidents have been granted lifetime pensions (raised in 1971 to $60,000 per year); also office space, an office staff, and free mailing privileges.

3. *Term of Office.* The President serves a four-year term.

> *(a)* Until 1951 there was no constitutional limit to the number of terms a President could serve. However, following the precedent set by George Washington, no President ran for more than two terms until the time of Franklin D. Roosevelt, who was elected four times.

(b) In 1951, the Twenty-second Amendment to the Constitution provided that henceforth a President can serve no more than two elected terms of his own, plus not more than two years of a term to which he may succeed as Vice President.

Presidential Succession. Under the Constitution, if a vacancy in the Presidency occurs, the Vice President takes over the office. Before 1947, the *Presidential Succession Act* provided that the President and Vice President were to be succeeded, if necessary, by the members of the Cabinet in the order of the creation of the various departments, starting with the Secretary of State. (See chart on page 107.) In 1947, the law was changed to place the Speaker of the House of Representatives and the President pro-tem of the Senate in the direct line of succession, *before* the members of the Cabinet.

The 25th Amendment. In 1967, the 25th Amendment was adopted to plug several constitutional loopholes by providing answers to questions such as the following: "What happens when a President is physically unable to perform the duties of his office?" "What happens if a President is unable to perform his duties but unwilling to give up his office?" "Who becomes Vice President if the man holding that office either dies or assumes the Presidency?"

1. In recent years, heart attacks suffered by both President Eisenhower while in office and by President Johnson before becoming President have caused great concern about the Presidential succession. The 25th Amendment declares specifically that the Vice President is to take over the Presidency whenever the President declares himself disabled. The amendment also provides for a take-over by the Vice President (with the approval of Congress and the Cabinet) whenever a disabled President cannot or will not yield his office.

2. The assassination of President Kennedy in 1963 left the nation without a Vice President until 1965. This was the sixth time in the 20th century alone that such a situation has occurred. The Twenty-fifth Amendment eliminated this gap by providing that the President is to nominate a Vice President whenever that office is vacant, subject to confirmation by both houses of Congress.

3. When Vice President Spiro Agnew resigned in 1973, President Nixon (under the terms of the 25th Amendment) nominated Gerald R. Ford to succeed him. When President Nixon in turn resigned in 1974, as a result of the Watergate scandal, Ford succeeded to the Presidency. Ford thereupon nominated Nelson R. Rockefeller to be Vice President.

Powers of the President. The President of the United States has vast powers. The Constitution gives him certain specified powers, such as the power to execute laws, make treaties, and approve acts of Congress. These powers have been expanded greatly over the years as a result of acts of Congress, decisions of the courts, and precedents set by vigorous Presidents.

1. *Executive and Administrative Powers.* As Chief Executive the President has the power and responsibility to enforce and administer Federal laws. In addition he must manage the machinery of government.

(a) He carries out these functions through heads of departments, bureaus, and other administrative and law enforcement agencies (*e.g.,* the Federal Bureau of Investigation and the Department of Justice). These agencies in turn supervise millions of civil service employees (see page 109). Congress often grants the President the right to issue regulations which have the force of law *(ordinance power).*

(b) Most important among the President's executive powers are his powers of *appointment and removal.* Today the President has the power, directly or through his subordinates, to appoint over two million employees of the national government. Some of these appointments, usually of higher officials, require Senate confirmation by majority vote; in this category are ambassadors, Cabinet members, diplomats, and heads of bureaus and commissions. The President also has broad powers of removal from office.

(c) Recently the courts have been called on to decide whether a President can claim *"executive privilege"* in order to withhold information about alleged criminal activities by his subordinates on the grounds that revealing such information would harm national security.

2. *Legislative Powers.* The President is often referred to as the "chief lawmaker" because of his important role in the legislative process.

(a) The Constitution gives him authority to call special sessions of Congress, to send messages to Congress, to recommend legislation, and to sign or veto bills.

(b) Among the more important Presidential message to Congress are the "State of the Union" address at the opening of Congress, the Budget Message, and the Report on Economic Conditions.

(c) Custom and tradition have given the President additional "extra-constitutional" legislative powers. He may use his power of appointment to reward faithful service (*patronage*). As a leader of his party he remains in close contact with party leaders in Congress and tries to carry out the party program. He may seek to gain popular support for legislative programs by direct appeal to the public.

3. *Judicial Powers.* The President's powers have been strengthened by his ability to affect the judicial processes of government.

(a) He appoints Federal judges, including Supreme Court Justices (with Senate approval).

(b) He can recommend changes in court organization (*e.g.,* by increasing the number of Federal judges or the size of the Supreme Court).

(c) He may enforce judicial decisions with or without vigor, depending on his philosophy of government.

(d) He has broad pardoning powers and can also issue *reprieves* (postponement of penalties) or *paroles* (releases from part of a sentence).

4. *Powers in Foreign Affairs.* The President directs the foreign affairs and shapes the foreign policy of the United States.

(a) As the nation's head and official spokesman, he issues statements on foreign policy and decides what the nation will do in a given situation.
(b) He directs the diplomatic service through the State Department and appoints ambassadors and other foreign representatives.
(c) He recognizes foreign governments by receiving their representatives or by issuing a proclamation of recognition.
(d) He commands the armed forces of the United States.
(e) The President may negotiate treaties and other agreements with foreign nations. (Treaties must be approved by two-thirds of the Senate.) He can also make *executive agreements* with foreign governments, without need for Senate approval.

5. *Military Powers.* As Commander-in-Chief of the armed forces the President has important military powers in war and peace.

(a) In wartime, the President helps determine strategy, appoints commanding officers, and issues emergency decrees. The President also receives emergency powers from Congress.
(b) Since he has the power to send units of our armed forces to danger spots anywhere in the world, the President can place the nation in a state of war, or virtually force Congress to declare war. For example, President Polk sent an expedition into Mexico in 1846 in response to a border dispute, thus helping to bring on the Mexican War. In 1950, President Truman involved the United States in the Korean War by sending American troops to Korea in support of the United Nations. In 1965, United States armed forces entered actively into the war in Vietnam, under the orders of President Lyndon B. Johnson, without a declaration of war.
NOTE: To prevent "another Vietnam" from occurring, and in an effort to regain some of its control over the warmaking process, Congress passed the *War Powers Act* of 1973 over President Nixon's veto. This law provides that the President must inform the Congress within 48 hours of any commitment of U.S. armed forces outside our territory, or of any substantial increase of our combat forces in a foreign country. Unless Congress authorizes such an operation within 60 days, the President must halt the military action.
(c) In peacetime, the President may use the armed forces, including the militia, to preserve order or prevent violence. For example, in 1958 President Eisenhower sent troops to Little Rock, Arkansas, to enforce a Supreme Court decision on desegregation of public schools.

6. *Emergency Powers.* Under the Constitution and laws of Congress, the President assumes emergency powers in times of crises. Such powers have been used by Presidents to take over industries for brief periods to protect the public *(e.g.,* in cases of strikes affecting the national welfare), to close banks, and to lend naval vessels to friendly nations.

Growing Importance of the Presidency. The President's overall role in American government has become increasingly important. Today the executive branch is probably more influential in relation to the two other branches than the founding fathers ever dreamed it would become.

1. *A National Symbol.* The President is considered the symbol of the nation. He is its spokesman in world affairs. He is the most respected citizen in the land.

2. *Strong Presidents.* The actions and policies of certain "strong" Presidents have contributed to the growth in importance of the executive branch. Among these Presidents are Washington, Jackson, Lincoln, T. Roosevelt, Wilson, and F. D. Roosevelt. In general, these Presidents believed that the President is the representative of all the people, and should lead rather than follow Congress.

3. *Controlled Powers.* Despite tremendous powers, no American President has sought to become a dictator. This is a tribute to the American way of life as well as to the principles of separation of powers and checks and balances.

The President's Assistants. With growing powers and duties has come the need for more and more help for the President. Without such help, his job would be impossible. Today the President of the United States is responsible for administering over 2000 agencies and for taking care personally of thousands of details of office. The fulfillment of many of these responsibilities is made possible through the *Executive Office of the President.* Among the agencies in the Executive Office are:

1. *The White House Office* consists of counselors, assistants, and special consultants and their staffs. Each concentrates on one or more aspects of the President's job and is a "troubleshooter" for him.

2. *The National Security Council* advises the President on matters of national security. It is composed of the President, the Vice President, and the Secretaries of State and Defense and is serviced by specialized agencies, such as the Central Intelligence Agency and the Joint Chiefs of Staff.

3. *The Domestic Council* formulates and recommends to the President policies designed to deal with domestic (internal) problems.

4. *The Council of Economic Advisers* reports to the President on the nation's economic health, advises him on economic policy, and helps prepare reports to Congress.

5. *The Office of Management and Budget* directs the preparation of the annual budget which the President submits to Congress, and aids the President in bringing about "more efficient and economical conduct of government service."

The President's Cabinet. Almost from the beginnings of government under the Constitution, the President has been assisted by a group of advisors known as the *Cabinet.* Each Cabinet officer heads one of the eleven major executive departments of the government.

1. *Result of Custom.* The Cabinet is not provided for by the Constitution. It originated when President Washington began to call upon the heads of executive departments for advice and information.

2. *Cabinet Meetings.* The President calls Cabinet meetings as often as necessary, and confers regularly with Cabinet officials on matters related to their departments. He may accept or reject their suggestions, as he sees fit. Other government officials, such as the Vice President, are often invited to attend Cabinet meetings.

3. *Cabinet and Congress.* Unlike the British Cabinet, which is directly responsible to Parliament, the President's Cabinet is responsible only to him. Members are appointed by the President with the consent of the Senate, but may not be members of Congress.

4. *Growth of Cabinet.* Congress has created executive departments as often as it has deemed necessary. The first four executive offices were created during Washington's administration (*Secretary of State, Secretary of Treasury, Secretary of War, Attorney General*). Since that time the number has grown to twelve. (In 1971, the Postmaster General ceased to be a member of the Cabinet when the Post Office Department became a semi-independent, non-profit corporation called the *U.S. Postal Service.*)

5. *Term.* Cabinet members have indefinite terms (that is, they serve at the pleasure of the President).

6. *Work of Executive Departments.* See chart on pages 107-8.

The first Cabinet. From left to right: President Washington, Secretary of War Henry Knox, Secretary of Treasury Alexander Hamilton, Secretary of State Thomas Jefferson, and Attorney General Edmund Randolph.

EXECUTIVE DEPARTMENTS AND THEIR RESPONSIBILITIES

DEPARTMENT AND YEAR ESTABLISHED	CHIEF OFFICER	RESPONSIBILITIES
State (1789)	Secretary of State	Handles foreign relations; supervises diplomatic and consular services; issues passports; protects rights of Americans abroad; publishes acts and resolutions of Congress, and executive orders and proclamations; supervises the machinery for electing the President and Vice President.
Treasury (1789)	Secretary of Treasury	In charge of government finances; supervises collection of revenues; handles disbursement of government funds; arranges loans and bond issues; reports to Congress on the government's financial situation; supervises the coining and printing of money; administers the Coast Guard and Secret Service.
Defense (1947)	Secretary of Defense	Established in 1947 by combining the old War Department (1789) and Navy Department (1798). A civilian Secretary of Defense administers the army, navy, and air force, each headed by a separate secretary of its own. The Department plans and executes the defense policies of the nation. The Joint Chiefs of Staff serve as military advisers to the Secretary of Defense, the President, and the National Security Council.
Justice (1789)	Attorney General	Represents the nation in legal affairs. The Attorney General is the chief law officer of the United States. The Justice Department gives legal advice to the President and heads of departments; investigates and uncovers violations of Federal laws; supervises United States marshals and attorneys; enforces Federal civil rights legislation. The Federal Bureau of Investigation (FBI) is an important part of the Department.
Post Office (1794)	Postmaster General	Handled nation's postal system until replaced in 1971 by independent agency called the U.S. Postal Service.

[Continued on p. 108]

Interior (1849)	*Secretary of* *the Interior*	In charge of Federal lands, Indian affairs, reclamation projects, mines, territories, and island possessions. Supervises Fish and Wildlife Service, National Parks.
Agriculture (1889)	*Secretary of* *Agriculture*	Concerned with agricultural improvements, including farming methods and output, farm credits, rural electrification, soil conservation, forestry, etc.
Commerce (1903)	*Secretary of* *Commerce*	Collects statistics and promotes foreign and domestic commerce, manufacturing, transportation, shipping, and fisheries. Takes National Census every ten years. Issues patents; registers trademarks.
Labor (1913)	*Secretary of* *Labor*	Promotes better conditions for working people; mediates labor disputes; collects and publishes labor statistics; supervises administration of Wages and Hours laws.
Health, *Education* *and Welfare* (1953)	*Secretary of* *Health, Education* *and Welfare*	Concerned with improving the health, education and social security systems in the country. Supervises agencies dealing with these matters.
Housing and *Urban* *Development* (1965)	*Secretary of* *Housing and* *Urban* *Development*	Handles and promotes housing, slum clearance, and other aid-to-cities programs.
Transportation (1966)	*Secretary of* *Transportation*	Develops a national transportation policy and coordinates the efforts of agencies in land, sea, and air transportation.
Energy (1977)	*Secretary of* *Energy*	Develops a national energy policy; coordinates public and private efforts to conserve energy and develop new sources.

The Independent Commissions and Administrative Agencies. Since 1887, when it established the Interstate Commerce Commission, Congress has created a large number of executive bodies (called *agencies, commissions, boards,* etc.) to assist the executive branch in the administration and enforcement of Federal laws. (These agencies are said to be "independent" because they are outside the regular executive departments.)

1. *Membership.* Members of these independent agencies and commissions are appointed by the President for fixed terms, with the consent of Congress. The term of service is usually seven years.

2. *Functions.* In some cases the independent agencies have taken over, completely or in part, functions formerly exercised by the executive departments. In other cases they have undertaken entirely new activities in which the government has become involved.

3. *Important Independent Commissions.* The independent agencies have become an important instrument for regulating the economic life of the country. Among the more important of these bodies are the following:

(a) The *Interstate Commerce Commission (ICC)*, created in 1887, regulates rail and motor transportation, and inland and coastal shipping.

(b) The *Federal Trade Commission (FTC)*, created in 1914, promotes free competition by controlling monopoly and discouraging unfair business practices.

(c) The *Federal Power Commission (FPC)*, created in 1920, licenses water-power developments on navigable rivers and draws up water-power policies.

(d) The *Securities and Exchange Commission (SEC)*, created in 1934, regulates the security markets and other organized exchanges, and checks fraudulent and unfair practices in the sale of securities.

(e) The *Federal Communications Commission (FCC)*, created in 1934, regulates telephone, radio, and television communication.

(f) The *National Aeronautics and Space Administration (NASA)*, created in 1958, is in charge of our program of space exploration.

4. *Powers.* These and other agencies, such as the *Board of Governors of the Federal Reserve System* (1913), the *National Labor Relations Board* (1935), and the *Atomic Energy Commission* (1946), are actually *regulatory agencies,* responsible to Congress, with *quasi-legislative* and *quasi-judicial powers.* They issue and enforce regulations which have the force of law. Though they aid in carrying out laws, they are largely independent of the President. In addition to these regulatory agencies, there are many other agencies with purely advisory service functions, such as the *National Agricultural Advisory Commission.* In recent years, it has been suggested that the powers and actions of this "fourth branch of government" be more carefully checked and limited than in the past.

The Civil Service. The United States *Civil Service* consists of all persons who work for the Federal government, exclusive of elected officials and members of the armed forces. The Civil Service System was established by the *Pendleton Act* of 1883. It is administered by the U. S. Civil Service Commission. There are many categories of civil service jobs.

1. *Appointive Positions.* The highest positions are usually appointive; that is, they are appointed by the President with the consent of the Senate. Included in this category are heads of departments, ambassadors, district attorneys, and members of the independent agencies.

2. *Non-classified Positions.* A second large group of civil service workers falls into the *non-classified* or "higher" civil service category. These positions are ordinarily filled directly by the President, the courts, or heads of departments. Included here are Presidential assistants, United States Marshals, and heads of bureaus.

3. *Classified Positions.* Most civil service employees fall into the third category, the *classified civil service.* Positions here are filled from lists established as a result of open competitive examinations. Government employees who receive jobs in the classified civil service keep their positions for life, unlike the appointive and non-classified job holders, who may be replaced after each election.

REVIEW TEST (Chapter 6 — Part V)

Select the number preceding the word or expression that best completes each statement or answers each question.

1. What has made the direct election of our President by the Electoral College outdated? (1) increase in population (2) passing of the "Lame Duck" Amendment (3) rise of political parties (4) rise of the "Solid South"

2. The number of electoral votes to which each state is entitled depends upon the number of (1) popular votes cast by the state in the last election (2) Senators and Representatives that the state has in Congress (3) native-born citizens in the state (4) electoral districts in the state

3. A person may not be elected President of the United States more than twice, according to (1) a provision of the original Constitution (2) an amendment of the Constitution (3) a law of Congress (4) custom

4. In his inaugural oath, the President of the United States swears (or affirms) to preserve, protect, and defend (1) the Constitution (2) democracy (3) the nation (4) the states

5. Members of the President's Cabinet remain in office (1) for a term of four years (2) for a term fixed by the House of Representatives (3) at the pleasure of the Senate (4) at the pleasure of the President

6. Which of the following persons is an employee of the Executive Branch of the United States government? (1) a page boy in the Senate (2) a secretary of a member of the House of Representatives (3) an Associate Justice of the Supreme Court (4) a representative of the State Department in a foreign city

7. Because of the treaty-making procedure provided in the United States Constitution, some Presidents have (1) negotiated executive agreements instead of treaties with foreign nations (2) vetoed proposed Constitutional amendments curbing the treaty power (3) obtained advisory opinions from the Supreme Court before submitting treaties to the Senate (4) referred treaties to the House of Representatives instead of to the Senate

8. According to the Constitution, responsibility for the conduct of foreign affairs is given to the (1) President (2) Secretary of State (3) President's Cabinet (4) Senate Foreign Relations Committee

9. As Commander-in-Chief of the armed forces, the President can (1) declare war (2) draft men and women into the armed forces (3) establish a treaty of peace (4) order the armed forces into foreign countries to protect American interests

10. A bill that has been vetoed by the President of the United States may become a law if it is passed by at least a (1) two-thirds vote in the Senate (2) three-fourths vote in each house of Congress (3) two-thirds vote in each house of Congress (4) two-thirds vote in the House of Representatives

11. In case of the death or removal from office of both the President and the Vice President of the United States, the official who shall become President is the (1) Chief Justice of the Supreme Court (2) Secretary of State (3) Speaker of the House of Representatives (4) President pro tempore of the United States Senate

12. All of the following Presidents significantly expanded the powers of the Presidency *except* (1) Abraham Lincoln (2) Theodore Roosevelt (3) Woodrow Wilson (4) Dwight Eisenhower

13. All of the following assist the Federal government in the enforcement of Federal laws *except* (1) the National Security Council (2) the National Labor Relations Board (3) the Federal Communications Commission (4) the Federal Trade Commission

14. Which of the following established the Civil Service System? (1) the Taft-Hartley Act (2) the Pendleton Act (3) the Morrill Act (4) the Tenth Amendment

15. Which of the following were elected by a minority vote in the elections indicated. (1) Rutherford Hayes (1876) and Woodrow Wilson (1912), (2) John F. Kennedy (1960) and Richard Nixon (1968), (3) none of the preceding, (4) all of the preceding

Name the individual who at present heads each Cabinet department described below:

1. This department plans the defense policies of the nation.

2. This department enforces civil rights legislation.

3. This department supervises the coining and printing of money.

4. This department supervises Indian Affairs, National Parks, and island possessions.

5. This department issues passports and protects the rights of Americans abroad.

Essay Questions

1. In the course of our history the Presidents of the United States have become more clearly recognized as democratically selected leaders of the American people. (a) Show how changes in nominating procedures have made nomination of the President more democratic. (b) Describe the part played by political parties following the nomination of a candidate in the election of the President. (c) Explain the major issues involved in one of the following election campaigns: (1) Franklin D. Roosevelt—Herbert Hoover (2) William McKinley—William J. Bryan (3) Woodrow Wilson—William H. Taft (4) John F. Kennedy—Richard Nixon (5) Barry Goldwater—Lyndon B. Johnson (6) Richard Nixon—George McGovern (7) James E. Carter—Gerald R. Ford.

2. Discuss fully the part played by the Electoral College in selecting the President of the United States.

3. Explain one criticism that has been made of (a) the Electoral College (b) the method of Presidential succession (c) independent regulatory agencies.

4. Discuss two ways in which the President may influence (a) legislation (b) foreign policy.

5. Explain, giving evidence, why each of the following statements has been made about the President of the United States: (a) He is the world's most powerful elected leader. (b) He derives his powers from both the written and unwritten constitutions. (c) His job is one of the most difficult in the world.

6. Show how amendments to the Constitution have affected the Presidency.

Part VI — THE FEDERAL JUDICIARY

The Federal judiciary is the third coordinate branch of our national government. The *jurisdiction* of the Federal courts (that is, their right to hear and decide cases) extends to cases concerning the Constitution, treaties with other nations, and laws of Congress. Because it is supposed to maintain a proper relationship between the executive and legislative branches of the Federal government, and also between the national and state governments, the Federal court system has been called the "balance wheel" of the Federal system.

Jurisdiction of the Federal Courts. Under Article III of the Constitution the Federal judiciary has specific responsibilities.

1. *Types of Cases.* The Constitution gives Federal courts jurisdiction over three types of cases.

    (a) Cases arising under the Constitution, laws, and treaties of the United States.

    (b) Cases related to the sea *(admiralty and maritime jurisdiction).*

    (c) Cases involving certain parties, such as: ambassadors, ministers, and foreign consuls; cases between states, or citizens of different states; and cases in which the United States is a party.

2. *Concurrent and Exclusive Jurisdiction.* Some cases, such as those involving ambassadors and patents, may be tried *only* in Federal courts; this is known as *exclusive jurisdiction.* Other cases, such as those between residents of different states, may be heard in both state and Federal courts; this is known as *concurrent jurisdiction.*

3. *Original and Appellate Jurisdiction.* Some Federal courts, notably the District Courts, have only *original jurisdiction.* In other words, they are courts in which cases are heard for the first time. Other courts, like the Courts of Appeals, may hear cases only on appeal from the lower courts *(appellate jurisdiction).* The United States Supreme Court has both original and appellate jurisdiction.

Civil and Criminal Cases. Both civil and criminal cases may be tried in Federal courts. *Civil suits* are concerned with individual rights and responsibilities — for example, a dispute between two persons over the terms of a contract. *Criminal cases* are those in which the state charges a person with a public offense (crime).

Organization of the Federal Court System. The Constitution provides for a Supreme Court and such lower ("inferior") courts as Congress decides to establish *(Article III, Section 1).* Under this power, Congress has created a national court system consisting of the Supreme Court, Courts of Appeals, District Courts, and a number of so-called special courts including the Court of Claims, the Tax Court, and the Court of Customs and Patent Appeals.

The judges who preside over the Federal courts are nominated by the President and confirmed by the Senate. In all the courts except the special courts, the judges serve for life or until retirement. They may be removed from office only by impeachment proceedings, based on formal charges of misconduct in office.

District Courts. The District Courts are the "lowest" Federal courts. There are 86 of them in the 50 states and one in the District of Columbia. The great majority of the civil and criminal cases involved in the Federal court system are tried in the District Courts. In about half of these cases, the United States government is a party — for example, in prosecuting persons accused of violating Federal laws.

Each District Court has jurisdiction over cases arising in a specific area of the United States or its territories. Each such area is called a *judicial district.* A case heard in a District Court may be appealed to a Court of Appeals. In some cases, appeals may go directly to the Supreme Court.

Courts of Appeals. The United States Courts of Appeals hear appeals from decisions of the District Courts and of Federal agencies, such as the Federal Trade Commission and the Interstate Commerce Commission. There are eleven of these courts, each of which considers appeals from the several District Courts located within its judicial circuit. In most cases, the Courts of Appeals have final jurisdiction, since Congress has decided that only cases involving the constitutionality of state or Federal laws and treaties of the United States and the constitutional rights of individuals may be appealed to the Supreme Court. When a Circuit Court hears a case, it may uphold or reverse the decision of the lower court or Federal agency.

The Supreme Court. The Supreme Court is the highest court in the land. It has been called "America's unique contribution to the theory of government."

1. *Size.* The size of the Supreme Court is fixed by Congress. At present, the Court has nine members—one Chief Justice and eight Associate Justices. The Chief Justice presides over the Court.

2. *Jurisdiction.* The Supreme Court has *original jurisdiction* in cases affecting ambassadors and other public ministers, and in those cases to which a state is a party. There are relatively few such cases. The Court has *appellate jurisdiction* in all other cases. Most of its work today consists of cases involving questions of the constitutionality of Federal and state laws, Federal treaties, and cases appealed from the highest state courts.

3. *Operation.* The Supreme Court has the power to decide which cases it will try. It selects the cases it wishes to hear from among those appealed to it. To do this it issues a *writ of certiorari,* which is an order directing the lower Federal or state court to send up its proceedings in the case for review. The Supreme Court's heavy burden of work forces it to turn down most requests for review.

4. *Decisions.* Supreme Court decisions are rendered by majority vote. The decision is usually written for the majority by one of the Justices. If a Justice agrees with the decision, but does not fully accept the reasoning behind it, he may issue a *concurring opinion.* In many cases, Justices on the minority side prepare *dissenting opinions* (opposing views).

5. *Judicial Review.* The Supreme Court has the power to declare unconstitutional all or part of any act of Congress, state constitution, state law, or local ordinance, if it feels that it is contrary to the U.S. Constitution. This power to decide on the constitutionality of laws is called the *power of judicial review.* This right was established by Chief Justice JOHN MARSHALL in the famous case of *Marbury v. Madison* (1803).

NOTE: When the Supreme Court declares a law unconstitutional, the law is no longer enforced. It is *not* annulled or repealed.

6. *Criticism of the Court.* Throughout the course of American history, the Supreme Court has had to take forthright positions on important national issues such as slavery, regulation of business, and civil rights. It has, therefore, been under constant criticism.

(a) At one time or another, the Court has been accused of being partial to property interests, of overemphasizing personal rights at the expense of public security, and of handing down decisions and orders which have the effect of law and thus infringe on the rights of Congress and the President ("judicial legislation").

(b) Among the suggestions made by critics for curbing the powers of the Court are: **(1)** increasing to six or seven the majority vote required to declare laws unconstitutional; **(2)** making the amending process simpler, so that Congress and the states will be in a better position to override unfavorable Court decisions by changing the Constitution; **(3)** amending the Constitution so that Congress can override an unfavorable Court decision by a two-thirds vote; and **(4)** providing for the election and recall of Federal judges.

(c) Defenders of the Supreme Court feel that its powers should not be curbed. They feel that the Court is the "balance wheel of the Constitution," and in recent years has become a defender of human rights. They argue that to limit its power would be to destroy the system of checks and balances.

Special Federal Courts. In addition to the regular Federal courts, Congress has created special courts to handle special kinds of cases.

1. *The United States Court of Claims* hears cases in which individuals claim that the Federal government owes them money. For example, a person injured by a government mail truck might bring suit in this court.

2. *The United States Customs Court* settles disputes over the value of goods imported into the United States, and other matters involving the United States Customs Service.

3. *The United States Court of Customs and Patent Appeals* hears appeals from the Customs Court and from the United States Patent Office.

4. *Territorial Courts* have been established by Congress in the United States territories of Puerto Rico, Guam, the Virgin Islands, and the Canal Zone. They are considered part of the Federal court system, and have the same jurisdiction as regular Federal District Courts as well as jurisdiction in local affairs (except for Puerto Rico, which has its own local courts, equivalent to state courts).

Relationship of State Courts to the Federal Court System. Each state has its own court system. These are in most cases completely independent of the Federal court system. In some instances, however, as we have noted, cases may be appealed from the highest state court to the United States Supreme Court. The Supreme Court from time to time has declared unconstitutional state laws and has overruled state court decisions.

Enforcing Court Decisions. Courts hear and decide cases brought before them. It is up to the executive branch of the government, however, to apply and enforce such decisions. Among the chief United States officials who help carry out decisions of the Federal courts are the following:

1. The *United States Attorney General,* who heads the Department of Justice, is a member of the President's Cabinet and is the government's chief law-enforcement officer. In cases of exceptional importance, he may appear personally before the Supreme Court to represent the government.

2. The *Solicitor General* is the chief assistant to the Attorney General. He ordinarily represents the government before the Supreme Court.

3. The *Federal Bureau of Investigation* (within the Department of Justice) investigates violations of Federal laws.

4. *Federal District Attorneys* and their staffs prosecute persons charged with violations of Federal laws and represent the government in civil actions.

5. There are a number of court officers, such as *United States Marshals,* who have the duty of enforcing Federal laws.

REVIEW TEST (Chapter 6 — Part VI)

Select the number preceding the word or expression that best completes each statement or answers each question.

1. The number of Justices on the Supreme Court is: (1) determined by its own membership (2) determined by Congress (3) stated in the Constitution (4) determined by the President

2. To declare an act of Congress unconstitutional the Supreme Court must render a decision based on (1) a unanimous vote (2) a majority vote (3) a two-thirds vote (4) a three-fourths vote

3. The right to set aside legislation on the grounds of unconstitutionality was (1) specifically granted in the original Constitution (2) voted by Congress (3) provided for by Constitutional amendment (4) assumed by the Supreme Court itself

4. In which instance would the Supreme Court have original jurisdiction? (1) New York State sues New Jersey over navigation on the Hudson River (2) the robbing of a national bank (3) violation by a citizen of the Federal income tax law (4) violation of a citizen's civil rights

5. What is the role of the United States Supreme Court in the legislative process? (1) Congress must receive an advisory opinion from the Court before it passes a bill. (2) A citizen does not have to obey a law until the court pronounces it constitutional. (3) The Court deals with legislation only when acting on a case. (4) The Court may act only on the constitutionality of laws affecting states.

6. The situation where a case may be heard in both the state courts and in Federal courts is known as (1) exclusive jurisdiction (2) concurrent jurisdiction (3) appellate jurisdiction (4) original jurisdiction

7. Which of the following statements is *not* true about Federal judges? (1) They are nominated by the President. (2) They are confirmed by the Senate. (3) They may be removed only by impeachment. (4) They must have first served in state courts.

8. To which court would a case on appeal from a District Court generally go? (1) the Supreme Court (2) a Court of Appeals (3) the Court of Claims (4) the highest state court

9. Of the cases sent to it for review, the Supreme Court is able to render decisions on (1) nearly all (2) about two-thirds (3) about half (4) much less than half

10. A foreign ambassador in the United States who felt that his rights had been jeopardized could have his case brought directly to (1) the Court of Claims (2) a Federal District Court (3) a Court of Appeals (4) the Supreme Court

State whether each of the following statements is true or false. If the statement is false, replace the word or phrase in **boldface type** *with one which will make it correct.*

1. The right of the Supreme Court to decide on the constitutionality of laws of Congress is known as **due process.**

2. In cases before the Supreme Court, the U. S. government is represented by the **assistant district attorney.**

3. Decisions and orders of Federal courts that have the effect of laws are referred to as **"judicial legislation."**

4. If one or more Supreme Court justices disagree with the majority they may file an **obiter dictum.**

5. The Federal Court of final jurisdiction in most cases that do *not* involve the constitutionality of laws or treaties is the **Court of Appeals.**

Essay Questions

1. Explain why the Federal court system has been called the "balance wheel" of the federal system.

2. Define: *original jurisdiction; appellate jurisdiction; concurrent jurisdiction.*

3. Discuss the role of each of the following in the Federal court system: (a) the United States District Courts (b) the Courts of Appeals (c) the Supreme Court (d) the Court of Claims (e) the Court of Customs and Patent Appeals.

4. By giving specific evidence, show how changing social conditions or philosophies are often reflected in decisions made by the United States Supreme Court.

5. The Supreme Court of the United States has (a) expanded the power of Congress (b) protected property rights (c) strengthened civil liberties. For each of the above show how a Supreme Court decision contributed to the effect indicated.

6. The Supreme Court has been under constant criticism throughout American history. (a) Explain why the Court has been a target for critics. (b) Describe three suggestions for curbing the power of the Court that have been made in recent years. (c) Explain why you favor or oppose limiting the Court's authority.

Part VII — EXPANSION OF THE CONSTITUTION

Nothing shows the genius and foresight of the framers of the Constitution more clearly than the fact that our basic law is as serviceable today in the "space age," as it was when adopted in the "horse and buggy age." Of course, the Constitution under which we are governed today is not exactly the same as the document which went into effect in 1789. The Constitution has been adapted to constantly changing conditions by means of several different processes, including amendments, acts of Congress, use of the elastic clause, Presidential actions, court decisions, and usage and custom.

Constitutional Amendments. Article V of the Constitution provides for formal changes through the amending process. The amendments adopted thus far have defined more clearly the relations between the Federal government and the states, have extended individual freedom, and have made modifications in the organization and structure of the executive and legislative branches.

1. *The Amending Process.* There are four methods of amending the Constitution, only two of which have thus far been used.

(a) An amendment may be proposed by a two-thirds vote of each house of Congress, and ratified (approved) by the legislatures of three-fourths of the states. All amendments except the Twenty-first have been adopted in this manner.

(b) An amendment may be proposed by a two-thirds vote of each house of Congress and ratified by conventions of three-fourths of the states. The Twenty-first Amendment was ratified in this fashion.

(c) An amendment may be proposed by a national convention called by Congress upon request of the legislatures of two-thirds of the states, and ratified by the legislatures of three-fourths of the states. This procedure has never been used.

(d) An amendment may be proposed by a national convention called by Congress upon request of the legislatures of two-thirds of the states, and ratified by conventions in three-fourths of the states.

2. *Criticism of the Amending Process.* Amending the Constitution is a difficult process. Of the thousands of amendments suggested throughout our history, only 26 have been adopted. Defenders of the present system maintain that it has met the needs of the country over the years, and that it has prevented hasty, ill-considered action. Critics argue that in most instances the process is too slow and difficult. (Defenders answer that an amendment strongly backed by public opinion may move through very quickly — *e.g.,* the 26th giving the vote to 18-year-olds, which was ratified in 1971 within six months after being approved by Congress.) Another criticism is that the present system is undemocratic, since the people neither propose nor ratify amendments directly. Moreover, a small minority of states (representing quite possibly a much smaller minority of the total population) may be able to block the will of the majority. Today, amendments must be approved by 38 states.

PROVISIONS OF THE AMENDMENTS

Amendments 1-10 (1791)

The first ten amendments are called the *Bill of Rights* because they guarantee rights similar to those in the English Bill of Rights of 1689. *Amendments 1 to 9* define and protect the rights of individuals against acts of the national government. These rights include: freedom of speech, press, religion, petition and assembly; freedom from unreasonable searches and seizures; trial by jury, with no excessive bail, fines, or punishments. *Amendment 10* reserves to the states powers not granted to the national government.

Amendment 11 (1798)

A state may not be sued by a citizen of another state without its consent.

Amendment 12 (1804)

Changed the method of choosing the President and Vice President by providing for separate voting for each in the Electoral College.

Amendments 13, 14, 15 (1865, 1868, 1870)

Sometimes called the "Civil War Amendments." *Amendment 13* (1865) abolished slavery. *Amendment 14* (1868) defined and guaranteed citizenship, thus extending it to former slaves. It also prohibited states from depriving anyone of "life, liberty, and property, without due process of law." *Amendment 15* (1870) extended to former slaves the right to vote by declaring that suffrage cannot be denied or abridged because of "race, color, or previous condition of servitude."

Amendment 16 (1913)

Gave Congress the power to levy income taxes.

Amendment 17 (1913)

Provided for the direct popular election of U. S. Senators.

Amendment 18 (1919)

Prohibited the national sale, manufacture, and transportation of intoxicating beverages (Prohibition).

Amendment 19 (1920)

Gave women the right to vote by providing that the right to vote cannot be denied because of sex.

Amendment 20 (1933)

Provided that the terms of the President and Vice President are to begin on January 20, instead of March 4. Also provided that the regular session of Congress is to begin each year on January 3. This eliminated the "lame duck" session of Congress in which Congressmen defeated for re-election in November continued to serve until following March 4.

Amendment 21 (1933)

Repealed the Eighteenth Amendment (Prohibition).

Amendment 22 (1951)

Limited a President's stay in office to two full terms, or not more than ten years.

Amendment 23 (1961)

Gave the residents of the District of Columbia (the national capital) the right to vote in national elections.

Amendment 24 (1964)

Prohibited the payment of a poll tax or other tax as a qualification for voting in elections for any Federal office.

Amendment 25 (1967)

Clarified the Presidential succession by authorizing the Vice President to take over whenever the President declares himself disabled. Also provided for the assumption of the Presidency by the Vice President when a disabled President is unable or unwilling to give up his office. In this case, Congress and the Cabinet must approve. Finally, authorized the President to name a Vice President (subject to confirmation by Congress) whenever that office becomes vacant. See page 102.

Amendment 26 (1971)

Gave the vote to qualified citizens who had reached the age of 18. (This applied to *all* elections, state and local, as well as Federal.) Previously most states had set the minimum voting age at 21. This amendment added 11 million potential voters to the electorate. Its effects on the nation's political life are still to be demonstrated.

The Unwritten Constitution. The original Constitution and its amendments provide only a basic framework of American government. To understand the American governmental system as it actually operates, we must study the ways in which the "written Constitution" has been expanded by laws of Congress, decisions of the courts, actions of the Presidents, and customs and traditions. These aspects of American government are often called the "unwritten Constitution."

1. *Expansion Through Acts of Congress.* In the more than 150 years since the adoption of the Constitution, Congress has passed many thousands of laws filling in the organization and structure of American government. Laws of Congress have created Federal departments, as well as hundreds of other agencies and commissions, have established Federal courts below the Supreme Court, and have brought into being such important features of American government as the United States civil service and social security systems. Congressional use of the *elastic clause* and *implied powers* has made possible a tremendous expansion in Federal powers.

2. *Expansion Through Judicial Interpretation.* As a result of the doctrine of *judicial review,* the Supreme Court has handed down decisions which have broadened the authority of the national government, reversed decisions of state courts, protected personal and property rights, and declared unconstitutional acts of Congress and the states.

3. *Expansion Through Presidential Action.* Presidents of the United States have also expanded and given shape to the Constitution and the Federal government. Presidents Washington and Monroe, for example, did much to determine the general direction of American foreign policy for a century. Presidents Jackson, Lincoln, Wilson, and F. D. Roosevelt built the tradition of strong Presidential leadership. Executive agreements with foreign governments have been repeatedly used (especially by recent

Presidents) to avoid the Constitutional restriction that treaties must be ratified by a two-thirds vote of the Senate.

4. *Expansion Through Custom and Tradition.* Many characteristics of American government are the result of custom and tradition.

(a) *The President's Cabinet.* Although the Cabinet is not mentioned in the Constitution, all Presidents since Washington have followed the practice of holding more or less regular meetings with the heads of the executive departments. The President is not required to follow the advice given by the Cabinet, although he is often guided by it.

(b) *Political Parties.* Political parties have grown out of the needs of American politics and have become an integral part of our political processes. They are not mentioned in the Constitution.

(c) *Committee System.* The committee system, perhaps the most important feature of Congressional organization, is based upon custom rather than upon any written legal requirements.

(d) *Senatorial Courtesy.* This refers to the practice whereby the Senate will not normally ratify an appointment unless the President has consulted the Senator or Senators of his party from the state affected. This, too, is a matter of custom, rather than law.

(e) *Two-term Tradition.* Until Franklin Roosevelt, who was elected four times, Presidents followed the custom established by George Washington, of not seeking more than two terms in office. This custom has now become part of the written Constitution through the Twenty-second Amendment.

REVIEW TEST (Chapter 6—Part VII)

Select the number preceding the word or expression that best completes each statement or answers each question.

1. The process of amending the United States Constitution is (1) part of our unwritten law (2) patterned after English practice (3) based on a decision of the United States Supreme Court (4) provided for in the Constitution itself

2. The Constitution of the United States provides that amendments may be proposed by (1) Congress (2) the President (3) Governors of the states (4) state conventions

3. The ratification of an amendment to the Constitution requires the approval of (1) the President and Congress (2) a majority of the United States Supreme Court Justices (3) legislatures or conventions in three-fourths of the states (4) a majority of the eligible voters

4. All of the following are methods of adjusting the Constitution of the United States to changing conditions *except* (1) direct amendment (2) loose construction (3) custom (4) initiative and referendum

5. Which of the following is an example of our unwritten Constitution? (1) a meeting of the President's Cabinet (2) the nomination of a new Justice to the U.S. Supreme Court (3) approval of a treaty by the U.S. Senate (4) delivery of the President's State of the Union Message to Congress

6. How many states can block the passage of an amendment? (1) 7 (2) 9 (3) 11 (4) 13

7. The first 10 Amendments to the Constitution of the United States limit the power of (1) state governments only (2) the Federal government only (3) both Federal and state governments (4) local governments only

8. The reason that an amendment was needed to levy a Federal income tax was that (1) the people opposed Federal taxation (2) it was a type of tax that had never been used (3) the states were already using this type of taxation (4) it was a direct tax, not apportioned according to population

9. Amendments to the United States Constitution intended to extend democratic practices, include provisions for all the following *except* (1) the right of women to vote (2) right of Negroes to vote (3) right of the people to elect members of the House of Representatives (4) abolition of the "lame duck" session of Congress

10. Which of the following is *true* for citizens living in the District of Columbia? (1) They elect representatives to Congress. (2) They do not pay personal income taxes. (3) They are ineligible for civil service positions. (4) They vote for Presidential electors.

Match each Amendment in Column A with the quotation in Column B that identifies it.

A	**B**
1. Amendment I	*a.* "No person shall be elected to the office of President more than twice"
2. Amendment XVII	*b.* "The Senate of the United States shall be composed of two Senators from each state elected by the people thereof"
3. Amendment XIV	*c.* "The eighteenth article of amendment . . . is hereby repealed"
4. Amendment XXI	*d.* "Congress shall make no law respecting an establishment of religion . . . or abridging the freedom of speech"
5. Amendment XXII	*e.* "Nor shall any person be subject for the same offense to be twice put in jeopardy of life or limb . . ."
	f. "Nor shall any state deprive any person of life, liberty, or property without due process of law . . ."

Essay Questions

1. For about 175 years the Constitution of the United States has been able to survive in a rapidly changing civilization. Giving specific examples, show how the original Constitution of the United States has been expanded by each of the following: (a) amendments (b) laws of Congress (c) decisions of the Supreme Court (d) custom and usage.

2. The United States Constitution is a living document. Describe briefly a circumstance that led to the adoption of one amendment to the Constitution in each of the following periods: (1) 1789–1815 (2) 1860–1875 (3) 1900–1930 (4) since 1930.

3. The amending process of the United States Constitution has been both praised and criticized. (a) Give one argument in favor of the present system. (b) Give one argument against the present system.

4. By giving specific examples, show how amendments to the Constitution have: (a) altered or improved the structure of American government and (b) contributed to the growth of democracy.

Part VIII — THE PROTECTION OF CIVIL RIGHTS AND CIVIL LIBERTIES UNDER THE CONSTITUTION

The protection of individual rights is one of the most cherished features of American life and government. The desire for protection of these rights was part of the concept of personal freedom and limited government brought to the New World by the colonists, and developed during the Colonial and Revolutionary periods. The rights and liberties guaranteed under the original Constitution have been expanded by laws, amendments, and court interpretations. The problem of their continued protection and expansion is an important issue in American life today.

> NOTE: In this book and elsewhere, the terms *civil rights* and *civil liberties* are often used interchangeably. There is, however, a distinction between the two terms that should be noted. Technically speaking, *civil liberties* are the individual freedoms protected by the Constitution against infringement and encroachment by the *government*; for example, freedom of speech and the right to protection of property. *Civil rights* are the individual freedoms that are protected (or that citizens think should be protected) against infringement and encroachment by other *individuals* or by *private groups;* for example, opportunities for equal education and housing. In many instances the terms overlap, and it is often difficult, and indeed unnecessary, to distinguish between them.

The Protection of Property. The desire to safeguard the rights of property holders was a major reason for the calling of the Constitutional Convention. The Constitution attempts to protect the rights of property in several ways.

1. *Restriction of the Power of Eminent Domain. Eminent domain* is the right of a government to take private property for public purposes — for example, to build a dam, housing project, or highway. The Fifth Amendment restricts the right of eminent domain by forbidding Congress to take private property *without* just compensation and due process of law.

2. *Restriction of the Power to Tax.* In order to prevent the government from favoring any single person, group, or section at the expense of another, the Constitution provides that direct taxes must be apportioned among the states according to their population. (*Article I, Section 9*). Also, excise taxes (for example, taxes placed on goods made in this country) must be uniform throughout the United States (*Article I, Section 9*); Congress may not levy taxes on exports (*Article I, Section 9*); no state may levy taxes on imports or exports (*Article I, Section 10*).

3. *Restriction of the Right to Issue Money.* To prevent states from passing laws that favored debtors at the expense of creditors, the Constitution declared that states may not issue paper money. Nor may states make anything legal in payment of debts (*legal tender*) except gold or silver (*Article I, Section 10*).

4. *Protection of the Right of Contract.* Under the Constitution, the states are forbidden to pass laws which impair the obligations of contracts; *e.g.*, laws interfering with the collection of debts (*Article I, Section 10*).

The Protection of Personal Liberties. In general, the Constitution aims to safeguard the freedom and security of the person, freedom of expression, and the right to fair treatment under the law. These rights are protected by limitations placed on the national government and the states. Some of these protective features are in the original Constitution, while others have been added since then.

Protection of Civil Liberties in the Original Constitution. Although the framers of the Constitution depended largely on the states to safeguard personal liberties, they wrote several safeguards directly into the basic law.

1. *No Ex-post-facto Laws.* Neither the Federal government nor any state may pass an *ex-post-facto law.* This is a law which makes a person liable to punishment for an act which was not considered a crime at the time it was committed (*Article I, Sections 9-10*). Also, a law may not increase the penalty for an act committed before the passage of the law.

2. *No Bills of Attainder.* Neither the Federal government nor any state may pass a law providing for punishment of an individual without a trial (*Article I, Sections 9-10*). Such a law is called a *bill of attainder.*

3. *No Suspension of the Writ of Habeas Corpus.* A *writ of habeas corpus* is a court order compelling the authorities to bring a prisoner into open court without delay and to prove that there are legal reasons for holding him in custody. The writ is intended to prevent unjust imprisonment. It may not be suspended by the Federal government except in times of rebellion or invasion.

4. *Careful Definition of Treason.* Under the Constitution, treason is limited to two offenses: **(a)** attempting to overthrow the government and **(b)** giving aid to its enemies (*Article III, Section 3*).

The Bill of Rights. When the Constitution was originally presented for ratification, there was a widespread feeling that it did not adequately protect individual rights. To meet this objection, the first ten amendments (the *Bill of Rights*) were added as a group in 1791. The Bill of Rights, particularly the first eight amendments, guarantees the basic rights and liberties of individuals. These are listed below. (As set forth in the Constitution, these guarantees apply to the Federal government only.)

Freedom of religion.

Separation of church and state.

Freedom of speech.

Freedom of the press.

Freedom of assembly.

Freedom of petition.

Freedom to keep and bear arms.

Freedom from quartering soldiers in private homes in times of peace.

Freedom of persons and property from unreasonable search and seizure.

Search warrants to be issued only with good cause.

Indictment for crime only by a grand jury. (An *indictment* is a formal accusation which requires that the accused stand trial. A *grand jury* is composed of from 12 to 23 citizens, set up to decide whether there is sufficient evidence to warrant an indictment.)

Freedom from double jeopardy (being tried twice for the same offense).

Freedom from self-incrimination (being forced to testify against oneself) in criminal cases.

No person to be deprived of life, liberty, or property without due process of law (*fair court procedures*).

Speedy, public trial in the district where the crime was committed.

Trial by jury in criminal cases or civil suits involving more than $20.

Right of the accused in criminal cases to be informed of the charges, to question witnesses, to call witnesses in his own behalf, and to have the assistance of counsel (a lawyer).

Freedom from excessive bail, fines, or cruel and unusual punishments.

Ninth and Tenth Amendments. The Ninth and Tenth Amendments protect personal liberties in a broad and general way. The *Ninth Amendment* states that a right possessed by the people but not mentioned by the Constitution still belongs to the people and may not be denied by the government. The *Tenth Amendment* declares that rights not delegated to the Federal government, nor prohibited to the states, are reserved to the states or to the people.

Later Amendments. Later amendments to the United States Constitution provide additional guarantees of civil rights.

Slavery and involuntary servitude are forbidden (*Thirteenth Amendment*).

Life, liberty and property may not be taken away by states without due process of law (*Fourteenth Amendment*).

All native-born and naturalized persons have *dual citizenship* — that is, they are citizens of both the United States and the state in which they reside (*Fourteenth Amendment*). Broad court interpretations of this amendment have "nationalized" the Bill of Rights, applying it to the states as well as to the Federal government.

The privilege of voting may not be denied because of race, color, or previous condition of servitude (*Fifteenth Amendment*).

The right to vote may not be denied because of sex (*Nineteenth Amendment*).

The right to vote for Federal officials may not be made to depend upon the payment of a special tax (*Twenty-fourth Amendment*).

State Constitutions. State constitutions contain listings of civil rights similar to those of the Federal Constitution. In many cases, the enumeration of rights is even more exhaustive.

Limitations on Individual Rights. Although civil rights are guaranteed under the Constitution, no person may do just as he pleases. For example, although we have the right of free speech, we do *not* have the right to yell "Fire!" in a crowded theater without cause. This would endanger the safety of others. Under the doctrine of *"police powers,"* the Supreme Court has recognized that the states have the right to protect the *health, safety, morals,* and *welfare* of the general public. The states have exercised these powers by forbidding gambling, by prohibiting child labor, by establishing traffic regulations, by requiring vaccinations, and by many other similar actions. Congress, under its delegated powers, has been able to protect the public welfare by requiring safety devices on airplanes and trains, by regulating the sale of drugs, and, on occasion, by fixing wages and prices.

Recent Civil Rights Problems. In recent years the Supreme Court has had to deal with burning civil rights issues with increasing frequency.

1. *Right of Dissent.* During and after World Wars I and II, the problems of individuals and groups who sought to overthrow the government were paramount. In deciding this issue the Court has been faced with the problem of preserving the rights of dissenters and minorities without endangering the national security. In ruling on cases of espionage and subversion the courts have generally applied the *"clear and present danger"* doctrine set forth by Supreme Court Justice Oliver Wendell Holmes, Jr. in 1919 in the case of *Schenck v. U.S.* This rule holds that the test of legality of a person's words or actions is whether or not they create a clear and present danger to the security of the nation. In 1940, the *Smith Act* made it a crime to teach and advocate the violent overthrow of the government, or to conspire to teach and advocate such ideas. In *Noto v. U.S.* (1961), the Court ruled that belief in the desirability of the idea of the overthrow of the government did not in itself represent a "clear and present danger" to national security.

2. *Changes in the Supreme Court.* In the 1960s and 1970s, the Supreme Court continued its function of ruling on civil rights issues, as surveyed below. It is to be noted that from 1954 to 1969, the "Warren Court" (headed by Chief Justice Earl Warren) took a generally "liberal" position, often protecting the rights of individuals, including criminal suspects and defendants, against governmental action or inaction. More recently, the Court has handed down more "conservative" rulings in a number of cases involving constitutional issues, although certainly not *all* decisions have been of this nature.

(a) *Integration of Public Schools.* In 1954, in a landmark decision, the Supreme Court held in *Brown v. Board of Education* that segregation of public schools on the basis of race is unconstitutional. This led to an intensive, bitterly contested, and only partly successful campaign to integrate public schools and school systems in all parts of the

United States. In 1974, the Court ended a 20-year pattern of decisions favoring school desegregation when it ruled in a decision involving the city of Detroit (*Milliken v. Bradley*) that segregation in an urban school system cannot be alleviated by combining urban and suburban school districts unless *both* areas in question are involved in discriminatory practices.

(b) *Public Accommodations.* The Court has upheld the public accommodations section of the 1964 Civil Rights Act, guaranteeing black Americans access to such facilities as hotels, theaters and restaurants.

(c) *Rights of Defendants in Criminal Cases.* The Court has ruled that there must be prompt presentation of charges in criminal cases (*Mallory v. U.S.*, 1957). It has ruled that a state must provide free counsel for defendants who cannot afford a lawyer (*Gideon v. Wainright*, 1963); and that a defendant has a right to have his lawyer with him when he is being questioned (*Escobedo v. Illinois*, 1964). In the famous case of *Miranda v. Arizona* (1966), the Court ruled that a defendant must be given a fourfold warning before he is questioned: (1) that he may remain silent; (2) that anything he says may be used against him; (3) that he may have a lawyer present; (4) that, if he is unable to pay, he may have a lawyer without charge. In *Furman v. Georgia* (1972), the Court ruled that the death penalty, as it was then being administered in the United States, was cruel and unusual punishment, in violation of the 8th and 14th Amendments.

(d) *Separation of Church and State.* In a highly controversial decision, the Court in 1963 declared that Bible readings and all other religious exercises in the public schools violated the First Amendment and were thereby unconstitutional (*Engel v. Vitale*). In 1972, the Court ruled that Amish parents need not send their children to public school beyond the eighth grade.

(e) *Wiretapping.* The court has held, in a number of cases that wiretapping and other forms of electronic surveillance ("bugging") violate the Fourth Amendment prohibition against "unreasonable searches and seizures." Such covert operations are legal only in special circumstances, when authorized by a court order.

(f) *Executive Privilege.* In an historic decision in 1974, the Supreme Court ruled unanimously that President Richard Nixon could not withhold from the special Watergate prosecutor certain tape-recorded conversations between him and his aides. This ruling (*United States v. Nixon*) led directly to Nixon's resignation a few weeks later. The long-term significance of the decision was its impact on the division of powers within the Federal government. The Court agreed with the President that there was a need for *"executive privilege"* in order to protect the confidentiality of certain communications between a President and his aides. However, the courts have the final right to determine how this principle is to be applied.

(g) *Other Important Decisions.* Other decisions of the Court have limited the power of government bodies to censor books and movies, thus expanding the First Amendment guarantee of free speech. Also limited have been the rights of Federal and state governments to restrict travel, to deny employment to persons whose associations are deemed subversive, and to apply the laws of libel.

REVIEW TEST (Chapter 6 — Part VIII)

Select the numbers preceding the word or expression that best completes each statement or answers each question.

1. Protection of free speech and press is found in   (1) all of the first ten amendments   (2) none of the first ten amendments   (3) the Tenth Amendment   (4) the First Amendment

2. The Bill of Rights of the Constitution provides that   (1) Congress shall not prohibit the free exercise of religion   (2) the writ of habeas corpus shall not be suspended   (3) Congress must guarantee each state a republican form of government   (4) no citizen may be deprived of the right to vote

3. The Bill of Rights of the Constitution of the United States provides that   (1) "the accused shall enjoy the right to a . . . trial by an impartial jury . . ."   (2) the Constitution shall "secure the blessings of liberty to ourselves and our posterity"   (3) "all men are created equal"   (4) "all persons born or naturalized in the United States, and subject to the jurisdiction thereof, are citizens of the United States and of the State wherein they reside"

4. A basic safeguard of our liberties provided by the Constitution is the   (1) guarantee of equal suffrage for all   (2) system of checks and balances   (3) amendment limiting the term of office of the President   (4) plan of proportional representation in the United States Senate

5. Which of the following is specifically forbidden by the United States Constitution?   (1) child labor   (2) kidnaping   (3) a bill of attainder   (4) issue of fiat money by the Federal government.

6. In 1920 a man committed a murder in State X. In 1921 the penalty for murder in State X was changed from life imprisonment to death. In 1922 this man was convicted of this crime in a state court and sentenced to death. Under what provision of the United States Constitution might he appeal to a Federal court?   (1) due process of law clause of the Fourteenth Amendment   (2) double jeopardy clause   (3) bill of attainder provision   (4) *ex post facto* clause

7. A writ of habeas corpus would probably be sought by a person who has been   (1) charged with a crime and can't afford bail   (2) imprisoned without being charged with a crime   (3) tried and convicted   (4) tried twice for the same crime

8. The only crime defined in the Constitution of the United States is   (1) arson   (2) felony   (3) larceny   (4) treason

9. A function of a grand jury is to   (1) provide lists of jurors   (2) prosecute a case   (3) present an indictment   (4) impose a sentence

10. The right of the government to take private property for public use, providing just compensation is made, is known as   (1) bill of attainder   (2) eminent domain   (3) habeas corpus   (4) gerrymandering

Essay Questions

1. Show how the Constitution protects individual and property rights.

2. Give specific examples that show how political or civil liberties in the United States have been extended by   (a) constitutional amendments   (b) acts of Congress   (c) Supreme Court decisions.

3. Explain and illustrate the meaning of each of the following: (a) American citizens have responsibilities as well as rights.   (b) Civil rights are relative, not absolute.   (c) Civil rights are continually being defined and redefined.

4. Explain the meaning and importance of the "clear and present danger" doctrine as it applies to the "right of dissent." Why do you agree or disagree with this doctrine?

Part IX — THE CITIZEN'S RESPONSIBILITY IN GOVERNMENT

It is the duty and responsibility of all Americans to make democracy work.

Basic Definitions. *Democracy* is a form of government in which sovereign power rests in the hands of the people. In the words of Abraham Lincoln, a democracy is a "government of the people, by the people, for the people." The United States is a *representative democracy* in which the people rule through representatives of their own choosing. It is a *republic* because the voters elect their governing officials. It is a *democratic republic* because elections are fair and based on universal suffrage.

Role of the Citizen. In order to preserve and make more effective the democratic way of life made possible by the American form of government, there are several important things each citizen should do or believe.

1. *Equality.* The citizen should understand that democracy presupposes the fundamental equality of all men. Equality means that no man is privileged over other men in the eyes of the law, regardless of race, color, religion, or social or economic status.

2. *Patience.* The citizen should understand that democratic governments cannot act as swiftly (except in emergencies) as those of dictatorships because of their built-in system of checks and balances. Slow and deliberate decisions make possible greater justice for all.

3. *Self-restraint.* The citizen should appreciate the fact that although democracy rests upon individual liberty, "personal liberty ends where public injury begins." Each person must surrender something of the privilege to do as he pleases, in order to make organized society possible.

4. *Respect for the Law.* The citizen must understand that when we say democracy is "a government of law, not men" we mean that the liberty we enjoy is *liberty under the law.* No government can exist without obedience to the law. In a democracy this obedience should come out of respect for the law. Respect carries the responsibility of obeying the law, whether or not one approves of it.

5. *Duties as Well as Rights.* The citizen must understand that citizenship in a democracy implies duties as well as rights. Among the important duties of citizens are paying taxes, serving on juries, serving in the nation's defense, and keeping informed about public affairs.

6. *Participation in Public Affairs.* Beyond being informed about public affairs, the citizen should *participate* in public affairs. He can do this by working with the political party of his choice, by joining groups working for improved government, by writing to and visiting public officials to express his opinions, by taking part in public meetings and discussions, by voting intelligently, and by running for office.

7. *Intelligent Voting.* The citizen should try to vote intelligently, using reason rather than emotion in his consideration of issues and in his appraisal of the record and ability of the candidates.

8. *Fair Play.* The citizen must appreciate that good citizenship necessarily calls for fair play. Fair play means honesty and decency. It means loosing without anger and winning without gloating. It means protecting the rights of minorities.

9. *Family and School.* The citizen should demonstrate in family living and in school the same qualities that are essential for making democracy work. These include consideration of others, cooperation with parents and schoolmates, respect for rules and regulations, assumption of the responsibilities of family living, and participation in school affairs.

REVIEW TEST (Chapter 6 — Part IX)

Read the following selection. Then, for **each** *statement below, write the* **number** *of the expression that best completes that statement. Base your answers on the selection and your knowledge of history.*

Every now and then some American gets up and says that the United States is a Republic and not, as some suppose, a democracy. The Constitution does not say this is a democracy. It does say, "We, the people of the United States." The confusion perhaps lies between the old concept of a democratic community so small that it can be administered like a town meeting, and a Republic so large that the citizen must delegate some functions.

But there is no question as to the essence of democracy, which, as de Tocqueville said, "consists in the absolute sovereignty of the majority." There are limitations on this sovereignty, even in the United States. The decisions of the Supreme Court are among these limitations. But what the people want in a democracy, they can get."

1. Which title best expresses the main ideas of this selection? (1) Views on American democracy by foreign observers (2) The nature of democracy (3) The conflict between the majority and the individual (4) The transition from autocracy to democracy

2. It is the author's opinion that (1) the United States is a democratic republic (2) the functions of the United States Supreme Court should be restricted (3) the essence of democracy is respect for the individual (4) any limitation upon sovereignty is regrettable

3. According to the selection, restrictions on sovereign power exist in (1) other countries, but not in the United States (2) countries where the majority ignores minority rights (3) a country that neglects to hold town meetings (4) the United States, as well as in other countries

4. Which feature of United States government today is *least* in accord with de Tocqueville's viewpoint on the essence of democracy? (1) the preamble to the Constitution (2) the election of United States Senators (3) the election of the President (4) the election of members of the House of Representatives

Essay Questions

1. Discuss three responsibilities of the American citizen towards his government.

2. Explain with illustrations why "*do* democracy" is much more important than "*say* democracy."

3. As a high school student discuss three things *you* can do *now* to give real meaning to the ideals of American democracy.

REVIEWING UNIT TWO

Select the number preceding the word or expression that best completes each statement or answers each question.

1. The delegates to the Philadelphia Convention of 1787 were authorized to (1) write a new Constitution (2) limit the powers of the central government (3) increase the powers of the states (4) revise the Articles of Confederation

2. Who wrote detailed notes of the proceedings of the Constitutional Convention (1787)? (1) James Madison (2) Roger Sherman (3) John Hancock (4) George Washington

3. The "Great Compromise," which became a part of the Constitution of the United States, related to (1) slavery (2) tariff (3) representation (4) labor

4. The chief objection to the adoption of a federal constitution was that it (1) reserved too much power to the states (2) contained too many compromises (3) provided insufficient guarantees of civil liberties (4) required the approval of all states to amend

5. According to the Constitution of the United States, New York State is denied the power to (1) levy a tax on furs (2) enter into a treaty with Canada for development of electric power on the St. Lawrence River (3) authorize its State Troopers to inspect cars coming from Pennsylvania (4) regulate the working hours of New Jersey commuters employed in New York State

6. The "elastic clause" of the Constitution has made it possible for Congress to (1) issue patents (2) regulate wages in interstate industries (3) levy an income tax (4) enact naturalization laws

7. During the past few decades there has been in the Federal government an increasing tendency toward (1) government by commissions (2) weakening the power of the executive (3) limitation of the civil service (4) support of business interests by the Federal courts

8. The right to pass bills of attainder and *ex-post-facto* laws is (1) reserved to the states (2) delegated to Congress (3) permitted to both state and Federal governments under the Fifth and Fourteenth Amendments (4) denied to both state and Federal governments

9. The constitutional argument advocated by some sections of the South against action by the Federal government for integration in education is based upon (1) delegated powers (2) division of powers (3) the supremacy clause of the Constitution (4) the "elastic clause" of the Constitution

10. Which one of the following is basic to the idea of a federal system of government? (1) division of powers between the national government and state governments (2) creation of a strong executive branch (3) distribution of powers between the Senate and the House of Representatives (4) establishment of an independent Supreme Court

11. The Senate of the United States differs from the House of Representatives in that (1) the Senate is continuously in session (2) a two-thirds vote is required to pass bills in the Senate (3) one-third of the Senate is elected every two years (4) Senators must be 40 years of age or older

12. Which of the following headlines indicates the role of the Senate of the United States in making foreign policy? (1) **TREATY APPROVED; UNITED STATES JOINS NATO** (2) **KOREA INVADED; UNITED STATES SENDS TROOPS** (3) **RED MISSILES POUR INTO CUBA; UNITED STATES ESTABLISHES QUARANTINE** (4) **NEW POLICY ANNOUNCED; UNITED STATES INSISTS ON "OPEN-DOOR"**

13. In case of the death or resignation of a United States Senator, the vacancy is usually filled by (1) a temporary appointment by the Governor (2) vote of the state legislature (3) vote of the United States Senate (4) appointment by the United States Attorney General

14. The attempt of persons not members of the legislature to influence legislation is called (1) log-rolling (2) filibustering (3) lobbying (4) gerrymandering

15. The United States Supreme Court ruled that the distribution of seats in state legislatures should be based on population. This means that (1) the poll tax is illegal (2) rural political domination is likely to be upset in the near future (3) in many cases urban districts will soon lose control of state legislatures (4) Federal courts will determine the number of election districts in each state

16. According to the Constitution, without the consent of Congress no state can (1) tax business enterprises (2) regulate public utilities (3) enter into agreements or compacts with another state (4) establish a militia

17. Elimination of the Electoral College system for selecting the President of the United States would require a (1) Constitutional amendment (2) popular referendum (3) Presidential proclamation (4) Supreme Court decision

18. If the President, the Vice President, and the Speaker of the House were unable to serve as Chief Executive, who would succeed to the Presidency today? (1) the Secretary of State (2) the Chief Justice of the Supreme Court (3) the majority leader of the House of Representatives (4) the President pro tempore of the Senate

19. Drawing up the budget for the Federal government is the responsibility of the (1) Senate (2) House of Representatives (3) President (4) the Secretary of the Treasury

20. The number of Presidential electors for each state is determined by (1) the number of votes cast in the last election (2) the number of citizens voting in the primary election (3) agreement between the major parties (4) the Constitution

21. Only a natural-born citizen of the United States is eligible to hold the offices of the President of the United States and (1) Lieutenant Governor of New York (2) Governor of Arizona (3) Vice President of the United States (4) Chief Justice of the Supreme Court

22. As provided in the Constitution, the United States Supreme Court has original jurisdiction when it (1) tries a case originating in the lower courts (2) tries a case involving the interpretation of a Federal law (3) hears a case on appeal from a United States Court of Appeals (4) hears a case affecting an ambassador

23. The provision of the original Constitution that gave the voters the most direct participation in government dealt with the manner of choosing the (1) President (2) members of the House of Representatives (3) members of the Senate (4) Justices of the Supreme Court

24. The Fourteenth Amendment to the Constitution forbids states to (1) levy income taxes (2) pass bankruptcy laws (3) deprive any citizen of equal rights (4) coin money

25. The requirement that Presidential electors must vote separately for President and Vice President was provided in (1) the original Constitution (2) the Presidential Succession Act (1886) (3) a Supreme Court decision (4) an amendment to the Constitution

26. The document that defines the supreme law of our country is the (1) Declaration of Independence (2) Constitution of the United States (3) Bill of Rights (4) Articles of Confederation

27. The Senate can invoke cloture, or a curtailment of debate, by a (1) majority vote (2) two-thirds vote (3) unanimous vote (4) three-fourths vote

28. The clause ". . . the House of Representatives shall choose immediately by ballot the President" was the constitutional basis for the election to the Presidency of (1) John Quincy Adams (2) Andrew Jackson (3) James K. Polk (4) Martin Van Buren

29. A practice that has become a part of our "unwritten Constitution" is (1) the convention method of nominating Presidential candidates (2) Senate approval of Presidential appointments (3) the order of succession to the Presidency (4) the President's power to negotiate treaties

30. In a congressional election year the voters elect (1) the entire Senate and House of Representatives (2) two-thirds of the Senate and one-third of the House of Representatives (3) one-third of the Senate and the entire House of Representatives (4) two-thirds of the Senate and the entire House of Representatives

For **each** *governmental action in Column A, write the* **letter** *preceding the judgment in Column B that tells whether or not the action was or would probably be considered constitutional or unconstitutional.*

A	B
1. New York State grants Fulton a monopoly of Hudson River traffic	*a.* Constitutional: a delegated power of Congress
2. Southern states have operated segregated schools	*b.* Constitutional: the President is Commander-in-Chief of the Armed Forces
3. President Truman orders troops to Korea	*c.* Constitutional: a power specifically assigned to the Senate
4. Congress declares war on Japan	*d.* Constitutional: the President receives and sends ambassadors
5. United States rejects Treaty of Versailles	*e.* Constitutional: this may be done by a two-thirds vote of Congress
6. No candidate receives majority of electoral votes; Senate elects President	*f.* Unconstitutional: only Congress may make laws
7. President Franklin Roosevelt recognizes Soviet Russia	*g.* Unconstitutional: only the Federal government may regulate interstate commerce
8. Congress levies a tax on wheat being shipped to India	*h.* Unconstitutional: even a state may not break a contract
9. Taft-Hartley Act passed despite President's veto	*i.* Unconstitutional: no state may deny any person equal protection of the laws
10. State legislature cancels charters of private schools with registrations below 50	*j.* Unconstitutional: only the House of Representatives acts in such a situation
	k. Unconstitutional: tariffs cannot be levied on exports

Cartoon A   Cartoon B

Base your answers to the following questions on cartoon **A** *and on your knowledge of United States government.*

1. According to the cartoon which statement is true? (1) Southerners are the only ones who use the filibuster. (2) Northern Democrats and Southern Democrats have agreed to cooperate. (3) Liberal Democrats approve of filibustering by Southern Democrats. (4) Liberal Democrats are going to use a tactic used on some occasions by Southern Democrats.

2. The men in the cartoon are probably members of the (1) United States Senate (2) House of Representatives (3) United States Supreme Court (4) minority party in Congress

3. The filibuster is most frequently used to (1) gerrymander election districts (2) delay a vote (3) influence a Supreme Court decision (4) build up the power of the majority group

4. The effectiveness of the filibuster can be limited by skillful use of (1) reapportionment (2) cloture (3) a bill of attainder (4) a writ of mandamus

5. The most prolonged filibuster in recent years (1) blocked passage of an amendment to reduce the power of the Supreme Court (2) preceded the passage of the Civil Rights Act of 1964 (3) was over the issue of tax reduction (4) resulted in the passage of a law limiting the length of debate in the Senate

Base your answers to the following questions on cartoon **B** *and on your knowledge of United States government.*

1. The cartoon means that: (1) the Democratic Party controls the Senate and the Republican Party the House of Representatives (2) the Treasury is being plundered by our legislators (3) the nation has a Republican President and a Democratic Congress (4) both major parties are trying to capture the government

2. The principle of government that is best illustrated here is (1) checks and balances (2) federalism (3) division of powers (4) constitutional flexibility

3. Who was President when this situation last occurred? (1) F. D. Roosevelt (2) Truman (3) Eisenhower (4) Kennedy

4. The cartoonist's attitude seems to be one of (1) gentle criticism (2) bitter condemnation (3) enthusiastic praise (4) complete objectivity

5. At the present time the nation has (1) a Democratic Congress and a Democratic President (2) a Republican Congress and a Republican President (3) a Democratic President and a Republican House of Representatives (4) none of these political situations

Essay Questions

1. Define or explain the meaning of each of five of the following terms as used in the Constitution:

Habeas Corpus	Grand Jury
Treason	Delegated Powers
Impeachment	Quorum
Naturalization	Original Jurisdiction

2. Give one or two reasons for agreeing or disagreeing with each of the following statements: (a) A person disagreeing with the government's foreign policy has the right to destroy his draft card. (b) The law denying a place on the ballot to the Communist Party is a just law. (c) Public opinion should not influence the making of laws.

3. (a) State one specific provision of the Constitution that relates to each of five of the following: (1) treason (2) income taxes (3) making of treaties (4) power of the Supreme Court (5) civil rights (6) election of the President (7) succession to the Presidency. (b) Giving specific illustrations discuss a 20th-century problem related to one of the topics selected in answer "a."

4. Discuss each of the following statements concerning the Presidency of the United States: (a) Amendments to the Constitution have affected the Presidency. (b) Political parties play an important part in the nomination of the President. (c) The process of electing the President encourages candidates to concentrate much campaign activity in certain states.

5. The success of a President may often be measured by the laws passed during his administration (a) Explain two ways in which a President may influence Congress to pass laws in which he is interested. (b) Explain two ways in which members of Congress may make it difficult for a President's legislative program to be enacted. (c) Discuss the significance of one specific law passed by the present administration.

6. Much of the work of the Federal government is carried on through the activities of independent agencies and commissions. (a) Explain a circumstance under which one Federal regulatory commission or agency was established, and describe one of its major functions today. (No credit will be allowed for using a Cabinet department.) (b) Discuss one reason why Congress makes use of investigating committees, and describe the work of one such committee. (c) Discuss one criticism directed at regulatory agencies and one that has been directed at congressional investigating committees.

7. (a) Explain two ways in which the Constitution protects states' rights. (b) Discuss fully one specific controversy involving states' rights that at one time or another in the nation's history has developed over each of two of the following issues: (1) tariff (2) establishment of a bank of the United States (3) reconstruction (4) segregation (5) control of tidelands oil.

8. Explain an action taken in recent years by the U.S. Supreme Court on three of the following issues: the right of dissent; racial segregation; rights of defendants; separation of church and state; wiretapping; capital punishment.

THE YOUNG NATION
MEETS ITS FIRST CHALLENGES

CHAPTER 7 _____

The Federalists
Launch the New Republic

The government of the United States during its earliest years was in the hands of the Federalists. They set important precedents, came to grips with pressing domestic and foreign problems, and made lasting contributions to the young nation's development. During the *Federalist Era* (1789-1801) George Washington and John Adams served as Presidents.

Part I — ESTABLISHING THE NEW GOVERNMENT

The first task that faced the new government after its election was to breathe life into the Constitution by establishing governmental machinery and providing for financial stability.

The New Government Is Organized. The first government under the Constitution went into operation in 1789.

1. *Congress.* The Congress that had been elected in the first national elections of 1788 started its work in the temporary capital of New York in April, 1789. It was composed largely of "Federalists," or supporters of the Constitution.

2. *President and Vice President.* George Washington, who had been unanimously elected President by the Electoral College, was inaugurated on April 30, 1789. John Adams was sworn in as Vice President. Washington was esteemed and respected as the hero of the Revolution, as a man of character, and as a person of balanced judgment. Adams had been an outstanding colonial and revolutionary leader.

3. *Problems.* The new administration faced staggering problems. **(a)** Over half the population was known to oppose the strong central form of government set up by the Constitution. **(b)** The treasury was empty. **(c)** There were no Federal laws, no law enforcement officers, and no courts. **(d)** The Constitution had provided only a broad general outline of government; this now needed specific implementation. **(e)** The new nation did not have the respect or confidence of foreign nations.

4. *First Steps.* Congress took several steps to get the machinery of government started.

    (a) In order to set up executive departments to help the President, Congress created the departments of *State, Treasury,* and *War,* as well as the posts of *Attorney General* and *Postmaster General.*

    (b) Congress passed the *Judiciary Act* of 1789, which provided for the organization of the Supreme Court and lower Federal courts.

    (c) To raise revenue, Congress passed the *Tariff Act* of 1789, which set low duties on goods imported into the country.

    (d) To fulfill campaign pledges, Congress also approved the first ten amendments to the Constitution (the *Bill of Rights*), which were ratified by the states in 1791.

5. *First Precedents.* Nearly everything Congress and the President did at this time was a "first." Among the noteworthy precedents established during the first administration were these: **(a)** Congress decided to address the Chief Executive as "Mr. President," rather than by a more aristocratic title such as "Your Excellency." **(b)** The President chose able men as heads of departments — Thomas Jefferson as Secretary of State, Alexander Hamilton as Secretary of the Treasury, Henry Knox as Secretary of War, and Edmund Randolph as Attorney General. John Jay became the first Chief Justice of the Supreme Court. **(c)** Washington soon abandoned as too cumbersome the constitutionally prescribed practice of having department heads submit opinions to him in writing. He substituted meetings with the heads of departments which became known as "cabinet meetings."

The Inauguration of George Washington as first President of the United States, taken from an original painting.

Hamilton's Program Establishes a Sound Financial System. The outstanding achievement of Washington's first term as President was the adoption of the *Hamilton Program,* which Washington personally favored. ALEXANDER HAMILTON, brilliant young Secretary of the Treasury and supporter of strong central government and the interests of business, developed a four-point program designed to establish a sound financial system for the new nation.

1. *Hamilton's Program.* Hamilton proposed the following:

   (a) *Payment of the National Debt.* He urged full payment of the national debt, which consisted of money owed by the government to foreign nations and citizens and money owed to the people of the United States in the form of war bonds and obligations of the Confederation.

   (b) *Assumption of State Debts.* He advocated the assumption (taking over) by the national government of state debts incurred during the Revolution.

   (c) *Establishment of a Source of Income.* Hamilton urged that the Federal government raise funds through a system of import duties (tariffs), the sale of Western lands, and excise (internal) taxes on liquors.

   (d) *Organization of a Sound Banking and Currency System.* Hamilton proposed the minting of gold and silver coins, and the establishment of a strong national bank which would keep government funds, help sell government bonds, and issue a stable and uniform national currency.

2. *Support for Hamilton's Program.* Hamilton argued that payment of national debts was necessary to establish national credit, that assumption of state debts was a measure of justice and sound policy, that a national bank would be good for the country's business, that a protective tariff was needed to encourage home manufacturing, and that an excise tax would accustom the people to the taxing power of the Federal government. Support for his program came mainly from business interests and those who stood to benefit from specific parts of the program (*e.g.,* holders of bonds and debt certificates, and land speculators).

3. *Opposition to the Plan.* There was much opposition to Hamilton's plan, led by Thomas Jefferson and James Madison. Opponents argued: **(a)** that it was a program to benefit the rich; **(b)** that assumption of state debts was unfair because some states had already paid their debts or had only small ones; **(c)** that payment of the debt would result in increased taxes; **(d)** that redeeming bonds and debt certificates at face value (par) would benefit only those who had bought them up at a fraction of their stated value, rather than the original owners; and **(e)** that the proposed national bank would be an unconstitutional extension of Congress' power to regulate the currency.

4. *Adoption of the Hamilton Program.* Despite the opposition, Hamilton's suggestions were adopted.

(a) Provision was made for paying the debt in full, by issuing new bonds (*funding the debt*).

(b) The first *Bank of the United States* was chartered in 1791 for a period of twenty years with a capital of $10,000,000. It was to be organized and run privately, with the government to own one-fifth of its stock. The Bank was given authority to issue bank notes, to pay government debts and taxes, and to establish branches.

(c) The *Tariff Act of 1792* was passed to replace the Tariff Act of 1789. The purpose of the new tariff was not so much to raise revenue for the government (*revenue tariff*) as to *protect* American industry against foreign competition. The rates, however, were not high.

(d) A system of gold and silver coins (still in use) and a Mint to produce them were provided for.

(e) An excise tax was placed on whiskey distilled within the country.

(f) To help insure passage for his program of assumption of state debts, Hamilton asked Jefferson (a Southerner) to obtain the support of Southern Congressmen. In return, with Hamilton's support, a bill was passed establishing the national capital at Philadelphia for ten years, and then permanently in the South on the banks of the Potomac (Washington, D. C.).

5. *Results of the Hamilton Program.* Hamilton's program was a success. It had several important results.

(a) It established United States credit abroad, encouraged foreign trade, and stimulated national prosperity.

(b) The successful operation of the Bank attracted business support and insured the acceptance of the new national currency.

(c) By leading to the formation of the antifederalist *Republican Party,* the program helped bring about the development of parties.

(d) Swift and decisive action to put down the *Whiskey Rebellion* (1794) established the authority of the national government. The Whiskey Rebellion came about when a group of frontier farmers in Pennsylvania refused to pay the whiskey tax and threatened the tax collectors. When Pennsylvania hesitated to do anything about this defiance of Federal authority, Washington sent in a National Militia led by Hamilton and composed of units from four states. It easily captured several leaders and dispersed the rebellious farmers. Washington later pardoned those imprisoned.

REVIEW TEST (Chapter 7 — Part I)

Select the number preceding the word or expression that best completes each statement or answers each question.

1. Each of the following was a problem faced by the new government of the United States in 1789 *except* (1) an empty treasury (2) an unpopular leader (3) opposition at home to a strong central government (4) lack of respect abroad

2. The first Congress did all of the following *except* (1) select the President (2) enact an excise tax (3) establish a Mint (4) issue bonds to fund the national debt

3. Immediately following the adoption of the Constitution in 1788, political power was mainly in the hands of (1) Western farmers (2) men of property and wealth (3) veterans of the American Revolution (4) city workers

4. The suppression of the Whiskey Rebellion illustrated the (1) strength of the Indian confederacy in the Northwest Territory (2) ability of the new government to put down domestic uprisings (3) extent among workers of dissatisfaction with the Eighteenth Amendment (4) need for revising the Articles of Confederation

5. Alexander Hamilton based much of his financial program on his belief that (1) the success of the new government required the support of the propertied classes (2) the states should be discouraged from depending on the Federal government for help (3) speculation in government securities must be prevented (4) land was the most important source of wealth

6. The first Bank of the United States was (1) a private corporation chartered by the United States government (2) an institution owned and operated by the government (3) a private bank having no connection with the national government (4) an institution of which John Marshall was President

7. What proposal in Hamilton's financial program resulted in an expansion of the powers of the Congress under the Constitution? (1) a national bank (2) a revenue tax (3) payment in full of foreign debts (4) an excise tax

8. George Washington was sworn into office the same year that (1) the Constitution was ratified (2) the French Revolution began (3) Napoleon became Emperor of France (4) Abraham Lincoln was born

9. In 1790 most adult Americans were (1) veterans (2) hunters (3) tradesmen (4) farmers

10. The Hamilton program did *not* (1) establish United States credit abroad (2) provide for the establishment of a Mint (3) result in the passage of a high protective tariff (4) stimulate national prosperity

Select the item in each group that does **NOT** *belong with the others.*

1. Members of Washington's first Cabinet: Thomas Jefferson, Alexander Hamilton, Edmund Randolph, James Madison

2. Supporters of Hamilton's Program: bondholders, businessmen, small farmers, land speculators

3. First Bank of the United States: a 20-year charter, the government owned 20% of its stock, failed soon after being chartered, acted as financial agent for the Federal government

4. Capital cities in United States history: Chicago, New York, Philadelphia, Washington, D. C.

5. The First Congress of the United States: elected in 1788, composed largely of Federalists, established departments of Commerce and Labor, provided for an organization of a system of Federal courts

Essay Questions

1. Explain one way in which the United States in 1790 differed from the United States today: (a) politically (b) economically (c) socially.

2. Show how "life was breathed into the Constitution" by (a) President Washington and (b) the First Congress.

3. Alexander Hamilton has frequently been called a financial genius. By giving evidence defend or attack this viewpoint.

Part II — FACING FIRST CHALLENGES IN FOREIGN AFFAIRS

The new government inherited from the Confederation problems and controversies with France, Britain, Spain, and the border Indians. Its foreign problems were further complicated by the French Revolution and the resulting wars between France and the rest of Europe.

Problems with France. The first major test of foreign policy came with France.

1. *Divided Opinion on the French Revolution.* When the French Revolution broke out in 1789, most Americans were sympathetic to it. As leadership passed from the more moderate to the more extreme groups, with France declaring war on England in 1793, American opinion became sharply divided. The more conservative Federalists, with strong trade ties to Britain, lost sympathy for the revolution and bitterly condemned it for its excesses (beheading of the King and Queen, the Reign of Terror). The Jefferson-led Republicans continued to support the revolution, maintaining that some violence and bloodshed were necessary in the fight for human liberty.

2. *Citizen Genêt.* Upon hearing that war had broken out between Great Britain and France, and that a new French Minister, Citizen Genêt, would soon arrive to ask the United States as an ally of France to declare war on Great Britain, Washington was forced to make a decision on what American policy would be.

3. *Proclamation of Neutrality (1793).* After hearing opinions from the anti-French (and pro-British) Hamilton, and the pro-French Jefferson, Washington decided that the 1778 *Treaty of Alliance* with the former government of Louis XVI of France did not apply, since the final form of French government was still unsettled. In April, 1793, therefore, he issued a *Proclamation of Neutrality,* which announced a friendly but neutral policy toward all warring nations. Americans were warned not to engage in any hostile acts against either side. Washington felt that the nation could ill afford to become involved in a European war when it was still so young and weak. The Neutrality Proclamation was the first formal statement of American aloofness from Old World affairs.

4. *Recall of Genêt.* Citizen Genêt defied the Proclamation and attempted to appeal to the American people over the President's head by enlisting seamen and fitting out privateers. Although President Washington asked for Genêt's recall, he permitted him to stay on in the United States when he learned that Genêt would have to stand trial in France before a more extreme government than the one that had sent him here. Genêt later became an American citizen.

Problems with Britain. Strained feelings with Britain had continued even after the Revolution. During Washington's administration attempts to improve relations led to the *Jay Treaty* of 1795.

1. *Grievances.* Americans had several grievances against Britain:

   (a) The British had refused to evacuate the Northwestern fur-trading posts on the Great Lakes, as provided under the terms of the Treaty of Peace of 1783. They justified this on the ground that Americans had refused to return the confiscated property of Tories who had fled during the Revolution.

   (b) The British had also refused to allow American shippers to trade with British colonies.

   (c) It was claimed that the British were encouraging Indian attacks against American frontier settlements, a factor which hindered the westward movement of pioneers.

   (d) As a result of the war between Britain and France, which began in 1793, Britain seized American ships trading with the French West Indies, and "impressed" (forced) American seamen into British service on the grounds that they were Englishmen, or deserters from the British navy. The British policy was "once an Englishman, always an Englishman." This, of course, infuriated Americans, who were proud of their independence.

2. *The Jay Treaty, 1795.* In order to settle the disputes with Britain and to secure commercial privileges, Washington sent John Jay to England. Jay's discussions led to a treaty in which Britain agreed to: **(a)** surrender the Northwest posts; **(b)** open its ports in the East Indies to American vessels; **(c)** extend minor trading privileges in the West Indies; and **(d)** submit to arbitration commissions the questions of pre-Revolutionary debts owed to British creditors by Americans, and claims against Britain by American shippers.

3. *An Unpopular Treaty.* Although the Jay Treaty prevented a possible war with Britain, it was most unpopular with Americans because it did nothing about impressment, and did little to promote United States trade with the British West Indies.

Relations with Spain. Because Spain feared that the Jay Treaty would draw Britain and the United States closer together, she hastened to settle her outstanding differences with the United States. In 1795 Thomas Pinckney, a special envoy, negotiated the *Pinckney Treaty (Treaty of San Lorenzo)* with Spain. Spain **(1)** accepted the American claim to the 31st parallel as the northern boundary of Florida (the southern boundary of the United States); and **(2)** acceded to American pressure for free navigation on the Mississippi and the right of free deposit at New Orleans (permission to unload without payment of a duty).

Relations with the Indians. In 1795, the same year in which the Jay and Pinckney treaties were signed, General Anthony Wayne signed the *Treaty of Greenville* with the Indians of the Northwest, after decisively defeating them in the battle of Fallen Timbers in 1794. The treaty opened new frontier areas to white settlement. All three treaties eased pressure along the borders and encouraged western expansion. By 1800, Vermont, Kentucky, and Tennessee had been admitted as new states.

Washington's Farewell Address, 1796. Washington had been unanimously re-elected for a second term in 1792. Feeling that the government had been safely launched and desiring final retirement after more than 50 years of service to his country, he refused to be renominated for a third term. As his second term neared its end, he issued his famous *Farewell Address* (1796).

1. *Washington's Advice.* In the Farewell Address Washington urged the American people: **(a)** to be friendly with all nations; **(b)** to avoid foreign political entanglements and permanent alliances; **(c)** to restrain the evil effects of sectional and party conflict; and **(d)** to take advantage of our geographic isolation in order to develop peacefully.

2. *Importance.* The Farewell Address is considered one of America's most important historic documents. It chartered a sensible course for the young and still weak country, and its influence, particularly in its isolationist aspects, remained strong in American foreign policy until well into the 20th century. Indeed, it was not until 1945, after World War II, that the United States fully accepted a position of international responsibility.

REVIEW TEST (Chapter 7 — Part II)

Select the number preceding the word or expression that best completes each statement or answers each question.

1. President Washington's chief reason for issuing the Proclamation of Neutrality in 1793 was to (1) satisfy the Antifederalist leaders (2) safeguard our newly acquired independence (3) develop the interest of the American people in European affairs (4) fulfill our obligations in our treaty with France

2. Which provision of the treaty ending the American Revolution was not carried out by Great Britain until after the Jay Treaty went into effect? (1) evacuation of British troops from United States soil (2) settlement of the western boundary of the United States (3) sharing of the Newfoundland fisheries with the United States (4) recognition of United States independence

3. The Treaty of 1795 with Spain was most popular with (1) Western farmers using the Mississippi River for shipping (2) Northern fur trappers seeking the removal of British troops from the Northwest Territory (3) patriotic Americans attempting to stop the impressment of seamen (4) New England merchants seeking to reopen triangular trade.

4. At the time it occurred, which of the following aroused the strongest popular opposition in America? (1) President Washington's issuance of the Proclamation of Neutrality (2) signing of the Pinckney Treaty (3) recall of Citizen Genêt (4) ratification of the Jay Treaty

5. In his Farewell Address, George Washington advised the American people to do all the following *except* (1) avoid permanent alliances with foreign nations (2) maintain a large army and navy (3) encourage trade and commerce (4) avoid party strife

6. Which of the following treaties eased Indian pressures along the borders of the United States during Washington's administration? (1) Treaty of Greenville (2) Pinckney Treaty (3) Treaty of Paris, 1783 (4) Treaty of Ghent

7. The foreign policy shaped by Washington's Farewell Address was (1) imperialism (2) nationalism (3) isolation (4) collective security

8. All of the following events occurred during Washington's Presidency *except* (1) the Whiskey Rebellion (2) the recall of Citizen Genêt (3) Shays' Rebellion (4) beginning of the French Revolution

9. Which headline would have been most unlikely while Washington was President? (1) **REIGN OF TERROR KEEPS FRANCE IN TURMOIL** (2) **JEFFERSON ARGUES FOR SUPPORT OF BRITAIN AGAINST FRANCE** (3) **WAYNE DEFEATS INDIANS AT FALLEN TIMBERS** (4) **WASHINGTON URGES YOUNG NATION TO GO IT ALONE**

10. The impressment of American seamen aroused anger against (1) England (2) France (3) Spain (4) the Barbary Pirates

State whether each of the following selections is true or false. If the statement is false, replace the word or phrase in **boldface type** *with one which will make it correct.*

1. In Washington's administration, **Spain** granted the right of deposit at New Orleans.

2. The danger of war with Britain in the 1790's was lessened by the **Jay Treaty**.

3. In the struggle between Britain and France, Alexander Hamilton was **pro-French**.

4. Washington sent **John Adams** to negotiate national differences with Spain.

5. In his Farewell Address, Washington warned against conflicts between **sections** as well as between parties.

Essay Questions

1. "The great rule of conduct for us in regard to foreign nations is, . . . to have with them as little political connection as possible." (a) Show how the above advice given by George Washington in his Farewell Address fitted the needs of our Republic at the time it was given. (b) Discuss fully two important changes that have taken place during the 20th century that might make this advice no longer pertinent in our relations with Europe.

2. Discuss one problem President Washington faced with each of three foreign nations and describe the steps taken to solve each problem.

3. "Events abroad have frequently influenced the foreign policy of the United States." Explain how this applied to the United States in the period 1789-96.

Part III — THE DEVELOPMENT OF POLITICAL PARTIES

American political parties developed out of the financial and domestic policies and problems of Washington's first administration (1789-93). Some historians have attempted to trace the beginning of political parties in the United States to the struggle between the Federalists and Antifederalists over the adoption of the Constitution. Actually, however, these groups were *factions* rather than parties in the modern sense, since they came into existence for a special purpose and disbanded as soon as the struggle was over.

Federalists and Republicans. Disputes over Hamilton's program and over the question of support for Britain or France resulted by 1793 in the appearance of two organized political parties. The *Federalist Party,* led by Hamilton, made its appeal to the business and financial classes, including most former supporters of the adoption of the Constitution. The *Democratic-Republican Party,* led by Jefferson, appealed primarily to the middle class and less privileged groups, including most former opponents of the adoption of the Constitution.

1. *Hamilton vs. Jefferson.* Both Hamilton and Jefferson were gifted, dedicated statesmen who made outstanding contributions to the early development of the nation. Both were effective political leaders. In personality and philosophy of government, however, they were in sharp contrast. Hamilton was dynamic and aggressive, while Jefferson was quiet and unassuming. Differences in their points of view influenced not only the thinking and programs of the first political parties, but also the political and economic beliefs of opposing groups ever since.

2. *Federalist Principles.* The Hamiltonian *Federalists* believed: **(a)** The national government should be a powerful central government. **(b)** The government should be controlled by the "upper classes," who were aristocratic, wealthy, and well educated. **(c)** Too much democracy was to be feared since the "common man" was ignorant and untrustworthy. **(d)** The main aim of government was to safeguard property and preserve law and order. **(e)** Since the future of the nation was tied up with the development of industry, the government should encourage and support industry.

3. *Republican Principles.* The Jeffersonian *Republicans* believed: **(a)** The national government should be comparatively weak, with limited power. This was necessary to prevent tyranny. ("That government is best that governs least.") **(b)** The government should be run in the interests of all the people by well-informed leaders, regardless of class background. **(c)** The people were to be trusted and should be given an opportunity for education. **(d)** The main aim of government was the protection of liberty, not property. **(e)** The country would be better off if the population consisted mainly of independent, landowning farmers. Therefore, no special privileges should be extended to industry.

NOTE: The Republican Party of Jefferson's time should not be confused with the present-day Republican Party, which came into existence in 1856. As we have noted, Jefferson's party was also known as the Democratic-Republicans. It is usually regarded as the forerunner of the Democratic Party of our own day. (See chart on following page.)

COMPARISON OF FEDERALIST AND DEMOCRATIC-REPUBLICAN PARTIES

	FEDERALIST PARTY	DEMOCRATIC-REPUBLICAN PARTY
Leaders	Hamilton, Adams.	Jefferson, Madison.
Supporters	Manufacturers, merchants, bankers, holders of large estates. Strongest in Eastern and Middle states.	Small farmers, plantation owners, laborers, small shopkeepers (the non-propertied classes). Strongest in South and West.
Interpretation of Constitution	Broad interpretation; use of implied powers; strong central government.	Strict interpretation; states' rights; weak central government.
Views on Democracy	Opposed extension of democracy; distrusted the "masses"; favored rule by the "best people."	Favored expansion of democracy; desired rule for the masses by educated leaders; opposed to privilege and aristocratic rule.
Views on Specific Issues	Supported Hamilton's program, including a strong central bank, a protective tariff, and funding the national debt.	Opposed to Hamilton's program; in favor of state rather than central banking; against favors to industry (for example, opposed the protective tariff).
Foreign Affairs	Friendly to Great Britain; in sympathy with conservatism of the British government.	Friendly to France and the revolutionary tradition.

The Development of Party Rivalry. Although Washington himself was a conservative and in sympathy with the Federalist program, he opposed the growth of parties and of party conflict. Nevertheless, party organizations and rivalries developed early.

1. *Effect of Hamilton's Program.* The first "party battles" arose out of the issue of the creation of a national bank. Hamiltonians supported the Bank as a proper exercise of implied powers. Jeffersonians attacked the Bank as an improper extension of the power of the national government.

2. *Election of 1792.* The Election of 1792 showed growing opposition to the Federalist program. Though Washington was re-elected unanimous-

DEVELOPMENT OF OUR TWO MAJOR PARTIES

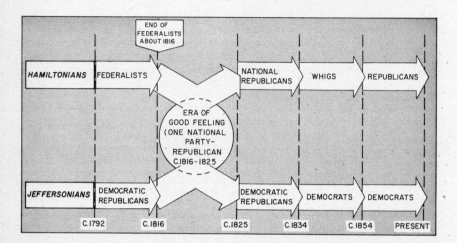

ly, the Federalists lost control of the House of Representatives, and Adams' electoral majority for the Vice Presidency was cut considerably.

3. *Organization of the Republican Party.* In 1793, Jefferson resigned from the Cabinet, brought together the groups opposing the Federalist program, and began systematically to build a Republican Party organization. Party rivalry was further sharpened by the differing points of view concerning the French Revolution.

4. *Election of 1796.* Party rivalry came to "full bloom" in the election of 1796. Each party put up its own slate of electors pledged in advance to vote for the party's candidates. (This has become a permanent feature of the electoral process.) The campaign was characterized by partisanship and bitterness. Even Washington was subjected to abuse and criticism. John Adams was chosen President by a narrow margin on the Federalist ticket. Jefferson, leader of the opposition Republican Party, became Vice President because a few New England electors refused to vote for Thomas Pinckney, the Federalist Vice Presidential candidate.

REVIEW TEST (Chapter 7—Part III)

Select the number preceding the word or expression that best completes each statement or answers each question.

1. In the United States, political parties appeared on the national scene shortly after the adoption of the Constitution because (1) Washington disliked Jefferson (2) the Constitution provides for the two-party system (3) England had a two-party system (4) differences arose over political and economic issues

2. According to the Jeffersonian Democrats, which group benefited least from Federalist policies? (1) bankers (2) farmers (3) manufacturers (4) merchants

3. All of the following were political ideals of Alexander Hamilton *except* (1) strong central government (2) liberal interpretation of the Constitution (3) faith in the political competence of the masses (4) reduction of state powers to simple, unimportant functions

4. In opposing Hamilton's policies, Jefferson favored (1) a loose interpretation of the Constitution (2) control of the government by the rich and well-born (3) states' rights (4) Federal control of banking

5. On which of the following issues were Alexander Hamilton and Thomas Jefferson in closest agreement? (1) establishing a national bank (2) locating the national capital in the South (3) supporting England in her war with France (4) favoring manufacturing over farming interests

6. Between 1789 and 1799 the Democratic-Republicans sympathized with the French Revolutionists because the Democratic-Republicans (1) hoped to buy Louisiana (2) were opposed to Hamilton (3) favored the farmers (4) held similar ideals of liberty

7. Who was in closest political agreement with Hamilton? (1) James Madison (2) Aaron Burr (3) George Washington (4) Samuel Adams

8. The first major issue to cause contention between the Federalists and Democratic-Republicans was (1) the request of French Revolutionists for American aid (2) the plan for establishing a national bank (3) the Whiskey Rebellion (4) the establishment of executive departments

9. In which elections did the Federalists suffer their first political defeat in Congress? (1) 1788 (2) 1792 (3) 1796 (4) 1800

10. The first bitterly contested Presidential campaign took place in (1) 1792 (2) 1796 (3) 1800 (4) 1804

Supply the word or expression that correctly answers each question.

1. Who was our first Vice President?

2. Who became Vice President when John Adams was elected President?

3. Which party won the Presidency in 1796?

4. Which political party had the support of most conservatives in the 1790's?

5. Which political party advocated a strict interpretation of the Constitution during the era of Federalist supremacy?

Essay Questions

1. Both Alexander Hamilton and Thomas Jefferson greatly influenced American history. Hamilton helped to lay the foundations for strong government and sound economic life; Jefferson developed important American ideals. (a) Discuss fully two major contributions of Hamilton to the nation. (b) Show fully how one important ideal developed by Jefferson has contributed to our American heritage.

2. Discuss two important issues over which Thomas Jefferson and Alexander Hamilton and the parties they represented had serious arguments.

3. Discuss one important cause and one important result of the rise of political parties in the United States.

4. By referring to specific issues, indicate which political party during Washington's Presidency had the program best suited to the needs of the emerging nation.

5. "Although Hamilton and Jefferson have long since passed from the scene, their conflicting points of view are very much alive today." Give evidence in support of this statement that is reflected by recent American political, economic, or social developments.

Part IV — THE DECLINE OF FEDERALIST POWER

During the administration of John Adams, the opposition to the Federalist program continued to grow. In 1800 the Republican Party captured the Presidency.

The Administration of John Adams (1797-1801). Although John Adams was honest, sincere, and able, he was not a popular President. He was handicapped by his record of favoring a central government dominated by the rich and well-born, by his feud with Hamilton for leadership of the Federalist Party, by difficult foreign problems, and by the fact that he had "stepped into Washington's shoes."

1. *The XYZ Affair (1797).* Throughout his administration Adams was faced by serious foreign problems, particularly with France. The *XYZ Affair* brought the nation to the verge of war.

(a) Angered by the lack of assistance from the United States, and by the Jay Treaty with England, France began to attack and seize American ships and cargoes. In addition, the authorities in Paris refused to receive the United States Minister.

(b) In order to avoid war, Adams sent three commissioners to France to negotiate (John Marshall, Elbridge Gerry, Charles Pinckney). They were met by three agents of the Directory, sent by Talleyrand, the French Foreign Minister. When the French agents, known as *X, Y,* and *Z,* asked for a $240,000 bribe from the United States in return for a favorable treaty with France, the American representatives left in anger.

(c) News of the insult infuriated Congress and outraged most Americans, including Jefferson and many Republicans. Congress authorized American vessels to attack French ships that interfered with their trade, and began to prepare for war. American sentiment was summed up in the challenge, "Millions for defense, but not one cent for tribute!" Between 1797 and 1800 a state of undeclared naval war existed between France and the United States.

(d) Although Adams and the French government continued to explore peace possibilities, the matter was not settled until Napoleon overthrew the Directory. Under the *Convention of 1800,* the two countries re-established friendly relations. France agreed to cease her attacks on American shipping, to accept the doctrine that "neutral ships make neutral goods," and to give up the Treaty of Alliance of 1778.

2. *The Alien and Sedition Acts (1798).* The Federalists tried to use the *XYZ* affair and the resulting ill-feeling with France to weaken the Republican Party and to silence opposition. Under the pretext that the national emergency required drastic action, the Federalists in 1798 persuaded Congress to pass a series of laws known as the *Alien and Sedition Acts.*

(a) *Provisions.* The *Naturalization Act* increased the residence requirements for citizenship from 5 to 14 years in the case of aliens. The
Alien Act gave the President power to imprison or deport (send out
of the country) any alien considered dangerous to the national peace
or safety. The *Sedition Act* permitted the arrest of citizens who opposed or criticized the President or government.

(b) *Purposes.* The real purposes behind the Alien and Sedition Acts were
(1) to make it more difficult for immigrants to become American
citizens (most immigrants were sympathetic to the Republican Party), **(2)** to check French influence, and **(3)** to prevent or limit
criticism by Republican newspapers of the President and Congress.

(c) *Results.* The Alien and Sedition Acts drew widespread protests from
all over the country, especially from Republicans. Republican leaders attacked the acts as violations of freedom of speech and press
guaranteed by the First Amendment, and issued the *Virginia and Kentucky Resolutions.* Under the Sedition Act about 70 persons were
jailed or fined, including several Republican editors and printers.

(d) *The Virginia and Kentucky Resolutions (1798).* The most noteworthy
reaction to the unpopular acts took the form of the *Virginia and Kentucky Resolutions,* drawn up by Jefferson and Madison, and adopted
by the legislatures of these states. The resolutions declared that:
(1) The Alien and Sedition Acts were unconstitutional, and therefore
null and void. **(2)** The Constitution was a compact (agreement)
drawn up among the states, granting the Federal government only
certain specified powers (the *compact theory of union*). **(3)** Each
state had the right to judge whether an act of Congress was unconstitutional. If a state judged an act unconstitutional, it did not have
to obey it (the *theory of nullification* or *states' rights*).

The Republicans Win the Election of 1800. In the bitterly contested
Presidential election of 1800, which took place soon after the Alien and
Sedition controversy, Jefferson defeated Adams for the Presidency. The
Republicans also captured both Houses of Congress.

1. *The Revolution of 1800.* The Republican victory in the election of
1800 has been referred to as "The Revolution of 1800," because it meant
repudiation by a majority of the voters of the aristocratic theory of government by "the rich, the well-born, and the able." Although Jefferson and
the Republicans did not advocate changing the organization or structure
of the government, they did bring into government the theory that it was
the *common people* who should rule, through their chosen representatives.

2. *Jefferson Elected by the House of Representatives.* Despite the fact
that Jefferson had been running for the Presidency, and Aaron Burr, an
astute New York State politician, for the Vice Presidency, each received
the same number of votes for the Presidency in the Electoral College. The
tie vote sent the election into the House of Representatives. Jefferson was
finally elected on the 36th ballot, after Hamilton and other responsible
leaders threw their support to him, as a man of better character than Burr.

(a) To prevent the recurrence of a similar situation, Congress and the states quickly adopted the Twelfth Amendment, which provides for the casting of separate ballots for President and Vice President.

(b) Although historical evidence does not support their view, Burr and his supporters were convinced that Hamilton had bargained secretly with Jefferson behind the scenes. The resulting ill-feeling on Burr's part was later to be one of the factors that caused Burr in 1804 to challenge Hamilton to a duel in which Hamilton was shot and killed.

3. *Reasons for the Defeat of the Federalists.* There were several important causes for the defeat of the Federalists in 1800. These include: **(a)** Republican criticism of the government for using force in the Whiskey Rebellion; **(b)** bitter resentment over the Alien and Sedition Acts on the part of foreign-born citizens and recent immigrants; **(c)** effective organization of the Republican Party, resulting from the tireless efforts of Jefferson; **(d)** party rivalries within the Federalist Party, particularly between Hamilton and Adams; **(e)** resentment over the Jay Treaty with England and the pro-British policy of Federalist leaders; and **(f)** growing democratic sentiment throughout the country, in opposition to the aristocratic beliefs of the Federalists.

Contributions of the Federalists. Although the Federalist Party continued to be an important political force until after the War of 1812, the *Federalist Era* of control of the national government came to an end with Jefferson's inauguration. Nevertheless, the Federalists must be given credit for several solid achievements during their period of supremacy:

1. They set the government in motion and established important precedents.
2. They created a sound financial system and established credit at home and abroad.
3. They established the power and authority of the national government.
4. Their policies promoted commerce, industry, and prosperity.
5. They maintained peace and won the respect of foreign nations.

REVIEW TEST (Chapter 7 — Part IV)

Select the number preceding the word or expression that best completes each statement or answers each question.

1. Which of the following had a unifying rather than dividing effect during the Administration of John Adams? (1) passage of the Alien and Sedition Acts (2) XYZ affair (3) the Genêt affair (4) Hamilton-Burr duel

2. The theory of states' rights, under which some Southern states have resisted desegregation, can be traced as far back in United States history as the (1) Hartford Convention (2) Whiskey Rebellion (3) Whig Party platform (4) Kentucky and Virginia Resolutions

3. The most objective account of the controversy over the Alien and Sedition Acts of 1798 would most likely to be found in (1) the diary of John Adams (2) the private papers of Thomas Jefferson (3) newspapers of the period (4) the *Rise of American Civilization,* a book written by two eminent historians in 1927

4. The election of which of the following Presidents revealed the need for separate balloting for President and Vice President? (1) James Monroe (2) Thomas Jefferson (3) James Madison (4) John Quincy Adams

5. In 1800 most people in the United States were actively engaged in making a living by (1) trading (2) manufacturing (3) farming (4) lumbering

6. The election of 1800 has been referred to as the "Revolution of 1800" because (1) rioting occurred in frontier settlements (2) basic financial policies of the previous administration were repealed (3) a shift in political power occurred (4) the incoming administration was more sympathetic to commercial than to agricultural interests

7. What was a major reason for the defeat of the Federalists in 1800? (1) Washington's refusal to run for a third term (2) the undeclared war with France (3) the Alien and Sedition Acts (4) the Hartford Convention

8. What party captured the Presidency in 1800? (1) Democratic-Republican (2) Whig (3) Federalist (4) Free Soil

9. Which of the following occurred first? (1) XYZ affair (2) election of John Adams as President (3) Alien and Sedition Acts (4) election of Jefferson as President

10. Jefferson's election in 1800 was made possible by the last-minute support of (1) Burr (2) Hamilton (3) Adams (4) Marshall

Select the letter of the item in each group that does **NOT** *belong with the others.*

1. Involved in XYZ affair: (a) John Marshall, (b) James Madison. (c) Charles Talleyrand

2. Purposes behind Alien and Sedition Acts: (a) to make it more difficult to obtain American citizenship (b) to limit criticism by Republicans (c) punish Federalist leaders for treason

3. Possible headlines during election of 1800: (a) HOUSE ELECTS JEFFERSON (b) BURR SECOND CHOICE IN ELECTORAL COLLEGE (c) REPUBLICANS CAPTURE PRESIDENCY AND CONGRESS

4. Contributions of Federalist Party: (a) the creation of a state banking system (b) the establishment of credit at home and abroad (c) expansion of the power of the central government

5. Reasons for defeat of Federalists in 1800: (a) resentment over the use of force during Whiskey Rebellion (b) growing democratic sentiment in the nation (c) Republican strength among the commercial and industrial interests

Essay Questions

1. Discuss one domestic and one foreign problem faced by the John Adams' administration, and show how each was handled.

2. "Defenders of civil rights, past and present, are unanimous in their condemnation of the Alien and Sedition Acts." Explain the reasons for such a point of view.

3. To what extent is it correct to refer to the election of 1800 as the "Revolution of 1800?"

4. Discuss three important reasons for the defeat of the Federalists in 1800.

5. Explain the debt of the nation to the Federalist Party.

CHAPTER 8

The Republicans Lead the Nation at Home and Abroad

In 1800, Thomas Jefferson, candidate of the Democratic-Republican Party, was elected President. This resulted in the first transfer of political power in the history of the United States. The peaceful nature of the change established an important precedent for the two-party system. Under Jefferson and Madison, the Democratic-Republicans accepted much of the Federalist program. They also introduced many democratic precedents and made important contributions to the nation's development. Like the Federalists, they had to wrestle with serious foreign problems, which were climaxed by the War of 1812 with Britain.

Part I — THOMAS JEFFERSON IN OFFICE

THOMAS JEFFERSON served two terms as President (1801–09). Jefferson was one of America's most remarkable public servants. He was a philosopher, scholar, architect, designer, inventor, scientist, and farmer, as well as a brilliant statesman. Like Washington, he gave over fifty years of public service to his country. His contributions include the writing of the Declaration of Independence and the Virginia Statute for Religious Freedom, as well as service as Minister to France, Secretary of State, Vice President, and President. The principles of Jeffersonian democracy are still a vital part of American life.

Jeffersonian Principles. Symbolic of the changeover in control of the government was the fact that Jefferson was the first President to be installed in office in Washington, D. C. The seat of government had been moved to the new capital from Philadelphia in 1800. Jefferson's *First Inaugural Address* is considered one of the finest ever written. In it he outlined his approach to government.

1. *Democracy and Government.* In his Inaugural Address, Jefferson restated his theory of democracy and government, which included belief in the common man, faith in the republican form of government, protection of civil and political liberty, equal justice and opportunity for all, popular education, economy in government, states' rights, and *laissez-faire* (minimal interference of government in agriculture and industry).

2. *Foreign Policy.* Jefferson also accepted the foundations of foreign policy laid down by Washington. He advocated "honest friendship with all nations, entangling alliances with none."

152

The Jeffersonian System. Jefferson never gave up his belief in democracy, limited government, and personal freedom. One of the first acts of Jefferson's administration was the freeing of a number of individuals still in jail under the *Sedition Act* — passed by the Federalists in 1798 (page 148). The Sedition Act was then allowed to expire. The *Naturalization Act,* which had increased the period required for naturalization of aliens, was repealed.

On the other hand, Jefferson was forced, like most Presidents since his time, to reverse or modify some of the policies he had championed while his party was out of power. Contrary to the fears of many Federalists that he would work for a radical overthrow of the established order, his program was one of peaceful change and moderate reform.

1. *Jeffersonian Simplicity.* Though Jefferson himself was a man of wealth and culture, he believed in simplicity in living and government. As President he dropped formal inaugural programs, aristocratic ceremonies, and stately receptions.

2. *Economy.* Jefferson's desire for economy in government resulted in such measures as repealing the excise tax on liquor, reducing military and diplomatic expenditures, reducing the national debt, and spending government funds with great care.

3. *Internal Improvements.* Jefferson's desire to meet the needs of Westerners for adequate transportation facilities caused his administration to support a program of internal improvements (roads, canals, harbors, etc.), despite the fact that such a program broadened the power and responsibilities of the national government. In 1808 the Republican Congress approved the building of a *National* or *Cumberland Road* from Cumberland, Maryland, to Wheeling, West Virginia.

4. *Replacement of Federalists.* As a believer in democracy, Jefferson wanted to have government officials who were responsive to the desires and needs of the people. As a party leader, he was anxious to reward his Republican supporters. Jefferson tried to achieve both purposes by replacing many Federalists with Republicans in the civil service. Federalist judges appointed by John Adams during the last hours of his administration (the "midnight judges") under the Judiciary Act of 1800 were dismissed, and the act was repealed. This set the stage for the later *Marbury v. Madison* case in the Supreme Court.

Two of Jefferson's noteworthy Cabinet appointments were JAMES MADISON, who helped shape foreign policy as Secretary of State, and ALBERT GALLATIN, who as Secretary of the Treasury was responsible for the government's sound financial policy.

5. *Federalist Policies Retained.* Jefferson did not want to, and in the case of the judiciary was not able to, sweep away all evidences of "Federalism." Much of Hamilton's program was kept, including the United States Bank and payment of the national debt. Many Federalist office holders were retained, in spite of much pressure on Jefferson to replace them. The courts also remained almost entirely in Federalist hands, despite Republican attempts to dismiss and impeach some Federalist judges. Also, it was during Jefferson's administration that JOHN MARSHALL became fourth Chief Justice of the Supreme Court. Marshall set forth the doctrine of judicial review and handed down decisions strengthening the national government at the expense of the states (See page 174.)

6. *Force When Necessary: The War with Tripoli.* Like his Federalist predecessors, Jefferson tried to pursue a policy of peaceful relations with foreign nations, and he opposed war when it could be avoided. However, he did not hesitate to use force to defend American rights, as in the *Tripolitan War* (1801–05).

 (a) Jefferson was determined to end the humiliating situation under which, for several years, the United States had been forced to pay an annual tribute to the rulers of the North African states of the "Barbary Coast" (Tunisia, Algeria, Tripoli) in order to prevent seizure of ships and cargoes by the Barbary pirates.

 (b) When the ruler of Tripoli, dissatisfied with the size of our payments, began hostilities in 1801, Jefferson sent a small squadron of American ships under Stephen Decatur into the Mediterranean. After several years of undeclared war, the United States subdued the Barbary pirates and secured a temporary peace treaty. Not until Commodore Decatur won a more decisive victory in 1812, however, was permanent peace established.

 (c) The Tripolitan War caused the Republicans, who had formerly favored a small navy, to increase the size and strength of the country's naval forces.

The Louisiana Purchase. The purchase of Louisiana in 1803 was the most significant achievement of Jefferson's first administration.

1. *Interest in Louisiana.* The Louisiana Territory, west of the Mississippi, had been given to Spain by France at the end of the French and Indian War. Americans were genuinely alarmed when it was discovered that Spain had transferred Louisiana back to France in 1800 by a secret treaty. Jefferson was so disturbed at the prospect of having a strong and aggressive nation like France as a neighbor that he began to consider a possible alliance with Britain. Western farmers were angered by Spain's withdrawal of the right of deposit in New Orleans in 1802. (France had not yet taken formal possession of Louisiana.) American expansionists were unhappy because they had hoped that Louisiana would become available for the future growth of the United States.

2. *Jefferson Purchases Louisiana.* When Jefferson heard that Napoleon planned to re-establish a French empire in America, he sent James Monroe and Robert Livingston to France to try to buy New Orleans. They were

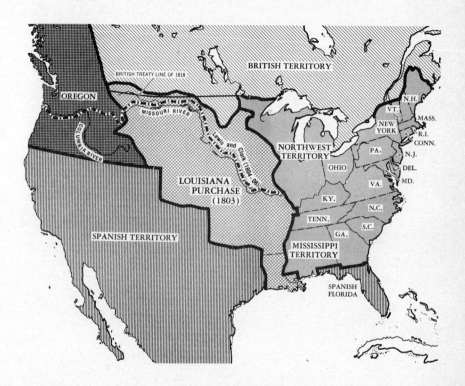

The Louisiana Purchase.

agreeably surprised by Napoleon's offer to sell *all* of Louisiana to the United States for $15,000,000, an offer which Congress and the President speedily accepted. Napoleon's action was in large part a result of a successful Negro revolt in Haiti against French control, which upset his dreams of American empire, and also of his need for funds to finance the expected renewal of war with Britain.

3. *Significance of the Louisiana Purchase.* The Louisiana Purchase, often called "the greatest land bargain in history," had many far-reaching results.

    (a) It doubled the area of the United States.

    (b) It increased tremendously the nation's store of natural resources.

    (c) It gave the United States control of the Mississippi down to its mouth, and ended rivalry with Britain, France, and Spain in the Mississippi Valley.

    (d) It strengthened national unity by making the Westerners grateful for the safeguarding of their interests by the Federal government.

(e) It promoted westward expansion.

(f) It forced Jefferson to modify his constitutional theory of strict construction of the powers of the national government because he realized the tremendous importance of this territory to the future of the United States. Also, he hoped that the rich farming lands acquired would insure the future of the United States as a great agrarian (agricultural) democracy.

(g) The purchase reduced further the prestige of the Federalists, who had strongly opposed such a step. (It should be noted that the Federalists, like the Republicans, reversed their constitutional principles here. Although they had previously called for a strong national government, they now maintained that the government had no power to make such a purchase.)

(h) Finally, the acquisition of Louisiana paved the way for a future struggle between North and South over the extension of slavery into new territories.

The Lewis and Clark Expedition (1804–06). The Louisiana Purchase also made possible the exploration of the western portion of the continent. At Jefferson's urging, Congress appropriated funds which enabled him to send MERIWETHER LEWIS and WILLIAM CLARK on an expedition to explore the vast region. Leading a group of about 50 men, Lewis and Clark set out at a point near St. Louis in 1804. They traveled northwest up the Missouri River into what is now North Dakota. Then they struck westward across the Rockies. They entered the valley of the Columbia River and finally reached the Pacific Ocean. The expedition returned to its starting point in 1806.

In addition to providing a great deal of valuable information, the *Lewis and Clark Expedition* became the basis for the later American claim to Oregon. Two years later (1806–07) another expedition led by ZEBULON PIKE, added to the knowledge of the central and southern portions of the Louisiana Territory.

REVIEW TEST (Chapter 8—Part I)

Select the number preceding the word or expression that best completes each statement or answers each question.

1. Which of the following was *not* part of Jefferson's theory of democratic government? (1) faith in the republican form of government   (2) territorial expansion United States (3) protection of civil and political liberty (4) economy in government

2. What characteristic of our country today may be considered a fulfillment of one of Jefferson's principles? (1) an industrialized society   (2) popular elections   (3) a large public debt   (4) a strong central government

3. Write the number of the *incorrect* choice. Thomas Jefferson strongly advocated (1) a democratic society of free, independent farmers   (2) widespread public education   (3) religious freedom   (4) a protective tariff to encourage manufacturing

4. Which of the following material concerning Thomas Jefferson would be likely to reveal most accurately his aims and objectives as President? (1) legislation enacted during his administration (2) an analysis of his administration by John Adams (3) his First Inaugural Address (4) the newspapers of his time

5. The primary purpose for the purchase of the Louisiana Territory was to (1) double the area of the United States (2) lessen the danger of Indian attack (3) insure an outlet for Western goods (4) aid the French

6. The Louisiana Purchase (1) established the western boundary of the United States at the Pacific (2) deprived Spain of her last possession in North America (3) included territory from Canada to the Gulf of Mexico (4) added all the territory between the Appalachians and the Rockies

7. All of the following were results of the purchase of Louisiana *except* that it (1) increased the power and prestige of the central government (2) set a precedent for the acquisition of new territories (3) led to the XYZ affair (4) gave the United States undisputed control of the Mississippi River

8. What state was formed from territory that was purchased by the United States in 1803? (1) Missouri (2) Oregon (3) Tennessee (4) Texas

9. Exploration of the Louisiana Territory and the Pacific Far West was accomplished in the early 19th century by (1) Lewis and Clark (2) Young and Jay (3) Hawley and Smoot (4) Lowell and Clay

10. On which issue did Thomas Jefferson reverse his opinion of strict construction of the Constitution? (1) the Bank of the United States (2) the purchase of the Louisiana Territory (3) the moving of the capital to Washington, D. C. (4) the payment of the national debt

Match each name in Column A with the item in Column B that is most clearly identified with it.

A

1. Albert Gallatin
2. John Adams
3. James Madison
4. Stephen Decatur
5. Zebulon Pike

B

a. Explored part of the Louisiana Territory

b. Jefferson's Secretary of State

c. Handled national finances for Jefferson

d. Appointed midnight judges

e. Part of a conspiracy to form an empire in the Southwest

f. Defeated Barbary Pirates

Essay Questions

1. Explain each of the following elements of "the Jeffersonian System": (a) Jeffersonian simplicity (b) internal improvements (c) economy (d) replacements of Federalists (e) retention of Federalist policies.

2. Jefferson was an advocate of peaceful relations with foreign nations, but used force where necessary. Show how this applied to the Tripolitan War of 1801–05.

3. "The principles of Jeffersonian democracy are still firmly embedded in American life." Discuss fully.

4. Thomas Jefferson's purchase of Louisiana is considered one of history's "most fateful decisions." Give evidence to support this statement.

Part II — JEFFERSON AND MADISON ATTEMPT TO PRESERVE THE PEACE

The temporary peace (1801–03) in the wars between Great Britain and France came to an end in 1803, when Napoleon began his conquest of Europe. The renewal of war set off a chain of events which helped bring on the War of 1812 between the United States and Britain.

The Napoleonic Wars. The chief antagonists in the Napoleonic Wars were France and England. In this struggle between "the tiger and the shark," France was supreme on land and Great Britain on the sea. Each tried to break the deadlock by destroying the trade of the other. **(1)** A series of *British Orders in Council* (1806–07) declared a blockade of Europe and forbade all neutral nations to trade with France in Europe, the West Indies, or India. **(2)** In retaliation, Napoleon issued the *Berlin and Milan Decrees* (1806–07), which declared a blockade of the British Isles and forbade all nations, including the United States, to trade with Great Britain.

Effects of Napoleonic Wars on the United States. The struggle between England and France had serious effects upon the United States. **(1)** It injured, though it did not destroy, the very profitable wartime trade that American merchants and shippers had carried on with the belligerents (fighting nations). **(2)** Resentment was greatest against Britain, who controlled the seas and could enforce her decrees effectively. **(3)** British naval vessels not only stopped, seized, and searched American ships and cargoes but also *impressed* American seamen into service in the British Navy. Strong official protests had no effect. **(4)** Especially humiliating was the *Chesapeake Affair* (1807). The British warship *Leopard* fired upon the lightly armed American frigate *Chesapeake*, killing three American seamen, and inflicting much damage. Four American sailors were forcibly removed on the grounds that they were British deserters.

Jefferson's Attempts to Avoid War. Like Washington and Adams before him, Jefferson wished to avoid war, if possible. When his repeated protests against violation of American neutral rights failed to bring results, he adopted a policy of "peaceable coercion."

1. *Peaceful Coercion: The Embargo Act (1807).* Jefferson reasoned that France and England needed American foodstuffs and raw materials so badly they would agree to respect our rights if faced with the threat of an economic boycott. At his urging, Congress passed the *Embargo Act* of 1807, which forbade the departure of all American merchant ships for foreign ports.

2. *Failure of the Embargo.* The Embargo Act failed to achieve its purposes and had to be repealed in 1809, just before Jefferson completed his second term. American commerce was nearly ruined. New England, especially, was hit hard as goods piled up on wharves and unemployment grew. Indeed, American merchants and shippers were hurt more than the British or French commercial classes. England and France both continued their blockades and refused to stop interfering with American shipping. Vigorous protests from all sections of the United States, including talk of secession in New England, alarmed both Congress and the President, and the Republican margin of victory in the elections of 1808 was decreased.

3. *Non-Intercourse.* In place of the Embargo, Congress substituted the *Non-Intercourse Act* of 1809, which reopened trade with all nations of the world, except Great Britain and France.

Madison as President. JAMES MADISON succeeded Jefferson in 1809 and served two terms as President. He came to the Presidency with a brilliant record, including activity during the Revolution, a prominent role in drawing up the Constitution and in writing the *Federalist Papers,* service in Congress, a leading place in the Republican Party, and service as Jefferson's Secretary of State and close adviser.

Madison, like Jefferson, attempted peaceful coercion and negotiation. Unfortunately, he did not provide vigorous executive leadership and was unable to handle successfully the problems of neutrality which he inherited from the previous administration.

1. *Failure of Non-Intercourse.* Widespread smuggling and evasion of the Non-Intercourse Act made it ineffective as a means of economic coercion, though it did in some measure help revive American trade.

2. *Macon's Bill.* In 1810, Congress passed a new measure, called *Macon's Bill Number 2,* which repealed the Non-Intercourse Act, reopened trade with England and France, and provided that if either nation ceased its violations of United States neutrality, non-intercourse would be revived against the other.

3. *Non-Intercourse Revived Against Britain.* When Napoleon announced his intention of repealing the Berlin and Milan Decrees, in order to take advantage of the Macon proposal, Madison announced that he was reestablishing non-intercourse against Great Britain, unless she revoked her orders. Later historians have criticized Madison for acting hastily and unwisely in accepting Napoleon's promise because once the United States resumed non-intercourse with Britain, the wily Napoleon again imposed restrictions on American trade.

4. *Declaration of War Against Great Britain.* After the Macon Bill, relations between the United States and Britain went from bad to worse. Not wishing to fight both Napoleon and the United States at the same time, and also aware that the British people and manufacturers were suffering from the lack of American food and markets, the British government in June 1812 finally decided to repeal its restrictions on American trade. Unfortunately, only two days after the British decision to repeal its restrictions, the United States declared war, and the announcement of the British reversal came too late to prevent hostilities.

REVIEW TEST (Chapter 8—Part II)

Select the number preceding the word or expression that best completes each statement or answers each question.

1. Before the war of 1812 the section most actively engaged in maritime commerce was the (1) Middle Atlantic States (2) Pacific Coast States (3) Southern States (4) New England States

2. What economic group in the United States most strongly objected to the Embargo Act of 1807? (1) New England shippers (2) Southern cotton growers (3) frontier farmers (4) Northern factory workers

3. What is a major reason why the United States declared war on Great Britain rather than on France in 1812? (1) France had aided the United States during the American Revolution. (2) France's democratic revolutionary principles were similar to those of the United States. (3) New England merchants wanted revenge for shipping losses. (4) Britain failed to repeal its trade restrictions in time to avert war.

4. Madison became President in (1) 1806 (2) 1807 (3) 1808 (4) 1809

5. The chief antagonists in the Napoleonic wars were (1) England and France (2) England and Russia (3) France and Germany (4) Spain and Portugal

State whether each of the following statements is true or false. If the statement is false, replace the word or phrase in **boldface type** *with one which will make it correct.*

1. United States citizens were angered by the impressment of American sailors by the **French.**

2. The Chesapeake Affair was humiliating to the **United States.**

3. The Embargo Act was replaced by **Macon's Bill Number 2.**

4. The nation that took most advantage of the repeal of the Non-Intercourse Act was **England.**

5. The policy of "peaceful coercion" was designed by **Napoleon.**

Essay Questions

1. How did war in Europe affect the United States between 1803 and 1812?

2. Show how Jefferson used economic measures in an attempt to avoid war. Explain why his policies were bitterly condemned.

3. "James Madison became heir to Jefferson's foreign problems." Explain what he "inherited," and how he tried to solve the problems of his inheritance.

4. What story might have been printed under each of the following newspaper headlines that could have appeared in the period 1800–12?

 a. STRUGGLE BETWEEN TIGER AND SHARK THREATENS TO INVOLVE THE UNITED STATES

 b. LEOPARD ATTACKS CHESAPEAKE. AMERICAN RIGHTS VIOLATED.

 c. ADMINISTRATION ADOPTS POLICY OF PEACEFUL COERCION

 d. MADISON ASKS FOR WAR

Part III — THE WAR OF 1812

The War of 1812, long celebrated as a great triumph for the United States, actually ended in a military stalemate, and in a peace treaty which did little more than bring an end to the fighting. The long-range effects of the war, however, were highly significant.

Causes of the War of 1812. The group that was most affected by the restrictions on American commerce, the New England shipping interests, was opposed to going to war with England in 1812. These merchants had continued to profit from wartime trade after the repeal of the Embargo. Why, then, did Madison feel compelled to ask Congress to declare war? Historians have suggested a number of reasons.

1. *Violations of Neutral Rights.* Americans in all sections resented British violations of our neutral rights, considering them an insult to our national honor. They were angered by the impressment of thousands of American seamen, the loss of American lives resulting from the firing upon American ships, and the search and seizure of American ships and cargoes.

2. *Economic Difficulties.* Southerners and Westerners blamed Britain (and also France) for causing an economic depression by closing European ports to their exports.

3. *Indian Troubles.* Already alarmed by Indian raids on the Northwest frontier, Westerners were convinced that the British were behind efforts of the Indian leader Tecumseh and his brother, "The Prophet," to organize a great Indian Confederation, designed to prevent further seizures of Indian lands by the whites. When General WILLIAM H. HARRISON won a victory over the Indians in 1811 at *Tippecanoe* (in Indiana) and reported the capture of English ammunition and rifles, Westerners clamored for war with Britain.

4. *Land Hunger and Expansionism.* Western and Southern leaders, particularly those from frontier areas, were anxious for the United States to expand into Canada and the Floridas. They demanded the acquisition of Canada, and supported war with Britain as a means of ending the Indian menace and gaining control of the valuable fur trade. They also insisted that the annexation of East and West Florida would end Spanish influence, remove border disputes, wipe out a refuge for runaway slaves, and give the United States control of valuable river outlets. In Congress, this program was loudly advocated by the *"War Hawks,"* a group of nationalistic young Republicans who had gained control of the House of Representatives in the election of 1810. Among the important War Hawk leaders were HENRY CLAY of Kentucky and JOHN C. CALHOUN of South Carolina. The theory behind the program of territorial expansion urged by the War Hawks was later to be called *Manifest Destiny.*

Lack of Preparedness for War. The United States was poorly prepared for war. It had only a small army and unreliable state militias, and it lacked military and Congressional leadership. In addition, the nation was weakened by financial disorders, caused by inadequate banking facilities and inflation. (These financial troubles resulted largely from the failure to recharter the United States Bank in 1811.) Such unfavorable conditions cancelled out the advantages gained from the fact that Britain did not carry on the war very actively, since her chief concern at the time was to defeat Napoleon in Europe.

The Hartford Convention. Perhaps the most important unfavorable factor for the United States was the national disunity caused by New England's opposition to the war. Referring scornfully to "Mr. Madison's War," New Englanders refused to buy war bonds; they sold supplies to the British in Canada; and they refused to allow the President to use their state militias outside their own borders. The high point of New England opposition came at the *Hartford Convention,* called in 1814 by Federalist leaders. This convention adopted a report condemning the war against England and supporting states' rights and the doctrine of nullification. A series of constitutional amendments was proposed which would have had the effect of limiting the powers of Congress and the President and of curbing the influence of the South and the West in the national government. (The war came to an end before any serious effort was made to act on these proposals.)

Military Events of the War of 1812. The War of 1812 has been called "America's worst fought major war." It produced no decisive victory on either side, and it ended in military stalemate. The tiny United States Navy, assisted by hundreds of privateers, did far better than the Army. The gallant and skillful fighting of our seamen against the mighty British fleet won the admiration of the world in spite of the fact that Britain was ultimately able to blockade the leading ports and to cut off most of our overseas trade.

1. In 1812, several United States land campaigns against Canada failed. The British defeated invading American forces led by General Hull and captured Detroit. American morale was boosted, however, by the brilliant victories of individual American naval vessels. Especially notable was the triumph of our warship *Constitution* ("Old Ironsides") over the British frigate *Guerrière.*

2. In 1813, the United States won a major naval victory on Lake Erie. Captain OLIVER HAZARD PERRY built a small fleet and engaged a British squadron that was guarding the important supply route along Lake Erie from Canada. After a short but spirited fight, Perry was completely victorious. He reported the victory to his superior, General Harrison, in the famous message, "We have met the enemy and they are ours . . . ." — words which have become part of the living tradition of the United States Navy.

This triumph gave the United States control of the Great Lakes and led to the British evacuation of Detroit. In the same year, General Harrison defeated the British and their Indian allies in a land battle. This made possible the recovery of the Northwest and a brief invasion of Canada.

3. In 1814, the British made a vigorous attempt to end the war. They raided the eastern coast of the United States and captured Washington, D. C., where they set fire to government buildings, including the Capitol and the White House. Then they attacked Baltimore. The heroic resistance of Americans to the bombardment of Fort McHenry, just outside Baltimore, inspired Francis Scott Key to write *The Star-Spangled Banner,* which became our national anthem.

Later in 1814, another British army made an attempt to push south from Canada along the Lake Champlain route. But an American squadron under Captain THOMAS MACDONOUGH defeated the British naval force on Lake Champlain. As a result, the British army had to retreat, and Americans marched into Canada from Niagara.

4. Early in 1815, came the greatest American land victory of the war. The British attempted to capture New Orleans but were repelled with severe losses by an American army commanded by General ANDREW JACKSON. Strangely enough, this bloody battle was fought after the treaty of peace had been signed. Because of poor communications, the news of peace had not reached the rival armies.

The Treaty of Ghent (1814). Both sides were eager for peace and the *Treaty of Ghent* (December, 1814) reflected the indecisive military situation. It provided merely for an end to the fighting and the restoration of conditions as they were before the war. Nothing was said about impressment or neutral rights, but provision was made for future settlement of questions of boundaries and fisheries by referring these matters to arbitration commissions.

Significance of the War of 1812. Although the causes of the War of 1812 were not removed by the peace treaty, the war had such important lasting results for the United States that it has often been called the "Second War for Independence."

1. *Foreign Respect.* The United States, a young and sparsely populated country, had showed the world that it would defend itself whenever its rights were violated by anyone, even a great power. Never again would the United States be treated as an insignificant weakling in the family of nations.

2. *End of European Involvement.* The war marked a turning point in American foreign relations. Our direct involvement in the affairs of Europe was virtually at an end, and it became possible for the United States to remain for the next 100 years generally isolated from European power politics. Thus, the United States was able to settle its political and economic problems undisturbed by European involvements.

3. *Nationalism.* The war resulted in a feeling of national unity. Americans felt proud of their country and eager to develop its national resources and power. For several years this feeling submerged sectional differences.

4. *Westward Expansion.* The war paved the way for a new surge of westward migration. This was made possible, in large measure, by increased attention to Western development and by the removal of the Indian menace east of the Mississippi. This resulted from the wartime defeats of the Indians in the northwest by Harrison and in the southwest by Jackson.

5. *Growth of Manufacturing.* The War of 1812 stimulated the growth of American industry and developed a sense of national self-sufficiency. During the Embargo and war years, Americans were forced to develop their own manufacturing industries, since they were cut off from English and European supplies.

6. *The Collapse of Federalist Influence.* Finally, the war resulted in the elimination of the Federalist Party as an important factor in American political life. When hostilities ceased soon after the Hartford Convention, the Federalists were severely criticized and discredited for their disloyal behavior during the war. After losing badly to the Republican Party in the election of 1816, the Federalists never again nominated a Presidential candidate.

REVIEW TEST (Chapter 8—Part III)

Select the number preceding the word or expression that best completes each statement or answers each question.

1. Reasons given for the United States Declaration of War on England in 1812 include all of the following *except* (1) nationalism (2) violations of neutral rights (3) European alliances (4) land hunger

2. Two Americans, known as "War Hawks," who were eager to acquire Canada by the War of 1812 were (1) Jackson and Madison (2) Webster and Clinton (3) Calhoun and Clay (4) Burr and John Quincy Adams

3. The defense of Baltimore on September 14, 1814, inspired Francis Scott Key to write (1) "America the Beautiful" (2) "The Star Spangled Banner" (3) "Battle Hymn of the Republic" (4) "America"

4. Which factor best explains why the United States was able to fight England to a military "draw" in the War of 1812? (1) Britain's chief concern at the time was Napoleon. (2) American generals consistently outmaneuvered the British. (3) American gun-boats shattered the British blockade. (4) American morale was high.

5. Which section of the United States was most strongly opposed to the War of 1812? (1) Middle Atlantic States (2) New England States (3) Southern States (4) Western States

6. Which was a result of the War of 1812? (1) The United States gained all remaining territory east of the Mississippi River. (2) Great Britain agreed to end the impressment of American seamen. (3) The Democratic-Republican Party lost its influence in United States politics. (4) The United States earned respect abroad.

7. A constitutional issue arising at the Hartford Convention was similar to the issue caused by (1) the XYZ affair (2) the Alien and Sedition Acts (3) the Second Continental Congress (4) Washington's Proclamation of Neutrality

8. Which of the following was a result of the other three? (1) Alien and Sedition Acts (2) disappearance of the Federalist Party (3) Hartford Convention (4) increase in the democratic spirit of the United States.

9. An important result of the War of 1812 was that it (1) strengthened the Federalist Party (2) introduced ironclad naval vessels (3) settled the Oregon boundary dispute (4) encouraged manufacturing in the United States

10. According to the Treaty of Ghent what question was left for future arbitration? (1) fishing rights (2) disarmament on the Great Lakes (3) neutral rights (4) evacuation of Canada by the British

Supply the word or expression that correctly completes each statement.

1. In the early 1800's Westerners firmly believed that the ..?.. were encouraging Indian raids along the northern and western borders.

2. In addition to desiring Canada the War Hawks were eager to secure ..?...

3. The military engagement fought after the Treaty of Ghent had been signed was the ..?...

4. Two significant American naval victories on the Great Lakes in the War of 1812 took place on Lake ..?.. and Lake ..?...

5. The American general who gained fame for his victories over the Indians before and during the War of 1812 was ..?...

Essay Questions

1. Discuss three important causes of the War of 1812?

2. New Englanders of the time called the War of 1812 "Mr. Madison's War." Why? To what extent do you agree or disagree with this point of view.

3. Many Americans have looked upon the War of 1812 as a glorious military victory for the United States. Give evidence which tends to support or refute this opinion.

4. Explain one immediate and three lasting results of the War of 1812.

5. Why has each of the following been considered a military hero of the War of 1812? Oliver Perry, Thomas MacDonough, William H. Harrison, Andrew Jackson.

REVIEWING UNIT THREE

Select the number preceding the word or expression that best completes each statement or answers each question.

1. Included in the initial steps of the first Congress to put the new government into operation were all of the following *except* (1) creation of the departments of State, Treasury, War, and also the posts of Attorney General and Postmaster General (2) Tariff Act of 1789 (3) approval of first ten amendments to the Constitution (4) Alien and Sedition Acts

2. During the war between France and England, Washington proclaimed the neutrality of the United States because (1) neutrality was promised in the Jay Treaty (2) Congress had abrogated the French treaty (3) a policy of neutrality was in the best interests of the country (4) the majority of the people of the United States were against England

3. The Whiskey Rebellion was a reaction to a Federal law. The law in question could not have been passed under the Articles of Confederation because the Federal government lacked the power to (1) control interstate commerce (2) control foreign commerce (3) collect taxes (4) levy tariffs

4. The Pinckney Treaty (1795) directly benefited (1) New England merchants (2) farmers in the Ohio Valley (3) Southern plantation owners (4) Atlantic coast shipping interests

5. The Kentucky and Virginia Resolutions were primarily concerned with the (1) doctrine of states' rights (2) system of checks and balances (3) Alien and Sedition Acts (4) Tariff of Abominations

6. Which one of the following events occurred *second?* (1) adoption of the Bill of Rights (2) Hartford Convention (3) ratification of the Constitution (4) Whiskey Rebellion

7. Alexander Hamilton's financial program helped to (1) prevent deflation (2) shift a fair portion of the debt to the states (3) strengthen the new national government (4) win the support of the small farmers to the Federalist Party

8. The Virginia and Kentucky Resolutions were written by (1) Adams and Clay (2) Jackson and Van Buren (3) Madison and Jefferson (4) Washington and Adams

9. "His Majesty will withdraw all his troops and garrisons from all posts and places within the boundary lines assigned by the treaty of peace to the United States . . ." These words are found in the (1) Jay Treaty (2) Pinckney Treaty (3) Rush-Bagot Treaty (4) Treaty of Ghent

10. During the first quarter of the 19th century, which of the following was a source of friction between the United States and Great Britain? (1) resolutions adopted at the Hartford Convention (2) activities of the Indians in the Northwest Territory (3) annexation of Louisiana (4) Shays' Rebellion

11. The "War Hawks" were (1) Indians (2) Congressmen (3) adventurers (4) explorers

12. An important economic result of the War of 1812 for the United States was the (1) encouragement given to manufacturing (2) establishment of "pet banks" (3) decrease in tariff rates (4) decline in industrial importance of the New England states

166

13. Which of the following groups contains three prominent members of the Federalist Party? (1) James Madison, Alexander Hamilton, John Jay (2) Thomas Jefferson, Aaron Burr, James Monroe (3) John Adams, John Marshall, James Madison (4) Alexander Hamilton, John Adams, John Marshall

14. What United States President had the political courage to oppose a declaration of war with France even though many in his political party wanted war? (1) John Adams (2) Thomas Jefferson (3) James Madison (4) James Monroe

15. All of the following were causes of the War of 1812 *except* (1) election of Madison (2) violation of America's neutral rights (3) Indian troubles (4) land hunger and expansionism

For each of the following events write:

W — *if it occurred when George Washington was President*

A — *if it occurred when John Adams was President*

J — *if it occurred when Thomas Jefferson was President*

M — *if it occurred when James Madison was President*

1. The Genêt affair.

2. War with the Barbary Pirates.

3. The XYZ affair.

4. Burning of the national Capitol by the British.

5. The Proclamation of Neutrality.

6. The Whiskey Rebellion.

7. The establishment of the first Bank of the United States.

8. The repeal of the Embargo Act.

9. The defeat of Tecumseh by General Harrison.

10. The Virginia and Kentucky Resolutions.

Match each person in Column A with the letter preceding the quotation in Column B with which he is most closely associated.

A	**B**
1. Thomas Jefferson	*a.* "We have met the enemy, and they are ours."
2. James Madison	*b.* "Then conquer we must, for our cause it is just."
3. George Washington	*c.* "We are all Republicans; we are all Federalists."
4. Oliver Perry	*d.* "The rule of conduct for us in regard to foreign nations is . . . to have as little political connection as possible."
5. Francis Scott Key	*e.* "Liberty and Union, now and forever, one and inseparable!"
	f. "British cruisers have been in the continued practice of violating the American flag . . . of seizing and carrying off persons sailing under it . . . our commerce has been plundered on every sea."

The statements below identify states that are located on the map. Write the **letter** *that indicates the location of that state on the map.*

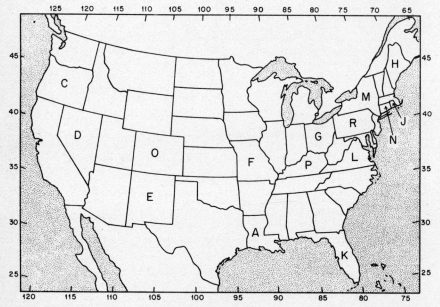

1. This state joined the Union soon after the inauguration of George Washington as President.

2. Western farmers insisted upon the right of deposit at a port in this state.

3. Of our first five Presidents, four were residents of this state.

4. A convention opposing the War of 1812 met in this state.

5. Here Zebulon Pike attempted to reach a mountain peak that bears his name.

6. The first capital of our nation, where George Washington was inaugurated April 30, 1789, was located in this state.

7. This state was first to join the Union from an area purchased by the United States.

8. Federal militia were used for the first time in this state to uphold United States law.

9. The Lewis and Clark expedition gave us a basis for our claims to this state.

10. This state, most of which lies west of the Appalachian Mountains, opposed the Alien and Sedition Acts in President Adams' administration.

Essay Questions

1. Discuss fully a major issue that arose between the President and the individual indicated: (a) President Washington — Citizen Genêt (b) President Jefferson — Napoleon I.

2. Explain the controversy arising over the issue indicated in each of the following instances: (a) George Washington — the excise tax (b) John Adams — the Alien and Sedition Acts (c) Thomas Jefferson — the Federalist System (d) James Madison — violation of American rights.

3. American public opinion has often been sharply divided over important issues or events. For each of the following indicate two persons or groups of persons holding differing points of view on the issue. Discuss one reason for this difference in viewpoint.

(a) Chartering of the First Bank of the United States.

(b) "The Revolution of 1800."

(c) Entrance of the United States into the War of 1812.

4. Who served his country better, Hamilton or Jefferson? Explain fully.

5. Political parties have long been an important feature of the American governmental system. (a) Discuss two conditions or ideas or issues that gave rise to political parties in the United States. (b) Show how Hamilton and Jefferson influenced the parties of which they were leaders. (c) If Hamilton were alive today which political party would he support? Why? (d) If Jefferson were alive today which political party would he support? Why? (e) Explain two advantages of the two-party system.

6. Explain, by giving evidence, why you agree or disagree with each of the following statements: (a) As President, Washington did not live up to the reputation he had earned as a general. (b) Alexander Hamilton was a financial wizard. (c) Thomas Jefferson's basic principles have long been outmoded. (d) The Louisiana Purchase was the world's greatest land bargain.

7. Some say the War of 1812 was caused by expansionism and land hunger; others say that it resulted from violations of our national honor and disregard of our maritime rights. Which point of view seems best substantiated by the facts of history? Explain.

8. Explain why the War of 1812 has been referred to as (a) the Second War for Independence, and (b) a significant turning point in American history.

9. Discuss two instances in which states' rights became an issue in the period 1789–1814.

| Unit Four | NATIONALISM AND SECTIONALISM |

CHAPTER 9

Nationalism and the Era of Good Feeling

The War of 1812 was a turning point in the history of the United States. From it there emerged a spirit of *nationalism*, or devotion to the interests of the nation as a whole. For several years after the war there was a burst of national pride, in which concern for national needs outweighed sectional or local interests. This development of nationalism in the United States took place at about the same time that nationalism was beginning to be an important force in 19th-century European affairs.

The "Era of Good Feeling" (1817-25). This period of nationalism in the United States was characterized by the ascendency of the Democratic-Republican Party in national politics. As we have seen, the opposition of the Federalist Party to the War of 1812, and its support of the unpopular position taken at the Hartford Convention (see page 162), led to its disappearance as a national party. Because of the lack of a well-organized national political party to oppose the Republican Party, the administrations of James Monroe (1817–25) have been called the *Era of Good Feeling*.

1. *James Monroe as President.* JAMES MONROE, who succeeded Madison in 1817, was re-elected almost unanimously by the Electoral College in 1820. Monroe was the last of the "Virginia Dynasty" of Presidents (Washington, Jefferson, Madison, Monroe). He was also the last of the Revolutionary generation to serve as President. Though he came to office with a long record of public service, he is not considered to have been an outstanding President.

2. *The "Nationalized" Republican Party.* The Republican Party went along with the new national spirit; it abandoned its earlier states' rights –strict interpretation policy, and it supported measures which strengthened the central government. Republican leaders in Congress **(a)** increased the strength of the army and navy, **(b)** chartered a Second Bank of the

United States (1816), **(c)** passed a protective tariff (1816), **(d)** recommended a national system of roads and canals, and **(e)** championed a vigorous foreign policy which resulted in the settlement of disputes with Britain, the acquisition of Florida, and the proclamation of the *Monroe Doctrine.*

Nationalism in Economic Affairs. The spirit of confidence in the nation's destiny was shown in the legislation passed by Congress to promote national development. The Republican Party, now strongly nationalistic, supported measures it had opposed during the Federalist Era. This new spirit was most clearly demonstrated in a program for economic development proposed by Henry Clay and adopted by the Republican Party in 1816. It became known as the *"American System."*

The "American System" proposed a program of three essential steps: **(1)** a protective tariff, behind which American manufacturers (situated mainly in the North) could develop and prosper; **(2)** establishment of a national bank, which would stabilize the currency and unite the country economically; and **(3)** use of the revenues gained from the tariff for internal improvements, such as transportation. This last would benefit the West particularly.

1. *Passage of the Protective Tariff of 1816.* In 1816, Congress enacted a protective tariff to safeguard the New England and Middle Atlantic states from the "dumping" of cheap British textiles on the American market after the War of 1812. Southern Congressmen, led by John C. Calhoun, supported the measure because they believed that the South would benefit from industrialism, and also because they felt that the nation should be economically as well as politically independent of Europe. Westerners supported the tariff because it fitted in with the "American System."

2. *Chartering of the Second Bank of the United States (1816).* To reestablish a sound banking system and a stable currency (one having the same value in all sections), Congress in 1816 chartered a *Second Bank of the United States.* The failure to recharter the first Bank in 1811 had led to serious financial difficulties. *Inflation* (a sharp rise in prices) had resulted from the unrestrained issue of unbacked paper money by state banks. Business in general was greatly hampered by the fact that state banknotes differed in value from state to state, and in many instances would not be redeemed in gold or silver by the issuing bank.

Like its predecessor, the Second Bank of the United States was given a 20-year charter, and was to be run privately, with 20% of its stock owned by the Federal government. Its capital stock was set at $35,000,000, about 3½ times that of the first Bank. President Madison, who had led the fight against rechartering the First Bank, did not oppose the Second.

3. *Internal Improvements.* Although little was actually accomplished in the way of enacting a program of internal improvements at national expense, Congressional action in the era after the War of 1812 showed a growing awareness of the need to knit the West more closely to the rest of the nation. **(a)** The *Cumberland (National) Road* was extended to Wheeling on the Ohio River. **(b)** Congress passed Calhoun's *Bonus Bill* of 1816, which provided for the use of the $1,500,000 "bonus" paid to the Federal government by the Second Bank of the United States (in return for the special privileges granted under its charter) as a revolving fund for internal improvements. However, President Madison vetoed the bill because he felt that Congress did not have the power to build and maintain roads. **(c)** Individual states attempted to fill the gap by granting financial assistance to private road- and canal-building companies, or by constructing their own roads and canals.

Nationalism in Foreign Affairs. The shaping of American foreign policy after the War of 1812 clearly showed the emerging nationalist spirit. Effective steps were taken to protect the nation's frontiers and interests in the Western Hemisphere.

1. *Protection Against the Indians.* As new areas opened to settlement in Ohio, Indiana, Illinois, and other new states, the national government attempted to safeguard settlers on the westward-moving frontier by signing additional treaties with the Indians, by fighting them when necessary (*e.g.* the *Seminole War* in 1817 with the Indians of the Southwest), and by putting them on reservations.

2. *Settlement of Disputes with Great Britain.* After the War of 1812, Great Britain adopted a more friendly and respectful attitude toward the United States, as can be seen in its willingness to settle remaining disputes amicably. This added to the young country's prestige and set a precedent for the peaceful settlement of disputes which has characterized relations between the two nations ever since. **(a)** The *Rush-Bagot Agreement* (1817) provided for reduction of armaments on the Great Lakes (complete disarmament was finally achieved in 1871, under the *Treaty of Washington*). **(b)** The *Treaty of 1818* safeguarded United States interests along the northwest border. It set the 49th parallel as the boundary between the United States and Canada, from the Lake of the Woods to the Rocky Mountains. It also provided for joint American-British occupation of the Oregon Territory for 10 years, subject to renewal, and it settled the question of offshore American fishing rights in Canadian waters (the Newfoundland fisheries).

3. *Purchase of Florida (1819).* In 1819 the United States rounded out its southern and eastern boundaries by obtaining Florida from Spain.

> (*a*) Despite Spanish protest, by the end of the War of 1812 West Florida had already been annexed by the United States; part in 1810 on the grounds that it was included in the Louisiana Purchase, and part in 1813 during the War of 1812, because Spain was an ally of England. Florida itself, or "East Florida" as it was then called, remained in Spanish hands and continued to be a refuge for hostile Indians (who made raids across the border), outlaws, and runaway slaves.

(b) As a result of border raids during the *Seminole War* of 1817, Andrew Jackson crossed the Florida border in pursuit of Seminole Indians. In addition to routing the Indians, he seized Spanish posts and executed two British traders guilty of inciting the Indians.

(c) To head off an international crisis because of Jackson's illegal actions, Secretary of State John Quincy Adams, in a series of negotiations, convinced the Spanish government that it ought to sell Florida to the United States, in view of the fact that Spain was unable to maintain order there. As a result, the United States obtained Florida in return for assuming $5,000,000 of claims against Spain by American citizens. In addition, Spain gave up its claim to Oregon, while the United States relinquished its claim to Texas as part of the Louisiana Territory. Thus, the Florida Purchase not only rounded out the United States' boundaries to the south and east but also strengthened our claim to Oregon and paved the way for the "cotton kingdom" to expand to the southwest.

The Monroe Doctrine (1823). The most impressive evidence of American nationalism in foreign affairs was the proclamation of the *Monroe Doctrine* in 1823.

1. *Background.* While Europe was engaged in the Napoleonic Wars and their aftermath, Spain's Latin American colonies revolted against the mother country and set themselves up as independent republics. The United States feared that the *Quadruple Alliance* (Russia, Prussia, Austria, France) would attempt to regain Spain's colonies by force. This would have the effect to cutting off our growing trade with Latin America. The United States was also disturbed by Russia's *Edict of 1821,* extending the boundary of Alaska south to the 51st parallel in the Oregon Territory, and by Russia's claim to what is now the Northwestern coastal area of the United States as a field for colonization. In addition to concern over these specific territorial and commercial interests, the United States government was genuinely alarmed by the prospect that European intervention in the affairs of the Western Hemisphere might set a dangerous precedent for possible future attacks upon the United States itself.

2. *Provisions of the Doctrine.* Great Britain also felt that its trade relations with Latin America would be menaced by European attempts to regain the Spanish colonies. Britain, accordingly, suggested a joint British-American policy to oppose intervention, but Secretary of State John Quincy Adams urged President Monroe to issue such a statement alone. Accepting the advice, Monroe proclaimed the famous "Monroe Doctrine" in a message to Congress (1823). It stated: **(a)** that the Western Hemisphere was no longer a field for future European colonization; **(b)** that the United States would not interfere with European colonies already established; **(c)** that any attempt on the part of a European power to intervene in the Western Hemisphere would be considered dangerous to the peace and safety of the United States; and **(d)** that the United States would not interfere in the internal affairs or quarrels of any European nation.

3. Significance of the Monroe Doctrine. Although it was no more than a Presidential statement of United States policy, the Monroe Doctrine had significant effects upon American development.

(a) European monarchs were angered rather than frightened, but they made no attempts to recover Spain's former colonies because of fear of England. In 1824 Russia signed a treaty with the United States agreeing not to trespass on the Northwest coast.

(b) The Doctrine was a forthright statement of American pride and patriotism. At a time when this nation would actually have had to rely upon the British Navy to repel foreign invasion, our government asserted its right to self-defense, and boldly warned Europe to leave the Western Hemisphere alone (*non-colonization; non-intervention*).

(c) The Doctrine was also a logical extension and reassertion of the policy of isolation set forth by Washington in his Proclamation of Neutrality and Farewell Address, by Jefferson in his First Inaugural Address, and by Madison in his war message to Congress in 1812.

(d) Finally, and most important, the Monroe Doctrine became a cornerstone of American foreign policy. Under various interpretations of its provisions, the United States remained aloof from European affairs, never willingly allowed a powerful nation to secure a foothold near its strategic Caribbean possessions, became the "watchman of Latin America," and used the Doctrine as an excuse for its own imperialism at the beginning of the 20th century.

Judicial Nationalism — The Decisions of John Marshall. American nationalism in the form of a strengthening of the Federal government received its most powerful impetus from the decisions of JOHN MARSHALL, Chief Justice of the Supreme Court. Marshall was appointed by President John Adams at the end of the Federalist Era, and served for over 30 years (1801–35). As noted earlier, he handed down decisions which increased the power of the national government, established the prestige of the Federal judiciary, and protected the rights of property. Marshall wrote over 500 decisions, many during the period of postwar nationalism, and their effects are still felt today. He is considered our greatest Chief Justice.

1. Establishing the Supremacy of the Federal Judiciary. In a series of notable decisions, the Marshall-dominated court established the authority of the Federal judiciary.

(a) In *Marbury v. Madison* (1803) the Court held it had the right to declare acts of Congress unconstitutional and void, if they were in conflict with the Constitution (*judicial review*). William Marbury, one of the "midnight judges" (see page 153) appointed by John Adams, applied to the Supreme Court for a *writ of mandamus* (a court order) to compel Secretary of State Madison to deliver his commission of office. The Court ruled that while Marbury was entitled to his commission, the Supreme Court had no authority to issue a writ of mandamus, and, furthermore, that the section of the Judiciary Act of 1789 which gave the Supreme Court this authority was itself an unconstitutional extension of the Court's original jurisdiction. Thus, for the first time, an act of Congress was set aside by the Supreme Court as being in violation of the Constitution and hence unenforceable.

(b) In *Fletcher v. Peck* (1810) the Supreme Court established its right to set aside a law of a state legislature if it conflicted with the United States Constitution, or the Federal government's laws and treaties. The Supreme Court declared that a land grant was a *contract* between a state and an individual, even if fraudulently secured. Since no state has the right to invalidate a contract, an act of the Georgia Legislature which repealed a land grant made by a previous session of the legislature (swayed by bribery) was unconstitutional.

(c) In *Martin v. Hunter's Lessee* (1816) the Court proclaimed its right to hear appeals from decisions of state courts, if the claim was made that such decisions conflicted with the Constitution. In a closely allied decision, in *Cohens v. Virginia* (1821), Marshall declared that the Supreme Court was superior to state courts in all questions relating to the powers of the Federal government.

2. *Strengthening the Federal Government.* Many of Marshall's famous decisions expanded the powers of the national government at the expense of the states.

(a) In *McCulloch v. Maryland* (1819) Marshall held that Congress could establish a bank under its implied powers and that a state could not tax a Federal agency since "the power to tax involves the power to destroy;" and this would make a state equal in power to the Federal government. He therefore ruled unconstitutional a law of the state of Maryland intended to destroy a branch of the Bank of the United States by imposing a heavy tax on its banknotes.

(b) In *Gibbons v. Ogden* (1824) Marshall ruled that Congress alone, and not the states, had the right to regulate interstate commerce. He forbade New York State from granting to a private concern a monopoly to operate steamboats on the Hudson River between New York and New Jersey, on the ground that such navigation is interstate commerce, and therefore subject only to Federal jurisdiction.

3. *Protecting Property Rights.* In other decisions, Marshall protected the rights of property against actions of state legislatures that seemed too radical. In *Fletcher v. Peck,* as indicated, Marshall held that states could not set aside legislative land grants, since they were contracts. In the *Dartmouth College Case* (1819) Marshall upheld a similar principle by ruling that a college charter was also a contract, and therefore could not legally be impaired. The decision voided an act of the New Hampshire Legislature which changed the pre-Revolutionary charter of Dartmouth College.

Nationalism and the Westward Movement. One of the most important influences upon the growth of American nationalism was the *Westward Movement.* The advance westward and the existence of a frontier for over three centuries were unique features of America's development, and they provide a key to the understanding of American history. (Some observers, such as the great historian of the frontier, Frederick Jackson Turner, have held that the frontier is *the* key factor in the history and development of the United States.)

1. *Westward Expansion.* Americans began to move West from the time of the first settlements. Some were eager for adventure. Others hoped to make their fortunes. Most were attracted by the abundance of cheap, fertile land and the chance to improve their lot in life. There were three major periods of westward migration before the Civil War.

> (*a*) The first wave took place during the Colonial Period. Pioneers from Eastern seaboard sections of the 13 colonies moved into the Western ("back country") regions as far as the Appalachian Mountains. By the time of the Revolution, frontiersmen like DANIEL BOONE, JAMES ROBERTSON, and JOHN SEVIER had established advance settlements on the other side of the mountains.

> (*b*) The second wave of westward migration occurred between the Revolution and the War of 1812. Some pioneers settled in the western portions of New England, New York, and Pennsylvania. Others pushed across the mountains and down the Ohio Valley into Ohio, Illinois, and southern Indiana. Western settlement also resulted in statehood for Vermont, Kentucky, Tennessee, Ohio, and Louisiana.

> (*c*) A third wave of pioneers moved westward between 1812 and 1860. This included settlers from the East and older frontier regions, and immigrants from Europe. By the time of the Civil War, they had settled the Old Northwest and Southwest, east of the Mississippi River, and had crossed into Iowa, Minnesota, North and South Dakota, the Oregon Territory, and California. Between 1812 and 1861, seventeen new states entered the Union.

2. *Government Land Policy.* The westward movement was helped by the land policy adopted by the government. The fact that the land was granted by the Federal government, not the original 13 states, made the Westerners particularly nationalistic.

> (*a*) To encourage more regular and more secure settlement, various ordinances provided for land surveys before settlers could secure titles. This also enabled the government to set aside lands for future sale or for specific uses, for example, education.

> (*b*) To make land available to small settlers, and to ensure that not too much would fall into the hands of large-scale land speculators, the government reduced the size and price of the minimum plot. By 1820, a settler could buy 80 acres of farm land for about $100.

> (*c*) To make it possible for settlers who were living on lands without titles (*squatters*) to keep their holdings, Congress passed a series of *preemption acts,* giving the squatters first chance to buy such lands at $1.25 an acre.

3. *How Settlers Went West.* The westward journey was a difficult one. It meant fighting the hazards of nature and, on occasion, hostile Indians. It took months, and in some cases, years. **(a)** The pioneers usually followed river valleys through the mountains, then pushed across the foothills, flatlands, and prairies. **(b)** Some settlers walked; some came on horseback; some traveled in large canvas-covered (*Conestoga*) wagons. Others came by stagecoach over rough roads, or used rafts and boats on rivers and canals. **(c)** Transportation facilities were never fully adequate, but they were gradually improved to meet the demand of Westerners for better means of traveling and transporting goods to and from the West.

4. *Types of Settlers.* Several types of settlers moved West. **(a)** Hunters, fur trappers, and Indian fighters (*frontiersmen*) pushed into the wilderness first and blazed new trails. **(b)** Pioneer farmers followed, clearing the forests and engaging in simple agriculture. Many of these "pulled up stakes" and moved farther west when they felt "crowded" by too many settlers. **(c)** Finally, permanent settlers arrived and established farms (homesteads) and plantations, or (later) villages and towns.

5. *Life on the Frontier.* Life on the frontier was primitive, hard, and lonely. Most pioneers were poor farmers who struggled to support their families. They lived in crude log cabins; made their own clothing, utensils, and furniture; and had few schools or churches. Gradually, as more settlers arrived and villages and towns developed, conditions began to improve.

Significance of the West in American History. The continuous movement of Americans westward had important effects upon American history.

1. *Nationalism.* The West stimulated a strong spirit of nationalism, especially in the period after the War of 1812. Westerners looked to the central government for land, protection, and internal improvements. They became advocates of national expansion.

2. *Sectionalism.* As the West grew, it developed its own sectional interest and point of view on such issues as tariff, internal improvements, and the acquisition of new territories. In addition, the question of the admission of slavery to newly acquired territories contributed to the bitterness between North and South that helped bring on the Civil War.

3. *Democracy.* The West also stimulated political and social democracy. Western life promoted self-reliance and individualism. Westerners believed in personal equality, individual freedom, and equality of opportunity.

4. *Economic Strength and Opportunity.* The agricultural resources of the West made it the granary of the nation. The exchange of Western farm produce for manufactured goods of the East promoted national unity, strength, and self-sufficiency. The presence of cheap, fertile land in the West attracted not only the restless and discontented of the East, but also millions of European immigrants.

REVIEW TEST (Chapter 9)

Select the number preceding the word or expression that best completes each statement or answers each question.

1. Who was a famous historian who did significant research on the importance of the frontier in United States history? (1) John Sevier (2) Henry Clay (3) Frederick J. Turner (4) Henry Adams

2. Which Supreme Court case did *not* involve a state law? (1) *Marbury v. Madison* (2) *Gibbons v. Ogden* (3) *Dartmouth College v. Woodward* (4) *Brown v. Board of Education of Topeka*

3. The main reason for the announcement of the Monroe Doctrine in 1823 was (1) fear that European countries would try to restore the former Spanish colonies to Spain (2) the desire to annex Texas (3) hostility to England (4) the belief that Washington's policy of not interfering in European affairs was no longer sound

4. The original Monroe Doctrine was proclaimed by (1) an act of Congress (2) a treaty with England (3) an executive statement of policy (4) an alliance with Latin America

5. The Monroe Doctrine was (1) a continuation of Washington's foreign policy (2) a reversal of Washington's policy (3) a concession to the Federalists (4) an attempt to open new territory to slavery

6. Which of the following was an important reason for the success of the Monroe Doctrine in the early 19th century? (1) economic aid by the United States to Latin America (2) United States control of the Panama Canal (3) United States influence in world affairs (4) British support of United States policy

7. The Monroe Doctrine might be applied in case (1) Japan invaded Siberia. (2) Russia violated the neutrality of Switzerland. (3) England and Canada made a trade treaty. (4) France tried to exert political control over Haiti.

8. Florida was acquired by purchase and conquest from (1) France (2) Russia (3) England (4) Spain

9. An important result of the Westward expansion of the United States was the (1) rise of industrial unions in the East (2) development of a strong political party opposed to Westward expansion (3) repeated reopening of the slavery controversy in Congress (4) restriction of immigration from the Philippine Islands

10. The Western pioneers contributed to American democracy by (1) establishing the first public elementary school system (2) serving as a symbol of economic opportunity and political equality (3) supporting the Federalist party after it declined in the East (4) opposing government involvement in internal improvements

Select the letter of the item in each group which does **NOT** *belong with the others.*

1. Characteristics of the period immediately following the War of 1812: (a) imperialism (b) internal improvements (c) nationalism (d) protective tariff

2. Provision of the Monroe Doctrine: (a) the Western Hemisphere is no longer open to European colonization (b) existing European colonies in the Western Hemisphere will not be interfered with (c) the United States will not intervene in Latin America to restore stability (d) the United States will not interfere with European affairs

3. Nations in favor of helping Spain recover her American possessions in 1823: (a) England (b) France (c) Russia (d) Austria

4. Influences on Latin American movements for independence during the early 19th century: (a) Russian Revolution (b) American Revolution (c) Napoleonic Wars (d) declining power of Spain

5. Trends in Supreme Court decisions in the first quarter of the 19th century: (a) strengthening the national government (b) establishing the supremacy of the Federal judiciary (c) protecting property rights (d) protecting civil liberties

6. Purposes of Clay's "American System" (a) linking East and West (b) stimulating manufacturing (c) encouraging immigration (d) unifying the nation

7. Characteristics of the "Era of Good Feeling": (a) abandonment of strict interpretation of the Constitution by the Republican Party (b) nearly unanimous re-election of James Monroe as President (c) democratizing of the Federalist Party (d) lack of well-organized political opposition to the party in power

8. Characteristics of Second Bank of the United States: (a) opposed by the Republican Party (b) 20% of its stock owned by the Federal government (c) greater capital than First Bank of the United States (d) a 20-year charter

9. Evidences of postwar cooperation between the United States and Britain: (a) reduction of armaments on the Great Lakes (b) settlement of the northern boundary between the United States and Canada (c) joint occupation of Oregon (d) yielding of United States claims to Texas

10. Features of the westward movement during first half of the 19th century: (a) generous government land policy (b) movement of the frontier beyond the Mississippi River (c) warfare between homesteaders and cattle ranchers (d) improved transportation facilities

Essay Questions

1. Why has the period of United States history after the War of 1812 been referred to as the "Era of Good Feeling"? Give evidence that supports this view.

2. Using specific illustrations, show how each of the following advanced the growth of nationalism in the United States: (a) War of 1812 (b) decisions of John Marshall (c) the westward movement.

3. Explain the causes, provisions, and results of the Monroe Doctrine.

4. Giving specific facts, show how each was a cause or a result of the westward movement of the 19th century: (a) growth of democracy (b) internal improvements (c) immigration from Europe (d) sectionalism.

5. Show how growing nationalism influenced relations between the United States and each of the following after the War of 1812: (a) Great Britain (b) Spain (c) Latin America.

6. (a) Why is John Marshall considered the greatest Chief Justice of the Supreme Court? (b) Explain the importance of each of the following of Marshall's decisions: (1) *Marbury v. Madison* (2) *McCulloch v. Maryland* (3) *Gibbons v. Ogden* (4) *Dartmouth College Case* (5) *Martin v. Hunter's Lessee* (6) *Fletcher v. Peck.*

CHAPTER 10

Economic Changes and the Rise of Sectionalism

Important economic changes which took place in the United States during the first half of the 19th century transformed the nation's economy and paved the way for the growth of sectionalism.

Part 1 — ECONOMIC TRANSFORMATION OF THE UNITED STATES BEFORE THE CIVIL WAR

The United States of 1850 was appreciably different from the United States of 1790. Underlying this transformation was a series of revolutionary changes in agriculture, industry, transportation, and communication.

Changes in Agriculture. Important changes in farm methods and implements, particularly during the second quarter of the 19th century, began an *Agricultural Revolution* which was to continue throughout the rest of the century.

1. *Farming in the Early 1800's.* At the beginning of the 19th century, farming in the United States was very similar to what it had been during the Colonial Period. Farm tools were simple, crude, and hand-made. Farm methods were primitive and the abundance of cheap fertile land encouraged wasteful cultivation.

2. *Changes on the Farm.* Beginning with the invention of the *cotton gin* by ELI WHITNEY in 1793, revolutionary changes in agriculture raised agricultural productivity, contributed greatly to the nation's wealth, and helped overcome the shortage of labor on the farms.

   (a) The cotton gin revolutionized cotton picking and made cotton growing profitable in the South by making it possible to separate mechanically seeds from raw cotton fiber. By mid-19th century cotton was the nation's leading export.

   (b) Better cultivation of the soil and the opening of new lands to agriculture followed the introduction of the *cast-iron plow,* perfected by JETHRO WOOD in 1819, and the *steel plow,* invented by JOHN DEERE in 1837.

   (c) The *McCormick reaper,* patented in 1834 by CYRUS McCORMICK, made it possible for Western farmers to cut grain (wheat) more easily and cheaply.

180

(d) Also introduced were such labor-saving devices as *horse-drawn rakes, mowing machines, threshers, grain drills,* and *seeders.*

(e) Farmers began to use *fertilizers, rotate their crops,* and experiment with *livestock breeding.*

(f) New agricultural information and knowledge was spread through agricultural societies, fairs, and magazines.

Despite this agricultural progress, many small farmers continued to cling to older methods, or found themselves unable to purchase the newer tools. It should also be noted that the magnificent land of the Middle West, and the advances in transportation which made it relatively easy to ship produce to the East, made it difficult for most Eastern farmers to compete. This was particularly true of New England where the land was generally poor.

Changes in Industry. The development of the Industrial Revolution in the United States during the first half of the 19th century produced changes even more dramatic than those in agriculture.

1. *Beginning of the Industrial Revolution in the United States.* The Industrial Revolution originated in England about 1750. It involved extensive substitution of machines for hand labor, and it changed the locale of production from the home (*domestic system*) to the factory. The Industrial Revolution began in the United States about 1790, with the construction of the first textile (cotton) mill by SAMUEL SLATER in Rhode Island. It gained real momentum in the early 19th century when New England merchants, unable to carry on trade because of the Embargo Act and the War of 1812, put their unused capital into industry. They were aided by cheap water power, abundant labor supply, and an excellent climate.

2. *Growth of the Factory System.* Although much manufacturing continued to be done by hand in small shops or in the home, especially in farm areas, the *factory system* of production by machines had become very important by 1850. The number of factories multiplied rapidly during and and after the 1820's, and the value of manufactured goods rose sharply. New England became the nation's leading industrial center, especially for the production of clothing and textile machinery. By mid-century, owners of industry were competing for power and influence with the older agricultural and commercial "aristocracy." Several important factors made this industrial growth possible, including: the expansion of the nation in size and population, the improvement of transportation facilities, and the transfer of investment capital from shipbuilding and commerce into industry.

3. *Inventions and New Sources of Power.* Another important reason for the growth and success of the factory system was the introduction of improved equipment and methods, resulting from ingenious inventions and new sources of power.

(a) The perfection of the *power loom* by FRANCIS LOWELL and PAUL MOODY in 1814 made possible the combining of spinning and weaving under one roof.

(b) The invention of the *sewing machine* by ELIAS HOWE in 1846 revolutionized the clothing, shoe, and leather industries.

(c) Better types of machinery were made possible by the introduction of *new and improved methods of making steel* from iron ore, by WILLIAM KELLY and others in the 1850's.

(d) The principle of *interchangeable parts* was introduced by ELI WHITNEY in the manufacture of firearms early in the 19th century, and soon spread to other industries.

(e) The introduction of *steam power* to replace water power made possible the establishment of factories away from streams and rivers.

4. *Results of Industrial Changes.* Changes in industry had significant results in the United States before the Civil War. **(a)** More and cheaper goods became available. **(b)** New work opportunities were opened to immigrants. **(c)** The growth of cities was stimulated as they became centers of factory production and markets for agricultural produce. **(d)** Two new classes emerged: factory owners (industrialists) and factory workers. **(e)** A new type of agriculture developed in the East to serve the cities — truck, dairy, and sheep farms.

Changes in Transportation. Changes in industry and agriculture were to a considerable degree made possible by improvements in transportation which overcame earlier travel handicaps.

1. *Better Roads.* During the first quarter of the 19th century (the *Turnpike Era*), thousands of improved roads and bridges were built, usually by private companies, and frequently with state aid. Most of these were toll roads (*turnpikes*). The *Cumberland Road,* the first important Federal road, was built from Cumberland, Maryland, to Vandalia, Illinois, between 1806 and 1852. For a number of years it was the nation's most important highway to the West.

2. *Introduction of Steamboats.* In 1807 America's first successful steamboat, the *Clermont,* built by ROBERT FULTON, traveled up the Hudson River from New York City to Albany in 30 hours. During the height of the *Steamboat Era* which soon followed (*c.* 1820–60), more than a thousand steamboats on the Mississippi, Ohio, and their tributaries carried a large part of the nation's freight, and reduced travel time and costs considerably.

3. *The Building of Canals.* Because of the low cost and the convenience of water transportation, producers were eager for continuous water transport facilities between East and West. This encouraged states and state-subsidized private companies to build canals between rivers and lakes, during the *Canal Era* (*c.* 1825–40). The most successful of all canals was

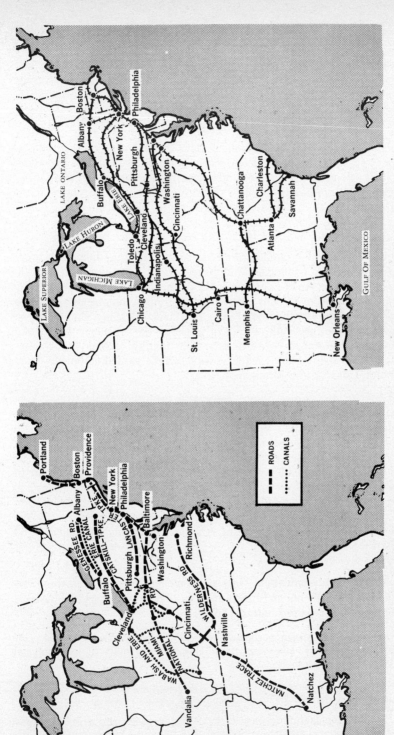

The map on the left shows the network of canals, roads, and turnpikes that linked the Eastern seaboard with the Middle West and South by the middle of the 19th century. The map on the right shows the system of railroads developed during this era to provide transportation from the Atlantic Coast to as far West as the Mississippi River.

the famous *Erie Canal* (1825), running between the Hudson River and Lake Erie in New York State. Built largely through the efforts of Governor DE WITT CLINTON, the Erie Canal made possible an all-water route from the port of New York to the interior of the country. It assured the prosperity of New York City as a center of commerce.

4. *The Development of Railroads.* The development of the railroad was made possible by the perfection of the steam locomotive. The first important railroad in the United States was the *Baltimore and Ohio Railroad.* It began operation in 1830 with horse-drawn coaches, but switched to the steam locomotive after the successful trip in 1831 of the *Tom Thumb,* a steam locomotive built by PETER COOPER. This made it possible for Baltimore to compete for Western trade with New York and Philadelphia.

Railroads multiplied rapidly, after early engineering difficulties were overcome and public confidence established. By 1860, there were 30,000 miles of railroad in America, most north of the Mason-Dixon line. They were the fastest and most convenient form of transportation, and began to compete successfully with other forms of travel. Because they were so expensive to build, the railroads received financial assistance from both the states and the Federal government. The uniting of many short lines into trunk lines in the 1850's made possible uninterrupted shipments from the Atlantic Coast to the Mississippi River.

5. *The Era of Clipper Ships.* Improved means of ocean travel kept pace with other forms of transportation. After the War of 1812, sturdy American "packet" sailing ships began to carry freight, passengers, and mails across the Atlantic on regular schedules. In the 1840's and 1850's they were joined by the speedy, graceful "Yankee Clippers," the fastest ships afloat, and often called America's greatest contribution to the art of shipbuilding. At the height of the "Golden Age of American Shipping" in the early 1850's, the United States merchant marine led the world. In the 1850's, the introduction of improved ocean-going iron steamers by the British brought about the decline of America's maritime supremacy and the end of the *Clipper Ship Era.*

Changes in Communication. Improved means of communication followed the improvements in transportation. There were several notable achievements in the period before 1860.

(1) SAMUEL F. B. MORSE perfected the electric telegraph in 1844, thus opening a new era in speedy communication. Thousands of miles of telegraph line were strung out in the 1850's.

(2) CYRUS FIELD laid the first successful cable on the floor of the Atlantic in 1858, the prelude to an era of rapid international communication.

(3) As the 19th century advanced, the use of the faster and newer means of transportation to carry the mails increased the volume and brought down the price.

REVIEW TEST (Chapter 10—Part I)

Select the number preceding the word or expression that best completes each statement or answers each question.

1. Which of the following was the most important export from the United States in 1850? (1) wheat (2) iron (3) manufactured goods (4) cotton

2. Which of the following factors was primarily responsible for the growth of the factory system in the United States? (1) mercantilism (2) immigration (3) formation of labor unions (4) new sources of power

3. Which of the following was the common means of travel between New Orleans and St. Louis in 1850? (1) stagecoach (2) railroad (3) steamboat (4) Conestoga wagon

4. Of the following which was a cause of the other three? (1) increase in Western migration and settlement (2) building of the Erie Canal (3) reduction of food prices on the Eastern seaboard (4) growth of New York City as the country's largest seaport

5. A major reason for the end of the Clipper Ship Era was the development of (1) coastwise canals (2) ocean-going iron steamboats (3) steam railroads (4) coast to coast highways

Match each of the numbered statements with a name from the list below.

Elias Howe   Samuel Morse   John Deere   Peter Cooper
Eli Whitney   Cyrus Field   Cyrus McCormick   Robert Fulton
Samuel Slater   Francis Lowell   William Kelly

1. I have been called "father of the American factory system" because I introduced use of machinery in the textile industry.

2. My most famous invention increased agricultural production by speeding up the process of harvesting.

3. My invention of the sewing machine revolutionized the clothing and shoe industry.

4. I introduced the principle of interchangeable parts into the manufacture of firearms, early in the 19th century.

5. I built America's first successful steamboat.

6. My "Tom-Thumb" made possible the era of steam railroads.

7. My invention of the wireless telegraph opened a new era of rapid communication.

8. My development of a successful underwater cable paved the way for speedy international communication.

9. My invention helped make possible the combining under one roof of the spinning and weaving processes.

10. My steel plow was a revolutionary step forward in its day.

Essay Questions

1. Show how two important inventions or changes helped transform American economic life before the Civil War, in each of the following fields: agriculture, industry, transportation, communication.

2. Discuss three results of economic changes in the United States during the first half of the 19th century.

3. Explain why the growth of the factory system in the United States during the first half of the 19th century is considered to be one of the more important developments of the period.

Part II — THE RISE OF SECTIONALISM

The economic changes of the first half of the 19th century caused the North, South, and West* to develop sectional interests based on their economic development. These interests began to make themselves felt during the political calm of the "Era of Good Feeling." By the mid-1820's, sectionalism had become strong enough to push aside the temporary surge of nationalism which followed the War of 1812. *Sectionalism* means devotion to the interests and needs of a particular state or section of the country, rather than to the nation as a whole. Sectional rivalry brought the "Era of Good Feeling" to an end and ushered in an "Era of Hard Feeling." It brought much bitterness to the national political scene.

Sectional Differences After 1820. Between 1820 and 1860, sectional rivalry became increasingly intense and created an atmosphere which made possible an attempt to divide the Union. The basis for this rivalry was provided by the economic developments which took place in the North, South, and West during this period.

Economic Interests of the North. After the War of 1812, the North was changing from a region of small farms and commercial cities, to one of factories and mill towns.

1. The rise of manufacturing in the North was made possible by several factors. There was *capital* available for investment, resulting from earlier profits in shipping and commerce. There was an abundant supply of *labor,* provided by farm women and children and by immigrants. There was *cheap power,* made possible by the swift-flowing streams of the seaboard and by newly discovered coal deposits in Pennsylvania. There were *markets* for manufactured goods opened by improvements in transportation and communication.

2. To support its industrial development the North adopted the following policies:

(a) It *advocated high (protective) tariffs* to choke off foreign competition.

(b) It *supported internal improvements at Federal expense* to open new markets and sources of raw materials in the West.

(c) It *championed the Second National Bank* to provide a sound currency, necessary for interstate business.

---

* In discussing sectional issues before the Civil War some writers prefer to call the North, the *Northeast;* the South, the *Southeast;* and the West, the *Northwest.* A glance at the map on page 215 shows the reason for this terminology. The West at that time included much that would be called the Middle West today.

(d) At first it *opposed territorial expansion,* since this might lead to the admission of new states and a resulting weakening of Northern influence in Congress. Later it *supported expansion* as a means of opening new markets for its manufactured goods.

(e) It *favored high-priced public lands,* since this would make difficult the emigration of Eastern workers to the West.

Economic Interests of the South. In the period after the War of 1812, the South rapidly shifted its major attention to the cultivation of *cotton.* Although such crops as tobacco, rice, sugar, hemp, corn, beans, and wheat continued to be grown in quantity, cotton became "king." Cotton production expanded so rapidly that by 1860 "King Cotton" accounted for 60% of the nation's exports. Also, cotton production exhausted the soil so rapidly that the center of cotton production moved steadily westward: first it was centered in South Carolina and Georgia; then it expanded into the rich "black belt" of Mississippi and Alabama; by the Civil War it was centered in the fertile "bottom lands" of the Mississippi and its tributaries.

1. The following were major factors in the expansion of cotton production.

(a) The invention and widespread use of the *cotton gin* made profitable the growth of short fiber ("upland") cotton.

(b) The *admission of new states* opened new territory to cotton planting.

(c) The use of *slave labor* made cotton a profitable plantation crop.

(d) The *increased demands of British cotton mills* encouraged planters to extend their holdings.

2. The South supported policies in Congress which would benefit the cotton and slave economy.

(a) After 1824, it *favored a low tariff* since a high protective tariff would raise the price of the manufactured goods it needed. It also feared that a protective tariff would lead to discrimination against American cotton in foreign markets. (Note: Before 1824, the South had favored a protective tariff because it had believed it would become a manufacturing region.)

(b) Southerners opposed the *Second Bank of the United States* and *supported state banking.* Planters were in constant need of capital for expansion, and disliked being in debt to Northern banks. They preferred doing business with banks they could control (that is, local and state banks).

(c) The South *opposed internal improvements at Federal expense.* It had a fine river transportation system of its own and was not interested in constructing roads and canals at Federal expense, particularly since its markets were not in the West.

(d) The South *favored territorial expansion,* preferably into territory suited to cotton and slavery, like Texas and California.

(e) Southern planters *favored cheap public lands* but opposed "squatters' rights," since squatters might keep them off the best lands.

Economic Interests of the West. Between 1820 and 1860 the "Old West" between the Appalachians and the Missouri River filled up rapidly. By 1850 half of the nation's population lived in this region, and some had already pushed west of the Mississippi. Like the South, the West was primarily an agricultural section. It was favored by fertile soil, adequate rainfall, and a growing season long enough to cultivate a variety of crops. Western farms were for the most part medium in size, and worked by pioneer families. Western farmers, particularly those who had emigrated from the North, were in general opposed to the expansion of slavery. Western corn and wheat began to be sent East and abroad in increasing quantities.

1. As already indicated, the development of the West was made possible by the continuing westward movement, the rising tide of immigration, improvements in transportation and communication, territorial expansion, and a liberal government land policy. (See page 176.)

2. As a farming area in need of markets, the West advocated policies best suited to its needs.

(a) It *supported a national policy of cheap public lands,* with squatters' rights, as this would promote rapid settlement and agricultural expansion.

(b) It *supported the protective tariff,* in the hope that this would expand the industrial cities of the Northeast and provide a market for Western crops.

(c) It overwhelmingly *supported the building of internal improvements at national expense,* since it needed canals and roads to get its goods to market, and could not afford to construct them itself.

(d) The Western farmer *opposed the Second Bank of the United States* since he was a debtor in need of credit, and preferred the easy credit policies of state banks to the stricter financial practices of the National Bank.

(e) The West also advocated a policy of *encouragement of European immigration,* in order to get settlers.

3. In the pre-Civil War rivalry between North and South, the West acted as a kind of "balance-wheel." It supported the South on the issues of cheap money and state banking. It supported the North on the protective tariff. In turn, the South, supported the West in its desire for cheap public lands, while the North backed the Western demand for Federal internal improvements.

Sectional Differences Not Rigid. Rivalry between the sections was often not as clearcut as it might seem at first glance. Groups and regions within each section often took an opposite position to the section's prevailing point of view. **(1)** The small farmers of the Southwest joined the farmers of the Northwest (the West) in seeking internal improvements at Federal expense. They saw eye to eye with the rest of the South on most other issues. **(2)** New England shipping interests joined the South in opposing high tariffs, since they stood to lose money if imports declined. They joined the other Northern interests on other issues. **(3)** Most people in the Northeast still lived on farms and backed policies favorable to farmers. At the same time, the Northeast became the country's manufacturing center, with its industrial interests strongly supported in Congress. **(4)** Commercial interests in leading Southern ports, like Baltimore and New Orleans, worked closely with Northern bankers and merchants.

Accordingly, it should be remembered that when the statement is made that the North or the South was "opposed to" or "favored" a particular course of action, what is really meant is that the *predominant group in Congress* from that section took a certain point of view on the issue under discussion.

POSITION OF THE SECTIONS ON MAJOR ISSUES BEFORE THE CIVIL WAR

ISSUE	NORTH (NORTHEAST)	SOUTH (INCLUDING SOUTHWEST)	WEST (NORTHWEST)
Cheap Public Land	Opposed	Favored	Favored
Internal Improvements at National Expense	Favored	Opposed	Favored
Protective Tariff	Favored	Opposed	Favored
Territorial Expansion	Favored (into Northwest)	Favored (into Southwest)	Favored
Second Bank of United States and Sound Currency	Favored	Opposed	Opposed
Extension of Slavery into New Territories	Opposed	Favored	Opposed

REVIEW TEST (Chapter 10 — Part II)

Select the number preceding the word or expression that best completes each statement or answers each question.

1. The section of the country that most consistently demanded internal improvements at Federal expense before the Civil War was (1) New England (2) the West (3) the Middle Atlantic States (4) the South

2. Why did New Englanders generally oppose a liberal policy in the sale of public lands? (1) They feared a migration from New England to the West. (2) The market for New England manufactures would be reduced. (3) Only slave owners wanted cheap lands. (4) The New England states had surrendered their claims to Western lands.

3. During the first half of the 19th century, which of these would have been most likely to support a protective tariff? (1) a Massachusetts textile manufacturer (2) a Virginia planter (3) a Nebraska homesteader (4) a New York retailer

4. All of the following were major factors in the expansion of cotton production from 1800–60 *except* (1) increased British demands (2) admission of new states (3) the establishment of the Second Bank of the United States (4) technological advances

5. Over which issue would small farmers of the Southwest in the period 1800–60 have differed most sharply from large plantation owners in the same region? (1) protective tariffs (2) internal improvements at Federal expense (3) state banking (4) cheap public land

*Select the item that does **NOT** belong with the others.*

1. Opposed to extension of slavery in new territories: North, South, West

2. Opposed to Second Bank of United States: North, South, West

3. Factors favorable to manufacturing in the North: investment capital, abundant labor supply, cheap money, expanding markets

4. Favored by Westerners: territorial expansion, slave labor, protective tariffs, liberal government land policy

5. Characteristics of agriculture in the West, 1820—60: the plantation system, variety of crops, fertile soil, abundant rainfall

Essay Questions

1. Describe two important economic developments in each of the following sections between 1800 and 1860: the North, the South, the West.

2. Explain how the economic interests of the North, South and West affected their attitudes toward political and economic issues in the first half of the 19th century.

3. Explain why it has often been said that the West was a "balance wheel" in the pre-Civil War rivalry between North and South.

4. Give two illustrations which prove that sectional differences before the Civil War were not clearcut.

Part III — SECTIONALISM BEGINS TO AFFECT NATIONAL POLITICS

Before 1815, sectionalism in politics occasionally showed itself in events such as New England's opposition to the War of 1812 at the Hartford Convention. In the 1820's, sectional issues began to make themselves more strongly and consistently felt on the national scene.

Panic of 1819. Sectional bitterness began to show itself during the business recession of 1819 (the *Panic of 1819*) and the depression which followed. In Congress, spokesmen of each section blamed the others for the hard times that prevailed.

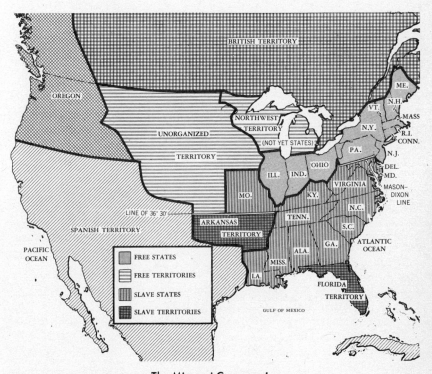

The Missouri Compromise.

The Missouri Compromise (1820). Slavery became a national political issue for the first time in 1818, when Missouri applied to the Union for admission as a slave state. At the time there were eleven slave and eleven non-slave states. After bitter debate, and in order to preserve the balance of power in the Senate, the *Missouri Compromise* was adopted in 1820. It was the first of a series of compromises worked out by HENRY CLAY, who became known as the "Great Compromiser." Central to the controversy was the question of slavery in the Louisiana Territory.

1. *Provisions.* Under the provisions of the compromise, Maine was admitted as a free state; Missouri was admitted as a slave state; and slavery was excluded from the Louisiana Purchase, north of the 36° 30′ line (the southern boundary of Missouri).

2. *Results.* The compromise temporarily restored the "Era of Good Feeling," for Monroe was re-elected in 1820 without sectional opposition. The compromise also temporarily settled the issue of expansion of slavery.

Election of 1824 Brings Sectionalism to Surface Again. Sectionalism affected national politics again in the Presidential election of 1824. The appearance of rival candidates within the Republican Party marked the end of the "Era of Good Feeling."

1. *Candidates.* Although the Republican Party was the only political party in the field in 1824, four Republican "favorite sons" ran for the Presidency, each with sectional support. HENRY CLAY and ANDREW JACKSON represented the West; WILLIAM H. CRAWFORD, picked by a Congressional caucus, was favored by the South; and JOHN QUINCY ADAMS was the candidate of New England.

2. *Election of Adams by the House of Representatives.* No candidate received a majority in the Electoral College. This placed the final choice in the House of Representatives, as provided by the Twelfth Amendment. The House chose John Quincy Adams as President, after Henry Clay, who had received the fewest electoral votes, threw his support to Adams.

3. *Results.* Jackson and his supporters were bitter over his defeat. Jackson had received the most electoral votes in the Electoral College, though not enough to elect him. When Adams made Clay his Secretary of State, it was charged that this was part of a "corrupt bargain" made to get Clay's support in the election. Though the charge was never proved, Adams was hurt by its constant repetition during his term in office.

Sectionalism and the Administration of John Quincy Adams. Though John Quincy Adams was one of the ablest men ever to sit in the White House, his administration was troubled and unsuccessful. Adams was a poor "politician," unable to compromise, and too cold and austere to win public support. His term in office is sometimes called the "Era of Hard Feeling" (1825–29).

1. *Adams' Program.* Adams proposed a broad nationalistic program which included: **(a)** internal improvements on a national scale, **(b)** promotion of the arts and sciences with Federal support, **(c)** the establishment of a national university, **(d)** participation with Latin American countries in an inter-American movement, and **(e)** protection of Indian rights.

2. *Failure of Adams' Program.* Adams was unable to win public or Congressional support for his program. Sectional rivalries in Congress made it impossible to line up support for a truly *national* program. Southerners and Westerners were antagonized by Adams' signing of the protective tariffs of 1824 and 1828, and by his attempt to prevent the Georgia Indians from being unjustly deprived of their lands. Also, pro-Jackson forces bitterly opposed and helped to block every part of Adams' program.

3. *Split in the Republican Party.* During Adams' administration the Republican Party split in two. The *Democratic-Republicans* (or *Democrats*) supported Jackson. They opposed high tariffs and centralization in government. They claimed to represent the common man. The *National Republicans* (later called *Whigs*) supported Adams. Like the earlier Federalist Party, they were in favor of a strong national government and a protective tariff. They received the support of the more conservative groups in the North and East.

REVIEW TEST (Chapter 10 — Part III)

Select the number preceding the word or expression that best completes each statement or answers each question.

1. What made slavery a national issue? (1) the election of Jackson (2) the Panic of 1819 (3) Missouri's desire to enter the Union (4) South Carolina's threat to nullify the tariff of 1828

2. All of the following were provisions of the Missouri Compromise *except* (1) Maine to be admitted as a free state. (2) Missouri to come in as a slave state. (3) Territory south of 36° 30' in Louisiana territory to be open to slavery. (4) Territory west of the Rockies to be closed to slavery.

3. Which of the following was true of the election of 1824? (1) The Republican Party was united in its support of John Quincy Adams for the Presidency. (2) There was clearcut sectional rivalry within the Republican Party. (3) Former Whigs threw their support to Andrew Jackson as Democratic candidate for President. (4) James Monroe was re-elected.

4. All of the following were true of the Presidency of John Quincy Adams *except* (1) He received the united support of the public and Congress. (2) He introduced a statesmanlike program of national development. (3) He was criticized by supporters of Andrew Jackson. (4) He was denounced by Southerners and Westerners for his attempt to see justice done to Indian tribes in Georgia.

5. What is true about the so-called "corrupt bargain" between Henry Clay and John Quincy Adams. (1) The charge was never proved but was good political ammunition for the anti-Adams forces. (2) It resulted in the selection of Jackson as President by the House of Representatives. (3) It showed that the North and West were working together against the South. (4) It resulted in a split within the Republican Party.

Essay Questions

1. Define (a) nationalism and (b) sectionalism, as they applied to national development in the period 1815–60.

2. Show how sectionalism was brought into national politics by (a) the Missouri question and (b) the election of 1824.

3. Why has the administration of President John Quincy Adams been called the "Era of Hard Feeling"?

CHAPTER 11

The Jacksonian Era

The quarter century from 1825 to 1850 has been called the time of the *"Rise of the Common Man."* It was a period of political and social ferment, and it was characterized by a forward surge of democracy. Because Andrew Jackson is closely identified with the period's spirit, ideals, and achievements, this era is also known as the *"Age of Jackson"* or *"Jacksonian Era."*

Part I — GROWTH OF DEMOCRACY IN THE AGE OF JACKSON

The election of Jackson in 1828 was evidence of the growth of democracy in the United States.

Election of Andrew Jackson. In the Presidential election of 1828 ANDREW JACKSON won a sweeping victory over John Quincy Adams. Jackson ran on the *Democratic* (Democratic-Republican) ticket, and he carried every Western and Southern state, as well as New York and Pennsylvania. The campaign was bitter and featured more "mudslinging" than real discussion of the issues.

1. *Reasons for Jackson's Victory.* Several factors help explain Jackson's victory.

   (a) His supporters had built a strong national and local party organization during the administration of Adams.

   (b) Jackson had been a popular national hero ("Old Hickory") ever since his military victory at New Orleans.

   (c) He was effectively pictured as the champion of the people, while Adams was denounced as their enemy.

   (d) For the most part, Jackson received the votes of most "plain people" of the nation (city workers, frontiersmen, small farmers), who preferred his humble origins to the more "aristocratic" and propertied background of Adams and supporters.

   (e) Jackson also received the support of small businessmen, who voted for him because he opposed business monopoly. Moreover, he enjoyed the backing of Southerners, who felt that as a slaveholder he would be in favor of states' rights and protection of slavery.

   (f) Jackson's victory was also made possible by the extension in the 1820's of the right to vote to thousands of common people who had hitherto been disenfranchised by property qualifications for voting.

2. *The "Revolution of 1828."* Jackson's election has been referred to as the "Revolution of 1828" because of its political and social consequences. Like Jefferson, whose election in 1800 was also called a "revolution," Jackson and his party introduced a more democratic approach to government. Jackson was the first President to be born in poverty. To this day, he is the only President who was the son of immigrant parents. He was the first President from a Western state, and his election was the first national victory for the "common man." The "common man" would no longer automatically accept leadership from the wealthy, educated, and semi-aristocratic class. It was also evidence of the shift in political power from the seaboard states of the East toward the newer states of the West.

NOTE: It should be kept in mind that the elections of Jefferson and Jackson were not "revolutions" in the sense of a violent overthrow of the existing order. They were, rather, marked shifts in political power. Nevertheless, neither Jackson nor Jefferson surrendered government to the "mob" as the wealthier classes feared would happen.

Jacksonian Democracy. Jackson was a symbol of the democratic changes that were taking place during the first half of the 19th century. The combination of his ideas on government and the democratic achievements of his times is called *Jacksonian democracy.* Jackson advanced, rather than introduced, the democratic gains of his age. In doing so he encouraged those who were fighting for reform.

1. *Jackson's Ideas on Government.* Andrew Jackson believed that a democracy should represent the will of the people. He looked upon himself as the champion of the masses, rather than as a representative of the privileged classes. His ideas, or philosophy of government, may be stated as follows:

(a) *Direct Government.* Jackson felt that all elected officials, including the President, should be directly responsible to the people.

(b) *Rotation in Office.* Jackson believed that any intelligent person was capable of holding any office. Frequent replacement of officials (*rotation in office*) would furnish incentives for ambitious individuals to enter government service, since more job opportunities would be provided. This would make all citizens feel they were part of the government as in ancient Athens.

(c) *The Spoils System.* Unfortunately, Jackson's support of the idea of rotation in office was linked to his acceptance of the political adage — "To the victor belongs the spoils." He discharged about one-fifth of the holders of Federal jobs, and replaced them with loyal party supporters, regardless of their qualifications.

NOTE: The spoils system had been used *before* Jackson, for example by Jefferson in the Federal government, and by numerous state and local officials. However, it is most directly associated with Jackson because he used it so extensively on a national scale. It set an unfortunate precedent for the future.

2. *Jacksonian and Jeffersonian Democracy Compared.* Although both Thomas Jefferson and Andrew Jackson strongly influenced the American democratic tradition, their approach to the nature of democratic government differed in a number of important respects.

JEFFERSON AND JACKSON COMPARED

IDEAS OF JEFFERSON	IDEAS OF JACKSON
1. Government should be in the hands of experienced, educated leaders.	**1.** All citizens are fit for office, regardless of background.
2. Central government should be weak. "That government is best which governs least."	**2.** Central government should be strong. Business should be controlled if necessary.
3. A weak central government will protect the country from the evil effects of minority rule.	**3.** A strong central government will make it possible to check the power of a favored few.
4. Concentration of power in any single branch of government is dangerous. There should be a separation of powers in government.	**4.** The executive branch of the government should provide leadership for the nation. The President is the representative of *all* the people.
5. The independent farmer is the backbone of nation. City workers cannot be fully trusted in politics since they may be swayed by unscrupulous power seekers (demagogues).	**5.** The common man is the backbone of the nation. The city worker, the farmer and the small businessman can all be trusted to assume responsibility for the general welfare.

Democratic Advances During the Age of Jackson. In the "Age of Jackson" there was a marked extension of the political rights of the ordinary citizen and a greater concern for his economic and social welfare. Government came closer to the people. The ferment of the time was due largely to the rapid economic changes and to the activities of small businessmen and organized workers, who were seeking a position of greater influence in the society. The following developments illustrate why the Age of Jackson is often called the era of the "Rise of the Common Man."

1. *Suffrage Extended.* There was a rapid increase in the number of people who voted. Between 1830 and 1850, the number of voters tripled. Remaining property and religious qualifications for voting were abolished in nearly every state.

2. *Increase in Number of Elected Officials.* A growing number of states, especially in the West, provided for an increase in the number of elected officials and for the direct election of the governor.

3. *Change in Nominating the President.* The nomination of Presidential candidates was taken out of the hands of the Congressional "caucus" of party leaders in Congress, and placed in the hands of *nominating con-*

ventions. The first nominating convention was held by the Anti-Masonic Party in 1831. The major parties soon adopted the practice of nominating conventions and *written party platforms,* another innovation of the Anti-Masonic Party.

4. *Change in Selecting Electors.* Popular election of the members of the Electoral College replaced selection by state legislatures.

5. *More Liberal State Constitutions.* The new Western states that entered the Union usually had liberal state constitutions. Typical provisions included abolition of property and religious qualifications for voting, popular control of the executive and judicial branches, and more frequent elections. Eastern states adopted similar reforms.

6. *Growth in Political Power of the Working Class.* In this period there was a growth in the influence of the working class. The working-class vote helped elect Jackson. Labor unions and workingmen's parties helped to enact such reforms as abolition of imprisonment for debt and free public schools.

7. *Humanitarian Reform.* The Age of Jackson was an age of humanitarian reform. Much was done to improve the lot of the sick and unfortunate. (See page 208 for a further discussion of these reforms.)

8. *Separation of Church and State.* The movement to end compulsory taxation for church support (separation of church and state), begun during the Revolutionary Era, was completed during the Age of Jackson. In addition, nearly all states dropped their religious qualification for voting. Many new religious sects appeared, especially on the frontier.

9. *Influence of the West.* The growth of the West, with its emphasis upon equality and its opposition to aristocracy and privilege, had a democratizing effect upon the nation as a whole.

REVIEW TEST (Chapter 11 — Part I)

Select the number preceding the word or expression that best completes each statement or answers each question.

1. A factor that contributed to the election of Andrew Jackson to the Presidency in 1828 was (1) the electoral votes of the New England states (2) Jackson's approval of the Second Bank of the United States (3) the lowering of property qualifications for voting (4) the aid given to Jackson by Henry Clay

2. What was Andrew Jackson's attitude toward the spoils system? (1) that civil service laws should be strengthened (2) that rotation in office was a good thing (3) that the spoils system was bad but he could do nothing about it (4) that only highly educated persons should hold positions in the government

3. Which of the following statements concerning the national nominating conventions for the Presidency is true? (1) They are provided for in the Constitution. (2) They preceded the congressional caucus as a nominating procedure. (3) They have been the basic Presidential nominating procedure since the early 1830's. (4) They are not held when a President seeks re-election.

4. During the Jacksonian Era, members of the Electoral College began to be selected directly by (1) the President (2) Congress (3) state legislatures (4) the voters

5. During the first half of the 19th century, the right to vote was most generally extended by (1) lowering the voting age (2) removing property qualifications (3) outlawing poll taxes (4) amending the Constitution

6. The Jacksonian Era is generally considered to include the (1) 1st quarter of the 19th century (2) 2nd quarter of the 19th century (3) 1st half of the 19th century (4) 2nd half of the 19th century

7. In relation to the democratic changes that were taking place while he was President, Jackson's main attitude was that of (1) innovation (2) opposition (3) encouragement (4) unawareness

8. Jefferson and Jackson agreed on all of the following *except* that (1) the rights of the individual should be protected (2) privilege and monopoly in government are undemocratic (3) the power of government rests upon the consent of the governed (4) all citizens are equally fit for office

9. Which of the following principles was Jacksonian rather than Jeffersonian? (1) City workers, small farmers, and small businessmen constitute the backbone of the nation. (2) "That government is best that governs least." (3) A central government of limited power will best protect the country from the evil effects of minority rule. (4) City workers cannot be fully trusted in politics, since they may be swayed by demagogues.

10. Because of its nature the "Age of Jackson" may also be called the era of (1) Big Business (2) the Rise of the Common Man (3) International Anarchy (4) Whig Supremacy

Indicate whether each of the following statements is **true** *or* **false**. *Give one fact or reason in support of each true statement, and reword correctly those statements which are false.*

1. While Jackson was President religious and property qualifications were abolished in every state.

2. The "Revolution of 1828" brought about a shift in political power.

3. During the Jacksonian Era workingmen began to exercise political influence.

4. The separation of church and state was an aim which reformers were unable to achieve until after the Civil War.

5. A characteristic of the "Age of Jackson" was the adoption of more democratic state constitutions.

Essay Questions

1. "Jackson's election was both a cause and a result of the growth of democracy in the United States." Give evidence in support of this statement.

2. (a) Explain why the election of Andrew Jackson as President in 1828 has been called "the Revolution of 1828." (b) Why do you agree or disagree with this interpretation?

3. Discuss three ways in which Jacksonian democracy was like Jeffersonian democracy, and two ways in which it differed.

4. Explain three ways in which political democracy was extended during the Jacksonian Period.

Part II — JACKSON FACES THE SECTIONAL AND NATIONAL ISSUES OF HIS TIME

Few American Presidents appealed more to the popular imagination than Andrew Jackson. When he was inaugurated in 1829, he was the idol of the masses, who looked upon him as a self-made man, a defender of democratic ideals, and a dynamic innovator. (Actually, by the time he became President, Jackson was no longer the rough, hot-tempered frontiersman of his early years. He had become a wealthy planter, with gentlemanly manners.)

On the other hand, Jackson aroused fear and resentment among the conservative groups in the nation, who regarded him as the symbol of "King Mob" in the White House. To his opponents, Jackson's vigorous actions and policies earned him the title of "King Andrew" and "King Veto."

Jackson's Principles as President. Although Andrew Jackson did not come to office with a carefully worked out program, his actions were for the most part guided by three principles. **(1)** He believed that the government must be run in the interests of the majority. **(2)** He believed that the interests of the nation as a whole came before the interests of any single group or section. **(3)** He believed that it was the President's job to lead the country as a kind of "Tribune of the people."

Jackson, a Strong President. Andrew Jackson is considered a "strong" President. He vigorously attempted to lead the country in national affairs.

1. Jackson took outspoken positions and direct action on the major issues that confronted him in office.

2. He never bothered to establish close working relations with Congress.

3. He increased the personal power of the President by open use of patronage, by the development of a favorable party press, and by his use of the veto. (Jackson vetoed 12 bills, more than all Presidents before him combined; he also was the first to use the *pocket veto*.)

4. He preferred to rely for advice more on an unofficial "inner circle" of close associates (the "Kitchen Cabinet"), than upon the Cabinet.

5. He ended political ties with Vice President John C. Calhoun, who, next to himself, was the most influential man in his first administration. In 1831 Jackson ended Calhoun's influence in the administration by completely changing his Cabinet, many of whom were Calhoun supporters. For these and other reasons (see below), Calhoun resigned the Vice Presidency and became a Senator from South Carolina.

6. When Jackson considered it necessary, he disregarded or even defied the Supreme Court. In vetoing a bill to recharter the Second Bank of the United States, for example, Jackson ignored John Marshall's decision supporting the Bank's constitutionality. In addition, Jackson, who shared the dislike of many Westerners for Indians, refused to enforce Marshall's order that Georgia return certain lands to the Creek Indians. He is reported to have said, "Marshall has made his decision; now let *him* enforce it."

Jackson, the Tariff, and Nullification. As President, Jackson upheld the principle of *national supremacy*. This dismayed Southerners, who had believed that as a Westerner and champion of the small man, Jackson would support states' rights. The issue which caused him to take a firm stand was the threat of Southern planters to disregard national law in protest over the high protective tariff. This came to be known as the *nullification issue*.

1. *Tariff Rates Are Raised.* The protective tariff of 1816, imposed to protect United States manufacturers from the dumping of European goods onto the market after the War of 1812, was followed by yet higher protective tariffs in 1824 and 1828.

2. *Southern Opposition.* In 1816, the South supported the protective tariff, because many of its leaders believed the South would become an industrial section. By 1824, however, Southern leaders had become convinced that their future was tied to cotton growing and other forms of agriculture. They began to oppose protective tariffs on the ground that as an agricultural section the South did not need protection because it imported manufactured goods. To Southerners a high tariff meant high prices for the goods they had to buy. Although most of the "old" South's (east of the Mississippi) economic difficulties resulted from the fact that it could not compete in cotton production with the better lands of the Southwest, it blamed its ills principally on the tariff.

3. *The "Tariff of Abominations."* The very high rates of the *Tariff of 1828,* which was passed largely as a result of Northern and Western support and Southern miscalculation, alarmed and provoked the South to a rebellious mood. So deeply angered were Southerners that they referred to the law as the "Tariff of Abominations."

4. *The Exposition and Protest (States'-Rights Theory of Union).* The Southern answer to the Tariff of 1828 was set forth in the South Carolina *Exposition and Protest* (1828). This was a statement by Vice President Calhoun which was adopted by the South Carolina Legislature in 1828. It justified Southern opposition to the tariff on constitutional grounds, by reviving and extending the *doctrine of nullification,* set forth earlier in the Virginia and Kentucky Resolutions of 1798–99. (See page 149.) Calhoun stated the following premises on the relationship of the states to the Constitution and to the Federal government:

> (a) The Constitution is a compact (agreement) between sovereign states (the *compact theory*).

> (b) The states as a body are therefore superior to the Federal government.

(c) Each state, consequently, has the right to decide when a Federal law is unconstitutional (*states' rights*).

(d) If a state feels that Congress has exceeded its power, it has the right to declare a Federal law null and void within its borders (*doctrine of nullification*).

NOTE: One should not confuse Calhoun's doctrine of *nullification* with the later doctrine of *secession*. Calhoun believed in the Union and was not in favor of secession. Indeed, he thought that the right of nullification was necessary to hold the Union together because it would prevent any one section from taking advantage of another.

5. *Webster's Reply to Senator Hayne (National Theory of Union).* The clearest rebuttal to Calhoun's states'-rights theory of Union was given by DANIEL WEBSTER in a famous debate with Senator Hayne of South Carolina. This debate arose over the question of the sale of public lands. Webster, the greatest orator of his day, and the defender of New England's interests in the Senate, rejected the doctrine of nullification. Instead, he set forth the *national theory of Union*. His speech, considered one of the greatest ever delivered on the floor of the Senate, ended with the ringing phrase, "Liberty and Union now and forever, one and inseparable." The main points of Webster's argument are as follows:

(a) The Union is a creature of the people, *not* the states. ("WE, the people . . .")

(b) Congress is the *people's* government, made for the *people* and answerable to the *people*.

(c) No state has the power to declare an act of Congress unconstitutional. Only the Supreme Court may do this.

(d) If states could nullify acts of Congress, the Union would become a mere "rope of sand," and would soon dissolve.

6. *Jackson Takes the National Point of View.* A short while after the Webster-Hayne debate, President Jackson came out firmly in support of national supremacy.

(a) At a Jefferson Day dinner in 1830, President Jackson toasted the Union in the following words: "Our Federal Union — it must and shall be preserved!" Vice President Calhoun answered in a second toast, "The Union — next to our liberty most dear. May we all remember that it can only be preserved by respecting the rights of the States . . . ."

(b) Although Jackson's position surprised most Southerners, who had expected him to take the states'-rights position on nullification, it was really not inconsistent with his beliefs. Jackson did feel that the Federal government should have limited powers, and showed this in such acts as his veto of the bill for building the Maysville Road. On the other hand, he believed even more strongly that no state had the right to disregard Federal law.

7. *South Carolina Threatens to Secede.* The crises over the tariff and states' rights reached a climax when South Carolina threatened to nullify the Tariff of 1832. (Although this actually reduced some of the rates of the Tariff of 1828, it was still a high protective tariff.) The South Carolina Legislature, calling the tariff unconstitutional, recommended non-payment of customs duties within its borders after February 1, 1833, and threatened to leave the Union if the Federal government used force to collect duties. State troops were called up and began to drill for an emergency.

8. *Jackson Threatens to Use Force.* Jackson took active steps to cope with the challenge. He asked Congress to pass a "Force Bill" giving the President the right to use the army and navy to enforce the tariff act. He sent warships to South Carolina waters, and spoke out against nullification, saying "disunion by armed force is treason." He threatened to hang Calhoun from the nearest tree.

The fear and resentment that Jackson aroused in conservative groups in the country prompted them to depict him as a tyrannical Old World monarch. This poster, the work of Jackson's Whig opponents, derides him as "King Andrew the First." However, the common people continued to see Jackson as a defender of democratic ideals and a dynamic innovator.

KING ANDREW THE FIRST.

9. *Compromise Tariff of 1833 Ends Dispute.* Trouble was avoided by a compromise worked out by HENRY CLAY, and supported by Calhoun (who had resigned the Vice Presidency to enter the Senate). **(a)** Under the *Compromise Tariff of 1833,* tariff rates were to be gradually reduced, so that by 1846 they would reach the same levels as in 1816. **(b)** Both sides claimed victory; the South boasted that the Federal government had been forced to reduce the tariff; the nationalists were satisfied that national supremacy had been upheld both by Congress's passage of the Force Bill and by South Carolina's repeal of its nullification ordinance.

Jackson and the Second Bank of the United States. Jackson's belief in the supremacy of the Union did not prevent him from taking a sectional point of view on other public issues. Because of his background as a Southerner and a Westerner, Jackson opposed a national banking system and favored state banking. From the time he became President in 1829, he denounced the Second Bank of the United States, carried on a campaign against its existence, and finally destroyed it.

1. *Jackson Condemns the Second Bank.* As already described (page 171), the Second Bank of the United States had been chartered in 1816 for 20 years.

    (a) Jackson opposed the Bank as a "monopoly" of the "rich and powerful." He supported the views of small farmers, workers, and rising businessmen, who felt that it charged excessive interest rates, withheld credit, favored "big business" over small business, and interfered with the activities of small state banks. The directors of the Bank replied that it was merely insisting upon adequate security for loans — a sound banking principle.

    (b) Jackson also accused the Bank and its president, NICHOLAS BIDDLE, of attempting to influence legislation and of lending money to his political opponents.

    (c) In spite of the ruling of the Supreme Court in *McCulloch v. Maryland* (1819) that the Bank was constitutional, Jackson asserted that it was unconstitutional, and that the President could act independently of both Congress and the Supreme Court.

2. *The Bank and the Election of 1832.* The National Republicans made the Bank an issue in the Election of 1832 by persuading Nicholas Biddle to ask Congress for a renewal of its charter, four years before it expired. Both houses of Congress passed the recharter bill. As expected, Jackson rejected the bill with a vigorous veto message in which he declared that it was unconstitutional, monopolistic, and hostile to small banks. Henry Clay, who was nominated for President in 1832 by the National Republicans, campaigned in favor of rechartering the Bank. Jackson, as the candidate of the Democratic Party, ran for re-election in opposition to the Bank. Jackson's victory by a large majority in the Electoral College convinced him that he had the people's mandate (order) to destroy the Bank.

3. *Jackson Destroys the Bank.* In 1833, after his re-election, Jackson ended the effectiveness of the Bank by having his Secretary of Treasury, ROGER TANEY, remove government deposits from the Bank and redeposit them in certain carefully selected state banks, called "pet banks" by Jackson's opponents. Although the Bank continued to do business until its charter expired in 1836, it never recovered from the economic blow and loss of prestige caused by the removal of government funds.

Jackson Defends National Rights in Foreign Affairs. Jackson increased the prestige of the nation in foreign affairs. **(1)** Through friendly negotiations he persuaded the British to remove restrictions on trade with the West Indies. **(2)** In order to get France to pay for the damage done to American shipping during the Napoleonic Wars, Jackson threatened to seize French property in the United States and sell it to pay off the debt. France at first broke off diplomatic relations with the United States, but finally agreed to pay (at Britain's urging), when Jackson said he meant no insult by his action.

Van Buren and the End of the Jackson Era. MARTIN VAN BUREN, Secretary of State and Vice President under Jackson, succeeded him as President in 1837. Because Van Buren was Jackson's handpicked successor, and because he attempted to continue Jackson's policies, his administration is considered part of the Jacksonian Era. However, Van Buren's term in office was a troubled one. He was not a strong leader like Jackson. In addition, he inherited the growing opposition to Jackson, was faced with a severe depression, and suffered widespread dissatisfaction with his policies.

1. *The Panic of 1837.* The most serious problem faced by Van Buren was the Panic of 1837 and the long depression that followed it.

> *(a)* The depression actually started during Jackson's last year in office and reached its low point during the first two years of Van Buren's administration. It was the worst economic collapse in the nation's history to that time. Many state banks and other businesses failed, and there was much unemployment in the cities. Crop failures aggravated the hard times.

> *(b)* The Panic of 1837 developed largely as a result of overspeculation in Western lands and internal improvements (road and canals) in the 1820's and 1830's. State banks made things worse by granting too many unsecured loans and by issuing large quantities of unsecured paper money ("wildcat currency"). The speculative bubble burst in 1836, when Jackson issued an order, known as the *Specie Circular,* requiring that in the future all public lands be paid for in gold and silver coin (specie). The state banks were unable to meet demands for gold and silver in exchange for their paper banknotes. Alarmed by this, foreign banks and other creditors of state banks demanded repayment of loans. To raise funds, the state banks in turn called in their loans to American businessmen, thus creating a financial crisis throughout the country.

2. *The Independent Treasury System.* During the depression the government was forced to issue special Treasury notes to pay its bills, since its funds had been deposited in state banks. To avoid a repetition of this situation, Congress at Van Buren's urging took steps to safeguard government funds in the future. Under the *Independent Treasury System* which was established, the Federal government collected its taxes in gold and silver specie and stored its funds in subtreasuries (huge vaults) set up in large cities throughout the country.

Whig Victory in 1840. In 1840, Van Buren was defeated by the Whig candidate General WILLIAM HENRY HARRISON, an Indian War hero. This marked the end of the Jacksonian Era. The Whig Party had been organized in 1834 by Clay, Webster, and other opponents of Jackson. It had been defeated by Van Buren in the election of 1836.

1. *Election of 1840.* The 1840 election was one of the more exciting campaigns in United States history. The Whigs blamed Van Buren for the depression and criticized him for being an "'aristocratic Easterner." They captured both Congress and the Presidency, by using popular appeals to the voters — a technique begun by the Democrats in 1828 and 1832.

2. *A Hollow Victory.* The Whigs actually won a hollow victory. Harrison died shortly after his election, and JOHN TYLER became President. Tyler, who had been placed on the ticket only because of his opposition to Jackson, was actually an anti-Jackson Democrat, rather than a Whig. His opposition to policies proposed by Whig leaders caused his entire Cabinet to resign.

NOTE: Daniel Webster stayed on as Secretary of State only long enough to negotiate the important *Webster-Ashburton Treaty of 1842*, which settled the Maine boundary between the United States and Canada and fixed the boundary between both countries from Lake Superior west to the Lake-of-the Woods.

REVIEW TEST (Chapter 11—Part II)

Select the number preceding the word or expression that best completes each statement or answers each question.

1. Which one of the following maintained that the Union was more than a mere compact between the states? (1) Virginia and Kentucky Resolutions (2) Webster's reply to Hayne (3) report of the Hartford Convention (4) Exposition and Protest

2. The South Carolina Exposition and Protest was adopted as a result of (1) the "Tariff of Abominations" (2) the Hartford Convention (3) the Embargo Act (4) William L. Garrison's *Liberator*

3. President Andrew Jackson indicated disapproval of the states'-rights doctrine in the action he took concerning (1) civil service (2) the Seminole Indians (3) the tariff (4) the Supreme Court of the United States

4. A result of President Jackson's action in the nullification controversy was to (1) arouse the antagonism of the North (2) bring on the Panic of 1837 (3) contribute to Calhoun's election to the Vice Presidency in 1836 (4) strengthen the power of the national government

5. President Jackson removed the Federal deposits from the Bank of the United States because he claimed that the Bank (1) was supported by the plantation aristocracy (2) was responsible for the Panic of 1837 (3) discriminated against the farmer and the small businessman (4) had become unprofitable

6. One of the chief causes of the panic of 1837 was (1) building of factories (2) shortage of paper money (3) disappearance of the frontier (4) overspeculation in Western lands

7. In general, the Whig party was unified by its opposition to (1) James Polk's policy of "manifest destiny" (2) Andrew Jackson and his policies (3) internal improvements financed by the Federal government (4) the extension of slavery in the territories

8. The "Age of Jackson" came to an end with the election of (1) 1836 (2) 1840 (3) 1844 (4) 1848

9. What policy favored by George Washington was rejected by Andrew Jackson? (1) requesting the recall of a foreign ambassador (2) suppressing a rebellion of frontier farmers (3) chartering a national bank (4) issuing a statement of neutrality

10. In the matter of return of lands to the Creek Indians, Jackson (1) acted as a nationalist (2) favored a just settlement (3) thought as a frontiersman (4) used a pocket veto

Match each name in Column A with the letter of the item in Column B that is most clearly identified with it.

	A		**B**
1.	Andrew Jackson	*a.*	Accused by Jackson of lending money to his political opponents
2.	John C. Calhoun	*b.*	Placed government funds in "pet banks" at the President's request
3.	Daniel Webster	*c.*	"Our federal union—it must and shall be preserved."
4.	Nicholas Biddle	*d.*	Compromise Tariff of 1833
5.	Martin Van Buren	*e.*	Declared the Bank of the United States constitutional in a famous court decision
6.	William H. Harrison	*f.*	Independent Treasury System
7.	Roger Taney	*g.*	"Liberty and Union now and forever, one and inseparable."
8.	Henry Clay	*h.*	Successful Whig candidate for the Presidency
		i.	"The Union — next to our liberty most dear."

Essay Questions

1. Why was Andrew Jackson as President a most controversial figure?

2. Explain how Jackson handled the problems of (a) nullification (b) recharter of the Second Bank of the United States (c) speculation in Western lands.

3. Briefly explain the significance of each of the following during the Jacksonian Era: "Kitchen Cabinet"; Exposition and Protest; doctrine of nullification; Webster's reply to Hayne; Force Bill; "pet banks"; Specie Circular; Panic of 1837; Independent Treasury System; Webster-Ashburton Treaty; Whig Party.

4. Was Andrew Jackson a great President? Give three reasons for your answer.

5. Give specific evidence to show how each of the following was reflected in the actions of President Jackson: (a) nationalism (b) sectionalism (c) democracy.

Part III — SOCIAL AND CULTURAL PROGRESS IN THE AGE OF JACKSON

The period during and just after the Age of Jackson was one of the great reform eras in United States history.* Reformers worked actively in the 1830's and 1840's to rectify conditions they considered evil. There also were important cultural and scientific developments at this time.

Educational Reforms. Between 1820 and 1860 noteworthy advances were made in education. The United States became a world leader in extending educational as well as voting privileges to the common man.

1. *Free Public Elementary Schools.* As a result of the tireless efforts of crusaders like HORACE MANN and HENRY BARNARD, the public gradually accepted the idea of free public elementary schools. Mann is sometimes referred to as the "father of the public school in America." By 1860, tax-supported ("free") public elementary schools were provided by many states, particularly in the North. Most of these were of the one-room schoolhouse type, so familiar to later generations of Americans.

2. *Some Public High Schools.* Though most high schools of the period remained private "academies," Massachusetts and other New England states pioneered in the establishment of free public high schools. A small number were set up before the Civil War.

3. *More and Better Colleges.* Older colleges improved their curricula by setting up departments of law, medicine, and science. Several state universities were chartered.

4. *Education for Women.* Although girls, as a group, continued to receive little or no formal schooling, women won greater opportunities for education in this period. Emma Willard opened an academy (high school) for girls in Troy, New York, in 1821. *Wesleyan College,* established in 1836, was the first college for women. Mary Lyon founded *Mt. Holyoke Seminary* in 1837, which later became *Mt. Holyoke College.* Oberlin *College,* established in 1833, became the first college to admit women as well as men.

Women's Rights. In the 19th century, women were considered inferior to men in law and custom. In the early 1800's women could not vote or hold property. To protest against this, a vigorous women's rights or *feminist* movement was organized during the second quarter of the century.

1. *Feminist Leaders.* Leaders in the fight for women's rights included FRANCES WRIGHT, DOROTHEA DIX, EMMA WILLARD, MARY LYON, ELIZABETH CADY STANTON, and LUCRETIA MOTT. They persevered in spite of

---

* The other two major reform eras were the *Progressive Era* (1900–18) and the *New Deal Era* (the 1930's).

personal abuse and extreme unwillingness on the part of men to accept them as equals. They received the support of such outstanding men as the famous poet and essayist, RALPH WALDO EMERSON, the reformer and orator, WENDELL PHILLIPS, and the abolitionist poet, JOHN GREENLEAF WHITTIER.

2. *Results.* As a result of this feminist crusade, women were gradually given more educational opportunities. In addition, several states granted married women control over their own property.

3. *Seneca Falls Convention.* The world's first *Women's Rights Convention* was organized by Elizabeth Cady Stanton and Lucretia Mott at *Seneca Falls* (New York State) in 1848. The convention issued a ringing declaration of women's rights which stated that all men *and women* are created equal.

Humanitarian Reform. Reformers concerned principally with improving the welfare of the underprivileged and unfortunate are known as *humanitarians.* In the Jacksonian Era humanitarian reformers were active in many fields.

1. *Aid for the Physically and Mentally Handicapped.* Pioneer efforts were undertaken to help the physically and mentally handicapped. **(a)** The first schools for the blind and deaf mutes were established. **(b)** Dorothea Dix won international recognition for helping to improve the treatment of the insane. She was also a leader in the women's rights and prison reform movements.

2. *More Humane Treatment of Criminals.* As a result of the efforts of people like Dorothea Dix, important advances were made in the treatment of criminals. **(a)** Better facilities were provided in jails and workhouses. **(b)** The whipping of criminals was ended. **(c)** The death penalty for many crimes was eliminated. **(d)** Imprisonment for debt was abolished. **(e)** Greater emphasis began to be placed upon the rehabilitation (reform) of prisoners.

3. *The Temperance Crusade.* Reformers also fought against the evils of alcohol. The *American Temperance Society* was formed in 1826. In 1851 Maine became the first state to pass a prohibition law, as the results of the efforts of NEAL DOW. Other states followed.

Workingmen's Reform Movements. City workers and their leaders, desirous of improving their lot, eagerly joined the reform spirit of the times.

1. *Early Unions.* Small unions of skilled workers were established in several Eastern cities to combat low wages, long hours, and poor working conditions through collective bargaining. In 1837 the unions of six cities joined together in the *National Trades Union.*

2. *Workingmen's Parties.* Unions and their weapons (strikes, boycotts, picketing) were considered illegal during most of this period. Therefore, local *workingmen's parties* were established in several cities in New York and Pennsylvania to work for the legalization of unions and recognition of their demands.

3. *Labor's Demands.* The trade unions and worker's parties supported such reforms as: equal suffrage for all white male citizens; the right to organize, strike, and bargain collectively; a 10-hour day; restriction of child labor; free and equal public education; the breakup of "monopolies" like the Bank of the United States; sale of public lands in the West at low prices; and abolition of imprisonment for debt.

4. *A Short-lived Movement.* The labor movement of the Jacksonian period never grew very strong because of quarrels among leaders, division of opinion among reformers, and the "lure" of the growing Democratic Party. The trade unions of the 1820's and 1830's collapsed after the Panic of 1837.

5. *Successes of the Labor Movement.* Despite its short life, the workingmen's reform movement did achieve some measure of success. **(a)** The right to strike was recognized for the first time in Massachusetts in 1842 (case of *Commonwealth v. Hunt*). **(b)** Imprisonment for debt was abolished in most states. **(c)** Some workers and city employees won the 10-hour day. (In 1840, Martin Van Buren established a 10-hour day for all work done for the Federal government.) **(d)** A few states limited child labor.

Religion and the Growth of Democracy. The democratic spirit was promoted by religious developments of the era, and there was a noteworthy growth of religious tolerance.

1. *Separation of Church and State.* Religious equality was advanced by the abolition of religious requirements for holding public office, and the separation, by 1850, of church and state.

2. *The Church and Social Reform.* During this era the churches took an active interest in social reform. **(a)** Church organizations established schools, colleges, hospitals, and missions. **(b)** Churches encouraged the well-to-do to contribute money for the support of charitable organizations (philanthropy). **(c)** Churchmen became leaders in the temperance and prison reform movements. **(d)** Religious institutions also began to furnish such important social services as orphanages and homes for the aged.

Attempts to Establish Utopian Communities. Discouraged by the evils of the early Industrial Revolution, some individuals tried to establish a better world by forming "utopian" (ideal) communities based on the principle of voluntary cooperation (*utopian socialism*). ROBERT OWEN, a wealthy British manufacturer, established one such community at New Harmony, Indiana. Others were tried at Brook Farm (near Boston) and at Oneida, New York. The utopian communities were supported by such outstanding people as Emerson, British-American reformer Frances Wright, and the novelist, Nathaniel Hawthorne. Nearly all were short-lived. Lack of sufficient capital, unwillingness of all members to share the burdens, poor location, and such natural disasters as fires and plagues contributed to their failure.

The Early Peace Movement. Active concern for peace developed between 1820 and 1860. After the War of 1812, an anti-war movement developed and expressed itself in the organization of peace societies. WILLIAM LADD, ELIHU BURRITT, and others helped establish the *American Peace Society* in 1828. Ladd also urged the formation of an international peace organization and a world court. The Quakers were especially active in the peace crusade.

Growth of a Distinctively American Culture. An important feature of the first half of the 19th century was the development of a distinctively American culture. In 1800, Americans still looked to Europe for leadership in literature, the arts, and science. By 1850, Americans could boast of their own contributions in most of these fields.

The Rise of an American Literature by Midcentury. Particularly in the field of literature were the Americans able to achieve "cultural independence."

1. *Novelists.* Some of America's finest novelists wrote during the first half of the 19th century, and they frequently used the American past as their inspiration. Leading examples include the following: JAMES FENIMORE COOPER, WASHINGTON IRVING, HERMAN MELVILLE, NATHANIEL HAWTHORNE, and WILLIAM GILMORE SIMMS.

2. *Poets and Essayists.* A number of the great American writers devoted themselves to essays, poetry, and short stories. They also frequently took positions on the leading issues of the day. Some of the better known poets and essayists of this period were: RALPH WALDO EMERSON, HENRY DAVID THOREAU, WALT WHITMAN, JOHN GREENLEAF WHITTIER, JAMES RUSSELL LOWELL, WILLIAM CULLEN BRYANT, OLIVER WENDELL HOLMES, EDGAR ALLAN POE, and HENRY WADSWORTH LONGFELLOW.

3. *Historians.* American nationalism of the period was reflected in the works of able historians, several of whom wrote with pride and enthusiasm about the history of their own nation. Noteworthy were FRANCIS PARKMAN, GEORGE BANCROFT, WILLIAM PRESCOTT, and JOHN MOTLEY.

4. *Literary Centers.* Although all sections were represented, New York and New England were the leading centers of the "American literary renaissance."

5. *Newspapers, Magazines, and Public Lectures.* Newspapers, magazines, and public lectures became important forces in shaping American opinion and culture during this period.

(a) Important inventions like the *telegraph* and the *Hoe cylinder press* (1846) made possible the speedy collection and distribution of news, and the printing of thousands of newspapers daily. Newspaper circulation expanded as prices dropped from five or six cents, to a penny or two.

(b) Important new magazines printed articles, stories, and essays about current problems, as well as works by leading writers. Among the better known were the *North American Review,* the *Atlantic Monthly,* the *Southern Literary Messenger, Harper's New Monthly,* and the very popular *Godey's Lady's Book.*

(c) Public lectures, or *lyceums* as they were called, were important popular means of public education. The lyceums gave people in the smaller towns a chance to see and hear the intellectual leaders of the day.

Progress in the Other Arts by Midcentury. Progress in drama, music, and the fine arts lagged behind literary progress. Some highlights and significant developments, however, were noteworthy. **(1)** Well known actors like EDWIN FORREST and JOSEPH JEFFERSON toured the country, and presented American as well as English plays. With the coming of the steamboat and the railroad, traveling theatrical companies carried the drama to small towns as well as cities. **(2)** The *Hudson River School* of painters became famous for its landscapes (GEORGE INNESS, THOMAS COLE, and others). Also, the *Rocky Mountain School* became famous for its paintings of Indian and Western life (GEORGE CATLIN, ALFRED MILLER, and others). **(3)** Interest in music grew as a result of the formation of choral societies, the improvement of church music, and the introduction of music courses into the schools. Patriotic songs, in particular, had wide appeal, and minstrel shows helped to popularize such American tunes as STEPHEN FOSTER's *My Old Kentucky Home* and DAN EMMETT's *Dixie.*

The Growth of Science by Midcentury. Advances in the sciences were more notable than in the arts.

1. *Leading Scientists.* Several American scientists won national and international reputations. Among these were: LOUIS AGASSIZ and BENJAMIN SILLIMAN in *geology* (the study of the earth); ASA GRAY in *botany* (the science of plant life); JOHN AUDUBON in *ornithology* (the study of bird life); JOSEPH HENRY in *physics* (the study of matter); and MATTHEW MAURY in *oceanography* (the study of the oceans). Agassiz also made contributions in *zoology* (the study of animals) and Silliman in *chemistry* (the study of the changes in matter).

2. *Spread of Scientific Knowledge.* The establishment of the *Smithsonian Institution* in 1846, the increased publication of scientific periodicals, and the organization of scientific societies, all helped spread the new scientific knowledge.

3. *Applied Science.* Americans took the lead in the practical use of scientific knowledge and became the world's foremost *applied scientists.* They put science to work in many fields through practical inventions like the cotton gin, the reaper, the steamboat, and the railroad engine.

4. *Medicine.* Americans also contributed to practical advances in medicine during this period.

(a) Vaccination was introduced into the country about 1800 and spread rapidly, especially after a number of severe epidemics.

(b) Between 1810 and 1840, more than 25 medical schools were established.

(c) The physician CRAWFORD LONG in 1842 and the dentist W. T. G. MORTON in 1846 were the first to use anesthetics (ether) successfully in operations.

(d) In 1844, Dr. HORACE WELLS used gas (nitrous oxide) for the first time, in the extraction of teeth.

REVIEW TEST (Chapter II—Part III)

Select the number preceding the word or expression that best completes each statement or answers each question.

1. In the United States, all of the following were important concerns of the humanitarians of 1820–40 *except* the (1) abolition movement (2) treatment of the insane (3) public school movement (4) welfare of migrant laborers

2. The term "free" public schools means (1) schools open to all (2) tax-supported schools (3) the right of parents to send their children to either public or parochial schools (4) schools that are state-controlled rather than Federal-controlled

3. The Seneca Falls Convention was an important step forward in (1) the women's rights movement (2) the labor movement (3) the temperance crusade (4) better treatment for the insane

4. All of the following were major goals of the feminist movement of the 1830's and 1840's *except* (1) the right to vote (2) the right to hold property (3) the right to an education (4) the right of women to choose their own mates

5. Labor's demands in the 1830's and 1840's included all of the following *except* (1) the right to organize (2) the right to bargain collectively (3) the right to form workingmen's parties (4) the ten-hour day

6. Social reform activities of the churches in the pre-Civil War period included all of the following *except* (1) establishment of schools, hospitals, and missions (2) support of temperance and prison reform movements (3) sending missionaries to underdeveloped areas and countries (4) establishing utopian communities in frontier areas

7. In which cultural field did Americans make the most notable contributions in the period 1820–50? (1) architecture (2) literature (3) music (4) painting

8. The "Hudson River School" was the name given to a leading group of American (1) newspaper editors (2) sculptors (3) poets (4) painters

9. Who among the following was primarily an essayist and poet? (1) James Fenimore Cooper (2) Nathaniel Hawthorne (3) Ralph Waldo Emerson (4) Herman Melville

10. All of the following were important 19th-century historians *except* (1) George Bancroft (2) Walt Whitman (3) William Prescott (4) Francis Parkman

Indicate the letter of one or more fields listed below with which each of the persons named was actively identified.

A. Educational reform
B. Prohibition
C. Utopian socialism
D. International peace
E. Painting

F. Women's rights
G. Aid to the physically and mentally handicapped
H. Literature

.... **1.** Horace Mann
.... **2.** Elizabeth Stanton
.... **3.** George Inness
.... **4.** William Cullen Bryant
.... **5.** William Ladd

.... **6.** James Russell Lowell
.... **7.** Frances Wright
.... **8.** Dorothea Dix
.... **9.** Nathaniel Hawthorne
....**10.** Robert Owen

Select the letter of the item which does **NOT** *belong with the others.*

1. Noteworthy developments in music before the Civil War: (a) the writing of popular patriotic songs (b) introduction of music courses into the schools (c) the writing of great symphonies by American composers (d) an increase in the popularity of minstrel shows

2. Leading pre-Civil War American scientists: (a) Asa Gray (b) Joseph Henry (c) Isaac Newton (d) Louis Agassiz

3. Fields in which Americans made significant creative contributions in the period 1800–60: (a) architecture (b) literature (c) applied science (d) the writing of history

4. Associated with advances in medicine in the first half of the 19th century: (a) Matthew Maury (b) Crawford Long (c) Horace Wells (d) W. G. Morton

5. Associated with the American Theater before the Civil War: (a) Edwin Forrest and Joseph Jefferson (b) traveling theatrical companies (c) original musical comedies (d) a growing playgoing audience

Essay Questions

1. Why is the Age of Jackson called an Age of Reform? Discuss fully.

2. Discuss one important achievement in each of the following fields of reform activity in the pre-Civil War period: (1) education (2) women's rights (3) humanitarian reforms (4) trade unionism (5) religion (6) temperance.

3. Explain three results of the reform movements of the period 1830–60.

4. In 1820 an English critic wrote, "Who reads an American book or goes to an American play or looks at an American picture or statue? What does the world yet owe to American physicians or surgeons?" Select three of the areas indicated in this selection (such as literature, science, art, medicine), and, by giving evidence, indicate whether or not the opinion expressed in 1820 was equally true in 1860.

CHAPTER 12

Manifest Destiny and Territorial Expansion

The decade of the 1840's was an important one in the history of the United States because of the tremendous territorial growth which took place during this time. The United States acquired Oregon, Texas, and the present Southwest. It pushed its western boundary to the Pacific. More territory was gained in this single decade than ever before or since. As a result of this expansion, slavery became a national issue which no longer could be pushed aside.

Manifest Destiny. During the 1840's most Americans believed that the nation was destined by nature and Providence to expand from the Atlantic to the Pacific, and from Canada to the Rio Grande. This belief in expansion was known as *"manifest destiny."* Under the influence of manifest destiny the nation expanded to the Far West, and also came into conflict with its northern and southern neighbors, Great Britain and Mexico. Advocates of manifest destiny believed that expansion was necessary to: **(1)** obtain more land for farming, **(2)** eliminate European influence from the American continent, and **(3)** safeguard the national security by establishing "natural boundaries."

Early Territorial Growth of the United States. By the 1840's the United States had already begun to expand across the continent in "seven-league boots." The American Revolution extended the national boundary to the Mississippi (1783). The Louisiana Purchase pushed it to the Rockies (1803). The Florida Purchase brought it to the Gulf of Mexico (1819).

The Acquisition of Oregon (1846). In the early 19th century, Oregon was the vast territory west of the Rockies which extended from the parallel 54°40′ on the north (the southern boundary of Russian Alaska), to the 42nd parallel on the south (the northern boundary of Spanish territory).

1. *Conflicting Claims.* Although Russia and Spain also had laid claim to Oregon, the claims of Great Britain and the United States were strongest.

> *(a) Great Britain* based its claims on the late 18th-century explorations of Captain Cook in the Bering Strait and Captain Vancouver in the Puget Sound area, as well as upon the establishment of British fur trading posts in the Columbia River Basin.

> *(b) The United States* based its claims on the explorations of Captain Gray, who discovered the Columbia River in 1792; on the Lewis and Clark Expedition of 1804–06; and upon the establishment of a fur trading post near the mouth of the Columbia River by John Jacob Astor as early as 1811.

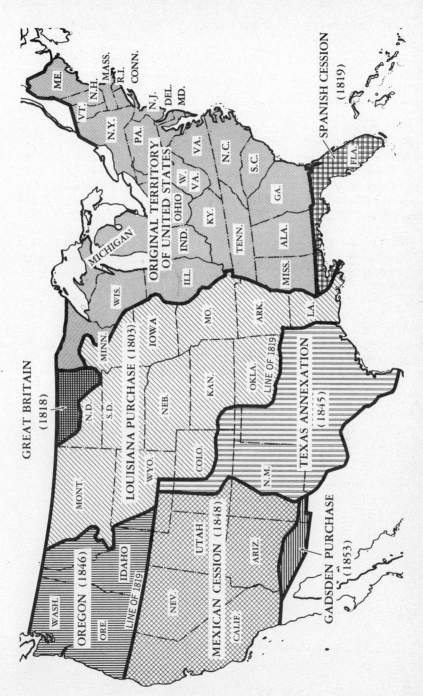

The territorial growth of the United States.

(c) *Spain* gave up its claim to Oregon in 1819, at the time of the Florida Purchase. *Russia* relinquished its claim in 1824, after the issuance of the Monroe Doctrine.

2. *Joint Occupation by Britain and the United States.* In 1818, as part of an overall settlement of the northern boundary dispute (see page 172), Britain and the United States agreed to *joint occupation* of Oregon for 10 years. This was renewed in 1827 for an indefinite period.

3. *American Settlement of Oregon.* During the 1830's and early 1840's a growing stream of Americans emigrated to the Oregon territory. Migration was stimulated by: **(a)** the propaganda of expansionists like Hall J. Kelley, who organized a society for the settlement of Oregon; **(b)** glowing reports about the territory's climate and soil by missionaries like Marcus Whitman and Jason Lee; **(c)** the establishment of overland wagon routes to the Oregon territory (the "Oregon Trail"); and **(d)** the foreclosure of many farms due to the Panic of 1837. By 1843 enough Americans had settled in Oregon to set up a provisional government and petition Congress for annexation.

4. *The Annexation of Oregon.* The demands of expansionists and settlers that the United States end its joint occupation led to the final acquisition of part of the Oregon territory by the United States in 1846.

(a) Expansion became an issue in the Presidential election of 1844. The Democrats and their candidate JAMES K. POLK campaigned for the acquisition of *all* of Oregon, with the slogans "Reoccupation of Oregon!" and "54-40 or fight!"

Bureau of Public Roads

1843 — The Oregon Trail.

(b) Fortunately, Polk's election as President did not cause a crisis with Britain. Because the United States was in the midst of a dispute with Mexico, our government was willing to accept a British offer to compromise. In 1846 both countries signed a treaty which divided Oregon between them, and fixed the 49th parallel as the northern boundary of the United States from the Rocky Mountains to the Pacific Ocean.

The Annexation of Texas. The spirit of manifest destiny was most clearly shown in the annexation of Texas. Texas was originally a Mexican province. After Mexico had revolted from Spain in 1821 and had secured its independence, the Mexican authorities encouraged American settlement in Texas by offering generous grants of fertile land. Following the lead of STEPHEN AUSTIN, who helped establish the first American colony in Texas, some 20,000 Americans had settled in Texas by 1830. Most were cotton growers from Southern states.

1. *Growing Opposition to Mexican Rule.* Although they had been given local self-governing rights, the Americans in Texas soon began to resent Mexican rule. **(a)** Many land grants were suspended by the Mexican government. **(b)** Mexico placed duties on goods imported into Texas from the United States. **(c)** In 1831, Mexico forbade the further importation of slaves. **(d)** In addition, the Mexican government began to challenge the desire of Texans to continue their customs, language, and traditions, and to maintain close relations with the United States.

2. *Texas Wins Its Independence.* In 1835, the Mexican President-dictator, Santa Anna, eliminated the possibility of continued local self-government by making Texas part of the state of Coahuila. The Texans reacted to this by declaring their independence. After a short but hard-fought struggle, General SAM HOUSTON led the Texan forces to victory over Santa Anna's troops in the battle of San Jacinto. Among the reasons for the victory was the Texans' intense desire to avenge the wiping out of a small force by a Mexican army at the *Alamo,* a fortified mission in San Antonio. "Remember the Alamo!" became the Texan war cry. Santa Anna agreed to recognize the independence of Texas.

3. *The Lone Star Republic.* Although the Mexican government refused to recognize Santa Anna's agreement, Texas organized itself into an independent state, the *Republic of Texas.* Sam Houston was elected the first president, and a request was made for annexation by the United States. In 1837, President Jackson recognized the new "Lone Star" republic, but took no action on annexation.

4. *Failure of Early Attempts to Annex Texas.* Early attempts to annex Texas to the United States were blocked by sectionalism. **(a)** Southerners favored annexation because it would extend the area open to slavery and increase the power of the South in the Senate. **(b)** Expansionists argued that the annexation of Texas would increase national wealth and power. **(c)** Northerners blocked the annexation, however, because they opposed the extension of slavery and the resulting increase in Southern power.

They also feared trouble with Mexico, which continued to lay claim to Texas. **(d)** In 1844, the anti-annexation bloc in the Senate defeated a treaty to annex Texas, despite the fact that it had the support of President Tyler and a strong lobby representing speculators in Texan bonds and land.

5. *Texas Is Annexed.* Texas was finally annexed to the United States in 1845. The Democrats campaigned for the "reoccupation of Oregon and the reannexation of Texas" in the election of 1844. They claimed that the United States had really occupied *all* of Oregon before joint occupation with Britain; they also claimed that Texas was part of the Louisiana Purchase. (Actually the United States had surrendered its claim to Texas as part of the Louisiana Purchase when it purchased Florida.) By linking Texas to Oregon as a campaign issue, the Democrats hoped to make its annexation more acceptable to Northern voters. Polk's election convinced Tyler that the country favored the acquisition of Texas. At Tyler's urging, Congress, by a close vote, passed a joint resolution annexing Texas. Tyler signed the resolution just before leaving office. In December, 1845, Texas became a state in the Union.

> NOTE: The use of the joint resolution, which requires a simple majority of each House, avoids the necessity of a two-thirds vote in the Senate, required for treaties.

The Mexican War (1846–48). The annexation of Texas by the United States caused Mexico to break off diplomatic relations and begin preparing for war. The Mexicans were bitter over the fact that the United States had encouraged the Texas revolution, and feared that a similar situation would develop in the Mexican provinces of California and New Mexico, where hundreds of Americans had already settled. Americans, in turn, had grievances against Mexico. They were angry over the mistreatment of American citizens, over the fact that Mexico had refused to pay the claims of American citizens for damages during the Texan revolt, and over the execution without trial of 22 Americans accused by Mexico of plotting a revolution (1835).

1. *A Boundary Dispute Leads to War.* War between Mexico and the United States developed over a dispute concerning the southern boundary of Texas. The United States claimed that the *Rio Grande River* was the southern boundary; Mexico insisted it was the *Nueces River*. President Polk's actions helped precipitate the war.

> (a) President Polk, an expansionist, had sent John Slidell to negotiate the Texas boundary dispute and purchase California and New Mexico for as much as 30 million dollars (the *Slidell Mission*).
>
> (b) When Mexico refused to receive Slidell, Polk ordered American troops under General ZACHARY TAYLOR into the disputed area between the two rivers.
>
> (c) Mexico declared war and sent troops across the Rio Grande to attack American forces.

(d) When skirmishes occurred between Mexican and American forces, Polk asked Congress to declare war on the grounds that Mexico had invaded United States territory and had shed American blood. War was declared on May 12, 1846.

2. *Mexico Is Easily Defeated.* Though there was much bitterly contested fighting, the United States easily defeated Mexico in hostilities that lasted about a year and a half (1846–48).

(a) American troops assumed and maintained the offensive.

(b) General ZACHARY TAYLOR invaded northern Mexico and defeated the Mexicans in the battle of *Buena Vista* (1847).

(c) At about the same time Colonel STEPHEN KEARNY marched into and took control of New Mexico. He then joined Colonel JOHN C. FRÉMONT and American naval forces in conquering California. (Frémont, a famous explorer of the Southwest, and known as the "Pathfinder," had already helped establish the independent "Bear Flag Republic" in California soon after the outbreak of the war.)

(d) In the final campaigns of the war, General WINFIELD SCOTT captured Veracruz on the east coast of Mexico, and then Mexico City (the capital) in September, 1847. Mexico sued for peace.

3. *The Peace Treaty.* The *Treaty of Guadalupe-Hidalgo* which ended the war in 1848 included the following main provisions:

(a) Mexico recognized United States title to Texas and accepted the Rio Grande as America's southern boundary.

(b) Mexico also ceded to the United States the territories of New Mexico and California (the *Mexican Cession*).

(c) The United States gave Mexico $15,000,000 and agreed to pay the claims of American citizens against Mexico (about $3,000,000).

4. *The Role of the United States in the War.* There has been much discussion of the question of whether or not the United States was justified in going to war with Mexico.

(a) *Critics* say the war was unnecessary and unjust. They point out that there was much opposition to the war in the North, especially among those who felt that acquiring new territory would help extend slavery. They criticize Polk for maneuvering the nation into war by sending troops into disputed territory. They argue that had he been patient the boundary dispute could have been negotiated.

(b) *Defenders* of the role of the United States argue that Mexico was unreasonable in not recognizing Texan independence, and in not entering into negotiations for the sale of New Mexico and California, in which there were already several hundred American settlers. They maintain that Mexico had never effectively governed these territories, and that sooner or later the settlers there would have insisted on joining the United States, as they did in the case of Texas. Some maintain that Mexico purposely sent troops across the Rio Grande in order to start a war it hoped to win.

5. *Importance of the War with Mexico.* The Mexican War had the following significant effects upon American history.

(a) It was a high-water mark of American expansion and a triumph for "manifest destiny." The United States gained territory amounting to about 25% of its present continental area and extended its southwestern boundary to the Pacific. (Five years later, in 1853, the *Gadsden Purchase* rounded off this boundary when the United States paid Mexico 10 million dollars for a small strip of land along the southern border of New Mexico. This land was particularly valuable because it offered the best route for a southern transcontinental railroad. Some consider the sum paid for the land to be "conscience money" for the territory gained in the war with Mexico.)

(b) A new West, rich in natural resources, was opened to settlers.

(c) The war gave military experience to soldiers who were later to become Civil War leaders.

(d) The war aroused fear and resentment against the United States on the part of Mexico and other Latin American republics — a feeling which persists to the present day.

(e) Finally, the Mexican War reopened the slavery controversy by making possible the renewal of the dispute over whether or not the newly acquired territory was to be open to slavery.

Settlement of the Far West. The acquisition of New Mexico and California hastened the settlement of the Far West.

1. *The Gold Rush in California.* The discovery of gold at *Sutter's Mill* in the Sacramento Valley in 1848, set off a great "gold rush" to California, which brought over 90,000 settlers (the "Forty-niners") to that territory within two years. In 1850 California drafted a Constitution and applied to Congress for admission as a free state.

2. *The Mormons.* The gold rush helped develop the Mormon settlements in Utah.

(a) The *Mormons* were a religious group founded by JOSEPH SMITH in New York around 1830. They were known officially as the *Church of Jesus Christ of Latter Day Saints.* Because they were persecuted for their religious beliefs, their social practices (like polygamy), and their abolitionist leanings, they were forced to move westward.

(b) In 1847 the Mormons were led by the able BRIGHAM YOUNG into the Great Salt Lake Valley, where they founded several settlements, including Salt Lake City. With great determination and industry, they irrigated the desert land and turned it into productive farms.

(c) The Mormon settlements were helped by the gold rush. They became a stop-over station along the overland route to California, and they were able to establish a prosperous trade. Within a few years they had attracted over 10,000 settlers. In 1850, the area entered the Union as the *Territory of Utah.* Brigham Young became its first governor. (Utah became a state in 1896.)

3. *The Movement of Settlers to the Far West.* The movement of settlers into the Far West was one of the greatest migrations in history. The trip from such "jump-off" points as Independence, Missouri, took several months to complete. Wagon trains made up of covered wagons ("prairie schooners") moved a few miles a day across endless plains, arid deserts, treacherous rivers, and winding mountain passes. Added to these natural hazards were the bitter winters and the hostile Indians. Hundreds perished along the Oregon and Santa Fe trails. The map on page 272 shows some of the important overland routes to the Far West.

REVIEW TEST (Chapter 12)

Select the number preceding the word or expression that best completes each statement or answers each question.

1. The policy of "manifest destiny" is best illustrated in the (1) Good Neighbor Policy (2) slogan "fifty-four forty or fight" (3) selection of the parallel 36° 30′ in the Missouri Compromise (4) granting of independence to the Philippines

2. In the campaign of which President was "manifest destiny" the principal issue? (1) John Q. Adams (2) Andrew Jackson (3) James K. Polk (4) Abraham Lincoln

3. A leader in the settlement of Oregon was (1) Stephen Austin (2) John C. Frémont (3) Zebulon Pike (4) Marcus Whitman

4. Which of the following was an argument used by the United States in the 1840's to support her claim to the Oregon territory? (1) American missionaries and fur traders had settled in the territory. (2) A provision of the Jay Treaty had ceded the territory to the United States. (3) France had ceded her claim to the territory to the United States. (4) Zebulon Pike's explorations had established United States claims to the territory.

5. What was the most important reason for Americans migrating to Texas during the 1820's? (1) to prospect for gold (2) to drive out the Mexicans (3) to live without restraint in the Lone Star Republic (4) to get cheap lands

6. One reason why Northerners opposed the annexation of Texas in 1836 and 1837 was (1) The balance of power in the Senate would be upset. (2) They feared interference with the negotiations for Oregon. (3) Texas was too expensive to purchase. (4) Texas was too sparsely populated with settlers from the United States.

7. An important result of the Mexican War (1846–48) was the (1) annexation of Texas (2) application of the Monroe Doctrine to Mexico (3) acquisition of Oregon (4) problem of extension of slavery in the new territory acquired

8. Which was the largest acquisition of territory by the United States? (1) Mexican Cession (2) annexation of Texas (3) purchase of Alaska (4) Louisiana Purchase

9. The state whose admission to the United States in 1850 marked the extension of the frontier to the Pacific was (1) Oregon (2) California (3) Washington (4) Utah

10. Which of the following was *not* true about the Mexican War? (1) Generals Taylor and Scott were military heroes. (2) The war was ended by the Treaty of Portsmouth. (3) As a result Mexico recognized the Rio Grande as the southern boundary of Texas. (4) United States forces helped overthrow Mexican rule in California.

The statements below identify territorial acquisitions of the United States. Match each statement with the letter indicating the location of that area on the map.

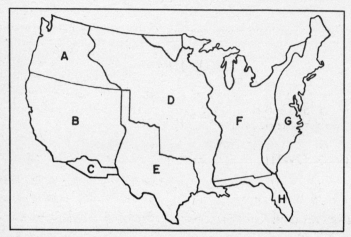

1. In 1803 the purchase of this territory from France doubled the area of the United States.

2. The dispute over the boundary in this area of the United States was settled by agreement with Great Britain in 1846.

3. In 1853 this area was purchased to aid in the development of a transcontinental railroad.

4. As a result of the demands of its leaders, this area was annexed to the United States in 1845.

5. In 1819 this territory was ceded to the United States by treaty with Spain.

Essay Questions

1. Nationalism and sectionalism have been parallel and often conflicting forces in United States history. (a) Explain how nationalism contributed to the acquisition of Oregon. (b) Show how nationalism and sectionalism entered into the debate over the admission of Texas into the Union.

2. The year 1846 has been called "A Year of Decision." (a) Explain one crucial problem facing the President of the United States in that year. (b) Show how the decision made by the President affected the history of the United States.

3. Explain one economic or one political condition that gave rise to the expression "Manifest Destiny" and indicate why the decade of the 1840's is considered *the* decade of manifest destiny.

4. Was the United States justified in going to war with Mexico in 1846? Explain your answer, giving facts and reasons to support your point of view.

5. Write the story that might have appeared under each of the following headlines in the 1840's:

MORMONS ESTABLISH SETTLEMENT IN SALT LAKE VALLEY

POLK ASKS FOR WAR WITH MEXICO

JOINT OCCUPATION OF OREGON COMES TO AN END

CHAPTER 13

Slavery Helps
Pave the Way to Disunion

The acquisition of new territory as a result of the Mexican War reopened the question of slavery in the United States. Bitter debate between North and South over the question of the extension of slavery took place in the 1850's, and aggravated sectional antagonisms. The election of Lincoln as President in 1860 caused the South to withdraw from the Union and was followed by the outbreak of the Civil War.

Part I — GROWTH OF SLAVERY IN THE UNITED STATES

In order to understand how slavery helped pave the way for disunion it is necessary to see how it became "the peculiar institution" of the South.

Slavery Becomes a Southern Institution. In the period before the Civil War, slavery became an important feature of Southern life and industry.

1. *Beginnings of Slavery in the United States.* The first Negroes in colonial America were imported into Virginia from Africa in 1619. At first, their legal status seems to have been that of *indentured servants* — that is, persons who were obliged to serve a master for a fixed number of years. During the 17th century, however, the institutions of slavery gradually developed. The various colonies adopted laws under which Negroes and their offspring were to be held in lifelong bondage. They and their offspring became, in effect, a form of property (*chattel slavery*).

2. *The Early Antislavery Movement.* In spite of its early growth, there were signs by the beginning of the 19th century that slavery might die out. It was not popular in the North, and it had not been particularly profitable in the South, except on large farms, such as rice plantations in Georgia and South Carolina. During and after the Revolution, many antislavery societies were formed. Their members opposed slavery on humane grounds and urged that the slaves be *emancipated* (freed). By the early 1800's, most Northern states had abolished slavery.

3. *Expansion of Slavery in the 19th Century.* The possibility that slavery would die out naturally vanished because of the tremendous growth of cotton culture in the first half of the 19th century. This expansion was made possible by Whitney's cotton gin, improvements in spinning and weaving, and an ever-increasing demand abroad for cotton textiles.

(*a*) By 1835, cotton had replaced rice and tobacco as the South's chief staple crop.

(*b*) Between 1820 and 1860, the number of slaves in the South grew from 1.5 million to nearly 4 million. In the same period, prices for a skilled slave field hand increased from about $400 to $500, to about $1200 to $1500.

4. *Slave Ownership.* In 1860, one of every two persons of the 14 million living in the South was either a slave or a member of a slave-holding family. However, it should be noted that fewer than one-third of all Southerners owned slaves. A few thousand large plantation owners held more than 50 slaves each. A greater number of smaller planters held 10 to 50 slaves. More than two-thirds of those who owned slaves had fewer than 10 slaves each.

Three-quarters of the Southern whites did *not* own slaves. Many were small farmers, occupying less fertile and less desirable land than the planters; some were poverty-stricken "poor whites" who eked out a bare living from worn-out land, and who were looked down upon as "shiftless" and "no-account." Southerners living in towns and cities owned relatively few slaves. Negroes there were used mainly as household servants. Some Negro slaves were employed in industry, transportation, and other non-agricultural pursuits.

5. *The Plantation System.* Although they were a small minority, the large plantation owners, and the plantation system they created, became the symbol of pre-Civil War Southern society. Large plantation owners dominated Southern politics and represented their states in Congress. They owned estates that varied in size from several hundred to several thousand acres, and they made large profits. On these plantations, hundreds of slaves raised the crops, did other necessary labor, and served as household servants.

Because many smaller Southern farmers hoped to become plantation owners, they usually accepted the slave system without question. The poor whites also tended to favor Negro slavery, perhaps because it gave them a social group to look down upon.

6. *Treatment of Slaves.* Slavery was a cruel, tragic, and immoral system. Families were often broken up as fathers were sold separately from wives and children. Slaves were housed and fed on a subsistence level. When they were ill, as occurred often, they usually received only the crudest medical attention.

That slaves resented and hated their condition is becoming increasingly clear. In desperation they often tried to run away to Northern states or Canada. Many did escape successfully. The right of the slave-owner to recapture "fugitive slaves" in free states became a burning issue between the North and South. In addition to running away, slaves sometimes committed sabotage or plotted revolts. Most of these uprisings were small and quickly repressed. One of the most noteworthy was the revolt led by NAT TURNER, a slave, in Virginia in 1831. Turner and some 70 followers rose against their masters and killed more than 50 whites before being put down by overwhelming force. (See page 227.) Some plots for revolt were betrayed and crushed before the rebels could strike. This was true of "Gabriel's Revolt" (Richmond, Va., 1800) and the uprising plotted by DENMARK VESEY (Charleston, S.C., 1820).

It is difficult to generalize about the treatment of slaves. There were undoubtedly many owners who were not cruel. Some masters felt it to be their duty to treat their "people" in a decent way. Others felt that mistreated slaves would not be good workers.

The other side of the picture is that slaves were often treated harshly by owners and were punished by flogging and branding. Under pressure by plantation owners to make a big crop and show fat profits, overseers often drove the black workers mercilessly.

The master-slave relationship, under which the slave was no more than a "chattel," or a form of property, was basically inhuman. Slavery must be condemned, therefore, as an undemocratic system, based on false ideas of racial superiority. It is often said that slavery tended to degrade the master as well as the slave. It also corrupted the society which tolerated it.

7. *The Profits of Slavery.* Historians are still debating to what extent slavery was economically profitable. Certainly, the big planters benefited from the advantages of large-scale production, made possible by slave labor. On the other hand, many smaller planters and farmers could not compete successfully, and found themselves in hopeless poverty, with a crushing debt burden. So much capital had to be invested in slaves and land that in "off years," when the crops failed or the price of cotton dropped, distress was widespread, affecting even the most prosperous planters. Economic hardships caused many thousands of Southerners to migrate to the North. It has also been argued that the existence of a large pool of cheap labor tended to retard economic and technological progress by reducing the need for labor-saving devices and for productive advances in general.

The Antislavery Movement. Friction between the North and South resulted from a growing antislavery crusade.

1. *Origins of the Antislavery Crusade.* Though the Quakers and others had been against slavery in the 18th century, an organized antislavery "crusade" first really began in the early 1800's, when some Southerners, such as BENJAMIN LUNDY, JAMES G. BIRNEY, and the GRIMKE sisters, began to criticize slavery and advocate emancipation. An increasing number of societies were formed to work for gradual emancipation. In 1816 the *American Colonization Society* was established to purchase slaves and send them to Africa. The Society was able to purchase the freedom of more than 1400 slaves and to send them to Liberia and Sierra Leone.

2. *The Abolitionist Movement.* In the 1830's the antislavery movement became more militant (aggressive). It turned its attention to the elimination of slavery as an institution. It drew inspiration from the emancipation of slaves throughout the British Empire in 1833. It included blacks as well as whites.

> *(a) Leaders.* Uncompromising leaders like WILLIAM LLOYD GARRISON demanded the immediate abolition of slavery. Black abolitionists like DAVID WALKER and HENRY GARNET also took this position.

More moderate leaders, like FREDERICK DOUGLASS, a former slave and perhaps the greatest black American of his generation, hoped to end slavery gradually, by means of the ballot box.

(b) *Abolitionist Arguments.* The abolitionists denounced slavery as a national disgrace, and a crime against humanity. They rejected the idea of compensated emancipation, since in their eyes the slave owner was a criminal, and certainly not entitled to payment for his "crime." In *The Liberator,* his weekly newspaper, Garrison denounced the Constitution for accepting slavery.

(c) *Spread of the Abolition Movement.* The abolitionist movement spread and gained momentum during the 1830's and 1840's, particularly in the Northeast and Northwest, where slavery did not exist. Outstanding leaders in addition to Garrison, were WENDELL PHILLIPS, THEODORE WELD, ANGELINA and SARAH GRIMKE, THEODORE PARKER, and LUCRETIA MOTT. It has been estimated that in the 1840's there were about 200,000 members in abolitionist societies.

(d) *Abolitionist Activities.* The abolitionists aroused public opinion by lecturing, writing, and sending antislavery petitions to state legislatures and Congress. They established the *"Underground Railroad,"* a well-organized series of escape routes over which more than 50,000 fugitive slaves were helped to escape to the North and Canada. Two black women who played heroic roles in this enterprise were SOJOURNER TRUTH, who helped escaped slaves settle in the North, and HARRIET TUBMAN, the most famous "conductor" on the Underground Railroad, who led over 300 black men, women and children to freedom.

Abolitionists formed the *Liberty Party* and ran JAMES G. BIRNEY for President in 1840 and 1844.

3. *Other Antislavery Points of View.* Although the abolitionists attracted most attention, there were other more moderate antislavery points of view. WILLIAM ELLERY CHANNING and others believed in gradual, voluntary emancipation through state action. ABRAHAM LINCOLN felt that by embittering the South the abolitionists were actually decreasing the possibility of emancipation. Most Northerners were opposed to the further extension of slavery, but considered it essentially a problem for the South to settle.

4. *Opposition to the Abolitionists.* Until the late 1850's, abolitionists were unpopular in the North as well as in the South. As time went on, however, their activities produced bad feeling between the two sections.

(a) Northern businessmen feared that abolitionist activities would be harmful to trade with the South.

(b) Northern workers feared the competition of free Negroes.

(c) Northern mobs drove abolitionist preachers from pulpits. The abolitionist editor Elijah Lovejoy of Illinois was murdered by a mob.

(d) Southerners blamed the abolitionists for the *Nat Turner Rebellion,* a slave-uprising in Virginia in 1831, which resulted in the death of over 50 white people. To prevent similar episodes, Southern legislatures established *slave codes,* which placed slaves under strict supervision. Stronger militia units and local patrols were set up in the Southern states.

(e) Relations between North and South worsened as a result of the "Underground Railroad." Northern Negroes were sometimes kidnaped and taken to the South in order to make up for the loss of Southern slaves who escaped. Northern states passed *personal liberty laws* which forbade this practice, and put obstacles in the way of apprehending runaway slaves.

(f) In 1836, Southerners in the House of Representatives secured the passage of the "gag rule," which prevented the reading of abolitionist petitions in Congress. John Quincy Adams, the former President, re-elected to the House, led an eight-year battle to repeal these resolutions because he considered them a violation of the Constitutional right of petition. They were repealed in 1843.

(g) Laws punishing the distribution of antislavery propaganda were passed by Southern legislatures.

Southern Defense of Slavery. At first the South tended to apologize for slavery as a "necessary evil." Roused to anger by the abolitionist attacks, however, Southerners began to defend slavery as a positive good. The Southern defense of slavery included the following arguments: **(1)** Slavery was a natural relationship between whites and blacks, and it was socially beneficial to both groups. **(2)** Slavery was ordained by God and accepted in the Bible. **(3)** Slavery brought Christianity and the benefits of civilization to Africans. **(4)** Slaves had more security and were treated more considerately than free workers in Northern factories ("wage slaves").

REVIEW TEST (Chapter 13 — Part I)

Select the number preceding the word or expression that best completes each statement or answers each question.

1. When was slavery introduced into the United States? (1) during the first quarter of the 17th century (2) during the second half of the 18th century (3) during the first decade of the 16th century (4) during the final third of the 19th century

2. Under the original Constitution (1) Slavery was recognized as a legal institution. (2) The importation of slaves was to be ended within 10 years. (3) Slaves were not to be counted for purposes of representation. (4) No provision was made for the return of fugitive slaves.

3. Which of the following was true about slavery in 1800? (1) It was expanding rapidly in all sections. (2) It had not yet proved to be very profitable. (3) There were fewer than 75,000 slaves in the nation. (4) The slave trade had been declared illegal by Congress.

4. Which were the South's chief staple crops before cotton became "king"? (1) indigo and corn (2) wheat and potatoes (3) tobacco and rice (4) peanuts and barley

5. In the first half of the 19th century most slaveowners owned (1) over 100 slaves (2) between 75 and 100 slaves (3) between 25 and 50 slaves (4) less than 10 slaves

6. Which of the following generalizations about Negro slavery in the United States before the Civil War seems most valid? (1) Most slaves were happy. (2) Many slaves tried to escape from bondage. (3) All slaves were subjected to extreme cruelty. (4) There is no evidence of slave insurrections.

7. The purpose of the American Colonization Society in the early 1800's was to (1) help slaves escape to freedom (2) purchase slaves and send them back to Africa as free men (3) establish slave settlements in the Far West (4) secure funds for the abolitionists

8. William Lloyd Garrison did all of the following *except* (1) supply vigorous leadership in the abolitionist movement (2) denounce the Constitution for accepting slavery (3) accept the Missouri Compromise as the best possible solution to the slave problem (4) publish *The Liberator*

9. All of the following were leading abolitionists *except* (1) Theodore Parker (2) Angelina Grimké (3) Abraham Lincoln (4) Elijah Lovejoy

10. John Quincy Adams led the fight to repeal the "gag rule" because (1) he was an ardent abolitionist in his later years (2) he believed it was unconstitutional (3) he opposed filibusters of any kind (4) he was proslavery

Supply the word or expression that correctly completes each statement.

1. The name given to the system of escape routes which helped thousands of slaves flee to the North and Canada was ..?...

2. The Presidential candidate of the abolitionist Liberty Party in the election of 1844 was ..?...

3. A former slave who became a leader in the move to eliminate slavery before the Civil War was ..?...

4. The first slaves were imported into the colony of ..?...

5. In order to put legal obstacles in the path of those who attempted to recapture runaway slaves Northern states passed ..?...

Essay Questions

1. Explain the geographic and economic factors which led to the growth of the plantation system and slavery in the South during the first half of the 19th century.

2. Explain the attitude toward Negro slavery in the United States taken by each of the following in the period 1830–50: (a) a Southern plantation owner (b) an abolitionist (c) a moderate antislaveryite.

3. Briefly discuss the role of each of the following in the crusade to end slavery: the American Colonization Society; William Ellery Channing, Nat Turner, Frederick Douglass, the Underground Railroad, Personal Liberty Laws.

Part II — SLAVERY AND EXPANSION

Sectional debates over the issue of slavery became sharper as the nation expanded.

The Missouri Compromise (1820). The first sharp sectional debate between North and South took place over the question of the extension of slavery. It led to the *Missouri Compromise* of 1820, under which as we have seen (page 191), Maine was admitted as a free state and Missouri as a slave state, with slavery prohibited north of 36° 30′ in the rest of the Louisiana Territory. As a result of the Missouri Compromise the question of the expansion of slavery in the Louisiana Territory was temporarily settled as a national issue, and Congress assumed the right to exclude slavery from the territories. Nevertheless, farsighted statesmen like Thomas Jefferson predicted that the issue could lead to the dissolution of the Union.

Territorial Expansion Again Makes Slavery a National Issue. It was soon made clear that the slavery question had been settled only temporarily by the Missouri Compromise. The antislavery crusade of the 1820's and 1830's kept the issue before the public and led to bitter feelings in both North and South. The acquisition of the Mexican Cession and the rapid growth of California brought the matter to national attention once again. The South wanted its share of the newly won land.

1. *The Wilmot Proviso.* Sectional feeling was aroused in 1846, during the Mexican War, when Representative David Wilmot, a Northern Democrat from Pennsylvania, introduced the *Wilmot Proviso.* This stated that slavery was not to be permitted in any territory acquired from Mexico by war or purchase. Although this resolution was passed in the House, it was defeated by Southern votes in the Senate.

2. *National Debate on Slavery.* After the Mexican War, national debate broke out over the question of what was to be done with the land acquired from Mexico. Four points of view were expressed: **(a)** Many in the North favored the Wilmot Proviso solution, barring slavery forever from the new territories. **(b)** President Polk and others favored extending the Missouri Compromise line to the Pacific. **(c)** Southerners, led by Calhoun, insisted that Congress had no right to prohibit slavery in the territories, despite the Missouri Compromise. **(d)** A group of Northern Democrats, led by Senators Lewis Cass of Michigan and Stephen A. Douglas of Illinois, argued that only the people of a territory could decide whether or not slavery could exist in the territory. Their point of view came to be known as *"popular sovereignty"* or *"squatter sovereignty."*

3. *Election of 1848.* The problem of slavery in the new territories was the burning issue in the Presidential election of 1848. The failure of both major parties to take a firm stand on slavery led to a split in the Democratic ranks, allowing General ZACHARY TAYLOR, the Whig candidate, to become President by defeating Lewis Cass, the Democratic standard-bearer, in a close election. In the election, the *Free Soil Party,* which opposed further extension of slavery in the territories, elected twelve Representa-

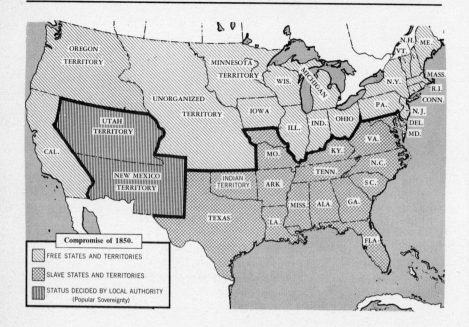

Compromise of 1850.

FREE STATES AND TERRITORIES

SLAVE STATES AND TERRITORIES

STATUS DECIDED BY LOCAL AUTHORITY
(Popular Sovereignty)

tives and gained a temporary balance of power in the House. The Free Soil Party attracted antislavery Whigs and Democrats as well as abolitionists. Its Presidential candidate was former President Van Buren.

Compromise of 1850. A national crisis developed in 1850, when Congress considered the application of California for entry into the Union as a free state. The possibility of a serious sectional split was avoided by the adoption of the *Compromise of 1850,* which was signed by MILLARD FILLMORE, who became President after Taylor's death in 1850.

1. *Provisions.* The *Compromise of 1850,* known also as the *"Omnibus Bill,"* was a series of five measures sponsored by Henry Clay. This marked the climax of a long career in which Clay had shown great political genius in the art of compromise and sectional accommodation.

(a) *California* was admitted into the union as a free state.

(b) The Mexican Cession was split into two territories, *Utah* and *New Mexico,* and the principle of *popular sovereignty* was to apply to both of them.

(c) Texas was paid $10,000,000 for giving up its claim to a part of New Mexico.

(d) A more effective *fugitive slave law* was enacted, compelling state and local officials to cooperate with Federal officials in capturing and returning runaway slaves.

(e) The slave trade (but not slavery) was prohibited in the District of Columbia.

2. *The Debate.* In the long bitter debate which preceded the adoption of the Compromise, the "Great Triumvirate" of the previous 30 years (Webster, Clay, and Calhoun) presented leading arguments on the slavery issue for the last time. Men who were to be the leaders of the 1850's, like Stephen A. Douglas of Illinois and William A. Seward of New York, also took an active part. Webster's support of the Compromise, as necessary for the preservation of the Union, (*Seventh of March Speech*) led to his bitter denunciation by his own section, New England, for "betraying" the interests of the North. Calhoun called for an end of antislavery propaganda in the North and for the safeguarding of the rights of slaveholders in the new territories.

3. *Results of the Compromise of 1850.* The most important result of the Compromise of 1850 was that it avoided secession and preserved peace for the time being. (In the long run, this helped the cause of the Union because when war did come, ten years later, the North was richer, better prepared, and more determined to preserve the nation.)

The Compromise of 1850 had other important effects.

(a) Each side felt that it had made an important gain: the North, through the admission of California as a free state; the South, because of the new fugitive slave law.

(b) As a result of the Compromise, the status of slavery in all of the territories was now clearly established by law. Many in both North and South believed optimistically that this marked a "final" settlement of the slavery issue.

(c) Business interests on both sides were beginning to benefit from a period of prosperity. This made them less inclined to reopen the slavery dispute and more favorably disposed toward the Compromise.

(d) The election of 1852 showed that the nation as a whole wanted to preserve the "sectional truce," in spite of the fact that extremists on both sides were unhappy with the Compromise. Both major party platforms accepted the Compromise as a "final" solution to the slavery question. Both of the Presidential candidates (Democrat FRANKLIN PIERCE and Whig WINFIELD SCOTT) avoided expressing themselves clearly on the slavery issue. Pierce won easily, largely because many Northern and Southern Whigs were dissatisfied with their party's "noncommittal" stand.

REVIEW TEST (Chapter 13—Part II)

Select the number preceding the word or expression that best completes each statement or answers each question.

1. The major reason for Northern opposition to the admission of Missouri as a slave state in 1820 was (1) the feeling that slavery was morally wrong (2) the belief that Congress had the right to exclude slavery from the territories (3) the fact that Missouri lay North of 36° 30′ (4) the fear that this would end the balance of power in the Senate

2. All of the following were provisions of the Missouri Compromise *except* (1) Maine was to be admitted as a free state. (2) Missouri was to be admitted as a slave state. (3) Slavery was to be forbidden in the Louisiana Territory north of 36° 30′. (4) Territory acquired from Mexico could be admitted on the basis of the principle of popular sovereignty.

3. Which of the following would have resulted if the Wilmot Proviso had been adopted? (1) Slavery would have been banned from any territory gotten from Mexico. (2) The Missouri Compromise line would have been extended to the Pacific. (3) Each state would have been allowed to determine the status of slavery within its boundaries. (4) The North would have been angered greatly.

4. Who most clearly favored the principle of popular sovereignty as the solution to the problem of slavery in the territories? (1) John C. Calhoun   (2) President Polk   (3) Stephen A. Douglas   (4) Martin Van Buren

5. Which of the following parties is correctly paired with the position it took in the national debate over slavery in the late 1840's (1) Democratic — slavery is to be banned West of the Mississippi (2) Whig — Congressional action to restrict slavery is unconstitutional (3) Free Soil — slavery shall not be extended further in the territories (4) Republican — the Constitution has to be amended to abolish slavery

6. Whom did the Free Soil Party nominate for the Presidency in 1848? (1) a Senator   (2) the Chief Justice of the Supreme Court   (3) a former President   (4) the Speaker of the House of Representatives

7. All of the following were provisions of the Compromise of 1850 *except* (1) Utah and New Mexico were admitted under the principle of popular sovereignty. (2) Texas was admitted as a slave state. (3) California came in as a free state. (4) The slave trade was prohibited in the District of Columbia.

8. The so-called "Great Triumvirate" of the period 1820–50 were Webster, Clay, and (1) Douglas   (2) Calhoun   (3) Seward   (4) Taylor

9. The victor in the Presidential election of 1852 was (1) Zachary Taylor (2) James Buchanan   (3) Franklin Pierce   (4) Henry Clay

10. In the bitter debate over the Compromise of 1850 who was angrily denounced for "betraying" the interests of his section? (1) William Seward   (2) Millard Fillmore   (3) John C. Calhoun   (4) Daniel Webster

State whether each of the following statements is true or false. If the statement is false, replace the word or phrase in **boldface type** *with the one which will make it correct.*

1. A state north of 36° 30′ in the Louisiana Territory that was permitted to enter the Union as a slave state was **Missouri.**

2. Zachary Taylor, the winner of the 1848 Presidential election, was a member of the **Free Soil Party.**

3. The description "Senator from Michigan, advocate of squatter sovereignty, and Democratic nominee for the Presidency" applied to **Stephen A. Douglas.**

4. In the election of 1852 **none** of the major parties supported the Compromise of 1850.

Essay Questions

1. Explain why the North and South each felt it had gained from (a) the Missouri Compromise (b) the Compromise of 1850.

2. Briefly explain the position or role of each of the following in the national debate over slavery and states' rights in the period 1820–50: Daniel Webster, Henry Clay, John C. Calhoun.

Part III — THE ROAD TO SECESSION AND WAR

The seeming calm that resulted from the Compromise of 1850 was merely "the lull before the storm." Although the North and South *outwardly* accepted the Compromise, there was continued dissatisfaction with the status of slavery. Northerners were bitter over the harshness of the new fugitive slave law. They held mass meetings of protest and evaded the law whenever possible, especially through their passage of state *personal liberty laws,* which forbade the use of local jails for housing recaptured fugitive slaves. Southerners resented the admission of California as a free state and supported the efforts of the Pierce administration to annex Cuba because that country offered possibilities for the expansion of slavery. The best known of these efforts was the *Ostend Manifesto* in 1854.

Kansas-Nebraska Act (1854). The *Kansas-Nebraska Act* of 1854 reopened the slavery controversy and aroused sectional hatreds by repealing the Missouri Compromise.

1. *Provisions.* The Kansas-Nebraska Act, which was introduced by Senator Douglas and which was passed by a narrow margin in Congress, included the following:

(a) The Act abolished the 36°30′ line separating free from slave territory in the original Louisiana Purchase (the territory between the western boundaries of Iowa and Missouri and the Rocky Mountains).

(b) This region was divided into two territories, *Kansas* and *Nebraska.*

(c) The Act provided for the admission of these territories as states, according to the principle of popular sovereignty.

2. *Effects.* The North was shocked by the Kansas-Nebraska Act, especially since the political status of slavery had been apparently settled by the Compromise of 1850, and also because the Act in effect repealed the Missouri Compromise and opened to slavery territory long considered free. Some have suggested that the Act was a result of Douglas' desire to be President, plus a Western desire to open up the new land for settlement. The Act increased sectional bitterness, led to a bloody struggle between proslavery and antislavery forces in Kansas, and caused Douglas to be denounced as a traitor by Northern antislavery interests. The passage of the Act also helped bring about the collapse of the Whig Party and the founding of a new Republican Party.

Formation of the Republican Party. A direct result of the Kansas-Nebraska Act was the formation of the *Republican Party.* Because both major parties (Whigs and Democrats) contained Northern antislavery and Southern proslavery "wings," neither party dared take a forthright position on slavery. Keen dissatisfaction with this state of affairs caused antislavery Democrats and Whigs to join with Free Soilers in 1854 to form the Republican Party, which was pledged to prevent the further expansion of slavery in the territories.

Civil War in Kansas. The Kansas-Nebraska Act also led to a bitter struggle for the control of Kansas in 1855–56. Proslavery and antislavery migrants poured into the territory and established two rival governments. Large-scale violence, amounting almost to bloody civil war, took the lives of many settlers. In the end, Federal troops had to be brought in to restore order. In 1857, Stephen Douglas blocked attempts by President Buchanan to bring Kansas into the Union as a slave state under a proslavery constitution (the *Lecompton Constitution*). Douglas felt that this constitution had been voted in fraudently, and that this violated the principle of popular sovereignty.

As a result, Douglas broke with the administration and lost Southern support. "Bleeding Kansas" became a symbol of the determination of both sides not to yield, and it did much to bring tempers to the boiling point. Not until 1861, after the Southern states had seceded from the Union, was Kansas admitted as a free state.

. Election of 1856. In the Presidential election of 1856, which took place at the height of the crisis over Kansas, JAMES BUCHANAN, the Democratic nominee, defeated JOHN C. FRÉMONT, the Republican candidate. The election clearly reflected the growing sectional division. The Democrats, supporting the Kansas-Nebraska Act and the principle of popular sovereignty, received most of their support from the South. The Republicans, opposing further extension of slavery in the territories, won 114 electoral votes, all of them in the North. This was really a surprisingly good showing for a party running its first Presidential candidate. The Whigs, who tried again to "straddle" the issue, came in a poor third. This marked their end as a national political party.

The Dred Scott Decision (1857). This famous Supreme Court decision brought the bitterness between North and South to a new high.

1. *Background of the Case.* Dred Scott was a slave who was taken by his master from Missouri, a slave state, to Illinois a free state, and then to Minnesota Territory, where slavery had been forbidden by the Missouri Compromise. Scott was then taken back to Missouri and was sold to a citizen of New York State. Scott sued in the Federal courts for freedom for himself, his wife, and their children, on the ground that residence in free territory had made them free. The suit was planned and financed by antislavery groups. Ultimately, the case reached the Supreme Court.

2. *Justice Taney's Decision.* Speaking for a majority of the Court, Chief Justice ROGER TANEY ruled: **(a)** Dred Scott did not have the right to sue in the Federal courts because, as a Negro slave, he was not a United States citizen. **(b)** Under the Constitution, a slave was property, essentially the same as any other property. Congress had no right to deprive a United States citizen (Scott's owner) of his property rights. Then, in an *obiter dictum* (a judicial statement not necessary to the exact issues being considered), Taney went on to say that the Missouri Compromise had been unconstitutional from the beginning. Congress had no right, under the Fifth Amendment, to limit property rights by forbidding a citizen to take slaves into any United States Territory.

3. *Results of the Dred Scott Decision.* The South was delighted with Taney's decision. It seemed to vindicate the Southern point of view and to open the way for the spread of slavery into the territories. The North was shocked and bitter. Antislavery spokesmen accused the Supreme Court of having conspired with Southern slaveholders.

The "Propaganda War" Heats Up. In the 1850's the "propaganda war" between North and South became more intense. It was both a cause and a result of the increase in ill-will between the sections on the slavery issue.

1. *In the North,* abolitionists sought to arouse emotions over the abuses of slavery. **(a)** One of their most potent weapons was the novel *Uncle Tom's Cabin* by HARRIET BEECHER STOWE. Published in 1852, Mrs. Stowe's book immediately became a sensational "best-seller." Its condemnation of the slave system was undoubtedly exaggerated and sentimentalized in some respects, but the book convinced vast numbers of Northerners that slavery was a moral evil which had to be uprooted. **(b)** Another influential book was *The Impending Crisis of the South* by HINTON HELPER, published in 1857. Helper, a Southerner, was not sympathetic to the Negro. He argued, however, that slavery benefited only a minority and retarded progress in the South. **(c)** Many were converted to the antislavery cause by HORACE GREELEY, who crusaded against slavery in the columns of the *New York Tribune*.

2. *In the South,* writers and speakers complained bitterly of "illegal conspiracies" against slavery. Southern "fire-eaters" accused Northern "Yankees," "Black Republicans," and "abolitionist fanatics" of trying to wreck the social and economic structure of the South and of trying to incite the Negroes to murderous uprisings.

The Lincoln-Douglas Debates (1858). In 1858, STEPHEN A. DOUGLAS, a Democrat, stood for re-election to the U. S. Senate from Illinois. He was challenged by his Republican opponent, ABRAHAM LINCOLN, to debate the slavery issue. The series of debates which followed marked one of the most notable political campaigns in United States history.

1. Lincoln emphasized an inconsistency in his opponent's position. Douglas was the champion of popular sovereignty. Yet, he also supported the Dred Scott decision. If Congress could not exclude slavery from a territory (under the Dred Scott ruling), then how could this be done by a territorial legislature, which received all its powers from Congress? Did not this make popular sovereignty meaningless?

2. Speaking at Freeport, Illinois, Douglas tried to get around this by answering that although the people of a territory could not legally *exclude* slavery, they might *discourage* it by refusing to pass laws supporting the institution. This so-called *Freeport Doctrine* was to cost Douglas the support of Southern Democrats. Lincoln, in contrast, forthrightly opposed slavery as "a moral, a social, and a political wrong" and advocated that Congress take action to prevent its further spread.

3. Douglas was re-elected to the Senate (by the Illinois Legislature). The debates, however, helped to bring Lincoln to national attention as a leading spokesman for the Republican Party.

John Brown's Raid (1859). JOHN BROWN was an ardent abolitionist and native of Connecticut who had fought with the antislavery forces in "Bleeding Kansas." He became convinced that the slaves could be freed only if they were enabled to use force against their masters. In October, 1859, Brown and a small band of followers seized the United States arsenal at Harpers Ferry, Virginia. Here he hoped to obtain arms and to distribute them for a slave uprising. The slaves, however, did not rally to Brown's "crusade," and his band was soon overpowered and captured by a detachment of U. S. Marines, commanded by Colonel Robert E. Lee. Severely wounded, Brown was tried for murder, conspiracy, and treason against the Commonwealth of Virginia. He was found guilty and hanged in December, 1859.

Southerners were alarmed and infuriated by John Brown's efforts to use force to bring about a slave uprising. Many in the North also condemned the raid, but many others looked upon John Brown as a martyr in the cause of freedom.

Lincoln Is Elected (1860). By the time of the election of 1860, the North and South were widely divided. Bitter disagreements over slavery existed within political parties and even in certain churches (for example, the Methodist, Presbyterian, and Baptist churches). The election of Lin-

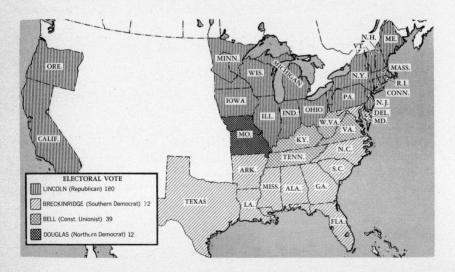

ELECTORAL VOTE
LINCOLN (Republican) 180
BRECKINRIDGE (Southern Democrat) 72
BELL (Const. Unionist) 39
DOUGLAS (Northern Democrat) 12

coln on the Republican ticket was probably made possible by a split over slavery in Democratic ranks.

1. *The Campaign.* Over the election of 1860 hung the threat of secession and civil war.

   (a) The Democratic Party chose STEPHEN A. DOUGLAS as its candidate on a platform supporting the *Freeport Doctrine.*

   (b) In anger at the failure of the party to adopt a proslavery platform, the Southern Democrats bolted the convention and nominated JOHN C. BRECKINRIDGE on a platform which advocated the protection and extension of slavery.

   (c) A third group, made up of former Whigs and Know-Nothings, formed the *Constitutional Union Party* and nominated JOHN BELL on a platform which called for maintaining the Union and compromise on the slavery question. (The Know-Nothings were a semi-secret political organization opposed to further immigration.)

   (d) The Republicans nominated ABRAHAM LINCOLN on a platform for preservation of the Union and exclusion of slavery from the territories. To win the support of Western farmers and Northern industrialists, they also supported a homestead act (distribution of free land), internal improvements, a stable currency, and a protective tariff.

   (e) Lincoln received a large majority of the votes in the Electoral College, but only about 40% of the popular vote. His support came almost exclusively from the Northern states.

2. *The South Secedes.* Lincoln's election led to the secession of the Southern States.

   (a) Led by South Carolina, the seven states of the lower South left the Union between December, 1860 and February, 1861 (South Carolina, Georgia, Florida, Alabama, Mississippi, Louisiana, Texas). They organized the *Confederate States of America,* adopted a Constitution, and elected Jefferson Davis as president of the "Confederacy." Davis had succeeded Calhoun in the 1850's as chief spokesman for the South in Congress.

   (b) The secessionists claimed that compromise was futile, that Southern rights had been violated, that the Republican Party was fundamentally opposed to their interests, and that the North was bent upon the destruction of both slavery and Southern civilization.

Outbreak of the Civil War. The secession of the Southern states started a chain of events that led to the Civil War.

1. *Buchanan Fails to Act.* Between the election of Lincoln, in November, 1860, and his inauguration, in March, 1861, President Buchanan failed to take decisive action against the seceding Southern states. Although he said no state had the right to secede, he also declared that the Federal government could not compel a state to stay in the Union against its will. Several efforts in Congress to work out a compromise met with failure. The

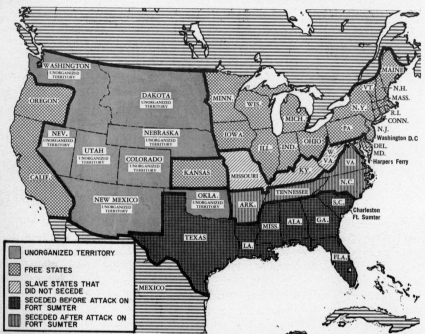

best known of these attempts were the proposals known as the *Crittenden Compromise,* under which the Missouri Compromise Line of 36° 30' would be renewed and extended to the Pacific, payment for escaped slaves would be guaranteed by the United States, and Congress would guarantee the protection of slavery where it was legal.

2. *Lincoln Takes Office.* When Lincoln took his oath of office, seven states had already seceded and had taken over Federal properties within their borders, including forts and arsenals. Only Fort Sumter in Charleston harbor, and three other forts in seceded territory remained in Union hands. Although the Confederates had fired upon a ship sent to bring men and supplies to Fort Sumter, and had forced it to turn back, Buchanan had taken no further action. Lincoln in his *First Inaugural Address* asked for patience on both sides and tried to calm the South by promising not to interfere with slavery where it existed. However, he indicated that as President he intended to maintain the Union, collect customs duties, and keep possession of all United States properties in the South.

3. *The Firing Upon Fort Sumter.* On April 6, Lincoln announced that he would send supplies to Fort Sumter. Fearing that he would send reinforcements as well, the Confederates called upon the fort to surrender. When its commander, Major Anderson, refused, the fort was bombarded for nearly two days, until it surrendered on April 13, 1861.

4. *War Begins.* The bombardment of Fort Sumter was the *immediate cause* of the Civil War. It ended Lincoln's hesitation about taking any action against the South which could be considered aggressive. On April 15, Lincoln issued a call for volunteers to put down the "insurrection." Jefferson Davis issued a similar call to the Confederacy. Volunteers on both sides enlisted in large numbers. War had begun!

5. *The Remaining Slave States Take Sides.* The call to arms forced the eight slave states of the upper South that had not yet seceded to take a stand. Led by Virginia, the middle tier of Southern states (Arkansas, Tennessee, North Carolina, Virginia) joined the Confederacy. The four *border states* (Delaware, Maryland, Kentucky, and Missouri) decided, after much discussion and opposition, to remain loyal to the Union. Strong opposition to secession in the western counties of Virginia caused this section to form the separate state of *West Virginia,* which voted to stay in the Union. It was admitted as a state in 1863 by Lincoln, as a war measure, since the Constitution prohibits the division of a state without its consent.

Basic Causes of the Civil War. For years, students of the Civil War have studied the question of what was responsible for the conflict. Regardless of one's conclusions, it can be said that the Civil War illustrates the fact that major historical events generally have many roots, some reaching far back into the past. In recent years, historians have suggested the following as the basic or underlying causes of the war. They have, however, been unable to agree on which, if any, was the *main* cause.

1. *Slavery.* More and more Northerners came to oppose slavery as a moral evil. Many accepted the idea of war as a necessary means of removing "the curse of slavery" and creating a better and more democratic nation. In recent years, a growing number of historians have pointed out that without slavery the war might not have come. Some have also pointed out that while the Northerners hated slavery, they offered no real solution to the race problem.

2. *Different Ways of Life.* Dissimilarities between the economic and social systems of the North and the South paved the way for misunderstandings. The North was an expanding commercial and industrialized section, whose economy was based on free labor. The South was a relatively stable agrarian society, whose economy was strongly influenced by slave labor and the plantation system. As time went on Southerners began to look upon the South as a distinct culture and civilization with needs and institutions of its own ("Southern nationalism").

3. *Sectionalism.* Differences in ways of life produced continued sectional friction over such issues as the protective tariff, centralized banking, the expansion of slavery into new territories, free land in the West, subsidies to railroads, and states' rights.*

---

* For many years the issue of states' rights was considered a major cause of the Civil War. Today it is considered a secondary cause rather than a primary cause; one used to *justify* rather than explain the secession.

4. *Declining Southern Influence in Government.* Southerners saw, with growing apprehension, that they were losing the struggle with the North for control of the Federal government. Already disturbed by the more rapid economic growth of the North, and by the end of the sectional balance in Congress resulting from the growing number of non-slave states, the South looked upon the victory of Lincoln and the Republican Party in 1860 as the "last straw." (Although the preceding Presidents, Buchanan and Pierce, were Northerners, their political ideas were acceptable to the South.) It was convinced that its interests would be sacrificed by the Federal government because the Republican Party not only represented Northern and Western industrial and agricultural interests but also was opposed to the further extension of slavery.

5. *Weaknesses in Leadership.* In the 1850's especially, there was less willingness on the part of national leaders than there had been in earlier years to compromise differences. In addition, extremist and often irresponsible agitators on both sides inflamed public opinion by distortions, exaggerations, and the creation of misleading issues. In recent years, some historians have suggested that with proper leadership the war might have been avoided.

REVIEW TEST (Chapter 13 — Part III)

Select the number preceding the word or expression that best completes each statement or answers each question.

1. Northern bitterness over the new fugitive slave law that was part of the Compromise of 1850 was shown by (1) the Ostend Manifesto (2) personal liberty laws (3) the Dred Scott Decision (4) the Wade-Davis Bill

2. Which of the following statements is true of the newer Congressional leaders of the 1850's? (1) They were led by Calhoun and Webster. (2) They were determined to spread slavery to the territories. (3) They were less willing to compromise than the leaders of the previous decades. (4) They supported the doctrine of nullification.

3. Presidents Pierce and Buchanan were (1) Southerners with proslavery sympathies (2) Southerners who supported abolition (3) Northerners with proslavery sympathies (4) Northerners who supported abolition

4. The Kansas-Nebraska Act revived sectional animosity by (1) dividing the Kansas-Nebraska territory into two sections (2) extending the 36° 30' line to the Pacific (3) permitting the use of force to end the "civil war in Kansas" (4) repealing the Missouri Compromise

5. Who succeeded Calhoun in the 1850's as leader of the proslavery forces in Congress? (1) Stephen A. Douglas (2) Jefferson Davis (3) Roger Taney (4) John C. Frémont

6. Did the Kansas-Nebraska Act contribute to the issues that brought about the present-day Republican party? Why or why not? (1) Yes, it extended the Missouri Compromise, which the abolitionists favored. (2) Yes, it permitted extension of slavery in the territories. (3) No, the act was passed after the Republican party was organized. (4) No, both Lincoln and Douglas supported the act.

7. In 1860 the Republican Party (1) favored the doctrine of states' rights (2) opposed the extension of slavery into the territories (3) opposed the protective tariff (4) favored squatter sovereignty

8. All of the following were results of the Lincoln-Douglas debates *except* (1) the re-election of Douglas on the Republican ticket (2) the growth of Lincoln's national reputation (3) the loss of Southern support for Douglas (4) the enunciation of the Freeport Doctrine

9. The meaning of the Dred Scott Decision was that (1) Congress could not prohibit slavery in the territories (2) only Congress could legislate to prohibit slavery in any part of the United States (3) slavery could not be prohibited in any state (4) the Fugitive Slave law was unconstitutional

10. The election of Lincoln in 1860 helped to bring about secession because (1) Lincoln had promised to free the slaves (2) a disappointed Douglas urged the South to revenge (3) the South had now lost control of both houses of Congress and the Presidency (4) Lincoln ordered an attack on Fort Sumter

Indicate the chronological order in which the events in each of the following groups occurred.

A

........Election of Taylor .. ..
........Election of Buchanan
........Election of Pierce

B

........Kansas-Nebraska Act
........Compromise of 1850
........"Bleeding Kansas"

C

........Lincoln-Douglas Debates
........Formation of Republican Party
........Dred Scott Decision

D

........John Brown's Raid
........Publication of *Uncle Tom's Cabin*
........Publication of *The Impending Crisis*

E

........Lincoln issues call for volunteers
........Bombardment of Fort Sumter
........Secession of South Carolina

Essay Questions

1. Show how changes in national leadership in the 1850's contributed to increasing bitterness among the sections.

2. Agree or disagree with the following statement, and give evidence to support your opinion: "If the Kansas-Nebraska Act had not been passed, the Civil War might have been avoided."

3. Show why each became a sectional issue: the Dred Scott Decision, John Brown's Raid, the Election of 1860.

4. Explain why each of the following has been considered a basic cause of the Civil War: (a) differing economic and social systems (b) sectionalism (c) slavery (d) declining Southern influence in government (e) weaknesses in leadership.

5. "The formation of the Republican Party was a sign of the times." Explain.

6. Some historians have argued that the Civil War was inevitable (the "Irrepressible Conflict"). Others have maintained that it could have been avoided (the "Repressible Conflict"). Some have blamed the Southern leaders for seceding. Others have argued that neither section can be blamed. Giving facts and reasons, explain fully how you feel about the coming of the Civil War.

REVIEWING UNIT FOUR

Select the number preceding the word or expression that best completes each statement or answers each question.

1. During the period 1815–60, United States foreign policy was chiefly concerned with (1) adjustment of boundaries (2) regulation of the importation of slaves (3) recognition of our rights as a neutral (4) formation of alliances with European powers

2. The history of the United States tariff between 1800 and 1860 shows that (1) President Jackson supported the South in its stand on the tariff (2) the South consistently opposed a protective tariff (3) the tariff issue contributed to the conflict between North and South over states' rights (4) the tariff was needed to restore American industry destroyed during the War of 1812

3. The Monroe Doctrine gave moral support to the actions of (1) Juan Peron (2) Simon Bolivar (3) Sam Houston (4) Napoleon III

4. The term "manifest destiny" is generally associated with United States' (1) territorial expansion in the 19th century (2) emergence as a world power in the 20th century (3) opposition to Japanese aggression in the Pacific (4) protective attitude toward South America

5. "Popular sovereignty" was a doctrine designed to settle the problem of (1) how a settler could get free land (2) whether slavery should be allowed to expand into new territories (3) whether industrial or rural areas should control state legislatures (4) what were to be the residence requirements for voting in new states

6. The Webster-Ashburton Treaty brought about a peaceful settlement of the controversy over the (1) Panama Canal tolls (2) boundary between Maine and New Brunswick (3) Alabama claims (4) trade with the West Indies

7. The state that had an independent government prior to admission into the Union was (1) Florida (2) Ohio (3) Oregon (4) Texas

8. To arrive at the most valid conclusions about the relations between the United States and Mexico in 1846, one should consult (1) editorials in periodicals published at that time (2) the diary of a soldier in General Taylor's army (3) an account of President Polk's message to Congress (4) the writings of several historians who have different points of view

9. The political philosophy of the Western frontier in the period 1800–50 was (1) opposed to the expenditure of public money for education (2) favorable to limitation of the suffrage (3) opposed to internal improvements at national expense (4) favorable to more democratic political institutions

10. The West supported all of the following *except* (1) the Second Bank of the United States (2) squatters' rights (3) internal improvements at national expense (4) cheap public lands

11. Before 1820 most farmers in the Ohio Valley sent their products to Eastern markets by way of the (1) Great Lakes (2) Cumberland Road (3) Erie Canal (4) Mississippi River

12. Which of the following men is paired with the field in which he was most prominent? (1) Samuel Slater — agriculture (2) Washington Irving — industry (3) Robert Fulton — literature (4) Henry Barnard — public education

13. Distinguished American writers of the early 19th century were: (1) Walter Lippman, Edna Ferber, William Allen White (2) Walt Whitman, Hamlin Garland, Carl Sandburg (3) Bret Harte, Nathaniel Hawthorne, Dorothy Canfield Fisher (4) Edgar Allan Poe, James Fenimore Cooper, Washington Irving

14. Which event occurred first? (1) completion of the first transcontinental railroad (2) invention of the telegraph by Morse (3) invention of the sewing machine by Elias Howe (4) opening of the Erie Canal

15. In which of the following was the second event a result of the first? (1) the XYZ affair — Whiskey Rebellion (2) Lincoln–Douglas Debates — "Freeport Doctrine" (3) Louisiana Purchase — signing of the Pinckney Treaty (4) Battle of New Orleans — outbreak of War of 1812

16. In which of the following was the second event a result of the first? (1) outbreak of the Napoleonic Wars — enactment of the Embargo Act (2) passage of the Missouri Compromise — Alabama claims (3) Tariff of 1828 — calling of the Hartford Convention (4) Homestead Act — establishment of "pet banks"

17. What American statesman held political and economic ideas most similar to those of Alexander Hamilton? (1) Thomas Jefferson (2) Andrew Jackson (3) Daniel Webster (4) William Jennings Bryan

18. Which of the following was most favorable to the proslavery interests? (1) Missouri Compromise (2) Northwest Ordinance (3) Dred Scott Decision (4) Compromise of 1850

19. The doctrine which stated that a state could refuse to permit a law of Congress to be enforced within its borders was (1) abolition (2) nullification (3) secession (4) expatriation

20. Many Southerners supported the Compromise of 1850 because it (1) contained a law for the return of fugitive slaves (2) prevented the admission of California (3) legalized slavery in Missouri (4) provided for a Southern railroad route

21. The theory that the Federal government was a compact or contract among the states was expressed in (1) Lee's Resolutions (2) the theory of Manifest Destiny (3) South Carolina's Exposition and Protest (4) Webster's reply to Hayne

22. In which case did a Supreme Court decision result in a clear need to define citizenship in the Constitution? (1) *Marbury v. Madison* (2) *Brown v. the Board of Education of Topeka* (3) *Dred Scott v. Sanford* (4) *McCulloch v. Maryland*

23. Sectionalism (1) disappeared after the Civil War (2) was advocated by the South only (3) still exists because of different economic and political problems (4) has been promoted by immigration

24. In 1860, 19 million bushels of corn went east over the railroads while 4.8 million bushels went south over the Mississippi-Ohio system. This statement helps to explain the (1) victory of canals over railroads in transportation (2) sympathy of the West for the South in the secession movement (3) dislike of Southern cotton farmers for the West (4) support given the North by the West in the Civil War

25. Westerners opposed the Bank of the United States because they (1) feared inflation (2) believed the Bank favored the debtor class (3) could not borrow money from it (4) believed that the moneyed class received most of the benefits

Select the letter of the item in each group that does **NOT** *belong with the others.*

1. National issues, 1825–60: (a) establishment of a United States Bank (b) levying a protective tariff (c) admission of new states (d) free coinage of silver

2. Leaders in westward expansion: (a) Meriwether Lewis (b) Charles Sumner (c) Joseph Smith (d) Marcus Whitman

3. Headlines of the period 1815–50:

(a) **TEXAS ANNEXED**   (c) **LEWIS AND CLARK RETURN**

(b) **JACKSON RE-ELECTED**   (d) **SECOND BANK CHARTERED**

4. Reformers of the "Age of Jackson": (a) Dorothea Dix (b) Horace Mann (c) Emma Willard (d) Clara Barton

5. Agreements or treaties with Britain: (a) Guadalupe-Hidalgo (b) Webster-Ashburton (c) Rush-Bagot (d) Joint Occupation of Oregon

On the time line, the letters **A** *through* **E** *represent time intervals, as indicated. For each event listed below, select the letter of the time interval during which the event occurred.*

	A		B		C		D		E	
1815		1825		1835		1845		1855		1865

1. *Uncle Tom's Cabin* is published.

2. Florida is purchased.

3. Buchanan is inaugurated.

4. The Mexican War ends.

5. The "Tariff of Abominations" is passed.

6. Oregon is annexed.

7. The Monroe Doctrine is issued.

8. The Whig Party captures the Presidency for the first time.

9. John Brown is captured and hanged.

10. The Specie Circular is issued.

Match each name in Column A with the letter of the item in Column B that is most clearly identified with it.

A	B
1. Henry Clay	*a.* "Reannexation of Texas and Reoccupation of Oregon"
2. John Marshall	*b.* An editor who urged young Americans to "go West" and opposed the extension of slavery
3. James Monroe	*c.* An essayist and reformer who campaigned for women's rights and urged self-reliance.
4. James Polk	*d.* A Supreme Court justice whose reasoning pleased the South
5. Andrew Jackson	*e.* A general who invaded Mexico
6. Horace Greeley	*f.* Senator, Secretary of State, Secretary of War, Vice President
7. Ralph Waldo Emerson	*g.* First a War Hawk and later a great compromiser
8. Roger Taney	*h.* "We should consider any attempt on their part to extend their system to . . . this hemisphere as dangerous . . ."
9. Winfield Scott	*i.* A military leader who became President
10. John C. Calhoun	*j.* Abolitionist editor murdered by a mob
	k. "The power to tax involves the power to destroy."

Essay Questions

1. Describe two developments during the period following the War of 1812 that illustrate the growth of nationalism.

2. Discuss briefly three issues that caused sectionalism to develop during the period 1820–60.

3. Explain two ways in which westward expansion in the United States was related to each of the following in the period 1800–60: (a) slavery (b) foreign policy (c) growth of democracy.

4. Discuss the following with respect to Andrew Jackson: (a) two activities that made him prominent before his election as President (b) one important domestic issue that arose during his administration (c) one lasting influence that he has had on the nation's history.

5. Each of the men below — although never President — nevertheless influenced significantly the history of the United States or of his state. Describe briefly an important influence of each upon the history of the United States or upon the history of his state.

Henry Clay   Stephen A. Douglas
Daniel Webster   John C. Calhoun
John C. Frémont   William Lloyd Garrison
Sam Houston   Brigham Young

6. In a democracy political differences are both inevitable and desirable. Below are listed three pairs of individuals who held opposite points of view on important issues in American history. For each of the pairs below, discuss one issue on which the persons differed, giving the point of view of each person. (a) John C. Calhoun — Andrew Jackson (b) Daniel Webster — Robert Hayne (c) Abraham Lincoln — Stephen A. Douglas.

7. Discuss one important political and one important economic result of the (a) War of 1812 and (b) Mexican War.

8. Discuss two reasons for agreeing or disagreeing with each of the following statements. (a) Reform movements of the Jacksonian Era were a failure. (b) Andrew Jackson deserved the nickname of "King Andrew." (c) The main responsibility for the Mexican War rests with Mexico. (d) The Civil War was inevitable.

9. Explain one way in which each of the following helped to bring about the Civil War: (1) the states'-rights theory (2) the tariff issue (3) the abolitionists (4) the Kansas-Nebraska Act (5) the Dred Scott Decision.

10. Explain five ways in which the United States of 1860 differed from the United States of 1815.

CHAPTER 14

The Civil War

The Civil War was a major turning point in American history. It established the permanence and supremacy of the Union and led to the complete abolition of slavery. It caused national attention to be shifted to new interests and developments. It was also a tragic episode, leaving wounds that still have not healed completely.

The different attitudes toward the Civil War are reflected by the different names given to it. At first the United States government called it the *War of the Rebellion,* and later the *Civil War.* Many Southerners have preferred to call it the *War Between the States* or the *War of Southern Independence.*

Union and Confederate Resources Compared. When the Civil War began, both the North and the South relied upon certain assets which each hoped would bring victory.

1. *Advantages of the North.* The advantages of the North appeared, in many respects, to be overwhelming.

(a) It had a well-established central government that was recognized abroad.

(b) It far surpassed the South in population, natural resources, financial wealth, and transportation facilities.

(c) It produced most of the nation's foodstuffs and manufactured goods (including iron and steel); it had nearly all the nation's mines.

(d) There was a large supply of skilled labor in the North.

(e) The North was in an advantageous position because it did not suffer from certain handicaps which limited the South, such as dependence on one crop (cotton), the need to import manufactured goods, and the new Confederate government's weaknesses (see pages 251-52).

2. *Advantages of the South.* The Confederacy based its hope for victory on a number of factors.

(a) Fighting a predominantly defensive war on their own soil, the Southerners might be expected to have higher morale than the Northern "invaders." Also, defensive operations on familiar terrain would require smaller numbers of troops than an offensive campaign.

(b) The Confederacy believed that its military leaders and soldiers were superior to those in the North.

(c) The South also expected its slaves to provide the food and supplies that would be needed, freeing the rest of the male population for military duty.

(d) It hoped that the border states would join the Confederacy, and that both France and England, its customers, would give it aid.

3. *An Unexpectedly Long War.* Despite the overwhelming superiority of the North, the war dragged on for four years (1861–65). There were several reasons.

(a) Neither side was well prepared for war. War supplies were lacking, and raw troops had to be trained rapidly.

(b) The South, as indicated, had the advantage of fighting most of the war on its own territory.

(c) At the beginning of the war, Northern armies were led by generals who lacked experience, ability, and fighting spirit.

The Strategy of the War. Each side had its own overall plan for victory.

1. *The Northern Plan.* The North hoped to defeat the Confederacy by "squeezing it to death," the so-called *anaconda policy.* This involved: **(a)** cutting off European assistance to the Confederacy by setting up a naval blockade along the Southern coasts; **(b)** cutting the South in two by seizing control of the Mississippi River; **(c)** driving into the heart of the South and capturing the Confederate capital, Richmond, Virginia.

2. *The Southern Plan.* The Southern plan was primarily defensive. Aside from attempting to capture Washington, D. C. by way of the Shenandoah Valley, and sending occasional raiding parties into the North, Confederate leaders hoped to defeat the Northern armies that invaded the South. Southern leaders believed that the South could win the war and establish its national independence simply by repelling Northern attacks. The North, in contrast, had to crush Southern resistance and occupy the territory of the Confederacy.

Military Highlights of the Civil War. Although it took longer than expected, the Northern plan of blockading, dividing, and crushing the South was in the end successful. The South surrendered in April, 1865. The war's more outstanding developments are outlined below.

The War on the Sea. Among the more important naval operations of the Civil War were the establishment of a blockade by the North and the use of foreign-built cruisers by the South.

1. During the war the Union maintained an effective blockade of Southern ports. It was established loosely at the beginning of the war and tightened as the war proceeded. The blockade was an important element in Northern victory, for eventually it cut off virtually all foreign aid to the Confederacy.

2. The most famous — though unsuccessful — effort to break the blockade took place in March, 1862. At that time, the ironclad Union vessel, *Monitor,* prevented the Confederate ironclad *Merrimac* from breaking the blockade at Hampton Roads, Virginia. This battle is said to have revolutionized naval warfare, as it foreshadowed the end of wooden ships.

3. Since the Confederacy had few warships or shipyards of its own, it secretly bought several cruisers from Great Britain. These preyed upon Northern commerce. The *Alabama, Florida,* and other armed cruisers of this type captured or destroyed many Northern vessels.

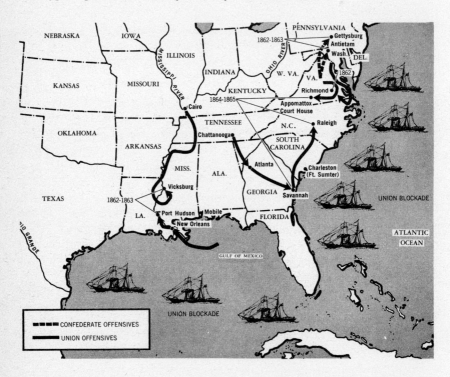

The campaigns of the Civil War.

The War in the West. The two major theaters of land warfare were the *West,* or the territory west of the Appalachians, and the *East,* particularly between the two capitals, Washington and Richmond. Although the Union lost battles in the West, it won all the major campaigns and thus was successful in cutting the Confederacy in two.

1. In 1861, Northern forces drove Southern troops out of the border states of *Kentucky* and *Missouri.* They thus prevented the use of the Ohio River as a Southern line of defense.

2. In 1862, the Confederacy was squeezed from both the north and the south. Led by General ULYSSES S. GRANT, Union forces drove south along the Mississippi River, winning a series of notable victories in battles at Shiloh, Fort Henry, Fort Donelson, and Memphis in western Tennessee. At the same time Admiral DAVID G. FARRAGUT captured New Orleans (April, 1862). Grant's brilliant and hard-won victory at *Vicksburg, Mississippi,* in July, 1863, gave the Union control of the Mississippi River and split the Confederacy, cutting the Atlantic coast off from much needed supplies.

3. In 1864, Grant became commander-in-chief of the Union armies and was succeeded in the West by General WILLIAM T. SHERMAN. In September, 1864, Sherman captured Atlanta and then marched 300 miles across Georgia to the sea. By December, Sherman had captured Savannah on the coast. Then the Union forces turned northward and invaded the Carolinas. As Sherman's army moved through the South, it lived off the land and laid waste or destroyed virtually everything that might be of value to the Confederate war effort. (Sherman felt that these tactics were necessary for victory. The Southerners, however, were extremely bitter over what they felt was needless destruction and brutality.)

The War in the East. In the Eastern theater, the Union suffered many defeats and disappointments before its greater resources made possible the final victory.

1. At the very outset of the war, Northern forces were humiliated by a Southern victory at the battle of *Bull Run* (Virginia). In the years that followed, Confederate Generals ROBERT E. LEE and T. J. ("STONEWALL") JACKSON outmaneuvered and outfought the larger Army of the Potomac. The Southerners won notable victories at the *Second Battle of Bull Run* (1862), *Fredericksburg* (1862), and *Chancellorsville* (1863). (All of these battles were in northern Virginia.)

2. Lee's attempts to exploit his victories by invading the North were less successful. He was checked at *Antietam* (Maryland) in 1862 and at *Gettysburg* (Pennsylvania) in 1863. The victory of the Union forces under General GEORGE G. MEADE at Gettysburg is usually considered to be a high point of the Civil War. The Confederate forces, repulsed with heavy losses, were never again able to invade Northern territory after Gettysburg. Foreign powers were now convinced that the Southern cause was hopeless. Moreover, this great victory, coming at the same time as Grant's triumph at Vicksburg, gave new confidence and spirit to the Northern armies and buoyed the morale of the home front throughout the North.

The War Comes to an End (1864-65). In 1864, President Lincoln put General Grant in charge of military operations in the Eastern theater of war. This action was based on the failure of such earlier commanders as McClellan, Pope, Burnside, and Hooker to defeat Lee, as well as upon Grant's victories in the West. Grant brought final victory to the Union.

1. Grant continued to hammer at Lee's forces. The *Wilderness Campaign,* which began late in 1864, was very costly to both sides. Although Lee put up strong resistance, he could not replace the men and equipment he lost. As the exhausted Southerners retreated, Petersburg, the "back door" to Richmond, was taken. Then Grant entered Richmond itself.

2. While Grant was moving south, Sherman was moving north. Caught in a squeeze, and unable to escape westward, Lee surrendered to Grant at the little village of *Appomattox Court House,* Virginia on April 9, 1865. In a generous gesture, Grant allowed Lee's troops to go home upon their giving their word not to fight again.

3. By May, 1865, all other Confederate armies had surrendered, and the Civil War was at an end.

Characteristics of the Civil War. The following were noteworthy characteristics of the Civil War.

1. *The Use of Cavalry.* Cavalry played an important role, perhaps for the last time in a major war.

2. *The Role of Women.* Women took an active role behind the lines. They manned factories in the North and plantations in the South, to release men for active duty. They served as nurses on both sides. Led by Clara Barton, who later became the first president of the American Red Cross, women provided welfare services for soldiers, widows, and orphans.

3. *The Role of Negroes.* More than 185,000 Negroes fought in the Union Armies and made a major contribution to the final victory. President Lincoln and other leaders paid tribute to the valor and ability of these Black fighters.

4. *The First Modern War.* The Civil War has been called the first modern war. **(a)** It was the first war in which *railroads* were important. **(b)** It introduced *trench warfare,* later to be used in World War I. **(c)** It was a *"total war"* in the sense that civilians shared the burdens of war with the military, especially in the war-torn South. In addition, Union armies adopted a "scorched earth" policy of laying waste areas through which they marched. Casualties were extremely heavy on both sides.

Wartime Problems of the North and South. Both sides had to meet serious problems during the Civil War.

1 *Financial Problems.* Each side resorted to emergency measures to raise sufficient money to fight the war.

    (*a*) The *North* financed the war by increasing the protective tariff (*Morrill Act* of 1862); by raising internal revenue duties; by issuing unbacked paper money (*greenbacks*), which fluctuated rapidly in value according to the success of the Union forces; by selling bonds; and by collecting taxes on incomes. To hasten bond sales, Congress in 1863 set up the *National Banking System.* Under this system, any state bank or any five persons with adequate capital could organize a National Bank, provided they invested one-third of the minimum capital in government bonds. The bonds were to be deposited in the United States Treasury. The National Banks thus established were then allowed to issue National Banknotes, first up to 90%, and later up to 100% of the value of the bonds deposited. This system was highly successful in raising money for the government.

(b) The *South* had more serious financial problems than the North. When the war broke out, the Confederate government had only limited funds. Hopes of raising funds through the sale of cotton to Europe were thwarted by the blockade. In desperation, the Confederate government sold bonds, levied heavy taxes, and issued paper money. The bonds and paper currency declined rapidly in value as the war went on. Taxes became increasingly difficult to collect.

2. *Production Problems.* In large measure the North defeated the South because the war stimulated, rather than hindered, its production facilities.

(a) Northern factories turned out an abundance of arms, munitions, uniforms, and other equipment. Northern and Western farms produced sufficient food for home consumption, as well as surpluses which were sold abroad.

(b) In contrast, the South lacked adequate production facilities. Though it managed to provide sufficient arms and ammunition, other necessities were continually in short supply. As the war progressed, serious shortages of food, clothing, and sanitary facilities developed on both the military and home fronts.

3. *Problems of Government.* To raise armies and provide effective government, the governments of both the Union and the Confederacy had to resort to extraordinary measures.

(a) Both governments had to draft soldiers into the army (*conscription*), since volunteers were insufficient to fill the ranks after the first few months. In the North, a provision allowing for exemption from service upon payment of $300 to the government aroused opposition to the draft, and helped bring on serious *draft riots* in New York City in 1863.

(b) Both governments also assumed broad wartime powers. In the South, for example, the Confederate government forced citizens to contribute foodstuffs, slaves, mules, and wagons. In the North, the government took over and ran the railroads in and near war zones.

(c) Both Lincoln and Davis exercised so much power as wartime leaders that they were accused of being dictators. Lincoln called for volunteers, expanded the army, and spent money before it was appropriated by Congress. In order to combat subversive activities by individuals and groups sympathetic to the Confederacy ("Copperheads"), he restricted civil liberties. Among such measures were: suspension of the writ of habeas corpus in certain districts, authorization of trial of civilians by military courts, and limitations on freedom of speech and press. Lincoln defended these moves by asserting that they were essential for swift and decisive action in a time of great national crisis. It has also been pointed out, in answer to Lincoln's critics, that he made no attempts to interfere with free elections, to reduce the authority of Congress, or to build up a private military force that would perpetuate his own power. The sole aim of all his actions and policies was the triumph of the Union cause.

(d) The effectiveness of the Confederate government was seriously weakened by anti-Confederacy feeling, especially in West Virginia, the Carolinas, and Alabama. In North Carolina and Georgia, states'-rights feelings often caused these states to ignore requests of the central government of the Confederacy.

Foreign Relations During the Civil War. During the Civil War, there were important diplomatic involvements with Great Britain, France and Russia.

1. *Relations with Britain.* When the Confederacy went to war, it hoped to receive all-out British support. Britain was considered to be absolutely dependent on Southern cotton. Moreover, British manufacturers might be expected to favor Southern independence on the grounds that such a country, with a rural economy, would be less likely than the Union to levy a protective tariff on incoming British goods. In addition, British aristocrats feared American democracy and favored the South. Although Great Britain did recognize and aid the Confederacy, especially in the early years of the war, it remained officially neutral, contrary to Southern hopes.

(a) *The Trent Affair.* The *Trent Affair* caused hard feelings between Britain and the North early in the war. In 1861, a Union warship stopped a British steamship, the *Trent,* in the Caribbean Sea, and removed two Confederate diplomats, Mason and Slidell. The British government demanded their release on the ground that Britain's rights as a neutral (freedom of the seas) had been violated. Feeling ran high until Lincoln released the Confederate agents.

(b) *The Alabama Claims.* Later in the war, the North repeatedly protested the sale of British-built cruisers to the Confederacy, especially since these were used to destroy Northern commerce. The complaint was that Britain had violated its neutrality. After the war the United States government requested payment for damages to its shipping (the *Alabama Claims*). In 1872, the United States was awarded $15,500,000 by an international board of arbitration — a sum which Britain promptly paid.

(c) *Britain Fails to Give All-Out Support to the South.* Despite its general sympathy towards the South, the British government refrained from officially abandoning its neutrality and openly supporting the Southern cause. **(1)** British manufacturers were able to get cotton from other sources. **(2)** British manufacturers made unexpected profits selling war materials to the North; also, British importers needed American wheat. **(3)** The British working classes looked upon Lincoln as the champion of democracy and were opposed to slavery.

2. *Relations with France.* The United States was antagonized by French actions during the Civil War. Emperor Napoleon III of France took advan-

tage of the fighting between North and South to extend the French Empire: he sent an army into Mexico and placed Austrian Archduke Maximilian on the throne. During the war the United States could do nothing but protest this action as a violation of the Monroe Doctrine. After the war, however, our government indicated that it was prepared to use force to expel the invaders. Napoleon thereupon withdrew the French troops, and the Mexicans captured and executed Maximilian.

3. *Relations with Russia.* Unlike France and England, Russia remained friendly to the North throughout the war. In 1867, when Russia offered to sell *Alaska* to the United States, we purchased it for $7,200,000, largely as a gesture of gratitude. (Alaska was considered all but worthless.) Secretary of State William Seward, who supported the purchase, looked upon Alaska as a strategic means of expanding United States power in the Pacific.

Lincoln's War Aims. Lincoln's stated aim at the beginning of the war was "to save the Union"; it was not his purpose at the time either "to save or destroy slavery." He was keenly aware that if antislavery measures were taken too early in the war, the Union might lose the support of the border states and also impair unity of purpose throughout the North.

Later in the war, Lincoln decided to free the slaves. His purposes were to give greater meaning and moral purpose to the war, to satisfy growing sentiment in the North in favor of emancipation, and to gain public support in Great Britain. Lincoln announced his intention to emancipate the slaves after the Union forces defeated Lee at Antietam, late in 1862 (page 249).

The Emancipation Proclamation. By the *Emancipation Proclamation,* issued on January 1, 1863, all the slaves in Confederate-held territory were declared free. It should be noted that the Proclamation did not immediately free a single slave because it applied *only* to areas not controlled by the Union. The Proclamation, however, became of great importance as a symbol. Thereafter, most of the people in the North considered themselves to be fighting a war to end human bondage and remedy a great social evil. Moreover, as the Union forces took over Southern territory, the slaves in those areas were freed.

The Thirteenth Amendment (1865). To free the slaves in areas where the Emancipation Proclamation did *not* apply (for example, in the border states and in Southern territory conquered before 1863), Congress drafted the *Thirteenth Amendment,* which was ratified in 1865. It abolished slavery throughout the United States.

Lincoln as Wartime Leader. As a wartime leader, President Lincoln faced many critical and difficult challenges.

1. *Opposition to Lincoln's Prosecution of the War.* Almost from the beginning, Lincoln's conduct of the war was under continued attack. At first he was bitterly criticized for not making the abolition of slavery a war aim. He was also blamed for early Union defeats. In addition, he was called a tyrant and would-be dictator for exercising extraordinary powers (page 251). During the Congressional elections of 1862, when Union armies were losing battles, the Democratic Party increased its strength in the House of Representatives.

2. *Election of 1864.* In 1864, Lincoln was re-elected on a platform of no compromise with the Confederacy. Though his popular majority was small, he won an overwhelming majority in the Electoral College, since he carried nearly every state still in the Union. In this election, the Republicans formed an alliance with pro-Union Northern Democrats, and Lincoln actually ran as the candidate of the so-called *Union Party*. ANDREW JOHNSON, a Unionist Democrat from Tennessee, was his running mate. (During Lincoln's first term, the Vice President was Hannibal Hamlin.)

(a) Lincoln's opponent on the Democratic ticket was the popular General GEORGE B. MCCLELLAN, whom the President had twice removed from the command of the Army of the Potomac. The Democrats opposed the war as a bloody failure, and called for immediate steps to end it by negotiation.

(b) Until shortly before the election it was not certain that Lincoln would be re-elected. However, a series of Union military victories, and the general feeling that it was unwise to "swap horses in midstream," helped make his re-election possible.

3. *The Death of Lincoln.* Shortly after the end of the war, at the beginning of his second term, President Lincoln was assassinated by a half-crazed, fanatical actor, John Wilkes Booth (April 14, 1865).

The Greatness of Lincoln. Lincoln's reputation as a President and as a man has grown enormously since the end of the Civil War. How is it that a President subjected to so much abuse during the war has ever since been considered one of America's greatest leaders? Several factors help to explain this.

1. *His Leadership Qualities.* Lincoln emerged as a dynamic and devoted wartime leader. Though he lacked experience in executive office when the war began, he grew in stature as the war progressed. He proved to be patient, tactful, and firm. He showed marked ability to interpret and lead public opinion. Despite increasing pressures within his own party and among Northern Democrats to end the war early and let the South have its independence, Lincoln insisted that it be fought to the bitter end. He played an important role in guiding military strategy and in providing national leadership.

2. *His Personal Qualities.* Lincoln's personal qualities won him the trust and admiration of most of his countrymen. He was affectionately referred to as "Old Abe" and "Father Abraham."

(a) Lincoln showed an unusual sense of *forbearance*. He accepted personal abuse and attacks of Northern critics with good humor rather than bitterness. He never expressed hatred of slaveholders as individuals, although he believed deeply that slavery was wrong.

(b) He displayed a high degree of *forgiveness* toward the Confederacy. In his famous *Second Inaugural Address* delivered on March 4, 1865, shortly before the end of the war, Lincoln called for "malice toward none," "charity for all," and care for *all* the victims of the war, including soldiers, widows, and orphans on *both* sides.

(c) In his famous *Gettysburg Address* and other utterances, Lincoln expressed the noblest ideals of American democracy with matchless eloquence. He described the United States in unforgettable terms as ". . . a new nation conceived in Liberty and dedicated to the proposition that all men are created equal." The war, as he saw it, was being fought to make sure that ". . . government of the people, by the people, for the people shall not perish from the earth." Hating violence and bloodshed but compelled to use military force to save the Union, Lincoln called on the nation to ". . . highly resolve that these dead shall not have died in vain."

(d) Lincoln was *charitable* toward his enemies. He granted generous surrender terms to the defeated armies of the Confederacy. He also called for *moderation*, rather than hatred in restoring the South to the Union.

(e) Lincoln's personal *kindness* and *compassion* were illustrated by tender letters of condolence written to Union parents who had lost sons in battle, and by his concern for captured and wounded Confederate soldiers.

3. *His Assassination.* Lincoln's assassination at the moment of victory and height of his fame made him a martyr. The North mourned him as a war hero and national leader who had held the Union together. Southerners recognized more and more, as time went on, that Lincoln was the one person who might have curbed the bitterness and hatred which characterized the postwar years. Much later, Jefferson Davis ventured the opinion that, "next to the destruction of the Confederacy, the death of Abraham Lincoln was the darkest day the South has known."

Results of the Civil War. The Civil War had many significant results.

1. *Heavy Losses in Life and Property.* About 1,000,000 men were killed or wounded in the Civil War. In addition, it has been estimated that the cost of the war in military expenses and destroyed property was over 15 billion dollars. The South, which suffered most, lost the flower of its young manhood, and had its farms and cities laid waste.

2. *Preservation of the Union.* The war preserved the Union and brought to an end the challenges of *state sovereignty, nullification,* and *secession.* The supremacy of the national government was assured.

3. *Expansion of the Constitution.* As a result of the assumption of increased powers by both the President and Congress, the war contributed to a broader interpretation of the Constitution.

4. *Emancipation of the Slaves.* The Civil War resulted in the emancipation of the slaves. The *Thirteenth, Fourteenth,* and *Fifteenth Amendments* gave the Negro freedom, citizenship, and the right to vote.

5. *Industrial and Commercial Expansion in the North.* The war contributed to the industrial and commercial expansion which had begun in the 1850's. The needs of the fighting forces greatly stimulated production in the North. The postwar industrial and agricultural boom in the North and West benefited from such wartime developments as the passage of a *protective tariff* (1862) and the establishment of a *National Banking System* (1863).

6. *Growth of the West.* Actions taken during the Civil War also helped pave the way for the development of the West. The government offered free land to settlers under the *Homestead Act* of 1862. It gave public support to agricultural colleges under the *Morrill Act* of 1862. It established a policy of generous assistance for the building of transcontinental railroads. In addition, wartime manpower shortages hastened the introduction of labor-saving machinery on the farms.

7. *End of the "Old South."* The war undermined the economy and social system of the *"Old South."* The plantation system was destroyed, and many former plantation owners were reduced to poverty. The newly freed Negroes and many poor whites found themselves without means of livelihood. Former Southern leaders were, for a time, excluded from political power.

8. *The Reconstruction Period and the Rise of a "New South."* The war was followed by a tragic and bitter period of *Reconstruction* in the South. During this time, the Southern states were gradually readmitted to the Union, and the foundations of a new political, social, and economic system were laid down.

REVIEW TEST (Chapter 14)

Select the number preceding the word or expression that best completes each statement or answers each question.

1. The immediate cause of the Civil War was the   (1) attack on Fort Sumter   (2) Dred Scott Decision   (3) the Thirteenth Amendment   (4) Battle of Bull Run

2. The major purpose of the blockade during the Civil War was to prevent   (1) English volunteers from going to the South   (2) export of cotton to Europe   (3) Confederate officials from going to Europe   (4) the Russian fleet visiting the South

3. During the Civil War, which of the following aroused the greatest open opposition on the part of Northerners?   (1) suspension of the writ of habeas corpus   (2) issuance of greenbacks   (3) military draft   (4) levy of an income tax

4. The Emancipation Proclamation was   (1) a law passed by Congress   (2) an amendment to the Constitution   (3) a Presidential order   (4) a joint resolution of Congress

5. What group in England showed the most sympathy for the Union cause during the Civil War in the United States?   (1) large landowners   (2) governing classes   (3) factory workers   (4) merchants

6. Why did the Trent Affair cause tension between the United States and Great Britain? (1) The British had enforced the practice of impressment. (2) The United States had violated British neutral rights on the high seas. (3) The *Trent* had broken the Union blockade of the South. (4) The *Trent* had been built for the Confederacy by the British.

7. In 1865, President Lincoln applied the Monroe Doctrine in resisting foreign interference in (1) Mexico (2) Venezuela (3) Santo Domingo (4) Cuba

8. The major purpose of the Homestead Act of 1862 was to (1) create future slave states (2) raise revenue for the Federal government (3) encourage settlement of public lands for farming (4) provide "favored" land companies with new lands

9. The Morrill Act of 1862 aided education by giving (1) to each state the right to control its own schools (2) to colleges funds for research (3) to each state public land from which the income was to be used for agricultural colleges (4) to the central government a grant of money to set up a Federal office of education

10. A long-lasting effect of the Civil War in the South was the (1) continuance of a "one-crop economy" (2) protection of civil rights of Negroes (3) reduction of racial tensions (4) development of a changed pattern of economic and social relationships

Select the letter of the item in each group which does **NOT** *belong with the others.*

1. Nations committing acts unfavorable to the Union cause during the Civil War: (a) Russia (b) England (c) France (d) Mexico

2. Southern military leaders in the Civil War: (a) Stonewall Jackson (b) George F. Meade (c) Robert E. Lee (d) J. E. B. Stuart

3. Related to the Alabama Claims dispute: (a) destruction of Northern commerce (b) sale of British-built ships to the Confederacy (c) final payment of damages to the United States (d) removal of Confederate agents Mason and Slidell

4. Advantages of the North in the Civil War: (a) larger population and greater resources (b) more manufacturing facilities (c) outstanding generalship throughout the war (d) a well-established, recognized government

5. Northern military successes during the Civil War: (a) the blockade of Southern ports (b) the battles of Bull Run and Chancellorsville (c) the battles of Vicksburg and Gettysburg (d) the campaigns of Sherman in Georgia and Grant in Virginia

Essay Questions

1. Explain why the Civil War has also been called: the *War Between the States,* the *War of the Rebellion,* the *War of Southern Independence.*

2. Compare the advantages of North and South at the beginning of the Civil War.

3. Discuss briefly the role or importance of each of the following during the Civil War: (a) *Battles:* Bull Run, *Monitor* vs. *Merrimac,* Vicksburg, Gettysburg. (b) *Military leaders:* Ulysses Grant, Robert E. Lee, "Stonewall" Jackson, George Meade, David Farragut.

4. Discuss steps taken by each side in the Civil War to solve the following problems, and indicate why they were successful or unsuccessful: (a) wartime finances (b) wartime production (c) stable and effective government.

5. Explain how either the Union or Confederacy became involved with the following foreign nations during the Civil War: (a) Britain (b) France (c) Russia.

6. Discuss the personal qualities and actions that contributed to Lincoln's greatness during the Civil War.

7. Discuss one important *political,* one *economic,* and one *social* result of the Civil War.

CHAPTER 15

The Era of Reconstruction

The period after the Civil War, during which the Southern states were restored to the Union, is known as the *Reconstruction Era*. The period (1865-77) was one of painful readjustment, the consequences of which are still felt to this day.

The Immediate Problems of Reconstruction. The end of the Civil War posed serious problems for the nation.

1. *Economic Problems.* The economic life of the South had to be rebuilt on the new basis of free labor. The South was suffering from war devastation, social and economic disorganization, and lack of food and other necessities of life. Plantations were in ruin, and thousands of Negroes wandered from place to place without homes or jobs. During the war, many whites had abandoned their homes and farms. Factories, bridges, railroads, and other facilities had been largely wrecked.

2. *Political Problems.* The Southern states had to be brought back into the Union and civil (*nonmilitary*) government, lacking in most Southern states since the end of the war, had to be reestablished.

3. *Social Problems.* In the midst of an atmosphere of hate and bitterness, a new set of relationships between whites and Negroes had to be worked out, and the status of the newly freed Negroes had to be clarified.

Presidential Reconstruction. President Abraham Lincoln and his successor, Andrew Johnson, believed that the South should be restored to the Union quickly, with as few penalties as possible.

1. *Lincoln's 10% Plan.* Lincoln insisted that the war was a mere rebellion, and that the Southern states had in fact never left the Union. Accordingly, he proposed to treat the Southern states as "erring sisters," without bitterness, and to restore them speedily to full and equal status within the Union. His plan for Reconstruction, announced in December, 1863, provided for: **(a)** an amnesty (pardon) for all Southerners who took an oath of loyalty to the Union, except for high leaders of the Confederacy; and **(b)** recognition by the President of any state government established by 10% of the voters as of 1860, if the state accepted the abolition of slavery and repudiated the principle of secession.

2. *Johnson Adopts Lincoln's Policies.* Johnson adopted Lincoln's plan with minor changes. He immediately recognized the governments of Arkansas, Louisiana, Tennessee, and Virginia, which had been set up under Lincoln's plan. By late 1865, when Congress reconvened, every Southern state except Texas had met Johnson's requirements that the ordinance of secession be repealed, that the state constitution be amended to abolish slavery, and that it repudiate the Confederate war debt. Southern delegates awaited admission to Congress.

> NOTE: Neither the Lincoln nor the Johnson plans called for recognition of the rights of Negroes, or for giving them the vote.

3. *Congress Rejects Presidential Reconstruction.* When Congress met in December, 1865, it rejected the Lincoln-Johnson plan, refused to seat the Southern delegates, and withheld recognition of the new state governments. Congressional leaders maintained that the Southern states had in fact left the Union, and that Congress alone could readmit them under its own conditions. House-leader THADDEUS STEVENS argued that the ex-Confederate states should be treated as "conquered provinces." Senate-leader CHARLES SUMNER believed that the Southern states had committed "suicide" when they seceded and could be treated as Congress saw fit.

Congressional Reconstruction. The *Congressional Plan of Reconstruction* was harsher to the South than the Lincoln-Johnson plan. Between 1865 and 1867 Congress took vigorous action to carry out its program.

1. *Aims of the Radical Republicans.* The leaders of the dominant group in Congress, called *Radical Republicans,* intended **(a)** to restore the powers of Congress, which had been overshadowed by those of the President during the war; **(b)** to punish Southern leaders; **(c)** to maintain Republican supremacy in Congress by keeping Southern Democrats out as long as possible; and **(d)** to protect the rights of the freed Negroes against abuse by Southern whites. The Radicals were angered, as were most Northerners, by the passage of a series of laws by Southern legislatures which restricted the rights of Negroes. These *Black Codes* imposed fines and jail penalties on Negroes without jobs, allowed jailed Negroes to be hired out to whites in order to work out their fines, and limited the civil rights of the freedmen. The Black Codes varied in severity from state to state.

2. *The Freedman's Bureau.* In 1865, before the war ended, Congress established the *Freedman's Bureau.* In 1866, the Bureau's powers were extended, over Johnson's veto. (Johnson was opposed to control of such an agency by the military.) The Bureau gave food, clothing, and medicine to poverty-stricken Negroes and whites, and helped them rent land and find jobs. Southerners accused the Bureau of raising false hopes of free land among the freedmen ("Forty acres and a mule").

3. *Civil Rights Act (1866).* In 1866, Congress passed the *Civil Rights Act,* over the President's veto. It gave citizenship to the Negroes, and guaranteed them equal treatment under the law.

4. *Fourteenth Amendment (1866).* In 1866, Congress passed the *Fourteenth Amendment* and referred it to the states for ratification. This amendment **(a)** granted citizenship to the Negro, **(b)** proclaimed that states would have their representation in the House of Representatives reduced if there was discrimination against Negroes as voters, and **(c)** excluded former Confederate officials from holding office.

5. *Military Reconstruction (1867).* The Radical Republicans were encouraged by their victory in the Congressional elections of 1866, which increased their strength in both houses. Angered by the rejection of the Fourteenth Amendment by ten Southern states in late 1866 and early 1867, they passed a series of *Military Reconstruction Acts* in 1867 providing for military government of the South until the Southern states were readmitted into the Union. These laws were passed over Johnson's vetoes. The *Reconstruction Acts* provided for the following:

(a) The ten "unreconstructed" states were to be divided into five military districts, each under the supervision of an army general, who was to act as military governor.

(b) To gain readmission into the Union, each Southern state was required: **(1)** to call a new constitutional convention elected by universal manhood suffrage, **(2)** to establish a state constitution and a government which guaranteed Negro suffrage and disqualified former Confederate leaders from voting, and **(3)** to ratify the Fourteenth Amendment.

Readmission of the Southern States. By the end of 1868, seven Southern states had complied with the conditions of Congress, and were readmitted to the Union. Mississippi, Texas, and Virginia did not go along immediately; they were readmitted in 1870, by which time they were required to accept the Fifteenth as well as the Fourteenth Amendment. (The *Fifteenth Amendment,* adopted in 1870, was intended to guarantee the Negro the right to vote.) Upon readmission, the military governors turned over the administration of government to new state and local officials. Federal troops, however, continued for several years to be stationed in the Southern states.

Congress Impeaches Johnson. From the beginning of his Presidency, a feud developed between Johnson and Congress. Radical Republican leaders opposed Johnson's proposals for lenient treatment of the South, were angered by his vetoes, and distrusted him as a Southern Democrat before the Civil War. Johnson was a self-made man with a long record of public service in state and national government. He was also a person of ability and integrity. However, he lacked the tact and the prestige of Lincoln. His blunt and often angry remarks frequently antagonized both Congress and the public. The feud was climaxed by Johnson's impeachment by Congress.

1. *Tenure of Office Act (1867).* In order to restrict Johnson's powers and lay the groundwork for possible later impeachment, Congress passed the *Tenure of Office Act* in 1867. The Act prohibited the President from removing government officials without the consent of the Senate. Johnson declared the act unconstitutional.

2. *Johnson Removes Stanton.* In 1868 Johnson removed his Secretary of War, Edwin M. Stanton, from the Cabinet. Stanton had opposed Johnson's Reconstruction policies and had consistently sided with the President's Radical Republican opponents.

3. *Impeachment of Johnson.* The House of Representatives immediately passed a resolution calling for the President's impeachment for "high crimes and misdemeanors in office." Chief Justice Salmon P. Chase presided at the trial before the Senate in 1868.

4. *Johnson's Acquittal.* Johnson was found not guilty of the charges, after two months of debate, during which time it became evident that there was no clear legal ground for his removal. Despite the weakness of the case against him, Johnson was narrowly acquitted by a vote of 35 for impeachment and 19 against. This was just one vote short of the necessary two-thirds majority required for removal from office.

5. *Decline in the Influence of the Radical Republicans.* The attack of the Radical Republicans on Johnson, as well as other policies of theirs, began to turn public opinion against them. This was made evident in the Presidential election of 1868 by the comparatively small majority of the popular vote won by the Republican candidate, ULYSSES S. GRANT. It was clear that the Republicans might have lost the election without the Negro vote. It was partly for this reason that the Radicals in Congress introduced the Fifteenth Amendment, guaranteeing that the right to vote should not be denied to United States citizens because of "race, color, or previous condition of servitude."

Reconstruction in the South (1867-77). The decade of Reconstruction in the South was a period of great change. Because of the confusion and bitterness which prevailed, it has been called a "tragic era."

1. *Establishment of the Reconstruction Governments.* The new state legislatures established under the *Military Reconstruction Acts,* with Negroes voting, were made up for the most part of Northern "carpetbaggers," Southern "scalawags," and Negroes. The "carpetbaggers" tended to dominate these bodies because of the inexperience of the Negro legislators. They were Northerners who had moved to the South after the war — some for political gain, some for business opportunities, and some with a real desire to help the newly freed Negroes. Many "carpetbaggers" were undoubtedly unscrupulous and self-seeking, but they did include people of integrity with humanitarian and idealistic instincts. Southerners who joined the "carpetbaggers" in their activities were referred to by other Southerners as "scalawags." For a number of years, particularly in the earlier period of Congressional Reconstruction, the "carpetbaggers" in effect controlled many Southern state governments.

2. *The Record of the Reconstruction Governments.*

(a) *Accomplishments.* On the positive side, the Reconstruction governments established and expanded free public school systems; built needed roads, bridges, and other public facilities; provided various forms of aid for the needy and handicapped; and reorganized and improved local governments, courts, and tax systems. Negro legislators were, for the most part, moderate in their demands. Some were men of outstanding ability, including JOSEPH RAINEY and HIRAM REVELS, who were later elected to the House of Representatives and the U.S. Senate, respectively.

(b) *Weaknesses.* On the negative side. Reconstruction governments were sometimes guilty of extravagance and corruption. Dishonest officials handed out "favors" in return for bribes, looted state treasuries, and squandered large sums of money on questionable projects. Taxes rose rapidly. (It should be noted, however, that the post-Civil War period was an era of corrupt state and local government in *all* sections of the country. It is open to question whether the Reconstruction governments were conspicuously worse in this respect than other state governments at the time—or worse than some of the governments in the Southern states *after* Reconstruction.)

3. *Southern Whites Regain Control.* Angered and humiliated by what they considered the excesses of Congressional Reconstruction, the Southern whites resorted to violence to regain political control.

(a) *The Ku Klux Klan.* Many Southern whites became convinced that they would have to take the law into their own hands. They organized secret societies like the *Ku Klux Klan* and the *Knights of the White Camelia* to intimidate Negroes by threats and open violence. The general purpose was to frighten Negroes away from the polls and to keep them in an inferior position socially and economically. Freedmen who could not be easily terrorized were often beaten or even murdered. Even the passage of special *Force Acts* by Congress (1870–71), which outlawed the Klan and gave the President authority to use force to uphold the Fourteenth and Fifteenth Amendments, had little effect.

(b) *Home Rule Restored to the South.* White supremacy was gradually restored in the South between 1871 and 1876. "Carpetbag" legislatures were replaced by legislatures controlled by white Southern Democrats. The withdrawal of Federal troops from the South in 1877 by President Hayes marked the official end of Reconstruction. A number of factors led to the restoration of white supremacy. **(1)** Most Negroes did not vote. **(2)** The influence of the Radical Republicans declined, while a more tolerant "Liberal Republican" movement gained in power. **(3)** The *Amnesty Act* of 1872 restored political privileges to thousands of ex-Confederates. An increasing number of Northerners became convinced, for various reasons, that conditions in the South would have to be "normalized," and that this meant return of governmental power to the "natural rulers" of the region—that is, the upper-class whites.

4. *The Restriction of Negro Rights.* Though they had been forced to recognize the freedom of the Negro, most Southern whites were not willing to recognize his political, social, or economic equality. They also feared that the Negroes would support the Republican Party if allowed to vote freely. Northerners were tired of the war and its aftermath. They were much more concerned with industrialization and winning the West than with securing justice for the Negroes. Consequently, a pattern of segregation and discrimination developed in the South toward the end of the 19th century.

(a) *Poll taxes* were established, calling for the payment in advance of a small fee, in order to vote. Most Negroes (as well as many poor whites) could not afford to pay this tax.

(b) *Literacy tests* were made part of the requirements for voting. Would-be voters had to show that they could read, write, and interpret the state constitution. The tests for Negroes were made difficult enough to exclude them from the polls.

(c) *"Grandfather clauses"* were added to state constitutions to protect poor whites from discriminations aimed at the Negro. These gave the right to vote to all persons whose fathers or grandfathers could vote in 1867, even if such persons could not meet other voting requirements. Such clauses were not declared unconstitutional until 1915.

(d) *"Jim Crow."* After 1890, a whole series of laws, known as "Jim Crow" legislation, provided for the segregation of Negroes in education, housing, travel, and recreation. Not until the middle of the 20th century did the Supreme Court begin to declare such laws unconstitutional (see page 424). Also, the lives of Negroes were jeopardized by the spread of lynchings.

5. *The Solid South.* The attempt of the Radical Republicans to develop support for the Republican Party in the South by granting the suffrage to the Negro backfired completely. White Southerners were so bitter at Congressional and "carpetbag" Reconstruction that they voted solidly Democratic for more than fifty years, and still do in virtually all local elections.

(a) The term "Solid South" is used to describe the solid support traditionally given to the Democratic Party in the Southern states.

(b) Recent cracks in the Solid South occurred when several Southern states supported Republican Presidential candidates in the elections of 1928, 1952, 1956, 1960, and 1964. In such states as Virginia and Texas, a genuine two-party system seems at last to be beginning to emerge.

Economic Changes in the South During and After Reconstruction. The tremendous blow to the plantation system caused by the Civil War brought about a basic reorganization of Southern economic life during and after Reconstruction. The new economy which emerged is referred to as the "New South."

1. *End of the Plantation System.* After the collapse of the Confederacy, the Southern planter was faced with declining farm values, mounting debts, lack of cash, and a shortage of labor. As a result, most of the great plantations of pre-Civil War days were split up into smaller units and sold.

2. *Growth of Farm Tenancy and Sharecropping.* Some of the new owners operated their farms themselves, or hired laborers, usually freed Negroes or poor whites. Many rented their lands to *tenant farmers* in return for a fixed money rental. Most entered into a new arrangement with tenants known as *sharecropping*. Under the sharecropping system, the owner provided the land, fertilizer, seed, tools, farm animals, and cabin. The "cropper" furnished the labor. At the end of the season the owner took a fixed share of the crop; what remained — and it was often very little — belonged to the sharecropper.

 (*a*) Farm tenancy and sharecropping provided an immediate and needed solution to the main agricultural problem facing the South after the Civil War — the necessity of getting the land back under cultivation.

 (*b*) In post-Reconstruction years, however, farm tenancy and sharecropping had harmful effects on both the South and the nation. Most tenants and sharecroppers were forced to borrow at high interest rates from store-owners and merchants, and therefore remained permanently in debt. Under the *crop-lien system* they pledged their crops as security. Since merchants and moneylenders insisted that the farmers grow cotton (the "cash crop"), tenants and sharecroppers were unable to diversify or rotate their crops. This led to soil exhaustion, and the sharecroppers and tenant farmers became one of the most poverty-stricken groups in the nation. They were poorly housed and fed, debt-ridden, uneducated, and lacking in incentive.

3. *Agricultural Progress.* In spite of the drawbacks of the farm tenancy and sharecropping systems, Southern agriculture as a whole began to make considerable progress. **(a)** During the last quarter of the 19th century, improved farm machinery was widely introduced. **(b)** Several agricultural colleges were established. Better farming methods increased the per-acre yield of such basic crops as cotton, tobacco, sugar, and rice. Cotton continued to be the South's number-one crop. **(c)** Most important of all was the growing *diversification* of Southern agriculture. In addition to the traditional staple crops, fruit growing and market gardening (vegetables) became important in some areas. Peanuts became a major crop. A profitable beef cattle industry began to develop.

4. *Growth of Industry in the South.* Perhaps the most noteworthy characteristic of the New South in the post-Civil War era was the *development of industry*. The war had shattered the limited Southern industry developed before 1860. Not until the late 1870's did industry begin to revive strongly. Thereafter, remarkable progress took place in the last quarter of the 19th century and continued into the 20th.

(a) Between 1860 and 1900, the value of Southern manufacturing increased over 400%. Among the leading products were tobacco, textiles, iron and steel, and lumber and other wood products. A significant symbol of the New South was the rapid growth of the number and size of Southern textile mills. These produced unfinished goods which were sent North for finishing. This marked the beginning of the end of the position of the South as merely a supplier of raw materials for the North and East.

(b) Large cities like Atlanta, Richmond, and Nashville increased in size, largely as a result of industrial expansion. Birmingham, Alabama, which was not founded until 1871, became a leading iron and steel center (the "Pittsburgh of the South").

(c) The growth of Southern industry was made possible by large investments of capital (much of it from the North).

An Era of Public and Private Corruption. During the Reconstruction Era, a low tone of public morality characterized the nation as a whole. National economic expansion was accompanied by widespread graft and corruption.

1. *National Scandals.* ULYSSES S. GRANT succeeded Andrew Johnson as President and served two terms (1869–77). Grant had made a brilliant record as leader of the Union armies and was honest, well-meaning, and popular. As Chief Executive, however, he failed to provide strong leadership and is generally regarded as one of the nation's least effective Presidents. Grant reposed confidence in men who did not deserve it, and this paved the way for scandals which reached into his own administration.

(a) *The "Black Friday" Scandal.* Early in his first term, Grant foolishly allowed himself to be influenced by two financial speculators, Jay Gould and James Fisk. In their efforts to corner the gold market and make huge profits, Gould and Fisk actually persuaded the President to change the gold-selling policies of the U. S. Treasury. The episode led to a stock market collapse on "Black Friday," September 24, 1869. Many innocent persons, including financiers, businessmen, and workers, suffered as a result. A Congressional investigation showed that Grant had done nothing illegal or dishonorable, but many felt that he had been guilty of irresponsibility and poor judgment.

(b) *The Crédit Mobilier Scandal.* This came to light during Grant's second term (1873), although the scandal had its origin before Grant took office. It involved the construction of the Union Pacific Railroad (completed in 1869), which had received large-scale government assistance. The *Crédit Mobilier,* the company that built the railroad, had enjoyed extremely favorable treatment from Congress and had earned huge profits. It was revealed that several Congressmen had received stock of this company virtually as a "gift." Moreover, an attempt was made in Congress to block investigation of these suspicious dealings. The Vice President of the United States and other high public officials were involved in this ugly scandal.

(c) The "Whiskey Ring" Scandals. These involved several public officials, including Grant appointees and his private secretary. They were found guilty of having helped a ring of whiskey distillers to defraud the government of millions of dollars in taxes.

2. *Scandals in State Government.* During this same postwar era, there was widespread corruption in state government. One famous and typical scandal involved the financiers Daniel Drew, Jay Gould, and James Fisk, who bribed many members of the New York State Legislature in order to obtain "favors" for the Erie Railroad, which they controlled.

3. *Municipal Corruption.* Corruption in municipal or city government was worst of all. Most notorious was the political organization in New York City, known as the *Tweed Ring*. Through his political machine, Tammany Hall, "Boss" William M. Tweed controlled the government of New York City for two decades (the 1860's and 1870's). Tweed and his henchmen sold jobs, franchises, and charters, and handed out lucrative contracts to friends. The Tweed Ring stayed in power by providing jobs and other help to immigrants, by packing the ballot boxes, and by manipulating the vote in other ways. It is estimated that the abuses connected with Tweed cost New York City well over 100 million dollars.

Growth of a Reform Movement. Many Republicans were deeply disturbed by the corruption of the postwar era. In opposition to "Grantism," they formed the *Liberal-Republican Party*. This group was pledged to fight against graft and dishonesty, and favored civil service reform. In the Presidential election of 1872, the Liberal-Republicans backed HORACE GREELEY, who also received the Democratic nomination. Although Greeley was overwhelmingly defeated by Grant, more and more citizens reacted against the administration. In 1874, the Democratic Party gained control of the House of Representatives. As a result, both parties drew up "reform" platforms in the election of 1876.

Disputed Election of 1876. In 1876, the Republicans chose RUTHERFORD B. HAYES, reform Governor of Ohio, as their Presidential nominee. The Democrats selected SAMUEL TILDEN, reform Governor of New York, who had helped break up the Tweed Ring. The results of the election were so close that it has become known as the "Disputed Election of 1876."

1. *Election Returns.* The election returns showed that Tilden had received 250,000 more popular votes than Hayes, that the electoral vote was 184 to 165, in Tilden's favor, and that 20 electoral votes were in dispute.

2. *Disputed Votes.* Since Tilden's 184 electoral votes fell one short of the 185 needed for election, the disputed votes of four states (South Carolina, Florida, Louisiana, Oregon) were of crucial importance. In each state two different sets of returns had been filed.

3. *Election of Hayes.* Congress set up an *Electoral Commission* to judge the disputed votes. The Commission awarded all 20 such votes to Hayes, giving him an electoral majority of 185 to 184.

4. *Acceptance of the Results.* The Democrats roundly denounced the results because Tilden had a popular majority, and because the Electoral Commission had voted along strict party lines (8 Republicans, 7 Democrats). Nevertheless, they accepted Hayes' election.

> NOTE: Recent research has shown that part of the Democratic willingness to allow Hayes to be inaugurated was a result of a secret compromise between Republican leaders and Southern Democrats. The Democrats were willing to let Hayes become President in return for the promise of such concessions as the withdrawal of Federal troops from the South, the appointment of a Southerner to the Cabinet, and help in securing more Federal funds for improvement projects in the South.

Results of Reconstruction. The results of Reconstruction, already described, may be summed up as follows:

1. *Solid South.* In bitterness against Radical Republican Reconstruction, the South gave its political support to the Democratic Party.

2. *Negro Rights.* Guidelines for a new social system, based upon the guarantee of the rights of freedmen, were set forth in the Thirteenth, Fourteenth, and Fifteenth Amendments adopted during the Reconstruction. Although social custom was to keep Negroes in a subordinate position, the laws of the land now guaranteed him a measure of equality.

3. *Discrimination.* To get around Congressional attempts to legislate Negro equality, the Southern states imposed many kinds of discrimination upon the Negro. Racial tensions were heightened.

4. *New South.* A "New South" emerged out of the Reconstruction, characterized by tenant farming and sharecropping, and later by diversification of agriculture and the rise of industry.

5. *Public Corruption.* The "tragic era" in the South during Reconstruction was matched by a tragic era of corruption and graft in government and industry throughout the nation as a whole.

REVIEW TEST (Chapter 15)

Select the number preceding the word or expression that best completes each statement or answers each question.

1. President Lincoln's plan for reconstruction was based on the theory that the Confederate States (1) were to be treated as territories (2) could be readmitted to the Union by Congress only (3) had never actually left the Union (4) were to be occupied by Union forces for a period of 20 years

2. During the Reconstruction Period an important objective of Congressional action was to (1) destroy the economy of the South (2) maintain Republican domination of the national government (3) restore pre-Civil War conditions in the South (4) pardon Southern leaders for Civil War activities

3. All of the following actions were taken by Congress during the Reconstruction Period *except* (1) enactment of the Black Codes (2) passage of the Civil Rights Act (3) establishment of Freedman's Bureau (4) passage of the Tenure of Office Act

4. Which of the following was a requirement for Southern states that wished to re-enter the Union under the Congressional Plan? (1) Ten percent of the white voters had to accept the Thirteenth Amendment. (2) Southern states had to ratify the Fourteenth Amendment. (3) Military governors had to guarantee the rights of Negroes. (4) Federal troops had to be removed.

5. During the Reconstruction Era, Northerners who went South for political and economic opportunity or to help the Negro were called (1) scalawags (2) KKK's (3) carpetbaggers (4) copperheads

6. Sharecropping emerged in the post-Civil War South as a means by which (1) Southern planters exchanged crops for Northern manufactured goods (2) more than one crop shared the available land on the plantation (3) former slaves formed co-operative credit associations to share costs of entering farming (4) impoverished planters and former slaves supplied each other's need for labor and land

7. During the Reconstruction Period immediately following the Civil War, the former Confederate states in drafting their new constitutions usually reflected the (1) influence of the radicals in the Republican Party (2) need to reestablish the plantation system (3) desire to provide for gradual extension of Negro suffrage (4) principle of "separate but equal" facilities

8. What was a common purpose of the "grandfather clause," the Ku Klux Klan, and the poll tax? (1) to drive the carpetbaggers from the South (2) to prevent the Negro from voting (3) to keep the poor whites under control (4) to disenfranchise Southern leaders

9. The city that came to be known after the Civil War as the "Pittsburgh of the South" is (1) Birmingham (2) New Orleans (3) Galveston (4) Raleigh

10. In the economic development of the South since the Civil War (1) cotton growing has been abandoned, (2) the size of plantations has increased (3) agriculture has become more diversified (4) the system of sharecropping has been ended

Match each name in Column A with the letter of the item in Column B that is most clearly identified with it.

A	B
1. Thaddeus Stevens	*a.* Removed from office by President Johnson
2. Andrew Johnson	*b.* Radical Republican leader
3. Edwin Stanton	*c.* Linked with municipal political corruption
4. Rutherford B. Hayes	*d.* Withdrew Federal troops from the South
5. William Tweed	*e.* Responsible for the Crédit Mobilier scandal
	f. Supported Lincoln's Plan for Reconstruction

Essay Questions

1. Explain two differences between the President's plan of Reconstruction and the Congressional Plan of Reconstruction following the Civil War.

2. Describe one social result and one political result of the Reconstruction Period in the South.

3. Discuss two important factors that have promoted the industrialization of the South during the 20th century.

4. Explan briefly the role or significance of each of the following during or following the Reconstruction Era: Freedman's Bureau; Black Codes; Military Reconstruction Acts; Tenure of Office Act; carpetbaggers and scalawags; Ku Klux Klan; poll taxes and "grandfather clauses"; Jim Crow laws; the Solid South; the New South; Black Friday; Whiskey Ring; Tweed Ring; disputed election of 1876.

REVIEWING UNIT FIVE

Select the number preceding the word or expression that best completes each statement or answers each question.

1. Which of the following disputes involved the United States and France? (1) Florida boundary dispute (2) Alabama Claims (3) Trent Affair (4) Maximilian Affair

2. Which of the following had a different general purpose from that of the others? (1) Black Codes (2) Freedman's Bureau (3) Ku Klux Klan (4) "grandfather clauses"

3. A primary source for the study of the Civil War is (1) an American history textbook (2) the *Dictionary of American History* (3) *Abraham Lincoln: The Prairie Years* and *The War Years*, by Carl Sandburg (4) *The Blue and the Gray*, the *Story of the Civil War as Told by Participants*, edited by H. S. Commager

4. An important result of the Civil War was that it (1) ended the states'-rights issue (2) strengthened our tie with Great Britain (3) helped to make industry rather than agriculture the basis of our economy (4) established equality for the Negro in the South

5. The Radical Republicans in Congress after the Civil War were those who (1) favored Lincoln's ideas on Southern Reconstruction (2) regarded the Southern states as conquered territories (3) introduced pro-labor legislation (4) opposed civil rights for the Negroes

6. During the Civil War Congress did all of the following *except* (1) issue unbacked paper currency (2) establish the National Banking System (3) adopt a protective tariff (4) reverse national immigration policy

7. The purpose of General Sherman's famous march to the sea was to (1) trap General Lee (2) come to Grant's aid (3) split the Confederacy (4) capture valuable cottonland for the North

8. The "anaconda plan" aimed at: (1) seizing control of the Mississippi (2) driving into the North (3) capturing Washington, D.C. (4) securing as many foreign allies as possible

9. Hayes' rival in the Presidential election of 1876 was: (1) Jay Gould (2) Samuel Tilden (3) William Richardson (4) Hamilton Fish

10. As a general, Ulysses Grant is considered to have been brilliant and effective. As President, he generally is thought to have been (1) equally effective (2) corrupt and unscrupulous (3) well-meaning but weak (4) an outstanding innovator of new ideas and policies

11. Carpetbaggers and scalawags were most active from (1) 1860–65 (2) 1865–70 (3) 1870–75 (4) 1875–80

12. All of the following were related to corruption in government *except* (1) Crédit Mobilier (2) Tweed Ring (3) Black Friday (4) Ten per cent plan

13. Which of the following was an important post-Civil War trend? (1) disappearance of tenant farming (2) growth of industry in the South (3) decline in the number of industrial workers (4) shift to revenue tariff

14. Which pair of events involved the United States with the *same* country? (1) Alabama Claims — Maximilian Affair (2) Oregon boundary dispute — annexation of Texas (3) Chesapeake Affair — XYZ Affair (4) Rush-Bagot Agreement — Trent Affair

15. "Home rule" was restored to the South in the period (1) 1861–66 (2) 1866–71 (3) 1871–76 (4) 1876–81

Supply the word or expression that correctly completes each statement:

1. The civilian leader of the Confederacy during the Civil War was ..?...

2. The general who commanded the victorious Union forces at Gettysburg was ..?...

3. Serious draft riots took place in the North during the Civil War in the city of ..?...

4. During the war Lincoln restricted civil liberties in certain districts by suspending the writ of ..?...

5. A European power that was friendly to the North throughout the Civil War was ..?...

6. Slavery was abolished throughout the United States by the ..?...

7. The famous speech in which Lincoln called for "malice towards none" and "charity for all" was the ..?...

8. President Johnson was impeached by the ..?.. and narrowly acquitted by the ..?...

9. The Force Acts (1870–71) outlawed the ..?...

10. The party which benefited directly from the decision of the Electoral Count Commission in 1876 was the ..?.. Party.

Essay Questions

1. Students of American history continue to argue over the fundamental causes of the Civil War. Discuss fully three important causes of the Civil War.

2. It has been said that while wars may solve some problems, they also create other problems. Discuss this statement in relation to (a) one problem that was solved by the Civil War and (b) two problems that were created by the Civil War.

3. In word and deed Abraham Lincoln ranks with the greatest of Americans. (a) Give a brief quotation from one of Lincoln's speeches or writings and explain its significance. (b) Explain fully how Lincoln's policy on two of the following showed his wisdom or leadership ability: (1) the Emancipation Proclamation, (2) his plan for reconstruction of the South, (3) the Trent Affair, (4) the Maximilian Affair.

4. Discuss fully three of the following statements, giving historical evidence to support each: (a) The campaign to win a Senate seat in the state of Illinois made Abraham Lincoln a national figure. (b) Abraham Lincoln made bold use of his Presidential powers. (c) Lincoln's Gettysburg Address deserves the praise it has received. (d) Abraham Lincoln's views on slavery were moderate in comparison with those of other leaders of the period.

5. Why has the Reconstruction Era been called an era of *"confusion, bitterness, change* and *corruption"*? (a) To what event or events does each of the italicized words refer? (b) Why do you agree or disagree with the statement as a whole?

6. Write a brief story that might have appeared under each of the following headlines in the newspapers during or after the period of Civil War and Reconstruction.

NATION MOURNS LINCOLN'S TRAGIC DEATH
KLAN HELPS SOUTHERN WHITES REGAIN CONTROL
JIM CROW JEOPARDIZES 13th AND 14th AMENDMENTS
GRANT'S ADMINISTRATION HURT BY SCANDALS IN HIGH PLACES
SOLID SOUTH EMERGES OUT OF RECONSTRUCTION

EMERGENCE OF MODERN AMERICA

CHAPTER 16 _____

Economic and Social Transformation . of the United States.

After the Civil War, the United States transformed itself from an isolated, predominantly rural, and avowedly experimental democracy, to a great industrial republic with worldwide interests and commitments.

Part 1 — THE PASSING OF THE FRONTIER

An outstanding feature of the development of the United States after the Civil War was the settlement of the region known as the *Great Plains*.

Settling the Great Plains. By the time of the Civil War, the line of settlement had advanced to the states just beyond the Mississippi River and then had jumped from there to the Pacific Coast (California and Oregon). In between, stretching from the Mississippi to the Rockies, lay the vast and unsettled *Great Plains* region. Between 1860 and 1890, this "last frontier" was occupied and settled.

1. *Miners.* Miners led the way, attracted first by the discovery of rich deposits of silver in Nevada (*Comstock Lode*) and then of gold in Colorado (*Pike's Peak* area).

2. *Cattlemen.* Cattlemen were attracted into the Great Plains area after the Civil War by the vast open range and by the growing demand in the East for beef.

3. *Farmers.* The most numerous and important of the groups to settle the Great Plains were the farmers. In a single generation, from 1870 to 1890, they occupied more farm land than had been settled in *all* the preceding years of the nation's history combined. As the farmers fenced off their lands, they often came into conflict with the cattlemen, who needed an "open range" for their stock to graze on.

4. *New Inventions.* The settlement of the Great Plains was encouraged and, indeed, was made possible by new inventions and new methods of farming. Improved weapons helped the cattlemen in their wars against the

Plains Indians. The development of "dry farming" methods to conserve moisture, and of windmills to pump water, made agriculture possible on the plains, where rainfall was sparse and uncertain. The invention of barbed wire also aided the farmer in protecting his crops and cattle.

5. *Liberal Government Land Policy.* A generous Federal land policy helped increase significantly the amount of land brought under cultivation. Under the *Homestead Act* of 1862, any person 21 years or older who was a citizen, or who had declared his intention of becoming a citizen, could have up to 160 acres of land *free,* if he promised to occupy and improve the land for five years. A fee of only $10 was required to register under this law. By 1890, nearly 50 million acres had been distributed under the Homestead Act. (Much of the land ended up in the hands of speculators, railroads, and mining companies, who often used fraudulent means to obtain title.)

6. *Building of Transcontinental Railroads.* The first transcontinental railroad was the *Union Pacific,* completed in 1869. Within 40 years, seven transcontinental lines were in operation. These railroads brought new settlers to the West, kept the settlers in contact with other sections of the nation, opened millions of acres of farmland to cultivation, and lowered the cost of transported goods. The companies that constructed the transcontinental railroads received much government aid in the form of land grants, loans, and special privileges, such as the free right of way through public lands. (See map below.)

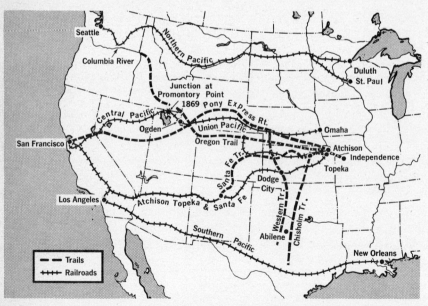

Defeat of the Indians. The westward movement into the Great Plains was accompanied by the crushing of Indian resistance.

1. The rapid advance of the settlers often carried them into lands legally set aside for Indian settlement, as well as other lands considered by the Indians to be rightfully theirs. Angered by this encroachment and by the destruction of the buffalo herds (a basic source of food and other necessities), the Indians rose in resistance. The "Indian Wars" that followed, lasting from 1865 to 1890, resembled modern guerrilla warfare. As late as 1876, a force of Sioux Indians wiped out a detachment of U. S. Army troops commanded by General Custer (at the Little Big Horn in Montana). In the end, the Indians had to yield to the numerical superiority of the whites and their use of trained troops armed with better weapons.

2. Beginning in 1869, the Federal government set aside areas called *reservations,* where Indians lived under government protection.

(a) Criticism continued, however, that the Indians were being mistreated and were economically, politically, and socially disadvantaged. Beginning in the 1880s, the U.S. government through the *Bureau of Indian Affairs* (BIA) has sought to help the Indians by providing schools, medical services, and economic aid. Under the *Dawes Act* (1887), Indians who chose to give up their tribal way of life were permitted to leave the reservations, to become citizens, and to acquire individual land holdings. In 1924, citizenship was extended to *all* Indians. In 1934, the *Wheeler-Howard Act* permitted tribes to buy land and engage in business.

(b) Today, many Indians live outside the reservations. They have settled in various parts of the country, where they engage in a wide range of occupations. Some have become prosperous and prominent in their communities. However, most Indians still live in poverty on reservations, somewhat removed from the mainstream of American life. High unemployment and underemployment are a major problem.

(c) In recent years, Indians have become more critical and militant, working through organizations such as the *American Indian Movement* (AIM). They maintain that the Indians themselves should have the power to make the social and economic decisions that affect their lives. They tend to be distrustful of the "white man's bureaucracy" of the Federal government, such as the Bureau of Indian Affairs. Some groups within AIM have sought to call attention to their cause by temporarily taking over government installations and other properties.

(d) The 1970 census revealed that between 1900 and 1970, the Indian population of the United States had roughly doubled, to a figure of about 800,000.

Effects of Settling the Great Plains. The settlement of the Great Plains had far-reaching consequences.

1. *New States.* The population of the area west of the Mississippi increased rapidly. From 1861 to 1890, nine new states entered the Union.

2. *Agricultural Progress.* The pre-Civil War "Agricultural Revolution" was continued and speeded up as a result of the need to develop the great

new farming areas in the West. New inventions, methods, and sources of power brought about many changes. (See page 330.)

3. *Passing of the Frontier.* The occupation of the Great Plains marked the end of the frontier as a constantly moving line of settlement.

4. *Results of the Closing of the Frontier.* The closing of the frontier affected national development in important ways. **(a)** It caused Americans to begin to see the need for conservation of their natural resources. **(b)** It contributed to overseas expansion by causing investors to look abroad for places to invest capital. **(c)** It contributed to the urbanization of the nation. Immigrants and workers no longer could look upon "going West" as a solution to their problems. More than ever, they tended to gather in the great cities of the country. **(d)** Finally, political leaders were forced to give greater attention to problems that were formerly solved by westward migration of dissatisfied persons and groups.

REVIEW TEST (Chapter 16—Part I)

Select the number preceding the word or expression that best completes each statement or answers each question.

1. The settlement of the West proceeded rapidly in the years following the Civil War because of the (1) Homestead Act (2) Carey Act (3) Resumption Act (4) Adamson Act

2. A weakness of the government's land policy in the West was that it did not (1) promote wise use of the land (2) lead to the development of transportation facilities (3) help promote a wider distribution of property (4) tend to develop a spirit of independence in the people

3. The policy of the Federal government toward the Indians in the period immediately following the Civil War was to (1) move them to reservations (2) drive them from the country (3) require those under 16 years of age to attend public schools (4) grant them full citizenship

4. A major cause of the disappearance of the frontier in the United States was the (1) adoption of a national conservation program (2) establishment of land-grant colleges (3) extension of railroads (4) growth of labor unions

5. The disappearance of the frontier has (1) increased the social and economic problems of the United States (2) decreased American investments abroad (3) raised the American standard of living (4) made conservation unnecessary

Essay Questions

1. Discuss three factors that contributed to the rapid settlement of the Great Plains.

2. Write a brief story that might have followed each of the following newspaper headlines during the period 1865–1900. Date each story.

COMPLETION OF UNION PACIFIC HAILED AS ONE OF CENTURY'S MOST MOMENTOUS ACHIEVEMENTS

CUSTER'S FORCE WIPED OUT BY SIOUX INDIANS

CENSUS BUREAU ANNOUNCES END OF FRONTIER

3. Explain two important results of the passing of the frontier.

Part II — INDUSTRIALIZATION OF THE UNITED STATES SINCE THE CIVIL WAR

After the Civil War the United States became an increasingly industrialized nation. In the 20th century, the United States became the industrial leader of the world.

The Continuing Industrial Revolution. The Industrial Revolution in the United States began with the emergence of the factory system in the first quarter of the 19th century (see page 181). By 1860, hundreds of small manufacturing establishments had been set up in the North and East. After the Civil War this "Age of Small Business" gave way to an "Age of Big Business" in which giant plants replaced small factories and large-scale production replaced small-scale production. In the 20th century, as industry has become nationwide, newer technological advances, sources of power, and methods of financing have made the Industrial Revolution a *continuing* process.

Industrial Growth After 1865. The evidences of the industrial transformation of the United States after 1865 are numerous.

1. *Mass Production.* In the decades after the Civil War, mass production became a characteristic of American industry. It was made possible by increased application of the principles of division of labor, standardized parts, and job specialization. Mass production increased the volume and variety of goods produced, and lowered their cost. It made possible a steady rise in the American standard of living.

2. *Increase in Output.* By 1900, the United States had become the world's greatest industrial nation. The value of its manufactured goods was double that of its farm goods. Between 1865 and 1900, the value of manufactured goods increased over 500%. The rate of increase in the 20th century has been even greater. By 1966, the *Gross National Product,* or total value of all goods and services produced, had risen to over 670 billion dollars.

3. *Growth of Big Business.* A growth in the size of companies doing business accompanied, and also helped to make possible, the nation's increased output. Giant corporations with many huge plants came into being across the nation. By 1940, thirty corporations had assets of over a billion dollars each. This trend to "bigness" has continued since then.

4. *Spread of Industry.* Although the concentration of industry remained greatest in the East, industry spread to the West and South as well.

5. *New Industries.* Continued industrialization created new industries. Within recent decades new industries such as electronics, plastics, and aerospace have grown to giant dimensions.

6. *New Methods of Merchandising.* Along with new industries there developed new methods of selling. Although the general store in rural communities and the small retail establishment of the city continued to exist into the 20th century, their future became increasingly threatened by the growth of large department stores, chain stores, mail-order houses, etc.

Causes of United States Industrial Growth. Among the more important reasons for the expansion of American industry are the following:

1. The United States was blessed with an abundance of natural resources, which were exploited with increasing efficiency.

2. A mounting tide of immigration helped to meet the labor needs of growing industry by providing cheap labor.

3. American and European investors were ready to provide the necessary investment capital for industry.

4. Military needs during the Civil War led to an increase in the number and size of factories; wartime profits made surplus capital available for postwar investment.

5. The government aided business by means of protective tariffs and various forms of subsidies (for example, the grants of land to transcontinental railroads). It also kept business regulation to a minimum until the end of the 19th century (*laissez-faire*).

6. Technological advances (the application of science to industry) made possible an unending stream of practical inventions and utilization of new sources of energy.

7. The growing population of the country and improved means of transportation and communication provided a ready and expanding market.

8. The corporate form of business made possible the financing of huge enterprises and their consolidation into industrial empires.

9. Farsighted business leaders took full advantage of the opportunities that appeared.

10. An increasingly effective banking system was developed to meet the needs of industry.

NOTE: The last five factors (6–10) mentioned above are treated at length in the following sections. (Factors 1-5 are discussed elsewhere.)

The Growing Role of Technology. An important reason for the United States' industrial growth in the late 19th and 20th centuries has been the continuing technological advances. This has been evidenced by new inventions, new methods of production, and new sources of power.

1. *Inventions.* A continuous stream of inventions since the Civil War has changed not only methods of production, but also methods of consumption. This can be seen in recent years in such inventions as the *electric stove,* the *refrigerator,* the *photoelectric cell, plastics,* and *synthetics.* Invention has become increasingly a matter of teamwork, in which scientists and inventors work together in large industrial or government research laboratories.

2. *Methods of Production.* New and improved methods of production have been an integral part of the technological advance. Techniques of mass production such as interchangeable standardized parts and division of labor, introduced in the 19th century, have been greatly advanced in the 20th. To these have been added labor-saving *automatic machinery, assembly-line production,* and, more recently, *automation* (the control of machines by other machines).

3. *New Sources of Power.* New sources of energy and power have contributed significantly to the nation's industrial and technological growth in the 20th century. From about 1890 to 1940, coal replaced wood as the nation's leading fuel. Today's leading fuels are oil and gas. At the same time, the nation has moved into an "Age of Electricity." *Electric power* began to compete with steam in the early 1900's and has since become the major energy source in home and factory. *Nuclear energy,* only recently introduced, and now in its early stages of development (submarines, power plants, etc.), may very well become one of the most important energy sources of the future.

4. *Thomas A. Edison — Symbol of the Age of Invention.* Outstanding among inventors of the new industrial age was THOMAS ALVA EDISON, who is often considered our greatest inventor. A "practical" rather than a "pure" scientist, Edison was able to put the principles of science to practical use in over a thousand important inventions or improvements. Notable among his contributions were the electric light bulb, the phonograph, the dictaphone, the storage battery, motion pictures, and the microphone. Edison's research laboratory at Menlo Park, New Jersey, was a forerunner of the great research laboratories of today, where teams of scientists and inventors pool their talents in "collective research."

Improved Means of Transportation and Communication. New and improved means of transportation and communication helped overcome the enormous size of the country.

1. *Advances in Transportation.* Among the significant advances in transportation were the rapid growth of railroads at the end of the 19th century, and the development of autos, trucks, buses and airplanes in the 20th century.

(a) *Railroads.* By 1900 railroads had become the country's biggest business, and the United States had the world's largest railroad network (237,000 miles). In the same period (1860–1900), steel steamships and freighters replaced the wooden vessels of earlier years.

(b) *Automobiles.* The development of the automobile and automotive industry in the early 20th century changed the transportation, industrial, and living patterns of the nation. It also stimulated the growth of scores of other industries (steel, road building, service stations, motels) and provided millions of jobs. HENRY FORD added the technique of assembly-line production to mass production, and made it possible to produce increasing numbers of cars at relatively low prices. In the second quarter of the 20th century, trucks and buses began to compete effectively with railroads in hauling passengers and freight.

(c) *Airplanes.* Since World War II, the airplane has cut down distances, tied together the nation and the world, and become a basic means of transportation. Recent inventions, such as radar and the jet engine, have increased the speed, safety, and comfort of air flight and have made the airplane the primary long-distance passenger carrier.

(d) *Rockets.* We are now moving into an age of space travel, made possible by the development of rockets during and after World War II. In the early 1960's the United States placed its first man-made satellites into orbit around the earth, sent its first unmanned rockets to the moon, and orbited its first astronauts.

2. *Advances in Communication.* Improvements in communication were as important as improvements in transportation.

(a) *Telegraph.* The telegraph became more important in the post-Civil War era of railroad expansion. It made possible the safe and efficient operation of railroads.

(b) *Transatlantic Cable.* Instantaneous communication with the rest of the world became possible with the laying of underwater cables stretching between the United States and other continents.

(c) *Telephone.* The invention of the telephone by ALEXANDER GRAHAM BELL in 1876 opened a new era of national communication. By the turn of the century, telephone lines were a common sight in the cities, and they were beginning to reach into rural areas.

(d) *Radio and Television.* The 20th century also gave birth to *radio* and *television.* By the middle of the century nearly every home in the country had at least one radio set. Television became popular after World War II. By 1960 it had become the favorite form of home entertainment and a major factor in the economic and political life of the nation. A new era in international communications opened in 1962 with the launching of the first successful communications satellite, making possible for the first time the worldwide transmission of television programs.

The Corporation Becomes the Dominant Form of Business. In the post-Civil War period the corporation became the dominant form of business organization. It made possible the rise of "Big Business."

1. *Large Amounts of Capital.* Increased adoption of the corporate form of business made possible the raising of large amounts of capital through the issuance of stocks and bonds.

2. *Growing Role of Corporations.* A steadily increasing share of the nation's business began to be conducted by corporations. Corporations combined to eliminate competition and provide economies in the manufacture, transportation, and marketing of goods. In many instances, particularly before World War II, United States firms joined international combinations (*cartels*) to divide world markets and control prices.

3. *Types of Combination.* Two types of business combinations that developed and are still much in evidence are the *horizontal combination* and the *vertical combination.*

(a) A *horizontal combination* refers to organization under one management of different producers of the same commodity. For example, General Motors, producing a number of different automobiles, is essentially a horizontal combination. If a horizontal combination is large enough, it may have substantial control over production and prices throughout an entire industry.

(b) A *vertical combination* refers to the organization under one management of various important steps in the production of a given commodity. For example, the Ford Motor Company owns mines, steamship lines, railroads, and other facilities by which it feeds raw materials into its factories. This makes possible independence from outside sources of supply and greater economic power.

4. *Methods of Combination.* Different methods of combining businesses were popular in different periods.

(a) *Pools* were popular in the 1870's, particularly among railroads. A pool was a "gentlemen's agreement" among business rivals to fix prices or divide profits or markets.

(b) *Trusts* became popular in the 1880's. Under the trust arrangement competing companies turned over their securities and power to a single board of trustees.

(c) *Holding companies* replaced trusts in the early 1900's. A holding company owns a controlling share of the stocks of other companies.

(d) In recent years, the favored form of business combination has been the *merger,* in which two or more companies combine. In the presently popular *conglomerate,* several companies in unrelated fields are merged (*diversification*).

5. *Continued Growth of Big Business.* Since the 1960's, businesses have grown bigger and the trend to consolidation has continued in spite of attempts by the Federal government to restrict concentration of ownership.

Industrial Leaders. The development of American industry owed a great deal to the existence of a skilled group of business managers (*entrepreneurs*) in the late 19th and early 20th century. These industrial pioneers, who developed and directed the nation's first large-scale industrial "empires," were able, energetic, daring, and often ruthless. They were formed in a highly competitive society and in an age where ideals of self-reliance and "survival of the fittest" were commonly accepted in business and society. Because they were men of foresight who developed new industries, improved business efficiency, and opened new opportunities for the investment of capital, they have been called "Captains of Industry." Because they became tremendously powerful, in many instances used their power to drive competitors out of business, and frequently resorted to underhanded or illegal practices, they have been called "Robber Barons."

Typical figures include CORNELIUS VANDERBILT, who developed the *New York Central Railroad;* ANDREW CARNEGIE, a Scottish immigrant, who became an outstanding leader of the iron and steel industry; JOHN D. ROCKEFELLER, a leader in the oil industry, who organized the first great trust — the *Standard Oil Company*; JAMES J. HILL, the greatest of the railroad builders, who constructed the *Great Northern Railroad;* and J. P. MORGAN, powerful banker and international financier, who helped set up the nation's first billion-dollar corporation, *United States Steel.*

Strengthening the Economy Through an Improved Banking System. An improved banking system contributed to the industrialization and growth of the nation after 1860.

1. *National Bank System.* As noted on page 250, the National Bank System was established during the Civil War (1863) to provide a sounder currency as well as a market for United States bonds. Although this system provided a uniform currency and therefore helped in the growth of the economy, two major defects became apparent as time went on.

> (*a*) The currency was *inelastic.* The amount of money and credit available depended upon the amount of bonds owned by the national banks, rather than upon business needs. In times of prosperity, when money and credit requirements of business increased, the banks cashed in some of their bonds because they could get a higher return elsewhere. This reduced the money supply. In times of depression, when less money and credit were required, the banks bought more government bonds (since the interest was relatively high), and thus expanded the money supply.

> (*b*) A second defect of the National Bank System was the *lack of provision for pooling of funds.* Most banks were concentrated in the financial and industrial sections of the North and East. In times of pressing need (such as planting or harvest time), Southern and Western farmers and businessmen could not secure additional funds locally, and often had to pay unduly high interest rates to Northern and Eastern banks.

2. *Federal Reserve System Replaces the National Bank System.* Following the financial *Panic of 1907,* during which the weaknesses of the National Bank System were particularly apparent, a new banking system, the Federal Reserve System, was established by Congress in 1913 at the recommendation of a National Monetary Commission and the urging of President Wilson. The Federal Reserve System is a central banking system. With some modifications in the 1930's, it has served well to meet the nation's money and banking needs. It is organized as follows:

> (*a*) The nation is divided into 12 districts, each with its own Federal Reserve Bank.

> (*b*) The Federal Reserve Bank in each district services the needs of the member banks in the district. Federal Reserve banks are "bankers banks"; that is, they deal with banks, not private individuals.

(c) All national banks must be members of the Federal Reserve System. State banks may or may not join. About two-thirds of the nation's banks have become members. They include virtually all of the larger banks, and they do most of the nation's commercial banking.

(d) The Federal Reserve System is supervised by a Board of Governors.

(e) Although the Federal Reserve Banks are owned by the member banks, the Federal government exercises a large measure of control over them through the *Board of Governors*, the members of which are appointed by the President.

3. *Advantages of the Federal Reserve System.* The Federal Reserve System has overcome the defects of the National Banking System by making possible the *pooling of reserves* and the creation of a *flexible currency* (explained below). Through its services, it has improved banking efficiency, helped curb inflation, contributed to meeting financial emergencies during World Wars I and II, and provided a market for the sale of government bonds. Federal Reserve Notes now constitute over 80% of our paper money. They are backed by gold certificates, government bonds, and commercial paper (promissory notes).

(a) *Pooling of Reserves.* Each member bank must keep a minimum reserve in the district Federal Reserve Bank, and most banks keep most of their reserves there. The proportion of reserves to total deposits is called the *reserve ratio*. It is fixed by the Board of Governors and changed from time to time. By requiring reserves to be kept in Federal Reserve Banks, the system makes possible the pooling of the reserves of individual banks in a central bank. Funds can be shifted easily from bank to bank in each district, and from district to district. The Reserve Banks thus act as "credit reservoirs" for the nation's commercial banks.

(b) *Flexible Currency.* Through its ability to regulate the amount of money and credit in circulation the Federal Reserve System has made possible a *flexible currency* — one that expands and contracts with the needs of business. This has been achieved by its ability to regulate the amounts of loans banks make to businessmen through: **(1)** *open-market* operations, **(2)** the *raising* or *lowering* of reserve requirements, and **(3)** the raising or lowering of the *rediscount rate*. These functions are described below.

(c) *Open-Market Operations.* Open-market operations occur when the Federal Reserve System buys or sells government securities in the open market. When it *buys* government bonds, the Federal Reserve System *expands* credit by putting more money into circulation. This money is deposited in banks, thereby increasing bank deposits. Increased bank deposits enable the banks to increase their loans, and thus extend more credit. When a Federal Reserve Bank *sells* government bonds in the open market, it *reduces* the amount of credit in circulation, since the purchasers pay for them by drawing checks on their banks. This reduces bank reserves and lessens the amount of loans that can be made.

(d) *Raising or Lowering Reserve Requirements.* By *raising* the reserve requirements (*reserve ratio*), the Federal Reserve System lowers the ability of banks to make loans, since more money must be kept in reserve. By *lowering* the reserve requirements the Federal Reserve System makes it possible for the banks to lend more money.

(e) *Raising or Lowering the Rediscount Rate.* By *raising* the rediscount rate, a Federal Reserve Bank makes credit more expensive for member banks and tends to discourage the extension of loans. By *lowering* the rediscount rate, the opposite effect is achieved. The *rediscount rate* is the per cent charge which a Federal Reserve Bank makes on loans to member banks. This helps to determine what the member banks will have to charge for loans to businessmen.

NOTE: The various steps which the Federal Reserve System may take to control the economy by expanding or contracting the supply of money and credit are known as *monetary policy.*

4. *Strengthening the Federal Reserve System.* The many bank failures that occurred after the *stock market crash of 1929,* and the depression that followed, showed that the Federal Reserve System had not solved *all* of the nation's money and banking problems. To strengthen the FRS the New Deal introduced the following changes in the 1930's.

(a) *Federal Deposit Insurance Corporation.* To prevent loss of deposits in the case of bank failure, a *Federal Deposit Insurance Corporation (FDIC)* was established to insure bank deposits up to a certain limit (now set at a maximum of $20,000 per depositor). The existence of the FDIC has helped greatly to increase the confidence of people in banks. Bank failures and losses to depositors have been held to a very low level.

(b) *Greater Capitalization Requirements.* To insure a stronger banking system, the minimum amount of capital required for the establishment of a national bank was raised.

(c) *Increased Powers of the Board of Governors.* The Board of Governors was granted increased powers over rediscount rates, reserve ratios, open-market operations, and margin requirements.

Results of the Industrialization of the United States. The following are among the more important results of the industrialization of the nation.

1. *National wealth was increased* by the expansion of industrial output.

2. *Standards of living were raised* to the highest in the world as more production made available increasing quantities of necessities and luxuries.

3. *Urbanization of the nation was speeded up* as the city replaced the country as the center of production, population, and influence.

4. *Immigration was encouraged,* since industrialization opened new job opportunities.

5. *Concentration of wealth and economic power in fewer hands* resulted from consolidation in industry. At the same time, however, most Americans came to enjoy higher incomes and improved standards of living, as noted earlier.

6. *Standardization of social life* occurred as industry made more uniform the ways in which people worked, dressed, ate, traveled, and spent their leisure time.

7. *The nation's early isolation from foreign affairs ended,* in large part because of the need of American industry for additional markets, sources of materials, and places to invest surplus capital.

8. *American nationalism was stimulated* by the emergence of the nation as the industrial leader of the world.

9. *A revolution on the farm* accompanied and resulted from the technological advances in industry.

10. *Serious problems resulted from industrialization.* These included business monopoly; labor discontent; the growth of slums, crime, and other problems in large cities; overproduction on the farms; and recurrent business cycles of booms and depressions.

Business Crises and Depressions. In spite of rapid growth, America's industrial development has been accompanied by periods of rising and falling business activity, known as *business cycles.*

1. *Nature of Business Cycles.* In the business cycle, a period of prosperity and expansion of business activity is followed by one of economic slowdown and depression. Economists have recognized four major phases of the business cycle: *prosperity, recession, depression,* and *recovery.* Causes of depressions have included overproduction, overspeculation, excessive credit, and lack of public confidence in business and banking.

2. *Attempts to Prevent Business Cycles.* The great depression of 1929–1933 caused the government to adopt new economic policies which it hoped would avoid serious depressions in the future. Among these "built-in stabilizers" are: the insurance of bank deposits; regulation of bank reserves by the Federal Reserve Board; the establishment of a *Council of Economic Advisers* to advise the President on the economic health of the nation; adoption of a public works program to stimulate industry and provide employment when necessary; and the use of taxation as an economic policy, to provide a stimulus to business or to help in checking inflation. The Social Security System, including the 50 state systems of unemployment insurance, is a major stabilizing force.

3. *Recent Recessions.* After World War II, economic expansion and national prosperity reached new heights. Nonetheless, ups and downs of economic activity have continued to take place, with relatively minor recessions in 1948, 1953, 1957, and 1960. Since the late 1960s, the United States has been going through the worst inflation in its history. In the 1970s, the nation's economy experienced a severe slowdown, leading to the highest rates of unemployment since the great depression. In the past, recessions have generally brought on lower prices, but in this case the decline was accompanied by more inflation. This condition—combined stagnation and inflation—has been called *"stagflation."*

REVIEW TEST (Chapter 16—Part II)

Select the number preceding the word or expression that best completes each statement or answers each question.

1. Which of the following pairs was chiefly responsible for the industrialization of the United States? (1) technology and invention (2) protective tariff and excise taxes (3) mercantilism and government subsidies (4) *laissez-faire* and reciprocal trade agreements

2. Which one of the following inventions had great influence in the 19th century? (1) airplane (2) automobile (3) motion pictures (4) steam engine

3. Mass production in America brought about all of the following *except* (1) more leisure time (2) an increased percentage of skilled workers in industry (3) increased labor-management problems (4) a higher standard of living

4. Which of the following statements about corporations is true? (1) They were not in existence before the Civil War. (2) Small businesses seldom incorporate. (3) Businesses form corporations to secure discounts on large purchases. (4) During the 20th century, corporations have become a dominant form of business organization in manufacturing.

5. By which of the following techniques have most business consolidations been brought about in recent years in the United States? (1) pooling agreement (2) merger (3) monopoly (4) trade association

6. John D. Rockefeller's most significant contribution to business enterprise in America was his (1) elimination of wasteful competitive practices (2) introduction of assembly-line techniques (3) introduction into business of applied ethics (4) promotion of peaceful settlement of labor disputes

7. What is a significant result of the Great Depression of 1929? (1) elimination of the business cycle (2) establishment by the Federal government of certain safeguards against extreme fluctuations (3) failure of the Republican party to win the Presidency since that time (4) sharp increase in the proportion of Americans engaged in agriculture

8. Which of the following was an advantage of the National Bank System? (1) It prevented economic depressions. (2) It provided backing for state bank notes. (3) It established a uniform national currency. (4) It provided for the pooling of bank reserves.

9. The Federal Reserve System was an improvement over the previous banking system in that the Federal Reserve System (1) makes bank failures impossible (2) provides for the free coinage of silver and gold (3) provides for elasticity of currency (4) is supervised by the Treasury Department

10. If the Federal Reserve System wished to cut down on the loans made by member banks, it could (1) lower margin requirements (2) lower the rediscount rate (3) raise the reserve requirements (4) order all loans stopped

*Select the letter of the item which does **NOT** belong with the others.*

1. 19th-century inventions: (a) typewriter (b) phonograph (c) radio (d) telephone

2. Reasons for United States industrial growth: (a) abundance of natural resources (b) government management of business (c) technological progress (d) an effective banking system

3. "Captains of Industry": (a) Thomas A. Edison (b) Andrew Carnegie (c) Cornelius Vanderbilt (d) James J. Hill

4. Methods of business combination: (a) pool (b) trust (c) industrial empire (d) merger

5. Results of the continuing Industrial Revolution: (a) larger business units (b) growth of unions (c) greater output (d) fewer technological changes

Supply the word or expression that correctly completes each statement.

1. The National Bank System was established to help finance the ..?...

2. Under the National Bank System the volume of currency depended upon the value of ..?.. held by national banks.

3. Federal Reserve notes are backed by gold certificates, government bonds, and ..?...

4. The name given to the purchase or sale of government securities by the Federal Reserve Banks is ..?...

5. The FDIC insures bank deposits fully up to the amount of ..?...

Essay Questions

1. Show how each of the following contributed to making the United States an industrial nation after the Civil War: (a) natural resources (b) inventions (c) industrialists (d) the Federal government (e) new sources of power (f) new methods of production.

2. "Big Business" has played a significant role in the affairs of the United States for the past 100 years. (a) Explain why the period after the Civil War was marked by great industrial expansion. (b) Discuss two specific problems created by the rise of "Big Business."

3. Listed below are five important events in the technological development of the United States. Show specifically how each of these brought about changes in the American way of life. (a) 1903 — first story portrayed in motion pictures. (b) 1903 — first powered flight at Kitty Hawk. (c) 1909 — manufacture of the model-T Ford. (d) 1920 — start of commercial broadcasting at radio station KDKA. (e) 1945 — first successful release of atomic energy.

4. Giving evidence to support your opinion, discuss the truth or falsity of each of the following statements: (a) The Industrial Revolution in the United States ended with the introduction of automation. (b) Serious depressions in the United States are now a thing of the past. (c) Industrialization has standardized American life.

5. Show how the Federal Reserve System remedied three weaknesses of the National Bank System.

6. Discuss two ways in which the Federal Reserve System can (a) act as a stimulus to the economy and (b) act as a brake on inflation.

Far-reaching social and cultural changes since the Civil War have helped make a new America. With the industrialization of the nation, Americans have had the wealth and leisure to develop their own culture and to make important contributions in every field of endeavor. Some of the more important developments in this area are outlined below.

Education. (1) Rapid expansion of elementary education. (2) Growth of high schools to replace the pre-Civil War private academies (90% of adolescents now enrolled in secondary schools). (3) Rapid increase in number of colleges in 20th century, more professional schools and university research schools and university research centers, recent growth of community and junior colleges. (4) Growth of educational opportunities for adults: lectures (*Chautauqua Movement*), libraries, colleges. (5) Recent problems: increasing enrollment and lack of teachers and classrooms, the dropout problem, integration in education.

Role of Women. (1) Continued battle for women's rights in 19th and 20th centuries. Passage of the 19th Amendment. Leaders: Anna Shaw, Susan B. Anthony. (2) Rise of women to positions of eminence (Clara Barton — Red Cross; Frances Perkins — first woman Cabinet member; Eleanor Roosevelt — international affairs and human welfare; Frances Willard — Prohibition Movement).

Literature and Theater. (1) Writers, poets, essayists, dramatists have best mirrored and reacted to changing America, its industrialization, and its effects on the individual and society. (2) *Local colorists* wrote lovingly of disappearance of rural America: Samuel Clemens (Mark Twain), Bret Harte, Edward Eggleston, Joel Chandler Harris. *Realists* described emerging industrial America and its problems: William Dean Howells, Hamlin Garland, Henry James, Willa Cather, O. E. Rolvaag, Edith Wharton. *Na-turalists* concentrated on the brutal and less pleasant aspects of society; Stephen Crane, Frank Norris, Jack London, Theodore Dreiser, Sinclair Lewis, F. Scott Fitzgerald. *Recent American fiction*: Ernest Hemingway, Sherwood Anderson, Thomas Wolfe, James T. Farrell, John Dos Passos, Pearl Buck, William Faulkner. *Poets*: Emily Dickinson, Sidney Lanier, Edwin Arlington Robinson, T. S. Eliot, Robert Frost, Edna St. Vincent Millay, Stephen Vincent Benet, Karl Shapiro, Marianne Moore, Wallace Stevens, Robert Lowell. *Playwrights*: Eugene O'Neill, Maxwell Anderson, Tennessee Williams, Arthur Miller. (3) Rise of modern newspaper and growing popularity of weekly and monthly magazines.

Painting, Sculpture, Architecture. (1) Until end of the 19th century American painting, sculpture, architecture imitated European models. (2) Many innovations in 20th century: growth in number of art museums and galleries, growth in wealth and leisure, growth in market for art. (3) Break with "genteel" tradition in painting in 20th century (impressionism, expressionism, abstractionism, cubism, surrealism, "pop art," "op art"). (4) Development of the skyscraper (America's unique contribution to architectural design). Also, development of new building materials — glass, aluminum, concrete, steel, etc. *Painters*: George Inness, Winslow Homer, Thomas Eakins, Maurice Prendergast, Robert Henri, Mary Cassatt, George Bellows, Grant Wood, Thomas Hart Benton, Andrew Wyeth, Jackson Pollock. *Sculptors*: Augustus St. Gaudens, Daniel Chester French, Gutzon Borglum, Alexander Calder, William Zorach. *Architects*: Henry H. Richardson, Louis Sullivan, Ralph A. Cram, Frank Lloyd Wright.

Music. (1) Last of the United States arts to achieve cultural independence. (2) 20th century music has increasingly departed from classical traditions. (3) Growth of vast musical audience, increase in symphony orchestras, introduction of folk music vogue and jazz. *Composers*: Stephen Foster, Edward MacDowell, Charles Ives, George Gershwin, Victor Herbert, Irving Berlin, Jerome Kern, Cole Porter, Richard Rodgers, Aaron Copland. *Performing artists*: Artur Rubinstein, Jascha Heifetz, Vladimir Horowitz, Marian Anderson.

Science and Medicine. (1) Americans have moved into the first rank in science and medicine; both pure and applied. (2) New views on life and matter were developed. (3) Advances in physics, astronomy, chemistry, checking of disease, new medicines, drugs, surgery. *Scientists*: Thomas H. Morgan, Albert Michelson, Robert Millikan, Arthur Compton, Ernest O. Lawrence, Harold Urey, Harlow Shapley, Josiah Gibbs, Albert Einstein, Isidor Rabi. *Men of Medicine*: Silas W. Mitchell, Edward Trudeau, Walter Reed, William and Charles Mayo, Harvey Cushing, Abraham Flexner, William Menninger, Jonas Salk, Albert Sabin, Selman Waksman.

Social Science. New ways of thinking about man, his society, and his behavior. *Leading social scientists*: William Graham Sumner, John Fiske, Edward Bellamy, Henry George, Lester Ward, Thorstein Veblen, Oliver Wendell Holmes, Louis Brandeis, William James, John Dewey, James Harvey Robinson.

New York State Department of Commerce

Philharmonic Hall in New York City's Lincoln Center for the Performing Arts. Communities throughout the nation are promoting similar cultural activities.

CHAPTER 17

Political Development of the United States Since the Civil War

Since the Civil War political parties and leaders have been concerned with solving the problems resulting from the industrialization and urbanization of the nation and from our changing role in world affairs. From time to time third parties and reform movements have emerged, generally because of the failure of the two major parties to offer solutions to pressing problems of the time.

Part 1 — POLITICAL DEVELOPMENTS (1865-1900)

Political developments between 1865 and 1900 took place against a background of rapid national change. Among the more noteworthy of these changes were the growing industrialization of the nation, the commercialization of farming, the movement of population to the Far West and Great Plains regions, the increased concentration of population in cities, and significant advances in transportation and communication. Problems faced by businessmen, farmers, and workers in this era were of national concern and tended to push foreign affairs into the background.

Political Conservatism (1865–1900). The decades after the Civil War were a period of political conservatism in which both major political parties supported the interests of big business and *laissez-faire*. Although it has become customary to refer to the era as one of "Republican supremacy" because the Republican Party captured the Presidency on nearly every occasion, this was in fact not so. Elections were very closely contested, and only twice between 1874 and 1894 were both houses of Congress controlled by the same party.

1. *Republican "Ascendancy."* In the post-Civil War era, from 1865 to 1900, the Republican Party elected every President but one (Grover Cleveland in 1884 and 1892). Republican candidates attracted votes by supporting policies that appealed to both the industrial East (protective tariffs and subsidies) and the agrarian West (free land). For two decades they also secured votes by *"waving the bloody shirt"*; that is, by reminding the voters that it was the Republican Party that had preserved the Union during the Civil War. (Republicans referred to their party as the GOP or "Grand Old Party.") For most of the period the "Stalwart" and the "Half Breed" factions fought for control of the party.

288

2. *Role of the Democrats.* Although the Democratic Party suffered in the public mind from its association with the "treason and rebellion" of the Civil War, it continued to play a major role in national politics, especially after it regained control of the South in the 1870's. Democrats vied strongly with Republicans in battles for control of Congress. With the noteworthy exception of tariffs, the Democrats took essentially the same position as the Republicans on most major issues. Moreover, though they usually supported low tariffs in their campaigns, they did little to lower the tariff when in control of Congress.

3. *Failure to Face Issues.* Because both parties feared losing the support of large blocs of voters, they avoided taking strong stands on the really important issues of the time, such as the conditions of the farmer and worker, the currency problem, and regulation of business. This failure to face up to important issues has led some historians to describe the period as one in which there was a "failure of party government." In campaigns the emphasis was on personalities rather than issues.

4. *Third Parties.* Since the major parties failed to come to grips with many important problems that faced the nation, third parties and reform movements advanced their own solutions to the nation's political, social, and economic problems. Although usually short-lived, these movements helped to bring significant problems to national attention.

(a) Sometimes the major parties took over an issue first championed by a third party. For example, in 1896 the Democrats came out in favor of free silver, a principle that until that time had been supported by the Populists. (See page 335.)

(b) Third-party movements also helped make local and national governments more aware of the growing need to curb economic and social abuses.

Presidents and Policies (1865–1900). With some exceptions, the political leadership of the nation was not particularly outstanding after the Civil War. Captains of industry earned more formidable reputations for ability to "get things done" than did most of the nation's Chief Executives. Indeed, it has been suggested that one reason for the lack of outstanding Presidents in this era was the fact that the ablest men went into business rather than politics.

NOTE: Most of the laws, events, and achievements that are mentioned briefly in this chapter are treated at greater length elsewhere in this book. The reader should consult the index freely whenever he wishes a fuller explanation of a particular event than the one offered here.

Andrew Johnson (Republican, 1865–69). ANDREW JOHNSON succeeded to the Presidency after the death of Lincoln. He was intelligent, forceful, and gifted, but also stubborn and hotheaded. His lack of tact and his decision to apply Lincoln's moderate plan of Reconstruction (with perhaps less realism and adaptability than Lincoln would have shown) aroused bitter opposition in Congress. In the forefront of this opposition were the "Radical Republican" leaders, who were determined to punish the South and extend rights to the freed Negro.

1. The Impeachment of Johnson. The battle between Johnson and Congress was climaxed by his impeachment in 1868, for violation of the *Tenure of Office Act*. Although most historians consider the Johnson acquittal by the narrow margin of one vote a triumph for justice, he has been criticized for poor judgment.

2. Noteworthy Events and Achievements of the Johnson Administration. Noteworthy events during Johnson's administration included: **(a)** military reconstruction in the South; **(b)** the establishment of "carpetbag" and "scalawag" governments in Southern states; **(c)** the adoption of the Thirteenth (1865) and Fourteenth (1868) Amendments; **(d)** the purchase of Alaska from Russia in 1867.

Ulysses S. Grant (Republican, 1869–77). ULYSSES S. GRANT was elected President in 1868 and re-elected in 1872. Although he had been a great general, Grant made a very poor President. He was unaware of the forces that were shaping the nation, showed poor judgment in making political appointments, and failed to exercise leadership within the Republican Party.

1. Political Developments. The political corruption in Grant's first administration so distressed the "Liberal" faction of the Republican Party that they supported the Democratic candidate, HORACE GREELEY, in 1872. Their failure to endorse Grant caused the Republican Party to do some "house-cleaning" and to begin to look favorably upon the idea of a merit system for the civil service.

2. Noteworthy Events and Achievements of the Grant Administration. In addition to widespread corruption and political scandals on all levels, the important developments that occurred during Grant's two terms of office included the following:

The *Panic of 1873* brought on hard times and serious unemployment.

The *Greenback Movement* tried but failed to get the government to inflate the currency.

Miners and farmers joined to demand the unrestricted coinage of silver (*free silver*).

Granger laws were passed by Middle Western states to curb railroad abuses.

The *Knights of Labor*, first important nationwide labor organization, was formed in 1869.

The first transcontinental railroad, the *Union Pacific*, was completed in 1869.

The *Fifteenth Amendment* was adopted.

Most Southern states were readmitted to the Union, and white supremacy was reimposed. The *Amnesty Act of 1872* restored political rights to most former Confederate leaders.

Rutherford B. Hayes (Republican, 1877–81). Grant's successor was RUTHERFORD B. HAYES, former Governor of Ohio, who gained office in 1876. Hayes was honest, able, and a reformer. However, he was unable to secure much constructive legislation as a result of opposition by his own party leaders and Democratic majorities in Congress. In addition, he lacked public confidence because of the disputed nature of his election.

1. *Political Developments.* Hayes had four difficult years as President. The Democrats controlled the House of Representatives and, from 1879 to 1881, the Senate as well. Conservative leaders of Hayes' own Republican party ("Stalwarts") were opposed to reform.

2. *Noteworthy Events and Achievements of the Hayes Administration.* A number of important events occurred while Hayes was President.

Hayes withdrew Federal troops from the South, formally ending Reconstruction.

Hayes selected office-holders on merit and resisted demands of party leaders that he replace thousands of office holders with party favorites. He believed in the principle: "He serves his party best who serves his country best."

Serious strikes broke out following years of depression after the *Panic of 1873.* The government was forced to intervene in the paralyzing railroad strike of 1877.

Congress yielded to the demands of free silverites and passed the *Bland-Allison Act* (1878), over Hayes' veto, providing for some silver purchases by the government.

Congress responded to growing anti-Chinese feeling by passing the *Chinese Exclusion Act* of 1881 over Hayes' veto.

James A. Garfield (Republican, 1881). JAMES A. GARFIELD succeeded Hayes as President. Garfield had been a college president and Civil War general, and was considered above average in ability. Unfortunately, he was assassinated by a disappointed office seeker several months after taking office.

1. *Political Developments.* Garfield was a "dark horse" nominee, selected as a result of a convention deadlock between ex-President Grant and James G. Blaine, the dynamic unofficial Republican Party leader. In the election of 1880, Garfield narrowly defeated General WINFIELD HANCOCK, the Democratic nominee.

2. *Noteworthy Events and Achievements of the Garfield Administration.* Garfield was in office only six months, and for a good part of that time he was incapacitated by an assassin's bullet. Although he had indicated interest in civil service reform before taking office, his extremely brief period of service prevented important steps in that direction. His appointment of Blaine as Secretary of State angered the conservative wing of the Republican Party, which sought the "spoils" of victory in the form of jobs. Blaine led the "Half-Breed" faction of the party, which (though spoils-conscious too) was mildly "reformist" in character. Garfield's assassin, Charles Guiteau, was a disappointed "Stalwart" office seeker.

Chester A. Arthur (Republican, 1881–85). Vice President CHESTER A. ARTHUR succeeded to the Presidency upon the death of Garfield. Since Arthur had never been more than a "machine" politician before becoming Vice President, little was expected of him. Arthur surprised everyone, however, by rising to unexpected heights as President. In the face of Presidential responsibilities, he turned out to be an able administrator, made sound appointments, and fought corruption and fraud in his administration.

1. *Political Developments.* Although Blaine resigned as Secretary of State, Arthur, a former Stalwart, disappointed and angered Stalwart leaders like Roscoe Conkling by not dropping *all* other Half-Breeds from office.

2. *Noteworthy Events and Achievements of the Arthur Administration.* Two notable events occurred while Arthur was President.

> (a) Congress appropriated money for building the nation's first steel warships. These became the basis of a modern navy, which shortly afterwards gave a good account of itself in the Spanish-American War.

> (b) Perhaps the most significant event of Arthur's Presidency was the passage of the *Pendleton Act* of 1883, which established a merit system for filling government jobs (the civil service) on the basis of competitive examinations. The Act affected only 10% of Federal employees when originally passed, but its coverage was extended by later Presidents. At present, about 90% of Federal positions (nonelective and non-military) fall within the system. The Pendleton Act was in part the result of Garfield's assassination at the hands of a spoils seeker, in part the result of the exposure of political scandals, and in part the result of Arthur's influence. It was the first major step in the battle to revise the spoils system that had developed since the time of Jackson.

Grover Cleveland (Democrat, 1885–89). GROVER CLEVELAND was the first Democratic President after the Civil War. Before attaining office, Cleveland had been Mayor of Buffalo and Governor of New York. His first administration (he also served as President from 1893 to 1897) was generally considered successful despite the fact that a Republican Senate was able to block many of his suggested programs. The traits that distinguished Cleveland as one of the nation's outstanding Presidents were courage, honesty, and a concern for public welfare. He tried hard to live up to his motto that "a public office is a public trust."

1. *Political Developments.* The campaign of 1884 was an outstanding example of an election in which personalities rather than issues were predominant. Though the Democrats called for tariff reduction, few fundamental differences separated the parties. Each attempted to "smear" the reputation of the rival party's candidate. JAMES G. BLAINE, the Republican standard bearer (referred to as the "Plumed Knight"), was accused of political dishonesty. Cleveland was accused of being a drunkard and of immoral conduct. In the end Cleveland won by a narrow majority. Among the reasons for the Democratic victory were **(1)** Blaine's association in the public mind with dishonest political maneuvers; **(2)** the desertion of the Republican Party by the "Mugwumps" — reformers who opposed Blaine's nomination; **(3)** several campaign blunders by Republicans, notably Blaine's failure to repudiate the charge by a Republican clergyman, that the Democratic Party was the party of "Rum, Romanism, and Rebellion," (which angered Roman Catholic voters); and **(4)** a business depression, which, as is usually the case, was blamed upon the party in power.

2. *Noteworthy Events and Achievements of the First Cleveland Administration.* Cleveland's first administration was characterized by the following developments.

Cleveland vetoed what he considered to be unjustified pension bills for veterans.

Cleveland was a moderate civil service reformer. Although he replaced some Republican office holders with Democrats, he did not make wholesale changes, despite the desires of party leaders.

Cleveland· was one of the first Presidents to champion conservation. He regained for the public domain over 81 million acres of land improperly acquired by railroads and ranchers.

The nation was faced with farm unrest resulting from the upset of the Granger laws by the Supreme Court's *Wabash Decision.*

Labor unrest was highlighted by the *Haymarket Affair* of 1886.

Congress passed the *Dawes Act* (1887) to help the Indians and the *Interstate Commerce Act* (1888) to curb railroad abuses.

Congress refused to support Cleveland's request for tariff reduction.

Benjamin Harrison (Republican, 1889–93). Cleveland's successor was BENJAMIN HARRISON, a former Union general, corporation lawyer, and Senator. Harrison was a man of honesty and integrity, but was also a loyal party supporter who preferred to follow rather than to lead Congress.

1. *Political Developments.* In the election of 1888, Cleveland received over 100,000 more popular votes than did Harrison. Harrison, however was elected because he received more votes in the Electoral College. At Cleveland's insistence, the Democrats supported tariff reduction. This cost them votes, since the Republicans argued that a protective tariff was necessary to protect American labor and insure a treasury surplus.

2. *Noteworthy Events and Achievements of the Harrison Administration.* These included the following:

The annual Federal budget topped the billion-dollar mark for the first time. Much of this was in the form of Civil War pensions.

The *Sherman Antitrust Act* of 1890 was passed to quiet the rising clamor against big corporations.

Congress passed the *Sherman Silver Act* of 1890, increasing government purchase of silver; it also boosted tariff rates to new highs (*McKinley Tariff*

of 1890). In a "log-rolling" compromise, Congressmen representing Western silver and farming interests agreed to support the protective tariff, in return for Eastern support for silver.

Labor dissatisfaction with wage cuts resulted in many strikes (for example, the *Homestead Strike* of 1892).

Continued farm unrest resulted in the formation of the *Populist Party.*

Grover Cleveland (Democrat, 1893–97). GROVER CLEVELAND was elected President for the second time in 1892. Cleveland was the only President to be re-elected after a defeat, the only one to serve two nonconsecutive terms, and the first to receive a popular plurality in three successive elections. The many different challenges that confronted the nation during Cleveland's second administration, particularly the Panic of 1893 and the resulting depression, made his second term more difficult than his first.

1. *Political Developments.* In 1892, tariff was again the main issue, with the Republicans upholding high tariff and the Democrats again calling for tariff reform. Among the factors contributing to Cleveland's victory over Harrison were popular resentment against the McKinley Tariff, and the use of troops by the Federal government against the strikers in the Homestead Strike. The election of 1892 was also significant for the remarkable showing of the Populist Party, which received over a million popular and 22 electoral votes for its candidate, General JAMES WEAVER.

2. *Noteworthy Events and Achievements of the Second Cleveland Administration.* Cleveland's second administration was marked by the number of noteworthy developments.

As a result of the *Panic of 1893* the nation plunged into a depression for which Cleveland was wrongly blamed.

To avoid damage to the value of the dollar resulting from a dwindling gold reserve, Cleveland persuaded Congress to repeal the *Sherman Silver Purchase Act* in 1893. (Under this act, silver certificates issued by the government were being exchanged for gold.) Cleveland also negotiated a loan for gold with a banking syndicate led by J. P. Morgan, in exchange for government bonds. Although these acts relieved the gold scarcity, Cleveland was denounced by silverites and debtors for "selling out to Wall Street."

Cleveland antagonized organized labor by issuing an injunction against the striking Pullman Car union. The imprisonment of union leader Eugene V. Debs convinced labor that the administration and the courts were "anti-labor."

Cleveland let the *Wilson-Gorman Tariff* of 1894 become a law without his signature because it resulted in only minor tariff reductions. However, he denounced it as a betrayal by the Democratic Party. The act contained (for the first time) a provision providing for an income tax on large incomes. This was declared illegal by the Supreme Court in 1895 for violating the "direct tax" clause of the Constitution.

Cleveland precipitated a crisis with Britain by charging her with violating the Monroe Doctrine in a boundary dispute with Venezuela (1895–96). A warlike atmosphere was ended by acceptance of Cleveland's plan to arbitrate the issue.

William McKinley (Republican, 1897–1901). WILLIAM MCKINLEY became President in 1896 as a result of an election considered to be a triumph for big business. A former Congressman and ex-Governor of Ohio, McKinley was able but rather rigorous and limited in his conservative outlook. He worked mostly with the Republican majority in Congress. His administration benefited from prosperity and supported big business. During McKinley's administration, the nation embarked upon a policy of territorial expansion (imperialism) that changed significantly the nature of United States foreign policy in the first quarter of the 20th century. McKinley was assassinated shortly after his inauguration in 1901 for his second term.

This poster of the 1896 election shows the partisan bitterness and personal ridicule that have often marked American Presidential campaigns.

1. *Political Developments.* In winning the Presidency in 1896, McKinley, the Republican standard bearer, defeated WILLIAM JENNINGS BRYAN, Presidential nominee of both the Democratic and Populist parties, who strongly urged the adoption of "free silver." McKinley's campaign slogan of the "full dinner pail" appealed to voters because of its emphasis on prosperity. ("See page 336 for full account of this election.)

2. *Noteworthy Events and Achievements of the McKinley Administration.* The following developments occurred while McKinley was President.

Prosperity returned to the nation after years of depression.

Congress passed laws placing the nation on a gold standard and raising the tariff (*Dingley Act* of 1897).

Businessmen dominated government. The antitrust laws were largely unenforced.

Foreign affairs overshadowed domestic events for the first time in over a quarter of a century. Hawaii was annexed. We also entered the *Spanish-American War,* and gained Guam, Puerto Rico, and the Philippines.

REVIEW TEST (Chapter 17—Part I)

Select the number preceding the word or expression that best completes each statement or answers each question.

1. Which of the following was a significant characteristic of politics in the United States during the quarter century following the Civil War? (1) abolition of the spoils system (2) greater Presidential concern for foreign affairs than for domestic affairs (3) disappearance of third-party movements (4) support of big business by both major parties

2. A political party that advocated the free coinage of silver was the (1) Republican Party (2) Federalist Party (3) Whig Party (4) Populist Party

3. I was victorious in a disputed election. I alienated my party by withdrawing the remaining Federal troops from the South and by supporting the motto, "He serves his party best who serves the country best." (1) Thomas Jefferson (2) Andrew Johnson (3) Rutherford B. Hayes (4) Ulysses S. Grant

4. In which of the following pairs did the first event lead directly to the second event? (1) formation of the Populist Party — rise of the Granger movement (2) purchase of Alaska — cold war with Russia (3) bombing of Pearl Harbor — annexation of Hawaii by the United States (4) assassination of President Garfield — passage of the Pendleton Act

5. I was the first Democrat elected to the Presidency after the Civil War. Tariff and currency problems occupied much of my time. I supported the principle that "a public office is a public trust." (1) Benjamin Harrison (2) Grover Cleveland (3) Chester A. Arthur (4) Woodrow Wilson

6. During my administration the United States was victorious in a short war and acquired an overseas empire. The slogan, the "full dinner pail" was used in one of my campaigns. (1) William McKinley (2) Theodore Roosevelt (3) William H. Taft (4) Woodrow Wilson

7. Which of the following was an outstanding issue in the Presidential campaign of 1896? (1) government ownership of railroads (2) monetary policy (3) imperialism in the Far East (4) removal of troops from the South

8. Two of the most controversial issues in the United States during the period 1875–1900 were (1) overseas expansion and the currency problem (2) slavery and antitrust legislation (3) states' rights and manifest destiny (4) immigration and internal improvements

9. Alaska was purchased during the administration of (1) Andrew Johnson (2) Ulysses Grant (3) James Garfield (4) William McKinley

10. The Liberal Republicans of 1872 opposed (1) political corruption in the Grant Administration (2) the annexation of Hawaii (3) the re-election of Hayes (4) the nomination of Tilden for the Presidency

For each President in Column A, write the letter of the event in Column B that occurred during his administration.

A	B
1. Ulysses Grant	*a.* Panic of 1873
2. Rutherford B. Hayes	*b.* Passage of Interstate Commerce Act
3. Grover Cleveland	*c.* First "billion-dollar Congress"
4. Benjamin Harrison	*d.* Passage of Bland-Allison Act
5. William McKinley	*e.* Annexation of Hawaii
	f. End of the Civil War

Essay Questions

1. For each of the following Presidents discuss one major domestic issue he faced, and the policy or program pursued by him in meeting this problem: Andrew Johnson, Ulysses Grant, Grover Cleveland, William McKinley.

2. Discuss each of the following in terms of political trends or developments in the period 1865–1900: (a) role of the Republican Party (b) role of the Democratic Party (c) role of third parties.

Part II — POLITICAL DEVELOPMENTS (1900–20)

The first two decades of the 20th century saw continued economic growth along lines begun in the post-Civil War period. As this growth speeded up, a new *industrialized* and *urbanized* America began to emerge. Agriculture slipped into a position of secondary importance. Businesses grew ever bigger, with consolidations proceeding rapidly, and manufacturing became the dominant form of economic activity. More and more Americans moved into the growing cities. In foreign affairs the Monroe Doctrine was given new meaning, the nation acquired overseas possessions, a Far Eastern policy took shape, and the United States was drawn into World War I. The problems and tensions resulting from these changes provided the key issues of American politics for decades to come.

The Progressive Era. The period between the Spanish-American War and World War I (*c.* 1900 to 1920) is known as the *Progressive Era*. It was a period marked by idealism and reform, as well as by significant economic growth. Its characteristics can best be understood by studying the Progressive Movement during the administrations of Theodore Roosevelt and Woodrow Wilson.

Progressivism was a movement designed to correct the abuses which reformers felt had crept into American society and government, as a result of industrialization and urbanization. In one sense, Progressivism may be considered a continuation of the reform movement of the late 19th century. In the early 20th century, however, the movement acquired new aims and methods.

1. *The Roots of Progressivism.* Progressivism was the outcome of a number of forces in American life. **(a)** The reform spirit of the 1880's and 1890's was still strong, despite the collapse of the Populist Party after the election of 1896. **(b)** After the hard times of the 1890's, many Americans were anxious for a better life and supported reforms intended to achieve this. **(c)** The middle class, frightened by the economic unrest of the 1890's and the actions of giant business organizations, was more willing to accept progressive reforms than it had been earlier. **(d)** After the quick victory in the Spanish-American War and the prosperity of the early 1900's, there was a new spirit of confidence in the nation's future. This provided a favorable climate for a reform movement intended to improve social conditions and to perfect our democratic institutions.

2. *Aims and Philosophy of Progressivism.* Progressives were disturbed by the graft and corruption that had become part of much of the nation's political life, particularly on state and local levels. Also, they were upset by the power of industrial monopoly and by the growing social problems of city life. The general aims of the Progressives were: **(a)** to extend political democracy by shifting control of government from the political bosses and powerful industrialists to the people; **(b)** to curb the power of big businessmen, in order to give greater economic opportunities to small business and labor; and **(c)** to eliminate the social ills of society through needed reforms.

Makeup of the Progressive Movement. Progressives came from many different groups. They shared a common desire for reform, improvement, and more democracy.

1. *Political Support.* Progressives came from both major parties, as well as from minor or third parties. Important political leaders in the movement included Presidents THEODORE ROOSEVELT and WOODROW WILSON, and Governors ROBERT LA FOLLETTE (Wisconsin), CHARLES EVANS HUGHES (New York), and HIRAM JOHNSON (California).

2. *Farm Support.* Although the Progressive Movement was for the most part an *urban* movement (just as Populism had for the most part been an *agrarian* movement), farm organizations and farm leaders were among those who pressed for reforms to give the voter a stronger voice in government. Such reforms, they hoped, would enable them to obtain favorable attention to farm problems (better roads, cheaper credit, lower taxes, etc.).

3. *Artists and Writers.* Progressivism received powerful support from artists and writers who through their works condemned the injustices of city life, the poverty of the times, and the inhumanity of an industrial society. Notable among these were: *realistic painters,* such as JOHN SLOAN, ROBERT HENRI, and GEORGE LUKS; *literary realists* like THEODORE DREISER, FRANK NORRIS, and JACK LONDON; *social workers, sociologists* and *economists* like JANE ADDAMS, LILLIAN WALD, FATHER JOHN RYAN, and JOHN SPARGO. Most influential of all were the *crusading journalists* (*"muckrakers"*), where sensational exposures in books, newspapers, and magazines laid bare the evils of monopoly and corruption. Eminent "muckrakers" included LINCOLN STEFFENS (exposed political corruption in the cities), IDA TARBELL (exposed monopoly practices of Standard Oil), UPTON SINCLAIR (exposed unsanitary practices in meat-packing), and FRANK NORRIS (exposed the great power and abuses of railroads).

4. *Intellectuals.* Important American intellectuals of the time, such as WILLIAM JAMES and JOHN DEWEY (philosophers), OLIVER WENDELL HOLMES (Justice of the Supreme Court), CHARLES A. BEARD (historian), and THORSTEIN VEBLEN (economist) called for new values and modes of thinking in regard to society.

5. *Urban Middle-Class Support.* Most Progressives were from the urban middle class — professionals, small businessmen, white collar men, intellectuals, artists, and writers. In general they felt their position and prestige threatened by the advancing forces of big business and machine politics. Some far-sighted "big business" leaders could also be counted among the Progressives; for example E. A. FILENE and GEORGE PERKINS.

Achievements of the Progressive Movement. The swelling chorus of protest aroused by the Progressives produced a number of significant reforms on national, state, and local levels. Responsible for initiating many of these advances were reform governors like ROBERT LA FOLLETTE, reform mayors like HAZEN PINGREE of Detroit and SAMUEL JONES of Toledo, and Presidents like T. Roosevelt and Wilson, who backed reform measures and brought the prestige of the Presidency to the cause of reform.

1. *Political Democracy Was Extended.* **(a)** Many cities and states adopted the *initiative* (popular introduction of laws), the *referendum* (popular vote on laws), or the *recall* (popular removal of officials), in order to give the citizen more direct participation in government. **(b)** The *short ballot* replaced the long ballot in many localities. Its purpose was to make possible more intelligent choice of candidates. **(c)** The *Seventeenth Amendment* (1913) provided for the direct election of U. S. Senators. **(d)** The *Nineteenth Amendment* gave the franchise to women (1920). **(e)** *Direct primaries* were adopted in a growing number of states to permit the selection of party candidates by registered voters. **(f)** New forms of city-government, particularly the *city-manager* and *commission* types were adopted as a means of ending municipal corruption.

2. *Curbs Were Placed on Trusts.* **(a)** Monopolies were prosecuted more vigorously for violation of the antitrust laws and decisions favorable to the government were handed down by the courts. **(b)** The movement to regulate business was strengthened by additional legislation, such as the *Clayton Act* (1914) and *Federal Trade Commission Act* (1914) and by the establishment of state public service commissions.

3. *Laws Safeguarding Labor and the Public Were Enacted.* Following the lead of pioneering states like Wisconsin and Oregon, national, state, and city governments took action along the following lines: **(a)** More adequate factory and building inspection codes were adopted. **(b)** Greater provision was made for sanitation and public health. **(c)** Minimum wage and workman's-compensation laws were enacted. **(d)** Congress enacted the *Pure Food and Drug Act* and the *Meat Inspection Act* in 1906. **(e)** In addition, the movement to conserve the nation's natural resources received active government support.

4. *Growing Concern for Social Reform.* **(a)** Settlement houses, public parks, playgrounds, and other recreational facilities mushroomed in the cities. **(b)** This growing spirit of *humanitarianism* also gave rise to many laws restricting child labor, and to new agencies for assisting young people (Boy Scouts, Campfire Girls, etc.). **(c)** Greater attention to the problem of discrimination led to the establishment of such organizations as the National Association for the Advancement of Colored People. **(d)** Attempts were made to improve housing conditions in the growing slums of the cities (for example, the *Tenement House Law* of 1902 in New York City).

Limitations of Progressivism. Although Progressivism injected a stream of idealism into American life that still influences present attitudes toward reform, the movement also had definite limitations.

1. *Some Unrealistic Beliefs.* For one thing, the Progressives were somewhat naive in their belief that once reforms were enacted the ills of democracy would disappear. It soon became apparent that reform "movements" were temporary, and that in most cases political bosses and machines were voted back into office as soon as enthusiasm for change had passed. Reformers soon realized, too, that some of the changes that were supposed to "purify" politics did not do so, for example, the attainment of women's suffrage.

2. *Some Undemocratic Attitudes.* In addition, it may be noted that some of the many reformers of the Progressive Era took positions that would hardly be considered democratic or liberal today. For example, many opposed immigration on the grounds that the new immigrants became the pawns of political bosses. Others opposed labor unionism, although sympathetic to the need for improved working conditions.

Presidents and Policies (1900–20). During the Progressive Era, political leaders and parties made more of an attempt to come to grips with the real issues facing the nation than had their predecessors.

Theodore Roosevelt (Republican, 1901–09). THEODORE ROOSEVELT, successor to McKinley, was one of the nation's most dynamic and influential Presidents. He came to office after a long career in public service, which included the offices of member of the U. S. Civil Service Commission, Police Commissioner of New York City, Assistant Secretary of Navy, Governor of New York State, and Vice President of the United States. Roosevelt was colorful, forceful, and popular. He provided dramatic leadership for the Progressive Movement by promoting reform, and increased national prestige and influence by aggressive conduct of foreign affairs.

1. *Election of 1900.* In the election of 1900, President McKinley (Republican) defeated William Jennings Bryan (Democrat), for the second successive time. Bryan and his supporters vigorously criticized "Republican imperialism" (referring to the acquisition of the Philippines, Guam, and Puerto Rico after the Spanish-American War). They also accused the Republicans of supporting the trusts. McKinley's victory by an even wider margin than in 1896 resulted in large measure from popular satisfaction with prosperity and business support of the tariff policy endorsed by the Republicans.

2. *Roosevelt Becomes President (1901).* McKinley was assassinated six months after his inauguration. Vice President Theodore Roosevelt became President at the young age of 42. Roosevelt's moving upward into the Presidency dismayed conservative Republican leaders, since he had been nominated as Vice President in order to get him out of New York State politics, where he had alarmed party leaders by his vigorous independence.

3. Re-election of Roosevelt in 1904. Roosevelt's record during his first term, together with his tremendous personal popularity, easily won him renomination and re-election in 1904. In defeating the Democratic nominee, Judge ALTON PARKER of New York, a "sound money man," Roosevelt carried every state outside the Solid South.

4. Noteworthy Events and Achievements of the T. Roosevelt Administration. Roosevelt's program of domestic reform is called the *Square Deal,* a term that developed from his promise to bring a "square deal" and "opportunity" to every man. His foreign policy rested upon his belief that the United States was destined to play an important role in world affairs in the 20th century (the *"new nationalism"*). The more noteworthy events and achievements of both of these phases of Roosevelt's Presidency are briefly outlined below.

In the *Anthracite Coal Strike* of 1902 Roosevelt showed his sympathy for labor by forcing the mine owners to accept arbitration.

Roosevelt's interest in curbing abuses of big business resulted in increased prosecutions of major corporations for violation of antitrust laws (*e.g.,* the *Northern Securities Case*). Facts about big business were gathered by a newly established *Bureau of Corporations.*

Congressional support of the Square Deal took the form of laws increasing the power of the Interstate Commerce Commission and protecting the public against inferior and unhealthy foods (*Pure Food and Drug Act* of 1906, *Meat Inspection Act* of 1906).

Roosevelt did much to promote conservation and arouse the nation to the necessity of preserving its natural resources. He sponsored conservation laws (*Newlands Act*), withdrew valu-able forest and mineral lands from public sale, appointed a *National Conservation Commission* and called the first Governors' Conference on Conservation in 1908. Many consider this conservation effort his surest claim to fame.

Roosevelt believed in an active role for the United States in foreign affairs. His policies, though often criticized as being "high-handed," increased the stature of the nation abroad. As President, Roosevelt built a strong navy, extended United States influence in the Caribbean (*Big Stick Policy*), acquired the Panama Canal Zone, and helped negotiate the *Treaty of Portsmouth* (1905) ending the Russo-Japanese War (for which he received the Nobel Peace Prize). He also mediated a dispute over Morocco between France and Germany, and initiated the Second Hague Disarmament Conference (1907).

The Importance of Theodore Roosevelt. Theodore Roosevelt made more of an impact upon national development than did most other Chief Executives. Because he brought new stature to the Presidency in the 20th century, T. Roosevelt has been called the "first modern President." It is with good reason that the years 1901–09 are often called the "Roosevelt Era."

1. *Progressivism.* Roosevelt did not start the Progressive Movement, nor go as far as many Progressives desired. Nevertheless, he was clearly a Progressive in his faith in progress, in his desire for greater justice for the average man, and in his desire to expose and drive from power the evil influences in society, including "corrupt politicians," "malefactors of great wealth," and "guilty labor leaders." Roosevelt's enthusiasm for reform gave respectability and strength to the Progressive Movement. His faith in democracy gave the common man respect for himself.

2. *Leadership.* Theodore Roosevelt believed in strong Presidential leadership. He thought of the President as "a steward of the people" who had "to do all he could for the people." The President's job, therefore, was to make proposals for solving the problems facing the nation and to win the support of both Congress and the people for his programs. As Chief Executive, Roosevelt made himself undisputed leader of the Republican Party by skillful political maneuvering and use of his power of appointment. His tremendous popularity with the voters held the more conservative members of his party in check.

3. *Respect for Intelligence.* Roosevelt was a learned man as well as an active one. As such he showed respect for brain-power and intellect. He called upon lawyers, economists, and labor leaders for suggestions. He also attracted to government service able advisors and subordinates.

William Howard Taft (Republican, 1909–13). WILLIAM HOWARD TAFT followed Theodore Roosevelt as President. As Roosevelt's able Secretary of War, Taft had been associated with the reform spirit of the administration. As President, however, Taft turned out to be a mild rather than a vigorous Progressive, with a record of commendable but cautious reforms. He was progressive in the sense that he saw the need for further social reform and for taking positive steps to curb big business and to promote conservation. He was a conservative, however, in his desire to go slowly and in his belief that the President should not actively attempt to influence legislation or Congress. The reform or insurgent wing of the Republican Party as well as former President Roosevelt were both disappointed with Taft's performance. The split between Taft and the *insurgents* contributed to an unhappy Presidency. (In 1921, Taft was appointed Chief Justice of the Supreme Court, thus becoming the holder of two of the highest offices on the American political scene.)

1. *Political Developments.* As Theodore Roosevelt's handpicked candidate, Taft defeated Bryan for the Presidency in 1908. (Bryan was the Democratic candidate for the third time.) Although the Republicans stressed prosperity and tariff revision, the Taft victory was essentially a victory for Roosevelt's popularity.

2. *Noteworthy Events and Achievements of the Taft Administration.* The following were among the more important events of Taft's Presidency.

The passage of the *Payne-Aldrich Tariff* (1908), which Taft failed to veto, angered the progressives in the Republican Party because rates were not reduced very much.

As a sincere conservationist, Taft withdrew additional mineral lands and water power sites from public sale. However, his support of Secretary of the Interior, Richard Ballinger, in a conservation scandal caused Progressives to condemn him for "selling out the public interest."

Among the reforms introduced by the Taft administration were: extension of the Civil Service system; establishment of the postal savings system; adoption of an 8-hour day for government employees; and the creation of a separate Department of Labor.

Taft's interest in world peace was shown by the signing of arbitration treaties with England and France and the final settlement (by arbitration) of a long-standing dispute with Great Brit-ain over the Newfoundland fisheries.

The reform or insurgent wing of the Republican Party joined with Democrats to curb the power of the Speaker of the House (Joseph Cannon) over the appointment of committee members.

Taft continued and extended the antitrust actions of T. Roosevelt and also extended the jurisdiction of the Interstate Commerce Commission.

Taft promoted a policy of *"dollar diplomacy"* in Latin America. Marines were dispatched to Caribbean countries on several occasions to protect American investments.

Dissatisfaction with Taft's policies caused the insurgent Republicans to form a *National Progressive Republican League* in 1911, led by ROBERT LA FOLLETTE. It also paved the way for Theodore Roosevelt's announcement that he once again would like to run for the Presidency. ("My hat is in the ring.")

Woodrow Wilson (Democrat, 1913–21). WOODROW WILSON, former college president and Governor of New Jersey, succeeded Taft as Chief Executive. Wilson was the second Democrat to reach the White House after the Civil War. He was an idealist, reformer, and student of government who believed that the President (like a Prime Minister) should provide leadership. His first administration was concerned primarily with domestic reform (the *New Freedom*), problems of neutrality, and trouble with Mexico. During his second term the United States became involved in World War I. Wilson helped frame the peace ending the war and was a chief architect of the League of Nations. The rejection by the Senate of both the League and the Treaty contributed to his physical breakdown and left him a disillusioned man.

1. *Political Developments.* Wilson's victory in the hotly contested *election of 1912* was made possible by a split in Republican ranks. Theodore Roosevelt led the newly formed Progressive ("Bull Moose") Party, consisting of Republican insurgents. Taft was renominated as the regular Republican candidate. The election of 1912 was a triumph of Progressivism. The Democrats and Progressives advocated reform and business regulation. Popular dissatisfaction with "stand-pat" government was indicated by the election returns, in which Taft ran a poor third behind Wilson and Roosevelt. The Progressives received nearly 3.5 million votes, and the Socialist candidate, Eugene V. Debs, polled close to a million votes.

2. *Noteworthy Events and Achievements of the Wilson Administration.* Wilson's years in office were years of challenge and accomplishment.

Wilson was a strong and popular President who controlled Cabinet and Congress.

During his first administration Wilson's *New Freedom* reform program took the form of legislation providing for downward tariff revision (*Underwood Act*, 1914), antitrust laws (*Clayton Act*, 1914), banking reform (*Federal Reserve Act*, 1913), improved conditions for railroad workers (*Adamson Act*), greater freedom for unions (*Clayton Act*), additional credit for farmers (*Farm Loan Act*, 1916), assistance to Federal employees (*Workingman's Compensation Act*, 1916), protection of consumers (*Federal Trade Commission Act*, 1914), and more self-government in American overseas territories.

Wilson rejected imperialism and dollar diplomacy. He refused to recognize governments set up by force or murder (*"Watchful Waiting"*). However, circumstances led Wilson to intervene actively in the affairs of Caribbean nations.

Wilson's re-election by a close margin in 1916 over Republican candidate Charles Evans Hughes (a Supreme Court Justice) was a personal victory over a reunited Republican Party. In the election, Republicans criticized the President's neutrality policies while Democrats adopted the slogan, "He kept us out of war."

During his second term in office Wilson was largely occupied with World War I problems. He furnished inspirational leadership and became spokesman for the Allied cause. Congress granted him extraordinary powers.

After the war, Wilson was a leader at the Versailles Conference and a champion of the League of Nations. Failure of the United States to sign the Versailles Treaty or to join the League disappointed him greatly and contributed to his physical breakdown.

The Significance of Wilson. President Woodrow Wilson left an indelible impression on the political life of the country.

1. *Progressivism.* Like Theodore Roosevelt, Wilson did not go as far as the Progressives in both parties wanted him to go. Nevertheless, he was clearly progressive in his desire for social justice, in his opposition to political and business corruption, in his desire to regulate business, and in the substantial reform record of his administration. (Note: In recent years leading historians like Arthur Link have come to believe that Wilson himself may not have been as progressive as was previously thought. It is felt that he was pushed into supporting many progressive laws — Federal Reserve Act, Clayton Act, etc.—by threatened revolts within his own party.)

2. *Leadership.* Like Roosevelt, Lincoln, and Jackson before him, Wilson strengthened and extended the Presidential power by strong leadership. To an extent exceeded by few Presidents, he thought of himself as the responsible leader of his party and of the entire country. Wilson furnished an example of moral as well as political leadership. His belief in humanity, his high idealism, and his moral dedication were clearly illustrated by his faith in American democracy, his desire for a peace without victory, and his work to establish a League of Nations to end war.

REVIEW TEST (Chapter 17 — Part II)

Select the number preceding the word or expression that best completes each statement or answers each question.

1. The Progressive Movement helped bring about   (1) the Bland-Allison Act (2) proportional representation in the election of members of Congress (3) increased popular participation in government (4) increased feeling against Germany before World War I

2. Wilson's political philosophy has been characterized as the   (1) New Deal (2) New Freedom (3) Square Deal (4) *laissez-faire* program

3. The principal factor responsible for the election of Woodrow Wilson to the Presidency in 1912 was   (1) his record of reform in New Jersey (2) his reputation as an educator (3) his progressive platform (4) the split in the Republican party

4. In which Presidential election was imperialism a major issue?   (1) 1900 (2) 1904 (3) 1908 (4) 1912

5. All of the following are associated with the Theodore Roosevelt administration *except* (1) "trust busting" (2) tariff reform (3) conservation measures (4) dynamic foreign policies

Select the letter of the item in each group which does **NOT** *belong with the others.*

1. Positions held by Woodrow Wilson: (a) college president (b) governor (c) Senator (d) President of the United States

2. Achievements of the Wilson administration: (a) downward tariff revision (b) laws benefiting labor (c) successful neutrality in world affairs (d) strengthened antitrust program

3. Associated with both Theodore Roosevelt and Woodrow Wilson: (a) candidates of the Democratic Party (b) belief in strong Presidential leadership (c) personal popularity (d) progressivism

4. Muckrakers: (a) Ida Tarbell (b) Upton Sinclair (c) Frank Norris (d) Theodore Roosevelt

5. Democratic reforms of the Progressive Era: (a) initiative (b) Twenty-second Amendment (c) direct primaries (d) city-manager form of municipal government

Essay Questions

1. The period from about 1900 to the First World War is commonly called the "Progressive Era." Why is or isn't this an appropriate title? Explain.

2. (a) Give two reasons for the emergence of the Progressive Movement. (b) Discuss two results of this movement.

3. Should Theodore Roosevelt and Woodrow Wilson be called Progressives? Explain fully.

4. Briefly identify each of the following: recall, short ballot, referendum, commission form of city government, Pure Food and Drugs Act, Bureau of Corporations, "stewardship theory of the Presidency," Richard Ballinger, Speaker Joseph Cannon, dollar diplomacy, "the insurgent revolt," Eugene V. Debs, Underwood Act, "watchful waiting," the "New Nationalism," Charles Evans Hughes.

Part III — POLITICAL DEVELOPMENTS IN THE 1920's

The period 1920–32 was marked by political conservatism, economic prosperity, rapid cultural and social change, and an attempt to stay out of foreign involvements.

Characteristics of the Period 1920–32. The major characteristics of the era may be summed up as follows:

1. *Political Conservatism.* During the 1920's, Progressivism as a movement came to an end. Although reforms continued to be enacted on state and local levels, there was a general reaction against "liberalism" in politics and economics, plus a desire to return to "the good old days" when things were less hectic and the nation not so actively involved in world affairs. Those who took this attitude called it the *"return to normalcy."*

> *(a)* An important cause of the political conservatism of the era was the disillusionment with World War I. The war casualties, the disorganization of life during the war years, and the feeling that the war had not "made the world safe for democracy" caused the public to look upon reformers with suspicion.

> *(b)* The generally hostile attitude toward protest and reform was strengthened by the "Red Scare of 1919–20," in which hysterical fear of a communist conspiracy against the United States government caused Attorney General Palmer to arrest thousands of alleged "agitators and radicals," often in violation of constitutional rights. Palmer's raids were duplicated by local police and self-appointed guardians of the law across the entire country.

2. *Economic Conservatism.* During the 1920's, conservative Republicans dominated national politics. Presidents Harding, Coolidge, and Hoover favored closer relations between business and government. They favored *"laissez-faire"* and "rugged individualism." The pre-World War I government campaign against big business monopolies slackened considerably.

3. *Boom and Bust.* After a brief postwar boom and depression, the nation moved into a period of unparalleled economic growth and prosperity. Most groups shared in the rise in the nation's standard of living, with the noteworthy exceptions of the farmers and unskilled workers. The businessman became the national hero. The rosy glow of the "Golden Twenties" came to an end in 1929, when, after an unprecedented stock market crash, the nation slid into its longest and most disastrous depression.

4. *Cultural Change.* The 1920's were also characterized by rebellion against traditional standards, new forms of cultural expression, and important advances in science and thought.

5. *A Mixed Foreign Policy.* The nation's foreign policies in the 1920's reflected the division of opinion between those who favored isolation and those who preferred international cooperation. Thus, while the United

States did not join the League or World Court, it participated in disarmament conferences and treaties, and helped sponsor a pact to outlaw war.

Presidents and Policies (1920–32). The administrations of Presidents Harding, Coolidge, and Hoover gave expression to the tone and philosophy of the 1920's. Harding and Coolidge, in particular, felt that the role of the Chief Executive was to enforce the laws of Congress, rather than to assume national leadership.

Warren G. Harding (Republican, 1921–23). United States Senator WARREN HARDING was elected to succeed Woodrow Wilson. Harding, a "dark horse" at the convention, had been a newspaper editor and had had a relatively inconspicuous political career. In the Senate, he had been a member of the anti-League group. Much of Harding's term of office, which ended in his sudden death in 1923, was occupied with problems of postwar adjustment. Because of his general lack of leadership and the many scandals that were uncovered in high office, Harding is considered one of the nation's least effective Chief Executives.

1. *Political Developments.* In the election of 1920, Republicans Harding and CALVIN COOLIDGE defeated Democrats JAMES COX and FRANKLIN D. ROOSEVELT. Harding won by a landslide, and by capturing Tennessee's electoral vote broke the "Solid South" for the first time since Reconstruction. The Republicans also increased their majority in Congress. In the campaign, the Democrats advocated that the United States join the League of Nations, while the Republicans backed its rejection by the Senate. Although the Republicans interpreted their victory as a vote of confidence in their position on the League, a more significant factor in their success was desire to get "back to normalcy" after two decades of Progressivism and wartime idealism.

2. *Noteworthy Events and Achievements of the Harding Administration.* Following are the important events of Harding's administration.

A *Veterans Bureau* was created in 1921 to handle claims of veterans for compensation and hospitalization. It has since become the *Veterans Administration (VA).*

A *Bureau of the Budget* was established to assist the President to draw up an accurate prediction of national income and expenditures.

A broad tax reduction program, sponsored by Treasury Secretary Andrew Mellon, was enacted and pleased big business.

Congress adopted severe restrictions on immigration to choke off a postwar surge to the United States (Acts of 1921 and 1924).

President Harding signed a separate peace treaty with Germany (1923).

At Harding's invitation leading world statesmen attended the *Washington Disarmament Conference* in 1921–22 and drew up plans for naval disarmament.

Harding refused to sign a bonus bill for veterans in 1920 on the ground that Congress had not provided funds.

Like the Grant administration, the Harding administration was plagued by scandal and corruption. Director of the Veterans Bureau, Charles Forbes, was found guilty of waste and misconduct; Alien Property Custodian Thomas Miller was found guilty of cheating the government; Attorney General Harry Daugherty was accused of favoritism to employees; and Interior Secretary Albert Fall was involved in an oil reserve scandal (*Teapot Dome*). Harding's loyalty to his friends and his anxiety over these scandals are said to have contributed to the exhaustion that preceded his unexpected death in 1923, while returning from a trip to Alaska.

Calvin Coolidge (Republican, 1923–29). Upon Harding's death, Vice President CALVIN COOLIDGE became President and went on to serve an additional term in his own right. Before taking national office, Coolidge had won fame as Governor of Massachusetts for ending a Boston police strike. Coolidge was a popular President. His administration coincided with the prosperity of the 1920's and the materialism and frenzy of the "Jazz Age." Coolidge believed in *laissez-faire* and economy in government.

1. *Political Developments.* In 1924, Coolidge easily defeated Democratic nominee, JOHN W. DAVIS. In the campaign, the Democrats condemned the Harding era for its corruption and "isolation," while the Republicans emphasized prosperity. The election was enlivened by the vigorous campaign of Senator ROBERT LA FOLLETTE ("Fighting Bob") on a new Independent-Progressive ticket. La Follette's candidacy was supported by the Progressives, the American Federation of Labor, and the Socialists. He received nearly 5 million votes, more than any other third-party candidate in American history. The Progressives advocated government ownership of public utilities (including railroads), restriction of the power of the Supreme Court (in behalf of labor), and aid to the farmer.

2. *Noteworthy Achievements and Events of the Coolidge Administration.* Coolidge's administration was comparatively uneventful. It was characterized by a reduction in taxes and the national debt, the ending of a dispute with Mexico over threatened seizure of American oil properties, the drafting of several arbitration treaties, and the signing of the *Kellogg-Briand Pact* to outlaw war. In addition, Congress passed a veterans' bonus bill over Coolidge's veto, which provided increased benefits at the end of twenty years. Like Harding, Coolidge was unsuccessful in getting the Senate to approve United States entry into the World Court.

Herbert Hoover (Republican, 1929–33). President Coolidge chose not to run for the Presidency again in 1928. Secretary of Commerce HERBERT HOOVER succeeded him in the White House. Before his election, Hoover had achieved a considerable reputation as a humanitarian, an administrator, and a mining engineer. Like his immediate predecessors, Hoover favored a minimum of government intervention in business and was a strong supporter of "rugged individualism." His administration began in a glow of prosperity, and ended with the nation deep in depression. To cope with depression problems Hoover was forced to modify his *laissez-faire* philosophy and to introduce programs of government assistance.

1. *Political Developments.* In the election of 1928, Hoover defeated the popular Democratic Governor of New York State ALFRED E. SMITH. Smith attacked the Republicans for lack of achievement, and called for the end of Prohibition. Hoover emphasized "Republican prosperity" and preached "rugged individualism." Hoover's landslide victory cracked the Solid South by capturing five Southern states. It was a result of Hoover's personal prestige, national prosperity, support of Prohibition, and an irresponsible whispering campaign against Governor Smith because he was a Catholic.

2. *Noteworthy Events and Achievements of the Hoover Administration.* The "Hoover years" were eventful and were marked by important developments.

Immigration was further restricted by the beginning of the quota system based on national origins.

Congress made an initial attempt to purchase farm surpluses through the *Agricultural Marketing Act* of 1929. It also, with Hoover's endorsement, passed the highest tariff in the history of the nation, the *Hawley-Smoot Tariff.*

In foreign affairs, the Hoover administration established a moratorium on war debts owed to the United States, participated in the London Disarmament Conference, renewed attempts to bring the United States into the World Court, vigorously opposed Japanese imperialism in China, and took important steps to end the long-standing policy of United States intervention in Latin America.

The many accomplishments of the Hoover administration, especially in foreign affairs, were overshadowed by the stock market crash of 1929 and the *Great Depression* which followed it. At first, Hoover took the position that the depression would soon end. ("Prosperity is just around the corner.") As poverty and unemployment grew steadily worse, however, the President was reluctantly forced to accept the doctrine that the welfare of the people in a national depression was the direct concern of the Federal government. Emergency steps taken to combat the spreading economic collapse included the establishment of the *Reconstruction Finance Corporation* to lend money to business, the beginning of a program of public works to provide employment (for example, Boulder Dam), and the levying of new taxes to pay for the additional government expenditures.

Growing public bitterness against Hoover and his administration for doing "too little too late" enabled the Democrats to take control of the House of Representatives in the election of 1930, and to capture the Presidency in 1932.

REVIEW TEST (Chapter 17—Part III)

Select the number preceding the word or expression that best completes each statement or answers each question.

1. In the 1920's the domestic policies of the Federal government were primarily concerned with (1) protecting business interests (2) furthering social reform (3) negotiating reciprocal trade agreements (4) improving the national banking system

2. The "Palmer raids" have come to symbolize (1) FBI vigilence (2) conservation scandals (3) wartime espionage (4) postwar political "jitters"

3. Which of the following is most commonly associated with the Presidencies of Ulysses S. Grant and Warren G. Harding? (1) business depression (2) public corruption (3) humanitarian reforms (4) territorial expansion

4. Both Presidents Van Buren and Hoover faced problems resulting from (1) a business depression (2) the enforcement of the Monroe Doctrine (3) a policy of high protective tariffs (4) the sale of Western lands

5. Which of the following does *not* apply to the decade of the 1920's? (1) conservatism in national politics (2) attempted isolationism in world affairs (3) noteworthy political reform in government (4) rebellion against traditional social and cultural standards

6. President Harding's administration was responsible for all of the following *except* (1) tax reductions (2) a separate peace treaty with Germany (3) calling the Washington Disarmament Conference (4) ending United States intervention in Latin America

7. The most significant aspect of the election of 1924 was that (1) John W. Davis was defeated (2) Senator Robert La Follette received nearly 5 million votes (3) the Progressives lost (4) Calvin Coolidge, the successful candidate, had been the former Vice President

8. Which of the following is associated with the Coolidge administration? (1) continued crises at home and abroad (2) opposition to United States entry into the World Court (3) economy in government (4) frequent Presidential "fireside chats" with the American people

9. Herbert Hoover believed in all of the following *except* (1) rugged individualism (2) *laissez-faire* (3) low tariffs (4) social reform

10. The slogan, "Prosperity is just around the corner" is linked to the name of (1) Warren Harding (2) Calvin Coolidge (3) Herbert Hoover (4) Alfred E. Smith

By writing the name of the correct President, indicate whether each of the following headlines is associated with the election or administration of Harding, Coolidge, or Hoover

1. PRESIDENT ANNOUNCES DEBT MORATORIUM

2. SMITH SUBJECT OF VICIOUS WHISPERING CAMPAIGN

3. BUREAU ESTABLISHED TO HANDLE VETERANS AFFAIRS

4. PRESIDENT REFUSES TO RUN FOR RE-ELECTION

5. NATION SADDENED BY UNEXPECTED DEATH OF CHIEF EXECUTIVE

Essay Questions

1. Show how each of the following was related to the administration of Warren Harding: "return to normalcy," the "Red Scare," naval disarmament, corruption in high offices.

2. "Coolidge was right for the country and the country was right for him." Explain why you agree or disagree with this comment on "the Coolidge years."

3. There has been considerable dispute over whether or not Herbert Hoover was an able President. Why? Explain your feelings in the matter.

4. "The period of Republican ascendency in the 1920's was a period of political conservatism in the national affairs." Give your reasons for agreeing or disagreeing with this statement.

Part IV — POLITICAL DEVELOPMENTS (1933–45)

The period during which FRANKLIN D. ROOSEVELT was President of the United States constituted a distinct era in American history. During the first part of this period, the nation was seriously involved with problems of depression and recovery. Later the country was plunged into World War II, a struggle for survival as a free nation. The United States that emerged from the war was vastly different from the nation that was so sorely beset by economic and social calamity in 1932. Roosevelt's election also began a 20-year period of Democratic control of the Presidency. A review of the undertakings and achievements of his administration makes clear the meaning and significance of this important period of American history.

The Election of Franklin D. Roosevelt. Franklin D. Roosevelt became President by defeating the renominated Herbert Hoover in the election of 1932. The Democratic landslide gave Roosevelt seven million votes more than Hoover and the electoral votes of all but six states. There were also unprecedented Democratic victories in Congress and on state and local levels.

1. *Issues in the Election of 1932.* The chief issue in the election was the depression. The Democrats blamed the Republican administrations of the 1920's for bringing on the depression. The Republicans commended President Hoover for his attempts to halt the depression and for other positive achievements. The Democratic platform also proposed United States entry into the World Court, the repeal of the Eighteenth (Prohibition) Amendment, stricter enforcement of the antitrust laws, and tariff revision. In the campaign, Roosevelt promised "justice" and a "New Deal" to the "forgotten man." His election was clearly a vote of no-confidence in Republican leadership and a hopeful turning to the Democrats to pull the country out of its economic difficulties. Although he was later to surprise them by his effectiveness, FDR was considered by many at the time of his election to be an "amiable aristocrat," who might not be much of a "doer."

2. *Roosevelt's Background.* Before becoming President, Roosevelt (a distant cousin of Theodore Roosevelt) had experienced a long career in public office. He had been a member of the Legislature of New York State and Assistant Secretary of Navy under Wilson. In 1920, he had been the unsuccessful Democratic candidate for the Vice Presidency. When elected President he was completing his second term as Governor of New York State. In the 1920's, his career was interrupted by a serious attack of infantile paralysis which crippled him for the remainder of his life.

3. *Roosevelt and the New Deal.* Roosevelt's program for restoring the nation's prosperity and eliminating the abuses which had helped bring an economic collapse was known as the *New Deal*.

Aims of the New Deal. The New Deal was a gigantic program of *relief, recovery* and *reform*. Its main objectives were to end the depression,

311

to bring back prosperity, to restore the purchasing power of the mass of people, and to introduce permanent large-scale reforms into the structure of American society. It attempted to achieve these aims by: **(1)** providing relief for the unemployed; **(2)** giving aid to homeowners to prevent foreclosures; **(3)** improving housing and slum conditions; **(4)** stimulating business and employment by public works projects; **(5)** encouraging a "partnership" of business and government to eliminate abuses in business and industry; **(6)** regulating the stock market, banking, and money in order to avoid situations that caused depressions; **(7)** raising wages and prices; **(8)** providing aid to the farmer by improving credit facilities, curtailing production, and raising prices; **(9)** safeguarding the rights of labor by guaranteeing collective bargaining; **(10)** providing insurance against old age and unemployment; **(11)** curbing child labor; **(12)** conserving and developing natural resources for the nation's benefit; **(13)** stimulating international trade by removing trade barriers; **(14)** adopting a "good-neighbor" policy in foreign affairs.

New Deal Emergency Measures. Many New Deal actions were emergency measures, taken in 1933 for the most part, to prevent disaster and to provide immediate relief. Included among such actions were: **(1)** the declaration of a brief national *bank holiday* in 1933, until the banks could reorganize and reopen; **(2)** the establishment of a *Civilian Conservation Corps (CCC)*, to provide jobs for needy youth, and a *Public Works Administration (PWA)* and a *Works Progress Administration (WPA)*, to provide jobs for unemployed adults; **(3)** grants of several billion dollars to states to provide direct relief to destitute families; **(4)** extension of credit to farmers and homeowners to prevent mortgage foreclosures; **(5)** the repeal of Prohibition and the enactment of a sales tax on alcoholic beverages to provide additional Federal income; **(6)** the creation of a *Federal Deposit Insurance Corporation (FDIC)* to insure bank deposits up to an individual limit of $5000; **(7)** the drawing up of "codes of fair competition" *(NIRA)* and establishment of public works projects to stimulate business and heavy industry.

Permanent Reforms of the New Deal. In addition to its emergency measures, the New Deal enacted more permanent reforms to correct long-existing abuses and to provide a sounder economic and social system. These more permanent reforms included the following:

1. *Agriculture.* To raise farm prices and reduce crop surpluses Congress enacted the *Agricultural Adjustment Act (AAA)* of 1933, the *Soil Conservation and Domestic Allotment Act* of 1936 and the *AAA* of 1938. Other laws extended credit facilities to the farmer.

2. *Industry.* After first trying to establish a "partnership" between government and business through the establishment of NIRA codes of fair competition (declared unconstitutional by the Supreme Court), the New Deal turned its attention to regulating business and restoring freer competition. The *Wheeler-Rayburn Act* (1935) regulated public utilities; the *Motor Carriers Act* (1935) extended the authority of the Interstate Commerce Commission; a *Securities Exchange Commission* was established to regulate securities exchanges and protect the investor.

3. *Labor.* The demands of labor for the right to bargain collectively and for better working conditions, higher wages, and shorter working hours were realized under the New Deal. The *Wagner Act* (1935) guaranteed collective bargaining and established the *National Labor Relations Board* to guarantee fair labor practices. The *Fair Labor Standards Act* of 1938 provided for minimum wages and maximum hours.

4. *Social Welfare.* New Deal legislation and agencies attempted to come to grips with some of the nation's social as well as economic needs. The *NIRA* codes and the *Fair Labor Standards Act* limited child labor. The *Home Owners Loan Corporation* (*HOLC*) and the *Federal Housing Administration* provided financial assistance to individuals and localities for improved housing. The *Social Security Act* of 1935 established a system of old-age pension benefits and unemployment insurance.

5. *Conservation.* The problems of the conservation of natural resources received increased attention under FDR. A *National Resources Committee* was created to plan conservation programs. The *Tennessee Valley Authority* (*TVA*) was created to provide flood control, irrigation, hydroelectric power, and regional redevelopment. A *Soil Conservation Service* was established to check the waste of land. Agencies like the *CCC* and *PWA* also provided meaningful conservation projects.

6. *Money and Banking.* The nation's financial institutions were strengthened under the New Deal to eliminate weaknesses and to provide against future crises. The *Banking Act of 1933* forbade commercial banks to make loans for speculative purposes. The *Banking Act of 1935* strengthened the Federal Reserve System. The gold standard was abandoned and a "managed" currency adopted. The *Silver Purchase Act* (1934) nationalized silver.

7. *Tariff and Trade.* To stimulate trade the New Deal inaugurated a reciprocal tariff program in 1934. Reciprocal trade agreements were signed with many nations.

8. *Other Measures.* Two other noteworthy New Deal measures were: **(1)** the passage by Congress of a veterans' bonus bill providing for immediate payment of the amount that was to have been paid to veterans in 1945; and **(2)** a general increase in taxes.

Planning and Administering the New Deal. Roosevelt's approach in the New Deal was experimental and practical. His philosophy, in his own words, was, "If it works, do it some more; if it fails, try something else." In consequence a vast complex of administrative machinery was created, and new programs replaced or overlapped older ones with startling rapidity.

1. *The "Brain Trust."* In drafting his program Roosevelt often relied on the advice of a group of experts in government and economics, mainly college professors. This inner group or "kitchen cabinet" became known as the "brain trust."

2. *Congress Under the New Deal.* During Roosevelt's first administration, Congress conferred extraordinary authority upon him. During the first three months (the "Hundred Days"), scores of bills became laws virtually without opposition. During his second administration, Roosevelt still continued to exercise a powerful influence upon Congress, but Congress became less willing to follow his lead unquestioningly. After the failure of Roosevelt's plan to enlarge the Supreme Court in 1937, conservative Southern Democrats became increasingly unwilling to follow the leadership of New Deal liberals. During World War II Congress accepted Presidential domination in foreign affairs, but actively opposed additional domestic reforms; on several occasions it passed laws over the President's veto.

3. *New Deal Agencies.* The administrative arm of the New Deal consisted of scores of agencies created for specific purposes. It became customary to refer to them by their alphabetical abbreviations — *NRA, WPA, PWA, CCC, TVA, SEC,* etc.

The Supreme Court and the New Deal. Toward the end of Roosevelt's first administration, a conservative majority on the Supreme Court began to declare unconstitutional important New Deal legislation. It argued that Congress had placed too broad an interpretation on the interstate commerce

Few events of the New Deal aroused more public concern than the Supreme Court's invalidation of important legislation. This cartoon, published in 1936 shortly after the Court held the Guffey Coal Act unconstitutional, suggested that the whole range of New Deal legislation might be nullified by the Court. During Roosevelt's second term, however, the Court sanctioned the major items of New Deal legislation that came before it. Changes in the membership of the Court (as a result of deaths and resignations) played a part in this.

Russell in the Los Angeles Times

and "due process" clauses and that it was interfering with states' rights and property rights. In 1935 for example, the Court voided the NIRA, and in 1936, it invalidated the AAA of 1933 and the Guffey-Snyder Coal Act.

1. *Roosevelt Attacks the Supreme Court.* President Roosevelt openly attacked the Supreme Court decisions and argued that human rights were more important than property rights. In 1937, early in his second term, he asked Congress to reorganize the Supreme Court by empowering him to appoint a new member whenever an incumbent Justice failed to retire upon reaching the age of 70. The maximum size of the Court was set at fifteen. What FDR hoped to do was to give the Court a liberal majority more friendly to his program. (Most of the conservatives were already over 70.) FDR was widely criticized for his "court-packing" plan. After weeks of debate the Senate turned down the plan.

2. *The Supreme Court Becomes More Liberal.* Although FDR lost his battle to enlarge the membership of the Supreme Court, death and resignations of Court members during the next few years gave him the opportunity to change its membership almost completely. During his second administration, the Court approved most New Deal measures (for example, it upheld the TVA), accepted Congress' broad interpretation of the due-process and interstate commerce clauses of the Constitution, and took a more liberal attitude toward social reform and civil liberties.

End of the New Deal. Although the New Deal, technically speaking, did not end until 1945, "reformism" came to an end about 1939. Thereafter, Roosevelt spoke of preserving what had already been done, rather than of introducing new reforms. Also, his preoccupation with World War II after 1939 pushed foreign rather than domestic affairs into the forefront.

Roosevelt Breaks the Two-Term Tradition. Franklin D. Roosevelt shattered the two-term tradition by serving more than three complete terms before his death in 1945. His continued re-election was a result of his leadership, the needs of the times, the real affection he aroused in the hearts of most Americans, and his fashioning of a "grand alliance" of political and economic groups, including Negroes, labor, minority groups, the South, and urban bosses. (This coalition has remained the basis of Democratic victories ever since. Although Dwight D. Eisenhower broke this alliance as an individual, the Democrats remained in control of Congress from 1954–60.)

1. *The Election of 1936.* By 1936, opposition to the New Deal had begun to be voiced. The President and the Democratic leadership in Congress were accused of moving toward socialism, of exercising dictatorial powers, and of spending too much money. Despite this fact, Roosevelt and his Vice President JOHN GARNER were re-elected by an even greater majority than in 1932. The Republican candidate, Governor ALFRED LANDON of

Kansas only carried two states. The Democrats again kept control of both Houses by large majorities. In the campaign, the Democrats argued that the New Deal had brought higher prices, rising farm incomes, and increased business activity.

2. *The Election of 1940.* In 1940, Roosevelt was renominated for a third term on the first ballot, despite the warning of his opponents that it would be dangerous to break the two-term tradition. Supporters of his candidacy argued that in view of the critical foreign situation it would be dangerous "to swap horses in mid-stream." HENRY A. WALLACE, Secretary of Agriculture was nominated for Vice President at Roosevelt's suggestion. Despite a whirlwind campaign by his Republican opponent WENDELL WILLKIE, Roosevelt captured 38 states and received nearly 5 million votes more than Willkie.

3. *The Election of 1944.* Roosevelt shattered the two-term precedent a second time by being re-elected for a fourth term in 1944, at the height of World War II. Senator HARRY S. TRUMAN served as Roosevelt's running mate and was elected Vice President. Roosevelt's re-election and his defeat of Republican Governor THOMAS E. DEWEY of New York gave evidence not only of his continuing popularity, but also of the feeling that at such a critical time the nation's foreign policy should be continued without change. Although the victory margin of less than 3 million votes was closer than in any other of Roosevelt's elections, the Democrats retained majorities in both Houses, and leading isolationists in Congress who had opposed the President's "internationalist" policies went down to defeat.

The Death of Roosevelt. Less than three months after he began his fourth term in January 1945, Roosevelt died suddenly of cerebral hemorrhage in April 1945, on the eve of military victory in World War II. He was mourned by freedom-loving people throughout the world.

The New Deal and Foreign Affairs. Because of the domestic crisis, the Roosevelt administration at first was too busy to devote much attention to foreign affairs. Despite this preoccupation, several noteworthy steps were taken to promote international good will, including the recognition of Soviet Russia, the development of a "Good Neighbor" policy in Latin America, the granting of independence to the Philippines, and the negotiation of reciprocal trade agreements with foreign nations. During the late 1930's, Roosevelt became actively involved in problems of maintaining the nation's neutrality in the face of growing Nazi aggression in Europe and the outbreak of World War II. From 1941, when the Japanese attacked the United States at Pearl Harbor, to 1945, when the war ended, the nation and its leaders were completely involved with the hostilities and problems of World War II. Together with Winston Churchill of Great Britain and Joseph Stalin of the USSR, Roosevelt helped map the grand strategy that resulted in the final defeat of the Axis. He also was one of the chief architects of the United Nations.

The Significance of Roosevelt and the New Deal. Despite bitter criticism by opponents, Franklin D. Roosevelt's place in history seems assured. He is considered to have been one of the most effective and popular Presidents of the United States. Roosevelt's long stay in office, his friendly smile, and his "fireside" radio chats helped make a whole generation of Americans feel that they knew him personally.

1. *Criticism of Roosevelt and the New Deal.* Roosevelt was bitterly accused by reactionaries and conservatives of introducing "creeping socialism," passing laws contrary to the Constitution, and squandering public funds. Liberals and radicals claimed the New Deal did not go far enough and had no clearcut philosophy. Economists pointed out that despite all New Deal efforts farm surpluses continued to grow, and unemployment remained high (9.75 million at the outbreak of World War II).

2. *Defense of Roosevelt and the New Deal.* Defenders of the New Deal argue: **(a)** It saved the nation from economic collapse. **(b)** It brought substantial gains to workers, farmers, and consumers. **(c)** It introduced the concept of Federal responsibility for relief to the needy. **(d)** It introduced reforms, such as Social Security, which on the whole have worked well and have become an integral part of the American way of life. **(e)** Many historians and economists have, in addition, suggested that the New Deal made it possible to abandon *laissez-faire* without adopting socialism, and thus saved the capitalist economic system. **(f)** They also point out that while many New Deal innovations were "revolutionary" in the sense that they were new, most of the New Deal was evolutionary — in the "reform without revolution" tradition of Thomas Jefferson, Theodore Roosevelt, and Woodrow Wilson. Among the "revolutionary" aspects were a shift in the focus of power from the states to the Federal government and the granting of power to minority groups.

REVIEW TEST (Chapter 17 — Part IV)

Select the number preceding the word or expression that best completes each statement or answers each question.

1. The primary issue in the campaign of 1932 was the (1) depression (2) tariff (3) "Good Neighbor" policy (4) national debt

2. All of the following were part of the New Deal *except* (1) a bank holiday in 1933 (2) a program to raise farm prices (3) legislation favorable to trade unions (4) a national program of medical insurance

3. During the New Deal Era, Congress refused to (1) regulate stock market listings (2) permit the President to establish codes of fair competition (3) change the membership of the Supreme Court (4) establish a system of old age insurance

4. Which of the following New Deal agencies is still functioning today? (1) WPA (2) NRA (3) TVA (4) CCC

5. All of the following served as Vice Presidents under President Franklin D. Roosevelt *except*   (1) John Nance Garner   (2) Wendell Willkie   (3) Henry A. Wallace   (4) Harry Truman

6. Which of the following did *not* occur while Franklin D. Roosevelt was President?   (1) the recognition of Soviet Russia   (2) the final defeat of Japan in World War II   (3) the beginning of insurance of bank deposits   (4) the negotiation of reciprocal trade agreements

7. An important reason for Franklin D. Roosevelt's election to the Presidency for a fourth term in 1944 was the   (1) strength of his running mate Henry Wallace   (2) support given him by powerful third parties   (3) ratification of the Twentieth Amendment   (4) reluctance of voters to change leadership in the midst of a great crisis

8. Woodrow Wilson and Franklin D. Roosevelt were both   (1) members of the Republican party   (2) in favor of creating an organization for world peace   (3) interested in passing a third-term amendment to our Constitution   (4) elected to the Presidency by the House of Representatives

9. Andrew Jackson, Theodore Roosevelt, and Franklin D. Roosevelt were similar in that all   (1) had difficulty in carrying through most of their legislative programs   (2) were elected by a small popular plurality   (3) were able to exercise great influence because of personal popularity   (4) felt that the President should be purely an executive officer

10. Abraham Lincoln, Theodore Roosevelt, and Franklin D. Roosevelt had all of the following policies in common *except*   (1) monopoly regulation   (2) expansion of executive powers   (3) more adequate provision for the national lands   (4) concern for the common man

Indicate whether each of the following statements is **true** *or* **false**. *Give one factor or reason in support of each true statement, and reword correctly those statements which are false.*

1. F.D.R. relied on a group of advisors popularly known as the "brain trust."

2. The Supreme Court did not begin to declare New Deal legislation unconstitutional until the end of Franklin D. Roosevelt's second term.

3. The New Deal introduced reforms in labor, banking, and agriculture, but not in conservation.

4. The New Deal represented a major step in the abandonment of *laissez-faire* in America.

5. Franklin D. Roosevelt was one of the most popular American Presidents.

Essay Questions

1. Discuss one permanent New Deal reform in each of the following areas: (a) agriculture   (b) industry   (c) labor   (d) social welfare   (e) conservation   (f) tariff and trade.

2. Why has the New Deal been called   (a) evolutionary?   (b) revolutionary?

3. Draw up a balance sheet of the successes and failures of the New Deal.

4. Franklin D. Roosevelt is generally ranked as one of the nation's greatest Presidents. Give three possible reasons for this estimate.

Part V—POLITICAL DEVELOPMENTS SINCE 1945

After World War II, the United States entered a new stage of economic growth and technological development. Following the conversion of the economy from a wartime to a peacetime basis, the nation entered a period of rising prosperity which (despite several economic recessions) has pushed the standard of living and production of goods and services to new highs. Accompanying these changes have been challenging problems of nuclear armament, the cold war with communist nations, relatively high unemployment in some areas, the need to improve living conditions in the nation's great cities, and the struggle of the Negro for full equality in American life. Our Presidents have had to deal with these problems.

Harry S. Truman (Democrat, 1945-53). Vice President HARRY S. TRUMAN succeeded Franklin Roosevelt as President after the latter's untimely death in 1945. Truman was re-elected in 1946. Before winning the Vice Presidency, Truman had held local offices and had served two terms as United States Senator from Missouri, in which position he had earned a reputation for efficiency and courage. President Truman faced the difficult problems of leading the nation through the remainder of World War II, of coping with problems of demobilization and reconversion, and of attempting to set new guidelines for the nation's future. In meeting these challenges, he displayed sincerity, purposefulness, and vigor, and built a record of positive accomplishment.

1. *Political Developments.* Truman's re-election in 1948 was a major political upset. He defeated Republican Governor THOMAS E. DEWEY of New York, who was running for the Presidency for the second time. The Democratic Party went into the election seriously split. Southern Democrats (*"Dixiecrats"*) had formed their own *States'-Rights Party,* because of opposition to the regular party's stand on civil rights. In addition, a new *Progressive Party* had been formed in opposition to Truman's foreign policy toward Russia, with former Vice President HENRY WALLACE as its candidate. Truman's surprising victory, by more than 2 million votes, was attributed to his vigorous campaigning and to overconfidence by the Republicans. The Democrats also recaptured both houses of Congress.

2. *Noteworthy Events and Achievements of the Truman Administration.* The "Truman years" were years of important developments and national undertakings, as outlined below.

Pent-up labor and consumer demands produced several waves of strikes and a rising price level. Congress passed the *Taft-Hartley Act* (1947) over Truman's veto to limit strike action and curb union abuses, Price controls were removed, but later restored in part to check inflation.

Quick demobilization and reconversion to a peacetime basis, combined with a worsening of relations with the Soviet Union, produced national challenges. Communist expansion after the war, plus threats of further aggression, caused the United States to extend economic and military aid to

319

Europe in the form of the *Marshall Plan* and *Truman Doctrine* in 1947. We also joined a military alliance for mutual defense (*NATO,* 1949), sent supplies to beleaguered Berlin (*Berlin Airlift,* 1948–49), and strengthened the nation's defenses. In the Far East, the United States joined with other UN nations to fight aggression in Korea.

Congress passed the *Internal Security Act* of 1950 (*McCarran Act*), requiring communist organizations to file membership lists and financial statements with the Attorney General.

Truman's domestic program of reform and improvements was called the *Fair Deal.* Fair Deal legislation provided for an expansion of Social Security benefits, the extension of rent controls, low-rental housing and slum

clearance programs, expanded reclamation and rural electrification programs, and increased FDIC coverage (to $10,000).

Other noteworthy events of the Truman administration included the establishment of a government monopoly over the production of fissionable materials (*Atomic Energy Act* of 1946); the passage of the *Presidential Succession Act* of 1947, putting the Speaker of the House first in line for the Presidency in case of Presidential or Vice Presidential death or disability; the *McCarran-Walter Immigration Act* of 1952 extending the quota system and adding safeguards against subversives; passage of the Twenty-second Amendment limiting the President's tenure to two terms; and the signing of a peace treaty with Japan in 1951.

Dwight D. Eisenhower (Republican, 1953–61). DWIGHT D. EISENHOWER, popular leader of the allied armed forces in Europe during World War II and postwar president of Columbia University, became the nation's 34th President. His victory ended twenty years of Democratic control of the White House. Though President Eisenhower favored more limited government and greater encouragement of business, he maintained in whole or in modified form most of the popular domestic programs introduced by his Democratic predecessors (Social Security, farm price supports, public housing, etc.). In foreign affairs Eisenhower continually faced crises arising out of the cold war.

1. *Political Developments.* Dwight Eisenhower was elected in 1952 and 1956, in each instance defeating ADLAI E. STEVENSON, the able Democratic ex-Governor of Illinois. Eisenhower's running mate for the Vice Presidency on both occasions was former Senator RICHARD M. NIXON. The Republican victory of 1952 was an overwhelming popular and electoral victory. It also gave the Republicans slim majorities in both houses and broke the Solid South for the third time. In 1956, Eisenhower was re-elected on the basis of "peace, prosperity, and popularity." However, his party failed to carry either house of Congress.

Despite a period of continuing prosperity, economic growth was slowed down by recessions in 1953, 1957, and 1960.

Eisenhower ended price and wage controls imposed during the Korean

War, and encouraged business by various policies. Eisenhower's program of *"Modern Republicanism"* provided for the continuation or extension of the New Deal and Fair Deal programs. At his urging, Congress established a new

Department of Health, Education, and Welfare, expanded the Social Security program, and provided more money for hospitals, medical research, and slum clearance and urban redevelopment. "Modern Republicanism" also included support for the UN, military aid to the nation's allies, and assistance to underdeveloped countries.

Labor made gains in the form of higher wages, additional fringe benefits, and the AFL-CIO merger. Congress passed the *Landrum-Griffin Act* of 1959, providing for greater democracy in union management.

In agriculture the Eisenhower administration adopted flexible farm supports and a *soil bank* plan to deal with the problem of surpluses.

Other noteworthy steps included: renewal of the *Reciprocal Trade Agreements Act,* appropriations for higher education, a noteworthy Supreme Court decision against segregation in public schools, the enactment of civil rights acts, and the admission of Alaska and Hawaii as states (1959).

Particularly dramatic during Eisenhower's first administration were the investigations by Senator Joseph McCarthy of Wisconsin, who brought sweeping and often reckless charges of communism against leading Americans, State Department employees, and Army personnel. McCarthy's influence declined as a result of a Senate vote of censure in 1954.

In foreign affairs, significant events included: the signing of a peace in Korea; negotiation of a Far East defense alliance (SEATO); issuance of the *Eisenhower Doctrine,* pledging aid against communist aggression in the Middle East; and several meetings at the "summit" between President Eisenhower and Soviet Premier Khrushchev. In addition, Eisenhower's "Atoms for Peace" plan led to the creation of the *International Atomic Energy Agency* within the UN.

John F. Kennedy (Democrat, 1961–63). JOHN F. KENNEDY became the 35th President of the United States in 1961. Kennedy was the first Roman Catholic, and at 43 the youngest man, ever to be elected to the Presidency. Prior to his election, he had served as Representative and Senator from Massachusetts. Unlike Eisenhower, who believed that the President should stay out of political battles, Kennedy believed in strong active Presidential leadership. President Kennedy used the term *"New Frontier"* to describe his program for economic and social progress and for competing with world communism.

1. *Political Developments.* President Kennedy was elected in 1960 by the narrowest of margins. Though Kennedy and his running mate, Democratic Senate Leader LYNDON B. JOHNSON, of Texas, received a solid majority in the Electoral College, their popular majority was only 118,000 votes out of a total of 69 million votes cast (one tenth of one per cent). The defeated Republican candidates were Vice President RICHARD M. NIXON and UN Ambassador HENRY CABOT LODGE. A highlight of the hard-fought campaign was a series of TV debates between Kennedy and Nixon. Factors that contributed to the Democratic win included: (a) an efficient political organization, built by Kennedy supporters; (b) the support of organized labor and the Negroes; (c) the favorable impression created by Kennedy in the television debates; and (d) the unifying influence of Senator Johnson, a Southerner, on the Democratic ticket.

2. *Noteworthy Events and Achievements of the Kennedy Administration.* The following policies, events, and achievements of the Kennedy administration were especially important.

To meet pressing economic problems the administration gave aid to distressed areas, provided for the retraining of unemployed workers, curtailed government expenditures abroad, cut income taxes to stimulate consumer demand, and called upon business and labor to hold prices and wage demands down.

The narrowness of his election victory, it is believed, caused the President, to follow a rather cautious middle-of-the-road policy in most domestic affairs. Congress adopted the following *"New Frontier"* legislation: assistance to economically distressed areas; increases in the minimum wage and in Social Security benefits; and increased Federal aid to housing.

The Kennedy administration tried to enforce civil rights legislation providing for voting guarantees, appointed Negroes to responsible positions, outlawed racial discrimination in Federally aided public housing, and pushed school integration.

Other noteworthy events included support and recognition of outstanding cultural and intellectual accomplishments by the President and his wife, the orbiting of the first United States astronauts in space, and increasing Negro demonstrations, for greater rights.

Serious challenges in foreign affairs included communist subversion in Southeast Asia; rising nationalism in Africa; a Soviet resumption of nuclear testing; the building of the Berlin Wall; and placing of missiles in Cuba by the Soviet Union.

To meet its foreign challenges, the Kennedy administration helped negotiate a truce in Laos, supported a UN peace force in the Congo, got Premier Khrushchev to remove Soviet missiles from Cuba, and negotiated a nuclear test-ban treaty with Russia. Other major steps were the initiation of a large-scale program of financial aid to Latin America aimed at raising the standards of living (*Alliance for Progress*) and establishment of a *Peace Corps* to send volunteer workers to underdeveloped nations.

A serious setback to American prestige under Kennedy was the failure in 1961 of a United States-backed invasion of Cuba by Cuban refugees.

On November 22, 1963, President Kennedy was assassinated in Dallas, Texas. The man accused of the slaying, Lee Harvey Oswald, was himself shot and killed as he was being moved from the city jail.

Lyndon B. Johnson (Democrat, 1963-69). LYNDON B. JOHNSON succeeded to the Presidency upon the death of President Kennedy in 1963. It was the climax of a long and successful career, which included service in the House of Representatives and the Senate, and as Vice President. President Johnson's program for national prosperity and progress was called the *"Great Society."*

1. *Political Developments.* In the election of 1964, President Johnson and his running mate for the Vice Presidency, Senator HUBERT H. HUMPHREY of Minnesota, won a landslide victory over the conservative Republican ticket of Senator BARRY GOLDWATER of Arizona and WILLIAM E. MILLER of New York. Democrats increased their majorities in both houses and ousted Republicans in many state and local contests. Despite this victory and though Mr. Johnson himself was a Southerner (Texas), five states of the "Deep South" went Republican. Early in 1968 Johnson indicated that he would not seek re-election. The unpopularity of the Vietnam War was believed to be largely responsible for this.

2. *Noteworthy Events and Achievements of the Johnson Administration.* President Johnson's major effort in foreign affairs was directed toward attempting to win the war in Vietnam. In the domestic field, he emphasized a progressive program of reform.

Several important civil rights laws were enacted to insure a greater measure of equality for Negroes. The *Civil Rights Act of 1964* prohibited discrimination in places of public accommodation. The *Voting Rights Act of 1965* attempted to end discriminatory practices in voter registration by providing for Federal registration where discrimination occurred. The *Civil Rights Act of 1968* banned discrimination in the sale or rental of housing on the grounds of race, religion or national origin. The *24th Amendment* (1964) forbids poll tax requirements in Federal elections.

As part of his Great Society program, Johnson persuaded Congress to adopt a number of social-welfare and economic measures. *Medicare,* a plan for hospital and medical care for the aged under Social Security, became law in 1965. This was later supplemented by *Medicaid,* a joint Federal-state program to pay medical bills for low-income persons and families.

In a *"war on poverty"* large sums were appropriated for better housing, assistance to the unemployed, increased welfare benefits, improved ed-

ucational facilities, manpower retraining and direct aid to depressed areas.

In 1965 Congress adopted a revised immigration law, bringing to an end the discriminatory policy of quotas based entirely on national origins.

To handle the growing problems of cities, two new Cabinet departments were created, *Housing and Urban Development* in 1965, and *Transportation* in 1966.

The Johnson administration faced many serious foreign challenges, foremost of which was the war in Vietnam. Our forces there rose to about 550,000 men. Large numbers of planes bombed North Vietnam until the President ordered a halt in 1968.

A new treaty was signed giving Panama greater control over the Canal Zone.

In 1965, American forces were sent to quiet a revolt in the Dominican Republic, and to prevent what the administration feared might be a communist takeover.

In 1968, the United States, Russia, Britain and 58 non-nuclear nations signed a "non-proliferation" treaty to prohibit the spread of nuclear weapons.

Richard M. Nixon (Republican, 1969-1974). Richard M. Nixon was elected the 37th President of the United States in 1968 and reelected in 1972. Before his election Nixon had been a United States Senator and Vice President under Eisenhower. His victory in 1968 was a dramatic comeback from defeat and political retirement. He had gone into private law practice after losing the Presidential election to John F. Kennedy in 1960, and then being defeated for the California governorship in 1962. As President, Nixon made major initiatives in foreign policy and negotiated a cease-fire in Vietnam, but his administration was less successful in halting growing unemployment and inflation and in countering a major economic recession in his second term in office. Nixon resigned the Presidency in August, 1974, in the aftermath of the so-called *Watergate Affair* (see below).

1. *Political Developments.* In 1968, Nixon appealed to the nation's discontent with the Vietnam War and its concern for preserving law and order. In one of the closest of Presidential races, he defeated the Democratic nominee, Vice President Hubert Humphrey, and also George C. Wallace, candidate of the American Independent Party. The Democrats retained control of both houses of Congress.

Nixon was reelected in 1972 in a landslide victory over Democratic Senator George McGovern, capturing 49 states and 60.7% of the vote. McGovern suffered the worst defeat ever experienced by a Democratic Presidential candidate.

2. *Noteworthy Events and Achievements of the Nixon Administration.* The Nixon administration faced challenging foreign and domestic problems.

Bold new initiatives in foreign policy were undertaken. The Nixon administration unexpectedly reversed this country's 22-year-old policy of opposition to the People's Republic of China (Communist China), and in 1971 voted to admit that regime to the United Nations. Nixon then reestablished limited diplomatic relations with China following a precedent-shattering visit to that nation.

Nixon also visited the Soviet Union as part of an effort to achieve an easing of relations with the USSR as well as Communist China — a policy known as *détente.* Cooperative relations with the USSR included a partial strategic arms limitation agreement on intercontinental missiles, increased trade, and provisions for joint space exploration.

In addition, the Nixon administration negotiated a cease-fire in Vietnam and began withdrawal of our forces.

Serious problems of unemployment, inflation, international trade deficits and economic recession occurred during Nixon's presidency. Devaluation of the dollar and international monetary agreements helped improve the position of the United States in foreign trade, but efforts to check growing inflation and unemployment, including a temporary wage and price freeze, were less successful.

Other noteworthy events on the domestic front included a dismantling of many of the anti-poverty programs of the previous Kennedy and Johnson administrations, the adoption of the 26th Amendment, which gave the vote to 18-year-olds, and the successful landing of astronauts on the moon.

The most dramatic occurrence of the Nixon administration was his resignation as President, as a result of the *Watergate Affair.* This many-sided scandal developed out of the discovery and arrest of five employees of the Republican Party's Committee to Reelect the President. These men had broken into the headquarters of the Democratic Party's National Committee in Washington, D.C. in June, 1972. As a result of committee investigations by both the Senate and House of Representatives and court trials, it became clear that top administration officials were involved in planning and attempting to cover up the Watergate operation. Evidence also revealed improper manipulation of the Internal Revenue Service and the FBI.

President Nixon insisted for more than two years that he had no knowledge of the affair. A decision of the Supreme Court in July, 1974 forced him to surrender secretly taped conversations with his closest aides, on the ground that "executive privilege does not apply to evidence for a criminal trial." The tapes showed that Nixon had known of and directed Watergate cover-up activities.

To avoid almost certain impeachment by the House and removal from office by the Senate, Nixon resigned on August 9, 1974. Many of his former advisers confessed to crimes or were indicted and convicted on criminal charges for their roles in the break-ins and cover-up. Nixon himself was granted an unconditional pardon by his successor, President Ford.

Also damaging to the prestige of the administration was the resignation of Nixon's first Vice President, Spiro Agnew, in September, 1973, after pleading "no contest" to charges of income tax evasion during his term as Governor of Maryland.

Gerald R. Ford (Republican, 1974-1977). Gerald R. Ford succeeded to the Presidency after Nixon's resignation. He had previously been nominated by Nixon as Vice President, following Agnew's resignation. Thus, Ford was the only man in our history to become Chief Executive without having been elected to either the Presidency or the Vice Presidency. Ford had a long record of service as a member of the House of Representatives from Michigan, and for some years had been the minority (Republican) leader in the lower house.

1. *Political Developments.* Defeating a strong bid by Ronald Reagan, former Governor of California, Ford won the Republican Party nomination for President in the 1976 election. His Democratic opponent was James E. (Jimmy) Carter, former Governor of Georgia. Carter won the election.

2. *Noteworthy Events and Achievements of the Ford Administration.* As President, Ford was challenged at home by continuing inflation, extensive unemployment, and a loss of public confidence in government. The Nixon pardon and the continuing recession impaired his early popularity.

Soon after becoming President, Ford offered amnesty to the approximately 28,000 draft dodgers and deserters of the Vietnam War period, provided they agreed to work in a public service job for up to two years. Few accepted the offer.

Ford clashed with Congress over national energy measures and questions of foreign policy and executive power. He vetoed most social welfare legislation passed by Congress as being inflationary.

Congress refused to appropriate funds requested by the President for military aid to stave off a final Communist victory in Cambodia and Vietnam. The United States in effect gave up its military effort in Southeast Asia.

In March, 1975, after Cambodian forces had seized a U.S. merchant ship, the *Mayaguez,* President Ford ordered an attack that succeeded in recovering the ship and its crew.

The Ford administration continued a policy of *détente* with the Soviet Union. We sold large quantities of grain to the Russians and purchased petroleum from them. In 1976, the two governments signed an agreement on the size and monitoring of underground atomic tests.

A notable diplomatic triumph of the Ford administration, negotiated by Secretary of State Henry Kissinger, was an agreement in 1975 suspending active conflict between Egypt and Israel. Under this pact, the United States agreed to station civilian contingents in the Sinai to monitor the terms of the agreement.

REVIEW TEST (Chapter 17 — Part V)

Select the number preceding the word or expression that best completes each statement or answers each question.

1. The first Republican to occupy the White House after Herbert Hoover was (1) Harry Truman (2) Dwight Eisenhower (3) John Kennedy (4) Richard Nixon

2. The "Fair Deal" was the name given to the domestic program of (1) Lyndon Johnson (2) John Kennedy (3) Harry Truman (4) Dwight Eisenhower

3. President Kennedy's "Alliance for Progress" Program was most consistent with the earlier Latin American Policy of (1) Abraham Lincoln (2) Franklin D. Roosevelt (3) Lyndon Johnson (4) Richard Nixon

4. An important achievement of the Lyndon Johnson administration was: (1) the censure of Senator Joseph McCarthy (2) the passage of Medicare (3) an end to the war in Vietnam (4) all-out aid to India to halt Chinese aggression

5. The first U. S. president to visit both the Soviet Union and Communist China, in an historic reversal of previous policy was: (1) Richard Nixon (2) John Kennedy (3) Dwight Eisenhower (4) Harry Truman

6. All of the following have served as Vice Presidents since World War II, *except* (1) Hubert Humphrey (2) Lyndon Johnson (3) Nelson Rockefeller (4) Richard Nixon

7. Direct United States military involvement in the War in Vietnam was ended by (1) Lyndon Johnson (2) Richard Nixon (3) John Kennedy (4) none of these

8. The landmark Supreme Court decision calling for desegregation of the public schools of the nation was handed down during the presidency of (1) F. D. Roosevelt (2) Harry Truman (3) John Kennedy (4) Dwight Eisenhower

9. All of the following events occurred during the administration of John F. Kennedy, *except* (1) the Cuban Missile crisis (2) establishment of the Peace Corps (3) the beginning of Social Security (4) the orbiting of the first astronauts into space

10. Which policy or event occurred during the administration of the Chief Executive with which it is paired? (1) adoption of Medicare—Truman (2) Devaluation of the dollar—Kennedy (3) East-West détente—Nixon (4) Civil Rights Act of 1964—Eisenhower

From the list below indicate the identifying letter of the President with whom each of the following ideas or events may be most correctly paired?

A. Harry S. Truman   D. Lyndon B. Johnson
B. Dwight D. Eisenhower   E. Richard M. Nixon
C. John F. Kennedy   F. Gerald R. Ford

1. End of the war in Korea
2. Watergate Affair
3. First Catholic President of the United States
4. Passage of the Taft Hartley Act over a presidential veto
5. Agreement with the Soviet Union on strategic arms limitation
6. United States joins NATO
7. The "New Frontier Program"
8. The "War on Poverty"

Essay Questions

1. List three important problems and three important achievements of each of the last four Presidents of the United States.

2. Briefly describe the nature of each of the following Presidential programs: Fair Deal, New Frontier, Great Society.

3. Discuss a common problem faced by Presidents Truman, Eisenhower, Kennedy, Johnson, Nixon, and Ford. Describe one step taken by each to handle or solve this problem.

REVIEWING UNIT SIX

Select the number preceding the word or expression that best completes each statement or answers each question.

1. From the Reconstruction Period to the present the Democratic party has been predominant in (1) the Southern states (2) the New England states (3) the Middle Western states (4) the states of the Pacific coast

2. Which of the following was true of the first session of Congress in Franklin D. Roosevelt's first administration? (1) A large number of investigating committees were appointed. (2) There were delays in committee on important measures. (3) An unusual amount of remedial legislation was passed. (4) Appropriations totaling 90 billion dollars were made.

3. With which period in United States history is the Progressive Movement associated? (1) 1830–45 (2) 1870–85 (3) 1900–20 (4) 1930–45

4. Which of the following Presidents is paired with an event that occurred during his administration? (1) Grover Cleveland — annexation of Hawaii (2) Theodore Roosevelt — Gentlemen's Agreement (3) Woodrow Wilson — Lend-lease Act (4) Franklin D. Roosevelt — Marshall Plan

5. The statement, "Like Franklin D. Roosevelt, this President concerned himself primarily with domestic reform during his first years in office, and with foreign affairs in subsequent years" applies most accurately to (1) Woodrow Wilson (2) Herbert Hoover (3) Harry Truman (4) Dwight D. Eisenhower

6. The administrations of Grant, Harding, and Truman were similar in that all three were (1) Republican-dominated (2) marked by a return to isolationism (3) followed by the election of a President from a different party (4) faced problems resulting from war

7. The names Oliver Wendell Holmes, Jr. and Felix Frankfurter are both important in the development of American (1) poetry (2) science (3) education (4) constitutional law

8. "Muckrakers" were (1) farmers who raised wheat (2) novelists of the Jacksonian era (3) early 20th-century writers who believed in political and economic reform (4) Theodore Roosevelt's Rough Riders

9. The initiative, the referendum, and the direct election of United States Senators are associated with the (1) New Deal (2) Age of Jackson (3) Progressive Era (4) Era of Good Feeling

10. The most important factor in the development of our economic life in the period since the Civil War has been (1) the growth of large-scale business organizations (2) the acquisition of new territory (3) reforms in government (4) reforms in banking

11. Both Andrew Carnegie and John D. Rockefeller, Sr. may be classified as (1) leaders in industrial consolidation in the 19th century (2) organizers of the Republican party (3) individuals favoring strict government regulation of railroads (4) opponents of the principle of philanthropy

12. The main reason why the United States had few investments abroad before 1890 was (1) The American people did not believe in imperialism. (2) Congress had prohibited all loans to foreign countries. (3) The development of the West offered a profitable field for the investment of capital. (4) Foreign countries did not need our capital.

13. Which of the following has had *least* influence on increasing general business prosperity since the end of World War II in the United States? (1) advances in technology (2) high farm productivity (3) large defense expenditures (4) rising employment

14. The author of the quotation "Whatever the long-term possibility that rapid economic growth could cover the rising need for both public and private expenditure, in the short run there is only one way to provide more funds for public needs — that is by lessening private spending" is probably trying to prove that (1) Taxes will hamper rapid economic growth. (2) Higher personal income taxes are essential to meet public needs. (3) Rapid economic growth will yield enough income to cover rising public needs. (4) Private spending will tend to lessen in the long run.

15. Between 1920 and 1957 the nation's gross national product more than doubled. This means the (1) amount of wages earned increased over 100% (2) total value of goods manufactured increased over 100% (3) total value of goods and services increased over 100% (4) Consumer Price Index rose steadily from 100 to over 200

*On the time line below, the letters **A** through **F** represent time intervals as indicated. For each of the following statements, write **first** the name of the President described, and **second** the letter that indicates the time interval during which this President's tenure of office occurred.*

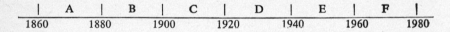

A	B	C	D	E	F
1860	1880	1900	1920	1940	1960	1980

Example: I became President during the worst economic collapse in our history and introduced a wide-ranging program of relief and reform.   F. D. Roosevelt D

1. The Federal Reserve Act and the lowest tariff in over 50 years were passed during my administration.

2. I was the first Republican President to break the "Solid South." I had to cope with the outbreak of the Great Depression.

3. After being re-elected to the Presidency by one of the widest margins in history, I was forced to resign as the result of a major scandal.

4. After gaining the Presidency by an extremely narrow margin of the popular vote, I sought, with my wife's help, to encourage the intellectual community and sponsor cultural activities in the White House.

5. My Civil War record helped me win the Presidency. During my administration, white supremacy was gradually re-established in the South.

6. After succeeding to the Presidency under the terms of the 25th Amendment, I ran as my party's candidate in the next regular election.

7. I succeeded to the Presidency after the death of the incumbent, and I became the only President to be impeached.

8. During my administration, American military participation in the Vietnam War was ended.

9. I became President of the United States after serving as top commander of the Allied Expeditionary Forces in Europe in World War II.

10. I became President as a result of the death of my predecessor; during my years in office the Marshall Plan and NATO became important parts of American foreign policy.

Essay Questions

1. Certain Presidential elections stand out in United States history for one or more of the following reasons: (a) personalities of the candidates (b) issues at stake (c) incidents associated with the election campaign (d) influence of a third party. For each of three of the above reasons choose a different Presidential election in the 20th century, and show how that election was influenced by the reason given.

2. Most Presidents of the United States have faced major domestic problems. For each of three of the following Presidents, discuss one major domestic problem he faced and the policy or program he adopted to solve that problem.

Andrew Johnson	Theodore Roosevelt	Richard M. Nixon
Grover Cleveland	Lyndon B. Johnson	

3. The business cycle has been a characteristic of economic life in the United States.

(a) Name one phase of the business cycle and describe the characteristic features of that phase.

(b) Explain two controls by which the Federal Reserve Board attempts to stabilize the economy.

(c) Describe two measures passed by Congress to meet the problems of the business cycle of the 1930's. (No credit will be allowed in *c* for repeating information given in answer *b*.)

(d) Explain why many economists today are suggesting that we abandon the use of the term "business cycle" in favor of "business fluctuations."

4. Presidential slogans often indicate a criticism of existing economic or political conditions. Each slogan below is paired with the name of the Presidential candidate who campaigned with that slogan. Explain *either one economic* or *one political* condition that gave rise to each of these slogans:

(a) William McKinley — the "Full Dinner Pail"

(b) Theodore Roosevelt — the "Square Deal"

(c) Woodrow Wilson — the "New Freedom"

(d) Warren G. Harding — the "Return to Normalcy"

(e) Franklin D. Roosevelt — the "New Deal"

(f) Harry S. Truman — the "Fair Deal"

(g) John F. Kennedy — the "New Frontier"

(h) Lyndon B. Johnson — the "Great Society"

PROBLEMS OF A CHANGING NATION

CHAPTER 18_____

The American Farmer
Since 1865

The farmer has always played an important role in the American economy. He has been a supplier of raw materials and food, and has provided a market for manufactured goods. After the Civil War the government was forced to give increasing attention to the farmers' problems. Today, the "farm problem" is one of the most perplexing of all economic problems faced by the American people.

Part I — THE AGRARIAN CRUSADE (1865–1900)

After the Civil War, the Agricultural Revolution continued on the farms. At the same time the economic position of the American farmer deteriorated. His efforts to improve his lot in the period 1865–1900 are often referred to as the *Agrarian Crusade.*

The Continuing Agricultural Revolution. Although noteworthy improvements in American agriculture had taken place before the Civil War (see page 180), it was not until after the war that the Agricultural Revolution really gained momentum. The most significant aspects have been the introduction of labor-saving tools and equipment, the application of science to agriculture, and the growing role of the Federal government in helping the farmer.

1. *New Tools and Equipment.* The introduction of labor-saving farm equipment after the Civil War brought to an end the era of hand labor on the farm. Hand tools gave way to horse-drawn machines; horses in turn gave way to tractors and power equipment. Included among the thousands of important new farm tools and machinery have been improved plows, corn huskers, hay loaders, cream separators, milking machines, cotton pickers, and gasoline tractors. So mechanized have many modern farms become that they have been called "factories in the field." Modern combines reap, thresh, clean, and bag grain in one continuous operation.

2. *The Application of Science to Agriculture.* The increased application of science to agriculture has been an important part of change on the farm since the Civil War. Introduced into farming by chemists, biologists, bacteriologists, and other scientists, were more efficient fertilizers; new and improved varieties of plants and livestock; and disease-resistant strains of grains, fruits, and vegetables. In addition, older agricultural methods, like crop rotation, were improved; new methods, like dry farming and contour plowing, were introduced; and new industrial uses for farm products were developed.

3. *The Role of the Government.* Much of the progress in scientific agriculture was a result of government aid. **(a)** The *Morrill Act* of 1862 granted land to the states for the establishment of colleges in which agriculture would be taught. **(b)** The *Hatch Act* of 1887 made provision for the establishment of agricultural experimental stations throughout the country. **(c)** The *Smith-Lever Act* of 1914 provided for county agents, who were to furnish useful agricultural and home economics information to farmers. **(d)** The *Smith-Hughes Act* of 1917 provided money for the support of agricultural and vocational instruction in public high schools. **(e)** The *Department of Agriculture,* established in 1862, rapidly became one of the largest of government agencies. It gives information and crop reports to farmers, encourages scientific farming methods, and runs experimental stations. **(f)** Government *irrigation* and *conservation* programs have also been a boon to agriculture.

Results of the Agricultural Revolution. The rapid changes on American farms since the Civil War have produced results of nationwide significance.

1. Much of the monotony, drudgery, and isolation of farm life has been eliminated.

2. Farm acreage and productivity per acre have risen sharply, leading to a tremendous expansion of production. Indeed, since the 1920's there has been overproduction of staple crops — *surpluses* which cannot be sold in the regular markets.

3. Farms have tended to become larger. In the 20th century particularly, large corporation-owned farms have increasingly replaced many "family-size" farms. More and more, farming has become "big business."

4. Farmers lost much of their economic independence as prices were increasingly set in national and international markets, rather than in local centers. Moreover, farmers became regular commercial consumers, buying innumerable commodities from businessmen, instead of producing most items on the farm itself. Many farmers today buy a large part of their food supply.

5. Increased productivity has led to a decline in the number of farmers. (The percentage of the nation's population engaged in agriculture dropped from 60% in 1860 to 40% in 1900, to 6% in 1969, and is still falling.)

6. There has been a decline in independent farm ownership and a corresponding rise in farm tenancy.

7. The diet of the American people has greatly improved.

The Changed Nature of American Farming After 1865. The farmers' problems after the Civil War were related directly to the transformation of agriculture by the Agricultural Revolution. After 1865, the self-sufficient farmer of pre-Civil War days, who raised just enough for his family's needs, gave way increasingly to the *commercial farmer,* who concentrated on raising one or two cash crops for profit. Although commercial farming made the farmer more a businessman and increased his chances of earning a better livelihood, it also exposed him to greater risks and economic hazards.

Agricultural Hardships After the Civil War. In addition to droughts, insect pests, and other adversities of nature, the farmers had many causes for complaint.

1. *Declining Prices.* The most serious of the farmers' problems was the decline of farm prices, which began soon after the end of the Civil War and continued almost until the end of the 19th century. Contributing to this decline was: **(a)** greatly increased agricultural production, resulting from new farm machinery and the addition of millions of acres of good farm land; **(b)** a scarcity of money in circulation; and **(c)** growing competition abroad from foreign nations, such as Canada, Australia, and Argentina.

2. *High Prices for Manufactured Goods.* In addition to receiving lower prices for what he sold, the farmer had to pay higher prices for what he bought. Because of protective tariffs and monopoly practices in industry, the farmer had to pay high prices for such needed articles as fertilizer, barbed wire, and farm machinery.

3. *High Middleman Costs.* Farmers complained that the railroads, commission merchants, stockyards, and other middlemen upon whom they were dependent for marketing their crops often exacted such high charges that there was little or no profit left for themselves.

4. *High Interest Rates.* As a group, farmers paid higher interest rates for loans than did manufacturers or merchants. In some sections of the West and South, interest rates might run as high as 20 to 50%.

5. *Unfair Tax Burdens.* One of the farmer's most pressing complaints was that he had to shoulder an unfair share of the nation's tax burden. Although it was often possible for the owners of new forms of wealth (industry, stocks, bonds) to evade, shift, or minimize their tax burden, the farmer had to pay all taxes placed on his land and livestock.

6. *Loss of Farms.* Falling prices, high middleman costs, and the other factors mentioned made it impossible for many farmers to pay their debts.

They were then forced to give up their farms and become tenant farmers, agricultural laborers, or wage earners in industry.

The Granger Movement. Made desperate by their many economic hardships, the farmers tried to get relief by calling for railroad regulation and currency inflation. The first organized widespread agrarian movement after the Civil War was the *Granger Movement*.

1. *Nature of the Grangers.* The Granger Movement was founded as a social organization called the *Patrons of Husbandry,* by Oliver H. Kelley in 1867. The hard times following the Panic of 1873 forced the Grangers to adopt a program of political and economic reform. They organized cooperatives, helped elect many officials in Western states, and influenced state legislatures, especially in the Middle West, to pass laws prohibiting abuses by railroads and grain elevator operators.

> (*a*) *Railroads.* For several decades after the Civil War the farmers were primarily concerned with abuses by railroads. In addition to charging higher rates because distances from markets increased as farmers moved West, railroads frequently resorted to unfair pricing practices. Transportation costs for *long hauls* between large cities, where several railroads might be competing, were often lower than for *short hauls,* between farm towns and city markets, where a single railroad might have monopoly control. Railroads also discriminated indirectly against farmers by giving *secret rebates* (partial refunds) to large industrial shippers.

> (*b*) *Other Middlemen.* Stockyards, grain elevators, and other companies that owned storage facilities at railroad centers charged exorbitant rates because they had little or no competition.

2. *The Granger Laws.* At first the *Granger laws* were upheld by the Supreme Court. In deciding cases like *Munn v. Illinois* (1876) the Court ruled that states had the right to regulate private property (for example, railroads) for the common good. However, railroads and other affected businesses fought the Granger laws in court until the Supreme Court reversed itself in the 1880's. In *Wabash v. Illinois* (1886) and in other cases, the Court declared that where railroads and other forms of commerce ran across state lines, the states could not restrict them, since Congress alone had the power to regulate interstate commerce. These decisions invalidated many of the Granger laws and led to a decline in the movement's influence.

3. *The Interstate Commerce Act (1887).* Although the Granger laws failed to achieve their purposes, public opinion forced both major political parties to help pass Federal legislation regulating the railroads. The earliest Federal action of this kind was the *Interstate Commerce Act* of 1887, which forbade pooling agreements, rebates, and other abuses. An *Interstate Commerce Commission (ICC)* was established to enforce the act. As originally passed, however, the enforcement provisions were weak, and had to be strengthened later (see page 372).

The Greenback Movement. Long before the Granger Movement declined the farmers turned also to inflation of the currency as a solution to the problem of decreasing farm prices.

1. *Withdrawal of the Greenbacks.* In 1866, the Federal government began to withdraw from circulation the unbacked paper currency ("Greenbacks") it had issued during the Civil War. Farmers joined other "cheap money" advocates in protesting vigorously. They claimed that the government's policy would not only cause prices to fall but would also force them to repay mortgage debts to Eastern bankers in dollars worth more than those they originally borrowed.

2. *The Resumption Act of 1875.* The Federal government agreed to stop retiring the Greenbacks and to reissue several million dollars worth. However the effect of this action was cancelled by the *Resumption Act* of 1875, in which Congress voted to make the Greenbacks redeemable in gold, starting January 1, 1879. In effect, this placed the "Greenbacks" on a par with other types of currency and ended their status as a form of "cheap money."

3. *The Greenback Party.* The Resumption Act caused supporters of cheap money to unite in 1876 to form the *Greenback Party,* which called for the issuance of more paper money. Although the Greenback Party secured over a million votes in the elections of 1878, it never became influential. Two factors account for this: in 1879 farm prices began to rise; in 1886, when farm prices began to decline, the farmers shifted their attention to another form of currency inflation, "free silver."

The Free Silver Movement. For over 20 years, from the mid-1870's to the late 1890's, the American farmer supported a movement to have as much silver as was brought to the mint coined into silver dollars (*free silver*). He hoped that this would swell the amount of currency in circulation, thereby lowering its value and raising the prices of farm products.

1. *Bimetallism.* Since its beginnings, the United States government had adopted a policy of backing its money with both gold and silver at a fixed ratio. Under this policy of *bimetallism,* it was, in the early 1870's, coining gold and silver without charge at a ratio of 16 ounces of silver to one ounce of gold ("free and unlimited coinage at 16 to 1").

2. *The Demonetization of Silver.* For many years before 1873, silver miners had stopped bringing their silver to the Mint for coinage because they could get a higher price for it from the silversmiths on the "market" than they received from the government. Since facilities for coining silver were lying unused, the government quietly stopped coining or *"demonetized"* silver dollars in 1873.

3. *The "Crime of '73."* In the mid-1870's, large silver deposits were discovered and mined in Nevada and Colorado. As silver poured onto the market, its value decreased rapidly. When miners who had formerly sold their silver to commercial outlets, tried to sell it to the Mint, they became painfully aware that silver had been demonetized. They now demanded that the government resume the free and unlimited coinage of silver, and denounced the demonetization act as the "Crime of '73." Farmers joined the silver miners because they were convinced that free silver would raise farm prices.

4. *The Silver Purchase Acts.* To meet the demands of the "silverites," Congress passed the *Bland-Allison Act* in 1878, providing for the purchase by the Treasury Department, for coinage into silver dollars, of 2 to 4 million dollars' worth of silver bullion each month. When this failed to halt the decline in the value of silver and the protests of the farmers, Congress passed the *Sherman Silver Purchase Act* of 1890, increasing government silver purchases to 4.5 million ounces per month. Payment for such silver was to be made in legal tender treasury notes, redeemable in gold or silver.

5. *Cleveland Displeases the Silver Interests.* During the Panic of 1893, holders of the silver certificates demanded gold. Alarmed at the shrinking gold reserve and the possibility that this would destroy faith in the soundness of the dollar and prolong the depression, President Grover Cleveland induced Congress in 1893 to repeal the Sherman Silver Purchase Act. In addition, to replenish the dwindling reserve, Cleveland in 1895 had the Treasury borrow a large sum of gold from an Eastern banking syndicate led by J. P. Morgan. Because the bankers made a large profit on the sale of the government bonds they received in exchange for the gold, Cleveland was bitterly denounced by the Western and Southern wings of his party (the Democratic Party). Populists and radical Democrats attacked the President as a "tool of Wall Street."

The Populist Movement. As the Granger and Greenback movements lost ground, new organizations, such as the *Farmers' Alliance* of the 1880's, took over leadership in the fight for free silver and against monopoly. In 1892, representatives of these agrarian groups met with representatives of labor and other discontented groups (Socialists, Single Taxers, ex-Grangers, etc.) to form the People's Party, known as the *Populists*.

1. *The Populist Program.* The Populist program was set forth in a statement of principles, known as the *Omaha Platform* (1892). It denounced both major parties as "tools of the capitalists," and called for: **(a)** free coinage of silver; **(b)** an increase in the amount of money in circulation; **(c)** a graduated income tax; **(d)** government ownership of *public utilities* (railroads, telegraphs, telephones); **(e)** tariff reduction; **(f)** an eight-hour working day; **(g)** direct election of Senators; **(h)** adoption of a secret ballot; **(i)** postal savings banks; **(j)** restriction of immigration; and **(k)** a single term for the Presidency.

2. *Populist Leaders.* Populist leaders like "Sockless" JERRY SIMPSON, MARY ELLEN LEASE, and IGNATIUS DONNELLY spoke heatedly against "international bankers" and "Wall Street monopolists." Though the Populists supposedly represented the interests of workers as well as farmers, the agrarian elements clearly dominated the Party and frequently denounced those who lived in cities as "urban parasites."

3. *Populist Strength Grows.* The Populist Party turned out to be one of the strongest third parties in American history. In the election of 1892, it polled over a million votes for its Presidential candidate, JAMES B. WEAVER, capturing the electoral votes of four Western states. It also sent several members to Congress. The split in the ranks of Western Republicans, caused by the Populists, made possible the victory of the Democratic Party and its standard bearer, GROVER CLEVELAND. In the Congressional election of 1894, the Populists increased their vote by 40%.

Election of 1896. Populism and the free silver movement reached their climax in the election of 1896. Led by Southern and Western leaders, the Democratic Party rejected Cleveland's sound money policy, and adopted a free silver platform calling for the free and unlimited coinage of silver at 16 to 1. WILLIAM JENNINGS BRYAN, a young Congressman from Nebraska, was chosen as the party's candidate for President after an impassioned plea for free silver (the *"Cross of Gold"* speech). Although they realized that it probably meant the end of the party as a separate organization, the Populists endorsed Bryan for President, hoping that this would make possible a victory for free silver. The Republicans nominated WILLIAM McKINLEY, former Congressman and Governor of Ohio, on a platform calling for a gold standard and a high tariff.

1. *The Campaign: Bryan v. McKinley.* In perhaps the most exciting campaign since the Civil War, Bryan carried the fight for free silver to all parts of the country, making hundreds of effective speeches, and appealing to the farmers, workers, and shopkeepers of the nation. McKinley conducted a quieter campaign, largely from the "front porch" of his residence

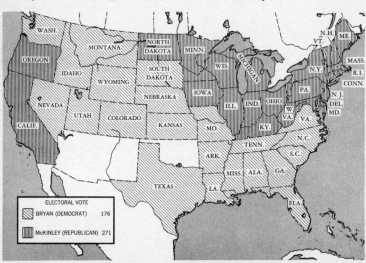

in Ohio. He appealed to the more conservative and propertied groups in the nation, and warned that free silver would rob citizens of their savings and cause further depression by debasing the currency. Speakers of both parties also appealed to and played upon class and sectional hatreds.

2. *McKinley's Victory.* McKinley won the election by a popular majority of over a half a million votes and an electoral vote of 271 to 176. Bryan's strength was greatest in the agrarian West and South; McKinley carried the industrial East. Among the important factors in the Republican victory were these: **(a)** McKinley's campaign was brilliantly organized and conducted with unlimited funds by Ohio industrialist Mark Hanna. **(b)** Republican leaders and businessmen appealed to people's fears by emphasizing that a Democratic victory would cause factories to close and jobs to be lost. **(c)** Because of tension and distrust between rural and urban areas, the working-class vote in many states went to McKinley. **(d)** The conservative and business elements of the country, including Eastern Democrats, lined up solidly behind McKinley.

3. *Results of the Election of 1896.* The election of 1896 had important results. It led to the temporary domination of the government by big business and financial interests. Also, it marked the end of the post-Civil War Agrarian crusade, since improved agricultural conditions after 1896 brought a temporary end to farm agitation. Although the *Gold Standard Act* of 1900 made currency redeemable in gold only, the discovery of new gold deposits in Alaska and South Africa increased the base for the national currency. Together with increasing demands for farm products at home and abroad, this increase contributed to higher farm prices.

Significance of Populism. Although it declined rapidly after 1896, the Populist Movement was significant in American development. **(1)** It fulfilled the traditionally important role of third parties in American politics — that of bringing new issues to national attention until they are adopted by one of the major parties. **(2)** It contributed to the growing demand for reform, which became the basis for the Progressive Movement of the early 1900's. (Some historians claim that it was the actual beginning of Progressivism. Others point out that after 1894, the Populists gave virtually all their attention to free silver and little to other "reforms.") **(3)** Most economists and historians today would agree that the Populists were overconcerned with currency reform. Although this phase of their program was a failure, nearly all of the other major demands of the Populist Party were enacted into law in the 20th century.

REVIEW TEST (Chapter 18—Part I)

Select the number preceding the word or expression that best completes each statement or answers each question.

1. The Homestead Act received the support of the farmer because it provided for (1) regulation of railroads (2) land on easy terms (3) conservation of the soil (4) low interest rates on mortgages

2. In the decades following the Civil War, what effect did the decline of farm prices have upon Western farmers? (1) It aided them by lowering the prices of manufactured goods. (2) It hurt them by forcing them to pay back a more valuable dollar than they had borrowed. (3) It helped them by creating a greater demand for their crops. (4) It had no effect upon them.

3. An organization active in the 1870's in securing state regulation of railroads was the (1) Grangers (2) Knights of Labor (3) Muckrakers (4) Populists

4. Which group most vigorously opposed the redemption of "Greenbacks" during the post-Civil War period? (1) manufacturers (2) silver mine owners (3) farmers (4) financiers

5. Cheap money enthusiasts favored all of the following *except* (1) the Bland-Allison Act (2) "Greenbacks" (3) Sherman Silver Purchase Act (4) the Gold Standard Act of 1900

6. Who gave greatest support to the Populist Party? (1) farmers and Radical Republicans (2) farmers and silver miners (3) bankers and steel manufacturers (4) railroad officials and union members

7. Which of the following policies was opposed by the Populists? (1) popular election of senators (2) the gold standard (3) a graduated income tax (4) government ownership of railroads

8. The mechanization of agriculture resulted in (1) a decrease in the number of small farms (2) a decrease in the amount of capital needed to begin farming (3) an increase in the cost of production per unit of output (4) curtailed production of surpluses

9. After the Civil War the farmers opposed all of the following *except* (1) secret rebates (2) high middleman costs (3) high tariffs (4) long-term loans

10. The "Crime of 1873" referred to (1) the backing of the "Greenbacks" with gold (2) free coinage of silver (3) demonetization of silver (4) the issuance of "Greenbacks" during the Civil War

State whether each of the following statements is true or false. If the statement is false, replace the word or phrase in **boldface type** *with one which will make it correct.*

1. The President denounced as a "tool of Wall Street" was **Grover Cleveland.**

2. The Populist candidate for the Presidency in 1892 was **William Jennings Bryan.**

3. In the election of 1896, McKinley's brilliant campaign manager was **Jerry Simpson.**

4. The "Cross of Gold" speech was an impassioned attack on **Free Silver.**

5. Many Populists later joined the **Progressive Movement.**

Essay Questions

1. Explain how the agricultural and industrial transformation of the United States affected the nature of American farming after 1865.

2. State two specific problems faced by the American farmer in the period 1865–90, and for each discuss one way in which either the farmer or the Federal government tried to solve this problem.

3. Show how each was related to the farm problem after the Civil War: Granger laws, Interstate Commerce Act, the protective tariff, the withdrawal of "Greenbacks," the demonetization of silver, free silver, the Populist Movement, the election of 1896.

Part II — FARM PROBLEMS IN THE 20th CENTURY

During the period from 1900 to 1920, the farm protest movements of the late 19th century gave way to a period of increasing farm prosperity. After World War I, however, a new and as yet unsolved farm problem developed, that of *overproduction* or *surplus*.

Agricultural Prosperity, 1900–20. During the period 1900–20, the American farmer shared in the general prosperity of the nation. The value of his property doubled and the prices of his crops increased almost 50%. Demand for agricultural commodities increased at home and abroad, especially during World War I (1914–18).

Hard Times for the Farmer After World War I. The farm prosperity of the early 1900's collapsed after World War I. During the war, rising prices and an almost unlimited demand for food and fiber had induced farmers to buy more land and equipment at high prices. The return of peace led to a decline in demand which sent farm prices and land values tumbling downward. Farmers were also faced with increasing competition from foreign nations, particularly Canada, Australia, and Argentina.

1. *Farm Depression.* Unlike industry, which recovered quickly after the war, agriculture remained in a state of depression and mounting surpluses. The depression of the 1930's added to the farmers' burden, as prices fell disastrously and overproduction became more acute. Thousands lost their farms and became farm tenants; others became farm laborers or *migratory farmers*. (Migratory farmers travel from section to section picking crops and serving as a pool of hand labor at harvest time. Since the 1930's, they have been one of the nation's most poverty-stricken groups.)

2. *Farmers' Efforts to Help Themselves.* As they had done in the 19th century, the farmers tried in the early 20th century to solve their problems by joint action.

(a) The *Non-Partisan League* was active in Western states from about 1915 to 1920. Its representatives gained control of several state legislatures, secured legislation favorable to farmers, and organized many types of farm cooperatives (banks, mills, warehouses).

(b) When the Non-Partisan League declined in the 1920's, farmers shifted their attention to organizing a *farm bloc* in both Congress and the state legislatures. (The farm bloc consists of legislators of both major parties who cross party lines, if necessary, to support legislation that helps the farmer.) Although the farm bloc secured legislation favorable to farmers in the 1920's, it could not prevent the farm depression.

(c) The farm bloc is still active, although perhaps not as influential as it once was. It is supported by the *farm lobby* which works in Washington and the state capitals in behalf of agricultural interests. Some of the organizations which support the farm lobby are the *National Grange,* the *American Farm Bureau Federation,* the *National Farmers' Union* and the *National Farmers' Organization.*

(d) Farmers also organized *cooperatives,* which undertake a variety of services for members, such as marketing crops, buying equipment and supplies, providing electricity, and extending credit. At present, about one-sixth of all the nation's farm products (by value) are marketed through "co-ops."

The Federal Farm Board. When it became increasingly clear that the farmers were unable to solve their basic problems by themselves, the Federal government took steps to aid the farmer. The *Agricultural Marketing Act* of 1929 established a 500 million dollar fund to be used by a *Federal Farm Board* for loans to farm cooperatives, to help them store surplus crops until prices became more favorable. The Farm Board also tried to raise prices by buying up surplus wheat and cotton. The attempt was a failure. Surpluses were so large that the available money was spent quickly, without halting the downward drop of prices.

The New Deal Tries to Revive Farm Prosperity. When Franklin D. Roosevelt became President in 1933, farm conditions were critical. Roosevelt's New Deal program included emergency agricultural measures which were to become the basis for the government's farm program in succeeding administrations. Most of these measures were concerned with surplus and credit.

1. *The AAA of 1933.* The *Agricultural Adjustment Act of 1933* attempted to raise prices by limiting production. Farmers were paid for cutting acreage of staple crops (wheat, corn, rice, tobacco). The funds for such payments were raised by a tax on the processing of farm products (for example, meat packing, and flour milling). Although prices of farm products began to rise, the Supreme Court declared the AAA of 1933 unconstitutional in the *Hoosac Mills Case of 1936.* The grounds cited were: **(a)** Farming is an intrastate industry; Congress, therefore, had infringed on the rights of the states. **(b)** The processing tax was an improper use of the Federal tax power, since one group was being taxed for the direct benefit of another.

2. *SCADA of 1936.* In order to limit production without running into the difficulties met by the AAA of 1933, Congress passed the *Soil Conservation and Domestic Allotment Act of 1936 (SCADA).* Under this act, which was upheld by the Supreme Court, farmers were offered *benefit payments* for conserving the soil by shifting production from staple crops to soil enriching crops (*e.g.,* clover, beans, alfalfa). The act served as a "stop-gap" measure until a more comprehensive program was established in 1938.

Agricultural Adjustment Act of 1938. The most comprehensive New Deal attack on the problems of crop surpluses, depressed prices, and reduced farm income took the form of the *Agricultural Adjustment Act of 1938.* This measure, which was upheld by the Supreme Court in 1939, placed emphasis upon marketing controls as well as on production controls. Its principles have become the basis of much of the Federal farm program since then.

1. *Acreage Allotments.* To prevent overproduction, farmers were asked to cut acreage devoted to staple crops, and to plant soil-conserving crops on the acres withdrawn from cultivation. Those who accepted these *acreage allotments* were to be given bounty payments by the government.

2. *Marketing Quotas.* If, despite acreage cuts, a surplus of crops was grown, the Secretary of Agriculture was authorized to establish *marketing quotas* for each crop, with the consent of two-thirds of the farmers involved. Farmers who accepted marketing quotas agreed to limit the quantity of each crop they placed on the market. The idea behind marketing quotas was that farm prices would be stabilized or even raised if surpluses were kept off the market. It has been difficult, however, to get two-thirds of the farmers producing a given crop, such as wheat, to agree to marketing quotas. They have rarely been used.

3. *Support Prices and Crop Loans.* The AAA of 1938 provided for the setting of minimum prices for various basic farm products. If the market price fell below these *support prices,* an agency of the Federal government, the *Commodity Credit Corporation,* offered the farmers loans on the basis of the "pegged prices." The CCC usually stored the crops thus acquired at its own expense. If the market price rose above the support price, a farmer cooperating in this program could sell the produce, pay off the loan, and pocket the difference. If the market price remained below the support price, the farmer allowed the CCC to retain the crops as payment for the loan. In either case, a minimum price was maintained for the farmer.

4. *Parity.* The formula still used in calculating the size of crop loans and the level of the support prices is called the *parity index. Parity* represents the level of prices the government thinks the farmers should receive to give them the same real income they had in the period 1909-14, when a "reasonable relationship" existed between the prices of what the farmer sold and what he bought. Each year the support or crop-loan price is established as a percentage of parity (the *parity index*). If the parity price of wheat is set at $1.30 a bushel and the support price is 90% of parity, a cooperating farmer can store his wheat crop (or any part of it he wishes) with the CCC, and receive a loan of 9/10 of $1.30 or $1.17 per bushel.

5. *Non-Cooperating Farmers.* Farmers who do not cooperate with the AAA program, or who exceed quotas, are not entitled to bounty payments or crop loans.

Other New Deal Farm Measures. The New Deal also extended financial aid to farmers. Between 1927 and 1932 alone, over 10% of America's farm property had been sold at auction for failure to meet mortgage payments. To deal with this situation, the Federal government created the *Farm Credit Administration* in 1933 to centralize financial assistance to the farmer and to extend emergency mortgage payment loans. In addition, in order to increase farm ownership again (by 1935, 42% of the nation's farmers were tenants), the government established the *Federal Security Agency (FSA)*. The FSA made long-term, low-interest loans to tenants, laborers, or sharecroppers who wished to buy farms; and short-term loans for the purchase of necessities such as seed, feed, and equipment. Aid extended by the FSA, expansion of electric facilities by the TVA and the Rural Electrification Administration, and other New Deal farm reforms helped to "revolutionize" farm life and added new comforts to what was often a dreary existence.

Results of the New Deal Program. As a result of holding surpluses off the market under the New Deal program, farm prices generally rose in the late 1930's, and farm income increased from 5 billion dollars in 1932 to 9 billion in 1939. In some measure, however, this was also due to the fact that as the nation gradually worked its way out of the depression, more money was spent for foodstuffs.

The New Deal was less fortunate, however, in solving the problem of surplus crops. Despite its attempts to curtail production, surpluses continued to grow. Between 1933 and 1941 total farm output grew over 20%. Farmers took their least fertile land out of production and cultivated the better land more intensively with the aid of better fertilizers and equipment.

Farm Prosperity During and After World War II. World War II, like other war periods, brought prosperity to the American farmer. Wartime demands at home and abroad pushed farm prices above parity in most cases, making government supports unnecessary. (These supports however, were fixed at 90% of parity during the war.)

Farm prosperity continued through the 1940's and early 1950's. It was stimulated by the *Marshall Plan* (1947–52), under which the United States gave food and other materials to war-torn European nations, and by the *Korean War* (1950–53), during which the needs of the armed forces expanded rapidly. Under the impact of this increased demand, surpluses that had piled up as a result of the government program were used up. Farmers were able to reduce or pay their mortgages in full. Farm income increased over 400% between 1939 and 1950.

Continued Assistance to the Farmer After World War II. When the high demand for farm commodities created by World War II and the postwar reconstruction period came to an end, American farmers were faced once again with the problems of surpluses, low prices, and low income. As a result, the Federal government continued its efforts to raise farm income by paying subsidies to farmers, by restricting acreage in order to avert oversupply, and by in effect (through crop loans) buying up part of the crop when necessary to keep prices from dropping below desired levels.

Criticism of the Farm Program. For many years serious criticism was leveled at the government's price-support program to farmers. Critics claimed the following: **(1)** The purchase and storage of crops and the direct payments to farmers were costing the government about 4 billion dollars a year. **(2)** The benefits of the program were going mainly to the big farmers and farm corporations ("agribusiness"). **(3)** The support program did not solve the surplus problem. Rather, it encouraged farmers to produce more on fewer acres, in order to qualify for government subsidies. **(4)** The overall effect was to raise the prices of foods and other farm goods to consumers.

Ending Production Controls — The New Farm Program. In 1973, in a long-delayed response to criticisms and to changing conditions, Congress adopted a new farm program to replace the structure of price supports and production controls that had been in effect for some 40 years. The 1973 law, authorized for four years, was designed to support *farm income* (rather than crop prices) and to *expand* (rather than to hold down) overall production. Such expansion was urgently needed to meet mounting food needs in the United States and throughout the world, resulting from rising population, higher living standards, crop failures and famines, and other emergency factors.

1. *Provisions.* The central purpose of the Farm Act of 1973 was to encourage American farmers to bring all suitable land under cultivation and to maximize production. All acreage controls were dropped. At the same time, certain safeguards for farm income were provided. **(a)** A new system of "target prices" was established for the main commercial crops — wheat, feed grains, and cotton. **(b)** Farmers will sell their crops at market prices, without government interference. **(c)** If prices fall below the "target" levels, the government will pay subsidies to farmers to make up the difference.

2. *Operation of the New Farm Program.* Under the new program, American farmers have in general been producing record harvests. Farm exports have been increased, including vast grain sales to the Soviet Union. In 1975, the United States and the Soviet Union signed an agreement for wheat and corn sales through 1980. American food has been going to many parts of the world to relieve human distress, to help restore our overall balance of international payments, and to serve as an instrument of the nation's foreign policy.

Subsidy payments to farmers have dropped from about 4 billion dollars in 1972 to under 1 billion dollars in 1976. There were virtually no payments for wheat and corn, and in view of the tremendous world demand, it was not expected that any such payments would be needed at least for some years. Although food prices in the United States continued to rise, it was emphasized that without the increase in production, prices might have been even higher.

However, various observers, including consumer groups, are wary of the new program. They say that the farmer is still being "over-protected" by government at the expense of everyone else. They fear huge costs to the taxpayer if crop surpluses and falling farm prices should reappear. In this connection, they point out that crop failures in the Soviet Union and elsewhere, resulting in an abnormal demand, cannot be expected to recur. They point to the raising of some "target prices" at various times since 1974 as evidence of the continued strength of the farm lobby in Washington.

Farm Problems Today. New problems have appeared in the farm situation in this country.

1. *Declining Numbers of Farms and Farmers.* During approximately the last 20 years, the numbers of farms and of farmers in the United States have been cut roughly in half — from 6 million to 3 million farms; and total farm population, from 20 million to less than 10 million. This has taken place in spite of government action to preserve the traditional "family farm." Increasing mechanization and other developments have made it possible to produce more and more with fewer farmers. Tenants and sharecroppers have been replaced by large farm enterprises which operate with hired labor ("agribusiness"). Many small farms have been consolidated into larger farms. Other farms have simply been abandoned or have become sites of housing developments, airports, highways, etc.

Many observers consider this an unhealthy trend in our society. Thousands of small farm communities have died or are dying. Large numbers of formerly self-employed farmers have had to give up their independent operations and become "hired hands," migratory farm laborers, or wage workers in the cities.

2. *Rural Poverty.* Poverty has become widespread in rural America, and the farm-assistance program has apparently done little to improve conditions. Today it is estimated that there are 14 million "rural poor" in the United States — about 40% of all Americans living in poverty. Entire rural communities are poverty-stricken. In recent years more than 20 million people have left the land seeking employment in the big cities. (Many of them have been former sharecroppers from the Deep South.) This mass "in-migration" has added greatly to problems in our urban centers.

REVIEW TEST (Chapter 18 — Part II)

Select the number preceding the word or expression that best completes each statement or answers each question.

1. A serious result of the application of scientific methods to agriculture in the United States has been (1) rapid exhaustion of the soil (2) elimination of submarginal land (3) periodic overproduction (4) increased cost of production

2. Which of the following periods was characterized by general farm prosperity? (1) 1865–80 (2) 1880–96 (3) 1900–14 (4) 1920–30

3. From 1920 to 1940, the condition of agriculture in the country may be said to have been characterized by (1) increased tenancy and the production of crop surpluses (2) increased land ownership due to steadily declining land values (3) much greater increases in farm prices than in labor costs (4) a vast extension of the foreign market for farm goods

4. The "farm bloc" in Congress is a group of (1) Congressmen who oppose favorable farm legislation (2) Republicans from the East who are unsympathetic to the farmers' demands (3) Congressmen who combine to vote for laws beneficial to farmers (4) Democrats from the West who favor the present farm policies

5. During the 1930's, tenant farming in the United States (1) existed only in the South (2) almost disappeared (3) increased in almost every part of the country (4) was confined to the New England states

6. The Agricultural Adjustment Act of 1933 was declared unconstitutional because (1) President Roosevelt felt the farmers were demanding too much (2) there was a great demand for farm products (3) the Secretary of Agriculture ordered little pigs killed (4) the Supreme Court ruled that the law was a violation of the rights of states

7. The purpose of the parity program for farmers was to (1) set maximum prices for farm products (2) protect the economic position of farmers (3) insure farmers against loss by floods (4) make credit available to farmers at low interest rates

8. Which of the following has declined in recent years? (1) farm size (2) farm surpluses (3) yield per acre (4) use of machines in agriculture

9. The Non-Partisan League was strongest in the (1) North (2) South (3) East (4) West

10. A basic reason for introducing the new farm program for 1974-78 was (1) increased world demand for food (2) loss of political influence by farmers (3) sharply declining price levels (4) elimination of poverty

Select the letter of the item in each group that does **NOT** *belong with the others.*

1. New Deal farm program: (a) Agricultural Adjustment Acts (b) Agricultural Marketing Act (c) Farm Credit Administration (d) Soil Conservation and Domestic Allotment Act

2. Provision of the AAA of 1938: (a) acreage quotas (b) marketing quotas (c) soil bank (d) crop loans

3. Features of Farm Act of 1973: (a) ending of 40-year price-support program (b) response to increased food needs (c) 'target prices" for main crops (d) sharp restriction of acreage

4. Efforts of the farmers to solve their own problems: (a) farm cooperatives (b) National Farmers' Union (c) Commodity Credit Corporation (d) the National Grange

Essay Questions

1. Explain the purposes and the actual effects (both good and bad) of the following: (a) the various farm price support programs in effect from 1933 to 1973; (b) the four-year farm income support program introduced in 1973.

2. Discuss the truth of each of the following statements, giving facts and illustrations to support your judgment: (a) Wars have often helped the American farmer. (b) The prosperity of farmers is of great importance to the United States.

3. Compared with other leading agricultural nations, the United States has an extremely small proportion of its population engaged in farming. Is this desirable or undesirable? Explain.

CHAPTER 19

The American Labor Movement

The industrialization of the United States was accompanied by the growth of labor unions. Since the Civil War, the role of organized labor in the economy has been a growing one. Problems related to workers and unions are among the more important economic issues today.

Part I — THE DEVELOPMENT OF THE AMERICAN LABOR MOVEMENT

The history of labor unions in the United States is closely related to the nation's economic development. It has taken over a century for organized labor to become as important as it is today.

Unions Before the Civil War. Unions are formed when employees feel that bargaining with the employer as a group will bring greater advantages than bargaining as individuals. When unions representing workers discuss the conditions of employment with employers the process is called *collective bargaining.*

1. *Hardships of the Early Factory System.* The early unions in the United States were established to improve the unsatisfactory conditions that developed with the rise of the factory system in America.

    (a) *Hours Were Long.* A work day of 12 to 14 hours was not unusual before the Civil War; even as late as the 1870's workers labored 11 or 12 hours a day, six days a week. (The 12-hour day, *seven days* a week, did not end at U. S. Steel until 1923.)

    (b) *Wages Were Low.* Even as late as the early 1900's, unskilled workers received $1 to $1.25 a day; skilled workers got up to $2 a day; and women and children received $2 to $4 a week.

    (c) *Working Conditions Were Poor.* In the early factories and other industrial establishments, workers faced such handicaps as poor lighting, inadequate sanitary facilities, and machinery without safety devices. Industrial accidents were blamed on the workers. As factories grew in size, employers lost personal contact with their employees and the conditions under which they worked.

2. *Other Labor Problems.* Other difficulties faced by workers in factories included domination of "company towns" by factory owners; periodic unemployment resulting from depressions and the introduction of labor-saving machines (technological unemployment); and lack of sympathy for the poor conditions of workers by government and industry. (Throughout

KNIGHTS OF LABOR 347

the 19th century, strikes were looked upon by many as illegal, unpatriotic, and even treasonable.)

3. *Early Labor Unions.* Although the first union in the United States was formed during Washington's administration (Philadelphia shoemakers, 1794), most pre-Civil War unions were established during the Jacksonian Era. They were made up primarily of skilled laborers (carpenters, printers, shoemakers, etc.). These early unions were for the most part weak and short-lived. Few survived the Panic of 1837. Among the reasons for their weakness were the competition of immigrants willing to work for lower wages and the difficulty of organizing women and children. In addition, until the case of *Commonwealth v. Hunt* in Massachusetts, in 1842, unions were regarded by the courts as illegal "conspiracies."

The Growth of Nationwide Labor Organizations. During and after the Civil War, labor began to organize on a national basis. At first, unions in the same trade combined into national unions (bricklayers, carpenters, cigar-makers, etc.). Later, federations of national unions were established. Several factors help explain the rise of this national labor movement. **(1)** As industry developed on a national scale, labor did the same, in order to bargain more effectively. **(2)** With the passing of the frontier, and the crowding of workers and immigrants into cities, opportunities arose to organize labor on a large scale. **(3)** Labor leaders believed that stronger organization was necessary in order to prod the government into taking action to help working people.

Knights of Labor (1869). Several attempts were made in the 1860's and 1870's to establish a national labor organization. The first to achieve any kind of success was the *Knights of Labor.* Organized in 1869 by Uriah Stephens and a group of tailors, the Knights developed rapidly into the nation's first important labor organization.

1. *Aims and Structure.* The Knights of Labor aimed to organize all workers into "one big union." All workers, skilled and unskilled, were admitted. The Knights advocated an eight-hour day, abolition of child labor, government ownership of public utilities, the exclusion of Chinese immigrants, and the establishment of cooperatives. It placed more faith in education and political persuasion than in collective bargaining. Its most able and influential leader was Terence V. Powderly.

2. *Growth and Decline.* At first, the Knights of Labor was organized as a secret society to prevent its members from being blacklisted by employers. The Knights dropped its policy of secrecy in 1881 and soon after won a number of big strikes. This helped it grow rapidly to a peak membership of 700,000 in 1886. Thereafter, it declined just as rapidly in numbers and influence, for several reasons. **(a)** It was (unjustly) associated in the public mind with the violence of the *Haymarket Affair* (see page 358). **(b)** It began to lose important strikes. **(c)** Most of its cooperatives failed. **(d)** It was weakened by constant quarrels over aims and methods between skilled and unskilled members, and between moderate and militant elements. **(e)** Its leadership became less effective. **(f)** It lacked sufficient financial reserves (for a "strike fund").

American Federation of Labor (1881). The *American Federation of Labor (AFL)* replaced the Knights of Labor as the nation's leading labor organization. It is still the most important element of the American labor movement.

1. *Origins.* The AFL was formed in 1881 as a rival of the Knights of Labor. It took its present name and elected its first full-time officers in 1886.

2. *Structure.* Unlike the Knights of Labor, which included nearly everyone and was centrally run, the AFL was a "union of unions," consisting primarily of skilled workers organized by crafts into a national federation. (Cigar-makers were in the Cigar-Makers Union, musicians in the Musicians Union, carpenters in the Carpenters Union, and so on.)

3. *Aims and Methods.* The AFL, like most of the American labor movement, was non-revolutionary. It accepted the private enterprise system and worked for change through established channels. Unlike the Knights of Labor, which favored persuasion and education, the AFL emphasized improving the status of labor through collective bargaining.

> *(a) Business Unionism.* The AFL stressed aims that were immediate and achievable ("business unionism"), including higher wages, shorter hours, and improved working conditions. It supported the idea of "job ownership" (security in employment), and advocated immigration restriction, relief from technological unemployment, enactment of favorable labor legislation, and the abolition of child labor.

> *(b) The AFL and Politics.* Though it urged its members to be politically active, and to vote regularly, the AFL did not support the formation of a separate labor party. It urged, instead, the support of candidates of existing parties who favored labor.

4. *Growth of the AFL.* The AFL grew rapidly. Skilled members of the Knights of Labor were among the first to join. Its membership rose to 500,000 in 1900, to 4 million in 1920, and to 8 million in 1940. At its peak in 1955, before merging with the CIO, the AFL had 10 million members in over 100 national unions organized primarily by crafts. Among its larger unions were the United Brotherhood of Carpenters and Joiners, the International Brotherhood of Teamsters, and the International Ladies Garment Workers Union.

5. *Leaders of the AFL.* The first and most outstanding leader of the AFL was SAMUEL GOMPERS. Gompers helped to organize the AFL, and then served as its first president for over 40 years (1882-1924). He won the respect of Presidents and businessmen. During World War I, he was called upon by President Wilson to head a *War Labor Committee* to promote national labor unity. Gompers is often considered America's greatest labor statesman. He was succeeded as president of the AFL by William Green and George Meany (the present head of the AFL-CIO).

Congress of Industrial Organizations (CIO). In the 1930's, a split took place in the ranks of the AFL, and a powerful rival federation emerged, the *Congress of Industrial Organizations (CIO).* The CIO was formed because of dissatisfaction with AFL policies on the part of some of its younger, more militant members. They were disturbed by a drop in AFL membership in the 1920's, and also with the failure to organize the semi-skilled and unskilled workers in the new mass production industries like automobiles and steel. They called for the formation of additional *industrial unions,* such as the United Mine Workers. In 1938, after being suspended for their organizing activities, the industrial unions within the AFL left the federation to form a new national labor organization, the CIO.

NOTE: Most AFL unions were *craft unions* (horizontal unions). A craft union is organized to include workers within a given trade, who may be employed in many different industries. Thus, there are craft unions of plumbers, carpenters, printers, electricians, etc. Some carpenters may work in steel plants, some in building construction, and some in the automobile industry, but they all belong to the same craft union. An *industrial union* (vertical union) includes all workers within an industry or plant regardless of whether they are skilled, semiskilled, or unskilled. Under this arrangement the skilled machinists, semiskilled truck drivers, and unskilled porters of a single plant are members of the same union.

1. *Growth of the CIO.* The CIO grew rapidly in numbers and strength. Successful organization drives in mass production industries during and after the New Deal Era (the 1930's) increased total membership to 5 million by 1955. Among the largest CIO unions were the United Automobile Workers, the United Steel Workers, and the United Textile Workers. John L. Lewis, president of the United Mine Workers, became the CIO's first president. He was succeeded by Philip Murray and Walter Reuther.

2. *Merger of the AFL and CIO.* In 1955, after 20 years of rivalry, the two labor federations agreed to reunite into a single organization and to end their raiding of one another's memberships, as well as to put a stop to *jurisdictional disputes.* (These are disputes in which unions of both federations try to organize and represent the same workers.)

American Federation of Labor and Congress of Industrial Organizations (AFL-CIO). The AFL-CIO is the largest and most powerful labor federation in the nation's history.

1. *Organization and Structure.* The AFL-CIO consists of over 140 national and international unions, and more than 60,000 locals. It has at present about 12.5 million members.

2. *Leaders.* George Meany, head of the former AFL, became the first president of the AFL-CIO. Walter Reuther, head of the former CIO, became vice president in charge of the Industrial Union Department.

3. Problems After Unification. Although organized labor gained in strength from reunification, expected gains in total membership have not materialized. (The reasons for this are discussed on the next page.) In addition, there have been some instances of jealousy and bickering among craft and industrial leaders, continued jurisdictional disputes between rival AFL and CIO unions, and violations of the "no-raiding agreement."

Independent Labor Unions. A substantial portion of organized labor always remained outside the big labor federations. At present there are about 4.3 million workers in "independent" labor unions.

1. Some nationwide unions, such as the large and well-organized Railroad Brotherhoods (membership about 500,000), have always been unaffiliated. (*Exception:* In 1956, the Locomotive Firemen and Enginemen joined the AFL-CIO.)

2. Some unions, like the United Mine Workers, which helped organize the CIO, and the United Auto Workers, have voluntarily left the parent organization.

3. Others have been expelled from the major federation. For example, the United Electrical Workers was expelled from the CIO in 1949 for communist domination; the International Brotherhood of Teamsters was thrown out of the AFL-CIO in 1957 because of corruption and racketeer influence.

GROWTH OF UNION MEMBERSHIP   PERCENT OF LABOR FORCE IN UNIONS

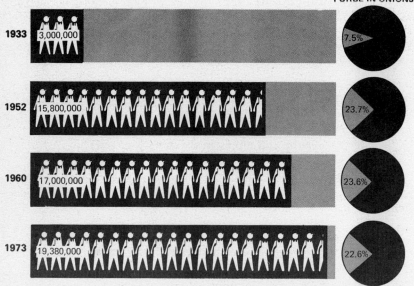

1933	3,000,000	7.5%
1952	15,800,000	23.7%
1960	17,000,000	23.6%
1973	19,380,000	22.6%

Membership in American labor unions from 1933 to 1973. Note that figures are given for total membership, and for membership as a proportion of the total labor force. (Figures from U. S. Bureau of Labor Statistics.)

4. From time to time radical union movements have developed that have opposed the capitalist economic system. The socialist-dominated *International Workers of the World (IWW)*, strong among the lumbermen of the Northwest in the early 1900's, denounced American government and society, and conducted violent strikes. The communist-dominated *Trade Union Unity League* of the 1920's and early 1930's first tried to establish independent unions under a policy of "dual unionism"; later (after its dissolution), it advised its members to "bore from within" in regular unions in order to persuade them to adopt radical economic and political programs.

Unorganized Workers. Despite the growing importance of organized labor, the membership of labor unions has never been more than about a quarter of the total working population. At present there are approximately 16.8 million union members in a civilian labor force of about 78 million. Several reasons help explain why most workers have not joined unions. **(1)** Workers in certain industries have traditionally preferred to remain independent (for example, agriculture, wholesale and retail trade, the professions, and personal services). Some of these "unorganized" industries, such as personal services, have grown far more rapidly in recent years than organized industries. **(2)** In a number of instances, unions have kept their doors closed to new members through restrictive policies. **(3)** It would also appear that many workers in the United States are reasonably well satisfied with their conditions of employment and feel no need for union representation or collective bargaining. **(4)** Opposition of employers and public officials to union organization has also been a factor, especially in certain sections of the country, such as the Deep South.

REVIEW TEST (Chapter 19—Part I)

Select the number preceding the word or expression that best completes each statement or answers each question.

1. The case of *Commonwealth v. Hunt* is important in labor history because (1) unions were guaranteed collective bargaining (2) unions were declared not to be conspiracies (3) the general strike was outlawed (4) picketing was legalized

2. An important reason for the decline of the Knights of Labor was the (1) organization of the Socialist Party (2) high cost of membership (3) conflict in interests between skilled and unskilled workers (4) passage of anti-labor laws by the Federal government

3. Samuel Gompers attempted to win gains for the labor movement by (1) uniting skilled and unskilled workers into one union (2) organizing industrial and vertical unions (3) forming craft unions of skilled workers (4) campaigning actively for the election of AFL members to public office

4. Which of the following was an important reason for the growth of labor unions in the latter half of the 19th century? (1) passage of the Sherman Antitrust Act (2) indifference of business to the welfare of employees (3) radical leadership of some unions (4) increase of women employed in industry

5. Throughout most of its history the American Federation of Labor has tried to achieve its aims by (1) organizing as an independent labor party (2) voting the Democratic ticket (3) supporting candidates who favored labor (4) encouraging immigration

6. The most influential leader of the CIO during the early years of its existence was (1) William Green (2) Samuel Gompers (3) John L. Lewis (4) Phillip Murray

7. Before their merger, the controversy between the AFL and the CIO was caused by (1) the antagonism between craft unions and industrial unions, (2) labor's attitude to the wage-and-hour bill (3) CIO support of the New Deal (4) the Clayton Antitrust Act

8. Industrial unionism grew most rapidly during the administration of (1) Andrew Jackson (2) Franklin D. Roosevelt (3) Theodore Roosevelt (4) Woodrow Wilson

9. Which statement concerning trade union membership in the United States is true? (1) It has steadily increased since the 1930's. (2) It includes over 50% of the labor force. (3) It has sharply increased since the AFL-CIO merger. (4) It has declined slightly in recent years.

10. The industry that is least unionized is (1) automobiles (2) steel (3) plumbing (4) agriculture

Supply the word or expression that completes each statement.

1. The first great national labor organization was the ..?...

2. The most able and influential leader of the labor organization referred to in question 1 was ..?...

3. The present head of the AFL-CIO is ..?...

4. A union that includes all the workers in a factory regardless of their degree of skill is called a(n) ..?.. union.

5. A union consisting primarily of skilled workers in the same occupation is known as a(n) ..?.. union.

Essay Questions

1. Show how the industrialization of the United States helped bring about the growth of unions.

2. Compare or contrast the Knights of Labor, the American Federation of Labor, and the Congress of Industrial Organizations as to (a) organization and (b) achievements.

3. Why has each of the following been considered a labor "statesman"? Terence Powderly, Samuel Gompers, John L. Lewis, Walter Reuther, George Meany.

4. Explain the status or role of independent labor unions within the labor movement.

5. Discuss the truth or falsity of each of the following statements: (a) Most workers are in unions. (b) The AFL-CIO has strengthened and unified the American labor movement.

Part II — THE AIMS AND METHODS OF
LABOR AND MANAGEMENT

Because the aims of labor and management often differ, labor disputes have become a characteristic feature of American industrial development. Most disputes are settled peacefully. When peaceful negotiation fails, however, each side resorts to more forceful "weapons."

Aims of Labor. Workers in general, and labor unions in particular, have always had the same basic objectives. In recent years newer aims have been added to the traditional ones.

1. *Traditional Aims of Labor.* Labor has always sought **(a)** *higher wages,* **(b)** *shorter hours,* **(c)** *improved working conditions,* and **(d)** *legal recognition* (collective bargaining).

2. *More Recent Aims.* In addition to their basic aims, unions in recent years have tried to secure the following: **(a)** *fringe* or *welfare benefits,* including such things as paid vacations and holidays, and pension and insurance programs; **(b)** *job security,* or the right of workers to hold jobs as long as there is work to be done, and as long as their work is satisfactory; **(c)** *seniority,* or acceptance by employers of the principle that workers with the longest employment records should be last to be fired and first to be considered for promotion; **(d)** *guaranteed annual wage,* a program under which the company would pay the worker a minimum annual wage, regardless of how many weeks a year he works; **(e)** the *checkoff,* or collection of union dues by the employer, or a regular payroll deduction; and **(f)** greater consideration for workers as human beings.

Aims of Management. Management or ownership has traditionally been interested in: **(1)** *good profits;* **(2)** *greater efficiency; and* **(3)** *freedom to manage,* which would include the right to hire and fire without interference. In addition, in recent years employers have become more interested in **(4)** *better relations with employees,* to keep morale high; and **(5)** *contract observance by unions,* in order to assure continuous production.

Peaceful Settlement of Labor Disputes. Despite the fact that strikes have always received more publicity, most disputes between labor and management have been settled without resort to forceful methods. In recent years, both sides have come to recognize that peaceful negotiation is to be preferred to bitter "warfare," because strikes are injurious to labor, management, and the public. Several well-established methods for peaceful negotiation have developed over the years. They are outlined below.

1. *Collective Bargaining.* The most important of all processes for ironing out labor differences is *collective bargaining.* This is the method by which employees negotiate with their employers through union representatives. Successful collective bargaining results in a *trade agreement* or *union contract.* Present-day contracts include rates of pay, basic hours, overtime pay, holidays, vacations, rest periods, seniority, safety and health provisions, apprenticeship rules, grievance machinery, employment and discharge procedures, union recognition, and length of contract.

2. *Mediation.* If collective bargaining does not solve a labor dispute, both sides may resort to *mediation* or *conciliation.* In this procedure a third party explores the issues and makes compromise proposals. Neither side is bound to accept the decisions of the mediator. An important United States agency that provides such services when serious strikes threaten or occur is the *Federal Mediation and Conciliation Service.* States and cities have also set up similar agencies.

3. *Arbitration.* Arbitration may occur after collective bargaining and mediation have failed. It is a procedure under which a new third party examines both sides of the dispute, and hands down a decision (called an *award*) that both parties agree to accept in advance. The suggestion that there be *compulsory arbitration* of labor disputes has been opposed by both labor and many segments of management. Labor feels that compulsory arbitration would be a threat to its ability to exert pressure in bargaining by going on strike. Management generally views it as a step toward the determination of prices by a "third party." It considers price determination a basic managerial function. In 1963, Congress passed the first compulsory arbitration law in United States history to head off a threatened nationwide railroad strike. (See page 367.)

4. *Fact-finding Boards.* In recent years, government officials have appointed *fact-finding boards* to investigate the facts and make recommendations in disputes that affect the public or national interest.

Weapons of Labor. When peaceful methods have failed to resolve a dispute, labor has resorted to more forceful means of achieving its objectives.

1. *Strikes.* Labor's strongest "non-peaceful" weapon is the *strike.* When a strike is declared, the employees stop working and refuse to return to work, in order to force the employer to yield to their demands. There are many types of strikes in addition to the normal work stoppage. Most of these are illegal today.

> (a) In a *sitdown strike,* workers stop working, but refuse to leave the plant. The sitdown strike was declared illegal by the Supreme Court in 1939.

> (b) In a *wildcat strike* union members go on strike without the approval of the union leadership. Such strikes were outlawed by the *Taft-Hartley Act* of 1947.

> (c) The *slowdown* is a more subtle form of work stoppage. Sometimes workers slow down by "throwing the book at the employer." That is, they interpret the rules and regulations in such a way as to slow down production or services.

(d) A *sympathetic strike* occurs when unions in plants not involved in a work stoppage go on strike in support of another union involved in a labor dispute.

(e) In a *general strike* all the unions of a given region (or even a nation) go on strike at the same time. This form of strike, considered extreme, has been less popular in the United States than in Europe, and has been frowned upon by most of American labor.

2. *Picketing.* Striking workers usually *picket* their place of employment. The pickets march up and down in front of the premises carrying signs that charge the employer with being unfair. Unions engage in picketing to discourage customers from buying, to prevent workers from entering, to bar the delivery or removal of goods, and to win public sympathy. *Mass picketing* occurs when many pickets march in a "picket line" at the same time. In most cases picketing is peaceful. In general, union workers will not cross picket lines set up by other unions. On occasions pickets have used force or violence to prevent the picket line from being broken up by police or employer-hired "strikebreakers."

3. *Boycotts.* Strikes are frequently accompanied by boycotts. A labor boycott is an attempt to persuade others not to purchase, transport, or work on products sold by a particular firm. Most boycotts are *primary boycotts,* in which striking workers refuse to patronize their employer and try to get others to do likewise. A *secondary boycott* takes place when a union boycotts firms not directly involved in the strike but which continue to do business with the place of business against which the union has already established a primary boycott. Secondary boycotts have been declared illegal by the *Taft-Hartley Act.*

4. *Closed Shop and Union Shop.* In the past, labor unions have tried to get employers to accept a closed shop. In a *closed shop,* the employer agrees to employ only workers who are already members of the union. Labor felt that this arrangement gave them strength in collective bargaining as well as great influence over hiring and firing. Since 1947, when the Taft-Hartley Act outlawed the closed shop and legalized the union shop, labor has fought for acceptance of the union shop. In a *union shop* an employee does not have to be a member before getting a job but must join the union within a specified period of time after being hired. Labor now accepts the union shop, though it once opposed it, because it has found that in practice the union shop gives nearly all the advantages of the closed shop.

(a) Labor spokesmen argue that the union shop prevents an employer from weakening a union by hiring workers whom he knows to be anti-union or who have promised not to join a union. Another argument is that under a union shop, an employee can not get a "free ride" by sharing in the benefits of a union contract without assuming any of the burdens of union membership, such as paying dues.

(b) Many employers argue that the union shop gives the union too much power and deprives the worker of his freedom by forcing him to join a union to keep his job. In recent years many states have passed *"right-to-work laws,"* forbidding the establishment of a union shop.

5. *Sabotage.* Occasionally in the past, but very rarely in recent years, angry workers have resorted to *sabotage.* Sabotage is deliberate damage or destruction of the employer's property (for example, destroying equipment). It has always been illegal, and has always been opposed by responsible labor leaders.

6. *The Union Label.* As a means of strengthening their position, unions urge the public as well as their own members to buy only union-made goods identified by a *union label.*

7. *The Checkoff.* In order to assure themselves of automatically paid-up members, unions aim to include the *checkoff* system in labor contracts, under which union dues are deducted from wages by the employer and sent to the union.

8. *Publicity.* In recent years, labor has tried to win public support by various forms of publicity such as newspaper advertisements during strikes, the publication of labor newspapers and magazines, the sponsoring of radio and television newscasts, and the sponsoring of scholarships. A major purpose of such publicity is to counteract anti-labor publicity put out by management.

Weapons of Management. Employers have also used powerful weapons to win labor disputes that cannot be settled peacefully.

1. *The Lockout.* Under certain circumstances, usually when workers threaten to go on strike, employers shut down their plants and refuse to let the workers go back to work. This practice, called the *lockout,* is based on the employer's belief that he can stand the financial loss longer than his workers can, and that he therefore can force them to accept his terms in the end. Lockouts were fairly frequent in the days when most plants were independently owned, but are rarely employed today.

2. *Injunctions.* For many years one of management's strongest weapons was use of the *injunction* against labor. The injunction is a court order in which a judge orders an individual or group to cease certain actions. Employers asked for and frequently received injunctions in order to break strikes, on the ground that harm was being done to their property. Failure to obey an injunction is considered "contempt of court" and may result in a fine or jail sentence. The use of the injunction against labor was greatly limited by the *Norris-La Guardia Act* of 1932.

3. *The Open Shop.* Many employers have tried to curtail union activity by maintaining an *open shop.* In theory an open shop is a business in which both union and non-union members may be employed. In practice, union members are not usually hired.

4. *The Blacklist.* A common practice among anti-union employers was to discriminate against or fire workers who joined or organized unions.

The names of such workers were placed on a *"blacklist,"* which was circulated among other employers. Blacklisted employees found it hard to get jobs. Although blacklists are now illegal, unions maintain that in certain cases they are still being used.

5. *Strikebreakers.* Occasionally, employers have tried to keep production going during a strike by hiring replacements for striking workers. Unions refer to such workers and to workers who stay on the job during strikes as "scabs" or "strikebreakers." Importing strikebreakers across state lines was outlawed in 1936.

6. *Labor Spies.* In the past, employers sometimes had their "spies" join unions for the purpose of helping to break them up by causing trouble, reporting on their tactics, etc. Much evidence about labor spies came to light in the 1930's. This practice has since been made illegal.

7. *"Yellow-dog Contracts."* In the past, when workers applied for jobs, some employers used to require them to sign an agreement not to join a union. This was a condition of employment, and it was understood that a worker who did join a union would be immediately discharged. This type of "yellow-dog contract," as it was called by union spokesmen, was declared unenforceable by the *Norris-La Guardia Act* of 1932.

8. *Company Unions.* For many years, employers tried to weaken the influence of regular unions by organizing *company unions* in their own plants. The employer usually had effective control of such unions. Company unions were declared illegal by the *National Labor Relations Act* of 1935.

9. *Welfare Capitalism.* To prevent unions from being organized, employers have offered workers the same type of benefits that unions seek, such as higher wages, medical and pension programs, recreation facilities, and paid holidays. This practice has been called *welfare capitalism.*

10. *Employers' Associations.* To promote their own interests, industrialists have formed industry-wide and national employers' associations. The *National Association of Manufacturers (NAM)* and the *United States Chamber of Commerce* have been among the most powerful of such organizations. One of the aims of such employers' associations has been the curbing of union strength.

11. *Publicity.* Management has always tried to win public support by publicity in the form of newspaper advertisements, editorials, and television and radio programs. Because most of the media of communication, such as newspapers and magazines, have been owned by business interests, management has usually had more success than labor in putting its point of view before the public. Today, however, this advantage is less marked than it used to be.

Struggle Between Labor and Capital Since the Civil War. Early struggles between labor and capital were marked by more violence and property destruction than those in recent decades.

1. *Era of Bitter Struggles (1865–1914).* From the Civil War to World War I, the struggle between labor and management was especially violent. Management had the advantages of greater financial strength and the general support of the courts and the public.

(a) In the *Railroad Strike* of 1877, Federal troops were used to break a strike for the first time.

(b) The *Haymarket Affair* of 1886 demonstrated the anti-labor and anti-radical feelings of the times. A bomb explosion that killed several policemen during a strike against the McCormick Harvester Company in Chicago led to the conviction for murder of a few anarchists. This was in spite of the fact that the actual bomb-thrower was never identified. Although the Knights of Labor was not involved in the bombing, the union was blamed for the violence.

(c) The *Homestead Strike* of 1892 saw the use of armed private detectives ("Pinkertons") as well as the state militia against the steel union.

(d) In the famous *Pullman Strike* of 1894, the courts began to use the Sherman Antitrust Act against labor unions. The head of the American Railway Union, Eugene V. Debs, was sent to jail for violating an injunction forbidding strike activities on the ground that interstate commerce was being interrupted.

(e) The *Danbury Hatters Strike* of 1902 also illustrated the use of the Sherman Antitrust Act against a union. The Hatters Union was crippled by a court award of triple damages against it for organizing a boycott that illegally "restrained trade" under the Sherman Act.

(f) The *Anthracite Coal Strike* of 1902 was the first notable instance in which the Federal government intervened in a labor dispute on the side of the union. President Theodore Roosevelt, acting "in the public interest," intervened in order to force the employers to accept arbitration because of an impending coal shortage during the bitter winter.

2. *Labor-Management Disputes Become Less Violent After World War I.* Despite occasional periods of bloody strikes after World War I, violence in labor-management disputes gradually declined, and was followed by a greater willingness to negotiate disagreements at the conference table. Among the important reasons for this increasing willingness to settle disputes peacefully have been: **(a)** growing understanding of the problems of workers by government and the general public; **(b)** protective state and Federal labor legislation; **(c)** the guarantee by law of the right of unions to bargain collectively with management; **(d)** the growing power of organized labor; **(e)** a more positive governmental role in attempting to avoid as well as to settle crippling strikes; and **(f)** growing recognition by the parties involved of the heavy costs of prolonged industrial work stoppages to both sides, and to the public.

REVIEW TEST (Chapter 19—Part II)

Select the number preceding the word or expression that best completes each statement or answers each question.

1. Organized labor has been most hostile toward the writ of (1) habeas corpus (2) assistance (3) mandamus (4) injunction

2. When labor and management agree in advance to accept the decision of a third party in a dispute, they are relying upon (1) the checkoff system (2) conciliation (3) secondary boycott (4) arbitration

3. When a dispute arises in an important industry, the government agency that tries to settle the dispute and prevent a strike is the (1) Federal Trade Commission (2) Department of Justice (3) Federal Mediation and Conciliation Service (4) Interstate Commerce Commission

4. Which of the following is a present goal of organized labor? (1) compulsory arbitration (2) right-to-work laws (3) guaranteed annual wage (4) abolition of featherbedding

5. Advantages that workers may obtain in addition to wages, as a result of collective bargaining, are known as (1) "sweetheart contracts" (2) trade agreements (3) escalator clauses (4) fringe benefits

6. Which of the following demands of labor is of most recent origin? (1) higher wages (2) improved working conditions (3) increased pension benefits (4) shorter working hours

7. A strike in which union members stop work without the approval of the union leadership is a (1) wildcat strike (2) sympathetic strike (3) general strike (4) sitdown strike

8. The use of a Federal injunction against strikers under the Sherman Antitrust Act took place during the (1) Railroad Strike of 1877 (2) Pullman Strike of 1894 (3) Anthracite Coal Strike of 1902 (4) Haymarket Affair of 1886

9. The first compulsory arbitration law in United States history was passed to avoid a crippling strike of the nation's (1) auto workers (2) teamsters (3) railroad workers (4) airplane pilots

10. What proportion of labor-management disagreements in the United States today are settled peacefully? (1) most (2) very few (3) less than half (4) about half

Select the letter of the item in each group which does NOT belong with the others.

1. Methods employed by organized labor to obtain its goals: (a) strikes (b) picketing (c) blacklist (d) slowdowns

2. Peaceful methods of settling industrial disputes: (a) conciliation (b) mediation (c) blanket injunction (d) arbitration

3. Methods employed by management to win labor disputes: (a) publicity (b) open shop (c) scabs (d) boycott

4. Practices now considered illegal: (a) secondary boycotts (b) closed shop (c) "yellow-dog contract" (d) union label

Essay Questions

1. Which of labor's aims have remained fixed over the years. Which have changed?

2. "The differing aims of labor and management make strikes inevitable." Discuss the truth or falsity of this statement.

3. Explain: (a) 3 weapons of labor that are considered legal; (b) 3 weapons of management that are considered legal; (c) 4 former weapons of labor or management that are now prohibited by law.

Part III — LAWS THAT HAVE HELPED LABOR

Since its beginnings, organized labor has called upon the government to pass laws to help improve its status and conditions. Especially significant in advancing the cause of labor were laws passed during the Progressive Era (1900–20) and the New Deal (1933–45).

Early Laws Favorable to Labor (1865–1900). Although Congress was not particularly sympathetic to the cause of labor after the Civil War, a number of measures that benefited workers were enacted. **(1)** The *Chinese Exclusion Act* of 1882 prohibited Chinese immigrants from continuing to enter the country. Labor had complained that Chinese immigrants were willing to work for lower wages than American workers. **(2)** The *Contract Labor Law* of 1885 ended the importation of contract laborers into the United States. These were foreign workers imported temporarily to work at low wages for American employers. **(3)** A *Bureau of Labor* was established in 1884 to collect labor statistics and make recommendations for improving working conditions. It developed into a Cabinet-rank *Department of Labor* in 1913. **(4)** In 1842, the eight-hour day, six-day week became standard for government employees.

Labor Gains in the Progressive Era. Under the stimulus of the reform movement of the Progressive Era, the Federal government began to pass laws protecting the rights of labor.

1. *Employer's Liability Act of 1908.* In 1908, Congress made employers of workers on interstate railroads responsible for payment for injuries received in industrial accidents.

2. *Clayton Antitrust Act (1914).* As a result of mounting pressure by labor and other reform groups, Congress amended the antitrust laws so as to prevent their application to labor activities. The *Clayton Antitrust Act* of 1914 declared that labor was not a "commodity." This meant that unions could not be prosecuted as "conspiracies in restraint of trade" under the anti-monopoly laws. The Clayton Act also limited the use of injunctions except to prevent "irreparable damage" to property. In addition, the Act provided for jury trials in contempt of injunction cases and prohibited injunctions against peaceful picketing. Unfortunately for labor, the phrases *irreparable damage* and *peaceful picketing* were not defined in the law, and conservative judges continued to hand down injunctions in labor disputes to prevent strikes and picketing.

3. *La Follette Seamen's Act (1915).* The *La Follette Seamen's Act* called for improved safety and working conditions for the sailors in the United States merchant marine.

4. *Adamson Act (1916).* To head off a railroad strike in 1916, during World War I, Congress passed the *Adamson Act,* which guaranteed the eight-hour day for all railroad workers. This paved the way for general acceptance by industry of the eight-hour day, six-day week, in the period after World War I.

5. *Attempts to Regulate Child Labor.* In this period, Congress attempted to restrict child labor **(a)** by prohibiting the shipment in interstate commerce of products made by children under the age of 16, and **(b)** by placing a 10% tax on the profits of goods made by children under 16, if shipped across state lines. Both laws were ruled unconstitutional.

6. *Norris-La Guardia Act (1932).* During the 1920's, labor continued to charge that even in spite of the labor clauses of the Clayton Act, judges were taking the employers' side by issuing injunctions in labor disputes. Congress acted to further restrict the use of the injunction by passing the *Norris-La Guardia Act* of 1932. The law provided that: **(a)** injunctions could not be used to enforce "yellow-dog contracts" or to prevent picketing; and **(b)** in contempt of court cases, the accused must be given a jury trial before a judge *other* than the one who issued the injunction. (The law applied only to Federal courts.)

Labor Comes of Age Under the New Deal. Labor finally "came of age" during the New Deal. President Franklin D. Roosevelt and his advisors believed that a strong labor movement was necessary to achieve higher wages, which in turn would provide the mass purchasing power needed for economic recovery. New Deal labor laws brought new strength and status to the labor movement.

1. *National Industrial Recovery Act (1933).* A milestone in labor history took place in 1933 with the inclusion of *Section 7a* of the *National Industrial Recovery Act (NIRA).* This section guaranteed labor the right of collective bargaining. This was the first time that employers were required by law to deal with unions.

2. *National Labor Relations Act (1935).* Section 7a of the NIRA became inoperative when the NIRA was declared unconstitutional in 1935. The right of collective bargaining was reaffirmed in this same year, however, with the passage of the *National Labor Relations Act (Wagner-Connery Act,* 1935). The Wagner Act was hailed as "Labor's Magna Carta."

> *(a)* It prohibited certain "unfair" employer practices, such as discrimination against union members, hindering the organization of unions, establishing company unions, and refusing to bargain collectively with employees.

> *(b)* The Wagner Act also provided for the establishment of a *National Labor Relations Board (NLRB),* which was designed to enforce the Act and to hold elections to determine which union (if any) was to be recognized as the exclusive bargaining agent for the workers of a given establishment.

3. *The Fair Labor Standards Act (1938).* The *Fair Labor Standards Act,* or *Wages and Hours Act* of 1938, established a minimum wage of 40 cents an hour, and a maximum work week of 40 hours for all workers in interstate commerce (or in the production of goods for interstate commerce). Work beyond 40 hours a week had to be paid at "time and a half," or 1.5 times the basic rate. In addition, the employment of children under 16 in interstate industry (18 in dangerous industries) was prohibited. Since 1938 the "floor" under wages has been raised several times, and is now $2.30 an hour in interstate industry (lower within many states).

4. The Social Security Act (1935). The *Social Security Act* of 1935 resulted from the growing belief that it was the responsibility of *society* to protect workers against unemployment and other economic misfortunes beyond their control. The Act established a vast program of national social insurance. Since 1935, it has been revised several times and its benefits increased to keep up with the rising cost of living. New groups not covered by the original law have been admitted to the program (for example, agricultural laborers, members of the armed forces, government employees not protected by a retirement plan, domestic workers, and the self-employed). As a result, most American workers, including the self-employed, are now protected by "social security."

The Social Security Program. The social security program is administered by the *Social Security Administration,* which is now part of the Department of Health, Education, and Welfare. It consists of four main parts, as outlined below.

1. *Old Age and Survivors Insurance (OASI).* Under this phase of the program, workers insure themselves against old age, death, and disability by paying a percentage of their weekly earnings into the OASI Fund. Employers must match these contributions. At age 65, employees can retire and receive a monthly pension for life (based on earnings, total contributions, and number of dependents). Provision is made for payments to a worker's survivors and dependents, in case of death or disability.

(a) When the program began, employers and employees each contributed 1.5% of the employee's weekly salary, up to $3000 a year. Retired workers received monthly payments of $10 to $85.

(b) Program benefits have been repeatedly improved. Cash benefits have been raised several times, and in 1972 were tied to increases in the cost of living, as measured by the Consumer Price Index. By 1978, the highest monthly benefit for a worker retiring at age 65 after 30 years of work was $553; for a retired couple, $804. Most retirees received much less than this. To pay for this, Social Security payroll deductions rose rapidly. By 1979, the maximum rate stood at 6.13%, applied to the first $22,900 of annual earnings.

2. *Unemployment Insurance.* The Social Security Act provided for establishment of unemployment insurance programs by each state. In nearly every state, the program is financed by a payroll tax on employers only (about 3.4%). Of this, about 90% is returned to the states to be paid out in unemployment benefits if programs meet Federal standards. The remainder is used to administer the program. The system is managed jointly by the states and the national government. Under existing programs, unemployed workers receive a weekly benefit for a limited number of weeks, providing they have been employed for a certain amount of time and are willing to take a suitable job if one is available.

(a) Details of the various programs differ quite widely from state to state. In 1979, the average benefit paid throughout the nation was about $80 a week. The maximum for an individual unemployed worker was $160 a week (in the District of Columbia). In some states, additional payments were made for dependents.

(b) Most states provide benefit payments for up to 39 weeks of unemployment. During periods of high unemployment, this limit has been extended to as much as 65 weeks.

3. *Aid to the Needy and Unfortunate.* The Social Security Act also makes provision for financial assistance to the needy. Under the program, the Federal government matches state appropriations for maternal and child health and welfare services and appropriations for aid to the elderly unemployed (not covered by OASI), the blind, and dependent children. Federal grants-in-aid for this purpose have increased over the years.

4. *Federal Health Insurance (Medicare).* In 1965, the Social Security program was expanded by the passage of a law providing for medical insurance for persons over 65. As explained on page 404 in greater detail, this "medicare" program provides payments for hospitalization, nursing home care, and outpatient services. It is considered the most ambitious expansion of Social Security since the program's inception.

State Laws Aiding Labor. Like the Federal government, the states slowly abandoned a hands-off attitude toward labor-management problems.

1. *Nineteenth-Century Beginnings.* In the period between 1865 and 1900, a few laws were passed limiting the hours of work for women and children in factories, and regulating safety and working conditions in mines, laundries, and other establishments. Although inadequately enforced, they paved the way for stronger legislation in the 20th century.

2. *Early 20th-Century Legislation.* Between 1900 and 1932, an increasing number of state laws were passed to protect labor. States pioneered in limiting working hours of women in industry, regulating or banning child labor, enacting factory inspection codes, compelling employers to compensate workers injured on the job (*workmen's compensation*), and raising the age of compulsory education. The state of Massachusetts took the lead in many of these reforms.

3. *Since the New Deal.* During and since the New Deal, most states have increased the protection and benefits extended to labor. This increased protection has taken the form of child-labor and wages-and-hours legislation, unemployment insurance, improved factory inspection, collective bargaining, better housing, and aid to the needy.

REVIEW TEST (Chapter 19—Part III)

Select the number preceding the word or expression that best completes each statement or answers each question.

1. The Norris-La Guardia Act (1) exempted labor unions from antitrust laws (2) forbade the use of injunctions against unions opposing "yellow-dog contracts" (3) regulated wages and hours (4) abolished child labor

2. One provision of the Clayton Act concerning labor resulted from (1) opposition of the AFL to the Taft-Hartley Act (2) failure of the Landrum-Griffin Act to end union racketeering (3) declaring the National Industrial Recovery Act unconstitutional (4) injunctions issued against labor under the Sherman Antitrust Act

3. Which of the following was a significant result of the Wagner Act of 1935? (1) It led to a rapid increase in labor union membership. (2) It led to a marked decline of the closed shop. (3) It encouraged the use of injunctions by employers. (4) It made legal the use of strikes and picketing.

4. The original Federal Social Security Act (1935) provided for all the following *except* (1) medical service and hospitalization (2) aid to blind and crippled persons (3) unemployment insurance (4) old-age insurance benefits

5. Within the next decade, the Social Security tax paid by employees is scheduled to (1) increase (2) decrease (3) be paid entirely by the employer (4) remain fixed at the present level

6. Which of the following laws provided for a minimum wage and a maximum work week? (1) Norris-La Guardia Act (2) Social Security Act (3) Fair Labor Standards Act (4) Adamson Act

7. The present Federal law prohibiting the employment of children under 16 in interstate industry was passed in the period (1) 1865–1900 (2) 1901–18 (3) 1921–32 (4) 1933–45

8. Collective bargaining was first guaranteed by (1) Section 7a of the NIRA (2) National Labor Relations Act (3) Clayton Act (4) Social Security Act

State whether each of the following statements is true or false. If the statement is false, replace the word or phrase in **boldface type** *with one which will make it correct.*

1. The **Adamson Act** established better working conditions in the United States merchant marine.

2. Section 7a of the National Industrial Recovery Act was **repealed** by a provision of the Wagner Act.

3. An original provision of the Fair Labor Standards Act set the floor on wages in interstate commerce at **forty cents** an hour.

4. Today the minimum age at which Social Security payments may begin is **65.**

Essay Questions

1. Show how each of the following helped improve the conditions of workers in unions: (a) Clayton Act (1914) (b) Norris-La Guardia Act (1932) (c) National Labor Relations Act (1935) (d) Fair Labor Standards Act (1938).

2. Discuss the following in regard to the present Social Security program: (a) the purposes of social security (b) how the law provides for old age and unemployment benefits (c) whether or not Social Security benefits should continue to be increased (d) whether or not health insurance should be provided under Social Security for persons *under* as well as over 65.

3. Why does organized labor look upon each of the following as periods of labor progress? (a) the Progressive Era (b) the New Deal.

Part IV — RECENT LABOR PROBLEMS AND DEVELOPMENTS

Since World War II, organized labor has been confronted with many challenges and problems.

American Labor During World War II. For the most part there was close cooperation among government, labor, and management during World War II. The latter two agreed to avoid strikes and lockouts for the duration of the war and to settle disputes peacefully through a War Labor Board. Labor was reassured by cost-of-living wage increases up to 15%, and by price controls and rationing. Though labor kept its "no-strike" pledge for the most part, a strike by the United Mine Workers in defiance of the President and the WLB caused Congress to pass the *Smith-Connally Anti-Strike Act* in 1943. The law provided fines and imprisonment for anyone encouraging strikes or lockouts in plants under government supervision and called for a 30-day notice by workers in private plants before going on strike.

Criticism of Labor After World War II. After World War II, labor came under increasing criticism. Critics complained of long and costly strikes, of the use of violence by union members, of public losses and inconvenience, of jurisdictional disputes among unions, of communist domination of some unions, and of wildcat strikes in defiance of contracts. Also criticized were certain job protection practices, such as *featherbedding* (insisting that employers hire workers for jobs not considered necessary by management). In addition there was much condemnation of undemocratic practices in some unions, including the restriction of union membership, and control by union "bosses" and racketeers.

New Laws Regulating Labor. Dissatisfaction with bitter postwar strikes and growing demands for limitation of certain labor abuses caused Congress to enact new legislation forbidding unfair labor practices.

1. *The Taft-Hartley Act (1947).* The *Taft-Hartley Act* was passed over President Truman's veto in 1947. It has been a most significant and controversial law.

> (a) *Certain Labor Rights Upheld.* The law reaffirmed labor's right to collective bargaining and forbade a number of unfair management practices.

> (b) *Certain Labor Practices Forbidden.* Various labor practices considered undesirable were forbidden, including jurisdictional strikes, featherbedding, secondary boycotts, high initiation fees, and the closed shop. (The union shop, however, is permitted.) In addition, in order to receive the assistance of an enlarged National Labor Relations Board, unions were required to provide data about their by-laws and finances, and union officers were required to swear they were not members of the Communist Party (the non-communist affidavit).

(c) *New Procedures for Preventing Strikes Introduced.* New procedures for dealing with actual or threatened work stoppages were established. (1) Unions are required to bargain in good faith for 60 days before the expiration of an existing contract. During this "cooling-off period" no strike or lockout is permitted. (2) If the President considers an actual or threatened strike a menace to national health or safety, he may obtain an injunction forbidding the strike for an additional 80 days. During this time fact-finding boards and the Federal Mediation and Conciliation Service try to bring both sides together.

(d) *Reaction to the Taft-Hartley Act.* For a number of years labor fought bitterly against the Taft-Hartley Act, denouncing it as a "slave labor" law. When it became clear that labor's strength was continuing to grow, despite the law, controversy gradually died down. Labor's demand for repeal of the law still continues however.

2. *The Landrum-Griffin Act (1959).* Criticism growing out of exposures of labor racketeering and corruption in some unions caused Congress to pass the *Landrum-Griffin Act* of 1959. Especially singled out for criticism were the leaders of the Teamsters Union, Dave Beck, and his successor, James Hoffa. Practices brought to light included stealing from union treasuries, control of unions by "strong-arm" methods, and secret agreements between labor officials and management ("sweetheart contracts").

(a) *Provisions.* The law attempts to insure democracy *within* unions by declaring embezzlement of union funds a Federal crime, by requiring the filing of annual reports on union finances with the Secretary of Labor, and by guaranteeing the secret ballot in union elections, plus regularly scheduled meetings. In place of the Taft-Hartley non-communist affidavit, there is a provision stating that it is illegal for communists or convicted criminals to serve as union officers for at least five years after severing connections with the party or leaving prison. Cases involving too few workers to be handled by the NLRB may be tried by state labor boards.

(b) *Operation of the Law.* Many observers believe that the Landrum-Griffin Act has in some measure helped clean up labor corruption, and has given rank-and-file workers a greater voice in union operations. Critics of the law maintain that it has hampered the legitimate operations of labor unions without doing much to correct abuses or to control the powers of union "bosses."

The Growing Role of Government in Labor-Management Disputes. Since World War II, the Federal government has played an increasingly active role in labor relations where collective bargaining has broken down. It has intervened frequently in major labor disputes, citing the "public interest" as its reason for doing so. In these disputes it has played the roles of peacemaker, referee, and balance wheel. Several noteworthy examples of such actions are mentioned below.

1. In 1952 the Federal government seized and briefly operated the nation's steel mills to avoid a steel strike during the Korean War. (The Supreme Court declared President Truman's action unconstitutional.)

2. Presidents Eisenhower and Kennedy issued Taft-Hartley injunctions to forestall steel and maritime strikes.

3. In 1963, Congress passed the first anti-strike law in the nation's history in order to impose arbitration on railroad management and the Operating Railroad Brotherhoods. Presidents Kennedy, Johnson, and Nixon have also had to intervene actively in railroad strikes by invoking an extended cooling-off period under a Taft-Hartley injunction. In 1971, at the request of President Nixon, Congress passed a law ordering railroad workers back to work to prevent a transportation crisis.

The Government and Fair Employment Practices. Since World War II, both state and Federal governments have taken steps to discourage discriminatory practices in the hiring of labor. **(1)** A number of states have passed legislation similar to the *New York State Anti-Discrimination Act of 1947 (Ives-Quinn Act)*, which makes it illegal for employers to practice racial or religious discrimination in employment. **(2)** Since World War II, the Federal government has included in its contracts a "no-discrimination" clause regarding the employment policies of firms with which it does business. **(3)** In 1962, as a result of the pressure of the Federal government and anti-segregationist groups, the AFL-CIO pledged to end discrimination against the admission of Negroes into its unions. **(4)** The *Civil Rights Act of 1964* contained broad provisions forbidding discrimination in employment and in admission to labor unions.

Labor-Management Relations Since World War II. Several trends in labor-management relations since World War II should be noted.

1. *Decline in "Industrial Warfare."* There has been a greater willingness than ever before to settle disputes peacefully. The overall time lost through work stoppages has been declining, although many damaging strikes do continue to occur.

2. *Industry-wide Bargaining.* There has been a trend toward *industry-wide bargaining,* in which employers negotiate trade agreements for a whole industry or for a large segment of the industry.

3. *Increasing Wages.* In recent years labor has attempted not only to keep up with the rising cost of living but also to share more fully in the national wealth. By bargaining and strikes, unions have been able to raise the real wages of workers (purchasing power) as well as the actual pay received in dollars. A notable exception to this trend was the period of the 1970s, when inflationary price rises nullified most pay increases and in some cases actually cut down on real wages, as compared with the late 1960s. In 1976, the average worker in manufacturing industries was earning wages at the rate of $200 a week before taxes. A growing number of unions have tried to meet the problem of the rising cost of living by linking wages to prices through an *"escalator clause"* in labor contracts. Such clauses provide that wages will rise or fall in relation to the Consumer Price Index published by the Bureau of Labor Statistics.

4. *Broadening Aims of Labor.* In recent decades, the aims of unions have gone beyond wages, hours, and working conditions. Labor has become concerned with the future security of its members as well as with their immediate gains. **(a)** Labor has asked for and received increased fringe benefits, such as paid vacations, life insurance, and medical and hospital care. **(b)** Some unions have asked for a *guaranteed annual wage.* (In 1967, Ford workers were guaranteed 90% of their wages during layoffs.) **(c)** Some firms, such as American Motors, have entered into profit-sharing arrangements with unions as a means of adding incentive for greater productivity. **(d)** Unions have also set up elaborate programs of social benefits for members, including health services, insurance, recreation, education, housing, pensions, and cultural activities. Unions also play a constructive role in general community affairs.

Recent Challenges to Labor. Organized labor faces many problems as the nation enters the last third of the 20th century.

1. *Static Union Membership.* In spite of increasing population and work force, total union membership in recent years has risen only slightly. In the early 1970's, it was slightly over 19 million. (See graph on page 350.) As a percentage of the total work force, union membership has actually showed a small decline.

2. *Disunity.* Reunification of the AFL-CIO did not bring true unity to the American labor movement. Jurisdictional disputes and power struggles between top union leaders have continued to occur. In 1968, the strong United Auto Workers Union withdrew from the AFL-CIO as a result of a power struggle between Walter Reuther, UAW president (also a Vice President of the AFL-CIO) and President George Meany of the Federation.

3. *Pressure for Curbing Major Strikes.* In recent years, national strikes have sometimes crippled important industries, such as steel, shipping, railroads, and aerospace. There have also been damaging strikes by public employees. As a result, there has been growing public pressure for laws that would prevent such stoppages.

4. *Automation.* Labor has become seriously concerned over the effects of automation. The rapid introduction of machines that control other machines or that do jobs formerly requiring many employees has drastically cut down on the number of workers needed in some fields of production. However, the fact is that the national economy has continued to grow, and that automation has made possible expansion of some industries and even the creation of new industries. In some fields (*e.g.,* banking, telephone service), it would be all but impossible to continue operations without automation. As a result, labor's fears of the possible disastrous effects of automation have tended to decline.

5. *Unemployment.* Unemployment has been a major problem for the American economy since the late 1950s, and particularly in the 1970s. In 1975, unemployment stood at about 9% of the nation's labor force—the highest figure since the great depression of the 1930s. A major cause of such high unemployment was the severe economic slump of 1973-75, during which industrial output dropped by almost 14%. Another contributing factor was the anti-inflationary program of the Federal government, which sought to "cool off" the economy by cuts in Federal spending and by monetary policy (control of credit). The Ford administration, although deeply concerned over the high unemployment, rejected suggestions for the creation of a huge Federal jobs program, similar to the New Deal measures of the 1930s. The administration seemed to be willing to tolerate a relatively high rate of joblessness, if necessary to control inflation.

All administrations since World War II have emphasized control of unemployment. In 1946, the *Council of Economic Advisers* was set up to make recommendations to the President for achieving full employment. Steps taken in the past few years to deal with unemployment include: (1) extending the number of weeks during which unemployment insurance is paid; (2) providing vocational training and retraining to the unemployed to give them marketable skills (Manpower Development Act of 1962 and later extensions); (3) giving help to regions with "chronic unemployment" (over 6% of the labor force in the area); (4) increased attention to the problem of eliminating the "pockets of poverty" that still exist in the nation; (5) several temporary reductions in income taxes.

REVIEW TEST (Chapter 19—Part IV)

Select the number preceding the word or expression that best completes each statement or answers each question.

1. In demanding that an employer hire only union members a union may be asking the employer to violate the   (1) Clayton Act   (2) Taft-Hartley Act   (3) Wagner Act   (4) Fair Labor Standards Act

2. In the case of a strike that threatens the national health and safety, the President of the United States may   (1) forbid the calling of such a strike   (2) permit the use of injunctions to halt such a strike temporarily   (3) provide for compulsory arbitration of such a dispute   (4) provide for government operation of plants threatened by such a strike

3. A major purpose of the Landrum-Griffin Reporting and Disclosure Act was the desire to   (1) reestablish the closed shop   (2) replace the injunction provisions of the Taft-Hartley Act   (3) strengthen the position of the AFL-CIO   (4) promote democratic operation within labor unions

4. State right-to-work laws have been opposed most vigorously by   (1) business managers   (2) consumers   (3) farmers   (4) trade unionists

5. An "escalator clause" in a labor-management contract is usually designed to (1) protect seniority rights of workers in the event of unemployment   (2) provide for a periodic increase in pension benefits   (3) keep real wages reasonably stable   (4) protect collective bargaining rights not guaranteed by state or Federal governments

6. A generally accepted long-range effect of automation on the labor force is that there will be   (1) a decrease in its total size   (2) a decrease in the percentage of skilled workers   (3) an increase in the percentage of unskilled workers   (4) an increase in the percentage of professional and technical workers

7. Which of the following is a true statement about organized labor?   (1) All large unions are affiliated with the AFL-CIO.   (2) The 1950's and early 1960's saw the most rapid membership increase in labor's history.   (3) Less than one-third of the labor force belongs to unions.   (4) Craft-industrial union rivalry ceased to be a problem with the merger of the AFL and CIO.

8. The author of the quotation, "Steamship companies could save $6,000 a month if the unions would permit them to eliminate the jobs of two engineers and five unlicensed personnel, which could be done without endangering the safety of the ships," is probably trying to prove   (1) Unions are blocking automation.   (2) The closed shop is a valuable protection for labor.   (3) Many steamship companies are owned by labor unions.   (4) Featherbedding is expensive.

9. The Consumer Price Index, computed by the Department of Labor, is extremely important because it   (1) is used to justify price increases   (2) reflects the volume of consumer credit   (3) has become a part of many wage agreements   (4) shows how consumers are spending their money

10. Which of the following represents an effort by a state to reduce racial and religious discrimination in employment?   (1) Smith-Connally Act   (2) Taft-Hartley Act   (3) Keating-Owen Act   (4) Ives-Quinn Act

Indicate whether each of the following statements is true or false. If the statement is false, replace the word or phrase in **boldface type** *with one which will make it correct.*

1. During World War II strikes were limited by the **National Defense Act.**

2. In the 1950's the Supreme Court held unconstitutional the seizure of the nation's steel mills by President **Eisenhower** to avoid a crippling nationwide strike.

3. Under profit-sharing arrangements worked out with management by a number of labor unions, workers receive a **guaranteed annual wage.**

4. Unemployment continues to be a major problem among **members of certain minority groups.**

5. In 1963 Congress passed a law providing for compulsory arbitration of a labor-management dispute in the **railroad** industry.

Essay Questions

1. Explain the purposes and provisions of two Federal laws affecting organized labor that have been enacted since World War II.

2. Discuss two events or episodes in recent years that illustrate the growing role of government in labor-management disputes.

3. Discuss two important challenges faced by labor unions today.

4. Explain why labor has favored or opposed the following: fringe benefits; guaranteed annual wage; profit sharing; right-to-work laws; automation; compulsory arbitration.

CHAPTER 20

Government Regulation of Big Business

Until the 1880's, the United States government maintained a *laissez-faire* attitude toward business. It was believed that such a policy encouraged individual initiative and promoted efficiency, competition, and prosperity. In addition to refraining from any control of business, the government helped industry by means of protective tariffs, favorable banking laws, and subsidies of land and natural resources. For various reasons, beginning in the late 1880's, the Federal government gradually abandoned its "hands-off" policy and began to regulate business in order to maintain competition.

Reasons for the Beginning of Government Regulation of Big Business. Government regulation of big business resulted from problems created by industrial development.

1. *The Trend Toward Business Combinations and Monopolies.* After the Civil War, business corporations combined to cut costs and eliminate competition. Through pools, trusts, holding companies, and other arrangements, they often established monopolies that harmed the small businessman through unfair methods of competition, and the consumer through high prices.

2. *Public Concern.* Increased public concern over the "abuses" of big business was voiced by writers and reformers, who called for government protection of economic opportunity.

> *(a)* Notable among the writers who protested against the evils of monopoly and harmful effects of *laissez-faire* were Henry George *(Progress and Poverty)*, Henry Demarest Lloyd *(Wealth Against Commonwealth)*, and Edward Bellamy *(Looking Backward)*.

> *(b)* Third parties like the *Grangers, Socialists,* and *Populists* began to call for regulation of big business. They were supported by farmers, workers, and reformers.

3. *The Failure of State Regulation.* Another factor that caused the Federal government to take action was the fact that the states proved unable to regulate business abuses effectively. After the Civil War, the courts held that corporations were "persons" in the eyes of the law. As a result, they declared illegal many state laws that regulated business on the ground that such legislation violated the Fourteenth-Amendment guarantee that a state could not deprive a *person* "of life, liberty, or property without due process of law."

371

Regulating the Railroads. Railroads were the first industry to be affected by direct government regulation. After the Civil War, railroad combinations charged high rates, gave secret rebates to favored shippers, discriminated against small shippers and out-of-the-way places, and often issued stock in excess of their real assets *(watered stock)*. Their monopoly power and unfair practices hurt the small businessman, the farmer, and the consumer. Failure of state attempts to regulate these abuses (the *Granger laws,* see page 333) caused the Federal government to intervene.

1. *The Interstate Commerce Act (1887).* In 1887, Congress passed the *Interstate Commerce Act,* which outlawed pools, rebates, and other railroad abuses. It also established the *Interstate Commerce Commission (ICC)* to investigate complaints and enforce the act. At first the ICC was ineffective. The law was significant, however, because it was the first important step taken by the Federal government to regulate industry.

2. *Railroad Regulation Becomes More Effective.* During the Progressive Era of the early 20th century, the powers of the ICC were greatly strengthened and railroad regulation became more effective. By 1920, the Commission had the power to regulate both maximum and minimum rates and to supervise the issue of railroad securities.

3. *The Railroads Become a Sick Industry.* After World War I, the increasing competition of automobiles, trucks, buses, airplanes, and internal waterways and pipelines, caused railroad revenues to decline seriously. By 1933, over 20% of the nation's railroads were in the hands of receivers.

4. *Government Aid to the Railroads.* Because of their financial difficulties the Federal government has, since the 1920's, given considerable financial aid and other assistance to the nation's railroads. It has encouraged consolidation, permitted railroads to eliminate unprofitable passenger services, approved rate increases, and regulated competing forms of transportation. (For example, in 1935 the authority of the ICC was extended to interstate trucks and buses by the *Motor Carriers Act.* In 1938, the *Civil Aeronautics Authority* was established to regulate the air lines. In 1940, the ICC was given power to regulate coastal and interstate shipping.)

5. *AMTRAK.* In 1971, Congress set up a government corporation commonly called AMTRAK to manage and operate most of the interurban rail passenger service in the United States. Functioning through contracts with the privately owned railroads, AMTRAK has been making a vigorous effort to upgrade passenger service, to get rid of poorly patronized runs, and to "sell" the public on the advantages of modern rail travel.

The Sherman Antitrust Act (1890). The beginning of government regulation of the railroads in 1887 was soon followed by steps against business monopoly in general. In the Presidential election of 1888, both Republicans and Democrats included an antitrust plank in their party platforms. In 1890 both parties supported the passage of the *Sherman Antitrust Act.*

1. *Provisions.* The Sherman Act: **(a)** declared all monopolies illegal; **(b)** outlawed all contracts, combinations, and conspiracies in the form of trusts or otherwise, that were "in restraint of trade"; and **(c)** allowed the injured party to collect triple damages.

2. *Weaknesses.* At first the Sherman Act proved to be ineffective. There were several reasons for this.

> *(a)* The law was too general. It did not define such terms as *restraint of trade* and *monopoly.*
>
> *(b)* It was not enforced vigorously by Presidents Harrison, Cleveland, or McKinley.
>
> *(c)* Court interpretation of the law was more favorable to big business than to the Federal government. For example, in 1895 the Supreme Court declared that the American Sugar Refining Company was not a monopoly despite the fact that it controlled 95% of the nation's sugar refining.
>
> *(d)* Many combinations dropped the "trust" form of combination to get around the wording of the Sherman Act, and reorganized as holding companies, interlocking directorates, or other forms of consolidation.

Stricter Regulation of Business at the Turn of the Century. In the first decade of the 20th century, during the *Progressive Era,* Presidents Theodore Roosevelt and William Howard Taft, both Republicans, took more vigorous action to restrain monopoly. These Presidents were undoubtedly influenced by the "muckrakers," a group of writers who set out to expose the evils of unrestrained industrial power.

1. *Accomplishments Under T. Roosevelt.* Although President Roosevelt himself coined the term "muckrakers" for the crusading writers because he felt they were too busy "digging up dirt" to see the benefits of big business, he was, nevertheless, greatly disturbed by the conditions they revealed. He became a powerful advocate of reform and business regulation.

> *(a)* Under Roosevelt's *Square Deal* program the following was accomplished: **(1)** The Interstate Commerce Commission was strengthened. **(2)** A *Department of Commerce and Labor* was established, and within it a *Bureau of Corporations* to investigate the activities of big business was set up. **(3)** A *Meat Inspection Act* (1906) provided for Federal inspection of meat shipped in interstate commerce. **(4)** A *Pure Food and Drug Act* (1906) made illegal the interstate shipment or sale of misbranded or adulterated food or drugs.
>
> *(b)* Roosevelt distinguished between "good" and "bad" trusts. He tried to break up the "bad" ones; that is, those that restrained competition or engaged in unfair trade practices. Enthusiastic supporters of Roosevelt called him the "trustbuster." Over 40 antitrust suits were begun while he was President. The most famous of these resulted in a Supreme Court decision that caused the breakup of the *Northern Securities Company* (1904). This was a railroad holding company that monopolized transportation in the Northwest.

2. *Accomplishments Under Taft.* The administration of President Taft was even more active in enforcing the Sherman Act. Two important decisions handed down in 1911 by the Supreme Court while Taft was President ordered the breakup of the *Standard Oil Company of New Jersey* and the *American Tobacco Company* on the grounds that both were in unreasonable restraint of trade. Most important was the *rule of reason* established in the Standard Oil and American Tobacco cases. Under this "rule," the Supreme Court distinguished between "reasonable" and "unreasonable" restraint of trade. Only trusts in "unreasonable" restraint of trade were thereafter considered in violation of the Sherman Act.

The Antitrust Laws Are Strengthened Under Wilson. Under President WOODROW WILSON (1913–20), the antitrust campaign was waged with even more vigor. Liberals were encouraged by Wilson's pledge in the election of 1912 to give a *"New Freedom"* to the small businessman by attacking the unfair practices of big business more vigorously. Wilson, a Democrat, advocated a return to free competition and a powerful attack on monopoly power. However, he believed in the regulation, rather than in the breakup, of big business. Under his New Freedom program, the language of the Sherman Act was made more definite and certain loopholes were eliminated.

1. *The Clayton Antitrust Act (1914).* The *Clayton Antitrust Act,* passed in 1914, with Wilson's backing, provided the following: **(a)** Certain specific business practices were declared illegal, including price cutting to reduce competition, purchasing stock in competing corporations to reduce competition or to create a monopoly, and the establishment of interlocking directorates among competing firms. **(b)** Labor and farm organizations were exempted from the antitrust laws on the grounds that "the labor of a human being is not a commodity."

2. *The Federal Trade Commission (1914).* In that same year, a *Federal Trade Commission (FTC)* was established to enforce the antitrust acts. The FTC was empowered to investigate illegal and unfair business practices, and to call for the ending of such activities through "cease-and-desist" orders. The agency was also given authority to request corporations to reorganize, as a means of making prosecution unnecessary. If a business refused to cooperate, the FTC could recommend government prosecution under the antitrust laws.

> *(a)* The FTC became increasingly influential in safeguarding the interest of the public. As a result of its activities, a large number of unfair business practices have been outlawed by the courts. These include misbranding, adulteration, false or misleading advertising, and harmful or untrue statements about competitors. In cooperation with industry, the FTC has also held many "fair trade conferences" and worked out sets of fair trade practices for different industries.

> *(b)* Unfortunately, and despite government action, some business firms continue to evade the antitrust laws or to get around FTC restrictions.

Continued Growth of Big Business. In the 20th century, in spite of the attacks on monopoly, big business has continued to grow in size, numbers, and power. An increasing share of the nation's wealth and production has been concentrated in fewer hands. By 1960, nearly half of the country's corporate wealth was owned by the 200 largest corporations. Of these, 60 firms controlled assets of over a billion dollars each. The following factors contributed to this concentration of ownership and control.

1. *Interpretation of the Antitrust Laws.* The courts continued to rule that the antitrust laws applied to unfair *trade practices* rather than to the size of a business. For example, in 1920, the United States Steel Company was held *not* to be in restraint of trade, although at the time it controlled over 50% of the nation's steel production.

2. *The Rise of New Forms of Combination.* To get around restrictions on "trusts," businesses developed new forms of combination such as holding companies, gentlemen's agreements, trade associations, and mergers, more recently of the *conglomerate* and *multinational corporation* types.

3. *Exemptions From the Antitrust Laws.* Congress sometimes contributed to the general weakness of the antitrust program by granting exemptions to the requirements of the laws. In 1918, for example, export associations were exempted from the antitrust laws (*Webb-Pomerene Act*). In 1922 agricultural cooperatives received a similar exemption (*Capper Act*).

4. *Relaxation of the Antitrust Program in the 1920's.* During the 1920's, antitrust action was much less aggressive and effective than during preceding administrations. This was the result largely of the *laissez-faire* and pro-big business attitude of Presidents Warren Harding (1921–23), Calvin Coolidge (1923–29), and Herbert Hoover (1929–33), all of whom frequently appointed big businessmen to the regulatory commissions.

Business Regulation Continues Under the New Deal. The New Deal administrations of Franklin D. Roosevelt (1933–45) adopted a "double-barreled" approach to big business. On the one hand, in order to help business recover from the depression, the Federal government temporarily suspended certain provisions of the antitrust acts. On the other hand, it exercised increased vigilance in preventing unfair business practices by strengthening the power of such regulatory agencies as the FTC and the ICC. Unlike the Republican administrations of the 1920's, which championed *laissez-faire,* the Roosevelt administration supported the principle of a growing and active role of government in economic affairs. The New Deal program of business regulation is outlined briefly below.

Regulation of Prices. The New Deal attempted to stimulate business by making it possible to fix prices.

1. *National Industrial Recovery Act (1933).* This law exempted business associations from the antitrust laws by permitting them to draw up codes of fair competition, subject to Presidential approval. In 1935, the

NIRA was declared unconstitutional on the grounds that Congress did not have the right to delegate lawmaking power to the President and business.

2. *Robinson-Patman Act (1936).* The *Robinson-Patman Act* of 1936 made it illegal for manufacturers and wholesalers to discriminate against small purchasers by selling to large buyers at lower prices. Chain stores and mail order houses protested vigorously against this law.

3. *Miller-Tydings Act (1937).* The *Miller-Tydings Act* of 1937 exempted manufacturers of nationally advertised articles from price-fixing prohibitions under the Sherman Act. Manufacturers of such goods were given permission to fix their resale prices to the public. The act became known as the *"fair trade"* law.

> NOTE: "Price fixing" became less popular, and less effective, in the 1950's as a result of unfavorable Supreme Court decisions and the rise of "discount houses" that sold goods below "list."

Protection of the Consumer. At the same time that it took steps to help the manufacturer set prices, the New Deal took steps to protect the consumer against dishonest commercial practices.

1. *Securities and Exchange Act (1934).* A law passed in 1933, amended by the *Securities and Exchange Act* of 1934, attempted to protect purchasers of stocks and bonds by requiring corporations to file with a newly created *Securities Exchange Commission (SEC)* relevant information regarding the purpose and nature of their securities issues. The SEC was also given power to establish rules for trading on stock exchanges.

2. *Federal Food, Drug, and Cosmetic Act (1938).* The *Federal Food, Drug, and Cosmetic Act* of 1938 (*Wheeler-Lea Act*) made the earlier act of 1906 more effective by prohibiting the sale in interstate commerce of harmful food, drugs, or cosmetics. The law extended the authority of the FTC by giving it power to forbid false and misleading advertising and to require more complete and accurate information on labels.

Regulation of Transportation and Communication. The New Deal extended government controls in transportation and communication, often in order to help businesses in these industries.

1. *Railroads.* The New Deal tried to aid the railroads by temporarily establishing a *Coordinator of Transportation* (1933–36) to recommend operating economies and necessary railroad consolidations and mergers; by granting the ICC power to regulate *motor vehicles* (trucks, buses, passenger cars) in interstate commerce (*Motor Carriers Act,* 1935); and by extending ICC jurisdiction to inland and coastal water carriers.

2. *Communications.* In 1934, the Federal government extended its regulation to all forms of communication, by establishing the *Federal Communications Commission (FCC).* The FCC was given power to regulate rates, services, and operation of the telephone, telegraph, radio, and (more recently) television industries.

3. *Merchant Marine.* In 1936, a *United States Maritime Commission* was created to exercise control over shipping activities to foreign countries. Its purpose was to encourage the expansion of the American merchant marine and to provide loans for shipyards and steamship companies.

4. *Aviation.* In 1938, a *Civil Aeronautics Authority* (*CAA*) was created, and given broad powers over the establishment and operation of airlines.

Regulation of Public Utilities. *Public utilities* refer to privately owned businesses that have a monopoly or semi-monopoly status and are clearly tied up with the public interest. Usually, they are industries that perform essential services for the public and which must be run as monopolies in the interests of efficiency. They include railroads, bus lines, electric power companies, telephone and telegraph companies, privately owned water supply systems, etc.

1. *Public Utility Holding Companies.* Like other businesses, many public utilities in the 1920's combined into holding companies. Because public utility holding companies consisted of non-competing firms, often in different states, they could not be declared in restraint of trade under the Clayton Act. Also, because their operations often extended beyond state lines, the states were unable to regulate them effectively.

2. *The Wheeler-Rayburn Act (1935).* The collapse of the holding company empire of Samuel Insull in 1929 wiped out the investments of over 175,000 stockholders and led to an exposure of utility holding company evils. As a result, in 1935, the *Wheeler-Rayburn Public Utilities Holding Company Act* was passed. This act had the following provisions: **(a)** It outlawed all holding companies beyond the *second degree.* In other words, one holding company might control the stock of a second holding company that controlled the companies providing the actual services, but the "pyramiding" could not go beyond this to still another holding company. **(b)** The SEC was empowered to abolish all holding companies which it considered unnecessary. **(c)** *The Federal Power Commission* (*FPC*) was empowered to regulate the rates and practices of utility companies doing business across state lines.

Tennessee Valley Authority. In 1933, the New Deal ended a long controversy over private versus public ownership of the hydroelectric power facilities at Muscle Shoals, Alabama, by establishing the *Tennessee Valley Authority* (*TVA*). The facilities had been set up during World War I to help meet wartime needs for power.

1. *Establishment of TVA.* The TVA was established as a government corporation that had the right to build dams, reservoirs, powerhouses, and transmission lines in a seven-state area (the valley of the Tennessee River), and to sell electric power to states, municipalities, businesses, and individuals.

2. *TVA Operations.* Within a few years, TVA built dams and power plants and began to sell electricity at lower prices than private utilities in the region. Private competitors protested that the TVA "yardstick" (that is, the cost to TVA of producing electricity) was a false one, since TVA did not make adequate allowances for taxes, interest, or depreciation.

3. *TVA Upheld by the Courts.* In 1936, the Supreme Court in the *Wilson Dam Case* upheld the right of TVA to construct dams and power plants on the grounds that Congress had the right to provide for national defense, prevent floods, control navigation, and conserve soil. In other decisions the Court also upheld the right of TVA to purchase private power and transmission facilities. As a result TVA bought the facilities of some private companies. (For further details on TVA see page 409.)

Private vs. Public Ownership of Public Utilities. Although the controversy over TVA died down after World War II, the general question of government ownership of public utilities continues to be debated.

1. *Arguments in Favor of Government Ownership.* Those who favor government ownership and operation along the lines of the TVA advance the following claims:

(a) Government-owned utilities can charge lower rates than private enterprises. This applies not only to Federal projects like TVA but also to state and local agencies.

(b) Government-owned utilities can provide services in underdeveloped areas which would not be profitable fields of operation for private facilities.

(c) Government enterprises can use their facilities for several coordinated purposes — such as power, irrigation, navigation, flood control, and erosion control. Thus, the planned development of an entire region (such as the Tennessee Valley) may be undertaken. In contrast, private utilities are concerned only with providing a single profitable service.

(d) Several states may join forces to construct and operate facilities such as tunnels, bridges, and airports. The New York Port Authority, in which New York and New Jersey participate, is an example of such an *interstate compact.* This kind of successful interstate cooperation is not open to private utilities.

2. *Arguments Against Government Ownership.* Opponents of government ownership of public utilities argue as follows:

(a) It is not true that government agencies can provide electric power and other facilities more cheaply than private enterprise. Government ownership only *seems* to be able to do this because of accounting methods which do not allow adequately for taxes (paid by all private utilities), interest, and depreciation.

(b) If the government in effect subsidizes an underdeveloped area by providing power and other services at uneconomically low rates, the nation as a whole must pay for this in the form of higher taxes.

(c) We live under a private-enterprise economy. It should be our policy to limit sharply the "public sector" of the economy and to maximize the area in which private enterprise operates. It is private enterprise that has made us the richest and most powerful nation in the world. Our system must not be undermined by "creeping socialism."

The New Deal Attacks Monopoply. In the late 1930's, the New Deal began to take more direct action against restraint of trade. A *Temporary National Economic Committee* (*TNEC*) conducted a lengthy and intensive investigation (1938–41) into business concentration and monopoly. Its final report recommended extensive overhauling and strengthening of the antitrust laws.

The Antitrust Program Since World War II. Since World War II, the government has continued its antitrust program.

1. *The Federal Trade Commission* has continued to issue "cease and desist" orders against such unfair practices as forcing retailers to push certain brands, selling below cost to weaken competitors, false or misleading advertising, and adulteration or misbranding. However, FTC and other regulatory agencies have often been accused of being too favorable to big businesses and of not taking sufficiently swift or vigorous action against them. More and more, antitrust actions are being initiated by individual businesses accusing other businesses of monopolistic abuses.

2. The *Antitrust Division* of the U.S. Department of Justice has continued to take action against violators of the antitrust laws by filing suits against them in the Federal courts, or by obtaining from businesses voluntary agreements to discontinue certain practices (consent decrees).

(a) After World War II, the government forced the breakup of agreements (*cartels*) between American and foreign firms to curtail production, limit competition, or raise prices.

(b) Antitrust rulings in the 1950's and 1960's cut down on "horizontal mergers" (between competitors) and, to a lesser extent, on "vertical mergers") (with suppliers or customers). Recently, however, *conglomerate* mergers have been on the increase. A *conglomerate* is a combination of essentially unrelated or diversified businesses. The most recent challenge to antitrust controls has been the trend among business giants to form *multinational corporations* of the conglomerate type. These businesses carry on a great variety of operations in many different countries, with the result that they may be largely free of effective control by national governments.

3. The *Supreme Court* has continued to apply the "rule of reason" in interpreting the antitrust laws. It continues to uphold the doctrine that monopoly is shown by unreasonable restraint of trade, *not* by size alone.

4. *Recent Action to Protect the Consumer.* In recent years, because of loopholes and the unearthing of unethical practices, new laws have been added to strengthen existing legislation relating to foods, drugs, and cosmetics. Laws have also been passed by Congress forcing manufacturers to disclose the nature of the materials used in fabrics, clothing, and furniture fillings. The *"Truth in Lending Act,"* which went into effect in July, 1969, requires that consumers be informed of the complete cost of credit, including disclosure of "true" annual interest rates on charge and installment buying accounts. Agencies to protect the consumer have also been created in state and city governments, and the findings of consumer advocates like Ralph Nader have been publicized widely.

Future of the Antitrust Program. What is the future of the antitrust program?

1. Many authorities believe that the antitrust laws should be made stronger and more precise and enforced with greater vigor.

2. There is, however, a widespread opinion that the antitrust laws are unenforceable because they are no longer relevant to present-day economic conditions. It is argued that our entire economy is based on giant enterprises with monopoly or semimonopoly status.

3. In addition, economists have pointed out that although the old-style free market competition is disappearing in some areas of our economy, competition is by no means dead. The giants of big business, for example, may no longer compete in terms of prices, but they do compete on the level of *quality, services,* and *advertising.* This can be seen in such industries as automobiles, gasoline, and soaps. Moreover, there is active competition *between industries.* In recent years, for example, steel has faced increased competition from building materials that are lighter, cheaper, or more suitable for particular purposes (*e.g.,* aluminum, magnesium, paper, cement, glass, and a wide range of man-made plastics).

Courtesy, Dorman H. Smith (Collier's Magazine)

This cartoon represents one point of view on the antitrust laws. Express this point of view in your own words. What answer might be made by those who feel otherwise about the antitrust laws?

The Government Is Not Against Big Business. This emphasis on the efforts of government (national and state) to regulate big business should not give us the impression that the government is *against* big business. On the contrary, our government recognizes clearly today, as it has in the past, that the rise of big business has been a vital factor in making the United States the world's greatest industrial power and in giving our people the world's highest living standards.

Accordingly, the government has aided business (both large and small) by strengthening the banking system and by adopting tariffs and other trade laws favorable to business development. Business has been aided by subsidies and tax incentives (special deductions). Government also carries on research and collects statistical data and other types of information of great interest to business.

The antitrust program as it operates today is designed not to destroy or hamper big business but to prevent certain abuses and thus to preserve the free enterprise system so essential to democratic capitalism.

REVIEW TEST (Chapter 20)

Select the number preceding the word or expression that best completes each statement or answers each question.

1. The inability of the Granger laws to achieve their purpose led to (1) Federal legislation regulating railroads (2) a government program of farm supports (3) the end of protective tariffs (4) the introduction of the gold standard

2. The Interstate Commerce Act of 1887 forbade all the following *except* (1) rebates (2) pooling (3) tariffs on goods going from one state to another (4) higher rates for short hauls than for long ones

3. An important effect of the Sherman Antitrust Act was that it (1) restored active competition (2) was a factor in the establishment of the National Banking System (3) corrected the weakness of the Clayton Antitrust Act (4) was a cause for change in the forms and techniques of business combinations

4. The Federal Trade Commission has power to (1) regulate railroad rates (2) settle labor disputes (3) set the price of agricultural products (4) order corporations to cease unfair business practices

5. The National Industrial Recovery Act was declared unconstitutional on the ground that (1) Congress has no right to regulate intrastate commerce (2) Congress has no right to regulate interstate commerce (3) no emergency existed (4) Congress has no right to delegate law-making power to the President and business

6. Which of the following statements best represents the Federal government's attitude toward "trusts" during most of the Progressive Era? (1) Good "trusts" should be allowed to exist, but the government should be ready to curb abuses. (2) There should be no interference with the organization of "trusts." (3) The Federal government should encourage the formation of "trusts" because of their benefits to the consumer. (4) All "trusts" should be abolished because they stifle competition and inevitably lead to economic abuses.

7. Early antitrust laws attempted to protect the public against the activities of big business by (1) establishing government regulation of wages and hours (2) encouraging government ownership of business (3) maintaining competition (4) confining activities of business within the boundaries of a single state

8. The economic concept of the "yardstick" is most frequently associated with (1) minimum wages (2) income tax rates (3) public utility rates (4) Social Security payments

9. Since World War II, a number of railroads have been granted permission by the Federal government to (1) organize holding companies (2) engage in pooling (3) merge competing systems (4) combine with airlines

10. Of the following Federal agencies, the first to be established was the (1) Federal Communications Commission (2) Federal Trade Commission (3) Interstate Commerce Commission (4) Securities and Exchange Commission

Select the letter of item in each group which does **NOT** *belong with the others.*

1. Effects of monopoly: (a) concentration of control (b) unfair competition (c) low taxes (d) high prices

2. Attacks on Big Business: (a) Henry George (b) Henry Demarest Lloyd (c) Calvin Coolidge (d) Edward Bellamy

3. Achievements of Theodore Roosevelt: (a) Meat Inspection Act (b) Wheeler-Rayburn Act (c) Department of Commerce and Labor (d) Pure Food and Drugs Act

4. Achievements of the New Deal: (a) Robinson-Patman Act (b) Miller-Tydings Act (c) Securities and Exchange Act (d) Clayton Act

5. Trends since World War II: (a) many Supreme Court decisions upholding restraint of trade (b) continued business concentration and combination (c) fairly active application of the antitrust laws by the Federal government (d) decline of "fair trade" price fixing

Essay Questions

1. Explain three reasons for the beginning of government regulation of big business in the closing decades of the 19th century.

2. Discuss the provisions and results of each of the following legislative acts dealing with big business: (a) the Interstate Commerce Act (b) the Sherman Antitrust Act (c) the Clayton Antitrust Act (d) the Wheeler-Rayburn Public Utilities Holding Company Act (e) the National Industrial Recovery Act.

3. During the past century railroads in the United States have been both aided and regulated by the Federal government. (a) Explain two ways in which the Federal government aided in the construction of railroads. (b) Discuss two reasons why it became necessary for the Federal government to regulate the railroads. (c) Discuss two reasons why so many railroads are now facing serious financial difficulties.

4. Indicate with supporting data or reasoning why you agree or disagree with the following statements:

(a) The nation would be better off without big business.

(b) The Federal antitrust program has been effective.

(c) Public ownership of public utilities should be extended.

(d) The present administration is opposed to big business.

CHAPTER 21

Tariffs and Trade
in United States History

Tariffs are duties or taxes on imports. They can be levied as a percentage of the imported goods (*ad valorem duties*) or as a specific amount of money per item (*specific duties*). Tariffs have been an important issue in American public life since the founding of the Republic. The questions have been whether tariffs should be levied at all, and, if so, whether they should be high or low and how they should be applied. In early years the tariff was closely linked to sectionalism. In more recent years tariff problems have been linked with problems of world trade and foreign policy.

Advantages of Foreign Trade. A nation's foreign trade consists of what it sells or *exports* to foreign nations and what it buys or *imports* from them in return. International trade has several important advantages: **(1)** It permits nations to specialize in the production of things for which they may be best suited (*international specialization*). **(2)** It can raise living standards by making it possible for nations to obtain a greater variety of goods and services at lower cost than if each had to produce for itself everything it needed. **(3)** It forces home industries to become more efficient because of competition from abroad.

Tariffs and Trade. From ancient times to the present, governments have set up barriers to unrestricted trade across their borders. There have been various purposes for this: to make possible a greater degree of national self-sufficiency, to protect or encourage certain industries, to raise revenues, and to insure sources of supply in case of war. The most common and most important of these trade barriers have been, and are, tariffs, or taxes on imports. There are two general types of tariffs — *revenue* and *protective*.

1. A *revenue tariff* is a tariff that aims at raising money for a nation. Since it does not aim to discourage imports, the rates are kept relatively low. Revenue tariffs generally do not restrict international trade.

2. A *protective tariff* is a tariff that aims to protect certain domestic industries against competition from abroad. The rates are normally higher than those of revenue tariffs. We sometimes distinguish between *low protective tariffs and high protective tariffs*.

3. *Free trade* is the absence of tariffs, or the existence of tariffs for revenue only.

The Debate Over Protective Tariffs. In the course of its history, the United States has joined other nations in levying tariffs. The argument over whether or not to impose protective tariffs has gone on since the nation's beginning, and is still a subject of debate among economists. The following chart outlines the major arguments given by supporters and opponents of protective tariffs.

PROTECTIVE TARIFFS — PRO AND CON

ARGUMENTS IN FAVOR OF PROTECTIVE TARIFFS

1. They build up a "home market" by reducing dependence on other areas.

2. They protect new or "infant" industries until they are able to compete with foreign producers.

3. They guard American business and labor against the competition of cheap foreign labor.

4. They protect industry against the *"dumping"* of surplus goods from abroad at ruinously low prices.

5. They encourage a variety of industries and thereby give us a better balanced economic life.

6. They help to maintain industries which are essential in time of war.

ARGUMENTS AGAINST PROTECTIVE TARIFFS

1. They lead to a decline in exports as well as imports, since other nations cannot buy from us unless they earn the necessary dollars by selling to us.

2. They are not really necessary to protect American workers and industry against cheap foreign labor. The greater efficiency and high per-capita rate of production of the American worker have in the past more than compensated for low labor costs abroad.

3. They lower the American standard of living because protection of domestic industry from foreign competition reduces productive efficiency and leads to an increase in consumer prices.

4. "Infant" industries in too many cases never grow up. They continue to demand protection long after they are strong enough to stand on their own feet.

5. They lead to such undesirable practices and developments as monopolies, log-rolling, and lobbying.

6. They lead to international ill-will and retaliation.

NOTE: Few economists today regard themselves as either all-out protectionists or unqualified advocates of free trade. It is generally recognized that in some areas of our economy protection is needed, but that it is also essential to promote a healthy flow of international trade. The argument today is not between "protectionism" and "free trade" in the abstract, but rather over specific questions of what tariffs should be applied, when and where they should be reduced or eliminated, and what concessions can be obtained from foreign countries for making such reductions.

Our Changing Tariff Policy. At different periods in its development the United States had adopted different tariff policies. These policies, their causes, and their purposes are outlined below. Some have already been discussed in earlier sections of the book.

Tariff for Revenue (1789–1815). From 1789 to 1815, United States tariffs were for revenue, mainly. The nation was primarily an exporter of foodstuffs and raw materials to Europe. The United States depended upon Europe, particularly Great Britain, for most of its manufactured goods. Despite the urgings of Alexander Hamilton and other protectionists, the tariffs of 1789, 1791, and others that followed did not attempt to discourage foreign imports.

Protective Tariffs and Sectionalism (1816–61). In the period between 1816 and the Civil War, the nation began to adopt protective tariffs. Sectional objections, particularly from the South, kept the protective tariffs low from 1843 to 1861. The sectional nature of the tariff disputes both before and after the Civil War caused many to refer to the tariff as a "mirror of sectionalism."

1. *Tariff of 1816.* The nation's first protective tariff in 1816 was adopted to protect the newly developing industries of the nation against the "dumping" of European goods after the War of 1812. It had the support of all sections of the country.

2. *"Tariff of Abominations" (1828).* Congress adopted higher tariffs in 1828 (the "Tariff of Abominations") and again in 1831. The South protested strongly against these tariffs; indeed, South Carolina threatened nullification and secession (see page 200). Southern planters argued that high tariffs forced them to pay inflated prices for manufactured goods at the same time that they had to sell their cotton in a world market at prices determined by free competition. As a result of this sectional opposition, tariff rates were gradually reduced after 1833. They remained fairly low until the Civil War.

Higher Tariffs After the Civil War. From the Civil War to World War I, the United States abandoned the low protective tariffs of the pre-Civil War era and adopted a policy of high protective tariffs. Congress passed high protective tariffs to help the rapidly expanding manufacturing industries of the North. The triumphant Republican Party, representing industrialist-protectionist interests, exerted a controlling influence on tariff-making during this period.

It was not until 1913 that the first real step was taken to reduce the protective tariff. The *Underwood Tariff,* passed in 1913 under the leadership of President Wilson and the Democratic Party, was the first tariff after the Civil War to lower the general level of tariff duties. However, the outbreak of World War I (1914) prevented this tariff from having its desired effect.

High Tariffs After World War I. Following World War I, tariffs reached the highest level in American history.

1. *Politics of the Tariff in This Period.* In the 1920's, Republican majorities in Congress, encouraged by the support of Presidents Harding, Coolidge, and Hoover, raised tariff duties to unprecedented levels. They believed that high tariffs would not only benefit industry but also help the farmers, who were suffering from low prices after World War I.

2. *The Fordney-McCumber Act (1922).* The *Fordney-McCumber Tariff* of 1922 raised tariff rates on both agricultural and manufactured goods to new highs. Although the President was given authority to lower as well as raise tariff rates up to 50% (following a recommendation by the newly established *United States Tariff Commission*), very few duties were lowered, and many were raised. In retaliation, over sixty foreign nations had raised their own tariffs against United States goods by 1928.

3. *The Hawley-Smoot Tariff (1930).* The *Hawley-Smoot Tariff* of 1930 brought United States tariff rates to the highest point in our history. They raised the rates on dutiable imports from an average of 30% to an average of 59%. The Act was passed in spite of strong opposition from European nations and many American economists. It brought further European retaliation in the form of higher tariffs on American exports.

NOTE: It should be noted that even under protective tariffs, many imports come in "duty-free" on what is called the *free list*. Products on the free list are those for which protection is considered unnecessary because foreign competition does not present a threat to home industry. Even under the Hawley-Smoot Tariff, over 60% of United States imports were on the free list.

Tariffs and World Trade After World War I. After World War I, our tariff policies conflicted with the new status of the United States as a *creditor nation*. This contributed to a decline of world trade.

1. *Creditor and Debtor Nations.* A *creditor nation* is one that has a favorable balance of payments; that is, it receives more in payments from foreign nations and citizens than it pays out to them. A *debtor nation* is one with an unfavorable balance of payments. To settle an unfavorable balance of payments, a nation may have to borrow money or ship out some of its gold reserves.

2. *A Debtor Nation Before World War I.* In the years before World War I, the United States was a debtor nation. Large European investments in American industry earned Europeans more than enough dollars (in the form of interest and dividends) to pay for their excess of imports from the United States. Under such conditions, it was only natural for us to sell more to European nations than we bought from them.

3. *A Creditor Nation After World War I.* After the war, the United States became a creditor nation, for several reasons. **(a)** The United States made large loans to Allied European governments to help them pay for the war and the rebuilding of Europe after the war. **(b)** A large part of the European investment in American industry was liquidated to help pay for the war. **(c)** After the war, United States investments abroad increased. As a result of all these developments, the United States began to receive greater payments from abroad than it had to pay out.

The high protective tariffs passed by Congress after World War I conflicted with our new creditor status. As a debtor nation before the war, the United States had made up for its debts by exporting more to Europe than it imported. After the war, European nations, as debtors, could not do likewise because high United States tariffs sharply restricted the sale of their goods to this country. To make it possible for Europeans to buy our goods in the 1920's, we had to make additional loans to Europe.

4. *The Decline in Trade in the Early 1930's.* World trade declined sharply in the early 1930's. Because of the depression, United States loans to Europe ended, and American investments abroad were curtailed. The result was that European nations could no longer buy from us, for lack of dollars, nor could they sell to us, because of the United States protective tariffs.

> *(a)* In desperation the European nations adopted policies of *economic nationalism.* They tried to produce as much as possible at home and buy as little as possible abroad. Tariffs were raised, imports restricted, and foreign trade rigidly controlled.

> *(b)* The decline in world trade that resulted had international consequences. Industries declined and unemployment increased. The United States lost a major portion of its markets abroad for such leading exports as wheat, cotton, automobiles, and machinery.

The Reciprocal Trade Program. In order to stimulate industry at home and halt the decline in world trade, the United States reversed its policy of high protective tariffs in the 1930's. It adopted a new policy of lowering tariff barriers through *reciprocal* (two-way) *trade agreements.* Reciprocal trade is still a key part of the nation's trade program.

1. *The Reciprocal Trade Agreements Act of 1934.* The reciprocal trade program was begun by the *Reciprocal Trade Agreements Act* of 1934, passed in large measure as a result of the efforts of CORDELL HULL, Secretary of State under President Franklin D. Roosevelt.

> *(a) Purpose.* The purpose of the Reciprocal Trade Act was to expand United States foreign markets by lowering our tariff barriers on foreign goods, in return for similar reductions on American goods by other nations.

> *(b) Provisions.* Under the *Reciprocal Trade Agreements Act:* **(1)** The President was given the authority to negotiate reciprocal trade agreements with other nations. **(2)** He was permitted to lower duties on specific foreign imports up to 50% (later 75%), in return for similar reductions by foreign nations.

2. *Results of Reciprocal Trade.* Under the Reciprocal Trade Act, as renewed and extended between 1934 and 1962, agreements were signed between the United States and more than 50 nations. Under the *"most favored nation"* clause of these agreements, each nation agreed to give all other nations with which it had similar pacts the same reduced rates.

The Reciprocal Trade policy had far-reaching results. Our tariff barriers were reduced from an average of 59% in 1931, to about 12% in 1961. The value of our international trade (both imports and exports) increased substantially. Under the "most favored nation" agreements many other nations benefited. Much of this expansion took place within the framework of the *General Agreement on Tariffs and Trade,* commonly called *GATT,* negotiated in 1947.

3. *Modifications in the Program.* Because business, labor, and agricultural interests claimed that they were being injured by foreign competition under reciprocal trade, Congress, in the late 1940's, limited the rate-cutting authority given the President in two ways:

> *(a) The "Peril-Point" Clause.* Under this provision, the United States Tariff Commission was given the right to advise the President not to lower rates beyond a level where specific industries would be harmed.

> *(b) The "Escape Clause."* If an industry claimed that rate reductions already in effect were causing it "undue hardship," the Tariff Commission was empowered to investigate. It might then recommend cancellation of these reductions.

4. *Weaknesses of the Program After World War II.* In the late 1950's and early 1960's, it was recognized that the original Reciprocal Trade Act was no longer adequate to meet the needs of the United States. Advocates of revision of our trade program advanced the following arguments:

> *(a)* Congress had placed too many restrictions on the President's authority to negotiate.

> *(b)* The United States was still continuing to erect unnecessary barriers to trade. For example, "Buy American" laws dating from the depression era required government agencies to give preference to domestic suppliers, even when foreign goods were available more cheaply. In addition, United States quotas had been put on the importation of oil, coal, lead, zinc, and a number of agricultural products.

> *(c)* United States industry was meeting serious new challenges from the expanding exports of European and Japanese producers.

> *(d)* The nations of the European Common Market were threatening to set up a unified tariff wall against all outside nations.

Recent Acts to Expand Trade. Recognizing the need to place the United States in a better position to build trade with other nations, Congress has enacted a number of laws to help our foreign commerce.

1. *Trade Expansion Act of 1962.* Passed at the urging of President Kennedy, this law gave our government new resources to negotiate trade agreements with other nations, particularly the European Common Market. The President was empowered for five years to raise or lower our tariff rates by up to 50%, and to eliminate entirely tariffs on goods for which the United States and Western Europe accounted for 80% or more of world trade. Provision was also made for aiding industries that might be hurt by such reduction of trade barriers. (These provisions were later extended.)

2. *Trade Reform Act of 1974.* This law renewed and expanded the President's powers to encourage foreign trade by negotiating agreements with other nations. The President was authorized not only to reduce or eliminate tariffs but also to eliminate or "harmonize" non-tariff trade barriers, such as import quotas and restrictive health and safety codes. The President could also retaliate against unreasonable foreign barriers to our exports by *raising* tariffs or placing other restrictions on the offending nation's goods. In such actions, the President utilizes determinations made by the newly organized U.S. International Trade Commission (successor to the former U.S. Tariff Commission). The ITC may also recommend aid to industries hurt by the lessening of trade restrictions.

3. *Results of the Trade Legislation.* The increased flexibility in our trade policies brought about by the acts of 1962 and 1974 has enabled the United States to participate effectively in the General Agreement on Tariffs and Trade (GATT) and in other cooperative programs with more than 50 nations. The pacts arranged in this way have substantially increased the volume of our foreign trade, including our sales abroad. Under these policies, the nations of the world have generally steered clear of ruinous "trade wars" which make use of such weapons as competitive restrictions on imports and subsidization of exports. All nations have benefited as a result of this.

Efforts to Stimulate World Trade After World War II. It was clear to the United States and its allies that the efforts of each government to manage its own currency and trade without regard to the policies and interests of other nations had, in the period of the 1930's, brought on trade wars that contributed not only to the rise of fascism but to World War II itself. Accordingly, in addition to its own reciprocal trade program, the United States has since World War II worked to promote trade and economic stability through international economic cooperation and foreign aid. These efforts are described below.

1. *Bretton Woods Agreement (1944).* At a conference in Bretton Woods, New Hampshire, in 1944, the United States and its allies drew up a plan to regulate world trade cooperatively. The *Bretton Woods Agreement* (1944) aimed to abolish trade wars that resulted in part from currency juggling and trade quotas. Under the agreement, the value of every important currency was fixed or "pegged" to the value of the U. S. dollar. The United States agreed to convert dollars into gold when presented by foreign nations, banks, and individuals. The belief was that, since the gold-backed dollar was stable in value, it would contribute to the stability of other currencies and thus remove barriers to world trade caused by fluctuations in the value of currencies.

2. *International Monetary Fund.* In 1946 the UN set up a specialized agency the *International Monetary Fund (IMF),* which carried a large part of the responsibility for making the Bretton Woods system work. Nations with weak or failing currencies have been granted loans by the IMF in the form of the more desirable or "hard" currencies (usually dollars or pounds).

3. *World Bank.* In 1946, the United States joined in the creation of another UN specialized agency, the *International Bank for Reconstruction and Development.* The *World Bank,* as it is usually known, makes loans to nations in currencies needed to help finance large-scale industrial projects and other worthwhile undertakings. Many loans have been granted to underdeveloped nations, thus stimulating international trade.

4. *GATT.* In 1947, the United States helped draw up the *General Agreement on Tariffs and Trade* (GATT). This is a multilateral (many-sided) trade agreement among 37 nations who do about 80% of the free world's trade. Through negotiation, GATT members have reduced tariffs on over 3500 types of goods in world trade. They have also, with less success, attempted to eliminate such trade barriers as import quotas, trade embargoes, and currency restrictions.

5. *The European Common Market.* The United States strongly backed the formation of the *European Economic Community* or *Common Market* in 1958. The original members were France, Italy, West Germany, the Netherlands, Belgium, and Luxemberg. They were joined by Britain, Ireland, and Denmark in 1973.

The Common Market aims to eliminate all trade barriers among the member nations, thus creating a vast free-trade area in Western Europe, comparable to the free trade area of the United States. As a result of phasing out of tariffs, ending of import quotas, and other forms of economic cooperation, Market members have already achieved a remarkable rate of economic growth and prosperity. Market members set common tariffs on imports from all outside nations, including the United States.

6. *U. S. Foreign-Aid Program.* Since World War II, the United States has given or loaned over 155 billion dollars to help the recovery of war-torn nations, to strengthen the free world against expanding international Communism, to raise living standards, and to help revive world trade.

The United States and World Trade Crises Since World War II. The new system of international trade born at Bretton Woods made possible a great growth in the volume of world trade. Nevertheless, it did not prevent continuing world monetary problems and crises. As a result of the crisis of 1971, during which the United States was forced to devalue the dollar, the Bretton Woods system was, in effect, scrapped in favor of a new system for currency regulation and exchange. The events behind this important change are outlined below.

1. *The Postwar Dollar Gap.* For nearly a decade after World War II, nations with which we normally do most of our foreign business had to import heavily from the United States in order to rebuild their war-shattered economies. Their lack of dollars to pay for these imports was referred to as the "dollar gap." To help bridge this "gap" the United States extended large-scale financial aid. After the early 1950's, the problem disappeared. Western European nations and Japan rebuilt their economies and emerged as strong competitors of the United States in world markets.

2. *The Vanishing U. S. Trade Surplus.* For over 75 years the value of goods exported from the United States exceeded the value of goods imported, giving this country a so-called favorable balance of trade. In the late 1960's, however, the picture began to change because of the growing competition of European and Japanese products in world and American markets, especially in such industries as shoes, textiles, steel, electronics, aviation, photography, and automobiles. In 1971, the United States experienced a balance of trade *deficit* (of about 2 billion dollars). Over the years, American goods had become more and more expensive for foreign buyers as a result of high labor costs and inflation; meanwhile the goods produced by such countries as Japan had become relatively cheaper and more attractive to consumers.

3. *Our Growing Unfavorable Balance of Payments.* A nation's *balance of payments* consists of the total of all its transactions with the rest of the world, of which imports and exports are only one part. Despite the fact that our country had a favorable balance of trade until 1971, it had an *unfavorable balance of payments* after 1957. This resulted from tourist expenditures, foreign business investments by American firms, expenditures for our armed forces overseas (including the war in Vietnam), and foreign-aid programs. As a result, for many years we have been paying out to foreign nations more than we collect from them. In 1967 alone, our foreign spending exceeded our earnings from abroad by over 3.5 billion dollars. One result of this was that many billions of U. S. dollars accumulated in the hands of foreign banks and other holders.

4. *The Gold Drain.* Under the postwar international exchange system foreign nations had the right to exchange American dollars for gold in the United States at $35 an ounce. As large quantities of foreign-held dollars were turned in for redemption beginning in the late 1950's, U. S. gold reserves began to shrink — from a postwar peak of 25 billion dollars in 1949 to 10.5 billions in 1971.

5. *The Monetary Crisis of 1971.* Thus, as 1971 opened, the United States had less than 11 billion dollars in gold to meet potential demands of about 30 billion dollars in foreign hands. By the summer of 1971, it became clear that in addition to the continuing unfavorable balance of *payments,* the United States would for the first time since 1893 be facing an unfavorable balance of *trade.*

As the balance of payments situation worsened, foreign banks and businessmen refused to accept American dollars at the official exchange rates. Fear spread throughout world financial circles that the United States would be unable to fulfill its obligation to exchange gold for dollars. The gold outflow accelerated steadily as nations and businessmen all over the world began to try to get rid of surplus American dollars. The value of the dollar in "unofficial" markets fell steadily. A major crisis seemed to be in the making.

6. *The United States Acts to Meet the Crisis.* In August 1971, convinced that decisive action had to be taken, the Nixon administration: **(a)** imposed a 10% surcharge on imports, to cut down on foreign imports; and **(b)** declared that the dollar was no longer convertible into gold.

7. *Devaluation of Dollar in 1971.* Shortly afterward in 1971, with a crisis still threatening, the United States and other leading monetary powers worked out the *Smithsonian Monetary Accord.* **(a)** The U.S. dollar was devalued by 8%, by raising the price of gold from $35 to $38 an ounce. **(b)** The value of the U.S. dollar (in terms of foreign currencies) was hereafter to be set by international agreement. **(c)** The U.S. dollar was to remain inconvertible into gold for an indefinite period. **(d)** The United States agreed to end the 10% import surcharge, imposed earlier. The aim of the devaluation was to lower the value of the U.S. dollar in relation to the currencies of major trading nations, like West Germany and Japan. It was hoped that this would help improve our balance of payments by making our exports cheaper, and at the same time making imported products more costly to American buyers.

8. *Devaluation of Dollar in 1973.* Early in 1973, President Nixon unexpectedly devalued the U.S. dollar, by an additional 10%. The aim again was to make American goods more competitive with those of foreign nations. This action upset world monetary markets for several months, as the value of the U.S. dollar abroad dropped sharply. Unable to agree on a new monetary system or on the fixing of new currency exchange ratios, as called for under the 1971 agreement, the leading nations compromised on a temporary system of *"floating"* exchange rates, under which the dollar price of the German mark, French franc, British pound, Japanese yen, and other currencies would be set by supply and demand.

9. *International Trade and Finance after Dollar Devaluation.* By the mid-1970s, it appeared that the dollar devaluations of 1971 and 1973 had achieved their purpose. The lowered cost of American goods abroad (resulting from devaluation), plus a sharp rise in worldwide demand for our food products, gave the United States a trade surplus and reduced its unfavorable overall balance of international payments.

One significant exception to this favorable trend occurred in 1974, as a result of the policies of the Organization of Petroleum Exporting Countries (OPEC). These major petroleum producers, mainly in the Middle East, suddenly quadrupled the price of their crude oil late in 1973. As a result, the dollar trade balance of the United States was seriously disrupted for a time. Similar effects were experienced by other oil-importing nations.

Meanwhile, the trading nations of the world have continued to operate on the system of floating currency rates. Disagreements and conflicts have occurred, but for the most part they have been successfully compromised. In 1974, a new law authorized Americans to acquire gold bullion for the first time since 1933. The fact that there was no "gold rush" to convert paper dollars into gold was another indication of the stability of the currency and foreign exchange system worked out by the United States and other leading nations.

REVIEW TEST (Chapter 21)

Select the number preceding the word or expression that best completes each statement or answers each question.

1. In the United States, a *tariff* is a tax on (1) exports only (2) imports only (3) both exports and imports (4) goods produced and sold within the United States

2. A protective tariff is intended primarily to provide protection for (1) consumers in the home market (2) consumers in foreign countries (3) producers at home (4) multinational corporations

3. The main purpose of reciprocal trade agreements is to (1) protect consumers within the United States (2) prevent foreign producers from "catching up" with advanced American technology (3) cxpand our foreign trade (4) make the United States more nearly self-sufficient

4. The United States enters into a trade agreement with Nation *A*, giving it "most-favored-nation" status. As a result, (1) Nation *A* gets a monopoly of U.S. trade (2) all U.S. exports are allowed to enter Nation *A* duty-free (3) the United States is guaranteed a favorable balance of trade with Nation *A* (4) U.S. tariff rates on many imports from Nation *A* will be reduced

5. Which of the following is now fully within the control of the U.S. government? (1) fixing the amount of gold represented by a dollar (2) fixing the market value of the dollar in terms of foreign currencies (3) creating a favorable overall balance of payments (4) making U.S. goods competitive with those of foreign nations

Essay Questions

1. Explain two arguments *for* and two arguments *against* protective tariffs.

2. Prepare a chart showing the overall trend of tariff rates in U.S. history. Include the following periods: (*a*) 1789-1815, (*b*) 1816-1861, (*c*) 1920-1933, (*d*) 1934 to date.

3. With regard to the devaluations of the U.S. dollar in the 1970's, explain (*a*) the conditions creating the need for this move, (*b*) the way in which the devaluation was carried out, (*c*) the results.

4. Explain how the trade and/or tariff policies of the United States have been affected by (*a*) the rise of the Common Market, (*b*) the industrial development of Japan, (*c*) the growth of world population, (*d*) the energy crisis.

CHAPTER 22 _____

Our Pluralistic Society
_____

In less than two centuries, the population of the United States has grown from nearly 4 million (1789) to over 200 million today. This fifty-fold increase was made possible in large measure by a continuous flow of immigrants to our shores in the 19th and early 20th centuries. In recent years immigration has been sharply restricted by the government. However, recent population trends have presented new challenges and problems.

Part I — IMMIGRATION AND ITS RESTRICTION

The United States is a "nation of immigrants." More than 24 million people from other nations have come to our shores—more than to any other nation on earth. Except for the American Indians, the entire population consists of immigrants or their descendants.

Largely as a result of this immigration, the people of the United States show a wide diversity of cultural, ethnic, and religious backgrounds. We express this by saying that the United States is a *pluralistic society*.

Hardships Faced by Immigrants. Most immigrants who came to the United States faced extreme hardships. In addition to a long ocean voyage under crowded and unsanitary conditions, the newly arrived immigrant was given the lowest paying jobs and was forced to live in slums if he stayed in the cities. If he went West, he had to face the rigors of life on the frontier. Also, most immigrants arrived virtually penniless.

Reasons for Immigration. Despite the hardships they faced, the majority of immigrants were eager to come to this country. They came for (**1**) economic improvement, (**2**) religious freedom, and (**3**) political freedom. America was looked upon as a land of freedom and opportunity. (It must be noted, of course, that Negro slaves did not come voluntarily.)

The Flow of Immigration. Because more immigrants have come to the United States in some periods than in others, it has become customary to refer to "waves" of immigration.

1. *Immigration in the Colonial Period.* Most of the immigrants to the original 13 colonies were Englishmen. However, there were also large numbers who came from Ireland, Scotland, and Germany. In 1750, three-quarters of the population were descendants of settlers from England or Ireland (the British Isles).

2. *Immigration from 1790 to 1830.* During the first half century of the Republic, fewer than 3,000,000 immigrants arrived. Immigration was temporarily slowed down by the American Revolution, the Napoleonic

394

Wars, and the War of 1812. Immigrants also found that land was expensive, and that jobs for unskilled laborers were few.

3. *Immigration from 1830 to 1860.* The first big wave of immigration to the United States occurred between 1830 and 1860. Nearly 5 million immigrants came from Ireland, Germany, France, and Great Britain.

(a) Most of the immigrants in this period came because land was becoming cheaper and because of the rapidly expanding job opportunities in factories, railroads, and the canal-building industry.

(b) Bad crops in the British Isles drove many farm workers to the United States. To escape starvation nearly a million Irish emigrants left for the United States after the failure of the potato crop in 1846.

(c) Unsuccessful revolutions in Europe in 1830 and 1848 brought thousands to the United States in search of economic opportunity and political freedom. The failure of the Revolution of 1848 in Germany caused leading German liberals and professionals to emigrate to the New World.

(d) Most of the immigrants of this period settled in cities. Many, however, became farmers. The German settlers tended to become pioneer farmers. The Irish went into factory work and construction projects.

4. *Immigration from 1860 to 1890.* The economic development of the United States after the Civil War created many new job opportunities. Encouraged by railroad builders and manufacturers, and driven by poverty at home, nearly 11 million immigrants entered the United States from 1860 to 1890. As in the pre-Civil War era, most came from the countries of Northern and Western Europe (the British Isles, Germany, France, the Scandinavian countries).

5. *Immigration from 1890 to 1914.* The high-tide of immigration to the United States took place between 1890 and World War I. In that period, over 16 million immigrants came to our shores.

(a) Whereas most immigrants before 1890 were from Northern and Western Europe, most of these "newcomers" came from Southern and Eastern Europe (Austria, Hungary, Poland, Russia, Italy, the Balkans). Many came from the Orient.

(b) Because of their extreme poverty, most of the "new immigrants" of this period moved into crowded city tenements. They worked for low wages, often under conditions worse than those they had left at home. Many were unskilled and illiterate and found it more difficult to adjust to the new way of life than had the earlier immigrants (the "old immigrants").

6. *Immigration After World War I.* The adoption of a restrictive immigration policy after World War I sharply reduced the flow of immigrants to the United States (see page 398). As a result, immigration no longer plays as significant a role in American life as it once did.

Impact of Immigration on American Life. Immigrants have contributed to the development of American civilization in many different ways.

1. *Democratic Ideals.* The immigrants were naturally eager to be free of the political, economic, and social restrictions typical of the Old World. Thus, they contributed heavily to shaping and strengthening the American democratic traditions of liberty and equality under the law.

2. *Economic Development.* Immigrants helped to settle the West and played a major part in the nation's agricultural and industrial growth. The hard work and specialized skills of these newcomers made possible development of resources and improved methods of production in many fields.

3. *Language and Culture.* Immigrants also contributed to the language and culture of most regions in the United States. Today, for example, Spanish influence is strong in the Southwest; French influence, in Louisiana; Scandinavian influence, in the Midwest; and German influence, in Pennsylvania. In most instances, the native customs brought from abroad were fused with those found here. In other cases, pockets of native culture were perpetuated in the nation's cities in the form of "Chinatowns," "Little Italys," and the like. The religious, cultural and family life of America shows clearly the effects of immigrant backgrounds and "life-styles."

4. *Leaders.* Only a few of the more notable "greats" among United States immigrants are listed in the chart below.

DISTINGUISHED IMMIGRANTS TO THE UNITED STATES

SCIENCE

Louis Agassiz (Switzerland)	Edward Teller (Hungary)
John Audubon (Haiti)	Alexander Graham Bell (Scotland)
Albert Einstein (Germany)	Charles Steinmetz (Germany)
Enrico Fermi (Italy)	

MUSIC

Arturo Toscanini (Italy)	Leopold Stokowski (Great Britain)
Igor Stravinsky (Russia)	Rudolf Friml (Germany)
Bruno Walter (Germany)	

LITERATURE AND JOURNALISM

Thomas Mann (Germany)	Jacob Riis (Denmark)
Lin Yutang (China)	Joseph Pulitzer (Hungary)
George Santayana (Spain)	

LABOR ORGANIZATION

Samuel Gompers (Great Britain)	Philip Murray (Scotland)

OTHER FIELDS

Painting: Ben Shahn (Russia)	*Law:* Felix Frankfurter (Austria)
Sculpture: Augustus Saint-Gaudens (Ireland)	*Theater:* Ferenc Molnar (Hungary)
	Politics: Carl Schurz (Germany)
Business: James J. Hill (Canada)	John Peter Altgeld (Germany)

Opposition to the Immigrant. For the first decades of the nation's history, immigrants were generally welcome. Thereafter, immigrants whose language, customs, or ways of living were different faced problems of hostility and discrimination, as well as of adjustment. Reasons for prejudice and opposition were economic, political, social and psychological. (1) As early as the 1790's, political distrust of foreigners by the Federalists resulted in the *Alien and Sedition Acts*. (2) In the 1850's the *Know-Nothing Party* opposed immigration for religious (anti-Catholic) and economic (job-competition) reasons. (3) Anti-Jewish prejudice and discrimination (*anti-Semitism*) surfaced in the 1880's and has still not wholly disappeared. (4) In the 1920's, the Ku Klux Klan vigorously voiced its opposition to further immigration (see page 398 for reasons). (5) More recently, newcomers from Puerto Rico have been victims of prejudice. (It should be noted that minorities like the American Indians and Negroes—as slaves and as free men—were subject to the same kinds of discrimination as immigrants.)

Immigration Restriction Becomes a National Issue. Until the end of the 19th century, the Federal government made no attempts to cut down on immigration. By the 1880's, increasing public sentiment against this *laissez-faire* policy caused Congress to begin to restrict immigration. Thereafter, our immigration policy became increasingly selective and restrictive. The matter became a national issue for many decades. Arguments given in opposition to unrestricted immigration included the following:

1. *Fear of Job Competition.* Workers and unions feared that immigrants would take away jobs. (It should be noted that in most cases immigrants were offered only the lowest paying jobs.)

2. *Opposition to the "New Immigrant."* Arguments were advanced against the "new immigrants." It was claimed: **(a)** that they came from nations whose customs and traditions were different from those prevailing in the United States; **(b)** that they were easily influenced by unscrupulous politicians; and **(c)** that they could not easily be "Americanized."

Selective Immigration (1882-1920). In response to the demands of labor and other groups, Congress passed laws excluding certain groups from entering the country to become citizens.

1. *Exclusion of Asians.* Asians were the first to feel the effects of the new policy of selective immigration.

> *(a) Chinese Exclusion Act (1882).* The *Chinese Exclusion Act* of 1882 barred Chinese laborers from entering the country for a period of ten years. It was later renewed, and in 1904 made permanent. Chinese laborers had been coming to the United States for a half a century, to work on the railroads and other construction projects. By the end of the century many had settled on the Pacific Coast, and labor unions complained that their low standard of living was forcing wages down.

> *(b) Gentlemen's Agreement (1907).* The ban on Chinese laborers was extended to Japanese laborers in 1907. Under the *Gentlemen's Agree-*

ment, negotiated with Japan by Theodore Roosevelt in 1907, Japan agreed to stop the emigration of Japanese laborers to the United States. In return, Roosevelt persuaded a San Francisco school board to withdraw an order barring Japanese children from public schools. This order had resulted from rising ill-will against Japanese farmers and laborers who had settled on the West Coast. Despite the Gentlemen's Agreement, several West Coast states continued to restrict Japanese land purchases. This caused Japan to accuse the United States of bad faith.

2. *Other Laws Discouraging Immigration.* Other laws of the period 1882-1920 excluded certain undesirable groups from the United States. These included criminals, the mentally defective, contract laborers, anarchists, and radicals who believed in the overthrow of the government by force. In 1917, Congress passed a *Literacy Act* over President Wilson's veto. It required that all immigrants be able to read or write English or some other language.

Reasons for Restriction of Immigration. After World War I, the United States immigration policy became restrictive as well as selective. Laws were passed limiting the number of immigrants who could enter the country in any one year. Several factors, some old and some new, contributed to the increased severity of our program. (1) It was recognized that restrictions attempted before and during World War I had not substantially reduced the tide of immigration. (2) There was a sharp rise in the number of immigrants who came to the United States immediately after the war. (By 1920 this number was nearly a million a year.) (3) Many believed in the theory (proved to be false) that immigrants from Northern and Western Europe were "superior" to those from Southern and Eastern Europe. This was known as the doctrine of *Nordic supremacy.* (4) Related to the "Nordic supremacy" theory was the belief that many Southern and Eastern Europeans (Poles, Russians, Italians, Jews, etc.) had not "Americanized" rapidly enough. Many were disappointed over the fact that the United States had not so much been a "melting pot" as a "mixing bowl"; that is, that newer immigrants often tended to retain many European customs and traditions. (5) There was the still-continuing fear that unrestricted immigration jeopardized the jobs of American workers.

Restrictive Immigration Legislation. The result of these fears and attitudes was a series of laws that sharply reduced the numbers of immigrants to the United States and (until 1965) discriminated in favor of the "old immigrants" from Northern and Western Europe (British Isles, France, Scandinavia, Germany, etc.) and against the "new immigrants" from Central and Eastern Europe (Italy, Poland, Greece, etc.). Immigration from Asia was severely limited.

1. *Acts of 1921 and 1924. The Emergency Quota Act of 1921* set the number of immigrants at 3% of the number that had come to the United States from each country by 1910. The *Johnson-Reed Act of 1924* cut the national quotas to 20% of the number living here in 1890, and excluded all Orientals, including Japanese.

2. *National Origins Clause (1929).* The *National Origins Clause* went into effect in 1929. (**1**) A total of no more than 150,000 "quota immigrants" were to be admitted each year. (**2**) Each country was assigned a quota or share of the 150,000 in accordance with the number of persons of its national stock living in the United States in 1920. (**3**) The minimum quota for each country was set at 100. (**4**) Immigrants from Asia were excluded completely. (**5**) No quotas or limitations were applied to the Western Hemisphere (Canada and Latin America).

3. *McCarran-Walter Act (1952).* The *McCarran-Walter Act* of 1952 continued the national origins system: (**1**) A total of 156,000 quota immigrants were to be admitted annually, with each nation outside the Western Hemisphere assigned a minimum quota based on national origin. (**2**) The exemption for persons born in the Western Hemisphere was continued. (**3**) A token quota of 2000 was assigned to the Far East and Pacific areas. (**4**) Present or former members of communist or other totalitarian groups were barred. Provision was made to deport subversives.

4. *Refugee and Displaced Persons Acts.* Occasionally, Congress made exceptions in the restrictive immigration policy. Provisions were made to admit limited numbers of refugees from Nazi Germany before World War II, displaced persons (refugees) after World War II, and Hungarian refugees after the 1956 revolt against Soviet Russian domination.

Present Immigration Policy. In 1965 steps were taken to eliminate basic discriminatory features of our immigration policy.

1. *Criticism of the National Origins System.* The national origins system as expressed in the Johnson-Reed and McCarran Acts came under

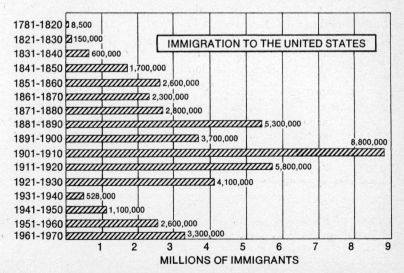

Years	Immigrants
1781-1820	8,500
1821-1830	150,000
1831-1840	600,000
1841-1850	1,700,000
1851-1860	2,600,000
1861-1870	2,300,000
1871-1880	2,800,000
1881-1890	5,300,000
1891-1900	3,700,000
1901-1910	8,800,000
1911-1920	5,800,000
1921-1930	4,100,000
1931-1940	528,000
1941-1950	1,100,000
1951-1960	2,600,000
1961-1970	3,300,000

IMMIGRATION TO THE UNITED STATES

MILLIONS OF IMMIGRANTS

bitter criticism. Among the charges made were: **(a)** The law was based essentially on racist thinking because it deliberately gave preference to migration from the countries of Western and Northern Europe. **(b)** The law was unfair because large unused quotas assigned to nations such as Great Britain were not transferable to other countries *(e.g.,* Italy, Greece) with small quotas and long lists of would-be migrants.

2. *Immigration Act of 1965.* The basis of our present immigration policy is the *Immigration Act of 1965.* This law repealed the quota system, attempted to correct the most discriminatory aspects of existing policy, and set new guidelines for control of immigration. **(a)** The national origins plan was ended as of July 1, 1968. **(b)** A ceiling of 170,000 persons was set on admissions from outside the Western Hemisphere, with a maximum of 20,000 from any one country. **(c)** First preference was to be given to certain "preference categories," including persons with talents and skills needed in American life. **(d)** Exempted from the ceilings were immediate relatives (children, spouses, parents) of persons already living in the United States, as well as certain "special immigrants" (for example, resident aliens returning from abroad). **(e)** For the first time, a ceiling was placed on the number of immigrants from within the Western Hemisphere (120,000 annually), but without national limitations as such.

Changing Immigration Patterns. The *Immigration Act of 1965* allowed, for the first time since the 1920's, large-scale immigration from countries outside of Northern and Western Europe.

Although total numbers have not risen greatly since 1965, many more immigrants have been coming from regions and countries which formerly had low quotas. They include particularly: **(1)** Southern and Eastern Europe (Italy, Greece, Portugal); **(2)** Asia (the Philippine Republic, China, Korea, India); **(3)** the West Indies (Jamaica, Haiti); and **(4)** Africa. At the same time, immigration from former "high-quota" areas, such as Northern Europe and Canada, has declined sharply. In recent years nonwhite immigration has reached significant proportions for the first time in the 20th century. Over the last few years the largest numbers of immigrants have come from Mexico, the Philippines, the West Indies, and Italy.

REVIEW TEST (Chapter 22 — Part I)

Select the number preceding the word or expression that best completes each statement or answers each question.

1. .Why were very few restrictions placed on immigration during the 19th century? (1) The native birth rate was low. (2) There were no organized labor groups. (3) There was a great need for cheap labor. (4) Most immigrants could speak English.

2. The percentage of Americans who trace their national origin to the British Isles (1) is higher today than it was a century ago (2) is lower today than it was a century ago (3) has changed little over the years (4) is insignificant

3. The period in which the greatest number of German and Irish immigrants came to the United States was (1) duing the American Revolution (2) between 1783 and 1800 (3) between 1845 and 1860 (4) since 1920

4. Congressional regulation of Chinese immigration began a few years after (1) the building of the Erie Canal (2) the construction of the first transcontinental railroad (3) the coal strike of 1902 (4) World War I

5. Which of the following opposed unlimited immigration during the 19th century? (1) steamship companies (2) promoters of Western railroads (3) the United States Steel Corporation (4) the American Federation of Labor

6. From 1890 to 1920, the majority of the immigrants to the United States (1) were from Southern, Central, and Eastern Europe (2) settled in the West (3) wished to escape religious persecution in Europe (4) avoided the cities because they disliked city life

7. The McCarran-Walter Immigration Act (1952) provided for (1) the introduction of literacy tests for immigrants (2) the exclusion of all Asiatics from the United States (3) elimination of the quota system of admission (4) a screening process to keep out subversives

8. The number of immigrants admitted to the United States from each country under the McCarran-Walter Act was based, in general, upon (1) treaty provisions (2) national origins of our population (3) population of the foreign countries (4) the form of government of the foreign countries

9. The Immigration Act of 1965 provides for all of the following *except* (1) an annual limit to the number of immigrants from the Western Hemisphere (2) a quota system based on national origins (3) a ceiling of 170,000 immigrants from outside the Western Hemisphere (4) an allowance for spouses, minor children, and parents of immigrants to be admitted without regard to numerical ceilings

10. When did United States immigration policy first become *restrictive* as well as selective? (1) in the 1860's (2) in the 1890's (3) in the 1920's (4) in the 1940's

Select the letter of the item in each group that does **NOT** *belong with the others.*

1. "Favored" nations under immigration laws from 1920 to 1965: (a) Brazil (b) Mexico (c) Czechoslovakia (d) England

2. Foreign-born American citizens: (a) Philip Murray (b) Albert Einstein (c) Samuel Gompers (d) Robert Kennedy

3. Laws whose purpose was to restrict immigration: (a) Gentlemen's Agreement (b) National Origins Act (c) Displaced Persons Act (d) Chinese Exclusion Act

4. Unopposed as a group to increased immigration quotas: (a) United States Presidents since World War II (b) labor unions (c) naturalized citizens (d) manufacturers

5. Favored restricted immigration to the United States: (a) President Wilson (b) Ku Klux Klan (c) Know-Nothing Party (d) Alien and Sedition Laws

Essay Questions

1. Explain the government's policy toward immigration from 1789 to 1870 and indicate why it pursued this policy.

2. Discuss briefly two causes for adopting restrictions on immigration during the period 1890–1930.

3. Explain two changes made in our immigration program since 1940. Are these basic changes? Explain.

4. Give arguments (a) favoring and (b) opposing our present immigration policy.

5. Show with illustrations how immigrant groups have enriched American life.

With the decline of immigration, new population patterns and problems have developed.

Immigration and Population Growth. Although the total number of immigrants has risen slowly each decade since the 1930's, immigration no longer plays as significant a role in the nation's population growth as it once did. At its peak (1910-20), immigration accounted for about 55% of the population growth of the United States. In the decade 1960-70, the corresponding figure was only 2%.

Recent Population Trends. The industrialization and urbanization of the nation in the past century have been accompanied by a number of population trends, some of which have created major current problems. The following are among the more significant of these changing patterns:

1. *A Growing Population.* The population of the United States grew from 30 million in 1860 to 76 million in 1900, to 190 million in 1960, and passed the 200 million mark in 1967. It is estimated that by 1980 our total population will have risen to between 245 and 280 million.

(a) Despite the large population rise of the last three decades, there are increasing signs of a slowdown in growth. The nation's percentage growth of 13% during 1960-70 was the smallest since the depression decade of the 1930s. The birth rate has continued to decline in the 1970s.

(b) The increase in the population of the United States is part of a worldwide *population explosion.* This has already increased the world's population from 2 billion to nearly 4.2 billion within 40 years. At present growth rates, the figure will be nearly 8 billion by the year 2000. The desirability of such an increase is now widely questioned, in view of worldwide political and racial tensions, environmental pollution, and diminishing natural resources.

2. *A Shifting Population.* Significant population shifts have resulted from changes in the economy, transportation developments and new social patterns.

(a) Americans have become highly mobile. In 1970, for example, one person out of five changed his place of residence every year.

(b) The increased mobility of the population has been reflected also by regional population shifts. Most noteworthy have been movements from: **(1)** South to North, **(2)** East to West, **(3)** Puerto Rico and other Caribbean islands to mainland, **(4)** farm to city, **(5)** cities to suburbs, and **(6)** established areas to newly developing areas. In recent years, there has been a sharp population rise in the "Sunbelt" region that stretches across the United States from Southern California to the East Coast, where it extends from Florida as far north as Virginia.

(c) In 1980, about 80% of the population of the United States lived in urban areas (including suburbs), as compared with 70% in 1960, and 64% in 1950.

3. *A Longer-lived Population.* Continued advances in public health, sanitation, and medicine have resulted in a longer life span for the average person. In 1850, the average American could expect to live to 40. In 1900, average life expectancy was 48. Today it is over 70 years.

4. *An Aging Population.* Because Americans are living so much longer, the proportion of older people in the total population has increased rapidly. In 1900, approximately 4% of the nation's population was over 65 years of age. By 1950, the number in this age category had risen to 8.5%, and by 1970 to about 10% (roughly 20 million persons).

5 *Occupational Changes.* Noteworthy shifts in occupation have accompanied the other changes in our population makeup.

(a) There has been a sharp decline in the proportion of the population engaged in agriculture. In 1850, about 64% of the total labor force worked on farms. This dropped to 22% in 1930, and to 10% by 1960. Today, it is only 4.5%.

(b) Another noteworthy trend has been the increase of persons employed in the so-called service industries — the professions, clerical work, advertising and sales, repairs and maintenance, recreation, the "beauty" industries, etc.

Population Problems. Many problems and challenges, as well as opportunities, have resulted from the changing population patterns.

1. *Food and Other Resources.* Although the United States is not an overpopulated country, if population growth continues at the present rate, there may be a population-resources "squeeze" by the 21st century. This may offer a threat to living standards and to "quality of life" in general.

2. *Transportation.* The mobility, spread, and shifts in population have placed a severe burden on our transportation facilities. Providing and maintaining adequate roads and highways has become one of our most serious transportation problems. Because of the continued sharp increase in auto, bus, and truck traffic, road systems soon become obsolete, and vast sums are being spent by Federal, state, and local governments to build roads for tomorrow. Where there has been a flight to the suburbs in urban areas, problems of local transportation have become difficult and complex.

3. *Housing.* The rapidly growing and shifting population of the nation, plus its steadily rising standard of living, has created pressing housing problems in many areas. Local, state, and city governments have had to become increasingly involved in helping to provide adequate housing for all. (See page 417.) With the growth of urban population slum problems have become even more acute, and crime and illness rates have risen.

4. *Education.* School enrollment has grown steadily with the increase in population. In 1976, there were 59 million enrolled in the public and private schools, and the nation was spending nearly 119 billion dollars a year on education—8% of the gross national product. Most noteworthy has been the sharp rise in enrollments in colleges and universities in roughly the last decade to over 11 million. A mounting problem of the

1970's is finding the necessary funds to maintain and improve the education system. Sharply rising costs, including higher teacher salaries, have led to financial crises for many of the nation's schools and colleges. Public schools have been forced to drop staff and cut services; parochial schools are struggling to keep open; and many private colleges and universities face a severe budgetary squeeze.

5. *Business and Employment.* Generally speaking, the increase in population has been a stimulus to industry and employment. New industries have developed to meet the needs of the growing numbers of people, and old industries have expanded. Production of goods and services has increased rapidly. The working force has increased to over 95 million. At the same time, because of changing population needs and patterns, some formerly important industries have declined in importance (for example, coal mining, inter-city railroad passenger service). In addition, although the total number of jobs has increased, the nation has faced in recent years a relatively high rate of unemployment resulting from a sluggish economy, competition from foreign nations, and technological changes.

6. *Our Older Citizens.* At the beginning of the century, one of every 25 adults was 65 years of age or older. Today, as a result of advances in medicine, sanitation and living standards, about 26 million Americans, nearly one out of every 10, have reached that age. This group of "senior citizens" presents society with a number of problems. Among them are **(a)** unemployment, **(b)** lack of planned retirement, **(c)** inadequate housing, **(d)** low income, and **(e)** need for medical care.

Medicare. In 1965, Congress passed the *Medicare Act* providing for medical care for the aged under Social Security. Although the program at first was considered "controversial," it has quickly become an accepted part of the nation's Social Security and health facilities because most Americans over 65 cannot afford to pay for adequate medical care. Benefits have already been raised several times to keep up with rising costs.

1. *Provisions of Medicare.* The basic provisions are as follows:

(a) The Basic Plan. Coverage (financed by Social Security) is available to all persons over 65. Each patient is entitled to receive hospitalization for up to 90 days, with the individual paying the first $144 of hospital charges, and after 60 days an additional $36 daily. Other services include nursing care for up to 100 days, with the patient paying $18 daily for the next 80 days; home nursing for up to 100 visits a year after discharge from a hospital or nursing home; and various out-patient tests and diagnostic services.

(b) Other Provisions. **(1)** Patients have a free choice of hospital, doctor and nurse. **(2)** Extended coverage for doctor's fees and other health expenses is available for an additional premium of $8.20 a month (as of 1979). **(3)** The program is financed by an increase in Social Security taxes paid by wage earners and employers. **(4)** Older persons not covered by Social Security are included in this program.

2. *Achievements of Medicare.* The Medicare program has grown rapidly. Approximately 98% of the nation's hospitals and nearly all its physicians are participating. There have been some complaints regarding rising doctor's fees and some evidence of fraudulent billing, but on the whole there is general agreement that Medicare has worked well.

3. *Medicaid.* Under this program, the states have set up *Medicaid* plans to provide medical benefits for various types of relatively low-income families. It applies also to older people (over 65) whose needs for some reason are not met by Medicare. The Federal government matches state payments on a sliding scale for medical and dental care. All of the states have adopted such plans. A great many needy people have benefited, although there has been evidence of need for tighter administration to prevent a minority of unscrupulous practitioners and suppliers from exploiting patients and "ripping off" public funds.

REVIEW TEST (Chapter 22 — Part II)

Select the number preceding the word or expression that best completes each statement or answers each question.

1. At present the population of the United States is closest to (1) 60,000,000 (2) 400,000,000 (3) 150,000,000 (4) 200,000,000

2. The U.S. "population picture" in the 1970s has been marked by (1) stable population (2) declining birth rate (3) fewer "senior citizens" (4) a shorter life span

3. The most densely populated area in the United States is (1) the Southern states (2) the states of the Pacific coast (3) the Western Mountain states (4) the Northeastern states

4. A significant population trend from 1890 to 1920 was (1) a great surge of population from the East to the West (2) a back-to-the-farm movement (3) a decline in urban population (4) continued and rapid growth of cities

5. Compared to colonial times, the proportion of older people in the population of the United States today is (1) much smaller (2) slightly smaller (3) about the same (4) larger

6. All of the following have been recent population movement trends in the United States *except* (1) South to North (2) cities to suburbs (3) West to East (4) Puerto Rico to the United States

7. At present the working force of the nation is between (1) 30–40 million (2) 50–60 million (3) 70–80 million (4) 90–100 million

8. Under the Medicare program (1) Persons 55 years of age and over are entitled to free hospital care. (2) Patients have a free choice of hospital, doctor, or nurse. (3) Financing is provided for by a special 3% tax on employers. (4) Only government employees will benefit.

Essay Questions

1. Describe three important population trends in the United States.

2. Discuss three problems that have resulted from the changing population pattern.

3. Explain why the nation is becoming increasingly concerned about the welfare of its aged population.

4. What have been the achievements of Medicare and Medicaid? What problems have appeared in these programs?

CHAPTER 23

Current Problems of
American Democracy

No nation's problems are ever fully solved. In this chapter we will examine several important problems facing American democracy today. The ability of the country to meet these challenges, and the way in which it handles them, will affect the future of all of us.

Part I — CONSERVING OUR NATURAL RESOURCES

Conservation is the protection and wise use of a country's natural and human resources—its *topsoil,* its *forests,* its *wildlife,* its *minerals,* its *water,* its *grazing lands,* and its *people.* Conservation of our *natural environment* is an increasingly urgent 20th-century challenge.

Tradition of Waste. Because of seemingly inexhaustible natural resources, Americans developed a "tradition of waste" in the 18th and 19th centuries that resulted in needlessly rapid using up of the nation's resources. This same attitude has in the 20th century led to widespread pollution of the air, water and land upon which man depends for life.

1. *Causes of Waste.* The chief causes of the waste of natural resources included: (**a**) the clearing or burning of forests without the replanting of trees, at first by pioneers, and later by lumber companies; (**b**) unscientific methods of farming, such as failure to rotate crops; (**c**) grants of large sections of mineral-rich and timber-rich lands by the government to private companies; (**d**) wasteful mining practices in the case of metals and fuels; (**e**) imperfect industrial processes, such as inefficient coal or other fuel-burning furnaces, or failure to use by products sufficiently; (**f**) failure to develop water power resources to compensate for dwindling coal, oil, and timber supplies; (**g**) careless disposal of waste products, such as the dumping of chemicals and sewage into rivers; and (**h**) in recent years, indiscriminate use of newly discovered insecticides and plant fumigants such as the widespread dusting of crops with DDT.

2. *Results of Waste and Careless Use.* Because of this tradition of waste the United States in the *first half of the 20th century* found that: (**a**) It had changed from a timber-rich to a timber-poor nation. (**b**) Much valuable topsoil was being lost because of erosion. (**c**) "Dust-bowls" developed in regions where grass had been stripped from land that should never have been cultivated in the first place. *More recently,* we have found that: (**d**) Water supplies are not keeping up with new demands. (**e**) Industrial and human wastes, poured into the nation's waterways and atmosphere, are poisoning fish, contaminating drinking water, and polluting the air around large cities. (**f**) The overuse of chemical insecticides (pesticides) is endangering the health of the nation's people and wildlife. (**g**) An energy crisis has resulted from increasing use and dwindling supplies of petroleum and natural gas.

Beginnings of Conservation Movement. Government concern for conserving the nation's resources appeared late in the 19th century.

1. *Reasons.* In the 1880's and 1890's, soil, mineral, and forestry experts observed with alarm that the nation was in danger of exhausting many of its natural resources if it continued to exploit them as wastefully in the future as it had in the past. They urged that positive steps be taken to conserve the country's natural resources.

2. *First Steps.* In the 1890's, Congress took its first actions with regard to protecting the nation's resources.

    (*a*) The *Forest Reserve Act* of 1891 authorized the President to set aside parts of the national domain as reserves for the future. A *Division of Forestry* was created in the Department of Agriculture to develop plans for caring for the nation's forests and for fighting forest fires. Presidents Harrison and Cleveland were the first to set aside reserves (called "national forests") under this act.

    (*b*) The *Carey Act* of 1894 granted Federal lands in arid regions to Western states, on condition that the states reclaim them through irrigation projects. Few states applied for such lands because of the costs involved.

Conservation Movement Under Theodore Roosevelt. Conservation became a nationwide movement in the 20th century, particularly as a result of the leadership of Theodore Roosevelt and, later, Franklin D. Roosevelt. Theodore Roosevelt was the first to get the nation as a whole interested in conservation.

1. *Newlands Act.* At Roosevelt's urging Congress passed the *Newlands Reclamation Act* of 1902, which remedied the weakness of the Carey Act by providing that the proceeds from the sale of Federal lands in Western states could be used for irrigation projects. Many reclamation projects were begun under this law.

2. *Inland Waterways Commission.* In 1907, Roosevelt appointed an *Inland Waterways Commission* to study problems relating to navigation and flood control on the nation's rivers, lakes, and canals.

3. *White House Conference.* In 1908, Roosevelt called the first national Conservation Conference at the White House. Cabinet members, business leaders, conservation experts, and most governors attended. They drew up resolutions calling for active efforts to fight forest fires, improve inland waterways, eliminate waste in mining, and conserve water power facilities. The Conference made conservation a national project.

4. *State Cooperation.* As a result of the recommendations of the Inland Waterways Commission and the Governor's Conference, state conservation commissions were established in 41 states, and Federal-state cooperation in conservation procedures was begun.

5. *National Conservation Commission.* In 1909, Roosevelt established a *National Conservation Commission* with Gifford Pinchot as chairman. This commission was charged with drawing up long range plans for preserving the nation's national resources. It put together an inventory of the nation's resources, plus a list of estimates of their probable duration.

6. *Withdrawal of Land From Public Sale.* With the advice and counsel of Gifford Pinchot, one of the nation's leading conservationists, Roosevelt withdrew from sale, and set aside as national reserves and parks, approximately 235 million acres of Federal lands rich in timber, minerals, and natural wonders.

Conservation Before the New Deal. Other Presidents "between the two Roosevelts" made noteworthy contributions to the cause of conservation.

1. *President Taft.* Taft promoted conservation by persuading Congress to grant greater authority to the President to withdraw public lands from sale. Taft set aside over 60 million acres of coal and timber lands.

2. *President Wilson.* During Woodrow Wilson's Presidency, Congress passed the *Mineral Leasing Act* of 1920, which provided that mineral-bearing public lands could be leased on a long-time royalty basis but not sold outright.

3. *President Hoover.* During the Presidency of Herbert Hoover, Congress authorized the construction of the *Hoover (Boulder) Dam.* When completed in 1936, the dam controlled floods on the Colorado River, produced hydroelectric power, and irrigated a vast area in the West.

Conservation Scandals. In several instances those who were entrusted with safeguarding the nation's resources became involved in scandals.

1. *Ballinger-Pinchot Controversy.* The Ballinger-Pinchot controversy arose during Taft's administration. Pinchot (head of the Forestry Division) and others accused Secretary of Interior Richard Ballinger of favoring private interests by reopening for sale valuable coal, water-power, and forest reserves. Taft supported Ballinger and dismissed Pinchot. However, public sentiment in favor of Pinchot caused Ballinger to resign in order to spare the administration further embarrassment. (Later evidence showed that Ballinger was not guilty of the charges levelled at him.)

2. *Teapot Dome.* In the "Teapot Dome Scandal," which broke during President Harding's administration, evidence was uncovered that the government-owned Teapot Dome and Elk Hills oil reserves, in Wyoming and

California respectively, had been leased by Secretary of the Interior Albert Fall to oil executives Harry Sinclair and Edward Doheny. It was charged that Fall had been given a cash gift by Doheny for granting the lease. Fall resigned, but was fined and sentenced to prison after a trial. (This is the only example in the nation's history of the criminal punishment of a member of the Cabinet.) The Supreme Court ordered the return of the reserves to the government on the ground that the leases had been obtained by fraud.

Conservation Under Franklin D. Roosevelt. Conservation received another important stimulus during the Presidency of Franklin D. Roosevelt.

1. *Civilian Conservation Corps (CCC).* The *Civilian Conservation Corps*, established to relieve unemployment, made valuable contributions to the conservation effort between 1933 and World War II. It built dams, fought plant diseases, replanted forests, and checked forest fires.

2. *National Resources Board.* A *National Resources Board,* appointed by Roosevelt in 1934, made a comprehensive report in 1935 which for the first time showed the close relationship of the country's land, water, and mineral problems. The report made clear the continuing need for additional conservation efforts.

3. *Soil Conservation Service.* As a result of the tragic waste of land that resulted from the dust storms of 1934, which turned large sections of the West into a "dustbowl," Congress in 1935 established the *Soil Conservation Service* as an independent agency. (It later became part of the Department of Agriculture.) In cooperation with state agencies and individual farmers, the Soil Conservation Service helped to check and prevent erosion on many millions of acres of land in the United States.

4. *Tennessee Valley Authority (TVA).* The most dramatic conservation program under the New Deal was the one undertaken by the *Tennessee Valley Authority* in the 1930's (see page 378 for background). The TVA built "multi-purpose" dams (such as the Norris Dam and the Wilson Dam) that checked floods in the Tennessee Valley, improved navigation, and furnished electricity. It taught farmers to conserve their land by farming scientifically, including the widespread use of synthetic fertilizers produced and distributed by TVA. It promoted public health, encouraged low-cost housing, provided recreational facilities, and helped develop local industries. Although there was much discussion about the right of the government to build and operate the TVA, there was no question as to its success in rebuilding and raising the standard of living in an entire region. TVA became an example of area development for the entire world.

5. *Multi-Purpose Dams.* In addition to the TVA, other major multi-purpose dams begun or completed during F. D. Roosevelt's Presidency included the *Grand Coulee Dam* on the Columbia River in Washington, the *Bonneville Dam* on the Columbia River in Oregon, and *Shasta Dam* on the Sacramento River in northern California. As a result of these and other projects completed earlier, more than 30 million acres in 17 western states were being irrigated by 1945.

6. *Other New Deal Conservation Programs.* Other important steps taken under the New Deal included: **(a)** the *Taylor Grazing Act* of 1934, which provided for the regulation of grazing on public lands; **(b)** the *Connally Act* of 1935, which prohibited interstate and foreign shipments of oil in excess of state limitations; and **(c)** the *Flood Control Act* of 1936, which introduced a nationally coordinated policy of flood control.

The Continuing Need for Conservation. Certain developments during and after World War II have kept alive and even intensified the need for continued conservation efforts.   **(1)** Wartime needs drew heavily on our essential mineral resources, and caused government officials to be concerned over the availability of such resources for the future.   **(2)** Persistent floods in many areas of the nation continued to cause concern over the waste of soil, water, and power (as well as lives and property). **(3)** Serious water shortages began to develop throughout the nation because of a sharp rise in water consumption for irrigation, industrial, and drinking purposes.   **(4)** Increasing population and expanded industrial needs have led to shortages of many basic materials, particularly fuels, such as petroleum and natural gas.   **(5)** Since the 1960's, there has been intense and growing concern over *environmental pollution.* The problem has been dramatized for the average citizen by heavy blankets of air pollution over urban centers, waterways that have become all but "dead"—incapable of supporting organisms, and oil spillages that have ruined beaches and killed supporting organisms — and oil spillages that have ruined beaches and killed wildlife.   **(6)** From a long-term point of view, perhaps the most important single factor in coping with the *ecological* (environmental) problem is our rapidly increasing population with proportionately greater demands on a fixed resource base.

Efforts to Preserve Our Environment. To deal with the conservation problem, government agencies have continued programs begun before World War II and have also embarked on new programs. Such projects have received the active encouragement of all recent Presidents.

1. *Government Actions.* The conservation activities of the Federal government, in many instances in cooperation with similar state actions, have in recent years included the following:

> (a) *Flood control* is being tried through watershed management, the dredging and widening of river beds, and the building of huge multi-purpose dams and river-basin developments (for example, the Fort Peck Dam on the Missouri River and the Hell's Canyon Project on the Snake River).

> (b) *Irrigation and reclamation projects* have been established to make arid lands fertile. These are operated, and in many instances built, by the United States *Bureau of Reclamation.*

(c) *Soil Conservation* practices have been promoted by the *Soil Conservation Service* (page 409). Over a million farmers have been taught to apply scientific conservation practices to their land. These include: *contour plowing,* or plowing across the side of a hill or slope instead of up or down; *strip cropping,* or raising different crops in alternating strips; *terracing,* or the building of ridges or embankments of soil across sloping fields to check the flow of water; and *land retirement,* or the planting of grass and trees on worn-out or badly eroded land.

(d) *Forest conservation* has been continued through creation of additional National Forests and Parks; and through scientific management of forests by the United States Forest Service.

(e) *Controlled leasing and sale of Federal lands* that contain timber water, minerals, and grazing land, has been conducted under the *Bureau of Land Management* in the Department of the Interior.

(f) *International cooperation* to improve navigation and develop power facilities became a reality (after 25 years of opposition by some railroad and private power interests, fearing ruinous competition), when the *St. Lawrence Seaway* was completed in 1959. The Seaway, which cost over a billion dollars, was jointly constructed by the United States and Canada. It has made it possible for ocean-going vessels to sail from the Atlantic Ocean into the Great Lakes, through a series of newly constructed locks. Ships using the Seaway pay tolls to defray the construction costs. Most of the power produced by power plants on the American side is sold by New York State to private utility companies and industrial plants.

(g) *Pollution.* Federal, state and local governments have begun to adopt measures aimed at eliminating or correcting practices that have polluted our air, water, and land. Such measures include: more careful waste disposal; banning or strict control of the use of certain pesticides; and mandatory use of special devices to control the wastes emitted from automobile exhausts, industrial plants, and furnaces. (The automobile industry is under government order to develop a "pollution-free" engine by 1978.) The *Environmental Protection Agency* (EPA) was set up by the Federal government in 1970 to work with and set standards for state and local governments, as well as with private business, in order to "abate and control" pollution of air and water and to deal with problems involving pesticides, solid wastes, radiation, and noise. The *(Federal) Resource Recovery Act* of 1970 emphasizes the recycling of solid wastes, such as metals. Federal-state programs have been developed to further the cleaning up of our waterways; particular attention is now being given to prevention of thermal pollution (injuriously high temperatures) and to the banning of the dumping of substances known to be health hazards, such as asbestos fibers.

2. *Non-Governmental Actions.* Public pressure, as well as mounting concern by scientific groups, industry, and private organizations specifically concerned with the environment, have led to expanded efforts on a non-governmental level to fight pollution and promote conservation.

(a) Much has been done to promote scientific farming, so that the soil can be conserved and more food raised on less land.

(b) To compensate for shortages (actual or potential) of various raw materials there has been increasing use of synthetics. New energy sources, especially atomic power plants, are being used. This will both conserve fossil fuels and prevent air pollution. (However, use of atomic energy involves pollution problems of its own.)

(c) Planned *reforestation* is being undertaken by leading lumber companies. This involves restricted cutting and planting of young trees to replace those cut down.

(d) Science, industry, and government have been cooperating to develop fuller utilization of the mineral and food resources of the sea.

Further Needs in Environmental Protection. In spite of the steps already taken we are continuing to waste our resources and foul our environment in alarming fashion. National concern over pollution of our environment has mounted steadily to almost "crusade" proportions.

1. *Forests.*   While it is believed that present supplies of timber are sufficient to meet immediate needs, it is estimated that more than twice as much will be needed to meet the estimated United States population of 300 million in the year 2000. Experts have urged extensive reforestation and stepped-up campaigns against forest fires.

2. *Water.*   We are now being warned that there may be a disastrous shortage of water by 1985 because of our growing population, increased industrial needs, and accelerating pollution of streams, rivers, lakes, and oceans. Experts are recommending that all levels of government undertake programs that will: (**a**) create water storage basins for the future by constructing more dams and reservoirs; (**b**) end pollution of bodies of water by eliminating "dumping" of untreated wastes, including detergents and chemicals; (**c**) ban industrial practices, such as the discharge of heated water, which along with water pollutants, has begun to disrupt the "balance of life" in our streams and lakes; (**d**) construct giant desalination plants for large-scale purification of salt water (tried in few places, but as yet too costly for practical use).

3. *Air.*   There is greater recognition of the urgency of immediate steps to cut down the fouling of our atmosphere with poisonous fumes from autos, industrial plants, domestic furnaces, and improper incineration of garbage. These steps include: requirement of air-purification devices on exhausts and chimneys; bans on the use of high-sulfur fuel oils; more careful incineration of garbage; and restrictions on the burning of certain chemicals by industry near population centers.

4. *Soil.*   In addition to continued erosion control and scientific farming, there is a great need to deal with the problem of excessive application of nitrogenous fertilizers that are poisoning our soil, as well as chemical pesticides like DDT that are threatening to destroy plants, insects and other elements necessary in the life-cycle.

5. *National Parks and Wildlife Preserves.* There has been growing recognition of the need to set aside areas where Americans can enjoy nature in its unspoiled state, and where certain rare species of animals can be preserved. Starting with Yellowstone National Park in 1872, the U.S. government has developed a magnificent system of National Parks and of other recreational areas, such as Wildlife Preserves. Many states have also set up systems of state parks.

6. *River and Power Development.* There has been continued interest in building additional regional river-basin projects, comparable to TVA, to provide an integrated power-development and flood-control program.

7. *The Energy Problem.* A world-wide "energy crisis" has developed in recent years, caused by a sharp rise in population, expanded industrialization, demands for higher living standards, and depletion of energy resources. In the United States, which is the world's largest user of energy, the "crisis" has been marked by increased dependence on foreign sources of supply. By 1975, about 18% of all our energy materials (particularly petroleum) were being imported, and the figure was rising yearly. Production of petroleum and natural gas in the United States has been decreasing at an annual rate of about 8%. Output of coal (our most abundant energy resource) has been increasing, but not sufficiently to meet our needs.

Among the steps proposed and (in some cases) adopted to help solve our energy problems are the following: **(a)** development of more efficient fuel-burning engines; **(b)** controlling the use of energy through rationing and economy measures, such as the use of public transportation in place of private automobiles; **(c)** increased coal production; **(d)** more extensive drilling for oil, including offshore deposits; **(e)** extraction of oil from deposits of shale rock; **(f)** more production of nuclear power; **(g)** intensive efforts to develop new sources of power including solar energy (direct utilization of the heat of the sun), use of geothermal energy (from the interior of the earth), and the harnessing of tidal power (the rise and fall of the ocean tides).

Major problems are connected with the development of new energy sources. Huge investments may be required, and the cost of the energy thus provided is likely to be very high. This might apply, for example, to oil derived from shale. Proposals for greatly expanding the number of nuclear power plants have been widely attacked on the grounds that there is an unacceptable chance of catastrophic accidents, and also that no safe method has been developed to dispose of radioactive wastes. Environmentalists oppose *strip-mining* of coal, a technique which involves removing surface layers of soil to get at the coal deposits underneath. Efforts to pass a tough Federal law requiring coal operators to restore land which has been "stripped" in this way have not yet been successful.

REVIEW TEST (Chapter 23 — Part I)

Select the number preceding the word or expression that best completes each statement or answers each question.

1. An early 20th century champion of environmental conservation was: (1) Grover Cleveland (2) Richard Ballinger (3) Harry Truman (4) Theodore Roosevelt

2. Gifford Pinchot was a pioneer in (1) nuclear fission (2) solar energy development (3) forest conservation (4) extraction of oil from shale

3. Which of the following played a role in drawing national attention to the need for conservation? (1) Conference of Governors, 1908 (2) Hague Conference, 1907 (3) Potsdam Conference, 1945 (4) Munich Conference, 1938

4. The TVA has (1) eliminated private ownership of public utilities (2) depopulated several states (3) discouraged private enterprise (4) raised living standards

5. The conservation programs of both Theodore Roosevelt and Franklin D. Roosevelt provided for (1) building a St. Lawrence Seaway (2) giving subsidies for soil conservation (3) reclamation and flood control (4) protection of oil resources

6. Land reclamation through irrigation was provided by the (1) Newlands Act (2) Northwest Ordinance (3) Interstate Commerce Act (4) Homestead Act

7. A person discussing Hell's Canyon, and Grand Coulee would probably be concerned with (1) contour plowing (2) recycling of waste (3) forest conservation (4) river-basin development

8. A conservation problem not considered serious until fairly recently is (1) erosion (2) environmental pollution (3) flood control (4) forest fires

Indicate whether each of the following statements is true or false. If the statement is false, replace the word or phrase in **boldface type** *with one which will make it correct.*

1. Federal irrigation programs are supervised by the **Bureau of Reclamation.**

2. The Teapot Dome scandal was embarrassing to **President Kennedy.**

3. Desalination plants are associated with **coal** conservation.

4. Our oldest national park is **Grand Canyon.**

5. Discharging heated liquids into rivers and streams results in **thermal pollution.**

Essay Questions

1. Explain fully President Lyndon Johnson's statement, "Conservation's concern is not only for man's enjoyment, but also for man's survival"

2. Describe *five* programs undertaken by the Federal government in the 20th century to overcome the "tradition of waste" established in previous centuries.

3. Show how *two* Presidents have advanced the cause of conservation.

4. Indicate two problems involving protection of the environment that face the United States today. State briefly a possible solution for one of these problems.

The most important natural resource of a nation is its people. In the past half century we have become more aware of the need to conserve the well-being and happiness of the nation's people as a source of national strength. This section deals with three important problems in the area of human conservation, namely, urban living, housing, and poverty.

Problems of Our Cities. The growth of huge urban population centers and the ever-increasing difficulties of living in these cities have presented the United States with some of its most serious contemporary social problems.

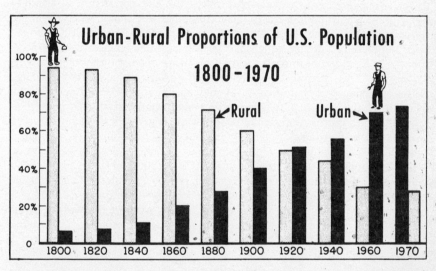

Urban-Rural Proportions of U.S. Population 1800-1970

This graph shows the steady shift of the United States population from rural areas to urban areas. Note that the urban-rural proportion virtually reversed itself in the period from 1880 to 1970. By 1980, the urban population reached 80% of the total.

1. *Cities in the 19th and Early 20th Centuries.* Since the Civil War, the proportion of the nation's population living in cities has increased greatly. As cities grew in numbers and in size in the 19th and early 20th centuries, they faced many difficult problems, such as providing adequate supplies of food, water, and other necessities; police and fire protection; safeguarding of health; education of vast numbers of children and young people; and local transportation. Steps taken to meet these challenges included: **(a)** adequate water-supply systems, with special provisions for purification; **(b)** use of railroads (and later trucks) to bring in supplies;

(c) larger and more efficient police and fire-fighting organizations; (d) public-health programs; (e) greatly expanded educational systems; and (f) use of trolleys, subways, and buses to provide rapid transport within the city.

As squalid and unhealthful slums developed in our great cities, social reformers began to demand that the city governments take corrective action. One of the most influential of these reformers was the New York City journalist JACOB RIIS, author of *How the Other Half Lives*. As a result of such agitation, city and state governments passed housing laws setting minimum standards for ventilation, fire protection, sanitary facilities, etc. Nevertheless, virtually every city continued to have huge areas of substandard housing. Perhaps the leading figure in combating social evils in American cities during the late 19th century was JANE ADDAMS, who established the nation's first settlement house in Chicago (1889).

2. *Present-day Problems of Cities.* In recent decades the problems of urban living have grown even more massive. The population of the nation's great "metropolitan areas" has continued to expand. The distribution of population, however, has changed markedly. After World War II, large numbers of families which had been living in the cities moved to the suburbs in the hope of finding improved housing and generally better living conditions. This "surburban explosion" has brought about a crisis in transportation because of the necessity of moving large numbers of people into and out of the central city every day. Also, many of the families that moved to the suburbs represented people with relatively high incomes, good educational background, and lively interest in civic affairs. At the same time, the cities received a population influx consisting largely of Negroes from the South and other minority groups, such as Puerto Ricans in New York City. These were generally people of low educational background and of limited earning capacity, because of lack of training and opportunity. These newcomers to the large cities soon found themselves living in "ghettoes" that rapidly deteriorated into blighted slum areas. The situation of *"de facto* segregation" in housing led to similar segregation in schools.

The costs of welfare, crime control, and other public services in these depressed neighborhoods have put a severe financial strain on our large cities. American cities today are still struggling with the multiple problems of decaying "downtown" neighborhoods, inadequate transportation, segregation in housing and education, and financial needs that tend to outrun revenues.

3. *Attempts to Meet City Problems.* Recently, the Federal and state governments have been giving greater attention to the hard-pressed cities where so large a proportion of Americans now live. In 1965, a *Department of Housing and Urban Development* was set up to coordinate Federal programs that are designed to give help to the cities. Among the measures already initiated to improve living conditions in our large cities are the following: (a) With Federal and state aid, *urban-renewal* and *model cities* programs have been undertaken to tear down slum dwellings and replace them with decent, modern housing and other needed facilities. **(b)** Increasingly large sums are being spent on development of highways, more adequate rapid transit systems, and modernized railroads for carrying commuters to and from the suburbs each day. **(c)** Strenuous efforts are being made to improve educational systems by such measures as smaller classes, higher teacher salaries, improved learning materials and instructional methods, and racial integration. Higher expenditures are required for all these purposes. **(d)** Some cities have also been developing effective programs for control of air and water pollution.

The urgent need for carrying out these and related programs on a truly national scale is reflected in the creation of a top-level *Council for Urban Affairs* by President Nixon, soon after taking office. The Council coordinates the activities of the three Cabinet departments directly concerned with cities and their needs—Health, Education and Welfare; Housing and Urban Development; and Transportation.

The Housing Problem. National population growth, regional population shifts, the doubling of the urban population within the past three decades, a rising standard of living, and continued pockets of poverty have in the past few decades made housing a pressing national concern.

1. *Nature of the Problem.* It is estimated that one out of every five Americans is "ill-housed." Substandard or inadequate housing generally means living quarters that are overcrowded, lacking proper sanitary facilities, and in poor physical condition. With well over two-thirds of the nation's population living in urban communities, the problem is most severe in the "blighted" slum areas of the nation's cities. It also exists in farm areas and small towns, where over 3 million families are inadequately housed. Both urban and rural slum areas have been a threat to the national welfare, since they have high rates of crime and disease.

2. *A National Challenge.* Although private housing developers have in recent decades produced more housing than ever before, they have been unable, even with mass-produced homes at lowered prices, to meet the national need for adequate housing, particularly for low- and middle-income groups. Unfortunately, even the growing national low-cost public housing program, financed by Federal, state, local, and private agencies, has been hampered by the rising cost of construction and credit.

3. *Recent Public Housing Programs.* Beginning with the passage of the *National Housing Act* in 1934, the Federal government, in cooperation with state and local governments, has played a very active role in the field of housing. Since World War II, government housing efforts and programs have been expanded considerably. Today, the national government has a wide range of programs for families with low or moderate incomes, coordinated by the *Housing and Home Finance Agency*.

    (a) Low-Cost Housing. The Federal government has continued to provide financial assistance to local agencies that build public housing

developments for low-income families. At present Federal agencies provide about 90% of the cost of such projects, and state and local agencies the remainder. The *Housing and Urban Development Act* of 1968 provided rental subsidies for low-income families, to enable them to obtain better housing. The *Housing and Community Development Act* of 1974 broadened this rental assistance program, making it available to families in the "moderate" income range.

(b) Housing Loans. Through *FHA (Federal Housing Authority),* the Housing and Home Finance Agency guarantees loans for constructing and improving homes. The loans are actually made by private sources, and the construction is done by private builders. Through the *Veterans Administration (VA),* FHA guarantees home loans for veterans.

(c) Cooperative Housing. By 1976, about 4 million middle-income Americans were living in apartments purchased in *cooperative* or *condominium* housing developments. Many of these developments were made possible by state subsidies to private construction firms under such laws as the *Mitchell-Lama Act* of New York State.

4. *Slum Clearance and Urban Redevelopment.* One of the major tasks undertaken in recent years by Federal, state, and local agencies, cooperating with private interests has been the tearing down and rebuilding of "blighted" (deteriorated) areas and slum sections throughout the nation.

(a) Urban Renewal. In the 1950s and 1960s, over 800 cities and communities demolished buildings in deteriorated areas and replaced them with *urban renewal* housing and "civic improvement" programs and developments. The funds came largely from government loans and grants.

(b) Model Cities. Urban renewal came to be strongly criticized because some rebuilt areas deteriorated rapidly into "subsidized slums" and in addition resulted in the uprooting of thousands of families from established neighborhoods. To counteract these weaknesses, the government in 1967 initiated *Model Cities* program, under which about 150 localities were given funds to mount a coordinated attack on urban problems in their communities, including housing, health, transportation, education and employment.

(c) Under charges of waste and unduly high costs, the Model Cities program was phased out by 1973. Since then, the Federal government has undertaken a less costly program of upgrading both public and private housing to help stop the deterioration of neighborhoods.

Poverty. Although the United States is the richest nation in the world millions of Americans are still living in poverty.

1. *Persistence of Poverty in United States.* Families are considered to be living in poverty when their income is too small to provide basic needs of food, shelter, and clothing, according to American standards. Most of these poor have to depend on some form of outside assistance to get along. Poverty was declared a national problem in the 1930's by President F. D. Roosevelt. Forty years later, the problem is still with us.

(a) *Extent of Poverty.* According to recent estimates, about 11.3% of all Americans, or roughly 24 million persons, are poor — that is, are living on incomes of less than $5500 (for a family of four). This figure is considered the absolute minimum for providing the essentials of life according to American standards.

(b) *Poverty-stricken Groups.* Our poor people are made up primarily of the following groups: (1) the aged poor, (2) unskilled workers, (3) the unemployed, (4) members of various racial and ethnic minorities, as detailed below.

(c) *Minorities and Poverty.* Poverty and unemployment are highest among certain minority groups. About 28% of all black families now have poverty-level incomes. The average (American) Indian family living on a reservation — a category comprising about a half million persons — earn less than $4000 a year. Puerto Ricans, Mexican-Americans (Chicanos), and other minorities are also close to the bottom of the economic scale. (Of course, some members of all such groups are prosperous, and even wealthy.)

2. *Causes of Poverty in the United States.* The following are considered to be the main causes of poverty in the United States.

(a) *Lack of Education and Training.* More than half of the poor have family heads with less than an 8th-grade education and without specialized vocational training.

(b) *Economically Depressed Areas.* In some areas, plants or industries have shut down, contracted their activities, or moved to other communities, leaving hundreds of thousands of unemployed and/or poverty-stricken behind. The worst of such "pockets of poverty" is *Appalachia,* a name given to the mountainous region, cutting across ten states from Pennsylvania to Alabama, where over a quarter of a million coal miners became unemployed.

(c) *Poor Health.* Poor health contributes to much of our poverty. Many men and women cannot hold down regular jobs because of inability to meet minimal physical standards.

(d) *Racial Discrimination.* Unfair discrimination by some employers, labor unions, and society generally has done much to keep black Americans and other minorities out of the more desirable jobs. Earnings of blacks in the United States are on the average only 70% of those of whites. The rate of unemployment for blacks is much higher than that for whites.

(e) *Unfavorable Economic Conditions.* Many people become unemployed and may sink into poverty as a result of adverse economic conditions. A low level of economic activity with rising unemployment may affect a region (as indicated above), an industry (for example, aerospace when government expenditures were cut in the 1970s), or even the entire nation, as in a severe recession or depression. The sharp economic turndown of the early and mid-1970s brought unemployment and distress to millions of Americans.

3. *The Cycle of Poverty.* The tragedy of poverty is that the poverty-stricken have become increasingly unable to break out of their impoverishment. Because they are ill-educated and unskilled, they cannot get jobs. Those who do get jobs receive low wages. They are the first to be fired and the last to be hired. Many become lonely, isolated, and even hostile. Many stop trying to earn a living because it all seems so hopeless. Their children, brought up under such conditions, start life with a crushing handicap.

4. *Steps Taken to Help the Poor.* In recent years, the nation's poor have been helped in a variety of ways.

(a) Federal, state, and local agencies are spending over $10 billion a year in direct relief payments *(income-maintenance program).*

(b) The Federal government provides large quantities of surplus foods.

(c) State and local communities have, with Federal assistance, established job-training programs for unemployed workers.

(d) Slum clearance and community rebuilding programs have been undertaken on a large scale.

(e) Special help has been given to children of poor families (free lunches, compensatory educational programs, etc.).

5. *The "War on Poverty."* Elimination of poverty has been a major national goal since the early 1960's.

(a) *Kennedy Administration.* Anti-poverty programs of the Kennedy administration included economic redevelopment of depressed regions *(Area Redevelopment Act)* and training programs to give marketable skills to the unemployed.

(b) *Johnson Administration.* Under the leadership of President Johnson a "War on Poverty" was launched. About 6.5 billion dollars was spent from 1965 to 1969 on a variety of programs, mostly administered by the *Office of Economic Opportunity* (OEO). **(1)** A *Job Corps* provided over 100 job-training centers for unemployed young people. **(2)** The *Neighborhood Youth Corps* provided jobs for boys and girls of high school age, to supplement family incomes. **(3)** *"Operation Head Start"* offered pre-kindergarten schooling for children from underprivileged homes. **(4)** VISTA *("Volunteers in Service to America")* was a so-called "domestic Peace Corps" that placed about 5000 volunteer workers in slums and other areas in need of such help. **(5)** *Community Action Programs* enabled local people to organize neighborhood facilities to provide job counseling, as well as legal, health, and other services for the poor. **(6)** Under *regional development programs,* the Federal government allotted funds to rebuild the economic life of depressed regions, such as Appalachia.

(c) *Nixon Administration.* Under President Nixon, most of the anti-poverty agencies set up by Johnson were dismantled, and their functions transferred to other bodies, such as HEW. Many programs considered wasteful or ineffective were simply eliminated. The *food stamp program,* however, was expanded. (Under this program, families qualifying for aid may purchase special food stamps at prices below their face value and use them like money to buy food.) The Nixon administration placed greater emphasis on voluntary action at community levels to deal with poverty problems.

(d) Like Nixon, President Ford considered much of the antipoverty program to be ineffective, and he sought to spend less on such activities, while returning greater responsibilities to state and local agencies. In 1975, Ford approved a bill creating a *Community Action Program* (as a replacement for the old Office of Economic Opportunity). The new program made available Federal grants and contracts to communities that instituted antipoverty measures meeting government standards. The law continued some funding for the *Head Start Program* for children from poor families, and also introduced a new pilot program exploring ways to help American Indians become economically and socially self-sufficient. A Ford proposal to raise the cost of food stamps was rejected by Congress.

(e) Evaluation. The antipoverty measures adopted since the early 1960s have cost vast sums of money, but it is undeniable that poverty on a large scale persists. Does this mean that the effort to eliminate poverty is hopeless and should be abandoned? Or does it suggest that we must continue, at great cost, to look for more effective ways to help the less fortunate members of our democratic society?

REVIEW TEST (Chapter 23 — Part II)

Select the number preceding the word or expression that best completes each statement or answers each question.

1. For what reason has the Federal government sponsored programs of public housing? (1) State housing programs do not exist. (2) There has been a surplus in the treasury. (3) There has been a growing need to provide adequate housing for low-income groups. (4) Private capital has not been used for housing.

2. Which of the following shows that poverty has not been eliminated in this country: (1) the soaring inflation of the 1970's (2) the nation's "welfare" program (3) the continued housing shortage (4) mismanagement of some antipoverty programs

3. Which of the statements about poverty in the United States is most accurate? (1) It does not exist in the North and East. (2) It affects nearly 30 million persons. (3) It is primarily a rural problem. (4) It is being wiped out rapidly by joint Federal-state action.

4. All of the following measures have been intended to help reduce poverty in the United States *except* (1) area redevelopment (2) reciprocal trade agreements (3) job training programs (4) direct financial assistance to family heads

5. "Appalachia" has in recent years been a national symbol of (1) integration in education (2) model housing for the aged (3) regional poverty (4) urban renewal

Essay Questions

1. Adequate housing is still a serious national problem. (a) Give two reasons that explain why the nation still suffers from inadequate housing. (b) Explain two steps taken in the past 10 years to help solve the housing problem by each of the following: the Federal government; the states or localities; private builders. (c) Explain why there is a debate over the role of the Federal government in public housing.

2. Explain: (a) *three* major causes of poverty in the United States (b) *three* recent steps taken to help eliminate poverty by Federal or local governments (c) *two* reasons for supporting or opposing these steps.

Part III — THE BLACK CIVIL RIGHTS MOVEMENT

As a result of the recent Civil Rights Movement of our time, black Americans have become increasingly "visible" in American life. Nevertheless, for most of our history, the Negro has been an "invisible man." Relatively few white Americans have been adequately aware of the fact that Afro-Americans, like other minorities, have helped build the nation, fight its wars, and contribute to its greatness and culture.

Achievement of Black Americans. Throughout our nation's history individual black Americans have made important contributions to national development. The names of some of these distinguished Americans are listed below. Some are well-known and others rarely mentioned. They are representative of a much larger number of individuals, whose names cannot be listed because of space limitations.

DR. CHARLES DREW was largely responsible for the development of the use of blood plasma in transfusions; DR. DANIEL HALE WILLIAMS performed the first successful heart operation; JAMES BECKWORTH discovered the pass through the Sierra Nevada Mountains that now bears his name; ELIJAH McCOY, 19th-century inventor, held more than 75 patents for mechanical devices; MARY McLEOD BETHUNE was a distinguished educator and an adviser to President Franklin D. Roosevelt; EDWARD BROOKE of Massachusetts is the first black U.S. Senator since Reconstruction, and THURGOOD MARSHALL is the first black Supreme Court Justice; ADAM CLAYTON POWELL represented a New York City district in Congress for over twenty years; ROBERT WEAVER was America's first black Cabinet member (Housing and Urban Development, in the Lyndon Johnson administration); SHIRLEY CHISHOLM became the first Negro woman elected to Congress and the first woman to run for the Presidency; CARL STOKES, RICHARD HATCHER, CHARLES EVERS, and THOMAS BRADLEY were among the first black Americans to become mayors of American cities.

JACKIE ROBINSON broke the "color line" in the big league baseball, making it possible for hundreds of other blacks to rise to positions of preeminence in the field of professional athletics. Among the vast number of outstanding black athletes are JOE LOUIS (boxing), WILT CHAMBERLAIN (basketball), WILLIE MAYS (baseball), JIM BROWN (football), JESSE OWENS (track), and ARTHUR ASHE (tennis).

A. PHILIP RANDOLPH became a national labor leader; IRA ALDRIDGE was a world-famous Shakespearean actor of the 19th century; ALAIN LOCKE interpreted the Negro "cultural renaissance" of the 1920's; DR. RALPH BUNCHE won the Nobel Peace Prize; CARL ROWAN was U.S. ambassador to Finland; GARRETT MORGAN was responsible for the invention of the traffic light; BENJAMIN BANNEKER was a many-sided man who made the first clock in America and helped design the city of Washington, D.C.; GWENDOLYN BROOKS was awarded the Pulitzer Prize for poetry; GEORGE WASHINGTON CARVER pioneered in developing industrial uses for the peanut; BOOKER T. WASHINGTON fought to upgrade Negro opportunities through vocational education at the end of the 19th century; WILLIAM E. B. DuBois urged militant action to end discrimination against blacks at the beginning of the 20th century; MARCUS GARVEY was an early 20th-century leader of a "Back to Africa" Movement.

Other eminent representatives of the Negro soul and intellect are included in the following listing: *Writers:* JAMES WELDON JOHNSON, RALPH ELLISON, JAMES BALDWIN; *Dramatists:* LORRAINE HANSBERRY, IMAMU AMIRI BARAKA (LEROI JONES); *Poets:* LANGSTON HUGHES, PAUL LAWRENCE DUNBAR, COUNTEE CULLEN; *Concert Artists, Musicians, and Performers:* MARIAN ANDERSON, LEONTYNE PRICE, LOUIS ARMSTRONG, DUKE ELLINGTON, SAMMY DAVIS, HARRY BELAFONTE; *Painters and Sculptors:* HENRY TANNER, AARON DOUGLASS, JACOB LAWRENCE, RICHARD BARTHE; *Actors:* SIDNEY POITIER, ETHEL WATERS.

The Continuing Problem of Discrimination. A major reason for lack of appreciation of Negro achievements and contributions to the mainstream of American life has been prejudice and discrimination. This continued long after the slaves were freed, and in the second half of the 20th century produced a "Negro Civil Rights Movement" that is affecting our lives today. The causes, nature, and results of this movement are traced below.

Discrimination Against Blacks After the Civil War. When Reconstruction ended and Federal troops were withdrawn, Southern states attempted to defeat the purpose of the Thirteenth, Fourteenth, and Fifteenth Amendments by imposing upon the Negroes political, social, and economic restrictions not specifically forbidden by the Constitution (see page 263). Black Americans also faced discrimination in the North and West, often in more subtle forms.

1. *"Jim Crow" in the South.* The pattern of discrimination in the South came to be known as "Jim Crow." Jim Crow laws required literacy tests (directly primarily against Negroes), poll tax payments, and property ownership for voting. In addition, blacks were sent to separate schools and compelled to ride in restricted sections of trolley cars, buses, and trains. They were discriminated against in hotels, places of amusement, restaurants, and waiting rooms of bus and railroad terminals. Such laws were upheld by the Supreme Court in the case of *Plessy v. Ferguson* (1896) on the ground that separation of the races was not unconstitutional so long as "separate but equal" facilities were provided for Negroes. In point of fact, however, the "separate" facilities available for blacks were often decidedly "unequal." By the end of the century, a large proportion of all blacks were born and raised in isolated Southern communities; and they lived and died in a state of inequality.

2. *Other Types of Discrimination.* Negroes were also limited in other ways. "White supremacy" organizations like the Ku Klux Klan continued to terrorize them. Court trials for blacks were often unfair. Many lynchings took place. Both in agriculture and in industry, Negroes were systematically limited, for the most part, to the hardest and poorest paying jobs. At first, most Negroes were sharecroppers, tenant farmers, or farm laborers. Many secured employment in cities as domestics or hotel, restaurant, and railroad employees. Others became unskilled workers in factories.

3. *Discrimination Outside the South.* Although the problem was most severe in the South, where most Negroes continued to live, discrimination also occurred in other sections of the nation. Even before the Civil War, the half-million Negroes of the North were subject to various forms of discrimination and segregation. This pattern continued into the 20th century. The problem became acute after World War I. During and after that war, Negroes began to migrate to the Northern cities in increasing numbers because of better job opportunities. Resentment over Negro competition for jobs led to race riots in Chicago, Tulsa, Detroit, and other cities. In addition, and despite the fact that they enjoyed greater political and legal rights than in the South, Negroes in the North were subject to discrimination in housing, employment, and social life (de facto segregation). They were forced to live in slum areas and to pay high rents. They received low wages. They were "last to be hired, first to be fired."

Action to Protect Negro Civil Rights During and After World War II. During and after World War II the Federal government took important first steps to extend and protect the civil rights of black Americans.

1. *Federal Action Against Employment Discrimination.* During World War II, a *Fair Employment Practices Committee (FEPC)* was established to enforce an executive order by President Franklin Roosevelt, banning job discrimination in plants working on Federal war contracts. Since the war, the ban has been extended to cover all work for the government.

2. *"To Secure These Rights."* Under Presidents F. D. Roosevelt and Harry Truman, important moves were initiated to end the segregation of Negroes in the military services. In addition, a committee appointed by President Truman made a comprehensive study of the problem of civil rights of minorities. Its report, *"To Secure These Rights"* (1947), showed that many minorities in the United States, including Negroes, Jews, Catholics, Orientals, and others, were still suffering from discrimination.

3. *Supreme Court Action.* Beginning in 1935, the Supreme Court issued a series of orders to the various states practicing segregation to open their graduate and professional schools to black citizens, unless they could provide separate facilities for blacks that were fully equal to those available to whites. Since it was usually too costly or impractical to provide such "separate but equal" facilities, a small but growing number of Negroes were accepted into institutions of higher learning. In 1944, the Supreme Court declared it unconstitutional to bar citizens from voting in primary elections because of race (*Smith v. Allwright*). In 1948 it declared "restrictive covenants" in real estate agreements to be unconstitutional and therefore unenforceable, thus cracking a main means of segregated housing (*Shelley v. Kraemer*). In 1954, in the *Brown v. Board of Education* decision, the Court outlawed segregation in public education. (See below.)

Segregation in Education Declared Unconstitutional. In 1954, the Supreme Court issued a momentous decision, declaring unconstitutional the principle of segregation in public schools, on the ground that it denied black Americans the equal protection of the laws guaranteed by the Fourteenth Amendment (*Brown v. Board of Education of Topeka*). The decision reversed the "separate but equal" doctrine established in *Plessy v.*

Ferguson. In 1955, the Court called for desegregating the schools "with all deliberate speed." Progress in desegregation of education has been relatively slow. In 1974, only 44% of Southern schools were integrated, and 70% of the black students were still attending all-black schools. Nevertheless, the decision proved to be a turning point in the history of the Black Civil Rights Movement in the United States.

Progress of the Black Civil Rights Movement. In the 1960's the frustration and impatience of blacks in America with the slowness of progress and reform expressed itself in a nationwide crusade for greater rights. This has sometimes been called the "Black Revolution of Our Times."

1. *Early 1960's.* In the early 1960's, with the aim of speeding up the granting of rights hitherto denied them, large numbers of blacks took part in many forms of protest across the nation, mainly non-violent. Such actions included sit-ins, picket lines, and boycotts — at segregated lunch counters, bus depots, beaches, churches, schools, housing projects, and elsewhere. Many willingly went to jail to dramatize their protest. In 1963, police brutality against Negro demonstrators in Birmingham, Alabama led to riots and focused world as well as national attention on the problem. Later in the same year (1963) the "Revolution" picked up new momentum, as widespread demonstrations were climaxed by a massive, peaceful, well-organized *Freedom March* of 200,000 blacks and whites on Washington, D.C., with the goals of "jobs and freedom."

2. *Late 1960's.* In the mid and late 1960's, the Black Civil Rights Movement took a more violent turn. Pent-up dissatisfaction in the "black ghettoes" in many of the nation's cities exploded into rioting, looting, arson, and clashes with the police. Acting independently in many cases, and jointly with whites in others, dissatisfied blacks also called for community control of education, meaningful desegregation, and school decentralization in large cities. This was accompanied by demands for black studies programs in high schools and colleges and for expanded admission of black students into colleges and universities. Demonstrations and occupations of school buildings dramatically caught the attention of the nation and resulted in some important changes.

3. *The 1970's.* The 1970's have seen a change in the nature of the Black Civil Rights Movement. The major goals continue to be more and better jobs, improved housing, greater educational opportunity, and more participation in political and economic decision-making. However, the movement is no longer unified and there has been a decline in "militancy" and in the influence of "black power" extremists. Instead of militant action many black leaders have been going into politics in increasing numbers, convinced that this is now the best way to achieve their goals. Others, like JESSE JACKSON, are concentrating on inducing white businesses to hire more blacks, and on getting blacks to patronize black-owned enterprises. There is also a growing sense of community in ghetto neighborhoods and an increase in self-help programs.

4. *Reasons for the Changed Nature of the Black Civil Rights Movement.* Major reasons for the changed nature of the Black Civil Rights Movement in the 1970's include the following: **(a)** The deaths of Dr. Martin Luther King, President John Kennedy, and Senator Robert Kennedy removed highly effective national spokesmen for the black cause. Most observers agree that the Nixon administration has been less active than its predecessors in sponsoring political, economic, and social action to increase the rights of blacks. **(b)** Black leadership on a national scale seems to have given way to local leadership. Of the many groups working for black progress in the 1960's, only the National Association for the Advancement of Colored People and the National Urban League remain highly influential. (See below.) **(c)** Growing numbers of blacks have become "middle class" and are more satisfied with their economic condition and less willing to engage in demonstrations and other forms of active protest. **(d)** Many blacks in urban ghettoes have been disillusioned by the fact that the civil rights victories and campaigns of the 1960's did not end discrimination or poverty. They are less inclined today to engage in organizational activities. **(e)** The many gains of blacks in the 1960's in education, upward economic movement, politics, and self-image have taken some of the "fighting edge" off the civil rights movement **(f)** The movement also suffered from the violence that accompanied the protests of the late 1960's, a fact that led to growing distrust and strained relationships between whites and blacks who had worked together in the early stages of the movement. Black leaders accused white sympathizers of "running out" on black problems before they were solved. Whites, for their part, found themselves increasingly excluded from the movement and became somewhat disillusioned or frightened by the "anger" of the newly militant black community. **(g)** Finally, there has been growing resistance to forced "integration." Attempts to break the pattern of segregation by busing school children or building low-income housing in white neighborhoods and suburbs have run into angry and sometimes violent opposition on the part of whites.

Leadership in the Negro Civil Rights Movement. Leadership in the Black Civil Rights Movement, particularly in the 1960's, was centered in the organizations and individuals noted below.

1. *Organizations.* The *National Association for the Advancement of Colored People* (NAACP) concentrated on winning legal rights; the *National Urban League* (NUL) stressed job opportunities; the *Congress of Racial Equality* (CORE) and the *Student Non-Violent Coordinating Commitee* (SNCC) prompted protest actions; and the *Southern Christian Leadership Conference* (SCLC) emphasized non-violent civil disobedience. Today, only the NAACP and the NUL are active and influential.

2. *Individuals.* For the most part the leadership of the movement has consisted of "moderates" who have favored legal and non-violent methods. Noteworthy among the moderate leaders have been ROY WILKINS, head of the NAACP, MARTIN LUTHER KING, founder of the SCLC; JAMES FARMER, for a time head of CORE; A. PHILIP RANDOLPH, President of the International Brotherhood of Sleeping Car Conductors; and WHITNEY YOUNG, late head of the NUL. In 1964, Martin Luther King was awarded the Nobel Peace Prize for his efforts to bring about a peaceful and constructive adjustment of racial differences. King's assassination in 1968 was a great loss not only to the black minority but to all the American people.

In the late 1960s, leadership of the Black Civil Rights Movement passed to some extent into the hands of militant and "angry" young leaders, such as Malcolm X, H. Rap Brown, Stokely Carmichael, and Eldridge Cleaver. In general, they opposed integration and cooperation with whites, and called increasingly for revolutionary changes in American life. In the 1970s, the influence of this extremist group declined markedly (see page 425). This did not, mean, however, that black Americans in general were satisfied with their status in the United States.

3. *Black Power.* At the height of the Black Civil Rights Movement in the 1960's the slogan "Black Power" was heard frequently. Black Power, with rather widely differing interpretations, came to be accepted by many leaders and organizations as a primary goal of the Black Revolution. To many it means organizing political and economic strength to achieve more nearly equal opportunity and the control by black Americans of the economic, political, and social institutions in their own communities. It also means the right of the Negro to chose his own mode of living — whether to live harmoniously in integrated groups, or to live among blacks in decent surroundings. In addition, it means recognition of an Afro-American cultural identity. To extreme "Black Nationalists," it means the establishment of a separate black nation. To militant firebrands in the late 1960's, it meant the overthrow of "white capitalism," the spurning of white America, and ever-increasing violence.

Results of the Movement for Full Equality. It is clear that while the Black Civil Rights Movement has not yet achieved its goals, it has resulted in noteworthy gains for the blacks in the United States. Major political, social, and economic advances are described in the following sections.

Recent Civil Rights Legislation. Growing pressure for legal equality for blacks resulted in the late 1950's and 1960's in a number of Federal laws.

1. *The Civil Rights Act of 1957* created a Civil Rights Commission to investigate interference with voting rights.

2. *The Civil Rights Act of 1960* made obstruction of integration of schools a Federal crime and set up Federal referees for voter registration.

3. *The Civil Rights Act of 1964* was initiated under President Kennedy and signed by President Lyndon Johnson. (a) It outlawed racial discrimination in hotels, restaurants, theaters, and other places of public accommodation. (b) It prohibited racial discrimination in employment. (c) It authorized the U.S. Attorney General to intervene on behalf of persons against whom discrimination is practiced. (d) It provided for the withdrawal of Federal funds from projects in which discrimination is practiced.

4. The *Twenty-fourth Amendment* (1964) outlawed all poll tax requirements for voting in Federal elections. This was extended by court interpretations to state and local elections.

5. The *Voting Rights Act of 1965* provided that state literacy tests could no longer be used to bar black citizens from the polls. Federal registrars were given authority to help register blacks for voting wherever there was evidence of discrimination and undue pressure. The law was extended for five years in 1970 and for another seven years in 1975. In the latter extension, the protection of the law was given to Spanish-speaking Americans and other "language minorities." This highly effective law has assured the vote to nearly 3 million black citizens and has brought Southern blacks into the "political mainstream."

6. The *Civil Rights Act of 1968* was passed in the wake of national shame resulting from the assassination of Martin Luther King. This "open housing" law banned discrimination in the sale or rental of housing on the grounds of race, religion, or national origin.

The Black Civil Rights Movement in the 1970's. The black civil rights movement in the late 1970's seemed to be groping for new leadership and direction. "Direct action" (such as protest marches and sit-ins), which had played so large a part in the black political thrust in the 1960's, had all but disappeared. There was much greater emphasis on peaceful, gradual, carefully planned action to improve the position of black Americans.

Black civil rights leaders and groups were continuing to widen their roles to include job programs, housing, and economic development. The *National Urban League,* headed by Vernon Jordan, was helping the hard-core unemployed by running Federal job training programs. *Operation PUSH,* headed by Rev. Jesse Jackson, aimed to get more black parents involved in schools, to induce more blacks to register and vote, and to encourage businesses to hire black employees, purchase products from black firms, and deal with black banks. *The National Association for the Advancement of Colored People* was concentrating on making sure that civil rights laws were being carried out. The NAACP has argued many court cases involving blacks, particularly in the areas of fair housing and school desegregation. It is particularly interested in helping to extend *affirmative action* programs that open up better jobs and promotions for blacks.

Black Gains in the 1970's. It was clear that blacks were continuing to make significant gains on many fronts in the 1970's.

Between 1970 and 1980, the number of blacks holding public office at all governmental levels increased three times. There was a modest increase in the number of black members of Congress—from ten in 1970 to seventeen in 1979. They were organized into a *"Black Caucus"* for more effective political action. Blacks were serving as elected mayors of such major cities as Los Angeles, Detroit, and Atlanta.

From 1970 to 1980, there was an increase of 10% in the percentage of young black people graduating from high school. In just seven years—from 1970 to 1977—the number of blacks attending college more than doubled.

Between 1958 and 1980, the proportion of black professionals, managers, administrators, and technicians more than doubled. In the same period, the proportion of black families moving into the top income brackets ($25,000 or over, in terms of 1977 purchasing power) increased from 1 in 100 to 1 in 9.

Unsatisfactory Aspects of the Black Situation. Despite gains such as those noted above, black people in the United States were concerned over many unsatisfactory conditions and developments.

As the 1980's began, the percent of black students reading on a level at least 2 years behind proper grade for their age was still well above the figure for whites. Despite wide-scale busing nearly half of the nation's minority children were attending segregated schools. (The biggest problem in achieving integration was in big cities, where black and Hispanic children often far outnumbered whites and where many whites had moved out of these cities or withdrawn their children from the public schools.)

Despite years of civil rights enforcement efforts and minority jobs programs, black unemployment at the end of the decade was more than double that of whites. It was estimated that the rate of unemployment among black teenagers was as high as 60% in some areas.

In addition, though income had risen, the median income level of black families in 1979 was still only 60% of the figure for whites. Black males were still being paid an average of 70% of white pay levels.

Despite the growth in political representation, black political power in the late 1970's seemed to be almost at a standstill. The momentum of a unified movement seemed to have come to a halt. Also, other civil rights groups—women, Hispanics, and the handicapped—were competing aggressively for public attention and support. Many black leaders were increasingly worried that some of their hard-won gains of recent years could slip away. In 1979 President Carter called upon black Americans to exercise their voting rights more diligently to help conquer "the cancer of racial injustice."

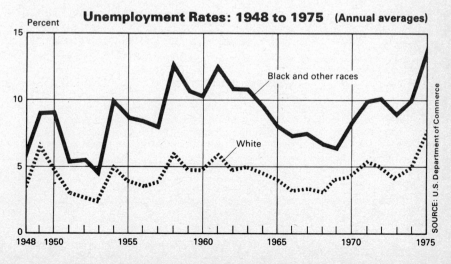

Percent **Unemployment Rates: 1948 to 1975** (Annual averages)

Black and other races

White

SOURCE: U.S. Department of Commerce

1948 1950   1955   1960   1965   1970   1975

REVIEW TEST (Chapter 23—Part III)

Select the number preceding the word or expression that best completes each statement or answers each question.

1. The term "Jim Crow" refers to post-Civil War discrimination against (1) Jews (2) Negroes (3) Catholics (4) Italians

2. Which of the following has fought for Negro rights longest? (1) the Southern Christian Leadership Conference (2) the Student Non-violent Coordinating Committee (3) the Congress of Racial Equality (4) the National Association for the Advancement of Colored People

3. All of the following tended to improve the status of the Negro *except* (1) the Black Codes (2) the Fifteenth Amendment (3) the Ives-Quinn Law (4) Tuskegee Institute

4. At present, poll taxes are (1) illegal in all elections (2) illegal in Federal elections (3) illegal in state elections (4) banned by the Twenty-third Amendment

5. *De facto segregation* results mainly from (1) court decisions (2) state laws (3) segregated schools (4) patterns of housing in the community

6. The Ives-Quinn Act in New York City attempts to increase opportunities for Negroes in (1) education (2) employment (3) labor unions (4) the armed forces

7. Which clause of the Fourteenth Amendment has been the basis for many recent Supreme Court decisions dealing with civil rights of minorities? (1) "All persons born . . . in the United States . . . are citizens of the United States . . ." (2) "No person shall . . . hold any office . . . who . . . shall have engaged in insurrection . . ." (3) ". . . nor shall any State . . . deny to any person . . . equal protection of the laws . . ." (4) ". . . Congress may, by a vote of two-thirds of each House, remove such disability."

8. Which of the following means of protecting the voting rights of Negroes was provided for by the Civil Rights Act of 1964? (1) the outlawing of literacy tests (2) bans discrimination against Negroes in housing rentals (3) reducing the number of Congressional representatives of a state that limits Negro voting (4) outlawing discrimination in places of public accommodation

Select the letter of the fields in which each of the following American Negroes has earned most fame.

1. Jackie Robinson	(a) EDUCATION
2. James Weldon Johnson	(b) CIVIL RIGHTS
3. Ralph Bunche	(c) GOVERNMENT
4. Booker T. Washington	(d) MUSIC
5. Martin Luther King	(e) LITERATURE
	(f) ATHLETICS

Essay Questions

1. Why would reference be made to each of the following in a history of discrimination in the United States? (a) Ku Klux Klan (b) Black Codes (c) Jim Crow (d) poll taxes (e) segregation in education (f) the Civil Rights Act of 1964 (g) *Brown v. the Board of Education of Topeka* (h) the Voting Rights Act of 1965.

2. Prove, using supporting evidence, the validity of the statement, "Black Americans made important contributions to our national life and culture."

3. Discuss the causes, nature, and results of the "Black Revolution" of the 1950s and 1960s. What changes have marked the movement in the 1970s?

4. Explain why the Black Civil Rights Movement is considered an important milestone on the road to complete civil liberty for all.

REVIEWING UNIT SEVEN

Select the number preceding the word or expression that best completes each statement or answers each question.

1. The earliest opposition to trade unions in the United States was based on (1) the conviction that unions were illegal conspiracies (2) destructive effects of nation-wide strikes (3) opposition to the violent tactics of unions (4) socialist influence in the unions

2. The author of the quotation, "We shall insist that management explore with us means to put an end to the hourly wage system from which so much of our member's insecurity stems," is probably trying to prove that (1) a piecework wage system should be adopted (2) a higher Federal minimum wage is essential (3) a guaranteed annual wage plan should be adopted (4) labor unions should work out wage scales with management

3. A major purpose of the Landrum-Griffin law is the desire to (1) assure democratic management of labor unions (2) replace the "cooling-off" period of the Taft-Hartley Act (3) establish the supremacy of the NLRB in labor-management disputes (4) re-establish the closed shop as a legal union activity

4. Most leaders of organized labor regard "right-to-work" laws as a (1) protection against unemployment (2) protection against discrimination (3) threat to the union shop (4) threat to lockouts and injunctions

5. The term "escalator clause" in labor-management contracts refers to (1) union representation (2) working conditions (3) seniority rights (4) wage adjustments

6. Under present labor legislation, the President can (1) stop any strike that has continued more than 80 days (2) decide when a strike endangers national health and safety (3) enforce compulsory arbitration in a major strike (4) issue an injunction against a strike in a defense industry

7. The Social Security Act was passed in 1935 to meet the problems of (1) racial and religious discrimination in employment (2) crime and juvenile delinquency (3) medical and hospital care for all Americans (4) unemployment and old age relief

8. Within the next decade, the Social Security tax paid by employees is scheduled to (1) increase (2) decrease (3) be paid entirely by the employer (4) remain fixed at the present level

9. A major purpose of the Soil Conservation Service is (1) to increase the amount of cultivated land (2) to encourage methods of farming that do not exhaust the land (3) to lower prices of farm products (4) to prevent dumping of farm products by foreign countries

10. In 1886, a Granger law then in effect was declared unconstitutional by the United States Supreme Court. This decision led to the (1) establishment of farm cooperatives (2) acceptance of acreage controls by the farmers (3) ratification of the Sixteenth Amendment (4) passage of the Interstate Commerce Act

11. The Interstate Commerce Act was significant in that it (1) introduced the commission as a regulatory device (2) reduced the number of court cases involving regulation of railroads (3) effectively reduced railroad rates (4) eliminated conflicting state laws

12. The Sherman Act of 1890 was designed to prevent (1) the sale of goods below cost (2) combinations in restraint of trade (3) holding companies (4) adulteration of goods

13. Under the quota system of immigration from 1952 to 1965, the United States (1) favored immigrants from Britain and Northern Europe (2) excluded all Asian and Pacific peoples (3) transferred unused quotas of some nations to other nations (4) accepted, outside of quota limits, all who established their status as "refugees"

14. The first tariff act with a considerable reduction in rates after the Civil War was enacted during the administration of (1) Woodrow Wilson (2) Warren G. Harding (3) Herbert Hoover (4) William McKinley

15. Tariff legislation passed by Congress in 1962 indicated (1) an increase in protectionist sentiment (2) willingness to move further on trade concessions (3) growing opposition to foreign aid (4) unwillingness to continue reciprocal agreements

16. Which of the following best summarizes United States tariff policy since 1934? (1) a tariff maintained for protection only (2) duties raised on agricultural products and lowered on manufactured goods (3) free trade established (4) reciprocal trade agreements made with other nations

17. Which of the following is true of population trends in the United States? (1) The closing of the frontier marked an end to major population shifts. (2) The population of the United States is characterized by immobility. (3) Population shifts have political effects. (4) Economic development has had little effect on population trends.

18. During the 20th century, the commerce clause of the United States Constitution has been the general basis for (1) enacting legislation in the interests of labor (2) increasing the power of the states (3) limiting Federal-state relationships (4) expanding the taxing power of Congress

19. In the case of *Brown v. Board of Education of Topeka*, the United States Supreme Court declared segregation in public schools unconstitutional, under the (1) "privileges and immunities" clause of Article IV (2) "due process" clause of the Fifth Amendment (3) "equal protection" clause of the Fourteenth Amendment (4) "elastic clause" of Article I

20. The constitutional argument advanced by some sections of the South against Federal action for integration in education was based upon (1) delegated powers (2) division of powers (3) the supremacy clause of the Constitution (4) the "elastic clause" of the Constitution

Select the letter of the item in each group which does **NOT** *belong with the others.*

1. Affected by restrictions of the McCarran-Walter Act: (a) Puerto Rico (b) the United Kingdom (c) West Germany (d) Japan

2. Influential labor leader: (a) Samuel Gompers (b) Eugene V. Debs (c) William Jennings Bryan (d) John L. Lewis

3. Problems of the farmer: (a) declining production (b) parity prices (c) soil conservation (d) world markets

4. Civil rights highlights: (a) March on Washington (b) *Brown v. Topeka* (c) Hawley-Smoot Act (d) Twenty-fourth Amendment

5. Urban renewal: (a) slum clearance (b) rezoning (c) Medicare (d) improved housing

6. Legal business forms: (a) corporations (b) mergers (c) partnerships (d) trusts

7. Agricultural pressure-group organizations: (a) Non-Partisan League (b) Know-Nothings (c) Grangers (d) National Farmers' Union

8. Problems of international trade: (a) balance of payments (b) reciprocal tariff negotiations (c) quotas and subsidies (d) de facto segregation

From the following list, select the **letter** *of the topic with which each of the laws or persons listed below is most closely connected.*

A. The history of labor
B. The problems of the farmer
C. Immigration
D. Conservation

E. International trade
F. Business regulation
G. Civil rights

Laws	Persons
1. Sherman Antitrust Act	**6.** Terence Powderly
2. Newlands Act	**7.** Gifford Pinchot
3. National Origins Plan	**8.** Cordell Hull
4. Landrum-Griffin Act	**9.** Ida Tarbell
5. AAA of 1938	**10.** Earl Warren

Essay Questions

1. Problems in labor relations have been important in the United States since the end of the Civil War. (a) Discuss two factors that hindered the growth of organized labor in the United States during the period 1865-1930. (b) Describe two major gains made by organized labor as a result of Federal labor legislation in the 1930's. (c) State and explain two problems that organized labor faces today.

2. The government's attitude toward organized labor has changed from one of opposition, to one of protection, to one of regulation. Show which government attitude was reflected toward the labor unions in each of three of the following: Railroad Strike (1877); Anthracite Coal Strike (1902); Clayton Act (1914); Wagner Act (1935); Taft-Hartley Act (1947); Landrum-Griffin Act (1959).

3. Explain fully why and how the government has for over 30 years been helping farmers regulate production. Present two arguments for or against continuing this program.

4. Explain why each of the following is considered an unsolved problem of American democracy: *conservation; poverty; Black rights.* Describe three types of action now being taken by the government or society to solve one of these problems, and tell why you agree or disagree with the policy that is being followed.

5. Each of the acts listed below was a "first" in its field of legislation. For each of three of these acts, show two ways in which later legislation changed or added to the original law. (a) Interstate Commerce Act of 1887 (b) Sherman Antitrust Act of 1890 (c) Newlands Act of 1902 (d) Social Security Act of 1935 (e) Wagner-Connery Act (National Labor Relations Act) of 1935 (f) the Civil Rights Act of 1957.

6. Tariffs and trade have long been important related economic problems in United States history.
(a) Explain fully how the tariff was a controversial issue in the United States during each of two of the following periods: (1) from 1824 to the Civil War, (2) from the Civil War to 1913, (3) from World War I to 1933.

(b) Discuss briefly one reason why some businesses today support high tariffs, and one reason why some businesses oppose them.

(c) Describe United States tariff policy since 1933.

(d) Discuss what is meant by the statement that tariff policy demands a balancing of special interests against the national interest.

7. The immigration policy of the United States government has reflected trends in the development of our country. (a) State the government's policy in relation to immigration in each of three of the following periods:

(1) 1789–1870   (3) 1920–40
(2) 1880–1910   (4) 1945–60
            (5) Since 1965

(b) Explain the factors that influenced the government's policy in each period mentioned.

8. Give the economic reasoning of those advocating each of the following: (a) division of labor in industry, (b) utilization of byproducts in manufacturing, (c) parity supports for farm prices, (d) organization of industrial unions, (e) labor's demand for cost-of-living adjustment clauses in union contracts.

9. Different solutions have been advanced for each of the following economic questions that concern the economy of the United States. Show that you understand the issues involved by discussing two different points of view on each of three of the following economic questions. (No credit will be given for a second point of view that is merely the negative statement of the first point without explanation.)

(a) How should we meet a basic problem posed by automation?

(b) Is there too much "bigness" in American business?

(c) How can we best solve the problem of farm surpluses?

10. Write an editorial of 100-200 words for each of the following headlines:
**ENVIRONMENTAL PROTECTION — A TOP NATIONAL PRIORITY
AT LAST — A DEPARTMENT OF URBAN AFFAIRS!
DO WE STILL HAVE SECOND CLASS CITIZENS?
POPULATION EXPLOSION POSES SERIOUS PROBLEMS FOR NATION
THE "CRISIS OF THE CITIES" THREATENS AMERICAN LIFE**

Unit Eight

AMERICAN FOREIGN POLICY IN THE 20th CENTURY

CHAPTER 24

The United States Acquires an Empire

Throughout much of its history, and particularly in the 19th century, the United States attempted to avoid European involvements and to concentrate on its own internal development. This policy, known as *isolation,* was not so much a desire to achieve physical and economic separation from the rest of the world as it was an attempt to remain independent of European alliances and conflicts. For this reason some historians in recent years have preferred to call the policy "withdrawal" or "preoccupation" rather than "isolation." The physical separation of the United States from Europe made it easier for the nation to concentrate on its own affairs.

It should be emphasized, however, that the "withdrawal" was never complete, for the United States was involved repeatedly in world affairs throughout this period. These involvements included wars, such as the War of 1812, disputes over violations of our neutrality, the acquisition of small overseas possessions in the Pacific, and expansion of our territorial boundaries, which inevitably led to disputes with foreign countries.

Toward the end of the 19th century, the United States consciously abandoned its traditional aloofness from foreign involvement and began to acquire an overseas empire. The *Spanish-American War* was a turning point in this development and in American foreign policy as a whole. This war not only extended American influence beyond its borders but also presented the nation with the problem of governing overseas possessions.

Growing Interest in Overseas Possessions. Although the United States had shown some interest in the problems of Cuba, the Dominican Republic, and the Virgin Islands in the middle decades of the 19th century, it did not develop an *active* interest in overseas possessions until the last quarter of the century. Several factors contributed to this new interest.

1. *Economic Development.* As a result of the rapid expansion of American production, which tripled United States export trade between 1870 and 1900, American producers were anxious to find additional markets for their raw materials, foodstuffs, and fibers.

2. *National Pride.* Toward the end of the century, many Americans began to be seriously impressed by the overseas imperialism of European nations, and some were anxious for the United States to join in the race for colonies. To justify a policy of imperialism for the United States, they talked about "racial superiority," "national mission," and a "new manifest destiny." The doctrines of Captain Alfred Mahan became popular among nationalists, imperialists, and militarists. Mahan advocated that the United States build up a large empire based upon naval and commercial strength, in order to prevent itself from being outdistanced by European competitors.

Early Steps Toward Empire. The United States acquired the first territories outside its present continental boundaries without a conscious desire to establish a colonial empire.

1. *Alaska.* In 1867, we acquired Alaska as a gesture of friendship to Russia. At the time, the territory was generally considered of little value.

2. *Small Islands in the Pacific.* To provide coaling stations for its expanding trade and its navy, the United States took possession of over 50 small islands in the Central and South Pacific between 1867 and 1900. Most of these islands were sparsely populated or completely uninhabited. In 1867, the United States took possession of the Midway Islands. In 1899, it made permanent its temporary control of several of the Samoan Islands, by arrangement with Great Britain and Germany.

3. *Hawaii.* The Hawaiian Islands were the most important of the United States' early overseas possessions. American missionaries, planters, and merchants had begun to settle in these islands as early as the 1820's. In 1893, American residents, with some help by United States armed forces, led a successful revolt which resulted in the establishment of a Hawaiian republic. President Cleveland, an anti-imperialist, opposed a treaty of Hawaiian annexation to the United States. However, at the request of Cleveland's successor, President William McKinley, Congress by a joint resolution annexed Hawaii to the United States in 1898. This took place during the Spanish-American War. The value of the Hawaiian islands lies in their agricultural production and in their central position on the shipping lanes between the United States and the Far East.

The Spanish-American War. The Spanish-American War gave the United States an overseas empire, shattered its tradition of isolation, and involved it actively in world affairs.

1. *Underlying Causes.* The war arose out of an incensed public feeling against Spain for its treatment of Cuban revolutionaries.

   (a) *United States Interest in Cuba.* Together with Puerto Rico, the island of Cuba was the last remnant of the once vast Spanish Empire in America. Cuba was near our borders, had valuable resources, and was looked upon before the Civil War as a possible outlet for the expansion of slavery. Efforts by Presidents Polk, Pierce, and Grant to purchase the island from Spain failed. (The best known of these efforts was the *Ostend Manifesto* of 1854, in which the American ministers to Great Britain, France, and Spain — speaking on their own authority — suggested that the United States would take Cuba by force if Spain refused to sell it. The Manifesto was immediately repudiated by U. S. Secretary of State William Marcy.) Toward the end of the century, United States businessmen began to invest in Cuban sugar and tobacco plantations.

(b) *Sympathy for the Cuban Revolution.* Beginning in 1868, Cubans engaged in a series of revolts against Spanish misgovernment. Although both sides used savage methods and destroyed United States property, American sympathy was on the side of the Cuban insurgents.

(c) *The "Yellow Press."* Public opinion was whipped into a fury by the American press, a large portion of which exaggerated the atrocities of the Spanish and the suffering of the Cubans. Particularly noteworthy examples of this "yellow journalism" were William Randolph Hearst's New York *Journal* and Joseph Pulitzer's New York *World*.

(d) *Growing Demand for Intervention.* Several groups took advantage of the public anger against Spain and helped convert it into a growing desire for war. Many religious leaders and leaders of both major political parties began to call for intervention on humanitarian grounds, Imperialists, militarists, and extreme nationalists ("Jingoists") looked upon war with Spain as a means of achieving glory and empire.

NOTE: As a group, American businessmen did *not* join in the clamor for war. They felt that war might upset the business revival of the period. Even those with Cuban investments argued that they had more to lose from war with Spain than from continued rebellion in Cuba.

2. *Immediate Causes.* Although President McKinley tried, on entering office, to curb the "jingoists" and to halt the drift toward war, a series of fateful incidents precipitated the outbreak of hostilities.

(a) *De Lome Letter.* In February, 1898, the Spanish minister in Washington, Dupuy de Lome wrote a letter criticizing McKinley as a weak politician. This letter was intercepted and published by a New York newspaper. The public outcry was so great that even de Lome's resignation failed to smooth the ruffled feelings.

(b) *Sinking of the* Maine. War feeling came to a climax six days after the De Lome incident when the United States battleship *Maine* was blown up in Havana Harbor with a loss of 260 officers and men. Though the cause of the explosion was unknown at the time (and has never been ascertained), the "jingo" press held Spain responsible, and called for war, using the slogan, "Remember the *Maine!*"

(c) *War Is Declared.* President McKinley, who had not wanted war, was carried along with the new wave of war fever resulting from the sinking of the *Maine*. Although the Spanish government was attempting to reach a peaceful solution to the crisis, McKinley sent a warlike message to Congress which resulted in a resolution recognizing the independence of Cuba. Spain declared war on the United States on April 24, 1898. The United States declared war the next day.

3. *Leading Events of Spanish-American War.* The war produced a quick and unexpectedly easy victory for the United States. The hostilities lasted only 10 weeks.

(a) *United States Naval Successes.* The new and modern United States Navy, superior in all respects to the Spanish naval forces, won decisive victories. The Spaniards were defeated with heavy losses at *Santiago,* Cuba, by Admirals Sampson and Schley, and at *Manila,* in the Philippines, by Commodore Dewey.

(b) *United States Successes on Land.* The United States land forces, though not as well prepared and organized as the Navy, won the battle of *San Juan Hill* (in which T. Roosevelt participated) near Santiago, and occupied Manila. Troops under General Miles took possession of Puerto Rico.

(c) *End of the War.* Completely crushed, Spain asked for peace on July 16, 1898.

Results of the Spanish-American War. War casualties in the Spanish-American War were small in number. More deaths resulted from disease (especially typhoid, malaria, and yellow fever) than from combat. More significant was the peace treaty ending the war, and its effects upon United States development.

1. *Treaty of Paris (1898).* Under the terms of the treaty of peace, signed in Paris in December, 1898, the United States received *Guam* and *Puerto Rico* from Spain, and was also granted the *Philippine Islands* in return for payment of 20 million dollars. Spain also turned *Cuba* over to the United States for occupation. (Under the *Teller Resolution,* passed by Congress just before hostilities began, the United States declared that it had no intention of annexing Cuba.)

2. *Imperialism and the Election of 1900.* A national debate over whether the United States should acquire foreign territory took place during and after the signing of the peace treaty. Since the treaty had been ratified by a narrow margin, Bryan and the Democrats tried to make imperialism the "paramount issue" in the election of 1900. Though McKinley's re-election was due primarily to the national prosperity that followed the war, it was also evidence of a national acceptance of overseas expansion.

3. *Long-range Significance of the Spanish-American War.* The Spanish-American War was important far beyond its military events or immediate results. Secretary of State John Hay called it "a splendid little war."

(a) It marked a change in foreign policy from isolation to foreign involvement.

(b) It brought the United States into close relationships with Latin America and the Far East.

(c) It gave the United States a colonial empire.

(d) It marked the emergence of the United States as a world power in the Pacific and Caribbean, and a nation that had to be reckoned with in world affairs.

(e) It stimulated industrial activity and contributed to a new era of postwar prosperity.

United States and Problems of Empire. In the 20th century, the United States added to its territorial possessions by acquiring the *Panama Canal Zone* from Panama in 1903, the *Virgin Islands* from Denmark in 1917, and the *Pacific Trust Territories* from the United Nations in 1947. Together with the territories acquired before and immediately following the Spanish-American War, this "empire" presented new challenges of government to the United States.

1. *Status of the New Territories.* Since the new dependencies (territories) were outside the United States' territorial boundaries, and since they were inhabited by peoples of different races, religions, languages, and levels of civilization, the United States faced difficult decisions as to their status. The important questions to be answered were twofold. Should the new territories be kept permanently as colonies, admitted as states, or granted independence? Should their citizens be granted the same constitutional rights and privileges as citizens of the United States?

2. *Incorporated and Unincorporated Territories.* As a partial answer to these questions Congress established two categories of dependencies.

(a) *Incorporated territories* were those considered eligible for self-government and eventual statehood, specifically Alaska and Hawaii. Citizens of incorporated territories were granted full constitutional privileges.

(b) *Unincorporated territories* were those dependencies not considered eligible for complete self-government or statehood (all except Alaska and Hawaii). Citizens of unincorporated territories were to be granted limited constitutional privileges and varying degrees of self-government.

3. *The Insular Cases.* The right of Congress to govern United States territories as it saw fit and to distinguish between incorporated and unincorporated territories was upheld in a series of Supreme Court decisions known as the *Insular Cases.* The Court ruled that:

(a) The Constitution did not apply fully to overseas possessions.

(b) Inhabitants of United States territories could have only such constitutional rights as Congress granted them.

(c) Congress could apply tariff duties on imports from our dependencies, if it wished to do so.

4. *Enlightened Territorial Government.* Although Congress never worked out a uniform pattern of territorial government, it eventually granted a considerable degree of self-government to most of our territorial de-

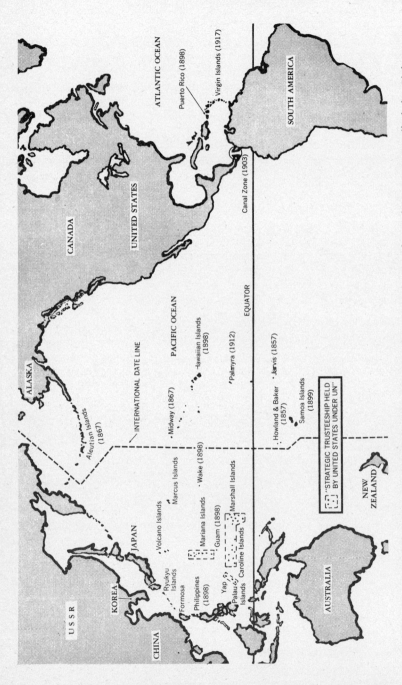

ATLANTIC OCEAN

Puerto Rico (1898)

Virgin Islands (1917)

SOUTH AMERICA

Canal Zone (1903)

CANADA

UNITED STATES

EQUATOR

ALASKA

INTERNATIONAL DATE LINE

PACIFIC OCEAN

Hawaiian Islands (1898)

Midway (1867)

Palmyra (1912)

Aleutian Islands (1867)

Howland & Baker (1857)

Jarvis (1857)

Samoa Islands (1899)

Marcus Islands

Wake (1898)

Volcano Islands

Mariana Islands

Guam (1898)

Marshall Islands

Yap

Palau Islands

Caroline Islands

Ryukyu Islands

Philippines (1898)

Formosa

JAPAN

KOREA

U S S R

CHINA

NEW ZEALAND

AUSTRALIA

"STRATEGIC TRUSTEESHIP HELD BY UNITED STATES UNDER UN"

Territories acquired by the United States. The Philippines are now an independent country called the Philippine Republic. The Hawaiian Islands have become one of the 50 states. The Pacific island groups held as a UN trustee-ship are moving toward self-government.

pendencies, including the unincorporated territories of Puerto Rico, Guam, and the Virgin Islands. The Philippines were given their independence; Puerto Rico became a self-governing Commonwealth; and Hawaii and Alaska were admitted as states. In the government of its empire, the United States established standards that may be considered advanced and enlightened, especially compared with most other imperialist nations.

United States and the Philippines. At first, the Philippines were not happy about trading one "master" for another. Once the United States took possession, however, our government established a record of achievement and liberal administration rarely equaled in the history of colonialism.

1. *First Military and Then Civilian Rule.* After putting down a revolt against American rule (led by Emilio Aguinaldo), the United States ended its military rule and replaced it with civilian government. This consisted first of a Commission and later of a legislature and governor.

2. *Steps Toward Self-Government.* The Philippines were given increasing measures of self-government. The *Jones Act* of 1916 granted the Filipinos full civil rights and the right to elect both houses of their legislature. It also promised eventual independence. The *Tydings-McDuffie Act* of 1934 provided for the establishment of a temporary self-governing *Philippine Commonwealth,* and for complete independence at the end of ten years. The act climaxed many years of agitation by Philippine nationalists and American liberals, who argued that the Filipinos were ready for self-government. They were supported by American sugar and fruit growers, who were hurt by the competition of Philippine imports, and by others who claimed the islands were costly to govern and too hard to defend in case of war.

3. *Full Independence.* Full independence was granted to the Philippines in 1946. Since independence, relations between the *Philippine Republic* and the United States have been generally cordial. The United States extended financial aid after World War II, and under the *Bell Act* of 1946 agreed to raise tariff duties gradually in order not to disrupt the new nation's economy. With Philippine consent the United States has maintained air, naval, and army bases in the islands. Though cooperation is still the keynote, there has recently been growing feeling against United States influence.

4. *The United States Record in the Philippines.* The United States made notable contributions to the welfare of the islands during its period of rule. Schools, hospitals, roads, and other public facilities were built. A modern system of communications and a national currency were established. Modern agricultural methods were introduced. Special low tariff duties were imposed on Philippine exports to the United States.

United States and Puerto Rico. The record of the United States in Puerto Rico, as in the Philippines, has been one of generally enlightened and liberal government.

1. *Steps Toward Self-Government.* The Puerto Ricans willingly accepted United States rule, and were rapidly advanced toward self-government. In 1900, Army rule was replaced by a popularly elected territorial legislature and a governor appointed by the President of the United States (*Foraker Act*). In 1916, United States citizenship was granted to the Puerto Ricans (*Jones Act*). In 1947, Puerto Rico was given the right to elect its own governor.

2. *Commonwealth Status.* In 1947, after years of nationalist agitation for full self-government, the Puerto Ricans were allowed by Congress to choose independence *or* statehood *or* Commonwealth status. They voted overwhelmingly for the creation of a Commonwealth. Under the constitution establishing the *Commonwealth of Puerto Rico,* which went into effect in 1952, the following relationships were established:

(*a*) Puerto Rico controls its own internal affairs and elects its own legislature and governor, like any state in the Union.

(*b*) Puerto Ricans are United States citizens, and are subject to Federal laws of the United States.

(*c*) Puerto Rico is represented in the House of Representatives by a Resident Commissioner, who may debate and serve on committees, though he may not vote.

(*d*) Puerto Rico remains within the United States tariff system and is granted free trade with the mainland.

(*e*) Unlike other United States territories, Puerto Rico is allowed to collect Federal taxes and to use the money for its own needs.

3. *United States Record in Puerto Rico.* Under United States rule, Puerto Rico has received many benefits, including significant improvements in health, education, agriculture, and transportation. Although English is taught in the schools, Spanish traditions, culture, and language are retained. The population of the island is increasing rapidly.

4. *Recent Attempts to Deal With Serious Problems.* In spite of an extraordinary record of progress during the half-century of United States control, Puerto Rico remains a depressed area. The island suffers from exhaustion of natural resources, absentee landlordism, low-wage levels, overpopulation, rural congestion, and unemployment. Under the leadership of Governor Muñoz Marín, its first Governor, Puerto Rico made vigorous and largely effective efforts to improve economic and social conditions. This policy has been continued by Marín's successors, Roberto Vilella, Luis Ferré, and Rafael Colon.

(*a*) *Operation Bootstrap.* Under a program of economic development, known as *Operation Bootstrap,* American businessmen have been actively encouraged to set up manufacturing plants and have been offered the advantages of relatively low-cost labor and low taxes. As a result of Operation Bootstrap, over a thousand new factories have already been established, and opportunities for employment have been greatly expanded.

(b) Other Reforms. In addition to Operation Bootstrap, the Puerto Rican Commonwealth has built schools and low-cost housing projects, has encouraged the diversification of agriculture, has begun to develop its hydroelectric resources, and has promoted the tourist trade.

(c) Results. The Puerto Rican standard of living has improved, and per capita income is among the highest in Latin America. In recent years, however, the economy of the Commonwealth has suffered some reverses, and unemployment has been high.

5. *Emigration to the Mainland.* Despite the new employment opportunities created by Operation Bootstrap, the population has continued to increase faster than jobs. Since the establishment of the Commonwealth, thousands of Puerto Ricans have been emigrating to the United States for greater economic opportunities. Where they have come in large numbers, as in New York City, serious problems have appeared, largely because of discrimination in housing and employment. Puerto Rican and United States authorities have cooperated to cope with such difficulties and to ease adjustment to the new environment.

6. *Question of Statehood.* Recently there has been increased interest in statehood for Puerto Rico. Advocates of such a change, including the former Governor, Luis Ferré, claim it would give Puerto Rico important economic and political gains. Opponents point out that the Island would lose the tax advantages that it now enjoys. A small group of Puerto Rican nationalists call for complete independence.

Alaska and Hawaii. Alaska and Hawaii both advanced rapidly to a status of self-government in the early part of the 20th century and were finally admitted into the Union as the 49th and 50th states.

1. *Alaska.* In 1912, Alaska became an incorporated territory and was given a territorial legislature. Its Governor continued to be selected by the President. In 1959, it entered the Union as the 49th state. Alaska is twice the size of Texas, and is rich in lumber, furs, fish, and minerals. Recently major oil deposits have been discovered.

2. *Hawaii.* Hawaii was given a territorial legislature and became an incorporated territory in 1900. Like Alaska and most other territories, its Governor was appointed by the President, and it sent a non-voting delegate to Congress. In 1959, it became the 50th state in the Union. Hawaii remains noteworthy for its sugar and pineapple plantations, the harmonious relations among the many racial and ethnic groups that make up the population, and the pleasant climate and beautiful scenery that have helped to create a flourishing tourist industry.

Smaller Possessions of the United States. The degree of self-government in the remaining dependencies of the United States varies widely. We continue to hold these dependencies mainly for strategic purposes. They are still considered unincorporated territories, ineligible for statehood.

1. *Guam* was annexed from Spain in 1898. Except for two years of Japanese occupation during World War II, it has been governed by the

United States Navy. In 1950, Guam received limited self-government in the form of a popularly elected single house legislature, a Governor appointed by the President, and a bill of rights. In addition, Guamanians were declared United States citizens. The tiny island is in the Marianas and is held primarily for its use as an air and naval base. (See map on page 440.)

2. The *Virgin Islands* were purchased from Denmark in 1917 for 25 million dollars to prevent Germany from buying them and thereby possibly "endangering" the Panama Canal. Since 1927, the islanders have been American citizens, and have elected their own legislature. The Governor, however, is still appointed by the President. The Virgin Islands consist of St. Croix, St. Thomas, St. John, and about 50 small and uninhabited islands east of Puerto Rico. They are valuable for their strategic location. (See map on page 440.)

3. The *Panama Canal Zone* is the strip of land, ten miles wide, through which the Panama Canal runs. Because of its highly strategic value the Zone is under the strict control of the United States Army. Its citizens, however, have been given the guarantees of the Bill of Rights. (See page 448 for a discussion of the United States and the Panama Canal.)

4. The *United States Trust Territory in the Pacific* consists of the *Marshall, Mariana* (except Guam), and *Caroline Islands* in the Pacific, east of the Philippines. (See map on page 440.) Held by Germany until World War II, the islands were assigned to the United States in 1947 by the UN Security Council, as a strategic trust territory. They are held for defense purposes, fortified as naval and air bases, and governed by a High Commissioner appointed by the President. In 1974, planning began to extend self-government to the Marshalls and Carolines. In 1975, the people of the Marianas voted to ask the United States for commonwealth status for their islands.

5. *Other Islands* in the mid-Pacific belonging to the United States and administered for defense purposes by the Navy or Interior Departments, include *Wake, Midway,* and the *Samoas.* Also, the United States still controls the Ryukyus under its post-World War II treaty with Japan. However, we returned Iwo Jima to Japan in 1967, and Okinawa in 1971. Under treaty agreement, Okinawa continues to serve as a strong U. S. Pacific base.

REVIEW TEST (Chapter 24)

Select the number preceding the word or expression that best completes each statement or answers each question.

1. One of the important reasons why some Americans became increasingly interested in overseas investment and activity in the period after 1890 was the (1) increased popularity of the mercantile theory of trade (2) "closing" of the American frontier (3) strong support for the policy of isolation (4) overpopulation of the American continent

2. The United States declaration of war on Spain (1898) is an example of (1) Presidential leadership in the face of Congressional disapproval (2) military maneuvers making war inevitable (3) the influence of the press on popular opinion (4) willingness of businessmen to provoke war for selfish advantage

3. An important result of the Spanish-American War was (1) It made Florida safe from Spanish invasion. (2) The United States acquired Cuba. (3) It gave the United States vital new interests in the Caribbean. (4) It increased rivalry between the United States and Great Britain.

4. Which event occurred *third?* (1) establishment of a self-governing Philippine Commonwealth (2) Philippine revolt against rule by the United States (3) sinking of the *Maine* (4) Treaty of Paris (1898)

5. Which of the following Supreme Court cases resulted from the acquisition of overseas territories? (1) Granger Cases (2) Insular Cases (3) Legal Tender Cases (4) New Deal Cases

6. A United States territory is represented in the United States Congress by (1) its governor (2) an elected commission of three (3) a delegate who may speak but not vote (4) two trustees

7. Hawaii is represented in the Congress of the United States by (1) senators and representatives (2) a territorial delegate without a vote (3) its governor (4) a commission elected by the voters

8. Since World War II, Alaska's strategic importance has increased primarily because of (1) the discovery of new gold mines (2) the large-scale mining of uranium deposits (3) the air routes across the Arctic (4) her admission as a state

9. The United States has purchased territory from all of the following *except* (1) Denmark (2) France (3) Italy (4) Russia

10. Which of the following is farthest from the United States mainland? (1) Puerto Rico (2) Guam (3) Virgin Islands (4) Panama Canal

Match each item in Column A with the letter of the item in Column B that is most closely associated with it.

A	B
1. Operation Bootstrap	*a.* Marshalls and Marianas
2. De Lome Letter	*b.* Hearst and Pulitzer
3. "Yellow Journalism"	*c.* A successful economic development program
4. Tydings-McDuffie Act	*d.* United States Control of Samoan Islands
5. Trust territory	*e.* Criticized President McKinley
	f. Commonwealth status for Philippines

Essay Questions

1. Describe the growing interest of the United States in overseas possessions in the quarter century before the Spanish-American War.

2. Discuss two causes, two military highlights, and two results of the Spanish-American War.

3. (a) Explain two problems faced by the United States as a result of acquiring overseas territory after the Spanish-American War. (b) Show how the United States attempted to solve these problems in the case of (1) the Philippines and (2) Puerto Rico.

4. Explain the extent to which you agree or disagree with the statement that "the United States has much to be proud of in its government of overseas possessions."

_____

CHAPTER 25

The United States Extends Its
Influence in the Western Hemisphere

In the 20th century, the United States has come into increasingly close contact with its neighbors in the Western Hemisphere.

Part I — THE UNITED STATES EXTENDS ITS INFLUENCE IN LATIN AMERICA

Latin America is the name given to the part of the Western Hemisphere that lies south and east of the United States. It consists of 23 independent nations, several European colonies, and one United States dependency (Puerto Rico). Most of the nations of Latin America, including by far the greater part of its population, are located in South America. There are six small republics in Central America, a number of island nations in the Caribbean, and one large country (Mexico) in North America.

The United States and Latin America. During the first three decades of the 20th century, the United States actively extended its influence in Latin America in order to protect its own growing economic, strategic, and territorial interests. The United States built the Panama Canal, expanded the Monroe Doctrine, established protectorates, and sent troops to the Caribbean to promote order and stability. By 1914, the Caribbean had become an American sphere of influence, and was referred to as a "United States Lake." Growing Latin American distrust of United States policies seriously weakened the *Pan-American Movement* for the improvement of relations between the nations of the Western Hemisphere. As a result, in the 1930's the United States abandoned its policy of active intervention in the internal affairs of Latin American republics and developed a *"Good Neighbor Policy."*

Latin American Backgrounds. To understand the history of the relations between the United States and Latin America, we must be familiar with the basic facts of Latin American geography and history.

1. *Geography.* Latin America is over twice the size of the United States in land area. It is situated for the most part in the tropics. Though it has a great wealth of natural resources, particularly tropical forests, minerals, and rolling prairies, these are largely undeveloped. The rugged terrain — mountains, jungles, and deserts — has held back economic development. Many Latin Americans still live in isolated villages, often out of touch with the modern world.

Latin America today.

2. *History.* Like the United States, the nations of Latin America were once colonial possessions, mainly of Spain and Portugal. Inspired by the successful American and French Revolutions, the natives of Latin America revolted against their European rulers and fought successful wars for independence in the period from 1791 to 1824. Leaders such as SIMON BOLIVAR, BERNARDO O'HIGGINS, and JOSE DE SAN MARTIN overthrew foreign rule and established independent republics in all of Latin America except Cuba. Unlike the United States, however, most Latin American republics have had unstable political histories. Governments have been frequently overthrown. Power has generally remained in the hands of a few wealthy landowners, aristocrats, and industrialists. Despite adoption of democratic constitutions, the peoples' rights have been largely ignored.

3. *The Latin American Way of Life.* Life in Latin America is considerably different from life in the United States.

(a) The population is composed of Indians, Whites, Negroes, and Mestizos. The *Indians* are the original inhabitants of Latin America. The *Whites* are descendants of the European settlers. The *Negroes* are the descendants of slaves brought to Latin America in the 16th century to work the mines and plantations. The *Mestizos,* or persons of mixed White and Indian descent, make up the largest population group in Latin America. In addition, in the deep jungles of the Amazon, there live tribes of primitive Indians, cut off from the rest of the world.

(b) Except for Portuguese in Brazil and a French dialect in Haiti, the official language of Latin America is Spanish.

(c) Most Latin Americans are Catholics, although state and church have been separated in most Latin American nations.

(d) Latin American culture has been strongly influenced by its Indian and Spanish backgrounds.

4. *An Underdeveloped Region.* Most of Latin America is underdeveloped. A small minority owns most of the land, industry, and other forms of wealth. Most people live in poverty. *Peonage* (sharecropping) is extensive. Class distinctions are rigid. Because educational opportunities have been limited to the wealthy, illiteracy is widespread. In most countries, the middle class of independent farmers, small businessmen, skilled craftsmen, professionals, and white-collar workers is small in numbers and weak in influence.

The United States Builds the Panama Canal. The building of the Panama Canal was both a cause and a result of more active United States participation in Latin American affairs.

1. *Early Interest in a Canal.* The United States was long interested in a canal across Central America. After the acquisition of Oregon and California, shippers urged a canal as a means of establishing a shorter route between East and West.

(a) *Treaty of 1846 with Colombia.* The United States received the right to build a canal or railroad across the Isthmus of Panama by a treaty with Colombia in 1846. (Until 1903, Panama was part of Colombia.)

(b) *Clayton-Bulwer Treaty* (1850). In 1850, the United States and Great Britain agreed to exercise joint control over any canal built by either across Central America *(Clayton-Bulwer Treaty).*

2. *Negotiations for a Canal.* The Spanish-American War influenced the decision to build a Central-American canal. During the war, the navy saw the need for a quick passage from the Atlantic to the Pacific Oceans. After the war, possession by the United States of new colonies in both the Caribbean and Pacific increased the need for a connecting link. Additional pressure for a canal came from manufacturers and farmers eager for cheap transportation and new outlets for their products at home and abroad.

(a) *Hay-Pauncefote Treaty (1901).* In 1901, the United States persuaded Britain to give up its right to joint control of a canal, and guaranteed in return that any canal built by the United States would be open equally to all nations *(Hay-Pauncefote Treaty).* Britain was willing to sign the treaty because of its involvements in Europe and the Boer War.

(b) *Purchase of French Properties and Facilities.* United States officials became interested in a canal across Panama rather than Nicaragua when, in 1902, a French company that had mismanaged an attempt to construct a Panamanian canal offered to sell its rights and properties to the United States for 40 million dollars.

(c) *Revolution of 1903 in Panama.* In 1903, Colombia refused to lease a strip of land across the Isthmus to the United States because of dissatisfaction with the terms offered by Congress. Soon after, a revolution broke out in Panama, which received the support of the Theodore Roosevelt administration. A new Republic of Panama was quickly formed and as quickly recognized by the United States.

(d) *The United States Acquires the Canal Zone (1903).* The new Republic of Panama quickly concluded the *Hay–Bunau–Varilla Treaty* with the United States. The treaty granted the United States a 10 mile-wide strip of territory across the Isthmus "in perpetuity," for the payment of $10,000,000 and an annual rental of $250,000.

3. *The Panama Canal Is Built.* Construction of the Panama Canal began in 1908 under Colonel GEORGE W. GOETHALS. It was completed in 1914. A great engineering feat, the Canal reduced the distance between New York and San Francisco from 13,000 to 5,000 miles. Colonel WILLIAM GORGAS did a noteworthy job of protecting the health of the 35,000 construction workers against yellow fever, malaria, and typhoid.

4. *The Role of Theodore Roosevelt.* President Theodore Roosevelt, an ardent supporter of American expansion and imperialism, was bitterly criticized at home and abroad for his diplomacy in acquiring the Canal Zone.

(a) During the 1903 revolution in Panama, Roosevelt sent two warships to Panamanian waters to protect American lives and property. Colombia protested that the ships were also used as a threat to prevent the landing of Colombian troops to put down the revolt.

(b) Roosevelt's actions aroused distrust and condemnation throughout Latin America. He later justified his role by stating, "I took the Canal and let Congress debate, and while the debate goes on the Canal does also." In 1921, after Roosevelt's death, the United States gave 25 million dollars to Colombia as a token reparation.

5. *The Canal Influences United States Foreign Policy.* The protection and control of the Panama Canal became an important part of United States foreign policy.

(a) Strong naval bases were built at Guantanamo Bay in Cuba and at Pearl Harbor in Hawaii, to safeguard the Canal. During the first decades of the century U.S. troops were sent to Latin American nations when revolutions threatened the security of the Canal.

(b) Since 1967, Panama and the United States have been trying to negotiate a new treaty that would give Panama greater immediate control over the Canal Zone, while allowing continuation of U.S. protection and operational control for the Canal itself. This status would continue until a designated date, when Panama would be vested with full sovereignty.

Use of the Monroe Doctrine in the 19th Century. In the 19th century, the United States used the Monroe Doctrine to check what it considered the extension of European *political influence* in the Western Hemisphere.

1. *Maximilian Affair.* During the Civil War, French Emperor Napoleon III established a puppet state in Mexico headed by Austrian Archduke Maximilian. Immediately after the war, when President Andrew Johnson condemned this as a violation of the Monroe Doctrine and threatened to send troops to oust the Emperor, Napoleon withdrew his French troops from Mexico. The puppet state was quickly overthrown by the Mexicans under the leadership of BENITO JUAREZ.

2. *Venezuelan Boundary Dispute.* In 1895, President Cleveland intervened in a boundary dispute between Venezuela and Great Britain. The difficulty resulted from the discovery of gold in a long disputed region on the border between Venezuela and British Guiana. Cleveland insisted that Britain submit the dispute to arbitration. His policy of "twisting the lion's tail" was based on the charge that Britain was violating the Monroe Doctrine by extending its political influence in Latin America.

(a) *Olney Doctrine Issued.* During the dispute, Secretary of State Richard Olney declared that the United States was "sovereign" in the Western Hemisphere and had the right to intervene whenever its own interests were involved. This statement became known as the *Olney Doctrine*.

(b) *Arbitration of the Dispute.* Although Britain refused to recognize the Olney Doctrine, it agreed to submit the matter to arbitration in order to avert a war. Subsequently the arbitration commission recognized the British claims.

Expansion of the Monroe Doctrine in the 20th Century. In the early part of the 20th century, the United States became increasingly interested in Latin America as a source of raw materials, a market for manufactured goods, and an outlet for surplus capital. In order to promote these economic interests, check further European economic penetration, protect our territorial interests, and safeguard the Panama Canal, the United States intervened actively in the affairs of Caribbean countries. It justified its actions by expanding its interpretation of the Monroe Doctrine.

1. *The Platt Amendment.* At the outbreak of the Spanish-American War, the United States guaranteed under the Teller Resolution that it would not annex Cuba. Though our government kept this promise, it persuaded Cuba after the war to add the *Platt Amendment* to its new Constitution of 1903. This clause gave the United States the right to intervene in Cuba in order to preserve order and independence, and also to establish naval and coaling stations there. Moveover, Cuba guaranteed not to yield territory to any other foreign power. In effect, the Platt Amendment made Cuba an American protectorate. During the next 30 years, the United States intervened frequently in Cuban affairs, as United States Marines were used to maintain order, protect American lives and property, and supervise elections.

2. *The Venezuela Debt Controversy.* In 1902, several European nations, led by Britain and Germany, blockaded Venezuela and actually fired on one of its villages when the country failed to pay its debts to them. Backed by an angry public, President Theodore Roosevelt persuaded both European nations to submit the matter to the Hague Court of Arbitration, which had been established in 1899 to promote the peaceful settlement of international disputes.

3. *The Roosevelt Corollary.* In 1904, when the Dominican Republic faced a similar threat of European intervention for non-collection of debts, Roosevelt proclaimed the *Roosevelt Corollary* (extension) of the Monroe Doctrine. He stated that the United States had the right to exercise "international police power" whenever Latin American republics were unable to maintain order or fulfill their obligations to other nations. The Corollary became known popularly as the *"Big Stick" policy*.

4. *"Dollar Diplomacy."* Roosevelt's successor, President William Howard Taft, helped expand United States influence by a policy of *"dollar diplomacy."* Under dollar diplomacy, United States bankers were encouraged by the government to invest in foreign areas of strategic importance to the United States, particularly in the Far East and in the Panama Canal area. In return, the bankers were assured that their investments would be protected by American diplomacy. Dollar diplomacy, it was felt, would give United States an economic stake in securing order and stability in areas considered important to the national interest. It would also prevent situations in which other major powers could take advantage of financial chaos in weak Latin American republics.

5. *Military Intervention in Latin America.* Roosevelt, Taft, and their successors used both the Roosevelt Corollary and dollar diplomacy to make virtual protectorates of several small Caribbean nations, as indicated below.

(a) *Dominican Republic.* In 1905, the United States assumed control of Dominican customs collections when that unstable republic defaulted on debt payments to European powers. This arrangement was surrendered gradually in the 1930s, under the Good Neighbor Policy (page 456). U.S. armed forces were stationed on Dominican soil from 1905 to 1907 and again from 1916 to 1924 to preserve order.

(b) Haiti. Political disorder in Haiti resulted in its occupation by marines from 1915 to 1930. Haiti was forced to sign a treaty agreeing to United States supervision of her political and economic affairs.

(c) Nicaragua. In 1912, at the request of the Nicaraguan President, marines were used to protect American lives and property. Thereafter, and until 1933, the United States intervened frequently in the political and economic affairs of Nicaragua. In 1916, the *Bryan-Chamorro Treaty* gave the United States the right to build a canal across Nicaragua, to lease the Corn Islands for military purposes for 99 years, and to establish a naval base in the Gulf of Fonseca.

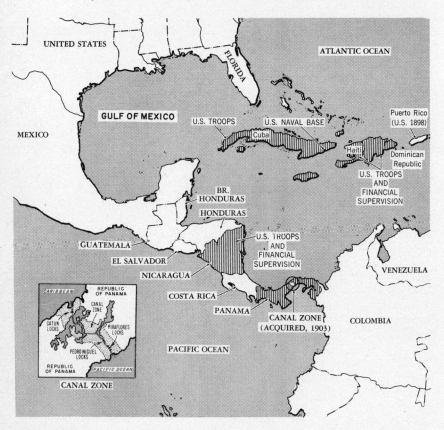

United States intervention in the Caribbean area in the early 20th century.

(d) Mexico. During the Mexican Revolution of 1911-18, the United States intervened militarily on two occasions. In 1914, United States troops landed at Veracruz in Mexico to protect American lives and property there. In 1918, a United States military expedition entered northern Mexico to end the guerrilla raids of General "Pancho" Villa along the Texas border. President Wilson also suspended diplomatic relations with Mexico during its Revolution because of political instability. (See page 460.)

The Caribbean — A United States Sphere of Influence. After the Presidency of Theodore Roosevelt, European governments generally recognized the "paramount interest" of the United States in the Caribbean, and ceased actively to challenge our leadership there.

1. *Naval Supremacy.* In return for United States support in the Far East and Europe, Britain withdrew most of its fleet from the Caribbean, leaving the United States in position of undisputed naval supremacy in the Western Hemisphere.

2. *Growing Economic Influence.* During the first quarter of the 20th century, United States businessmen invested heavily in Central and South American industry, trade, and government bonds. These investments gave them considerable economic and political influence.

3. *Latin American Distrust.* During the 19th century, Latin Americans had generally approved of the United States' applications of the Monroe Doctrine in their behalf. Dollar diplomacy and military intervention in the early 20th century, however, aroused suspicion, fear, and distrust. The United States became known as the "Colossus of the North," and its policies in Latin America were angrily denounced as "Yankee imperialism." In 1907, at the suggestion of Argentine Foreign Minister Luis Drago, the *Second Hague Conference* (see page 469) adopted a resolution opposing the collection of debts by force unless the debtor nation refused or rejected arbitration. This *Drago Doctrine* was aimed as much at the United States as at Europe.

The Pan-American Movement. At the same time that the United States extended its influence in Latin America, it also actively tried to improve its political, economic, and cultural relations with its hemispheric neighbors. This policy was called *Pan-Americanism*.

1. *Beginnings of Pan-Americanism.* The unofficial beginnings of Pan-Americanism go back to 1826 when the representatives of the independent Latin American countries met in Panama under the leadership of Simon Bolivar. The United States showed little interest in this and other early 19th-century conferences. The modern Pan-American Movement started *officially* with the meeting of the first *Pan-American Conference* in Washington, D. C., in 1889. This was largely a result of the efforts of United States Secretary of State JAMES G. BLAINE. The Conference established machinery for calling regular Pan-American conferences at scheduled intervals thereafter. At the second Pan-American Conference (1901–02), the *Union of American Republics* was established, with headquarters in Washington, D. C. Later (1914) its name was changed to the *Pan-American Union*. In 1948, the Pan-American Union was transformed into the present *Organization of American States (OAS)*. Canada was invited to join the movement, but she declined to do so because of her membership in the British Commonwealth. Nevertheless, Canada did send unofficial observers to many Pan-American meetings.

2. *Achievements.* Until the Organization of American States was created in 1948, the Pan-American Union acted primarily as a clearing house for the exchange of commercial, agricultural, and educational information among member nations. Members were considered equals.

(a) At regularly scheduled Pan-American conferences, the members considered such questions as tariffs, trade, finances, child labor, and the arbitration of disputes.

(b) The Pan-American Union gave concrete advice to member nations on the improvement of agriculture, the development of industry, and the use of natural resources. It also sponsored tours and exchanges of students, teachers, and artists. The *Inter-American Council of Jurists* advised on legal questions.

3. *Limitations.* Despite its usefulness as a means of international cooperation, the Pan-American Movement suffered from Latin American suspicion of United States aims and methods.

(a) Latin American leaders were angered by the Olney Doctrine, the "big stick," and dollar diplomacy.

(b) At Pan-American conferences, our Hemispheric neighbors also protested against the use of the Monroe Doctrine by the United States alone (*unilateral interpretation*). They asked for an equal voice in deciding upon the Doctrine's use and enforcement (*multilateral interpretation*).

(c) Some Latin American leaders tried to develop a movement known as "*Pan-Hispanism*," to promote Latin American unity and cultural relations with Spain. They not only angrily denounced the "big stick" and dollar diplomacy, but also reminded Latin Americans of the United States' annexations of Texas, the Canal Zone, and Puerto Rico.

(d) Until the late 1920's, the United States rejected Latin American protests and upheld its application of the Monroe Doctrine on the basis of international law. It argued: **(1)** that the Doctrine protected Latin America from the imperialist designs of European nations, and **(2)** that it had not been used as "an instrument of violence and oppression."

REVIEW TEST (Chapter 25 — Part I)

Select the number preceding the word or expression that best completes each statement or answers each question.

1. Which of the following occurred during the last quarter of the 19th century? (1) Maximilian Affair (2) Venezuela Boundary Dispute (3) Gentlemen's Agreement with Japan (4) Opening of the Panama Canal

2. Of the following, the factor that had the greatest influence on the decision of the United States to build the Panama Canal was the (1) success of the Erie Canal (2) discovery of gold in California (3) delay in the completion of the Union Pacific Railroad (4) development of the United States as a world power

3. The Panama Canal shortened the all-water route to (1) Buenos Aires (2) Capetown (3) Lima (4) Veracruz

4. Which of these groups of islands is closest to the Panama Canal? (1) Samoan Islands (2) Aleutian Islands (3) Hawaiian Islands (4) Virgin Islands

5. Theodore Roosevelt's corollary to the Monroe Doctrine provided for (1) freedom for all the colonies of European nations in the Western Hemisphere (2) the neutrality of the United States in case of European wars (3) the recognition of the American nations which have seceded from Spain (4) intervention by the United States in the affairs of Latin American countries to insure payment of debts by these countries

6. The Platt Amendment defined the relations between the United States and (1) the Philippines (2) Hawaii (3) Cuba (4) Panama

7. Theodore Roosevelt's point of view in regard to Caribbean affairs is best expressed by (1) "Peace at any price." (2) "Millions for defense, but not one cent for tribute." (3) "We are too proud to fight." (4) "Speak softly and carry a big stick."

8. Pan-Americanism is a movement to (1) unite all American countries under one government (2) bring about closer cooperation between the United States and Latin America (3) improve relations between the United States and Canada (4) bring all the American nations into the United Nations

9. Which of the following conferences laid the foundation for the establishment of the Pan-American Union? (1) Panama Conference, 1826 (2) Washington Conference, 1889 (3) Lima Conference, 1938 (4) Montevideo Conference, 1933

10. William Howard Taft is associated most closely with the beginnings of (1) dollar diplomacy (2) watchful waiting (3) brinkmanship (4) overseas expansion

Select the letter of the item in each group that does **NOT** *belong with the others.*

1. General characteristics of Latin America: (a) unstable government (b) high rate of illiteracy (c) universal suffrage (d) economy based on agriculture

2. Population groups in Latin America: (a) Negroes (b) Mestizos (c) Pampas (d) Indians

3. Latin American heroes: (a) Bernardo O'Higgins (b) Jose de San Martin (c) Dom Pedro (d) Simon Bolivar

4. Participants in the Maximilian Affair: (a) Archduke Maximilian (b) Grover Cleveland (c) Benito Juarez (d) Napoleon III

5. Policies developed by the United States in dealing with Latin America: (a) Roosevelt Corollary (b) Olney Doctrine (c) Pan-Americanism (d) Drago Doctrine

Essay Questions

1. Explain two important ways in which the geography of Latin America has affected its way of life.

2. Show how each of the following aspects of Latin American life is similar to or different from that of the United States: (a) government (b) economy (c) history (d) culture.

3. Show how each of the following helped make the Caribbean an American sphere of influence in the early part of the 19th century: (a) acquisition of the Panama Canal (b) the "big stick" (c) dollar diplomacy.

4. (a) Explain the nature and aims of Pan-American Movement during the first three decades of the 20th century. (b) Why do some claim that it was a success in this period while others consider it a failure?

5. Identify the role played by each in the history of relations between the United States and Latin America: Grover Cleveland, Richard Olney, William Howard Taft, William Gorgas, George Goethals, Theodore Roosevelt, James G. Blaine.

Part II — THE UNITED STATES TRIES TO IMPROVE RELATIONS WITH LATIN AMERICA

Since the late 1920's the United States has tried actively to improve its relations with its neighbors in the Western Hemisphere and to become itself a "good neighbor." In doing so, it has generally reversed earlier policies of one-sided intervention in Latin America.

Beginnings of the Retreat From Imperialism. The United States began its "retreat from imperialism" during the administration of Herbert Hoover. There were two basic reasons for this change in attitude. In the first place, there was growing recognition that in a rapidly changing and perilous world, the United States could no longer afford to make enemies in Latin America. Also, during the worldwide depression after 1929, many Americans suffered losses on their investments in foreign nations, including Latin America. This helped to produce strong sentiments against "economic imperialism."

The following significant reversals in policy toward Latin America occurred while Hoover was President.

1. *Rejection of the Roosevelt Corollary.* In 1930, the State Department published the *Clark Memorandum,* which officially rejected the Roosevelt Corollary in the following words: "The so-called Roosevelt Corollary . . . is not justified by the terms of the Monroe Doctrine, however much it may be justified by the application of the doctrine of self-preservation."

2. *Withdrawal of Marines from the Caribbean.* Under Hoover, the United States removed the Marines from Nicaragua in 1933 (after 20 years of almost continuous occupation) and promised to remove them from Haiti by 1934.

The Good Neighbor Policy. Franklin D. Roosevelt, Hoover's successor, built upon the foundation of his predecessor and inaugurated a new era of friendship with the United States' Latin neighbors. In his Inaugural Address in 1933, he pledged the United States to the policy of the "good neighbor." Roosevelt's program for Latin America, known as the *Good Neighbor Policy,* became an important part of United States foreign policy.

1. *"Pan-Americanization" of the Monroe Doctrine.* Under the Good Neighbor Policy, the United States "Pan-Americanized" the Monroe Doctrine, by abandoning its unilateral interpretation of the policy and agreeing to a multilateral approach. At the *Montevideo Conference* of 1933, Roosevelt declared that the United States was opposed to armed intervention in the Western Hemisphere by any nation and that such intervention was the *joint concern* of the entire continent. These principles were spelled out at the *Buenos Aires* and *Lima Conferences* of 1936 and 1938. In the *Declaration of Lima,* which became a symbol of the Good Neighbor Policy, all the American republics joined the United States in adopting the principle that any attack upon an American republic by a non-American nation would be considered an attack against all. The 21 republics also agreed that no state had the right to intervene in "the external or internal affairs of another." Finally, as a warning to the totalitarian states (Nazi Germany, Fascist Italy, and Japan), it was agreed that all American governments would consult to take joint action whenever the security of the Western Hemisphere was endangered.

2. *Abandonment of the Policy of Intervention.* United States actions under Roosevelt gave proof of United States abandonment of the policy of intervention in Latin America. **(a)** In 1934, the Platt Amendment, permitting United States intervention in Cuba, was repealed. **(b)** In the same year, the last United States Marines left Haiti. **(c)** In 1936, the United States renegotiated its position in Panama on terms more favorable to the tiny Central American republic. **(d)** The United States also refused to use force in 1938 when Mexico seized United States oil properties.

3. *The Reciprocal Trade Program.* The *Reciprocal Trade Program* of the Roosevelt administration (see page 387) also promoted good relations with Latin America. Reciprocal trade agreements between the United States and its sister republics of the Western Hemisphere increased exports as well as imports, and also improved both economic and political relations.

4. *Other Aspects of the Good Neighbor Policy.* Other elements of Roosevelt's Good Neighbor Policy included: **(a)** the granting of loans by a newly created *Export-Import Bank* to United States firms doing business with Latin America; **(b)** the establishment of the office of *Coordinator of Inter-American Affairs,* to promote increased cultural relations among the nations of the Americas, and **(c)** the beginning of the construction of a *Pan-American Highway,* with United States financial aid.

Inter-American Cooperation During World War II. The effectiveness of the Good Neighbor Policy was shown by the high degree of inter-American solidarity during World War II. After the Japanese attack on the United States in 1941, many Latin American nations immediately declared war on Japan. In contrast to World War I, when only eight Latin American states had joined the United States and its Allies, *all* twenty participated to some degree in the struggle against the Axis in the second World War. In 1945, all the American states adopted the *Act of Chapultepec,* guaranteeing the territory, sovereignty, and independence of all American nations against aggression from outside the Hemisphere.

NOTE: Argentina did not break off relations with the Axis until 1944. Among the important factors for this late action were: **(1)** pre-war suspicion of the Good Neighbor Policy; and **(2)** Nazi influence in Argentina, which had the support of German, Italian, and Japanese minorities in that country. Because of her position, Argentina was isolated diplomatically and economically by most Latin American nations during the war.

For relations between the United States and Latin America since World War II, see Chapter 30.

REVIEW TEST (Chapter 25 — Part II)

Select the number preceding the word or expression that best completes each statement or answers each question.

1. During whose administration did the United States first officially renounce the "big stick" approach in Latin America? (1) Calvin Coolidge (2) Herbert Hoover (3) Franklin D. Roosevelt (4) Harry Truman

2. Franklin D. Roosevelt's policy toward the Latin American nations may best be described as (1) aggressive imperialism (2) strictly "hands off" (3) Hemispheric cooperation (4) colonial expansion

3. The Good Neighbor Policy was promoted by the (1) Insular cases (2) "big stick" policy (3) Roosevelt Corollary (4) multilateral interpretation of the Monroe Doctrine

4. Which of the following was a part of the United States Good Neighbor Policy? (1) withdrawal of American troops from Haiti (2) assistance in outlawing communism (3) adoption of the Platt Amendment (4) organization of a United States Latin American bloc within the League of Nations

5. The last Latin American nation to break relations with the Axis powers during World War II was (1) Cuba (2) Brazil (3) Argentina (4) Panama

6. All of the following were aspects of the Good Neighbor Policy *except* (1) the Export-Import Bank (2) Office of the Coordinator of American Affairs (3) Pan-Hispanism (4) reciprocal trade agreements

7. Which of the following occurred *first?* (1) Clark Memorandum (2) abrogation of Platt Amendment (3) Act of Chapultepec (4) Declaration of Lima

8. The Good Neighbor Policy was begun in the (1) 1920's (2) 1930's (3) 1940's (4) 1950's

9. Which of the following occurred after the Japanese attack on the United States at Pearl Harbor in 1941? (1) Most Latin American nations declared their neutrality. (2) All Latin American nations pledged full support to the United States. (3) Many Latin American nations declared war on Japan. (4) Panama closed the Panama Canal to East-West trade.

10. Which of the following was a pre-World War II statement that proclaimed that an attack on any one American republic would be considered an attack on all? (1) Lima Declaration (2) Act of Chapultepec (3) Fourteen Points (4) Atlantic Charter

Essay Questions

1. Give two reasons that help explain the United States' "retreat from imperialism" in the Caribbean in the late 1920's.

2. Franklin D. Roosevelt called his Latin-American program the policy of the "Good Neighbor." By giving examples explain whether or not the actions of the United States during his administration actually made for better relations with the countries of Central and South America.

3. Discuss the meaning of the statement, "World War II was the first major test of the Good Neighbor Policy."

Part III — THE UNITED STATES AND ITS NORTH AMERICAN NEIGHBORS

The United States' relations with its two immediate neighbors, Mexico and Canada, have generally been good in recent years. In both cases, however, there have also been times of bitterness and tension, particularly in the early days of our Republic when the boundaries between the United States and its two neighbors were still uncertain.

United States and Mexico. Relations between the United States and Mexico have been similar to those between the United States and the rest of Latin America. In the past, there have been alternating periods of friendship and hostility. Since the adoption of the Good Neighbor Policy, relations between the two nations have become increasingly cordial. Today relations between the United States and Mexico are characterized by a high degree of cooperation.

The United States and Mexico in the 19th Century. Highlights of United States-Mexican relations in the 19th century were the *Mexican War* (see page 218), which left a heritage of ill-will, and the *Maximilian Affair* (see page 252), which resulted in improved feelings.

Growth of United States Investments in Mexico. Toward the end of the 19th century and during the early 20th century, United States investors and businessmen invested about a billion dollars in Mexican mines, railroads, oil wells, and ranches. Under the regime of PORFIRIO DIAZ, dictator of Mexico from 1877 to 1911, foreign businessmen, particularly from the United States, were encouraged to help develop Mexico's mines, land, and other industries.

The Mexican Revolution of 1911. Under Diaz, the living conditions of most Mexicans remained desperately poor. In 1911, under the leadership of FRANCISCO MADERO, a sincere liberal reformer, the Mexicans revolted and overthrew the Diaz regime despite the violent opposition of reactionary groups. Unfortunately for the United States, Madero was murdered by forces of VICTORIANO HUERTA, who in 1913 seized power and established a reactionary military dictatorship of his own.

"Watchful Waiting." President Wilson refused to recognize the Huerta regime on the ground that it had come to power by violence and did not represent the will of the people. He was convinced that a policy of non-intervention, which he called *"watchful waiting,"* would encourage the overthrow of Huerta. Wilson was bitterly condemned by businessmen, who called upon him to intervene in Mexico in order to protect their property, as the United States had done elsewhere under its policy of dollar diplomacy (see pages 451-52).

United States Intervention in Mexico. Wilson was soon forced to abandon "watchful waiting."

1. *The Veracruz Incident and Overthrow of Huerta.* In 1914, the Huerta regime arrested several American sailors at Tampico, Mexico. (They were attached to a naval squadron which had been sent to protect American lives and property.) Moreover, the Huerta government was known to be receiving German arms. In retaliation, the Wilson administration sent armed forces to seize the Mexican port of Veracruz. War was averted by the mediation of the "ABC" powers (Argentina, Brazil, Chile). Huerta fled the country and was succeeded by VENUSTIANO CARRANZA. When Carranza guaranteed to respect the lives and property of foreigners, the United States recognized his government and withdrew its forces.

2. *United States Expeditionary Forces Try to Capture Pancho Villa.* In 1916, the United States was forced to intervene actively for a second time. FRANCISCO (Pancho) VILLA, a rival of Carranza, resented United States recognition of the new regime. He seized and murdered several Americans in northern Mexico and raided American territory across the border. Villa also hoped that United States intervention would help unseat Carranza because of loss of prestige. With Carranza's reluctant permission, United States forces led by General JOHN J. PERSHING entered Mexico to punish Villa. Villa eluded capture, and the American troops were withdrawn early in 1917, because of the involvement of the United States in World War I.

Constitutional Government in Mexico Since 1917. Under Carranza, Mexico adopted a new liberal constitution in 1917, providing for democratic elections, land distribution, and social reforms. It also placed ownership of Mexico's natural resources in the hands of the people.

1. *Mexico's Social and Economic Revolution.* Under Carranza and his successors Mexico has undergone a genuine social and economic revolution.

(a) Large estates have been broken up and over 125 millions of acres of land distributed to the poor farmers.

(b) Thousands of schools and hospitals have been constructed.

(c) Improved transportation facilities (railroads, highways) have been introduced.

(d) New industries have been developed by the government.

(e) The rights of workers have been guaranteed.

(f) More land has been brought under cultivation as a result of large-scale irrigation projects.

(g) Church and state have been separated.

(h) Under the Constitution of 1917, Mexico owns and operates key industries such as electric power plants, oil fields, and railroads. Most business, however, is privately owned.

(i) Despite the nation's economic progress and rising standard of living, most Mexicans are still poor, with an average per capita income of $300. This is relatively high for Latin America, but it compares poorly with an average per capita income of $2500 in the United States.

2. Increased Political Stability. Since the late 1920's, Mexico's government has been one of the soundest and most stable in Latin America. Since 1929, all its presidents have been elected in regularly scheduled elections, and there have been no major attempts at revolution.

Recent Relations Between the United States and Mexico. In recent years, relations between the United States and Mexico have improved considerably.

1. Bad Feeling in the 1920's and 1930's. During the 1920's and 1930's, there was much opposition in the United States to the Mexican Revolution. Many Americans resented the confiscation of Church property and restrictions on Church influence. Businessmen were bitter over the imposition of new rentals and taxes by Mexico, and the collection of royalties on oil produced by foreign companies. In 1938, the confiscation by Mexico of foreign-owned oil properties aggravated the bad feelings and threatened the Good Neighbor program.

2. Improving Relations. Despite the near crises that developed, cordial relations were restored between the two nations. Especially outstanding in bringing about this reconciliation was the work of United States Ambassador to Mexico Dwight W. Morrow in the 1920's, and Secretary of State Cordell Hull in the 1930's. In the 1940's, after several years of negotiations, Mexico agreed to compensate the owners of the nationalized oil properties. In addition, under President Cardenas (1934–40), the government modified its hostile attitude toward the Catholic Church.

3. Cooperation Since World War II. Since World War II, relations between Mexico and the United States have been friendly. The two nations have worked cooperatively to attempt to solve a number of existing problems and disputes, including **(a)** the continuing illegal entry into the United States of seasonal migratory Mexican agricultural workers ("wetbacks"); **(b)** growing illicit drug traffic from Mexico into the United States; and **(c)** damage to Mexican crops resulting from the flow of U. S. industry-polluted Colorado River waters into Mexico during the past few years. The United States has also increased its aid to Mexico to help develop its industries and complete the Pan-American Highway.

United States and Canada. The history of relations between the United States and Canada has for the most part been one of increasing cordiality and cooperation. For over a century the two nations have shared the longest unfortified boundary in the world.

Canada as a Nation. Canada is a self-governing member of the British Commonwealth. It is the world's second largest nation in area. It is sparsely populated (about 19 million) and has a high standard of living. Canada is rich in natural resources, including farm lands, minerals, forests, and water power. In recent years, Canada's manufacturing industries have grown rapidly.

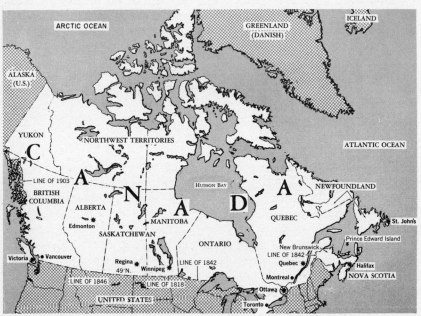

Brief History of Canada. The highlights of Canadian history may be summarized as follows:

1. *Taken from France by England in 1763.* Canada was wrested from France by Britain in the French and Indian War (1756–63).

2. *Rebellion for Home Rule in 1837.* Though loyal to England during the American Revolution and War of 1812, the Canadians (with the support of some American citizens) rebelled for more home rule in 1837. The rebellion was suppressed.

3. *Durham Report Recommends Self-Government.* In 1839, the *Durham Report* recommended self-government for Canada and other colonies capable of ruling themselves. This report has been called the "Magna Carta of the British colonies."

4. *Canada Becomes a Dominion (1867).* In 1867, the British *North America Act* combined the Canadian provinces into a federation called the *Dominion of Canada.*

5. *Canada Plays a Leading Role in the British Commonwealth.* Since 1867, Canada has developed into a democratic self-governing state within the Commonwealth. It has taken an active role in imperial affairs, and has come to Britain's aid during both World Wars.

6. *Role in UN and NATO.* Since World War II, Canada has been a leading spokesman for the anti-communist nations and an active member of the UN and NATO.

7. *Cooperation with OAS.* Because of its Commonwealth ties, Canada did not become a member of the Pan-American Union or the Organization of American States. It has, nevertheless, cooperated with these organizations and has sent unofficial observers to most conferences.

Relations Between the United States and Canada. There has from time to time been friction between the United States and Canada. For the most part, however, the United States has enjoyed good relations with Canada. Agreements such as the *Rush-Bagot Agreement* of 1817, demilitarizing the Great Lakes, and the *Webster-Ashburton Treaty* of 1842, which settled northeastern boundary disputes, paved the way for harmony.

1. *Common Bonds.* The two nations share an unfortified border 3,000 miles long. They also share a common language and a heritage of democratic rights and institutions. In addition, they are each other's best customers and cooperate in a program of joint defense.

(a) *Cooperation in World Wars.* Canada and the United States fought side by side in two world wars. During World War II, Canada permitted the United States to construct the Alcan Highway on Canadian soil, to facilitate shipment of arms and supplies to Alaska.

(b) *St. Lawrence Seaway.* After World War II, Canada and the United States cooperated to build the long delayed *St. Lawrence Seaway,* which has made it possible for ocean-going vessels to sail directly from the Atlantic Ocean to the Great Lakes. Finally completed in 1969, the Seaway has improved navigation, increased the volume of shipping and made possible development of hydroelectric power.

(c) *Joint Defense.* Because of the possibility of an attack over the North Pole in case of future war between Russia and the West, the United States and Canada have cooperated to build radar warning systems across the entire width of Canada. One of these is the *DEW (Distant Early Warning Systems),* operated by personnel representing both nations.

(d) *Recent Agreements.* In 1972, the two nations agreed to joint pollution control on the Great Lakes; in 1974, they set up procedures to deal with pollution from oil carriers and offshore drilling rigs. To curb airplane hijacking, terrorism, and narcotics traffic, a pact was signed in 1976 denying refuge to hijackers, and persons sought for murder, kidnapping, or assault on diplomats or heads of state.

2. *Problems and Disagreements.* In the 19th and early 20th centuries, the United States and Canada argued over such matters as boundaries, United States whaling rights off the west coast of Canada, and United States fishing rights in Newfoundland waters. All of the problems were eventually settled by negotiation. In recent years a number of new problems and disagreements have developed.

   (a) *Nuclear Weapons.* Although the United States has been reluctant to share its nuclear weapons with its European allies, it has urged Canada to accept defensive atomic weapons that could help protect the Hemisphere should there be a communist attack by way of the Arctic. Although Canada has agreed to accept such weapons, it has not been over-anxious to do so on the grounds they would be useless against a large-scale missile attack.

   (b) *Trade Problems.* Canada and the United States have for many years been each other's best customer. Because of the size, diversity, and great importance of this trade, problems have arisen frequently. For example, in 1973, at the height of the "energy crisis," Canada imposed severe restrictions on exports of crude oil and petroleum products. After sharp criticism in the United States, steps were taken to lower these restrictions. Similarly, strains have resulted from restrictions on Canadian-American trade in farm products.

   (c) *United States Control of Canadian Industries.* Canadians in recent years have been increasingly concerned over heavy American investments in Canada's industries, more than 40% of which are now controlled by United States citizens. For example, Americans own over 90% of the securities of Canadian auto firms. Although the Canadians realize that American investments have contributed to their country's industrial development, they would prefer to have their economic life more under the control of native businessmen and investors.

   (d) *Other Problems.* Recently, the United States has been concerned over Canada's decision to reduce its commitments to the North American Air Defense Alliance, as well as to NATO. Canadians argue that such defense groupings are becoming irrelevant in an era of intercontinental nuclear missiles. Criticism has also been evoked by the fact that Canada permitted thousands of young Americans opposed to the Vietnam War to live and work there, thus avoiding the draft.

REVIEW TEST (Chapter 25 — Part III)

Select the number preceding the word or expression that best completes each statement or answers each question.

   1. Which of the following incidents produced Mexican good will for the United States? (1) Mexican War (2) Maximilian Affair (3) Veracruz Incident (4) the expropriation of American-owned properties in 1938

   2. Which of the following attitudes was taken by the Mexican government toward United States businessmen seeking to invest capital at the beginning of the 20th century? (1) They were welcomed. (2) They were denied such privileges. (3) A United States loan was called for as a necessary condition for investment. (4) Mexico permitted but did not encourage such enterprises.

3. What was the attitude of reactionary groups in Mexico to the Revolution of 1911? (1) They supported it. (2) They opposed it. (3) They called on the United States for aid. (4) They offered reforms to the peons to delay it.

4. The "ABC" powers were called upon in 1914 to (1) end warfare between Mexico and Guatemala (2) iron out the domestic problems faced by the Mexican government (3) prevent communism from making further inroads (4) mediate a dispute between the United States and Mexico

5. The Constitution of 1917 in Mexico resulted in (1) a much higher standard of living for most people (2) restricted rights for workers (3) greater political stability (4) union of Church and State

6. Self-government for Canada was first recommended in the (1) Durham Report (2) statute of Westminster (3) Reform Bill of 1832 (4) the British North America Act of 1867

7. Canada is an active member of the (1) UN and NATO (2) the OAS and the UN (3) the League of Nations and the Common Market (4) NATO and the Common Market

8. All of the following statements about the St. Lawrence Seaway are true *except* (1) It was an example of cooperation between the United States and Canada. (2) It helps make possible an all water route through the heart of Canada. (3) It has increased the hydroelectric facilities of both Canada and the United States. (4) It was opposed for many years by railroads and private utilities in the United States.

9. The DEW and Pine Tree lines are (1) radar warning systems (2) Polaris missile installations (3) boundary lines established by treaties between the United States and Canada (4) sources of much friction between the United States and Canada

10. On which issue have the United States and Canada taken opposing positions in recent years? (1) a new Canadian flag (2) support of UN programs (3) American fishing activities in Canadian waters (4) Canada's contribution to NATO

Match each name in Column A with the letter of the item in Column B that is most clearly identified with it.

A

1. Porfirio Diaz
2. Woodrow Wilson
3. Francisco Madero
4. Pancho Villa
5. Dwight W. Morrow

B

a. negotiated Rush-Bagot Agreement
b. Mexican dictator
c. helped improve relations between Mexico and the United States in the 1920's
d. caused the United States to send troops into Mexico
e. Revolutionary leader
f. "Watchful Waiting"

Essay Questions

1. Explain three ways in which relations between the United States and Mexico in the 20th century have been similar to or different from relations between the United States and the rest of Latin America.

2. "Canada and the United States have set an example of good neighborliness for the rest of the world." (a) Give data to support this statement: (1) in the 19th century and (2) in the 20th century. (b) Discuss two exceptions to this general trend.

3. Show how each of the following has improved or hurt relations between the United States and its northern and southern neighbors (Canada and Mexico): "Watchful waiting"; the Webster-Ashburton Treaty; the activities of Pancho Villa; Mexico's 20th-century social and economic revolution; the Good Neighbor Policy; handling of the "wetback" problem; the St. Lawrence Seaway; the cold war; United States investments in Canada.

CHAPTER 26

United States Far Eastern Policy in the 19th and Early 20th Centuries

United States policy in the Far East has been shaped largely by commercial and military considerations. The development of our Far Eastern policy has centered mainly around China and Japan.

Origins of United States Interest in the Far East. For most of the 19th century, United States interest in the Far East was primarily commercial. Toward the end of the century, and in the period before World War I, strategic as well as commercial interests became important.

1. *United States Trade With the Far East.* Although we began to trade with China soon after the War of Independence, the Far East as a whole was not a major concern until the United States expanded to the West Coast and became a Pacific power. While our trade with the Far East continued to grow slowly in the 19th century, only 2% of our trade was with that region in 1900.

2. *Growth of a United States Empire.* Between 1867 and 1890, the United States took possession of many small and generally uninhabited or sparsely inhabited islands in the Pacific. Growing trade interests resulted from the annexation of Hawaii in 1898. After the acquisition of the Philippines and Guam, as a result of the Spanish-American War, United States interests became military as well as commercial. As the nation became a world power with an empire of its own, it became concerned with matters such as the *"status quo"* and the *"balance of power"* in Asia and the Pacific.

The United States and China in the 19th Century. In the 19th century, American relations with China became increasingly friendly, despite some friction over immigration toward the century's end.

1. *Extension of Privileges to the United States.* After the Opium War with Great Britain (1838–42), China was forced to open additional ports to foreign trade, and to extend extra-territorial rights to Western nations. The United States received these privileges along with other countries. Friendly relations with China were established as a result of the diplomatic efforts of Caleb Cushing, Anson Burlingame, and others.

2. *Chinese Immigration.* In 1868, in return for favorable trade privileges, the United States allowed Chinese citizens to enter freely as immigrants (*Burlingame Treaty*). Several years later, because of strong opposition to the importation of Chinese laborers (mainly to help build the transcontinental railroads), Congress passed the *Chinese Exclusion Act* (1882). It ended the migration of Chinese laborers to the United States. The Act was extended and made permanent in 1902, in spite of China's protests.

The "Open-Door" Policy. The United States did not participate in the imperialist scramble for concessions, privileges, and spheres of influence which, toward the close of the century, resulted in the "carving up" of China by Great Britain, France, Germany, Russia, and Japan. By the late 1890's, however, the United States began to fear that we might be cut out of Asiatic markets by foreign powers. This concern became more pronounced as we extended our empire to Hawaii and the Philippines. It led to the issuance of the so-called *"Open-Door" policy.*

1. *Provisions.* In 1899, United States Secretary of State, John Hay issued a "circular letter" to foreign powers asking them to accept formally the following principles: non-interference with special national rights ("spheres of influence") already established in China; treatment of all nations equally within each sphere of influence; extension to all nations of tariff concessions obtained from China; and a guarantee of China's territorial and administrative integrity. The purposes of this "open door" were: **(a)** to safeguard United States trade interests, and **(b)** to maintain China's independence and identity as a nation.

2. *Violation by Japan.* Although the great powers nominally accepted the principles of the "open door," they frequently ignored them. Japan, in particular, tried to close the "open door" and to establish hegemony (supremacy) in the Far East during the first three decades of the 20th century.

3. *Cornerstone of United States Policy.* Despite the fact that the policy of the "open door" did not bind other nations, it became the cornerstone of United States foreign policy in the Far East, and an essential element in the friendly relations between the United States and China in the early part of the 20th century.

The Boxer Rebellion. United States actions after the *Boxer Rebellion* promoted good relations with China.

1. *Outbreak of the Rebellion.* In 1900, the "Boxers," a patriotic, secret society of Chinese who deeply resented Western imperialism, rebelled against foreigners. They murdered nearly 300 Europeans (mainly missionaries and their families), and destroyed foreign property. Over 900 foreigners took refuge in the foreign legations in Peking.

2. *International Army Restores Order.* An international army of European, Japanese, and American soldiers rescued their besieged nationals, and restored order. Unfortunately, some of the troops also engaged in looting and unnecessary brutality.

3. *The United States Invokes the "Open-Door" Policy.* United States Secretary of State Hay invoked the "Open-Door" policy by asking the foreign powers not to punish China by further partition. This was accepted. However, Boxer leaders were punished, and China was required to pay a heavy indemnity.

4. *United States Returns Part of the Indemnity.* The United States won China's good-will by returning most of its share of the indemnity to China. It was used as a fund for sending Chinese students to study in American colleges.

United States Recognition of the Chinese Republic. In 1911, the reactionary Chinese monarchy was overthrown by liberal Chinese nationalists led by SUN YAT-SEN, who believed that China must modernize and Westernize in order for it to advance and throw off the yoke of imperialism. The United States was one of the first to recognize the new republic.

Early Relations Between the United States and Japan. Early contacts between the United States and Japan resulted in a period of friendly relations.

1. *The United States Helps Open Japan to the West.* Japan was opened to Western influence as a result of the naval expedition of Commodore MATTHEW PERRY. Perry led an expedition to Japan in 1853 to arrange for better treatment of American shipwrecked sailors and to obtain trade privileges. He impressed the Shogun (the ruler of Japan) with the superiority of Western civilization by firing the cannon on his warships and by showing samples of Western industry such as sewing machines and model railroads. As a result, the Japanese negotiated a treaty with the United States in 1854, granting better treatment to shipwrecked sailors, and the right to anchor and refuel in Japanese harbors. In 1859, the American envoy, TOWNSEND HARRIS, persuaded Japan to open one port to American commerce. Within several years similar rights were extended to other nations. For many years, the United States looked upon Japan with a "paternal" air, almost as a protege.

2. *Japan Modernizes.* Contact with Americans and Europeans convinced Japan's leaders that she could learn much from the West, and also that she would have to move fast to avoid Western domination. An amazing transformation took place between 1867 and 1914 during which Japan adopted and accepted Western ways with great skill. **(a)** The nobles deposed the Shoguns and united the country. Power was restored to the Emperor, and a constitutional monarchy was established, in which the army and navy retained much power. **(b)** Feudalism and serfdom were ended; land was given to the peasants; young people were sent abroad to study; and the Japanese army and navy were modernized along Western lines. **(c)** A Japanese industrial revolution produced a factory system, thousands of miles of railroad, a large merchant marine, an expanding cotton industry, and a fast-growing foreign trade.

Japan Becomes an Imperialist Aggressor. Japan also imitated European powers by embarking on a policy of imperialism in the Far East. China was her chief victim.

1. *Reasons for Japanese Imperialism.* Japanese imperialism resulted from economic, nationalistic, social, and military considerations. She wished to obtain markets and raw materials. Japanese militarists and patriots were anxious for prestige. The nation was overpopulated. Japan also wished to strengthen her military position in order to dominate the Orient.

2. *Sino-Japanese War (1894–95).* Utilizing her new army and navy, Japan defeated China in the *Sino-Japanese War* of 1894–95, a conflict caused by rivalry over Korea. As a result, Japan obtained Formosa and special rights in Korea.

3. *Russo-Japanese War (1904–05).* Japan's next major imperialistic move was directed against Russia. Around the turn of the century, both Japan and the Western powers became increasingly concerned over the growing influence and ambitions of Russia in the Far East. Japan felt that Russia's interest in Manchuria and Korea stood in the way of her own ambitions to expand on the mainland. Britain and the United States feared a change in the balance of power in the Far East. In 1904, Japan provoked a war with Russia and soon won military victories which startled the world.

The United States Mediates a Peace in the Russo-Japanese War. By 1905, both Russia and Japan desired peace: Japan, because her resources were severely strained; Russia, because of the costly losses and the outbreak of revolution at home. At Japan's request, President Theodore Roosevelt offered to help make peace. When Russia accepted, he called a peace conference at Portsmouth, New Hampshire, and helped negotiate the *Treaty of Portsmouth* (1905).

1. *Role of President Theodore Roosevelt.* At Roosevelt's suggestion both parties withdrew extreme demands. In return for giving up claims to a monetary indemnity, Japan was given the southern half of the island of Sakhalin. She also received control of Russian interests in southern Manchuria. President Roosevelt was awarded the Nobel Peace Prize in 1906 for his role in bringing the Russo-Japanese War to an end.

NOTE: Roosevelt's interest in international diplomacy was also shown by the calling of the *Second Hague Conference* in 1907, at his suggestion. The conference drew up an international agreement for more humane warfare. Unfortunately, this was scrapped when World War I broke out. The *First Hague Conference* in 1899 had established the *Hague Court of Arbitration.*

2. *Significance of the War.* The Russo-Japanese War marked the first time that an Oriental power had militarily defeated a European nation. This made the Japanese warlords feel that their nation could in the long run take control of the entire Far East. The war also marked the replacement of Russia by Japan as the major threat to the *status quo* in the Far

East, a fact which led to a worsening of relations between Japan and the United States.

Growing Friction Between the United States and Japan. The Treaty of Portsmouth marked the beginning of an era of growing tension between Japan and the United States. Friction developed when Japanese expansion began to challenge American interests in the Far East.

1. *The United States Begins to Consider Japan a Threat.* Until the Russo-Japanese War, the United States had looked with approval on Japan's development as a modern nation. When the war broke out, most Americans were sympathetic to Japan as the "underdog." Japan's quick victories, however, caused a reversal in America's attitude. President Roosevelt wound up trying to limit Japan's gains at the Peace Conference. Roosevelt's opposition to a Russian indemnity caused anti-United States riots in Tokyo. After 1905, United States policy centered on preserving the *status quo* and "balance of power" in the Far East. This included protection of the territorial integrity of China against the aggressive moves of Japan. We also began to fear for the safety of the Philippines.

2. *Anti-Japanese Feeling on the West Coast.* Fear of the Japanese "yellow peril" after the Russo-Japanese War brought anti-Japanese feeling in the United States to a head. Following a treaty in 1894 which allowed Japanese nationals to emigrate to the United States, several thousand Japanese came to California. These newcomers aroused the opposition of nationalist and labor groups because they tended to concentrate in certain sections, to dominate a few occupations (especially farming and fishing), and to work for low wages. The defeat of Russia by Japan and the resulting "yellow peril" scare caused an increase in prejudice and discrimination against the Japanese. When, in 1906, the San Francisco School Board ordered Japanese children in that city to attend a separate segregated school for Orientals, Japan lodged official protests.

3. *The "Gentlemen's Agreement."* President Theodore Roosevelt, who had opposed the action of the San Francisco School Board, attempted to work out a solution to the incident that would not only smooth Japanese feelings but also indicate that the United States did not intend to "appease" Japan. Under the so-called *"Gentlemen's Agreement"* of 1907, Roosevelt persuaded California to end discrimination against Japanese school children. Japan in return agreed to stop the emigration of Japanese laborers and their relatives to the United States. (Japanese were, however, still permitted to emigrate to Hawaii.)

4. *The Root-Takahira Agreement of 1908.* To preserve the balance of power in the Far East, Roosevelt made another "bargain" with Japan in 1908, known as the *Root-Takahira Agreement.* Under this agreement both nations agreed to preserve the "open door," and to respect each other's

Pacific possessions. In return for Japan's consent to these understandings, the United States indicated that it would no longer oppose further Japanese penetration of Korea. (Korea was annexed by Japan in 1910.) Soon after the Root-Takahira Agreement, Roosevelt sent the United States fleet to Tokyo on a "friendly visit," intended to impress the Japanese with our naval strength. Roosevelt recognized, more than did most Presidents up to that time, the importance of "power" in international relations.

5. *Friction Continues to Grow After World War I.* The continued friction between the United States and Japan paved the way for the Japanese attack on Pearl Harbor in 1941, which brought us into World War II. These developments are described in Chapters 28 and 29.

REVIEW TEST (Chapter 26)

Select the number preceding the word or expression that best completes each statement or answers each question.

1. American shippers began trading with China (1) after the "Open-Door" policy was announced (2) just prior to the Civil War (3) soon after the Revolutionary War (4) during the Administration of Theodore Roosevelt

2. An important factor in developing friendly relations between China and the United States was the (1) Four-Power Treaty (2) Gentlemen's Agreement (3) Opium War (4) indemnity settlement after the Boxer Rebellion

3. Perry's first visit to Japan was made primarily in order to (1) obtain Japanese markets for United States merchants (2) prevent the Japanese conquest of China (3) break the British monopoly on trade with Japan (4) settle a controversy over seal fisheries

4. During the last part of the 19th century, an important purpose for the modernization of Japan was to (1) improve living conditions of the peasants (2) drive European nations out of China (3) become strong enough to resist foreign domination (4) increase the power of the feudal lords

5. An important factor in Japan's emergence as a modern world power was her (1) involvement in World War II (2) participation in the technical assistance program (3) reliance on the teachings of Confucius (4) imitation of Western technology and other institutions

6. The "Open-Door" policy provided that (1) China and the United States would exchange immigrants (2) the United States would open her doors to Chinese immigrants (3) China would open her ports to trade with other nations (4) all nations would have equal trading privileges in China

7. In general, Secretary of State John Hay's interpretation of Europe's reaction to his "Open-Door" policy can best be described by (1) "Silence implies acceptance." (2) "Watchful waiting." (3) "Speak softly and carry a big stick." (4) "Open covenants of peace openly arrived at."

8. The Gentlemen's Agreement of 1907 was an (1) act of Congress preventing Chinese immigrants from entering the United States (2) act of Congress preventing Japanese immigration into this country (3) agreement among the Western nations not to attack Japan (4) immigration arrangement between the President of the United States and the Japanese government

9. President Theodore Roosevelt received an international peace prize for helping to negotiate a treaty ending conflict between (1) United States and Japan (2) Russia and China (3) England and China (4) Russia and Japan

10. History shows that American foreign policy in the Far East during the period 1900–14 (1) aroused Japanese resentment (2) encouraged German ambitions (3) produced a united China (4) weakened British influence

Indicate the chronological order in which the events in each of the following groups occurred.

A

.... Annexation of Hawaii.
.... Annexation of Philippines.
.... Spanish-American War.

C

.... Overthrow of shogunate in
        Japan.
.... Sino-Japanese War.
.... Perry's voyage to Japan.

B

.... Boxer Rebellion.
.... Chinese Exclusion Act.
.... Overthrow of Chinese monarchy.

D

.... "Open-Door" policy.
.... Gentlemen's Agreement.
.... Root-Takahira Agreement.

E

.... United States begins to consider Japan a threat.
.... Japan begins to industrialize.
.... Townsend Harris arrives in Japan.

Essay Questions

1. Giving reasons and supporting data, show how and why relations between the United States and China became increasingly friendly in the late 19th and early 20th centuries.

2. Discuss the effect of each of the following on relations between the United States and Japan before 1914: (a) Perry's voyages (b) the modernization of Japan (c) the Russo-Japanese War (1904–5) (d) Japanese emigration to the United States.

3. Identify each of the following in one or two sentences: Chinese Exclusion Act, Boxers, Sun Yat-sen, Treaty of Portsmouth, the "Yellow Peril," Gentlemen's Agreement.

CHAPTER 27

The United States and World War I

In 1917, the United States became involved in World War I, the greatest and most disastrous war in history up to that time. For America, World War I marked the end of one era and the beginning of another. It affected American society and history in many ways. Its effects are still felt today.

Outbreak of World War I. World War I broke out in 1914. It was waged by two opposing groups of nations: — the *Central Powers,* consisting of Germany, Austria-Hungary, and their allies (for example, Turkey and Bulgaria); and the *Allied Powers* (the Allies), consisting of Great Britain, France, Russia, and several other nations that came to their aid (*e.g.,* Italy).

1. *Immediate Cause.* The immediate cause of the war was the assassination of the heir to the Austro-Hungarian throne, Archduke Francis Ferdinand, by a Serbian patriot on June 28, 1914, in the Bosnian town of Sarajevo (then under Austrian rule). With the encouragement of Germany, Austria made extreme demands on Serbia, which was backed by Russia. When Austria declared war on Serbia, a "chain reaction" was set up which rapidly brought the members of the two major European alliances into conflict. Within a few months all the great powers mentioned above were involved.

2. *Fundamental Causes.* The assassination of the Archduke was merely the spark that set off the conflagration. The *roots* or basic causes of World War I went deep into the past. By 1914, the Balkans had become a "powder keg" of conflicting territorial claims, imperialistic rivalries, and nationalistic hatreds.

Military Highlights of World War I Before United States Entry. The United States did not enter World War I until April, 1917, nearly three years after the outbreak of the conflict. The following important military events occurred before American troops were sent into action.

1. *A "World" War.* World War I spread rapidly to all parts of the globe; although Europe was the main battleground, fighting also took place in Africa, the Far East, and the Middle East.

2. *The European Theater of Operations.* The most important theater of operations in Europe was the *Western Front.* In an effort to capture Paris, German armies overran Belgium and invaded France. They were finally stopped at the *Battle of the Marne* in France, in September, 1914. Despite bloody German drives and counterattacks by the Allies, the main battle line remained fairly stationary until 1918, when American troops entered the hostilities. Both sides had dug themselves into trenches along 600 miles of battlefront.

3. *The Eastern Front.* On the *Eastern Front* the Russians suffered disastrous defeats, after some initial successes. When the Czar was overthrown by the Russian Revolution of 1917, the *Bolshevik* (Communist) government signed the *Treaty of Brest-Litovsk* (1918) with Germany, which took Russia out of the war.

4. *Naval Warfare.* The war on the sea was highlighted by the effective blockade of Germany by Britain. This led to the naval *Battle of Jutland* (1916), when Germany tried unsuccessfully to break the blockade. Large-scale submarine warfare, introduced by Germany during the war, resulted in the destruction of more than 5000 Allied vessels.

5. *Seizure of Colonies of the Central Powers.* The Allies seized all German colonies in Africa and the Far East. They also freed Turkey's Near Eastern colonies of Mesopotamia, Palestine, Syria, and Arabia.

6. *New Weapons.* World War I differed from all previous conflicts in the large-scale application of science for military purposes, and in the mass production of weapons. Poison gas, submarines, tanks, airplanes and giant cannon were used for the first time.

United States Attempts to Maintain Neutrality. When World War I broke out, most Americans were relatively unconcerned. Europe seemed far away, and its quarrels unrelated to the United States. Americans in general, agreed with President Wilson's declaration that the war was one with which this nation "had nothing to do." In August, 1914, Wilson issued a *proclamation of neutrality* and urged a spirit of "impartiality" toward the belligerents in thought as well as actions.

As the fighting went on, however, many Americans tended to "take sides" in the great conflict.

1. *Anti-German Feeling.* For a number of reasons, public opinion in the United States was largely anti-German. **(a)** There was a sense of common heritage with Britain, and the memory of French help in the American Revolution. **(b)** Many Americans felt that, under the Prussian monarchy, Germany glorified war and accepted the idea that "might makes right." **(c)** There was fear of German aggression and expansionism. Memory of German threats against Venezuela in the debt dispute (page 451) were still fresh. **(d)** Finally, and perhaps most important, public opinion in this country was shocked by Germany's unprovoked invasion of Belgium early in the war, in open violation of a treaty guaranteeing Belgian neutrality.

2. *Pro-German Sentiment.* At first, there was also considerable pro-German sentiment, particularly among Irish-Americans, who were traditionally anti-British and among the 8 million Americans of German descent, who tended to favor their ancestral "fatherland." Some Americans refused to accept the charge of German "militarism" and "imperialism," in view of the great empires controlled by Britain and France.

United States Trade With the Belligerents. United States neutrality was made more difficult by the fact that this country rapidly became the greatest neutral shipper of supplies to both the Allies and the Central Powers. As in the Napoleonic Wars, each side wanted to buy American goods and at the same time to prevent the other side from trading with the United States. The United States was "caught in the middle."

British Violations of United States Neutrality. At the outset of the war, Britain declared a blockade against Germany and her allies, and warned neutrals against shipping war supplies (contraband) to German ports. Soon Britain began to force American ships into British ports for inspection and to seize cargoes going to Germany. (Some goods were being shipped directly; others were being sent indirectly through Denmark and other neutral nations.) President Wilson protested that these actions violated both the neutral rights of United States shippers and the doctrine of freedom of the seas. Britain replied that she had the right to enforce a blockade against the Central Powers even if this meant stopping American shipments to neutral nations, as long as the cargoes involved were destined for Germany, even if indirectly.

German Violations of United States Neutrality. Anger over violations of United States neutrality by Britain was outweighed by what most Americans considered to be even more serious violations by Germany. Since Britain controlled the seas, Germany decided early in the war to use submarine warfare to stop neutral shipments to the Allied Powers. In 1915, she declared a "war zone" around the British Isles, and warned that neutral vessels entering this zone might be torpedoed without warning (*unrestricted submarine warfare*). This zone was later extended to waters adjacent to France and Italy. In answer to United States protests against the violation of our rights as a neutral, Germany maintained that the United States was allowing Britain to violate American rights without reprisal, and it hinted that it might call off its submarines if the United States stopped furnishing munitions and supplies to the Allies.

1. *Sinking of the Lusitania (1915).* The horrors of unrestricted submarine warfare were brought directly home when a German U-boat (submarine) torpedoed and sank the *Lusitania,* a British ship en route to England from the United States. The lives of 128 Americans, including women and children, were lost. In answer to Wilson's vigorous protest and his demand for the safeguarding of the lives of non-combatants in war zones, Germany claimed that the *Lusitania* was carrying war supplies to Britain.

2. *The Sussex Pledge.* In March, 1916, the French vessel *Sussex* was torpedoed, three Americans aboard being injured. Instead of breaking off relations with Germany, as many urged, Wilson issued one last warning.

He threatened that unless Germany abandoned its unrestricted submarine warfare the United States would sever diplomatic relations. In the *Sussex Pledge,* the German government promised to end the sinking of merchant ships without warning and to make provision for safeguarding the lives of passengers. An offer was also made to compensate the Americans injured on the *Sussex.* (It is believed that Germany made the concession because she thought she would win the war within a few months, in which case submarine warfare would no longer be necessary.)

In the United States, the Sussex Pledge was considered a diplomatic triumph for Wilson and helped win his re-election in 1917. The Democratic Party campaigned on the slogan, "He kept us out of the war."

3. *Resumption of Unrestricted Submarine Warfare.* Soon after the Sussex Pledge, Germany came to realize that her victory was not inevitable. The British blockade had begun to cause severe shortages and hardships, and the Western Front had bogged down in a military stalemate. Accordingly, and fully aware that its action might bring the United States into the war, the German government in January, 1917, announced the resumption of unrestricted submarine warfare. Germany believed that should the United States enter the conflict, the Central Powers could win the war before American military aid to the Allies could become effective.

United States Declares War on Germany. The resumption of unrestricted submarine warfare led to the entry of the United States into the war on the Allied side. When Germany announced the renewal of unrestricted submarine warfare, Wilson broke off diplomatic relations. Between March 12 and March 17, 1917, four unarmed American merchant ships were sunk without warning by German submarines. Amidst mounting tension, Wilson called an emergency session of Congress and asked Congress to declare war (April 2, 1917). Four days later, on April 6, 1917, Congress declared war on Germany. The President's war message stressed the loss of lives and property and stated that our quarrel was with the military masters of Germany rather than with the German people.

Underlying Causes for United States Entry into World War I. The *immediate cause* of United States entry into World War I was the resumption of unrestricted submarine warfare by Germany, in March, 1917. The *basic causes* for its entry may be outlined as follows:

1. *Violations of Neutral Rights by Germany.* The most basic single factor in the decision to go to war with Germany was the violation of American neutral rights despite repeated United States insistence upon its unrestricted right to trade. The American people and their government were especially angered by the loss of lives that resulted from the torpedoing of ships without warning or provision for the rescue of those on board.

2. *Balance of Power.* Perhaps as important a cause as the above, and in the eyes of some historians even *more* important, was the fact that many

Americans felt that a German military triumph would threaten American security by upsetting the long-established balance of power in Europe.

3. *Idealism.* Many Americans agreed with President Wilson's statements in his war message which declared: "The world must be made safe for democracy," and "We are the champions of the rights of mankind." As the war continued, more and more Americans became convinced that a German victory would be a triumph for autocracy and a menace to American democracy.

4. *Economic Ties to the Allies.* The Allies were able to buy war materials and foodstuffs from the United States, whereas Germany could not because of the British blockade. There was some feeling that if the Allies were permitted to collapse, economic depression in America might follow due to the cessation of demands for war supplies. In addition, when Allied funds ran out, American bankers and investors had made war loans to the Allies. Many felt that Allied victory was necessary to insure the repayment of such loans.

5. *British Propaganda.* Skillful use of propaganda by the Allies contributed to the growth of anti-German feeling. Early in the war the British cut the transatlantic cable from Europe, and thereafter controlled virtually all war news. Americans were horrified by stories of German "atrocities."

6. *German Sabotage.* Germany blundered seriously by attempting sabotage in the United States in order to disrupt the flow of war supplies to the Allies. Notable efforts at sabotage included the destruction of a munitions barge in Seattle in 1915, and the blowing up of a munitions plant in Jersey City in 1916. Both of these incidents cost American lives and property. They resulted in the expulsion of high German officials from the United States.

7. *The Zimmermann Note.* The interception (by British agents) and publication of the *Zimmermann Note,* in March, 1917, aroused the entire nation just at the time that Germany broke the Sussex Pledge and resumed unrestricted submarine warfare. The "note" was a letter written to the President of Mexico, by German Foreign Minister Zimmermann. It suggested that if Mexico joined Germany in the event of war with the United States, Germany would return to her the territory that made up the states of Texas, New Mexico, and Arizona.

The Home Front During World War I. The United States faced huge and complex problems on the home and on the fighting fronts. It mobilized for war with amazing rapidity and made important contributions to final Allied victory.

1. *Finances.* About 33 billion dollars was spent on the war effort. Money was raised primarily by taxing and borrowing. Liberty Bonds and War Savings Stamps were sold. Taxes were levied on incomes, excess profits, and luxuries. Over 10 billion dollars was loaned to the Allies.

2. *Armed Forces.* In 1917, Congress passed a *Selective Service Act,* establishing a system for drafting men into the armed forces (conscription). Under this act (and others), nearly 4 million men entered the armed forces.

3. *Production and Transportation.* In order to mobilize its industrial resources efficiently, the government organized special boards and committees to coordinate the war effort, for example, the *War Industries Board,* the *Shipping Board,* the *Food Administration.* The railroads and telephone and telegraph lines were placed under government control. Citizens were urged to conserve food and fuel.

4. *Presidential Authority.* President Wilson was given almost unlimited authority by Congress to conduct the government during the wartime emergency, including the right to establish agencies, requisition necessary supplies, control agriculture and industry, and fix prices. In supervising the war effort, the President was helped by the assistance of able associates, such as Food Administrator HERBERT HOOVER, Secretary of War NEWTON D. BAKER, and War Industries Board Chairman BERNARD BARUCH.

5. *Public Opinion.* To win active public support and cooperation, a *Committee on Public Information* was created. It "sold" the war effort to the public through all sorts of publicity.

> *(a)* *Action Against Espionage and Sedition.* To prevent disloyalty and spying, Congress passed the *Espionage and Sedition Acts* which imposed severe penalties for treasonable or seditious activity. These laws were enforced with considerable vigor, and hundreds were jailed under their provisions, including Socialist leader Eugene V. Debs. Many Americans criticized the application of these laws for being over-severe and instigating intolerance.

> *(b)* *Anti-German Excesses.* Many Americans of German ancestry suffered from inflamed public opinion. The anti-German feeling resulted in many excesses, including the changing of street names, the banning of the teaching of the German language in the schools, and refusal to play music by German composers. The German word *Frankfurter* became "hot dog" and *sauerkraut* became "liberty cabbage."

Military Participation of the United States in World War I. Since the United States did not take positive steps to prepare for possible war until 1916, the rapidity with which it raised, trained, and sent over to Europe an American army of 2 million men amazed its friends and dismayed its foes.

1. *Arrival of United States Troops.* When the *American Expeditionary Force* (the *AEF*), under General JOHN J. PERSHING, arrived in France, in June, 1917, the Allies were in danger of defeat. The Russians had withdrawn from the war. The Italians had suffered reverses. The French had drained their manpower resources, and U-boats were sinking British ships at an alarming rate.

2. *The Military Defeat of Germany.* American forces helped to turn the military tide and make possible the final defeat of Germany.

(a) *On the Sea.* American naval forces were first to go into action. Led by Admiral Sims, they joined with British forces in convoying American troop ships and matériel to France and in destroying German submarines. By early 1918, the U-boat menace had been largely checked.

(b) *On Land.* In the battles of *Chateau-Thierry* and *Belleau Wood* American troops helped halt the German drive of 1918, which had pushed the Allies back.

(c) *Final Surrender.* In the battles of *St. Mihiel* and the *Argonne Forest,* the American forces helped the English pierce the German lines. Soon after, the formidable *"Hindenburg Line"* crumbled, and Germany surrendered and signed an armistice on November 11, 1918. Behind the final surrender was a decline in German morale caused by a collapse of the home front and the knowledge that millions of fresh American troops were on their way to the battlefields.

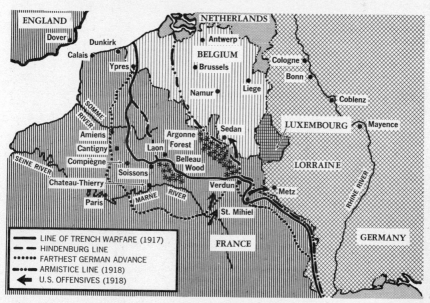

The Western Front in 1918.

Wilson's Program for Peace. Woodrow Wilson, an idealist in politics, fervently believed in peace. He became the moral leader and spokesman for the Allied cause.

1. *Patience and Firmness.* During the early years of the war, President Wilson was under increasing pressure to join the Allies. He refused, however, to be stampeded into a war declaration. Although he continued to insist firmly upon recognition of American rights, Wilson did all in his power to bring about peace between the warring nations. The President interpreted his re-election in 1916 as a "mandate for peace without victory" and continued to try to end the war by a negotiated settlement. Not until 1916, did he abandon his opposition to strengthening the United States military forces, as had been urged by such advocates of "preparedness" as ex-President Theodore Roosevelt and General Leonard Wood. Not until Wilson felt that the German leaders had finally rejected American friendship and had deliberately decided to bring the United States into the conflict, did he ask Congress to declare war.

2. *The "Fourteen Points."* In his war message to Congress Wilson said that the United States had no "selfish" purposes; and that it was fighting to make the world "safe for democracy," to insure the "rights and liberties of small nations," and to help establish a world organization to promote peace. In January, 1918, he converted these sentiments into a peace program, known as the *Fourteen Points*.

> *(a)* *Aims.* Wilson issued the Fourteen Points to inspire the weary Allies and to demoralize the enemy by holding out the attractive picture of a just peace.

> *(b)* *Provisions.* The more important of the Fourteen Points called for: **(1)** the abolition of secret diplomacy, **(2)** freedom of the seas, **(3)** the removal of barriers to international trade, **(4)** the reduction of armaments, **(5)** the adjustment of colonial claims, **(6)** independence and self determination for subject peoples and oppressed minorities (including the establishment of a Polish nation), and **(7)** the establishment of a *League of Nations* that could safeguard the peace and guarantee the independence and territorial integrity of all countries, large or small.

> *(c)* *Results.* Although the Fourteen Points were criticized by some as being too idealistic and impractical, they were effective psychological weapons for the Allies. They gave hope to oppressed and war-weary people throughout the world and helped undermine the resistance of the enemy. Observers felt that Wilson's peace aims contributed to the revolution in Germany that overthrew the Kaiser on November 9, 1918, two days before the Armistice.

Paris Peace Conference. The peace treaties following World War I were drawn up at the *Paris Peace Conference* held at Versailles in 1919. The Conference was dominated by the "Big Four" — Prime Minister DAVID LLOYD GEORGE of Britain, Premier GEORGES CLEMENCEAU of France, Premier VITTORIO ORLANDO of Italy, and President WOODROW WILSON of the United States. Wilson was hailed by the peoples of Europe who looked to him as a symbol of a better world ahead. The main terms of the treaties that were drawn up were shaped in part by Wilson's Fourteen Points, but in greater measure were the results of certain secret agreements made by the Allies during the war.

1. *Secret Treaties.* Britain, France, and some of the other Allies had made "secret" agreements and treaties to divide up the territories and colonies of the Central Powers according to their own needs and ambitions. For example, they promised to give certain non-Italian territories to Italy and to divide Turkey's territories into spheres of influence.

2. *Secret Treaties vs. the Fourteen Points.* Wilson was shocked to find, once the Paris Conference began, that his aims were in sharp conflict with those of Lloyd George and Clemenceau. Wilson found that the other members of the "Big Four" were far more concerned with dividing up the spoils of victory and punishing Germany than with framing a just peace. In order to win acceptance of the principle of a League of Nations (and also because his position at the conference had been weakened by a Republican victory in the mid-term elections of 1918), Wilson had to compromise most of his other aims in the Fourteen Points. Principles such as lower tariffs, disarmament, and a ban on secret diplomacy were ignored. The principle of the right of peoples to national self-determination was applied in some cases, but not in others.

3. *Treaty of Versailles With Germany.* Peace treaties were drawn up in 1919 with each of the defeated powers — Germany, Austria-Hungary, Bulgaria, and Turkey. The most important of these was the *Treaty of Versailles* with Germany. The main terms of the Versailles Pact were:

(a) An international peace organization, the *League of Nations,* was established.

(b) Alsace-Lorraine was returned to France; and the Saar Basin was put under League control for 15 years.

(c) Germany gave up Posen, West Prussia, and Upper Silesia to the newly created Republic of Poland. Danzig became a free city under the League of Nations. Northern Schleswig was given to Denmark.

(d) All the overseas possessions of Germany were taken away and divided among Britain, France, Japan, and Australia, as mandates.

(e) The German army and navy were greatly reduced in size, and fortifications were forbidden.

(f) Germany accepted responsibility for the war (the *war-guilt clause*) and agreed to pay reparations for war damages.

4. *Evaluation of the Treaty of Versailles.* The Treaty of Versailles has been both criticized and defended. *Critics* claim that Germany was treated too harshly. They say that the one-sided demilitarization of Germany and the loss of her entire empire paved the way for the rise of Hitler and for World War II. (The Nazis were later to win support by promising to revise the Treaty of Versailles.) *Defenders* of the Treaty argue that it was the best one possible under the circumstances. They point out that millions of minority peoples, such as the Czechs and Poles, were liberated from alien rule. They claim that the rise of Hitler was due not so much to the Treaty's provisions as to the failure of the Allies to enforce them properly.

United States Rejects the Treaty of Versailles. Although Wilson used his personal influence at home and abroad, safeguarding the peace proved more difficult than winning the war. The United States surprised the world by refusing to ratify the Treaty of Versailles. Strong opposition to further involvement in Europe, as well as partisan politics, contributed to the Treaty's defeat in the United States Senate.

1. *Opposition to the Treaty.* The nation debated the Treaty of Versailles for nearly six months. Although Wilson was supported by most of the press, most liberals, and most intellectuals, there was mounting opposition of the Treaty.

    (a) Republican Opposition. Many Republicans opposed the Treaty for partisan reasons. Some never forgave Wilson for failing to include leading Republicans in the peace delegation to the Versailles Conference. (Since the Republicans had captured both houses of Congress in 1918, most observers agreed that Wilson had committed a major political blunder by failing to include some of them in his delegation.)

    (b) Opposition to the League. Many opposed the Treaty because it included the Covenant (charter) of the League of Nations. They felt that the League would be an "entangling alliance" that might involve the United States in future European wars. A group of Senators, led by William Borah and Hiram Johnson (the *"irreconcilables"*), would have nothing to do with the League. Others, like Senator Henry Cabot Lodge, suggested safeguards or "reservations" before acceptance of the Treaty.

    (c) Other Opposition Groups. Some groups opposed the Treaty because they thought it too harsh, while others opposed it because they thought it was not harsh enough. Many Irish-Americans denounced the Treaty because they charged that the set-up of the League would give Britain and its dominions undue influence in world affairs (five votes).

2. *Defeat of the Treaty.* In 1919 and again in 1920, the United States Senate refused to ratify the Treaty of Versailles.

    (a) Lengthy Debate. Lengthy hearings and debates were held from July to November, 1919.

    (b) The Lodge Reservations. Leading the opposition was Republican Senator Henry Cabot Lodge. Lodge suggested "reservations" (conditions for acceptance) to the Treaty preserving the rights of the United States under the Constitution and Monroe Doctrine.

    (c) Defeat in the Senate. In November, 1919, and again in March, 1920, the Senate voted down the Treaty as amended by the Lodge reservations. Because Wilson asked "loyal" Democrats to join the "irreconcilables" in voting against the amended version, the Treaty failed to secure the required two-thirds vote for adoption. Wilson hoped that his position would be vindicated by a Democratic victory in the election of 1920 on a platform calling for adoption of the Treaty *without* reservations. Historians like Thomas Bailey believe that because of his unwillingness to compromise Wilson himself must share in the blame for the defeat of the Treaty of Versailles.

3. *Separate Peace With Germany.* Since the rejection of the Treaty of Versailles technically left the United States at war with Germany, in 1922 Congress formally declared peace by joint resolution. In 1923, under President Harding, separate peace treaties with Germany, Austria, and Hungary were ratified by the Senate. They did not contain the League Covenant. In its treaty with the United States, Germany agreed to pay damages for unrestricted submarine warfare; the United States agreed to pay for certain German property seized during the war.

Election of 1920. The rejection of the Versailles Treaty was made emphatic by the election of 1920. The Democratic platform endorsed the League of Nations. The Republican platform straddled the issue by not taking a firm stand. Though many internationalist Republicans had supported his election, the new President, WARREN HARDING, chose to interpret his victory as a defeat for internationalism and the League. Under Harding and his successors, the nation turned "back to normalcy" and away from "entangling foreign involvements."

Woodrow Wilson and the Fight for the Treaty. Woodrow Wilson campaigned strenuously for the adoption of the Treaty of Versailles and the League Covenant. He believed that a successful League would truly make World War I a "war to end wars." His physical exertions caused him to suffer a stroke, from which he never fully recovered. His illness weakened the fight for the passage of the Treaty at a crucial moment. Wilson hoped that the election of 1920 would be a *"solemn referendum"* in favor of the League. The Republican victory in that election left him a disillusioned and broken-hearted man. He died in 1924. His idealism, nevertheless, was to have lasting results.

REVIEW TEST (Chapter 27)

Select the number preceding the word or expression that best completes each statement or answers each question.

1. A basic cause of our entry into World War I was also a basic cause of our entry into the (1) Revolutionary War (2) War of 1812 (3) Mexican War (4) Civil War

2. A nation which gives aid to neither side in a controversy is said to be (1) a belligerent (2) a buffer (3) an aggressor (4) a neutral.

3. What policy did the United States government adopt officially when World War I broke out in Europe? (1) neutrality (2) belligerency (3) all-out aid to the Allies (4) pan-Germanism

4. Which of the following policies did President Wilson follow immediately following the sinking of the *Lusitania?* (1) He proposed a lend-lease plan for aiding the allies against Germany. (2) He presented his Fourteen Points as a basis for promoting world peace. (3) He refused to be stampeded into any hasty act leading to war. (4) He prohibited Americans from traveling on ships of belligerent nations.

5. The factor that most significantly caused the United States to declare war on Germany in April 1917 was (1) the sinking of the *Sussex* (2) the resumption of submarine warfare by Germany (3) the German invasion of Belgium (4) the interception and publication of the Zimmermann note

6. It has often been suggested that one of the main reasons for United States entry into World War I was that the United States (1) wanted to abandon her interests in the Caribbean (2) had become a creditor nation (3) sought territory in the Far East (4) had turned to the Republican Party for leadership in international affairs

7. Which of the following occurred *after* United States entry into World War I? (1) battle of the Marne (2) battle of Jutland (3) the re-election of President Wilson (4) the battle of Argonne Forest

8. The United States raised money to carry on World War I primarily by (1) high protective tariffs (2) sale of government-owned property (3) loans obtained from the American people (4) loans obtained from the allied nations

9. What principle of Wilson's Fourteen Points was incorporated in the Treaty of Versailles? (1) open diplomacy (2) removal of economic barriers (3) limitation on armaments for the victors as well as for the conquerors (4) a League of Nations

10. All of the following contributed to the rejection of the Treaty of Versailles by the United States Senate *except* (1) political blunders by Wilson (2) a resurgent spirit of isolationism (3) dissatisfaction with the Treaty's provision providing for a world peace organization (4) the election of Warren Harding to the Presidency

State whether each of the following statements is true or false. If the statement is false, replace the word or phrase in **boldface type** *with one which will make it correct.*

1. At the beginning of World War I, United States public opinion was aroused against **England** because of "atrocity stories" related to the fighting.

2. Socialist leader **Bernard Baruch** was sent to jail during World War I for violating the Espionage and Sedition Act.

3. General Dwight D. Eisenhower's military role in World War II was most like that of **General John J. Pershing** in World War I.

4. Wilson's plans for a "peace without victory" at Versailles were upset by the **Secret Treaties.**

5. In the debate over the Treaty of Versailles Senator **Henry Cabot Lodge** led the group opposed to the League, known as "the irreconcilables."

Essay Questions

1. Discuss three important reasons for United States entry into World War I.

2. Show how each of the following "home front" problems of the United States was handled during World War I: (a) financing the war (b) marshaling industry and transportation (c) raising troops (d) keeping civilian morale high.

3. Explain how American military participation in World War I helped make Allied victory possible.

4. Assume you were a United States Senator in 1917. (a) Explain, with reasons, why you would or would not have voted to support President Wilson's stand on the Versailles Treaty. (b) State two important arguments raised by those who would have opposed your point of view.

CHAPTER 28

United States Foreign Policy
Between Two World Wars

United States foreign policy between the two World Wars was influenced by the experiences of World War I, the nation's domestic needs and problems, and the actions of aggressors in Europe during the 1930's.

Part I — UNITED STATES FOREIGN POLICY AFTER WORLD WAR I

World War I influenced the American social and economic structure in many ways. It also had a powerful impact on United States foreign policy.

Postwar Readjustment. For several years after the end of World War I, the nation was largely occupied with the readjustment to peacetime conditions (the "return to normalcy").

1. *Demobilization.* The army was demobilized and drastically reduced in size. Provisions were made for veterans in the form of a "bonus certificate" payable in 20 years. The merchant fleet, which had been built at great expense during the war, was sold or scrapped. Wartime taxes were repealed, and other taxes were reduced. Railroads were returned to private control and given financial aid. War surplus materials were sold in the United States and abroad.

2. *Disillusionment.* During the war, public opinion had rallied to the support of the war effort. With the end of hostilities, a sharp reaction set in. As the nation counted its dead (117,000) and wounded (204,000), and struggled with the problems of postwar readjustment, a mood of disillusionment replaced the idealism of the war years. This mood was reflected in foreign affairs, as well as in other aspects of national life.

Foreign Policy After World War I. After World War I, our foreign policy appeared to be moving in two directions at the same time. On the one hand, because of national disillusionment about war, there was a strong effort to avoid political commitments, to stay out of European political entanglements, and to return to prewar isolationism. On the other hand, there were forces which made it impossible for the United States to escape its responsibilities as a world power and which brought about American cooperation in many efforts to preserve the peace.

Isolationist Trends. Many Americans wanted to return to the traditional policy of isolation, an absence of entangling alliances, and aloofness from shifts and changes in the power politics of Europe and the rest of the world. This isolationist aspect of American foreign policy was shown in the 1920's and 1930's by rejection of the Treaty of Versailles and the League Covenant, by repeated refusals to join the World Court, by a return to higher tariffs, by restriction of immigration, and by neutrality legislation.

1. *Rejection of the Treaty of Versailles and the League.* The first outward evidence of the wish to turn away from war and foreign involvement was the refusal of the United States Senate to ratify the Treaty of Versailles. After assuming office, President Harding declared that he would not take any steps to lead the nation into the League of Nations. Although pro-League advocates continued to urge United States entry into the world peace organization, no official steps were taken in this direction.

2. *Refusal to Join the World Court.* In 1921, the League established the *Permanent Court of International Justice (World Court).* Its function was to render advisory opinions and decisions on international questions and on disputes submitted to it. Despite much pro-Court sentiment, the Senate refused to allow the United States to join this body. In 1929, the Senate even rejected the *Root Formula,* under which the United States would have joined the Court with a special provision allowing it to withdraw if a dispute involving American interests was taken up without the consent of our government.

3. *A Return to Higher Tariffs.* In the 1920's, the United States joined many nations of the world in adopting policies of *economic nationalism.* To protect home industry, it adopted high protective tariffs.

4. *Restriction of Immigration.* World War I contributed to the reversal of the liberal immigration policies of the prewar period. Although there had been some restrictions on immigration before 1914 (see page 397), the nation had been proud of its "open-door" immigration policy. During the war, public opinion changed. Feeling ran high against German-Americans and other "hyphenated-Americans." Hate groups like the Ku Klux Klan stimulated this feeling, as did the "red scare" of 1919 (see page 306). Congress took drastic action early in the 1920's, in order to cut down the growing numbers of immigrants who began to pour into the country from their war-shattered homelands. Immigration was cut to a trickle by the *Quota Acts* of 1921 and 1924 and by the *National Origins Plan* of 1929 (see page 399).

5. *Neutrality Legislation.* During the early 1930's, the peace of Europe and the world was undermined by the aggressive expansion of Nazi Germany, Fascist Italy, and militaristic Japan. By the middle of the decade, Japan's invasion of Manchuria, Italy's attack on Ethiopia, and Germany's disregard of the Treaty of Versailles had made it clear that another major war was a distinct possibility. Because there was widespread feeling that United States involvement in World War I had been a "mistake," Congress passed neutrality legislation designed to keep us from becoming involved in any new European hostilities. The *Neutrality Acts* of 1935, 1936, and 1937 prohibited travel by American citizens on the ships of nations at war, placed an embargo on the sale or transportation of munitions to belligerents, forbade loans to nations at war, and provided that belligerent nations that wished to purchase materials from us would have to pay in cash and carry the goods in their own vessels ("cash and carry").

International Cooperation After World War I. In spite of the prevailing isolationist spirit, the United States was unable, because of its strength and position, to return completely to 19th-century isolationism. Even its refusal to become involved in European affairs helped shape the events of the 1920's and 1930's. In addition, there were positive American attempts to cooperate in international efforts to reduce tension and bring peace.

Cooperation With the League and the World Court. Though it never joined the League or the World Court, the United States cooperated with these organizations in many efforts.

1. *Attendance at Conferences.* Unofficial United States observers attended League conferences and worked with League agencies in such matters as aid to needy nations, the regulation of the opium traffic, and the improvement of international trade.

2. *German Reparations.* United States officials and bankers helped work out plans for repayment of German reparations.

3. *Sentiment for Joining the World Court.* Though repeatedly blocked by Senate isolationists, five American Presidents urged that the United States join the Court (Wilson, Harding, Coolidge, Hoover, and F. D. Roosevelt). In addition, eminent American jurists served as members of the Court (for example, John Bassett Moore, Charles Evans Hughes, and Frank B. Kellogg).

United States Leadership in Efforts to Restrain Japan and to Disarm. The Harding administration refused to become involved in European politics. Nevertheless, it took the lead in promoting international efforts to relieve tension in the Far East, which was caused by the growth of Japanese power.

1. *The Growth of Japanese Influence.* During World War I, Japan joined the Allies. While its partners were fighting in Europe, Japan strengthened its own position in the Far East. In 1915, the Japanese government presented the *Twenty-One Demands* to China. These called for recognition of Japan's paramount position in China, and for granting Japan special economic privileges in China and Manchuria. Though Japan's allies, particularly the United States, blocked some of these demands, Japan did obtain many economic concessions from the weak Chinese Republic. In addition, after the War, under terms of the Treaty of Versailles, Japan secured Germany's holdings in the Far East, including economic control of Shantung province in China, and islands in the North Pacific.

2. *Growing Western Concern Over Japan.* Growing United States concern over Japan's expansion and distrust of her future intentions were aroused by a dispute over the island of Yap, a cable station between the United States and the Philippines, and also by the failure of Japan to remove troops from Siberia after the war. Britain shared American fears. She was unhappy over her treaty of alliance with Japan (1902), since it could conceivably bring her into war with the United States. Also, Britain was apprehensive about the naval race into which it had been pushed by the growth of the United States and Japanese navies.

3. *The Washington Conference (1921–22).* In 1921, with British support, the United States State Department proposed an international conference to deal with problems of the Far East and disarmament. The major nations of the world attended, and helped draft several important treaties.

> *(a)* *Nine-Power Pact.* By the Nine-Power Pact, the signatory powers agreed to uphold the "open door" in China and to preserve that nation's territorial integrity and independence. Signers of the pact were Great Britain, the United States, Japan, China, Belgium, Italy, France, Portugal, and the Netherlands. (In accordance with the spirit of the Treaty, Japan also agreed to give up control of Shantung.)

> *(b)* *Four-Power Pact.* By the Four-Power Pact, Great Britain, France, Japan, and the United States agreed to respect one another's possessions in the Far East, and to confer if disputes arose. (This Treaty also ended the Anglo-Japanese Alliance of 1902.)

> *(c)* *Five-Power Pact.* A Five-Power Pact provided for *naval disarmament.* The United States, Great Britain, Japan, France, and Italy agreed to keep their fleets respectively at the ratio of $5:5:3:1.67:1.67$, on the basis of total tonnage. They also agreed to keep their fleets at 1921 levels by not constructing new capital ships (ships of over 10,000 tons) for ten years (the "naval holiday"). In addition, at the suggestion of United States Secretary of State Charles Evans Hughes, the United States, Great Britain, and Japan agreed to scrap over 60 battleships. In order to get Japan to agree to these restrictions on the size of her navy, the United States and Britain agreed not to strengthen their fortifications or bases in the Pacific.

4. *Results of the Washington Conference.* The Washington Conference was considered a diplomatic triumph for the United States, as well as a significant step toward world peace and disarmament. It also seemed to clear the air of existing problems in the Far East. As time went on, however, it became clear that the victory was only on paper. Land and air forces were not limited. French and Japanese dissatisfaction with their naval ratios under the Five-Power Pact contributed to the failure of later disarmament conferences (at London in 1930 and 1935, and at Geneva in 1927 and 1932). Moreover, while the United States and Britain refrained from building up their navies, Japan (and later her Axis partners) continued to add cruisers, submarines, and smaller vessels to their forces (as permitted under the Treaty). Finally, by the folly of not strengthening our Pacific outposts, the United States left Guam and the Philippines virtually defenseless. In effect, Pearl Harbor in Hawaii became our Pacific frontier. Meanwhile, Japan became the strongest power in the Far East.

The Attempt to Outlaw War (Kellogg-Briand Pact, 1928). In 1928, at the suggestion of French Foreign Minister Aristide Briand, supported by U. S. Secretary of State Kellogg, 15 nations signed an agreement renouncing war as "a means of settling international disputes" and calling for the settlement of all international disputes by peaceful means. Ultimately, 62 nations signed the pact. However, the *Kellogg-Briand Pact (Pact of Paris)* "had no teeth" because it provided no means for its enforcement, and events were to prove that it was not an effective instrument for preventing war. Nevertheless, it reflected at the time the desire of the United States to cooperate in preventing the recurrence of armed conflict.

Attempts to Solve Problems of War Debts and Reparations. The problems of *war debts* and *reparations,* which faced the United States and other nations in the 1920's, illustrated the difficulty in withdrawing from foreign involvements.

1. *War Debts.* During and immediately after the war, the United States lent 12 billion dollars to Britain, France, Italy, and other countries to help them pay the costs of war and reconstruction.

(a) The failure of international trade to revive after World War I (caused in part by the erection of tariff barriers by the United States) made it impossible for these countries to pay off their debts in goods and services. American attempts to get the loans repaid caused ill-will among our former allies, who felt that the United States, now the world's leading creditor nation, could afford to cancel them. Britain, France, and Italy insisted that they could not pay because Germany was not paying the war indemnities it owed to them (*reparations*).

(b) The United States was forced to scale down the debts and to accept token payments. In 1931, in addition, it declared a one-year moratorium (the "Hoover Moratorium") on debt payments.

(c) Despite these actions, by 1934 all the debtor nations, except Finland, had defaulted on their payments. In all, the United States collected about 10% of its loans. It considered the failure of its allies to pay these debts evidence of bad faith because many of these nations at the same time were spending large sums on armaments.

2. *Reparations.* The problem of *reparations* was closely linked to that of war debts, despite the United States' desire to keep them separate. Reparations were the indemnities that Germany had agreed, in the Treaty of Versailles, to pay to the Allies for war damages. They amounted to 33 billion dollars. However, unstable economic conditions prevented Germany from keeping up with her reparations payments. The problem disturbed Europe for over a decade. United States financial experts Charles Dawes and Owen D. Young helped work out plans to reduce reparations payments (*Dawes Plan,* 1924; *Young Plan,* 1929), but these programs failed to solve the problem. In 1931, Germany halted all payments of reparations because of severe economic difficulties. The *Lausanne Pact* of 1932 ended the need for future payments.

REVIEW TEST (Chapter 28 — Part 1)

Select the number preceding the word or expression that best completes each statement or answers each question.

1. An important result of World War I was that the United States (1) tried to avoid international entanglements (2) abandoned her interests in Latin America (3) began a policy of imperialism in the Far East (4) turned to the Democratic party for leadership in international affairs.

2. At the peace conferences following World War I, President Wilson advocated (1) the establishment of a League of Nations (2) harsh terms for reparations and indemnities (3) a United States of Europe (4) military occupation of Germany

3. During the 1920's the United States became the foremost advocate of (1) free trade (2) cancellation of war debts (3) military alliances (4) reduction of naval armaments

4. In 1922, nine nations meeting in Washington agreed to (1) respect the territorial integrity of China (2) request the United States to modify the anti-Japanese immigration laws (3) allow Japan parity in battleships with the United States (4) recognize Japan's claims to supremacy in the Far East

5. The Kellogg-Briand Pact of 1928 failed to accomplish its purpose because (1) the signers renounced war (2) too few nations signed it (3) there was no provision for its enforcement (4) it was rejected by the League of Nations

6. Which one of the following treaties was never ratified by the United States Senate? (1) the Kellogg-Briand Peace Pact (1928) (2) the Treaty of Versailles (1919) (3) the North Atlantic Pact (1949) (4) the Nine-Power Pact (1922)

7. European nations claimed they were unable to pay their debts because the United States (1) did not join the League of Nations (2) did not advance them more credit (3) raised its tariff rates (4) did not join the World Court

8. The Root Formula consisted of United States reservations in regard to the (1) League of Nations (2) World Court (3) Hoover Moratorium (4) Washington Conference on Naval Limitation

9. An important phase of United States foreign policy during the period 1920–29 was (1) active membership in the World Court (2) armed intervention in African affairs (3) complete disengagement from Far Eastern affairs (4) tendency toward isolation from European affairs

10. The problem of reparations after World War I ceased to be a cause of international bitterness after the (1) Dawes Plan (2) Lausanne Pact (3) Young Plan (4) Four-Power Pact

Essay Questions

1. Discuss briefly two reasons for each of the following: (a) the refusal of the United States to join the League of Nations and (b) restrictions placed upon immigration between 1920 and 1930.

2. A former Speaker of the House of Representatives once said, "I was ashamed of my country after World War I. We put our head in the sand and let the rest of the world go by." (a) Explain the developments that he probably had in mind. (b) Indicate the extent to which you agree or disagree with his point of view.

3. Show how each was related to, or part of United States foreign policy in the 1920's. (a) the "return to normalcy"; (b) the Root Formula; (c) economic nationalism; (d) the Washington Conference; (e) the Kellogg-Briand Pact; (f) war debts; (g) reparations.

Part II — THE UNITED STATES AND
THE RISE OF DICTATORSHIPS

In the 1930's the United States was forced to react to the aggressive moves of dictators both in Europe and Asia.

The Rise of Postwar Dictatorships. World War I paved the way for the rise of dictatorships in Europe by bringing about a situation of political instability and economic unrest. Military defeat, poverty, unemployment, and inflation helped bring the Communists to power in Russia, the Fascists to power in Italy, and the Nazis to power in Germany. In the 1930's, a military dictatorship was also established in Japan.

Axis Aggression in the 1930's. The 1930's were years of repeated crises brought on by the belligerent foreign policies of the dictatorships. Germany, Japan, and Italy, calling themselves "have-not nations," engaged in open aggression against weaker neighbors.

Japanese Invasion of Manchuria and North China. Japan took the first openly aggressive step in 1931 by seizing the rich Chinese province of Manchuria and renaming it *Manchukuo*. She took advantage of Chinese disunity and world concern with the problems of the Great Depression.

1. *Lytton Commission (1932).* The *Lytton Commission* of the League of Nations investigated the situation and condemned Japan's aggression (1932).

2. *Stimson Doctrine (1932).* The United States condemned Japan's action in the *Stimson Doctrine,* which stated that America would not recognize Manchukuo because it had been seized in violation of existing treaties. These treaties included the League Covenant, the Nine-Power Pact, and the Kellogg-Briand Pact.

3. *Japanese Aggression Continues.* Britain's unwillingness to support a United States proposal to impose economic penalties (sanctions) against Japan left Japan free to extend her political and economic influence in North China. From 1937 to 1939, Japanese armies overran China's northern provinces.

4. *Lack of Effective Action Against Japan.* Though world opinion was shocked by Japanese aggression in Manchuria and North China, which included the bombing of open cities and flagrant disregard for the rights of foreigners, no really effective counter-action was taken. In response to American indignation over the sinking of a United States gunboat, the *Panay,* in Chinese waters in 1937, Japan apologized and paid an indemnity. Because aggression was not halted when it first began in 1931 in Manchuria, some historians consider this the real beginning of World War II.

Hitler's Violations of the Treaty of Versailles. In 1935 and 1936, the Nazi dictator of Germany, ADOLF HITLER, boldly scrapped two sections of the Treaty of Versailles. In 1935, he announced the restoration of compulsory military service and began to build a strong air force. In 1936, he sent his troops into the demilitarized Rhineland. Though the League protested, no effective action was taken against Germany. Britain refused to go along with France's desire for strong measures.

The Italian Invasion of Ethiopia. BENITO MUSSOLINI, Fascist leader of Italy, was anxious to restore Italy to a position of power and glory. He planned to do this by re-establishing a Mediterranean Empire. He also hoped that expansion and conquest would take the minds of many Italians off their growing economic troubles. Consequently, in 1935, he invaded Ethiopia on a pretext, and quickly conquered that independent African nation.

1. *League Sanctions.* For the first time, the League took action against an aggressor. It imposed economic sanctions. Member nations were asked not to ship certain materials of war to Italy or to extend loans or credits to her.

2. *Failure of Sanctions.* Sanctions failed. Most nations did not abide by them, particularly because the United States and Germany, who were not members of the League, continued to ship oil and arms to Italy. The failure of League sanctions was a "go-ahead signal" to all the dictators, who now became convinced that the democracies were unwilling to take forceful action to stop them. In 1937, the *Rome-Berlin-Tokyo Axis* was formed to present a united front of dictators in making demands on weaker nations, and to frighten the democracies into inaction.

The Spanish Civil War. From 1936 to 1939, General FRANCISCO FRANCO led a revolt which in the end resulted in the overthrow of the Republican government of Spain. After seizing power, Franco set up a fascist-type dictatorship.

1. *Testing Ground for World War II.* The bitter Spanish Civil War was later looked upon as a "rehearsal" or "testing ground" for World War II. Hitler and Mussolini sent planes, tanks, guns, and troops to help Franco fight against the Republican armies (Loyalists). They claimed they were saving Spain from communism. Soviet Russia sent help to the Loyalists. In addition, volunteers from the United States and other nations joined with the Loyalists.

2. *The Non-Intervention Plan.* Great Britain and France realized that a Franco victory would surround France with anti-democratic governments and menace the British stronghold at Gibraltar. Nevertheless, rather than risk a world war by lining up with Russia against the Axis, Britain and France sponsored the so-called *non-intervention plan,* under which the big powers agreed not to send arms to Spain.

3. *Failure of Non-Intervention.* The plan was a dismal failure. While France and Britain observed the agreement, Italy and Germany continued to aid Franco. In addition, because of neutrality laws adopted by the United States, the Spanish Loyalists were unable to buy arms in this country.

Hitler's Bloodless Conquests. By 1938, Hitler had prepared Germany for war by mobilizing her war industries, building a line of fortifications to oppose the French *Maginot Line,* and enlarging, training, and equipping Germany's armed forces with the most modern weapons and the newest ideas in military science. In 1938 and 1939, a mere "show of force" enabled him to annex Austria, Czechoslovakia, and Memel in a series of "bloodless conquests."

1. *Annexation of Austria.* After stirring up trouble in Austria for several years, Nazi conspirators assassinated Austrian Chancellor Dollfuss. In March, 1938, German troops marched into Austria on the pretext that they were restoring order. They were unopposed. Austria was annexed and integrated into the Nazi state, although this was specifically forbidden by the Treaty of Versailles.

2. *Conquest of Czechoslovakia.* After World War I, Czechoslovakia had become one of Europe's most prosperous and democratic nations. After 1935, Nazi agents stirred up trouble in the Sudetenland, the westernmost section of Czechoslovakia, which had a large German-speaking population. In 1938, Hitler demanded self-determination for the Sudeten Germans on the ground that they were being "mistreated." To prevent Czechoslovakia from being invaded like Austria, Prime Minister Chamberlain of England and Premier Daladier of France met with Hitler and Mussolini at Munich in 1938 and negotiated the *Munich Pact.*

3. *The Munich Pact.* This agreement gave the Sudetenland to Germany in return for Hitler's pledge that he had "no further territorial ambitions" in Europe. This pact is considered the culmination of the policy of *appeasement,* which the democracies had adopted in the 1930's. (*Appeasement* in this sense means giving in a bit to an aggressor in the hope that he will eventually be satisfied enough not to continue his aggressions.) By making Hitler feel he was unbeatable, this policy of appeasement helped bring on World War II. Six months after the Pact, in 1939, Hitler violated his pledge and forced the rest of Czechoslovakia to become a German protectorate.

4. *Cession of Memel.* A week after absorbing the rest of Czechoslovakia, Hitler forced Lithuania to cede Memel to Germany. This was a piece of territory touching the border of East Germany on the Baltic. Half its population was German. It had been part of East Prussia before World War I.

Failure of Collective Security. The continued crises of the 1930's were a reflection of the post-World War I weariness and disillusionment of Europe, and of the breakdown of the collective security system established in the 1920's. This system had been based upon the League of Nations, the Washington Treaties, the disarmament movement, and agreements such

as the Locarno and Kellogg-Briand Pacts. The collapse of this peace structure left the world teetering on the brink of war.

United States Reaction to Axis Aggression. The United States reaction
to the aggression of the 1930's was shaped by its domestic problems, its
isolationist traditions, and its desire for security. At first the United States
tried to remain completely uninvolved. Later it was forced to abandon its
isolationist position, as described below.

Isolationist Sentiment in the United States in the Early 1930's. Several
factors contributed to a growth of isolationist feeling in the United States
in the early 1930's.

1. The nation was deep in the midst of a severe economic depression
and wished to concentrate on its own problems.

2. The rise of dictatorships in Europe, the problems of uncollected foreign debts, and the invasion of Manchuria by Japan convinced many Americans that World War I had not brought a stable peace, that the world had
not been made safe for democracy, and that, consequently, it would be
more than futile for the United States to assume a guiding role in world
affairs.

3. In 1934–35, disclosures made by the *Nye Investigating Committee*
of the United States Senate showed that American arms and munitions
manufacturers and American bankers had made large profits during World
War I by selling arms to the Allies. This information led to a widespread
belief that the United States had been "pushed into war" by these groups.

4. There was considerable feeling that we might have avoided entry
into World War I had we not insisted upon our neutral rights, had we not
sent arms to belligerents, and had we not made loans to the Allies.

The Attempt to Avoid War at All Costs. This mounting tide of isolationist sentiment strongly influenced public opinion and American policy
for most of the 1930's. At first, the nation attempted to avoid war at all
costs by strict isolationist and neutrality laws.

1. *Johnson Debt-Default Act (1934).* This law, passed in 1934, prohibited the sale in the United States of the securities of any nation that had
defaulted on its war debts to us. Congress felt that this would prevent the
United States from again becoming involved in helping any European
nation to finance its war preparations or expenditures.

2. *Neutrality Acts (1935–37).* The belief that the United States should
avoid involvement in Europe's wars resulted in the *Neutrality Acts* of 1935
and 1937. Under these laws American citizens were forbidden: **(a)** to
sell or transport arms or munitions to nations at war; **(b)** to make loans
to nations at war; or **(c)** to travel on ships of belligerents. In addition,
(d) under the "cash-and-carry" principle belligerents that wished to buy
goods other than munitions had to pay cash and carry the goods in their
own ships.

3. *Significance of the Neutrality Acts.* By enacting the Neutrality Acts, the United States indicated that it wanted to avoid war so badly it was willing not only to give up its traditional insistence on neutral rights and freedom of the seas but also to permit aggression to go unchecked in order to stay "uninvolved." United States neutrality, together with British and French appeasement, convinced the Axis powers that they had nothing to fear from the "decadent democracies."

Opposition to Strict Neutrality Begins to Develop. Between 1937 and 1939, President Franklin D. Roosevelt and many Congressional leaders began to feel that neutrality was a mistake, since, like appeasement, it had actually encouraged the aggressors.

1. *Roosevelt's Attitude.* President Roosevelt began to show that his attitude was changing in 1937 when, after the Japanese advanced into North China, he called upon the United States and other nations to "quarantine the aggressors," by economic boycott if necessary. Roosevelt permitted aid to be sent to China on the technicality that Japan had not declared war when she invaded North China. In 1939, after the Nazi seizure of all of Czechoslovakia, Roosevelt called upon Congress to repeal the arms embargo in order to enable Britain and France to arm themselves against Germany. When Congress refused, Roosevelt called upon Hitler and Mussolini to promise not to attack 31 nations he specifically listed. His proposal was spurned by the dictators.

2. *Lagging Public Opinion.* Public opinion moved more slowly than that of the administration. Many Americans were seriously disturbed by the fact that the United States Neutrality Acts had prevented the sending of aid to the Republican forces during the Spanish Civil War. Many more were frightened and alarmed by Mussolini's rape of Ethiopia and Hitler's bloodless conquests. Nevertheless, public opinion polls in the summer of 1939 continued to show that most people were still opposed to abandoning strict neutrality.

The Outbreak of World War II Leads to Abandonment of Strict Neutrality. With the outbreak of World War II in Europe, as a result of Germany's invasion of Poland (September, 1939), the United States began to reconsider and gradually to abandon its policy of strict neutrality. After first repealing the arms embargo and making it possible for Britain and France to purchase arms on a cash-and-carry basis, we gradually shifted to a policy of active aid to the Allies.

REVIEW TEST (Chapter 28 — Part II)

Select the number preceding the word or expression that best completes each statement or answers each question.

1. A development that characterized the period between World War I and World War II was the (1) lasting victory for democratic principles (2) rise of dictatorships in Europe (3) adoption of free trade policies (4) large-scale military disarmament by the big powers

2. Which statement concerning the Stimson Doctrine is true? (1) It led to a reduction in reparations after World War I. (2) It had little effect on Japanese aggression in the 1930's. (3) It helped settle the Venezuelan boundary dispute. (4) It extended the Monroe Doctrine to the Far East.

3. In 1934, the United States became a member of (1) the World Court (2) the League of Nations (3) the Munich Conference (4) the International Labor Organization

4. The use of the term "appeasement" in international affairs became well known as a result of the (1) Munich Pact (2) Fourteen Points (3) Stimson Doctrine (4) Statute of Westminster

5. United States neutrality legislation in the 1930's was evidence of a foreign policy most similar to that followed by the United States in the period (1) before the War of 1812 (2) after the War of 1812 (3) before World War I (4) after World War I

6. All of the following were evidences of an isolationist trend in the 1930's *except* the (1) cash-and-carry policy (2) Johnson Debt-Default Act (3) Lima Conference (4) the slogan "America First"

7. Which was an important political development in Europe during the period 1919–39? (1) change from the bloc system to the two-party system in France (2) development of multiple-party system in Soviet Russia (3) rise of the Liberal Party in Great Britain (4) development of a one-party system in Germany

8. In the 1930's the League voted sanctions against (1) Russia (2) Italy (3) Nazi Germany (4) Spain

9. The *"Panay* incident" involved (1) Germany and Austria (2) Russia and Great Britain (3) the United States and Japan (4) China and India

10. During the summer of 1939, when World War II started, what was the state of American public opinion? (1) Most people were strongly in favor of taking active steps to halt Hitler. (2) Most people were opposed to abandoning strict neutrality. (3) Most people supported the growing belief of President Roosevelt that strict neutrality was a mistake. (4) Most people called for League action to prevent the spread of military hostilities beyond the borders of Europe.

Essay Questions

1. Write the story that would have appeared under each of the following headlines of the 1930's:

U. S. CONDEMNS JAPANESE INVASION OF MANCHURIA
NEUTRALITY ACTS SHOW U. S. REACTION TO CRISES IN EUROPE
ROOSEVELT CALLS FOR QUARANTINING OF AGGRESSORS

2. Show how the United States reaction to the aggression of the 1930's was shaped by (a) its isolationist traditions (b) its domestic problems (c) its desire for security.

3. Discuss three reasons for the failure of collective security in the decade preceding World War II.

CHAPTER 29 ───

The United States and
World War II

───

World War II was brought about primarily because of the aggression of fascist dictators. After six years of fighting in Europe, Africa, the Far East, and on the high seas, the Allies won an unconditional victory over the Axis powers. As in the case of World War I, the United States did not enter the war until the conflict was well under way. The war was a "total war," involving civilian populations as well as armies, and requiring the mobilization of all the human and economic resources of the nations involved. Revolutionary new military weapons and tactics were developed. We are still feeling the effects of this great conflict.

World War II Begins. The immediate cause of World War II was Germany's attack on Poland in September, 1939. The Western democracies finally abandoned appeasement and formed a bloc to stop Hitler. When Poland was attacked, they declared war on Germany.

1. *The End of Appeasement.* When Hitler broke his promise not to seize any more European territory after acquiring the Sudetenland, Britain and France realized that the appeasement policy was a total failure. They saw also, that if they did not take a real stand against Hitler, they would be risking national disaster. In March, 1939, they promised to aid Poland if that country were attacked. In April, after Mussolini had seized Albania, they guaranteed assistance to Rumania and Greece. Negotiations to bring Russia into the anti-Axis pact failed because of mutual distrust. Despite their fears of further aggression, however, Britain and France still did not begin to arm rapidly.

2. *The Nazi-Soviet Pact.* The world was shocked in August, 1939, when Germany and Russia announced a 10-year non-aggression pact. Under the terms of this treaty the two nations secretly agreed to divide Poland, to allow Russia to take control of Latvia and Estonia, and to permit Germany to add Lithuania to its sphere of influence in Europe.

3. *The Invasion of Poland.* In March, 1939, Hitler demanded that Poland allow Germany to annex the Nazi-dominated free city of Danzig, and he demanded also that Germany be given control over a 25-mile wide zone of territory across the Polish Corridor. The Corridor was a narrow strip of land between Germany and East Germany, created by the Versailles Treaty to give Poland access to the Baltic Sea. Attempts by the Allies to persuade Hitler to negotiate with the Poles were unsuccessful. After signing the Nazi-Soviet Pact, which safeguarded his eastern border,

Hitler sent his air and land forces into Poland on September 1, 1939. Warsaw and other Polish cities were bombed. Britain and France declared war on Germany (September 3, 1939) when Germany ignored their demands to cease its attack and withdraw.

Basic Causes of World War II. Underlying the immediate causes of World War II were basic causes, which may be summarized as follows: **(1)** aggressive nationalism and imperialism on the part of Germany, Italy, and Japan; **(2)** the development of new alliances; **(3)** the collapse of collective security; **(4)** appeasement; **(5)** fascism and its doctrines of national aggrandizement, racism, violence, and disregard of human rights; **(6)** the failure of the United States to enter actively into European affairs in the 1920's and 1930's, and to help stop aggression.

Early Nazi Victories in Europe. For the first two years after the outbreak of war in 1939, the Nazis continued a nearly unbroken string of major military victories.

1. *Poland.* Poland was overrun in less than a month and partitioned between Germany and Russia, in accordance with secret terms drawn up in their mutual non-aggression pact.

2. *Scandinavia and the Low Countries.* In 1940, following a period of inactivity after the conquest of Poland, the Nazis invaded and occupied Denmark, Norway, Holland, and Belgium, without warning.

3. *France.* The Germans next invaded and conquered France, flanking the *Maginot Line* and driving the Allies back to the beaches at Dunkirk. Here the British forces on the Continent were evacuated to England in one of the most valiant episodes in military history. After Paris fell, France surrendered (June, 1940). It was divided into an occupied zone (two-thirds of France), controlled by the Nazis, and an unoccupied zone ("Vichy France") ruled by Henri Petain and Pierre Laval, two former French leaders who agreed to "collaborate" with the Germans.

4. *Battle of Britain.* In 1940–41, Germany launched an air assault against Britain. The great cities of Britain were bombed with devastating results, but the British people, under the inspiring leadership of WINSTON CHURCHILL, refused to quit. The small but heroic Royal Air Force held off the attackers.

5. *The Balkans.* After Bulgaria, Rumania, and Hungary had joined Hitler, German armies overran Greece and Yugoslavia (1941).

6. *Invasion of Russia.* In June, 1941, Hitler invaded Russia, in violation of their non-aggression pact. His goal, apparently, was to obtain the grain of the Ukraine, the coal of the Donetz Basin, and the oil of the Caucasus. German armies advanced to the gates of Leningrad in the north, to Moscow in central Russia, and to the Caucasus Mountains in the south. Hitler and much of the world felt that Russia was defeated.

Reasons for Early Axis Successes. There were two important reasons for these early Axis victories. **(1)** The Allies, or the *United Nations* as they came to be called, were caught off guard by the war. They were militarily unprepared. **(2)** The Nazis introduced a new type of "lightning" or *blitzkrieg warfare.* It involved close coordination of land and air forces; the bombing of plants, airfields, transportation centers, troop concentrations, and civilians; the use of spies, propaganda, and sympathizers behind enemy lines ("fifth columnists"); the use of armored (tank) and mechanized divisions; and the development of new tactics, emphasizing breakthroughs, speed, and movement, instead of the fixed battle lines and trench warfare of World War I.

Early Allied Victories in Africa. The earliest Allied victories were won in North Africa.

1. *Italian Armies Defeated.* In September, 1940, Italian forces invaded Egypt. British troops forced them back to Libya and overran the Italian colonies of Eritrea, Ethiopia, and Somaliland.

2. *The Battle of North Africa.* In 1941, German forces under General Rommel came to Mussolini's aid in North Africa. For over a year, a see-saw struggle took place between British and combined German and Italian forces. The climax came when the British, under General BERNARD MONTGOMERY, won a decisive victory at *El Alamein* in October, 1942.

Entry of the United States into World War II. Between September 3, 1939, when World War II began, and December 7, 1941, when Japan bombed Pearl Harbor, the United States gradually abandoned its policy of strict neutrality and moved closer to all-out war on the Allied side. The major events involved are outlined in the following sections.

"Cash and Carry." Immediately after war broke out in Europe, President Roosevelt asked Congress to ease the arms embargo so that arms could be sold to Britain and France. The *Neutrality Act of 1939:* **(1)** permitted belligerents to purchase materials of war on a cash-and-carry basis, and **(2)** banned American merchant ships from traveling in war zones, as designated by the President. Cash and carry actually aided Britain and France, because their financial resources and control of the seas enabled them to buy war materials in the United States and to carry such goods in their own ships. It marked a shift from isolation to pro-Allied neutrality.

Beginning of Active Aid to the Allies. The quick and unexpected fall of France to the Nazis in 1940 shocked most Americans out of their complacent attitude. They no longer were so sure that they could "sit this one out" as a neutral. President Roosevelt became convinced that Germany could not be permitted to become the dominant power in Europe, even if this meant direct American aid to Britain and France. Public opinion gradually shifted to support of "all-out aid short of war." Several significant developments in 1940 and 1941 indicated our growing concern and increasing involvement.

1. *The Draft.* In September, 1940, after intensive debate, Congress adopted the first peacetime draft in American history. The draft law made men between the ages of 21 and 35 liable for military service for one year.

2. *The Destroyers-For-Bases Deal.* In September, 1940, President Roosevelt also announced that the United States would exchange 50 over-age destroyers for 99-year leases on British sea and air bases in the Western Hemisphere (particularly in the Caribbean region and in Newfoundland).

3. *Re-election of Roosevelt in 1940.* During the campaign for the Presidency in 1940, the national debate over neutrality reached its height. Powerful isolationist groups, such as the America First Committee opposed any risks that could lead to war. Internationalist groups called for more active aid to the Allies. The nomination of internationalists for the Presidency by both major parties (WENDELL WILLKIE — Republican; FRANKLIN D. ROOSEVELT — Democrat) was evidence of the national shift toward intervention. President Roosevelt viewed his re-election as a vote of support for a program of greater preparedness and aid to the Allies.

The Lend-Lease Act (March, 1941). By December, 1940, public opinion polls showed that 60% of the American people favored helping Britain, even if it led to war. In March, 1941, therefore, while Britain alone withstood the Nazi onslaught, the United States Congress passed the *Lend-Lease Act.* The Lend-Lease Act empowered the President to "lend, lease, or exchange" war materials with nations whose struggle against aggression was considered necessary to American security. It made the United States the "arsenal of democracy," and it became a major factor in the final victory of the Allies.

Undeclared Naval War With Germany. The Lend-Lease Act led to a state of undeclared naval warfare with Germany. **(1)** In May, 1941, the United States established bases in Greenland and Iceland to help protect British and American convoys that were carrying goods and armaments to Britain (and later to Russia). **(2)** In the same month, Germany announced that American naval assistance to Britain would bring retaliation. **(3)** President Roosevelt quickly declared a state of unlimited emergency and announced that United States armed forces would be used to repel attack. **(4)** An American merchant ship, the *Robin Moor,* was torpedoed by a German submarine late in May, 1941. During the summer and fall of 1941, German subs sank several more United States ships. American naval vessels and merchantmen counterattacked and began to destroy German submarines. **(5)** By December, 1941, a state of undeclared naval war existed between the United States and Germany, and the United States was in effect an undeclared ally of Britain and Russia.

Japan Attacks the United States. A Japanese attack on Pearl Harbor in the Pacific on December 7, 1941 brought the United States into World War II as an active partner of the Allies.

1. *Japanese Expansion.* By 1941, the United States recognized that continued Japanese expansion in China was a major threat to our Far Eastern sources of raw materials (rubber, tin, oil), to our Pacific possessions, and to our national security.

2. *Embargo on Shipment of War Goods to Japan.* After Japan occupied French Indochina in July, 1941, the United States placed an embargo on oil and aviation gasoline to Japan. By then it had become obvious that Japan was preparing to attack the Dutch East Indies, in order to cut off vital resources from the United States, Britain and the Netherlands.

3. *Failure of Diplomatic Talks.* By the beginning of December, 1941, diplomatic talks between the United States and Japan appeared fruitless. The United States called for an end of the Japanese invasion of China and Indochina, while Japan asked for an end of aid to Chiang Kai-shek and the renewal of its trade treaty. The breaking of the Japanese code by the United States in 1941 convinced many of our high officials that war might soon come in the Pacific.

4. *The Japanese Attack on Pearl Harbor.* On December 7, 1941, while Japanese envoys Kurusu and Nomura were in the United States conferring about the embargo, a Japanese carrier force launched planes which attacked naval installations and ships at the United States base in Pearl Harbor, Hawaii. Several thousand Americans were killed or wounded. (Observers have noted that Japan's "sneak attack" was similar to its attack on Port Arthur at the beginning of the Russo-Japanese War.) Almost the whole United States Pacific fleet was damaged or destroyed. The attack on Pearl Harbor was part of a multi-pronged Japanese assault. Within 24 hours, Japan had also attacked Hong Kong, the Malay Peninsula, Borneo, and the United States outpost of Guam.

5. *The United States Declares War.* On December 8, 1941, at President Roosevelt's request, Congress declared war on Japan. Roosevelt called the attack "one which shall live in infamy." The United States in its declaration of war on Japan was joined by Britain, the Netherlands, and several Latin American nations.

6. *Axis Strategy.* On December 11, Germany and Italy declared war on the United States in accordance with their military alliance with Japan. Axis strategy was to engage and defeat the United States in the Far East before it could build up militarily, and thus deprive Britain and Russia of Lend-Lease aid.

War in Two Hemispheres. During World War II, the United States and its allies were engaged in fighting in two hemispheres. The basic military strategy agreed upon by the leaders of the United States, Great Britain, and the Soviet Union was to defeat Germany first, and then to defeat

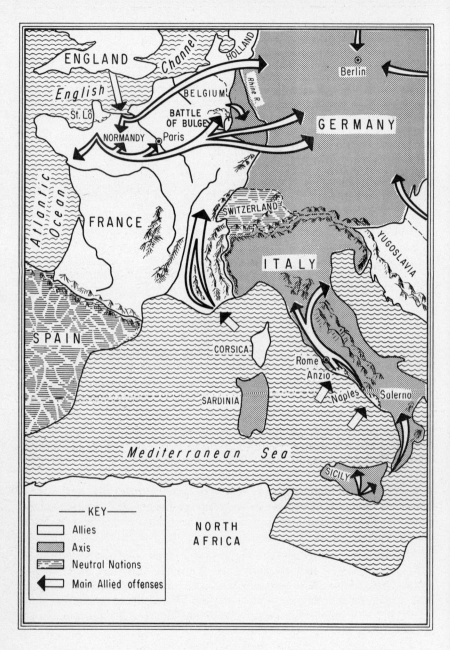

Principal campaigns in the Allied invasion of Europe and the defeat
of Germany.

Japan. President Roosevelt agreed to the strategy, although it was felt at the time that Japan was the greater menace to our security. The United States and Britain agreed to pool their resources and military equipment.

The War in North Africa. The first large-scale United States forces went into action in North Africa in November, 1942. An American expeditionary force under General DWIGHT D. EISENHOWER occupied Morocco and Algeria and advanced into Tunisia. Trapped between American troops on the west (Tunisia), British troops on the east (Libya), and Free French Forces on the south, the Germans and Italians were forced to surrender. (May, 1943). This victory, together with the earlier victory of General Montgomery at El Alamein in October, 1942, put the allies in control of the Mediterranean and paved the way for the invasion of Europe.

The Defeat of Italy. The Allies won a European foothold in Italy, and that country was the first of the Axis powers to be defeated.

1. *Invasion of Sicily.* Using their North African bases as a jumping off point, American forces invaded Sicily in June, 1943, and conquered it in five weeks.

2. *Overthrow of Mussolini.* In September, 1943, after months of air attacks, British and American armies landed in southern Italy, causing Mussolini to flee north. A new Italian government headed by Marshal Badoglio surrendered unconditionally. Rome fell in June, 1944.

3. *Final Defeat of the Germans in Italy.* Stiff German resistance in Italy made the Allied advance northward slow and costly. In May, 1945, the German armies were finally defeated.

4. *Importance of the Italian Campaign.* The primary value of the Italian campaign was that it pinned down large numbers of German troops, thereby preventing Hitler from using them elsewhere.

The Defeat of Germany. The final defeat of Germany in 1945 was the result of the successful invasion of Western Europe by Anglo-American forces and the large-scale victories of the Russians over the German armies in the East.

1. *Battle of Stalingrad.* The turning point of the war in Europe was the *Battle of Stalingrad* in the fall of 1942. The Russians held fast during a three-month siege, then counterattacked. In one of the great battles of history, the Nazis suffered a crushing defeat, losing almost their entire force.

2. *Russia Goes on the Offensive.* In 1943 and 1944, the Red armies went on the offensive. Fighting furiously and with tremendous power, they drove the Nazis out of Russia and back across Europe. Terrible casualties were suffered on both sides.

3. *Russian Victories.* By September, 1944, Russian forces had forced Rumania and Bulgaria to surrender and were at the gates of Warsaw in Poland.

4. *Invasion of Normandy.* The long-awaited and carefully prepared assault on Western Europe began on June 6, 1944 (*D-Day*). Anglo-American amphibious (land-sea) forces, under the supreme command of General Eisenhower, crossed the English Channel. Under a protective cover of thousands of airplanes, they landed on the coast of Normandy in France to open a *second front*.

5. *Nazi Defeats in Western Europe.* Aided by another United States army which invaded southern France (August, 1944), the Allied forces (British, Canadian, American) swiftly reconquered France and forced the Nazis out of Belgium, Holland, and Luxemburg.

6. *"Battle of the Bulge."* After a temporary delay caused by a German counter-offensive in December, 1944 (*"Battle of the Bulge"*), the Allies drove relentlessly onward, crossing the Rhine in March, 1945.

7. *The Advance into Germany.* As the Allies advanced into Germany, the Russians moved in from Poland, entered Vienna (Austria), and approached Berlin. On April 25, 1945, American and Russian armies met at the Elbe River, splitting Germany in two.

8. *The Defeat of Germany.* The war came rapidly to an end. As the German armies were cut to pieces and pounded mercilessly from the air, Hitler committed suicide, and Russian forces entered Berlin (May 2, 1945). On May 7, 1945, Germany surrendered unconditionally at Rheims in France. It was divided into British, American, French, and Russian zones of military occupation.

9. *V-E Day.* The United States celebrated the victory on May 8 (*V-E Day*), which President Truman declared to be a day of thanksgiving.

The War in the Pacific and the Far East. When the United States was attacked in December, 1941, all-out war in the Far East followed.

1. *Early Japanese Successes.* Japan was well prepared for war. While the United States was busy organizing her mighty resources, the Japanese war machine swept over the Philippines, the Malay Peninsula, and the Dutch East Indies.

2. *First United States Victories.* The turning point of the war in the Pacific area came in May and June, 1942, when the Japanese naval offensive was stopped in two major battles. **(a)** The *Battle of the Coral Sea* ended the threat to Australia. **(b)** The *Battle of Midway Islands* ended the threat to Hawaii. The Japanese forces suffered heavy losses.

3. *The Japanese Pushed Back.* During the next three years, the Japanese were slowly pushed back toward their home islands by a long series of amphibious operations, referred to as "island-hopping." The Gilbert, Marshall, and Mariana Islands were restored to Allied control. The Philippines were reconquered by General Douglas MacArthur.

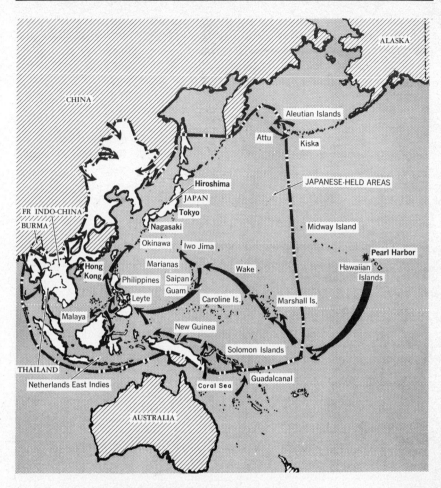

Principal Allied campaigns in the Pacific.

4. *The Assault on Japan.* By the middle of 1945, the United States was able to launch heavy aerial assaults against the home islands of Japan, from bases on the islands of Iwo Jima and Okinawa, as well as from aircraft carriers. General MacArthur and Admiral Nimitz laid plans to invade Japan.

5. *The China-Burma-India Front.* While driving Japan back in the Pacific, the Allies were making strenuous efforts to come to the aid of China. When the Burma Road was cut by the Japanese in 1942, General JOSEPH STILWELL, commander of the American forces in China, led American, British, and Chinese units back into northern Burma to construct another road. By 1945, after months of jungle warfare, supplies were again flowing to China over a new route. Meanwhile, British forces under Lord Mountbatten, reopened the original Burma Road.

6. *The Defeat of Japan.* Japan's final collapse came rapidly. Her forces were already in widespread retreat, her supply lines by sea had been completely disrupted, and the great cities of the home islands were being bombed more and more heavily. On August 6, 1945, an *atomic bomb* was dropped on Hiroshima by an American plane. It wiped out a large part of that city. On August 9, an atomic bomb wrecked Nagasaki. On August 8, Russia declared war on Japan and quickly overran Manchuria. On August 14, the Japanese government asked for peace. On September 2, 1945 (*V-J Day*), the articles of unconditional surrender were signed aboard the battleship *Missouri.* General Douglas MacArthur, the Supreme Allied Commander, began the occupation of Japan.

7. *Surrender Terms.* The surrender terms were based on the *Declaration of Potsdam,* issued by the Allies on July 26, 1945. **(a)** Japan was to be disarmed; war criminals were to be punished; Japanese territory was to be occupied by the Allies; all possessions outside the home islands were to be given up; and a democratic government was to be established. **(b)** The Japanese Emperor was permitted to retain his throne, but he was no longer to retain his divine status, and he was to take orders from the Supreme Allied Commander.

Allied War Aims. The Allies looked forward to a better world after the war. Their aims were best stated by President Roosevelt of the United States and Prime Minister Winston Churchill of Great Britain.

1. *The "Four Freedoms."* President Roosevelt outlined his plan for a brighter future by stating in a speech in January, 1941, that the world of the future should be founded on four freedoms: *freedom of speech, freedom of religion, freedom from want,* and *freedom from fear.* These ideals contrasted sharply with the fascist doctrines.

2. *The Atlantic Charter.* In August, 1941, shortly after the start of the Lend-Lease program, Roosevelt and Churchill met on board ship in Atlantic waters and drew up a joint statement of war aims. This *Atlantic Charter* was much like Wilson's Fourteen Points. It supported the following principles: **(a)** no territorial seizures by Britain or the United States, **(b)** self-determination for all nations and restoration of freedom to conquered nations, **(c)** creation of a lasting peace based upon freedom from fear and want, **(d)** freedom of the seas, **(e)** disarmament of aggressors, **(f)** international economic cooperation to raise standards of living, **(g)** peace based on collective security, **(h)** equal opportunities to all nations for trade and raw materials.

Military Conferences. Overall military strategy for winning the war was mapped by the top Allied leaders at a series of important conferences.

1. *Washington.* In Washington, on January 1, 1942, twenty-six nations signed the *Declaration of the United Nations,* pledging themselves to fight together as allies until the Axis had been defeated, and to seek a peace in accordance with the principles of the Atlantic Charter.

2. *Casablanca.* Unconditional surrender terms were agreed upon by Roosevelt and Churchill at the *Casablanca Conference* in January, 1942.

3. *Teheran.* Unified military action against Germany was agreed upon by Roosevelt, Churchill, and Stalin at the *Teheran Conference* in November, 1943.

4. *Yalta.* Plans for the defeat, disarmament, and occupation of Germany, and for the boundaries of a new independent Poland, were made at the *Yalta Conference* in February, 1945, by Roosevelt, Churchill, and Stalin. Russia secretly agreed to enter the war against Japan within three months after the defeat of Germany, in return for territory and privileges in the Far East.

5. *Potsdam.* Details of the occupation and administration of defeated Germany, and a declaration calling upon Japan to surrender, were drawn up by Truman, Stalin, and Attlee at the *Potsdam Conference* in July, 1945. (Clement Attlee had succeeded Churchill as British Prime Minister early in 1945. Truman assumed the Presidency after Roosevelt's death, also in early 1945.)

Characteristics of World War II. World War II was different from all other wars in several ways.

1. It was truly a *global war*. More nations took part than in any previous war. All continents and oceans were scenes of military action. Campaigns and supply lines stretched across the world.

2. It was a *total war*. The home front was as important as the fighting front. Civilians were mobilized for home defense and for war industries. Women entered the armed forces and industry in greater numbers than ever before. The population in areas under enemy rule took part in sabotage activities and organized underground resistance and guerrilla forces.

3. *New military methods* and *techniques* were introduced. These included *blitzkrieg* warfare, which was designed to split up enemy armies by combined use of planes, tanks, and motorized troops; the use of heavy bombardment to "soften up" fortifications before invasion or attack; the use of paratroopers; and amphibious landing operations.

4. Revolutionary *new weapons* and *devices* were employed for the first time. These included radar, guided missiles, and most important, the atomic bomb. The airplane (bombers and fighters) came into its own as a weapon of crucial importance.

The Home Front in the United States. The United States became more fully involved in World War II than in any previous effort. Never before had the Federal government so completely mobilized the nation's human and economic resources.

1. *Human Resources.* The human resources of the nation were fully committed. Eleven million men entered the armed forces; thousands of women also joined in non-combatant services. Thousands of civilians became air-raid wardens and aircraft spotters. Women by the thousands, as well as older citizens, entered the nation's booming war industries.

2. *Organization of Production and Industry.* Perhaps the most important factor in winning the war was the tremendous productive capacity of the United States. It truly became the "arsenal of democracy." Under Lend-Lease alone, the United States sent its Allies nearly 50 billion dollars in food, munitions, and other supplies. As in World War I, the Federal government directed and coordinated the war effort. The *War Production Board* (*WPB*) and the *Office of War Mobilization* directed war production by converting old factories, building new ones, and allocating scarce materials, including manpower. Existing industries, such as automobile and aircraft, were vastly expanded, and whole new industries were created (for example, synthetic rubber). Industrial production doubled, and agricultural output increased by over 30%.

3. *Role of Labor.* By 1944, nearly 50% of the nation's labor force had entered war industries, including millions of women and teenagers. A *War Manpower Commission* handled manpower questions and "froze" workers in necessary jobs. A *War Labor Board* handled disputes between labor and management and attempted to hold the line on wage increases to prevent sharp rises in prices. Organized labor agreed to limit its demands for wage increases and for the most part kept its "no strike" pledge. Congress, over the President's veto, authorized the Chief Executive to seize war plants threatened by strikes.

4. *Government Controls on Consumption.* Since the needs of the armed forces came first, restrictions were placed on the production of consumer goods, and price ceilings were established by the *Office of Price Administration* (*OPA*). The OPA also issued ration booklets to consumers to insure equal distribution of scarce commodities such as coffee, sugar, meat, and butter.

5. *Financing the War.* World War II cost the United States over 340 billion dollars, more than ten times the total cost of World War I. The government financed this tremendous war effort by increasing income taxes to their highest levels in history, by levying heavy excess profits taxes, and by issuing over 100 billion dollars in war bonds.

6. *Controlling Inflation.* During the war, the government took effective steps to control the inflationary pressures brought about by war expenditures, greatly increased payrolls, and a declining quantity of consumer goods on the market. As a result of increased taxes, wage and price controls, and rationing, prices were kept in check. Between 1941 and 1945, price levels rose only 30% (half as much as during World War I). Serious inflation was avoided.

7. *Civil Liberties.* By and large there were fewer violations and restrictions of civil liberties during World War II than in other wars. In general, conscientious objectors and pacifists were treated leniently and there was a minimum of discrimination against minorities. Negro rights and opportunities in industry were extended, and a *Fair Employment Practices Committee* (FEPC) was created to investigate and check job discrimination in defense industry. The one notable exception was the forced movement of Japanese-Americans from the West Coast into huge army-run relocation centers, early in the war. In view of the demonstrated loyalty of these citizens, and the fine performance of the Japanese *Nisei* units in combat, this action is now considered to have been ill-advised and unnecessary.

8. *Election of 1944.* As in the course of the Civil War, a national election was conducted in the midst of World War II. In the election of 1944, Franklin Roosevelt was re-elected for the fourth consecutive time, on an internationalist platform. His running mate was Senator HARRY S. TRUMAN of Missouri, a compromise candidate, who had won acclaim for his investigation of war contracts. Roosevelt defeated THOMAS E. DEWEY, the popular Republican Governor of New York State.

9. *The Death of Roosevelt.* Almost on the eve of final victory, President Franklin D. Roosevelt died suddenly on April 12, 1945. His death was mourned deeply throughout the world. At the time of his passing he was already thinking about planning for the peace.

The Results of World War II. World War II exacted a staggering cost in lives, physical destruction, and dislocation. Its *immediate results* are outlined below.

1. *War Costs.* World War II was the most tragic and costly war in history. (a) It was estimated that the war cost over a trillion dollars, plus an immense sum in property damages which is impossible to estimate. (b) War casualties included over 20 million dead and more than 30 million wounded. United States losses, greater than in any previous conflict, amounted to 292,000 dead and 670,000 wounded. (c) Abroad, millions of people lost their homes or fled into other areas. They became international refugees known as "displaced persons."

2. *Treatment of Defeated Nations.* The victorious powers were anxious to avoid mistakes in the peace settlement, such as had occurred in the Paris Peace Treaties after World War I. The major aggressors (Germany and Japan) were occupied by Allied troops, pending final peace treaty negotiations. In 1947, peace treaties with Germany's minor partners were drawn up.

> (a) Germany was divided into four zones to be occupied and administered by Britain, France, the United States, and Russia. The country was stripped of all war gains, reduced in size, disarmed, and demilitarized. Leading war criminals were tried by an international tribunal and sentenced to death or long prison sentences (Nuremberg Trials). Germany was to make heavy reparations payments in the form of goods, equipment, and money, especially to the Soviet Union.

(b) Japan was occupied by American forces under the Supreme Allied Commander, General MacArthur. Japan lost all territories outside her home islands. Leading war criminals were executed, notably Premier Tojo, who had been responsible for Japanese war atrocities.

(c) Peace treaties with the Nazi satellite nations were drawn up by a Council of Foreign Ministers and adopted in 1947. *Italy* was deprived of her colonies and demilitarized. She yielded territory to Yugoslavia (Venezia-Giulia). Trieste was internationalized as a free territory. Italy was required to pay 360 million dollars in reparations to the nations she had injured. *Rumania* yielded Bessarabia and Bukowina to Soviet Russia, and had to pay reparations. *Bulgaria* was forced to pay reparations to Greece and Yugoslavia. *Finland* lost the province of Petsamo to Russia and paid reparations.

(d) Austria was divided into four occupation zones (like Germany), and was ruled by an Allied Military Council. It was decided that since Austria had been forced into the war against her will, no punitive action would be taken against her.

3. *Problems of Reconstruction.* The nations of Europe, victors and conquered alike, faced the problems of restoring shattered industries; rebuilding homes, schools, hospitals, churches, roads and other facilities; and restoring normal trade activities. Some countries, like Belgium and West Germany, recovered rapidly; others, like France and Italy, recovered more slowly. The United States financed a large part of this postwar reconstruction.

The Significance of World War II. World War II contributed significantly to shaping the postwar world and its present-day tensions. It also had an important impact upon United States foreign policy. Its long-range results are outlined briefly below. (They will be discussed at greater length in the following chapter.)

1. *International Organization for Peace.* To eliminate the causes of war and to prevent future catastrophes, the statesmen of the world established a new international peace organization, the *United Nations (UN),* in 1945. An attempt was made in designing the UN to avoid the fatal weaknesses of the League of Nations. Since its creation, the UN has played an important role in world affairs.

2. *The Decline of Colonial Empires.* For the people in colonies, World War II became as much a war against colonialism as against fascism. During and after the war, the colonial peoples campaigned successfully for more self-government and independence. Japanese conquests early in the war showed colonial peoples that the white man was not invincible, and the Atlantic Charter and Four Freedoms held out promises of greater equality. Britain, France, Holland, and other colonial powers found it necessary to give in to the demands of colonial nationalism. The overall effect since the close of World War II has been the virtual liquidation of the major European colonial empires.

3. *The Cold War.* The United States and the Soviet Union emerged from World War II as the two most powerful nations on earth. Efforts of Russia to expand its political and economic system, and the determination of the United States to check communist expansion, brought on a *cold war* between the democratic (non-communist) and the communist nations of the earth. A new balance of power developed.

4. *The Atomic Age.* The development of the atomic bomb during World War II ushered in the age of atomic energy many years earlier than it might have come without the wartime emergency. Since the war, the nations have been experimenting with peaceful as well as wartime uses of the atom. It is predicted that the development of atomic energy to its maximum possibilities will revolutionize our way of life. At any rate, the question of nuclear disarmament has become one of the world's greatest problems.

5. *Abandonment of Isolation by the United States.* Postwar developments brought about by World War II have caused the United States to abandon isolationism and to assume the role of leader of the free world. Among the important factors which have brought about this commitment to internationalism in foreign policy are the following: the growth of communist power in Europe and Asia; the new defense requirements of an atomic age; the growth and development of the UN as a world peace agency; nationalism in Asia and Africa; the growing need for aid on the part of the developing nations of the world; and the realization that the old pattern of non-involvement had failed to keep the country at peace.

REVIEW TEST (Chapter 29)

Select the number preceding the word or expression that best completes each statement or answers each question.

1. Which of the following helps explain World War II but *not* World War I? (1) militarism (2) fascism (3) international anarchy (4) alliances

2. In 1941, the attitude of the United States toward Japan's new order in the Far East was (1) acceptance of Japan's domination of the Far East (2) abandonment of the "Open-Door" policy (3) indifference to Far Eastern questions (4) restriction of trade with Japan

3. The immediate cause for United States entry into World War II was the (1) German invasion of Poland (2) Italian invasion of Ethiopia (3) Japanese attack on Pearl Harbor (4) Russian attack on Finland

4. Before the United States entered World War II, Germany had conquered all of the following *except* (1) France (2) Denmark (3) Russia (4) Greece

5. In 1940, the United States leased naval bases in the Caribbean Sea from Great Britain to (1) cancel Great Britain's war debt (2) build adequate defenses in the Western Hemisphere (3) give its investors markets for exports (4) help England police her possessions in the area

6. Which of the following was true of the Draft Act of 1940? (1) It was the first peacetime draft in American history. (2) It made all men up to the age of 50 eligible for military service. (3) It applied to women as well as men. (4) It was passed over President Roosevelt's veto.

7. The battle considered to be the turning point of World War II in Europe was (1) Stalingrad (2) El Alamein (3) the "Bulge" (4) Berlin

8. The program under which the United States became the "arsenal of democracy" during World War II was made possible by (1) the Neutrality Act of 1939 (2) "Cash and Carry" (3) the Marshall Plan (4) the Lend-Lease Act

9. A widely adopted means of solving the manpower problem in the United States during World War II was to (1) use forced labor (2) increase the immigration quotas (3) employ large numbers of women (4) abolish all relief payments

10. Which of the following was a result of both World War I and World War II? (1) Japan lost all territories outside her home islands. (2) The United States joined her allies in collecting reparations. (3) Italy was forced to give up all her African colonies. (4) Germany had to give up her territorial holdings outside her borders.

Select the item in each group that does **NOT** *belong with the others.*

1. American victories in the Pacific: (a) battle of Coral Sea (b) battle of Midway Islands (c) invasion of Normandy (d) "island hopping" in the Gilbert and Marshall Islands

2. United States military commanders in World War II: (a) Montgomery (b) MacArthur (c) Stilwell (d) Nimitz

3. Military strategy conferences: (a) Casablanca (b) Yalta (c) Potsdam (d) San Francisco

4. World War II agencies: (a) War Production Board (b) Atomic Energy Commission (c) War Labor Board (d) Office of Price Administration

5. New weapons or tactics of World War II: (a) blitzkrieg warfare (b) use of paratroopers (c) amphibious landings (d) use of cavalry

Essay Questions

1. Show how each of the following led gradually to the abandonment of neutrality by the United States between 1939 and December, 1941, when we entered World War II: the Nazi-Soviet Pact, the Nazi invasion of Poland, the fall of France, the Battle of Britain.

2. In December 1941, the United States declared war on Japan. Describe our relations with Germany and Japan just before the Japanese attack on Pearl Harbor.

3. Some historians blame President Franklin Roosevelt for United States involvement in World War II. Present evidence for or against this point of view.

4. List and briefly explain *five* military highlights of World War II.

5. Discuss the United States contributions to the final defeat of (a) Germany and (b) Japan.

6. List four "home front" problems of the United States during World War II, and explain how each was handled.

7. Discuss two immediate and three lasting results of World War II on the United States and on the world.

CHAPTER 30

American Foreign Policy Since World War II

Since World War II, the United States has played a leading role in world affairs and taken an active part in the events of every hemisphere. *Collective security,* or the preservation of international order through united action of free nations, has become a cornerstone of American foreign policy.

Part I — THE UNITED STATES AND THE UNITED NATIONS

In contrast to its rejection of the League of Nations after World War I, the United States has attempted increasingly to work through the United Nations since World War II.

Origins of the United Nations During World War II. The United Nations was born during World War II. In addition to working together to defeat the enemy, the leaders of the Allied nations hoped to establish a system for permanent world peace after the close of World War II. At the same time that they met to map military strategy, they made plans for a postwar peace organization. The culmination was the *San Francisco Conference* of April, 1945, which drew up the *Charter of the United Nations.* It was adopted unanimously by the delegates of the 50 nations in attendance on June 26, 1945. (Poland was later admitted as a 51st "founding nation.")

UN — Purposes, Principles, and Membership. The purposes, principles, power, and structure of the UN are outlined in its *Charter.*

1. *Purposes of the UN.* The main aims of the UN are: **(a)** to maintain international peace and security; **(b)** to develop friendly relations among nations; **(c)** to further international cooperation in solving economic, social, cultural, and humanitarian problems.

2. *Principles and Powers.* Under its Charter, the UN can restrain nonmembers as well as members from violations of peace and security. It may not, however, interfere in the domestic affairs of any nation. UN members pledge themselves to do the following: **(a)** to respect the equality of all nations; **(b)** to carry out their obligations under the Charter; **(c)** to settle international disputes by peaceful methods; and **(d)** to refrain from using force or threats of force against other nations.

3. *Membership.* UN membership, according to the Charter, is limited to "peace-loving" nations. Fifty-one nations originally ratified the Charter in 1945. By 1976, membership had grown to 145, largely as a result of the admission of new African nations. In becoming the *first* nation to ratify the Charter, the United States gave clear evidence of its substitution of international cooperation for isolation as a basic national policy.

Organization of the UN. The UN is made up of six main organs or agencies.

1. *The General Assembly.* The General Assembly is composed of representatives of all the member nations. Each nation has one vote. The Assembly admits new members, votes on the UN budget, makes recommendations concerning world peace and security, and promotes international cooperation. It meets annually from September through mid-December. Because all nations have equal status in the Assembly and can discuss virtually any matter there, it has been called the "Town Meeting of the World."

2. *The Security Council.* The Security Council is made up of 15 member nations. Five are *permanent members* (United States, Soviet Union, Great Britain, France, and Communist China). Ten are *non-permanent members,* elected for two-year terms by the General Assembly and chosen on a regional basis. Under an amendment adopted in 1965 (which increased the Security Council membership from its original 11 members to 15 members), five Council seats are reserved for the Afro-Asian nations.

Under the Charter, the Security Council has the primary responsibility for protecting world peace. It may investigate dangerous situations and recommend diplomatic — or even military — action to prevent or end threats to world peace. The Council must approve the nomination of new members to the UN before the Assembly is called upon to vote on their applications for membership. The Council is considered to be in continuous session.

> (a) *Voting.* In the Security Council, decisions on important or "substantive" matters require an affirmative (yes) vote of nine members, including *all five* permanent members. Any one of the "Big Five" can prevent action by a negative vote or *veto.* Votes on less important "procedural" matters require the approval of any nine members of the Council.

> (b) *Use of the Veto.* Because of the cold war, the Soviet Union has used the veto frequently to block any action it considers opposed to its interests. It has invoked the veto on over 100 occasions.

3. *Economic and Social Council (ECOSOC).* This body is made up of 27 members, elected by the General Assembly. (Originally, ECOSOC had 18 members, but this figure was increased to 27 by an amendment adopted in 1965.) The Economic and Social Council is directly responsible to the General Assembly. It tries to find solutions to international economic and social problems such as poverty, illiteracy, and disease. It also coordinates the work of *specialized agencies* affiliated with the UN. These include the *Food and Agriculture Organization (FAO),* the *International Labor Organization (ILO),* the *United Nations Educational, Scientific, and Cultural*

Organization (UNESCO), the International Bank for Reconstruction and Development (IBR), and the World Health Organization (WHO).

4. *The Trusteeship Council.* The Trusteeship Council attempts to insure fair treatment for the peoples living in *trusteeships,* and to prepare them for eventual self-government. Trusteeships are the former colonies of defeated nations assigned to UN members. These *administering powers* submit annual reports to the Trusteeship Council. Under UN auspices, nearly all of the original trusteeships have received their freedom. The Trusteeship Council also tries to improve the conditions of non-self-governing peoples *not* under the trusteeship system (for example, those in the remaining dependencies of Britain, Spain, and Portugal).

5. *The International Court of Justice.* This court (often called the *World Court*) decides disputes between nations and gives advisory opinions on legal questions. It is made up of 15 judges selected by the Assembly for nine-year terms. UN members can submit disputes to the Court directly. Non-members may do so with the approval of the Security Council and Assembly.

6. *The Secretariat.* The Secretariat of the UN consists of a *Secretary-General,* appointed by the Assembly, and his staff. Members of the Secretariat maintain the UN headquarters, take care of clerical and financial matters, translate speeches, and engage in research. The Secretary General, considered the most important official of the UN, is chosen by the General Assembly for a five-year term, with the approval of the Security Council. He is the chief administrative officer of the UN. He draws up the agenda, submits reports, and supervises the staff of the Secretariat. Thus far, this position has been held by Trygve Lie of Norway, Dag Hammarskjold of Sweden, U Thant of Burma, and Kurt Waldheim of Austria.

United States Responsibility for the UN. Support of the UN has been a keystone of American foreign policy since the world body's creation in 1945. Before his death, President Roosevelt helped plan the basic design of the organization. The United States played host in San Francisco to the conference that drew up the UN Charter. Also, a generous gift of land in New York City by John D. Rockefeller, Jr. made possible the selection of New York City as the permanent headquarters of the UN. In addition, as the world's wealthiest nation, the United States has contributed more than any other country to the UN's financial support (over 30%).

United States Leadership in the UN. The United States has exercised leadership in many important UN projects and has been the free world's spokesman against communism in the cold war.

1. *"Uniting for Peace" Resolution.* Because Soviet vetoes had frequently stalemated the Security Council and blocked action on important issues, the United States introduced a "Uniting for Peace" resolution in the General Assembly in 1950. Under this plan, which was adopted by a large majority, the General Assembly can, in a crisis, be called into emergency session within 24 hours, at the request of any nine members of the Security Council, or by a majority of the member states. The Assembly can then recommend steps to meet the crisis, including use of armed force.

2. *Action Against Aggression in Korea.* When North Korea launched an attack against the Republic of South Korea in June, 1950, the United States sponsored resolutions in the Security Council calling for a cease-fire and assistance to Korea by UN members. The United States was the first country to send troops. It also led the combined UN forces until a final armistice was signed in 1953. (See page 553 for details of Korean War.)

3. *"Atoms For Peace."* Acting on the recommendation of President Eisenhower of the United States, the UN created an *International Atomic Energy Agency (IAEA)* in 1956. Its purpose is to establish a pool of fissionable materials to promote the peaceful use of atomic energy. Although cold war tensions have prevented the IAEA from making substantial progress, it has sponsored several international conferences at which members nations have exchanged useful information. The IAEA has also helped establish a number of small reactors in several European nations.

4. *Revolt in Hungary.* The United States took a leading part in the UN debates over the crushing by Russia in 1956 of a revolt in Hungary against the oppressive Soviet-supported regime. Through its UN Representative, Henry Cabot Lodge, the United States condemned the Soviet action as a threat to the peace. The Assembly adopted a resolution calling on Russia to cease its attack and withdraw its troops.

5. *Action Against the Suez Invasion.* The United States also played a leading role in helping to settle the *Suez Crisis* of 1956-57. This occurred after Egypt's seizure of the Suez Canal, which led Great Britain and France to send troops into Egypt to restore international control. (At the same time, Israeli forces invaded the Sinai Peninsula, which Egypt had permitted to be used for guerrilla raids against Israel.) The United States condemned the invasion and sponsored resolutions calling for a cease-fire and the end of military movement into Egypt. In response to an Assembly resolution, Britain, France and Israel pulled their troops out of Egypt. Their decision to withdraw was hastened by behind-the-scenes pressure by the United States, and a Soviet threat to send in "volunteers."

6. *Admission of Communist China into UN.* For many years, the United States led the opposition to the admission of Communist China into the UN. Our spokesmen argued that the Peking regime (the "People's Republic of China") represented an aggressor power that had seized territory on its borders (parts of India, Tibet) and had supported aggression (Korea, Vietnam).

Then, in an historic reversal in September, 1971, President Nixon declared that the United States would vote to seat Peking in the UN, although we would oppose the expulsion of Nationalist China. In October, 1971, the UN General Assembly voted overwhelmingly to seat the People's Republic. However, it also voted, in spite of strong United States opposition, to expel Nationalist China. The general position of the Nixon administration was that the realities of the world situation required us to seek to "normalize" relations with the world's most populous nation and to bring its government within the political structure of the world community.

7. *The Congo Crisis.* The UN played a leading role in helping to end civil war, violence, and disorder in the Congo, following that nation's independence from Belgium in 1960. In 1961, a United Nations Emergency Force helped to establish a national government in the Congo. After much bloody fighting, UN forces also brought about the forcible reintegration of secessionist Katanga province, which had, under Moise Tshombe, resisted joining a unified Congo. Secretary Dag Hammarskjold lost his life in a plane crash in 1962, while trying to arrange a cease-fire in the Congo.

8. *Active Support of the Work of UN Agencies.* The United States has been very active in supporting the work of the Economic and Social Council and the UN affiliated agencies that work with it, such as *UNICEF* (*United Nations Children's Fund*). It has also given more financial aid than any other nation to the UN *Technical Assistance Program* and to the *International Bank for Reconstruction and Development.*

9. *Arab-Israeli Conflict.* The United States has taken a leading role in negotiations in the UN (and elsewhere) concerning the explosive Middle East situation. American influence played a significant part in ending wars between Israel and the Arab states in 1967 and 1973, and in providing for the stationing of UN Observer Forces to monitor the truces. In 1975, the United States acted as an intermediary in getting Egypt and Israel to agree to disengage their forces in the Sinai Peninsula, while creating a UN-sanctioned buffer zone to separate the two powers. A key feature of this agreement was the stationing of 200 American civilian technicians at surveillance posts in two strategic passes, to monitor the cease-fire electronically.

10. *Recent U.S. Activities in the UN.* In recent years, the United States has continued its active role in the UN. **(a)** We joined with other Western nations in voting against a UN-adopted resolution that condemned Zionism as a form of "racism." Our representative has stood alone in the Security Council in vetoing resolutions that condemned Israel for "violence" in the Middle East, without any corresponding criticism of Arab policies. **(b)** Our government has played a major part in working out cease-fire agreements in the Middle East. **(c)** The United States has supported independence and majority rule in Southern Africa, and has condemned racial *apartheid,* especially in Rhodesia. **(d)** We have agreed to surrender our Pacific Island Trusteeships as soon as self-governing agreements can be worked out. **(e)** American diplomats have used the UN as a forum to debate and work out nuclear agreements, such as the non-proliferation pact of 1968.

In spite of such activities, it is widely believed that in recent years the United States has been showing "lessened enthusiasm" for the UN. To the extent that this is a genuine change of attitude, it may be attributed to the apparent indecisiveness and ineffectiveness of the UN in some situations, and also to the fact that the United States finds itself in an unaccustomed minority position in the UN General Assembly, where the "Afro-Asian bloc" now has a majority of the votes in many situations.

The Changing UN. The changing pattern of international relations since World War II has made the United Nations a considerably different type of organization from that which its designers expected it to be.

1. *Security Council Weakened by Russia's Use of the Veto.* The UN planners hoped that the Security Council would have available the combined armed strength of the Great Powers in the form of an international army. They believed that this would give the Security Council sufficient power to investigate and mediate disputes and, if necessary, to order sanctions, including the use of armed force. Though both the United States and the Soviet Union insisted on the inclusion of the veto, to safeguard their own national interests, it was felt that it would be only rarely used. The growth of cold war tensions has thus far shattered such hopes. Through its frequent use of the veto, the Soviet Union has stalemated Security Council action on many issues and in many critical situations. The international military force has never materialized, except for the "Emergency Forces" created for specific situations.

2. *Growing Strength and Importance of the UN General Assembly.* The repeated use of the veto in the Security Council has reduced the importance of that body as a peace-keeping agency. Consequently, the General Assembly has grown in importance and responsibility, and, in effect, has assumed much of the role that was originally intended for the Council. This has been evident in the activities of the Assembly in establishing the State of Israel, in helping to resolve temporarily some of the issues at dispute between Israel and the Arab states, and in carrying on discussions that led to the granting of independence to virtually all African colonies.

3. *Growing Voice of New Members.* Since 1945, the membership of the UN has more than tripled, with the great majority of the new members coming from Asia and Africa. Their growing influence, especially in the General Assembly, has led the world organization to pay more attention to such matters as decolonialization and aid to developing nations. The nations of the "Western bloc," including the United States, no longer dominate the General Assembly and are frequently outvoted by the "non-aligned" or "third world" nations of Asia and Africa.

4. *Bypassing of the UN.* On many occasions UN members have shown a certain reluctance to allow the UN to interfere in what they consider to be their purely internal affairs. **(a)** The United States and other members have reserved the right to decide in advance what is a matter of "domestic jurisdiction" before agreeing to accept the jurisdiction of the World Court. **(b)** France rejected UN attempts to help settle revolts in Algeria and Indochina, on the ground that these were purely "internal affairs." **(c)** South Africa has rejected UN attempts to get it to end its policy of racial discrimination (*apartheid*) on similar grounds. **(d)** The United States has dealt with successive international crises—in Cuba, Vietnam, the Dominican Republic—without actively involving the UN.

5. *Regional Groupings and Alliances Outside the UN.* Much of the world today is divided into regional groupings (Organization of American States, European Common Market, Arab League, etc.). The United States itself maintains mutual defense alliances with about 40 countries. Although the UN Charter permits regional agreements, their growing number has tended to diminish the UN's prestige, and to encourage the settlement of some disputes outside the world body.

Proposals for Changes in the UN. Many changes have been proposed to help the UN perform its functions of safeguarding the peace and working for better world conditions. Some would require additional and major revisions of the Charter.

1. *Abolition of the Veto.* Many have urged doing away with the Big Power veto, by substituting for it a majority or two-thirds vote in the Security Council.

2. *Weighted Voting in the General Assembly.* Some have recommended that the present "one nation, one vote" method of voting in the Assembly be replaced by a "weighted" system of voting, under which extra votes would be given to members on the basis of population, and economic strength.

3. *Changes in the Secretariat.* Because of the increasingly active role of the UN Secretary-General as a world "trouble-shooter," rather than as a mere administrator, there have been suggestions to change the nature of the Secretariat. Some would strengthen the Secretary-General's position by giving him more influence and assistance. At one time the Soviet Union sought to replace this key official by a three-man committee or *"troika."*

Financial Difficulties of UN. The UN has been plagued by financial problems. In the past major difficulties arose because the Soviet Union and France refused to pay their share of the cost of peace-keeping operations in the Middle East and the Congo. A World Court decision in 1962 declared that all UN assessments are binding. The United States thereupon insisted that delinquent nations pay the amounts due or suffer the loss of their votes in the General Assembly, as provided in the Charter. This nearly paralyzed the 1964-65 General Assembly session. Although the issue was "patched over," the larger problem of insuring adequate financing for the UN remains. The United States is still the largest contributor, although its share of the total has dropped from a high of 31.5% (in 1972) to about 25%.

Future of the UN. It is difficult to predict the future of the UN because we live in a rapidly changing world, with unstable and even critical conditions in many regions.

1. *Criticism of the UN.* Those who have to some degree lost faith in the ability of the UN to accomplish its goals point to the following: **(a)** The UN has not prevented wars in various parts of the world. **(b)** It has often been rendered helpless by the use of the Big Power veto in the Security Council. **(c)** It has no permanent military force of its own. **(d)** It has often been bypassed by the Big Powers in dealing with world problems in which they are deeply involved.

Another charge heard with increasing frequency in recent years is that the UN has been guilty repeatedly of a "double standard of morality." For example, the UN briefly applied sanctions to Israel in 1957 for failing to evacuate the Gaza Strip rapidly enough, but did not adopt similar measures against India for occupying part of Kashmir, or against the Soviet Union for crushing the uprising in Hungary in 1956. The third-world nations of Asia and Africa (supposedly "nonaligned" as between East and West) have been far quicker to condemn Western colonialism, which has all but disappeared, than communist imperialism, which is still in effect in many parts of the world.

2. *Defense of the UN.* Defenders of the UN admit its weaknesses, but emphasize its substantial achievements. They point to its many successes in settling, or at least easing, disputes (Iran, Indonesia, Korea, the Congo, the Middle East, etc.). They cite the many political, economic, and social accomplishments of the UN and its affiliated agencies. They insist that the weaknesses of the UN have resulted more from the cold war than from the institution's basic structure. They explain that the *Uniting for Peace Plan* has given the General Assembly power to act in a crisis if the Security Council is deadlocked by a veto. They feel that the existence of the International Court of Justice as part of the UN is a step toward the acceptance of international law as a substitute for war. They argue that the realization that nuclear war can destroy mankind has already caused East and West to relax cold war tensions in favor of a spirit of *détente*.

REVIEW TEST (Chapter 30 — Part I)

Select the number preceding the word or expression that best completes each statement or answers each question.

1. The United Nations can most accurately be described as (1) a court of international arbitration (2) a world state (3) a collective security pact (4) an association of sovereign nations

2. Which of the following statements concerning the organization of the United Nations is true? (1) The chief purpose of the Security Council is to keep peace. (2) In the General Assembly the number of votes a nation has depends on its population. (3) All members of the General Assembly are also members of the Economic and Social Council. (4) The non-permanent members of the Security Council are appointed by permanent members.

3. Which part of the United Nations provides a forum for the expression of public opinion by all members? (1) Security Council (2) Trusteeship Council (3) General Assembly (4) World Court

4. How is the Secretary-General of the United Nations chosen? (1) He is recommended by the Security Council and appointed by the General Assembly. (2) He is recommended by the World Court and appointed by the Security Council. (3) He is nominated by the Secretary-General and elected at a joint session of the Council and Assembly. (4) He is recommended by the Security Council and elected by a majority of the judges of the World Court.

5. In its dependence upon its member states for enforcing decisions, the United Nations closely resembles (1) the United States under the federal Constitution (2) the United States under the Articles of Confederation (3) France in relationship to her departments (4) Great Britain in relationship to her present colonies

6. One similarity between the League of Nations and the United Nations is that both (1) included all major nations as members (2) allowed each member nation a single vote in the Assembly (3) were dominated by the same "big five" powers (4) established an international police force

7. After World War II, the Trusteeship Council of the United Nations assigned to the United States control over the (1) Aleutian Islands (2) Philippine Islands (3) Marshall Islands (4) Bahama Islands

8. What has been an achievement of the United Nations? (1) establishment of a truce in Algeria (2) awarding of Kashmir to Pakistan (3) release of Hungary from the control of Soviet Russia (4) withdrawal of French and British troops from the Suez Canal Zone

Supply the word or expression that correctly completes each statement.

1. The present chief United States representative to the United Nations is . . ? . . .

2. In 1956, the United States took a leading part in condemning the crushing of a revolt in . . ? . . by Russia.

3. There are now a total of . . ? . . members in the United Nations.

4. The first UN military action to oppose aggression took place in . . ? . . (name of country).

5. The UN has condemned *apartheid* in . . ? . . (name of country).

Essay Questions

1. Many issues discussed at meetings of the United Nations have been of serious concern to the United States. Explain clearly the attitude of the United States toward each of the following issues: (a) use of the "veto" in the Security Council (b) the invasion of South Korea by North Korea (c) atomic energy control (d) financial support of UN peace-keeping forces (e) recognition by the UN of the Palestine Liberation Organization (PLO) as the representative of the Palestinian Arabs.

2. Explain how the United Nations helps meet the "collective security" goal of American foreign policy.

3. Indicate whether you agree or disagree with each of the following statements, and give two reasons for your answer. (a) The United Nations has successfully achieved its major aims. (b) The United States should withdraw from the United Nations. (c) The decision by the United States to end its opposition to Red China's entry into the UN was sound policy. (d) The present "one nation, one vote" system of voting in the General Assembly should be replaced by a "weighted" system under which extra votes would be given to certain members on the basis of population and economic strength. (e) The United States has not exercised sufficient leadership within the United Nations.

Part II — UNITED STATES AND RUSSIA — THE COLD WAR

Since World War II the United States and the Soviet Union have engaged in a *cold war.*

The Cold .War. The *cold war* is a struggle for supremacy between the communist nations, led for the most part by Russia, and the non-communist nations of the "free world," led primarily by the United States. It has been called a "cold war" because it has not involved large-scale fighting. Instead, there have been "hot" words, revolutions, and localized "brushfire" wars. Because each side has built large and powerful military forces, the peoples of the world (including a great many who feel themselves to be neutral in the cold war struggle) have been kept in a state of continuous tension. There is widespread fear that a relatively minor incident might spark a world war that could well destroy mankind.

Basic Causes of the Cold War. There are several basic reasons for the cold war.

1. *Communist Imperialism.* The major cause of the cold war has been communist imperialism and expansion. Since 1945, Russia and Communist China have brought under their control hundreds of millions of people and millions of square miles of territory outside their borders. This has been done either directly or through native communist parties and leaders trained by these two nations. The United States and its allies have tried to check this expansion.

2. *Contrasting Ideologies.* The cold war also results from sharply contrasting systems of beliefs or ideologies.

    (a) The democracies believe in a world of free and independent countries. The communists want to dominate the world through communist dictatorships in every nation.

    (b) The democracies believe in individual freedom. The communist dictatorships believe in the supremacy of the state and the restriction of individual freedom.

    (c) The democracies feel that living standards can rise more rapidly and efficiently under democracy than under communism. The communist powers are convinced that "capitalist democracy" is dying, that communism is more efficient and can outproduce capitalism, and that ultimately capitalism will give way to communism.

3. *Military, Economic, and Technological Rivalry.* A third important cause for the cold war is military, economic, and technological rivalry between the "free world" (popularly referred to as the *West*), and the communist world (referred to as the *East*). This rivalry has contributed to tension between East and West.

    (a) *Military Rivalry.* Each side has built up its military strength as rapidly as possible, particularly in the area of nuclear weapons. Through this *arms race,* both sides have attempted to reach a "balance of terror." This means that each side has tried to become so powerful that the other side will not dare attack it for fear of retaliation.

(b) *Economic Rivalry.* Both sides have also been stressing economic growth. Russia claims that it can and will outproduce the United States within a few years. The democracies have taken steps to boost their own production rates to prevent communist countries from "catching up."

(c) *Technological Rivalry.* Each side has also been spending tremendous sums on scientific and technological research in an effort to prove that its system is superior, and to improve its nuclear weapons, missiles, rockets, and space vehicles.

Russian Expansion After World War II. The outbreak of the cold war was not completely unexpected. Causes for distrust existed between Russia and the Western powers before the end of World War II. Then, when the war ended, the alliance went to pieces within a few years, primarily because of Soviet bad faith and ruthless expansion. The communists took advantage of the "power vacuum" created in Europe and Asia by the total defeat of Germany and Japan and the rapid withdrawal of United States forces from Europe.

1. *Central Europe and the Far East.* By keeping troops in Central Europe and the Far East when the war ended, the Soviet Union helped local communist parties take control of the governments of Bulgaria, Poland, Hungary, Yugoslavia, Albania, Czechoslovakia, East Germany, and North Korea. Because these new governments followed the lead of the Soviet Union, they were called Soviet "satellites."

(a) Opposition parties were eliminated as the communist party took over.

(b) Programs of forced collectivization of industry and agriculture were undertaken.

(c) Religious leaders in opposition to the government, like Cardinal Mindszenty of Hungary, were sent to jail.

(d) Russian troops were stationed in each satellite to help the government keep the people in line.

(e) Trade with Russia was expanded, while trade with Western Europe and the United States was kept to a minimum.

2. *Germany and the Far East.* Russia also sent supplies to the communists in China and stripped East Germany and Manchuria of vast quantities of industrial plants and equipment.

3. *Troops in Iran.* Only after vigorous protests by the United States and the UN, did Russia withdraw troops stationed in Iran during the war in joint occupation with the British (1946).

4. *Establishment of the Cominform.* In 1947, the Soviet Union re-established an international communist organization, the *Cominform,* to replace the *Comintern,* which had been dissolved during World War II.

5. *Maintenance of Armed Strength.* While the United States quickly demobilized its armed forces after World War II, Soviet forces were kept

at peak strength. (The United States was still not eager to shoulder the responsibilities of world leadership.)

6. *United States Protests.* The United States accused the Soviets of violating the Yalta Agreement, in which they had promised to permit free elections in Poland and the other liberated countries of Eastern Europe. The United States also protested the spread of communist propaganda in Europe and Asia and the use of violence in neighboring countries. Essentially, America called for a halt to "red imperialism."

7. *Russia's Justification of Her Actions.* Russia claimed that she was surrounded by hostile nations which were planning to attack her. Foremost among these was the "capitalist United States." Soviet leaders tried to justify repeated acts of aggression with the argument that they were only taking steps to safeguard their national security. (It should be noted that in expanding into adjacent territories, the Russians were also following a centuries-old policy established under the Czars.)

8. *The "Iron Curtain."* In 1946, Russia began to close down contacts between Soviet citizens and those of the non-communist world. Winston Churchill described this policy by stating that an *iron curtain* had been set up across Europe, from the Baltic to the Adriatic.

The Cold War Begins. The cold war broke out in earnest in 1947, when the United States took strong action to stop communist expansion. The situation which led the United States to adopt these policies may be described as follows: **(1)** Communist strength was growing in France and Italy, as the governments of these countries struggled with postwar reconstruction. **(2)** The Soviet Union had made threatening demands on Turkey for joint control and defense rights of the Dardanelles Strait. **(3)** Civil war in Greece had broken out between communist guerrillas and government forces. **(4)** Russia was making the Eastern Zone of Germany a communist satellite state. **(5)** Using violence, terrorism, and deceit, the communists took over the government of Czechoslovakia in March, 1947. This was a great shock to the West because it marked the first time that communism had triumphed in a country with strong democratic traditions.

The Truman Doctrine. United States action to resist further communist expansion took the form of military, financial, and economic assistance to nations threatened by communism. In 1947, Great Britain notified the United States that she was no longer financially able to maintain forces in Greece and the eastern Mediterranean to keep order there. The United States thereupon took action to check communism under a policy called the *Truman Doctrine.*

1. *Purpose.* In March, 1947, President Truman asked Congress to provide military and economic aid to nations threatened by communist expansion, particularly Greece and Turkey.

2. *Provisions.* Congress appropriated 400 million dollars for aid to Greece and Turkey. An American military mission was sent to Greece to advise the government on combating the rebels.

3. *Results.* As a result of our aid, the Greek government ended the communist menace and restored order. Turkey was able to resist Russian influence and demands. The Straits remained in Turkish hands.

4. *Containment.* Because the aim of the Truman Doctrine was to halt further communist expansion rather than to interfere with communism behind the iron curtain, it became known as a policy of *containment.*

5. *Break with Isolationism.* The Truman Doctrine marked a decisive break with the policy of isolation and non-interference in European affairs by the United States. Our country became the acknowledged leader of the non-communist world in the cold war. The containment of communism became one of the United States' most important foreign policy objectives in the postwar era.

Areas of Cold War Rivalry. The cold war has been fought with military, political, economic, and propaganda weapons. Both East and West have taken action along the following lines: military strategy, including alliances and military bases; foreign-aid programs; rivalry within the United Nations; attempts at disarmament and control of atomic weapons; atomic, missile, and space rivalry; propaganda; and espionage and subversion.

United States Military Strategy in the Cold War. Bases and alliances are part of the expanded American military effort since 1947 to contain communist powers and to halt communist expansion.

1. *Bases.* The United States has military bases in some 20 countries and territories outside its borders. As a group, they virtually encircle the Communist bloc. The number of such bases has decreased in recent years. One reason is the increased reliance on long-range ballistic missiles. Another is the opposition of newly independent nations to having such bases on their soil.

2. *Alliances.* The United States has made *collective defense* (military assistance) agreements with over 40 nations.

> (a) In Europe and the North Atlantic areas, the United States is allied to Canada, Iceland, and 12 nations of Western Europe in the *North Atlantic Treaty Organization (NATO).*

> (b) In Asia and the Far East, the United States has made individual (bilateral) alliances with Japan, South Korea, Nationalist China (Formosa), and the Philippines. It has also joined with Far Eastern nations in collective defense pacts: the *ANZUS Pact* consists of Australia, New Zealand, and the United States. The *Southeast Asia Treaty Organization (SEATO)* is made up of the United States, the United Kingdom, France, New Zealand, Australia, the Philippines, and Thailand. (Pakistan withdrew in 1972 because of the recognition of the independence of *Bangladesh* — formerly East Pakistan — by SEATO members.)

(c) In the Middle East, the United States has formal alliances with Turkey (also a member of NATO) and Pakistan. It also cooperates with the Central Treaty Organization (CENTO), made up of Turkey, Iran, Pakistan and Britain.

(d) In Latin America, the United States has, under the *Inter-American Defense Pact,* joined with the 20 Latin American nations in the *Organization of American States (OAS).* While the OAS has taken steps to check communism, it is the only United States alliance *not* originally formed to combat it.

Russian Military Strategy in the Cold War. The Soviet Union is strongly opposed to American overseas bases and has sought the removal of as many of them as possible. It has issued threats to governments that allow America to maintain bases on their territory. However, Russia itself has troops and bases in many of the countries of Eastern Europe, and has greatly expanded its fleet of nuclear-armed submarines. It has made a military alliance, the *Warsaw Pact,* with 7 East European countries (Bulgaria, Poland, Rumania, Czechoslovakia, Hungary, Albania, East Germany). In 1961, Albania was expelled from the alliance for backing Red China against the USSR. Recently relations between the USSR and Red China have deteriorated to the breaking point.

The United States Foreign-Aid Program. Since 1945, the United States has spent more than 143 billion dollars on foreign aid. Our aid program has been the greatest in the history of the world. Approximately two-thirds of this sum has gone for economic development, and the other third for military assistance. Recently there has been growing disillusionment with the results of the foreign-aid program and increased opposition to it.

1. *Mutual Security Program.* At first, the aid program, known as the *Mutual Security Program,* was extended only to military allies. Later, it was broadened to include all nations not considered threats to the West (including even communist Poland and Yugoslavia).

2. *Amounts of Aid.* At first most of the aid went to Western Europe to rebuild the war-torn economies of the Western Allies. More recently, most of our aid has gone to the developing new nations of Asia and Africa; aid to Europe has been cut considerably. By 1975, the total aid provided under various programs comprised about 52 billion dollars to Europe; 60 billion dollars to Africa, Asia, and the Middle East; and 13 billion dollars to Latin America. The graph on page 527 shows the amounts appropriated in recent years.

3. *Grants and Loans.* At first, most United States aid was in the form of grants that did not have to be repaid. The emphasis has now shifted to long-term loans at favorable terms.

4. *Major Aid Programs.* Major aid programs are outlined below.

(a) The *Marshall Plan* (1948-52) provided 12.5 billion dollars in economic assistance to 16 nations in Western Europe.

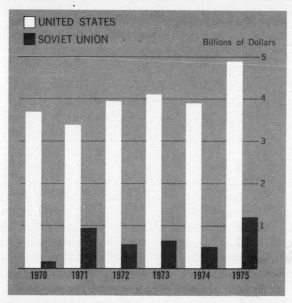

This graph shows the amount of economic aid extended to foreign countries by the United States and the Soviet Union, 1970-75. Other countries, such as West Germany, France, and Japan, also have foreign-aid programs, but the United States continues to be by far the largest single source of such funds. Another factor in this situation is the aid extended by agencies of the UN, such as the World Bank and the UN Development Program. (Source: U. S. State Department.)

(b) The *Point-Four Program*, initiated by President Truman (1949), extended hundreds of millions of dollars in technical assistance to less developed countries in Asia, Africa, and Latin America.

(c) The *Alliance for Progress* (1961-71) provided for United States participation in a 10-year, 20-billion dollar development program to raise standards of living in Latin America.

(d) The United States has also given aid to needy countries in the form of *development loans* for specific development projects (roads, dams, steel plants, etc.). This form of aid is presently coordinated by the *Development Loan Fund* (for public projects), and the *International Finance Corporation* (for private projects).

(e) In 1961, the United States began to ship surplus food stocks to other nations under an expanded *Food-for-Peace Program*.

(f) *Military aid* has taken the form of weapons, equipment, and military training and advice.

5. *Administration of the Aid Program.* Several different agencies have administered the foreign aid program since World War II. At present the administrative agency is the *Agency for International Development (AID)*, within the State Department.

6. *Limitations on Aid.* Most United States assistance has been extended with "no strings attached." In the past few years, however, Congress has provided that aid be withheld from nations that fail to take steps to compensate owners of American industry for property that has been nationalized: and also that United States aid should not be given for government-owned projects that compete with privately owned firms in other nations. (This restriction was imposed to encourage the growth of free enterprise in developing countries.)

7. *The Peace Corps.* A new departure in foreign aid was inaugurated by President Kennedy in 1961 when he introduced the idea of the *Peace Corps.* This is an organization made up of volunteers who agree to work for two years in underdeveloped lands on projects requested by the host nations. Corpsmen, primarily young men and women (although no age limit has been set), provide skilled assistance and instruction in various areas from language instruction to high-yield agriculture. Although Peace Corps volunteers are now serving in more than 50 nations, the popularity of the program has apparently been declining. There have been fewer volunteers, and several missions have withdrawn at the request of receiving nations.

The Soviet Foreign-Aid Program. The Soviet Union has also developed foreign-aid programs. Economic, technical, and military assistance has been given to underdeveloped nations, both allied and neutral. The scale of the aid has been growing, although it is still considerably smaller than that given by the United States. At first, the Soviet Union attached many "strings" to its aid, including requirements that recipients send certain products to Russia in exchange. More recently, Russia has been forced by Western competition and by the resentment of "client states" to grant its aid on more liberal terms.

Foreign-Aid Programs by Other Nations In addition to the United States and the Soviet Union, smaller aid programs have been undertaken by our Western allies, Japan, Communist China, and Israel.

Rivalry in Nuclear Weapons and Missiles. Since the start of the cold war, each side has spent huge sums on research to develop and improve its nuclear weapons, missiles and rockets.

1. *Nuclear Weapons.* The United States produced its first atomic bomb in 1945, and its first hydrogen bomb in 1952. The atomic arms race began when the Soviet Union tested its first atomic bomb in 1949. (Its first hydrogen bomb was exploded in 1953.) Each side has since produced large numbers of nuclear weapons of terrifying destructiveness; both now possess "overkill," or the ability to destroy each other many times over. France and the People's Republic of China (Communist China) have developed smaller nuclear capabilities.

2. *Missiles.* In addition, both the United States and the Soviet Union have developed many types of guided missiles, including surface-to-air missiles, air-to-air missiles, and underwater-to-surface missiles. Among the most powerful types of U. S. missiles are the *Minuteman,* launched from underground silos, and the *Polaris* and *Poseidon,* launched from submerged nuclear-powered submarines. It is believed that every major industrial target in both blocs now has an enemy missile constantly aimed at it, ready to be fired in case of emergency.

(a) Both the United States and the Soviet Union have recently developed long-range missiles capable of carrying several hydrogen bombs and dropping them on widely scattered targets. The American type is called MIRV (Multiple Independently Targeted Reentry Vehicle). The Soviets seem to have overcome an early American lead in this weapons category.

(b) In 1968, Congress agreed by a narrow margin to construct an *Anti-Ballistic Missile System.* The purpose of this ABM is to destroy enemy missiles in space before they can reach our Minuteman missile installations. Approaching enemy missiles would be hit by computer-programmed and radar-directed rockets. Although two ABM installations were planned, only one (in Grand Forks, Montana) has become operational, in accordance with agreements with the Soviet Union (see page 530). The U.S. defense effort has been modified to emphasize an "upgraded silo program," under which underground launching sites for our ICBM's (intercontinental ballistic missiles) are to be greatly strengthened to withstand any enemy attacks.

Disarmament and the Control of Nuclear Weapons. For a number of years after the beginning of the cold war, East and West engaged in disarmament talks aimed at developing plans for control of nuclear weapons. Serious disagreements over the best forms of control prevented significant progress until the early 1960's. Growing recognition by both sides of the possibility of mutual annihilation, plus the need to cut down the huge costs of the arms program, has provided a basis for working out a number of noteworthy agreements since the early 1960's. The growing climate of *détente,* or relaxing of strained relations, that seemed to be developing between the two "super-powers" in the 1970's, has also helped to widen the area of discussion to include limitation of strategic weapons, as well as nuclear arms control.

Although the issue of disarmament and nuclear arms control is still far from resolved, there is now agreement by both sides on the following goals: **(1)** the need to control nuclear weapons, stockpiles and means of delivery, and eventually to eliminate them entirely; **(2)** the need to prevent the spread of nuclear weapons to other nations, and to reduce the risk of war by accident, miscalculation or surprise attack; **(3)** the need for sharp reductions in armed forces and conventional weapons.

Steps toward Nuclear Arms Control and Disarmament. Noteworthy steps towards nuclear arms safeguards and disarmament that have taken place thus far include the following:

1. *Protecting Antarctica (1959).* In 1959, twelve nations, including the USSR, France, Britain, and the United States, agreed to prohibit military bases and nuclear weapons in the Antarctic.

2. *"Hot Line" (1963).* In 1963, the United States and the Soviet Union agreed to establish a "hot line" between Washington and Moscow. This is a direct communications link which can be used in crises, to prevent the use of nuclear weapons by misunderstanding, miscalculation, or surprise attack.

3. *Limited Nuclear Test Ban (1963).* In 1963, the United States, the USSR and Great Britain signed the Treaty of Moscow banning nuclear testing in the atmosphere, in space and under water. More than 100 other nations subsequently adhered to this treaty. (*Underground* testing, however, was not limited until 1974—see page 531.)

4. *Nuclear Non-Proliferation Treaty (1968).* Under a treaty approved by the UN in 1968, nuclear powers have agreed *not* to assist non-nuclear powers in securing nuclear weapons Non-nuclear signatories have pledged themselves not to acquire nuclear weapons The treaty was signed initially by the representatives of more than 80 nations, but it will not go into effect until *ratified* (formally accepted) by the governments of the United States, the USSR, Great Britain and 40 other nations. Although the "Big Three" have given their formal approval, the necessary number of ratifications has not yet been obtained. (France, Red China, and India, all of which are developing their own nuclear programs, have refused to ratify.)

5. *Seabed Test Ban (1970).* In 1970, with the concurrence of the "Big Three," the UN endorsed a treaty to ban weapons of mass destruction from the ocean floors and seabeds of the world.

6. *Outlawing Biological Warfare (1972).* Under a 1972 convention (agreement) on germ warfare, the United States and the Soviet Union pledged themselves not to use biological warfare, and to destroy existing stocks of such weapons. (President Nixon had already ordered destruction of our biological weapons in 1970.)

7. *Strategic Arms Limitation Talks.* In recent years, the United States and the Soviet Union have held extended discussions aimed to limit strategic arms. Several important agreements have resulted.

    (a) *SALT I.* The first round of *Strategic Arms Limitation Talks* (SALT) were begun in 1969 and resulted in 1972 in the first agreement between the two super-powers to limit strategic weapons. The general purpose of the agreement was to establish *parity* (equality) in the nuclear arms available to the Soviet Union and the United States, and thus to build a sound basis for bringing the competitive arms race under control. **(1)** The two nations agreed to limit the number of anti-ballistic missile (ABM) defense sites to *two* each, with not more than 100 missiles at each site. **(2)** The two nations agreed to a five-year freeze on the supply of strategic land-based intercontinental ballistic missiles (ICBM's) and submarine-launched ballistic missiles (SLBM's). This continued the existing Soviet lead in the number of ICBM's, but American experts were confident that this would be balanced by the greater efficiency of our weapons and by our superiority in long-range bombers and MIRV's.

(*b*) *Vladivostok Agreement and SALT II.* Negotiations for a second treaty began in 1972, but progress was slow. In 1974, President Ford and President Brezhnev, meeting in Vladivostok, agreed to an overall limit of 2400 "nuclear vehicles" for each power. This was an interim arrangement, intended to serve as a guideline for a new treaty. Such a treaty (SALT II) was signed at Vienna in June, 1979 by President Carter and President Brezhnev (page 598). (SALT I expired in 1977 but both sides agreed to abide by it, pending acceptance of a new treaty.)

8. *Test Ban on Underground Explosions (1974, 1976).* In 1974, the United States and the USSR agreed to limit the size of underground tests of nuclear *weapons* to 150,000 tons (150 kilotons). In 1976, a second agreement limited underground *non-military* explosions to 150,000 tons, but permitted a series of explosions totaling 1,500,000 tons (1.5 megatons). Whenever the 150,000 tons limit is exceeded by one of the powers, the other will be entitled to hold an on-site inspection. The treaty also provides for inspection by mutual agreement in cases of smaller explosions.

The United States at present has no plans to conduct non-military atomic explosions. The Russians are known to be interested in using such explosions for mining and river-diversion projects, but it is believed that they are likely to avoid explosions of such a size that the mandatory inspection agreement would be invoked.

Inclusion of the on-site inspection agreement, although severely restricted as to types of observations and equipment, is a provision that the United States has been seeking for two decades. However, critics of the agreement point out that the 150-kiloton ceiling, while hampering experimentation with very high-yield warheads of new types, still permits explosions with ten times the yield of the Hiroshima bomb used in 1945.

Space Rivalry. The Space Age opened in 1957, with the orbiting of the world's first satellite, Sputnik I, by Russia. Since that time both the United States and the USSR have made tremendous progress in the space field. **(1)** After first experimenting with orbiting space satellites around the moon, with the docking of manned spacecraft in space, and with "soft landings" of unmanned spacecraft on the moon, the United States successfully landed astronauts Neil Armstrong and Edwin Aldin, Jr. on the moon's surface in July 1969 *(Apollo 11).* By the time the "moon-shot" or Apollo program was completed in 1973, American astronauts had successfully landed on the moon six times, and both the Soviet Union and the United States had orbited space laboratories and sent space satellites toward Mars, Venus, and Jupiter. (2) Both nations have also developed space satellites that are now used for weather forecasting, surveillance, measurement of space radiation and intercontinental telephone, radio, and television transmissions. (3) In 1974, joint space experiments, involving rendezvous and docking activities, were carried out by teams of American "astronauts" and Soviet "cosmonauts."

War of Propaganda. Both sides have also used propaganda and psychological weapons in an effort to prevail in cold-war competition.

1. *Actions of the United States and Its Allies.* The United States and its allies have used various means to advance their cause and to counteract communist influence and propaganda. Powerful radio stations, such as the *Voice of America* and *Radio Free Europe,* have broadcast messages from the Western world to peoples of countries behind the Iron Curtain. Inhabitants of Soviet satellites have been encouraged to escape to freedom. Aid has been given to anti-communist and non-aligned (neutral) nations in an effort to win their sympathy and support.

2. *Actions of the USSR.* The USSR has made vigorous use of its own propaganda tactics. It has attempted to jam foreign broadcasts to people within the communist world. It has refused to permit its citizens to travel abroad. It has banned foreign books and literature. It has used Communist Parties outside its borders to stir up discontent. It has also extended economic aid to neutral nations.

Espionage and Subversion. Espionage and subversion have become important cold war tactics. Each side has set up extensive spy networks.

1. *Communist Tactics.* Communists have encouraged rebel and guerrilla movements in neutral nations. They have also tried to undermine, weaken and if possible overthrow existing governments in the Middle East, Latin America, the Far East and elsewhere. Cuban-trained communists have repeatedly attempted to stir up trouble in Latin America.

2. *Actions of the United States.* The United States government set up the *Central Intelligence Agency* (CIA) to coordinate intelligence-gathering activities, including espionage. Flights of planes and unmanned satellites have been directed over Soviet territory to conduct surveillance and gather intelligence. In some instances, the United States has encouraged uprisings against communist regimes (*e.g.,* "Bay of Pigs" invasion of Cuba, 1961).

United States Action Against Domestic Subversion. Shortly after the cold war began in the late 1940's, many Americans became alarmed over communist activities in the United States. Anti-communist hostility and in some cases "hysteria" reached its heights in the early 1950's.

The trials of Alger Hiss and of Ethel and Julius Rosenberg aroused national concern over communists in government. Hiss, a former State

Department official, was convicted in 1950 for perjury about his relations with communists before World War II. The Rosenbergs were convicted and executed (in 1953) for transmitting secret atomic bomb data to the Russians in 1945-46.

The Federal government also investigated many of its employees suspected of communist leanings or affiliations. It convicted a number of Communist Party leaders for violating the *Smith Act* of 1940, which outlawed advocating or teaching the overthrow of the United States government by force.

In 1954, Congress passed the *Communist Control Act,* outlawing the Communist Party as a legal political party. (Subsequent Supreme Court decisions have greatly limited the application of this law.) In the same year, however, Senator Joseph McCarthy of Wisconsin was censured by the Senate for disrespect shown to Congress in connection with his investigations of communist subversion. (For several years McCarthy had made spectacular but generally unsubstantiated charges about communism in the State Department and other government agencies.) In addition, in the 1950's and 1960's American labor unions took vigorous actions to curb communist influence inside their ranks.

The Soviet Union's Changing Tactics towards the West. Since World War II, Russia has for the most part been openly suspicious of and hostile to the West, especially the United States. From time to time, however, when it suited their purposes, Soviet leaders have been somewhat conciliatory and cooperative. Most recently, a new spirit of cooperation, negotiation, and easing of tensions, commonly called *détente,* has characterized relations. The *"Era of Détente"* has already produced important agreements between East and West. Although some observers feel that the cold war is in process of coming to an end, others suggest that the new approach may be a tactic designed to keep the West off balance. They suggest caution rather than over-optimism in relations with the Soviet Union.

1. *Hostility and Suspicion.* Russia's hostility has been illustrated in many ways, including the following: **(a)** She has created an anti-Western military alliance of communist nations (the Warsaw Pact). **(b)** Backed by the USSR, the East German communist regime has built a fortified wall dividing East Berlin from West Berlin, to prevent, among other things, the escape of East Germans to the West. **(c)** Periodically, traffic between East Germany and West Berlin has been shut off. **(d)** In the early 1960's, when Soviet-American rivalry seemed most intense, the USSR placed missiles in Cuba, posing a serious threat to the United States. In 1962, the world moved away from the brink of war when the Soviets withdrew their missiles in response to an American ultimatum. **(e)** Unrest and the danger of war in the Middle East have been intensified by Soviet military aid to the Arab states and by the bitterly antagonistic Soviet attitude toward Israel. **(f)** Soviet support of North Korea and North Vietnam helped prolong conflict in each of these regions. **(g)** The USSR has used the UN as a forum to denounce the West and to prevent action designed to restore or preserve the peace in crisis situations in Europe, Asia and the Middle East. **(h)** In 1960, Soviet Premier Nikita Khrushchev abruptly ended a summit conference with President Eisenhower, after an American surveillance (U-2) plane had been shot down over Soviet territory. **(i)** In 1975, the Soviet Union cancelled a 1972 agreement with the United States designed to lower trade barriers. This action was taken because our Trade Reform Act of 1974 had provided that an important tariff concession (most-favored-nation status) would be granted only if the Soviet government agreed to liberalize its emigration policies. (The aim of this was primarily to prod Moscow into allowing more Jews to leave the Soviet Union.) The Soviet position was that such American policies violated "the principle of non-interference in domestic affairs."

2. *Peaceful Coexistence.* From time to time, the USSR has shown a willingness to cooperate with the West, or at least to "sit down and talk." Premier Khrushchev called this *"peaceful coexistence."* **(a)** There have been several "summit conferences" between U.S. Presidents and Soviet leaders. Such discussions have had results of some significance, including the following: *(1)* agreements to establish and extend cultural, scientific and commercial exchanges; *(2)* agreements on the postwar status of Germany and Austria; *(3)* agreements to maintain closer communications, including the establishment of a "hot line" communications link between Washington, D.C., and Moscow; *(4)* an agreement to set up air travel between Washington and Moscow; *(5)* agreements to discuss limitation of conventional weapons, as well as nuclear disarmament; *(6)* agreements to work cooperatively on expanded trade and on prevention of hostile incidents at sea and in the air; *(7)* agreements to limit missile systems. **(b)** The USSR signed a peace treaty with Japan and restored diplomatic relations with West Germany. **(c)** The USSR has also accepted agreements banning the use of nuclear weapons in outer space and under the sea, and limiting space and underground nuclear testing. **(d)** Strategic Arms Limitation Talks (SALT) between the two nations have resulted in agreements to place limits on missiles and missile delivery systems. **(e)** An agreement relating to security and cooperation in Europe was reached at Helsinki, Finland in 1975, after a two-year effort involving 33 communist and non-communist European nations, plus the United States and Canada. The Western powers in effect accepted the territorial status quo in Europe, including the division of Germany. In exchange, agreements were made to permit freer flow of people, trade, and ideas between East and West.

Détente. Since the early 1970s, relations between the Soviet Union and the West (particularly the United States) have been changed significantly by the policy known as *détente.* This suggests a deliberate effort to relax tensions and to replace bitter opposition and conflict with a greater measure of acceptance and cooperation.

1. *Beginnings of Détente.* The major figures in introducing the spirit and policy of détente were President Richard Nixon, Chancellor Willy

Brandt of West Germany, and General Secretary Leonid Brezhnev of the Soviet Union. President Nixon met with Soviet leaders in Moscow and Washington. In an historic "about-face," he also visited and re-established relations with the People's Republic of China. Brezhnev has gone further than any other Moscow leader in seeking a normal relationship with the West. For example, he negotiated several purchases of huge amounts of grain from the United States and held friendly meetings with President Nixon and other top Western leaders. He also cooperated with Chancellor Brandt in the policy of *"Ostpolitik,"* which has led to resumption of West German relations with communist-dominated neighbors in Central and Eastern Eurpoe.

2. *Recent Evidence of Détente.* Various important developments in recent years are considered applications of the overall policy of détente. **(a)** During the 1972 visit of President Nixon to the USSR, the two nations reached agreements to freeze intercontinental missiles at their existing levels, to limit defensive missiles to 200 each, to cooperate on health and environmental problems, to stage joint ventures in space, and to set up commissions for scientific and trade cooperation. **(b)** The 1973 visit of Brezhnev to the United States resulted in additional agreements for cooperation in oceanography, agriculture, transportation, cultural exchanges, income-tax accommodations, atomic energy research, and trade. In addition, guidelines were drawn up for further arms-limitation negotiations. President Nixon visited Russia in June, 1974, and his successor, President Ford, met Secretary Brezhnev in Vladivostok in November of the same year. These meetings led to tentative agreements to limit underground nuclear explosions, antiballistic missile systems, and offensive nuclear weapons and delivery systems through 1985.

3. *Some Misgivings About Détente.* Although the cold war seems to have declined, many events continue to indicate that hostility and distrust between the two superpowers are far from completely overcome. **(a)** In 1972, the Soviet clearly had advance notice of the Egyptian-Syrian attack on Israel but failed to inform Washington, in the spirit of the Summit Conference of 1971. **(b)** The United States has complained of Soviet violations of recent agreements on strategic arms limitations. The USSR has made counter-charges. **(c)** The West has strongly criticized the Soviet Union for reneging on its agreements at the Helsinki Conference of 1975 to grant greater human rights. **(d)** In 1976, U.S. Secretary of State Henry Kissinger criticized Soviet action in support of one of the three factions in the civil war in Angola (Africa) as being "incompatible with a genuine relaxation of United States-Soviet tensions." **(e)** Critics also maintain that the Soviet Union has taken no positive action to help improve the critical situation in the Middle East, has supported insurgents in Southeast Asia and elsewhere, has continued abusive anti-United States propaganda, has moved quickly to exploit incidents of instability wherever they may occur, and has shown no signs of willingness to give up *anything.*

4. *Reasons for Détente.* Both sides have reasons for wanting to relax tensions and bring the cold war to an end. **(a)** In the *West,* there has been a growing belief that the old ideological issues of the cold war are no longer relevant and that a new era is emerging — one not dominated by the dogmas and deep distrust of the post-World War II period. **(b)** The Soviet Union, for its part, recognizes the superior productivity of the United States and the West, and evidently wants to share in its technological advances. At the same time, Soviet leaders have become increasingly concerned over Red China's growing strength, its entry into the UN, and its *rapprochement* with the United States. *Détente* with the West might make it possible in an emergency to concentrate Soviet military power in the East. Large-scale border clashes with China in 1969, and occasional border incidents since then, have deeply troubled Moscow. (In one of the most significant developments in recent years, the two communist giants and former allies have become bitter enemies. China has challenged the Soviet Union for the leadership of the communist world. China has denounced the USSR for abandoning "true Marxism" and for joining the United States in "imperialist designs" against small nations. The Peking regime has also laid claim to territory in Asia which, it claims, was unjustly taken from China by Czarist Russia.)

REVIEW TEST (Chapter 30 — Part II)

Select the number preceding the word or expression that best completes each statement or answers each question.

1. A factor *not* involved in the development of the cold war was (1) Soviet expansionism (2) ideological differences (3) competitive military buildups (4) improvement of Soviet living standards

2. The Truman Doctrine was issued in direct response to Communist threats to (1) Korea (2) West Germany (3) Egypt (4) Greece

3. Growing opposition within the United States to our foreign-aid program is attributable mainly to (1) the fact that most of the world is now prosperous (2) the refusal of other governments to extend foreign aid (3) some degree of disillusionment with the results (4) the success of the Marshall plan

4. Relations between the United States and the Soviet Union in recent years have been characterized by all of the following *except* (1) periodic "thaws" (2) competitive coexistence (3) economic and military competition (4) refusal to confer on limitations of nuclear weapons

5. The SALT agreements relate to (1) international action to conserve raw materials (2) improvement of dietary standards (3) population control (4) limitation of strategic weapons

6. Under the *Ostpolitik,* the Brandt regime in West Germany sought to (1) bring about immediate reunion with East Germany (2) reestablish Germany as a major military power (3) "normalize" relations with the Communist nations of Eastern Europe (4) strengthen NATO

7. Which of the following is *not* regarded as a reason for *détente* between the United States and the Soviet Union? (1) less emphasis on ideological differences (2) Soviet concern over the strength of China (3) Soviet desire to share in advanced Western technology (4) abandonment of Marxist ideas by Soviet leaders

8. A region in which the United States and the Soviet Union have been backing opposing nations involved in military conflict is (1) the Middle East (2) Western Europe (3) Africa (4) Eastern Europe

9. The abbreviation SALT indicates (1) a system of intercontinental nuclear missiles (2) a defensive system to intercept hostile missiles (3) a non-military use of nuclear energy (4) talks to limit strategic nuclear weapons

10. The attitude of most Americans toward the policy of *détente* can probably best be characterized as (1) cautious optimism (2) complete rejection (3) fear and despair (4) enthusiastic acceptance

Select the letter of the item in each group that does **NOT** *belong with the others.*

1. Attempts to control nuclear weapons: (a) Non-proliferation Treaty (b) Nuclear Test-Ban Treaty (c) SALT talks (d) Peace Corps

2. Important Soviet leaders since World War II: (a) Brezhnev (b) Lenin (c) Stalin (d) Khrushchev

3. Programs connected with U.S. foreign aid: (a) Point Four (b) Apollo II (c) Alliance for Progress (d) Agency for International Development

4. Steps taken in United States to halt domestic subversion: (a) trials of Communist leaders for violating the Smith Act (b) McCarran Act (1950) (c) *détente* (d) combating Communist influence in labor movement

5. Soviet subversive tactics: (a) making use of foreign Communist parties (b) encouraging free contacts between the Soviet people and people of Western nations (c) widespread use of espionage (d) efforts to undermine established governments

Essay Questions

1. Discuss two basic reasons for the cold war between the East and West after World War II.

2. Give data which show that the cold war has been characterized by all of the following (a) political rivalry (b) economic competition (c) military rivalry (d) psychological warfare.

3. Since 1947 both the United States and the Soviet Union have tried to solve the problems of disarmament and atomic weapons control. (a) Explain why a solution to these problems has not yet been fully reached. (b) Discuss two important agreements that have already taken place.

4. Discuss the policy of *détente,* including (a) its basic objectives and characteristics (b) the conditions which made it possible (c) the present status of the efforts to implement this policy.

5. Some observers feel that the cold war is now virtually over. Others are not so sure. Give your opinion of this question, citing at least three facts, interpretations, or points of view to support your judgment.

Part III — THE UNITED STATES AND EUROPE SINCE 1945

The cold war has re-emphasized the interdependence of the United States and Western Europe, and it has shaped America's policies with the rest of that continent.

Situation in Postwar Europe. World War II was followed by chaos and confusion in Europe. For a short while, it seemed that the disorganization of Western Europe might make possible the communist domination of that whole area.

1. *Economic Chaos.* World War II left Europe in ruins. The Western Allies were both militarily and economically drained by the war and in a poor position to defend themselves against military force or subversion by a new aggressor.

2. *Soviet Expansion in Eastern Europe.* The Soviet Union moved rapidly into the "vacuum" caused by the withdrawal and demobilization of the armed forces of its wartime allies. By keeping troops in Eastern and Central Europe when the war ended, the Soviet Union helped local communist parties take control of the governments of Bulgaria, Poland, Yugoslavia, East Germany, and Czechoslovakia. These were quickly converted into Soviet satellites. The Soviets also began to pressure Turkey for grants and concessions in the Dardanelles. In Greece, civil war broke out between communist guerilla forces and the government.

3. *Subversion in Western Europe.* Between 1945 and 1947, communist pressure and subversion in Western Europe created a dangerous situation. Communist parties in France and Italy were strong and seemed on the verge of coming to power either through the ballot box or by force.

4. *Economic Revival.* Western Europe, assisted at first by much United States aid, set about rebuilding its shattered cities, factories, transit facilities, and other economic resources. It was spectacularly successful, and, as a result, most Western European nations now enjoy unparalleled economic growth, and communist expansion and subversion have largely been "contained." The major factors in the revival of Europe are outlined below.

The Marshall Plan. In 1947, the Truman administration took a major step to check communist expansion and help rebuild Europe. The program came to be known as the *Marshall Plan.* It was first suggested by Under-Secretary of State Dean Acheson, but was brought to world attention in a speech by Secretary of State GEORGE C. MARSHALL in 1947.

1. *Purposes.* The Marshall Plan was based on the assumption that poverty, misery, and unemployment constituted a greater threat to Western Europe than outright military aggression. Accordingly, it was felt that the best way to fight communism was to help war-torn Europe rebuild, thereby reviving prosperity, giving hope for the future, and strengthening faith in democratic institutions. (See also Truman Doctrine, page 524.)

2. *Provisions.* Marshall proposed economic aid for postwar reconstruction to all European nations, including Russia and her satellites. In 1948, Congress set up the *European Recovery Program (ERP).* Under this program, popularly known as the *Marshall Plan,* about 12.5 billion dollars in food, machinery, raw materials, and other needed goods, was advanced to 16 European nations between 1948 and 1952.

3. *Results.* The Marshall Plan was remarkably successful. In four years, Europe's production increased 40% beyond prewar levels. Communist influence was weakened in France, Italy, and other countries. In addition, both the United States and Western Europe gained new insights into the advantages of close economic cooperation.

4. *Soviet Reaction to the Marshall Plan.* Russia refused to take part in the Marshall Plan and forced its satellites to refuse also, even though some of them were eager for aid. Soviet leaders tried to counteract the effects of the Marshall Plan by means of the "Molotov Plan" for economic cooperation within the communist bloc. This had the effect of cutting further the already shrunken trade between East and West. Although Russia agreed to extend economic aid on a large scale, events have shown that her capacity to deliver capital and many needed products was limited. Soviet satellites must pay, in one form or another, for all aid.

Early Growth of Economic Unity in Western Europe. The Marshall Plan paved the way for several significant steps toward economic unity.

1. *Benelux.* In 1948, Belgium, the Netherlands, and Luxembourg established *Benelux,* a customs union to reduce trade barriers.

2. *Council of Europe.* In 1949, twelve nations of Western Europe created the *Council of Europe,* the Council (now with 17 members) meets to exchange ideas on non-military matters.

3. *Coal-Steel Community.* In 1952, the Benelux nations, France, West Germany, and Italy agreed to pool their iron, coal, and steel resources and to create a free market for the exchange of these goods by eliminating trade barriers. This so-called *Schuman Plan* led to the formation of the *European Coal-Steel Community.*

The Common Market. The success of the Schuman Plan encouraged the formation in 1957 of the *European Economic Community (EEC)* or *Common Market.* The Common Market already has major achievements to its credit and may become one of the most significant developments of the 20th century. Its main features are outlined below:

1. *Purposes.* The Common Market was established under the *Treaty of Rome* in 1957 by the six members of the Coal-Steel Community (the "Inner Six"). French statesman JEAN MONNET played a chief role in planning the Common Market and convincing the six nations to join. The Market is a trading association which aims to unite the economies of the member nations in the near future, and at a later date to create some form of political union. At first, this is to be achieved by the gradual elimination of tariff barriers among members and the establishment of a single tariff policy toward other nations. The treaty also calls for the removal of restrictions on the movement of labor, capital, and business enterprises among the six members; for a common policy in agriculture; and for the coordination of monetary and fiscal policies.

2. *Achievements.* Since its inception, the Common Market has made highly impressive economic progress. Internal tariffs among member nations have been eliminated (as of July, 1968) and a common tariff applied to the rest of the world. Also, trade among member nations has more than doubled, and trade with nations outside the Market has jumped over 50%. In addition, the economic growth rate of Market nations (as measured by the value of goods and services produced) has risen over twice as fast as that of Britain and faster than that of the United States. Other noteworthy achievements include a sharp reduction in unemployment and an increase in living standards of member nations greater than anywhere else in Europe. In a highly significant step, the Common Market members admitted Britain into the Community in 1973, along with Ireland and Denmark. (France under De Gaulle's leadership had earlier twice vetoed Britain's application.) The expanded EEC has become the largest trading bloc in the world and one of its strongest economic powers.

3. *The United States and the Common Market.* The United States was among the earliest supporters of the Common Market, seeing it as essential to Europe's economic revival and as a bulwark against communism.

Problems have arisen for the United States, however, as EEC strength has grown and a common tariff has been set up against the goods of all nations outside the Market. American businessmen have complained that their products are being excluded from the Market area. (EEC members argue that the United States has imposed quotas on more products and on a greater volume of trade than the Common Market does.) Tariff negotiations between the United States and the EEC are continually under way and many mutual tariff reductions have already been arranged.

Attempts to Form an Atlantic Community. In 1961, the United States took the lead in helping to establish a 23-nation *Organization for Economic Cooperation and Development* (OECD). The OECD consists of the United States, Canada, and the Western bloc nations in Europe. Its aim is to promote economic growth in the "Atlantic Community" by working out beneficial economic policies, cooperative currency arrangements, and the like. In addition, the OECD has developed arrangements by which European nations are sharing with the United States a growing portion of the burden of aid to developing nations. The OECD is an outgrowth of the earlier *Organization for European Economic Cooperation,* formed in 1947 to handle Marshall Plan aid.

The Founding of NATO. Economic cooperation between Western Europe and the United States went hand-in-hand with military cooperation. This latter took the form of the *North Atlantic Treaty Organization*

(NATO), created in 1949. NATO has become an effective shield against communist aggression and expansion in Europe. When the United States joined NATO, it marked the first time our nation had taken part in a military alliance with foreign countries in peacetime.

1. *Beginnings.* NATO was the outgrowth of a series of collective security arrangements beginning in 1948, soon after the start of the cold war.

(a) In 1948, Britain, France, and the Benelux nations signed the *Brussels Agreement* creating a 50-year defense alliance, called *Western Union.*

(b) In 1949, Western Union was broadened into the *North Atlantic Treaty Organization.* At first its membership included Belgium, Canada, Denmark, France, Iceland, Italy, Luxembourg, the Netherlands, Norway, Portugal, the United Kingdom, and the United States. The addition of Greece and Turkey in 1951, and West Germany in 1954, made NATO a 15-nation alliance.

(c) Under an agreement called the *North Atlantic Pact,* an attack on any one NATO member is to be considered an attack on all.

2. *Organization.* NATO policies are set by the North Atlantic Council, which meets twice a year. Its main military headquarters, known as SHAPE (Supreme Headquarters, Allied Powers, Europe), is in Brussels. The first military commander of NATO was General Dwight D. Eisenhower, and every one of his successors in this post has been an American military man. NATO forces are equipped with nuclear weapons, including U. S. nuclear-powered submarines carrying Polaris and Poseidon nuclear missiles. Most NATO members have contributed some units to the permanent command. Other units take orders from their national governments, but are scheduled to fight under NATO command in time of war. The United States is the largest military power in NATO, with West Germany second.

NATO Policies and Programs. NATO's overall effectiveness may be reflected in the fact that since its establishment not a single piece of European territory has fallen under communist control. Nonetheless, the alliance has had its ups and downs.

1. *Unity in the 1950's.* At the height of the cold war, in the 1950's, enthusiasm for NATO was high among members, despite the fact that they never fully supplied their military quotas. Soviet threats and harassment gave NATO meaning and purpose.

2. *A Weaker Alliance in the 1960's.* By the beginning of the 1960's, a thaw in the cold war had set in. Western European leaders felt that Soviet aggression was no longer an immediate threat. They noted that communist satellite states, such as Rumania and Poland, were allowed increased measures of freedom from Soviet control. There seemed in their eyes to be less need for constant military readiness. This changed attitude was reflected in a weakening of NATO. Most members, including the United States, Britain and West Germany (the biggest contributors), reduced their troop allotments. Although France remained in the alliance, De Gaulle removed all French troops from the NATO command in 1966. NATO policy also shifted from "massive retaliation" to "flexible response."

3. *Effects of the Soviet Invasion of Czechoslovakia.* In 1968, Soviet forces (with contingents from several Warsaw Pact allies) invaded Czechoslovakia to crush that country's growing spirit of liberalism. To defend this action Leonid Brezhnev, head of the Communist Party, issued the *"Brezhnev Doctrine."* This asserted in effect that Russia's communist allies in the Warsaw bloc have only "limited sovereignty," and emphasized the right of the USSR to interfere in any socialist country to prevent "counter-revolution." This naked use of military force convinced NATO members that they must immediately rebuild their strength. To this end they pledged more money, more equipment, and better training for troops.

4. *Continuing Strains in NATO and Growing Independence of Western Europe.* Despite the general desire to strengthen NATO after the Soviet invasion of Czechoslovakia, the alliance still suffers from strains and disagreements. Members continue to fail to fulfill pledged contributions and differ over policy toward the communist world. European states still resent the refusal of the United States to share control of its nuclear weapons assigned to NATO. They openly question the willingness of the United States to come to their assistance with nuclear weapons if they should be attacked. The United States has been criticized, also, for failing to consult with other NATO members before its various summit and détente talks with the Soviet Union. This growing self-assertiveness of Western Europe has been enhanced by the overall success of the Common Market and the growing economic power of the members of that grouping.

In 1974, Turkey invaded the Greek island of Cyprus in the Mediterranean, with the stated purpose of protecting the interests of Turkish people on the island who want self-government. This military action and the Greek resistance to it created a serious difficulty for NATO. Until an uneasy truce was arranged with NATO help, the southern and eastern flanks of the alliance were jeopardized. When the United States placed an arms embargo on Turkey, that nation retaliated by taking over American bases in Turkey. (The embargo was later lifted.)

5. *NATO Strength.* Recent estimates place NATO forces at about 625,000 men in North and Central Europe, plus more than 7,500 nuclear weapons in its land, sea, and air commands.

The Warsaw Pact. After the inclusion of West Germany in NATO, the Soviet Union organized the Warsaw Pact (1955), a mutual defense alliance of the communist bloc nations in Europe. Warsaw Pact members include the Soviet Union, Bulgaria, Czechoslovakia, Hungary, Poland, Rumania, and East Germany. Unlike NATO, in which all members have some voice in shaping policy, Warsaw Pact decisions have been largely made by the Soviet Union, although there have been some signs of change.

1. *Strengths:* Warsaw Pact strengths include more combat troops, tanks and aircraft in Central Europe, plus a growing arsenal of long range missiles and an expanding submarine fleet. The Communists also have a strategic advantage in that they are concentrated geographically in a way that would facilitate delivering a powerful land-air blow at Western Europe before NATO forces could react.

2. *Weaknesses.* A counterbalancing factor is the fact that the United States continues to maintain its lead in deliverable nuclear weapons. The certainty of retaliation from this source serves as a deterrent to attack.

Growing Independence in Eastern Europe. It has become evident in recent years that although the Soviet Union continues to dominate its satellites in Central and Eastern Europe, they are increasingly inclined to make their own decisions and develop their own political and social patterns.

1. *Signs of Independence in the Communist Bloc.* Since the early 1960s, there have been more frequent and convincing signs that the Soviet satellites in Eastern and Central Europe are no longer willing to accept complete Soviet dominance. *Rumania* has openly resisted Soviet plans to limit its industrial development and to keep it a supplier of farm and raw materials. Instead, Rumania has moved to build industries and to develop trade with the West. Similar attitudes and policies have emerged in *Poland, Czechoslovakia,* and *Hungary.* Among the smaller countries, *Albania* has flatly rejected Soviet leadership, turning instead to Red China. *Bulgaria* has exchanged ambassadors with the United States.

2. *Other Challenges to Soviet Leadership.* The leaders of Communist Parties in Europe *outside* the "communist orbit" have increasingly asserted their right to determine their policies independently of Moscow. This principle was finally accepted by the Soviet leaders at an historic conference held in East Berlin in 1976. At this meeting, leaders of 29 Communist Parties in Europe subscribed to a document asserting that henceforward they would cooperate with the Soviet Union *voluntarily* and in accordance with "principles of equality and sovereign independence of each party, non-interference in internal affairs, and respect for their free choice of different roads in the struggle for social change." Among the strongest advocates of this policy were the leaders of Europe's largest national Communist Parties, in France, Spain, and Italy. This appeared to be a flat repudiation of the *Brezhnev Doctrine,* as set forth on page 542.

3. *Is Soviet Dominance a Thing of the Past?* In spite of the recent developments, there is no doubt that the Soviet Union remains the strongest communist state, and that it is still a potent force in Eastern Europe. Nonetheless, there is evidence that the political influence of the USSR is not as all-powerful as it once was, and that the communist movement, to some degree, is becoming decentralized, rather than dominated from Moscow. The Soviet leaders are now supreme only within their own borders. This trend has been compared with a decline in the political influence of the United States, which is less able than it once was to direct events outside *its* own borders. We may be coming to an end of the era when world events were dominated by two super-powers, as during the years of the cold war.

United States Aid to Yugoslavia and Spain. In attempting to prevent communist aggression in Europe, the United States and its allies have sought better relations with Communist Yugoslavia and Spain.

1. *Yugoslavia.* After World War II, a communist dictatorship under Marshal Tito was set up in Yugoslavia. After 1948, Tito refused to follow Soviet orders, and a split with Russia followed. Tito has insisted that Yugoslavia be permitted to take its own "path to communism" without Soviet domination. In recent years, the Soviet Union has stepped up its attempts to "woo" Yugoslavia back into its sphere of influence by offering substantial aid. The United States has extended economic and military aid to the Tito regime, although we recognize that it is firmly committed to its own brand of communism.

2. *Spain.* To strengthen the Western military alliance, the United States negotiated an agreement with Spain in 1953. Under this pact Spain has received military and economic aid in return for permitting the establishment of American naval and air bases on Spanish territory.

This agreement was bitterly criticized by many Americans, as well as by several allies (including France and England). It was claimed that Generalissimo Franco, the ruler of Spain, had been pro-Axis during World War II, and had established a fascist type of dictatorship. Defenders of the pact argued that Spain was an anti-communist nation which could furnish strategically located bases for the defense of Western Europe. The pact has been extended several times since 1953. The accession of King Juan Carlos I in 1975, following the death of Franco, seemed to favor extended cooperation between the United States and Spain.

The United States and Germany Since World War II. Since World War II, Germany has remained divided—a symbol of the cold war in Europe. Relations between the United States and West Germany have become increasingly close.

1. *Division of Germany* Repeated disagreements with the Soviet Union over the future of Germany caused the United States, Britain, and France to merge their occupation zones and to create the West German Republic with its capital at Bonn in 1949. (This is known as the *German Federal Republic.*) To counteract the establishment of the West German Republic, the Soviet Union established the East German Republic in the same year (the *German Democratic Republic*).

2. *Failure to Reunite Germany.* Cold war tensions have prevented the reunification of Germany. Western proposals for unification have been based on the principle of free elections throughout the entire country to choose representatives for a single central government. Soviet proposals have called for direct negotiations between the East and West German governments on the terms of unification, and the establishment of a confederation without abolishing the two separate governments. With each side fearful of unification on terms too favorable to the other, the situation seemed to be "frozen" for many years. In the early 1970's, however, under the leadership of Chancellor Willy Brandt, the two Germanys moved toward a limited measure of cooperation, although formal reunification still seemed to be far off.

3. Cold War Crises in Berlin. Berlin, the former capital of all Germany (and now of East Germany), was also split into two zones when Germany was divided after World War II. The former Russian zone (East Berlin) is part of East Germany. The former Allied-occupied zone (West Berlin) is now part of West Germany. Because Berlin lies wholly within East Germany, it has become a sensitive "trigger spot" in the cold war. Although the United States and its allies were guaranteed access routes into Berlin, as well as occupation rights, under the Potsdam Agreement, the communists have periodically tried to cut off or impede the use of these routes.

   (a) Soon after the West German Republic was established, the communists tried to starve out West Berlin by suddenly cutting off land transportation to Berlin (1948). The Allies overcame this Berlin blockade by organizing an "airlift" which transported food and other vital supplies into Berlin for over a year by air. The blockade was lifted in 1949. Periodically since then the East Germans have on various pretexts banned West Germans from using railroads and highways into Berlin.

   (b) The Russians repeatedly threatened to sign a separate peace treaty with East Germany unless the Western Allies left Berlin and accepted Soviet terms for a permanent all-German settlement.

   (c) In 1961, the East German government, with Russian support, constructed a wall (the "Wall of Shame") to separate East from West Berlin, in order to check the flight of East Germans to the West.

   (d) A four-power agreement on Berlin in 1971 helped to ease tensions. The Soviet Union, Britain, France, and the United States agreed that Berlin would become a responsibility of all four powers, with guaranteed access from West to East. This cleared the way in 1973 for East and West Germany to recognize each other officially and to open diplomatic relations.

4. The United States and West Germany. The cold war upset Allied plans to keep Germany de-nazified, de-industrialized, and demilitarized.

   (a) At first, top Nazis were tried and given long prison terms or sentenced to death. With the development of the cold war, less attention was paid to de-nazification. Though Germany's new top leaders remained anti-Nazi, many former Nazis were returned to positions of influence.

   (b) Plans to keep Germany industry weak were reversed as each side tried to win the backing of the German people. After the division of Germany, the United States helped redevelop German industry. It gave Marshall Plan aid and paid the costs of occupation.

(c) In 1955, sovereignty and independence were restored to West Germany. West Germany became a member of NATO and the European Common Market. It was also permitted to rearm.

(d) West Germany has made an amazing comeback. Today it is the most prosperous nation in Europe and the strongest power in NATO, next to the United States. It has also become the leading industrial nation of Europe, next to Russia.

(e) Under its first Chancellor, KONRAD ADENAUER, West Germany remained a firm supporter of the West and United States policies in the cold war. Adenauer's successors, LUDWIG ERHARD, KURT KIESINGER, WILLY BRANDT, and HELMUT SCHMIDT, have reaffirmed their nation's faith in American policies and military support. Under a policy of seeking to "normalize" relations with the communist nations of Eastern Europe (Ostpolitik), the Brandt government signed non-aggression pacts with the Soviet Union (1970), Poland (1970), East Germany (1972), and Communist China (1972). HELMUT SCHMIDT, who succeeded Brandt as Chancellor in 1974, continued his predecessor's basic policies of maintaining cooperative relations with the United States and other Western nations while developing closer relations with East Germany and other communist nations.

5. *The United States and East Germany.* East Germany has been a communist-dominated satellite of Russia. Living standards, although still below those of West Germany, are the highest in Eastern Europe.

In 1974, the United States established formal diplomatic ties with East Germany after years of non-recognition for fear of jeopardizing Western rights in West Berlin. Despite this recognition, our relations with the East German regime continue to be strained, with many major issues separating the two nations.

REVIEW TEST (Chapter 30 — Part III)

Select the number preceding the word or expression that best completes or answers each question.

1. All of the following are countries in Western Europe *except* (1) England (2) Italy (3) Poland (4) Belgium

2. All of the following are Russian satellites *except* (1) Yugoslavia (2) East Germany (3) Bulgaria (4) Hungary

3. In which of the following nations was the strength of communist parties greatest after World War II? (1) England and Spain (2) France and Italy (3) Norway and Sweden (4) Belgium and the Netherlands

4. Which of the following was an important result of the Marshall Plan? (1) It prevented the establishment of a communist bloc. (2) It helped in the reconstruction of Russia, as well as of Western European nations. (3) It helped contain communism. (4) It cast serious doubts on the values of economic aid.

5. The Common Market has achieved all of the following for its members *except:* (1) a reduction in tariffs (2) an increase in trade (3) higher living standards (4) political unity

6. Which nation is *not* a member of the Common Market? (1) the United Kingdom (2) France (3) Sweden (4) West Germany

7. A problem that has confronted the United States because of the Common Market has been: (1) a loss of military bases (2) the need to negotiate new trade relationships (3) the need to speed up atomic disarmament (4) rising African nationalism

8. All of the following statements about NATO are true *except* (1) West Germany is a key member of NATO. (2) France opposes United States influence in NATO. (3) All NATO top commanders have been U. S. generals. (4) In recent years unity among NATO members has increased.

9. All of the following statements about West Germany since World War II are true *except* (1) It has maintained friendly relations with the United States. (2) It has become one of Europe's most prosperous nations. (3) It has continued to refuse to recognize East Germany. (4) Its policy of *Ostpolitik* has caused continuance of the cold war.

10. Which of the following pairs an important national leader since World War II with the country he served? (1) De Gaulle—United Kingdom (2) Adenauer—West Germany (3) Franco—Italy (4) Churchill—Canada

On the time line, the letters **A, B, C, D** *represent time intervals, as indicated. For each event listed below, select the letter of the time interval in which the event occurred.*

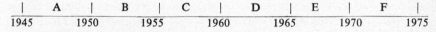

	A		B		C		D		E		F	
1945		1950		1955		1960		1965		1970		1975

1. Issuance of Truman Doctrine.

2. End of Marshall Plan.

3. Formation of Common Market.

4. Building of Berlin "Wall."

5. Entry of Britain into Common Market.

6. Soviet invasion of Czechoslovakia.

Essay Questions

1. Explain two important ways in which the United States has helped promote the economic development of Western Europe since World War II.

2. Describe one problem the United States has faced since World War II as a result of (a) the division of Germany (b) the fears of our NATO allies.

3. An important recent development has been the growing independence of the nations of Western Europe. (a) Explain the meaning of this statement. (b) Give two causes of this development. (c) Explain why the development has been favorable or unfavorable for relations between the United States and its allies.

4. Briefly identify each of the following: Brezhnev Doctrine, Alexander Dubcek, SHAPE, OECD, Jean Monnet, Willy Brandt, *Ostpolitik*.

Part IV — THE UNITED STATES AND THE FAR EAST SINCE 1945

Since World War II, Asia and the Pacific area in general have assumed new importance in world affairs. Because of the twin forces of *nationalism* and *communism,* the face of Asian politics has been radically altered. New nations have emerged, determined to be free of outside domination, and communism has gained a strong position in much of the Far East. The United States and the West are, naturally, most concerned with these new developments. In large measure, they are the result of the postwar surge of nationalism and of the changes in popular attitudes which have been called the "Revolution of Rising Expectations."

Twentieth-Century Nationalism. Nationalism in the 20th century is a complex idea, meaning many things. Principally, 20th-century nationalism refers to the desire of the peoples living in territories under foreign control to establish independent nations of their own. Efforts to achieve this goal are known as *colonial nationalism.* This movement of colonial nationalism reached its peak with the dissolution of the great European empires (French, British, Dutch, Belgian) after World War II. At present, the term *nationalism* generally refers to the efforts and policies followed by the world's newly emerging and developing nations in their attempts to gain unity, stability, and a higher standard of living.

The "Revolution of Rising Expectations." The "Revolution of Rising Expectations" refers to the desire and the determination of peoples living in the underdeveloped nations of the world to throw off their poverty and share in the abundance brought about by modern technology and science. As a result of cultural exchanges, motion pictures, radio, television, and other means of communication, the peoples of the underdeveloped regions have become aware of the fact that there are alternatives to the poverty, hunger, and disease that have always plagued them. They are determined to move toward the establishment of conditions that will mean longer, healthier, and more satisfying lives for the great mass of the people. In the United Nations and elsewhere, they are calling upon the more advanced nations of the world for assistance. The areas involved are mainly Africa, Asia, the Middle East, and Latin America. Adlai Stevenson, a former candidate for President and U.S. Ambassador to the UN, referred to the revolution of rising expectations as "the greatest challenge of our century." Nowhere is this "revolution" more evident or more important than in the Far East.

The Far East — An Underdeveloped Region. The Far East is one of the world's major underdeveloped regions. It has a population (now over 2½ billion) far greater than the combined populations of North America, South America, and Europe. Although the Far East produces many important raw materials and has huge resources that are still untapped, most of its peoples are illiterate, poor, hungry, and sick. The average life expectancy is about 40 years, and the per capita income is less than

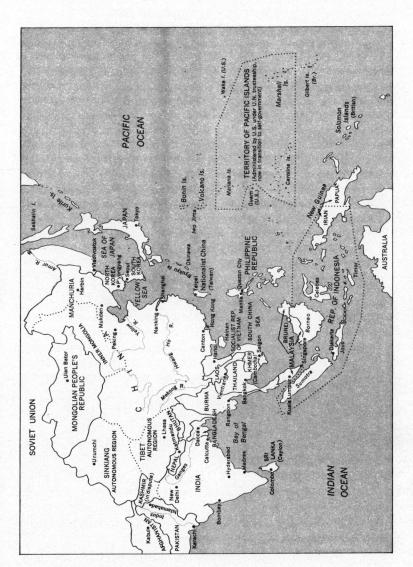

THE FAR EAST

$100 a year. Asia's major problem as an underdeveloped region lies in its exploding population, now growing at the rate of over 30 million a year. This has made it impossible for Asian nations to feed their people without outside assistance. Most nations of the region import food.

The "Asian Revolution." Three profound changes have taken place in Asia since 1945. These include: **(1)** the overthrow of the colonial powers, **(2)** the transformation of Japan, and **(3)** the emergence of Chinese communism. The impact of these changes has been so significant for the United States and the West that they are sometimes referred to as the *"Asian Revolution."*

The Overthrow of Colonialism. Faced with mounting demands for independence, and in some cases with open rebellion, the former colonial powers of Asia were forced in the postwar years to give up most of their colonial possessions. Britain freed India, Pakistan, Burma, Ceylon, and (later) Malaya. France was forced to give up French Indochina (Cambodia, Laos, and North and South Vietnam). The Netherlands had to grant independence to the East Indies (Indonesia). Japan, by virtue of its military defeat in World War II, was compelled to give up all its former colonies, including Korea and Formosa. The United States actually led the movement by granting independence to the Philippines in 1946, in accordance with a prewar promise.

The Transformation of Japan. After World War II, and up to 1952, the United States occupied Japan as the representative of the victorious powers. General Douglas MacArthur, Supreme Commander for the Allied Powers, was given authority to democratize and demilitarize Japan, and to rebuild her economic system. The reforms and changes introduced under American occupation amounted in fact to a revolution.

1. *New Constitution.* Under a new constitution (1947), the Emperor was stripped of his "divine" status and power but was kept as a symbol of national unity. The Cabinet was made responsible to a two-house legislature (*Diet*). In addition, many civil rights were granted for the first time; church and state were separated; and women were given the right to vote.

2. *Reforms.* Important economic and social reforms were enacted. These included the breakup of large estates and distribution of land to the peasants, the teaching of democracy in the public schools, and the establishment of labor unions with the right to strike.

3. *Trial of War Leaders.* Top Japanese war leaders were tried for war crimes by the Allies and were found guilty of atrocities and aggressive warfare. Some were executed, and others were given long prison sentences.

4. *End of the Occupation.* In 1951, the United States signed a lenient peace treaty with Japan, restoring her sovereignty, ending the occupation, and permitting her to apply for UN membership. Although American occupation ended in 1952, Japan, in a separate pact, allowed the United States to maintain troops and bases on her territory. In 1962, this mutual defense pact was renewed on even more liberal terms for Japan. Under its provisions either side can request withdrawal of the American bases at the end of ten years, and Japan must be consulted if American forces in Japan are to be used anywhere in the Far East.

5. *Japan's Re-emergence as a Prosperous Nation.* Since the occupation, Japan has re-emerged as the most prosperous nation in Asia and is now the world's third greatest industrial power. Economic growth has been amazing. Japanese products of good quality are now competing in the world's markets in such fields as textiles, steel, cameras, clothing, and electronic equipment. Large industrial combines have reappeared. The Japanese standard of living has risen rapidly in spite of sharp population growth.

6. *Recent U.S.-Japanese Relations.* Since the close of World War II the new Japan has been a firm ally of the West, and particularly of the United States. Nevertheless, each nation has at times been unhappy with certain policies of the other. **(a)** A large sector of Japanese public opinion is opposed to American military bases in Japan. **(b)** The Japanese were dissatisfied with United States occupation of the island of Okinawa, until it was returned to Japan in 1972. (Okinawa had been held by the United States after being captured in a bloody battle in World War II.) The United States retains a naval base on the island but has promised not to store nuclear weapons there. **(c)** To improve relations with the United States, Japan has in recent years accepted controls on the amounts of Japanese textiles and other goods sold here. **(d)** When the United States recognized the People's Republic of China in 1971, Japan moved to resume diplomatic relations and to expand trade with the communist giant on the mainland. However, Japan has severed diplomatic relations with Nationalist China (Taiwan), and its relations with the government of South Korea remain unsettled.

Emergence of Communist China. When World War II ended, the Nationalist (Kuomintang) government of China did little to restore the faith of the people in its leadership. The government included many corrupt and inefficient bureaucrats. Little was done about land reform. Wartime controls were not relaxed.

1. *Hostilities Between Nationalists and Communists.* Fighting had gone on before and during World War II between the Nationalists, led by Chiang Kai-shek, and the communists. After 1945, this developed into full-scale hostilities. Chiang was determined to wipe out communist resistance before starting to rebuild China. The communists were convinced that the weaknesses of the Nationalist government, plus growing inflation, made this the strategic time to overthrow Chiang's regime.

2. *United States Policies After World War II.* At first, the United States tried to help Chiang establish his military authority throughout all of China. When this failed, we attempted for nearly two years (1946-47) to bring about agreement between Chiang and his communist rival MAO TSE-TUNG. Despite the efforts of General George C. Marshall, Chiang refused to admit the communists into a coalition government, and the communists refused to disband their army as a condition for entry into such a coalition. By the end of 1947, civil war had broken out on a large scale.

3. *Communist Victory.* From 1947 to 1949, the communist armies won many major victories. They were aided by war materials captured from the Japanese and given to them by the Russians, as well as by the "power vacuum" created by the Japanese defeat. By 1948, they controlled Manchuria. By the end of 1949, they controlled most of China. Entire armies and villages surrendered or went over to the communists with minimal opposition. Much American equipment was seized by the communists. Finally, in 1949, Chiang and the remainder of his armies escaped to the island of Formosa (Taiwan) and made it the home of the Nationalist regime. In December, 1949, the communists set up the *Chinese People's Republic* on the mainland. In 1950, a Sino-Soviet mutual security pact was signed between the two communist giants, providing for broad areas of cooperation.

The Chinese Communist Republic. Under the leadership of the Chinese communists, led by Mao Tse-tung, mainland China was quickly converted into a one-party dictatorship along communist lines. Industry and agriculture were nationalized, and an ambitious program was introduced to transform the nation into a major industrial and agricultural power. Despite early failures and setbacks, there has been significant industrial progress in the production of coal, oil, steel, chemicals, and other goods. China also has developed a hydrogen bomb. However, China is still well behind the major world powers in technology and industrial output.

Despite the growing emphasis on industry, China remains primarily an agricultural nation. Under the *commune system* (large cooperative farms), agricultural production has been made more efficient, and mass starvation largely eliminated. Extensive social and cultural changes have accompanied these economic and political developments.

The Nationalist Regime on Taiwan. Since the triumph of the communists in 1949, the Nationalist regime of pre-communist China has continued to function on the island of Taiwan (Formosa), off the mainland coast. With the help of massive U.S. aid (ended in 1965), Taiwan has become a prosperous nation with a rapidly developing economy. Although disappointed at our recognition of the Chinese People's Republic (Communist China), Nationalist China still depends on American assistance for military security. (In return for Communist China's promise not to use force to regain Taiwan, the United States has agreed to reduce its forces on Taiwan, and to remove our naval units from the Formosa Straits, if tensions diminish.)

Foreign Policies of Communist China. Until recently Communist China adopted foreign policies considered aggressive, expansionist, and anti-Western. **(1)** Until recently, it threatened to retake Taiwan by force if necessary. **(2)** It actively aided North Korea in its fight against South Korea and the UN (1950-53). **(3)** It annexed Tibet on the pretext that it had always been part of the Chinese empire (1959). **(4)** It seized small pieces of territory on India's northern frontier (1963). **(5)** Its assistance helped nationalists and insurgents free Indochina from France (1950-54). **(6)** Chinese aid to communist forces and guerrillas prolonged the conflict in Vietnam, Laos, and Cambodia in Southeast Asia through the 1960s and into the early 1970s. **(7)** Since joining the UN in 1971, the People's Republic of China has been trying to build trade and other relations with the West. Although Chinese leaders have become less aggressive in foreign policy statements and actions, they have continued to promote revolutionary movements in Africa, Asia, and elsewhere. Although limited diplomatic relations were resumed with Russia in 1970, border differences and other issues have not been resolved.

United States Policy Toward Red China. From the time of the Chinese Communist takeover in China in 1949 until 1971, the United States actively opposed the Peking regime as an aggressor power. The two countries were openly hostile to one another. In 1971, in an historic policy reversal, the United States supported the admission of Red China to the UN and took steps toward normalization of diplomatic and trade relations.

1. *Containment Through Isolation.* During the 1950s and 1960s, the policy of the United States towards China was one of "containment through isolation." Our government formed military alliances, set up bases, gave military support to non-communist Asian countries, led the opposition to admitting Red China into the UN, carried on a total trade embargo, and continued to regard Nationalist China (Taiwan) as the legal government of China. Despite these policies, a growing number of nations, including Britain, France, Italy, and Canada, extended recognition to the regime on the mainland.

2. *Restoration of U.S.-China Relations.* In 1971, in a sharp reversal of United States policy, President Nixon recognized the communist regime of the People's Republic of China, and the United States voted to admit that government as China's representative in the UN. Nixon visited Peking in 1971 to reinforce the new relationship. The change in policy was a realistic recognition of the fact that the communist regime was in firm control of a vast land mass containing close to one-quarter of the world's population. It was also in accord with the recent tendency of the United States to avoid the role of a "policeman" or a "moral crusader" in its foreign dealings, particularly in the Far East.

    (a) Détente. The new relationship between the United States and the People's Republic of China is based on *détente,* or a relaxation of tensions. Some signs of improving relationships and understanding are: **(1)** High-ranking U.S. officials, including Secretary of State

Henry Kissinger have visited China. **(2)** Diplomatic envoys have been exchanged and "liaison missions" have been established in both countries. These are embassies in all but name. **(3)** Visits have been paid on both sides by scholars, journalists, artists, businessmen, athletes, etc. **(4)** Trade between the two nations has shown a substantial increase.

(b) Results of Détente. The United States has gained a number of specific advantages from the new policy. **(1)** By establishing ties with Peking, Washington has gained political "leverage" with both of the communist giants. Both China and the Soviet Union are apparently worried that the other may become "too friendly" with the United States. **(2)** China has agreed not to try to take over Taiwan by force. **(3)** China has reduced the flow of arms to North Korea and Vietnam. **(4)** Since the American pullout from Vietnam, neither China nor the Soviet Union has tried to exploit the new situation by taking openly aggressive action in the Far East.

The Korean Conflict (1950-53). The war in Korea turned the cold war "hot" and threatened the peace of the world. The United States became directly and fully involved.

1. *Joint Occupation of Korea After World War II.* Korea, a small country in northeast Asia, had been a Japanese colony for many years prior to World War II. After the defeat of Japan in 1945, North Korea was occupied by Russian troops, and South Korea by American troops. The 38th parallel was the dividing line between the two zones.

2. *The Division of Korea.* Separate governments were created for North Korea and South Korea when Russia refused to permit free elections supervised by the UN to set up a unified government. The United States and other nations recognized the government of South Korea, which had been elected in a UN-supervised election in 1948. SYNGMAN RHEE became the first President of the *Republic of Korea.* American occupation troops were withdrawn by 1949. A communist *"Democratic People's Republic"* was established in North Korea, and Russian troops were withdrawn in 1948.

3. *North Korea Invades South Korea.* In June, 1950, North Korean armies attacked and invaded South Korea without warning. The UN Security Council declared North Korea an aggressor and recommended that UN members send troops to repel the invaders. The Truman administration decided to commit the United States to the defense of South Korea, and ordered large-scale air, naval, and ground forces to Korea. Many other nations also responded to the UN request.

4. *The UN Army Goes into Action.* General Douglas MacArthur was made United Nations Commander-in-Chief. The UN army was made up of the forces of 20 nations, but was preponderantly American and South Korean. At first, UN forces were forced to retreat by North Korean armies. In September, 1950, however, MacArthur's forces went on to the offensive and pushed the North Koreans back.

5. *Entry of Red China.* When UN forces crossed the 38th parallel into North Korea in October, 1950 and approached the Yalu River (the border between Red China and Korea), a new phase of the war began. Large forces of well-equipped Chinese communist "volunteers" poured into North Korea and drove the UN forces back below the 38th parallel. The UN armies dug in and, strengthened by additional reserves, managed by the end of 1952 to move again close to the 38th parallel, where they remained in a military stalemate until the end of the conflict.

6. *The Armistice (1953).* As a result of lengthy negotiations, an armistice was signed in July, 1953, during the Eisenhower administration, providing for **(a)** the continued division of North and South Korea at approximately the 38th parallel (to correspond to the battle line at the time the fighting ended) and **(b)** the exchange of sick and wounded and other prisoners of war. (Over 20,000 North Korean and Chinese communists prisoners decided not to "go home.")

Aftermath of the Korean War. The Korean War had both immediate and long-range effects.

1. *How the War Affected the United States.* Coming only a few years after World War II, the Korean War was not received with much en-

Since the close of World War II, the United States has been involved in two major wars in Asia — in Korea from 1950 to 1953 and in Vietnam from 1965 to 1975. The maps above show the main areas of conflict.

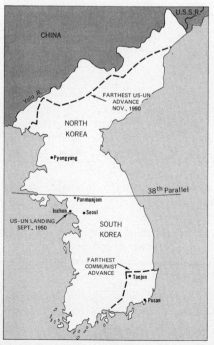 

thusiasm in the United States. Most Americans, however, understood the reason for the conflict and accepted it.

The war was a costly one. Our country suffered over 54,000 dead and 103,000 wounded. (Total casualties on all sides were over 3.5 million.) The United States alone spent 18 billion dollars on the war, plus more billions for relief and rehabilitation. The nation's armed forces were rapidly expanded to 2.2 million, and its defense program was completely revitalized after a post-World War II "slump."

2. *Significance of the Korean War.* The Korean War led to no immediate gains for the United States or the UN, since North Korea remained in communist hands. It was, however, important in several ways. **(a)** It showed that determined resistance under UN auspices could halt aggression. **(b)** It brought about the rebuilding of American armed forces and the strengthening of NATO. **(c)** It marked the beginning of Red China's expansion and aggression.

3. *Removal of General MacArthur.* In 1951, President Truman removed General MacArthur from his post as Supreme Commander of the UN forces because of his public criticism of the President's decision against bombing targets inside China itself.

4. *Recent Events in Korea.* Since the close of the Korean War, the United States has renewed its mutual Security Pact with South Korea (the Republic of Korea) and has provided military and economic assistance there. (North Korea has received similar support from Communist China.) Until 1972, when North and South Korea agreed to seek reunification by peaceful means, there were frequent military clashes along the demilitarized zone, and both side made charges of attempts at "infiltration." U.S. troops will remain in South Korea until that country's defenses can be made secure. However, our forces have been reduced, and there are now more Korean troops manning the armistice border.

The United States and India. India is the world's most heavily populated non-communist nation. Since 1947, when it received its independence from Britain, India has tried to develop its economy and reform its society largely through democratic means. It has remained for the most part "nonaligned" (neutral) in the contest between the West and the communist world.

1. *India's Problems.* India is one of the world's most important underdeveloped nations. It is so densely populated (over 500 million people in an area one-third the size of the United States) and so backward in some respects that poverty, disease, and starvation are major problems. To complicate matters further, India is made up of various peoples, languages, and religions (85% Hindu). In spite of some rich soil, food production can barely keep pace with population growth.

2. *India's Struggle for Progress and Stability* Since gaining independence, India has been trying to solve its massive economic problem through the development of a "mixed" economic structure. State-owned (socialized) and private enterprises exist side by side, while millions of peasants continue to work small farms which they own or rent. Through a series of Five-Year Plans, the Indian government has been working to develop industrialization, to increase farm production, to build factories, roads, dams, and other facilities, to reduce illiteracy, to educate future leaders, and to raise the overall standard of living.

India has become a leading producer of many industrial goods, such as textiles, steel, processed foods, and cement. Nuclear weapons have been developed, and nuclear power may eventually be widely used for constructive purposes. In spite of such progress, the level of living for untold millions is extremely low, by American standards.

In the late 1960s and early 1970s, there were major gains in food production, especially wheat. This was due to improved methods of cultivation, including irrigation, better seeds, and use of huge quantities of fertilizers. In the mid-1970s, however, the "Green Revolution" showed signs of faltering. One of the main adverse factors was the greatly increased cost of fertilizers derived from petroleum.

3. *Relations with the United States.* American aid to India in recent years has amounted to well over a billion dollars. This has been spent for desperately needed foodstuffs, community development projects, public health programs, etc. In the 1970s however, relations between the two nations have deteriorated markedly. India was angered by what it considered American criticism of the effort to help East Pakistan (Bangladesh) gain independence in 1971. (See below.) As a result, India has increasingly turned to the Soviet Union for both arms and economic assistance. The people and government of the United States continue to believe that India's survival as an independent, democratic, non-communist nation is essential to Asia's stability. Accordingly, public opinion in the United States was shocked when the government headed by Prime Minister Indira Gandhi in the 1970s began to restrict civil liberties and to choke off criticism and dissent by jailing thousands of political opponents.

Pakistan. The Republic of Pakistan was created as a Moslem state in 1947, when India gained its independence. Bitter disagreements between Hindus and Moslems made it impossible to join the two peoples into a single nation. Attempts to draw the boundaries on basically religious lines led to the division of Pakistan into two parts, separated by about 1000 miles of Indian territory.

1. *Position in International Affairs.* Pakistan joined both SEATO and CENTO and in general supported the West in the cold war. It received extensive military and economic aid from the United States. More recently, much aid has come from Red China.

2. *Hostility to India.* Relations between Pakistan and India remained strained. Fighting broke out in 1965, when Pakistani infiltrators crossed the UN truce line of 1949, dividing the disputed province of Kashmir into Indian and Pakistani zones. With the help of the USSR and the United States, the UN arranged a cease-fire, but the Kashmir issue remains unsettled until the present day.

3. *Civil War in Pakistan.* Bitter enmity developed between the West Pakistanians, who dominated the political and economic life of the nation, and the East Pakistanians, mainly Bengalis. The Bengalis (a majority of the total population) claimed they were being treated as "second-class citizens." Their efforts to gain self-rule for East Pakistan led to civil war in 1971, when a Pakistanian army (almost entirely West Pakistanian) entered East Pakistan to crush the independence movement.

4. *War with India.* India at first gave only limited military aid to East Pakistan. Then, as millions of Bengali refugees streamed into neighboring Indian territory, India intervened in full strength. Badly outnumbered by the Indian forces and cut off from their bases in West Pakistan, the Pakistanian forces were forced to surrender (December, 1971). Sheik Mujibur Rahman, leader of East Pakistan, became head of the new nation of *Bangladesh.* In 1973, India and Pakistan agreed to withdraw all troops on their common border, to exchange prisoners of war, and to repatriate war refugees. As a result, relations between the two nations have moved toward normalization.

5. *U. S. Policy.* Although the United States adopted an official policy of neutrality during the civil war and temporarily cut off arms to both sides, it "leaned" toward Pakistan in its attitude and was critical of Indian intervention in the war. As a result, relations with India deteriorated rapidly and have remained somewhat cool.

The Philippine Republic. Since the United States granted the Philippines independence in 1946, close relations have been maintained between the two countries. The United States has given the Philippine Republic aid and preferential tariff treatment. In 1947, the United States was authorized to maintain military bases on the islands. In 1951, the United States and the Philippines signed a mutual defense pact. In 1954, the Philippines joined SEATO. However, the American pullout from Southeast Asia after the close of the Vietnam War has caused much worry, and the Philippine government has been reassessing its defense agreements with the United States. The United States, in turn, has been concerned over the imposition of martial law by the administration headed by President Ferdinand Marcos, in order to curb rising discontent and opposition.

Indonesia. With a population of about 125 million and vast natural resources, Indonesia has become a major nation of Southeast Asia.

1. *Foreign Policy Shifts Under Sukarno.* Indonesia gained its independence from the Netherlands in 1947. Under its first President, Achmed Sukarno (1959-65), the young nation adopted a neutralist foreign policy and was able to gain aid from both sides in the cold war. However, when it became clear to Sukarno that the Western powers stood in the way of his plans for building an Indonesian empire, he moved closer to Communist China. The United States thereupon cut off aid. In late 1965, Indonesian military leaders smashed an attempted takeover by native communists and removed Sukarno from power. Close ties with Red China then ended. General Suharto became head of the Indonesian Republic and emerged as a foe of communist expansion in the Far East.

2. *Recent Developments.* The Suharto regime has attempted, with large-scale American aid, to restore economic stability. However the continued prevalence of poverty, unemployment, and inflation has led to increased opposition to the government. Following the communist triumphs in Indochina, and the virtual collapse of SEATO, Suharto asked the United States to maintain its naval presence in the waters of Southeast Asia.

The Small Nations of Southeast Asia. Relations between the United States and the small but strategically located nations of Southeast Asia have been strongly influenced by the struggle to contain communism.

1. *Thailand.* Thailand has been a consistent supporter of the West and has received much American aid. Because Thailand's leaders felt threatened by communist guerrillas operating out of Laos and feared a "war of liberation" inspired by Red China, they placed bases at the disposal of the United States. Since the close of the Vietnam War, U.S. forces have been withdrawn from Thailand, although the 1954 mutual-defense treaty continues.

2. *Malaysia.* The United States has been a supporter of the resources-rich *Federation of Malaysia.* The country was created in 1963, with the assistance of Great Britain, by uniting Malaya, North Borneo, Sarawak, and Singapore. (Singapore left the Federation in 1965.) Although the government of Malaysia has for the most part followed a pro-Western policy, and has opposed communist insurgency at home, it has recently sought better relations with communist powers, notably China.

3. *Burma.* Since gaining independence from Britain in 1948, Burma has generally played a neutral role on the international scene and has remained largely isolated from foreign contacts and influences. In recent years, Burma has faced problems of civil war and economic crisis. The military regime is anti-communist, but since the communist victory in Indochina, it has attempted to normalize relations with China.

The War in Vietnam. For most of the 1960s and into the early 1970s, Southeast Asia, particularly Vietnam, Laos, and Cambodia, continued to be a crisis area for the United States and the world.

1. *Origins of the Crisis.* Vietnam has been a troubled area since World War II, during which the French were unable to prevent Japanese occupation of the colony of Indochina. After the war, native Vietnamese forces rose in armed rebellion against a resumption of French control. The spearhead of the resistance was the *Viet Minh,* a guerrilla force led by Ho Chi Minh, an avowed communist. After much bloody fighting, the Viet Minh won a crushing victory over the French, climaxed by the fall of Dien Bien Phu in North Vietnam (1954).

The French then agreed to give up their former colony. The Geneva Agreements of 1954 had three main provisions: **(a)** Three states were created: *Laos, Cambodia,* and *Vietnam.* **(b)** Vietnam (the largest of the three) was divided at the 17th parallel into two parts. North Vietnam was to be under the control of the communist-led rebels, but the status of South Vietnam was left undetermined. **(c)** Elections were to be held within two years to elect a government for all of Vietnam. The United States, Russia, and other powers agreed to abide by the treaty.

In South Vietnam, power was wrested from the former emperor, a French puppet, by Ngo Dinh Diem, who then legalized his position by being elected President. Diem's regime, however, was undermined by increasing guerrilla action by the communist-dominated Vietcong, by growing opposition on the part of the Buddhists (the national religious majority—Diem was Catholic), by charges of corruption and undemocratic measures to repress opposition, and by a prolonged failure to hold national elections. In 1963, Diem was killed. After several years of instability, General Nguyen Van Thieu became President in 1967.

2. *United States Aid to South Vietnam.* After 1961, the United States gradually stepped up its military aid to South Vietnam. At first only supplies and military advisers were sent; then growing numbers of troops and increasing air and sea support. Responding to reports of an attack on an American destroyer in the Gulf of Tonkin by North Vietnamese patrol boats in 1964, Congress passed a resolution authorizing President Johnson to take any steps required "to maintain the peace and security of Vietnam" *(Gulf of Tonkin Resolution).*

3. *Escalation of the War in Vietnam.* By early 1965, the South Vietnamese forces appeared to be on verge of final defeat. To deal with this crisis, U.S. forces took over the major burden of the fighting. Ground and air combat became increasingly bitter. North Vietnam gave all-out support to the Vietcong, while Communist China and the Soviet Union stepped up their flow of supplies to both North Vietnam and the Vietcong.

4. *De-escalation and Withdrawal.* Strong opposition developed in the United States to or continued participation in the Vietnam War. In 1969, Johnson was succeeded in the Presidency by Richard M. Nixon, and the latter soon began to withdraw U.S. ground forces from Vietnam. As our units were pulled out, South Vietnamese forces replaced them and gradually took over the major burden of the fighting. By early 1973, our forces in Vietnam, which had once numbered about 543,000 men, were down to fewer than 50,000.

5. *A Cease-fire in Vietnam.* After years of fruitless attempts at peace talks, a cease-fire agreement was finally accepted by both sides in 1973. This provided for an immediate end to the fighting in Vietnam, the withdrawal within 90 days of remaining U.S. troops (there were still about 23,000 of our men in Vietnam), and the return of about 600 U.S. prison-

ers held by the Vietcong and the North Vietnamese. In accordance with
these terms, the United States soon removed all its combat forces and in
1974 Congress forbade further military aid to South Vietnam.

6. *The Final Communist Victory.* The truce was a failure, with mounting violations and active fighting by both sides. Early in 1975, North
Vietnam launched a massive attack, designed to impose a military solution
on the situation. As the South Vietnamese forces were routed, the Thieu
government collapsed, and a final surrender took place on April 30, 1975.
In 1976, the country was formally reunited under Communist rule.

7. *Costs of the War.* The United States was involved in combat in
Vietnam longer than in any other military conflict in our history. More
than 56,000 Americans died in the fighting, and some 300,000 others
were wounded. The South Vietnamese lost more than 200,000 men in
combat, and civilian casualties may have numbered a million. In addition,
the United States spent more than 140 billion dollars during the 14 years
(1961-75) of our involvement in this bitter struggle.

In addition to the tragic loss of life and the vast expenditures of money,
the war eroded the spirit of national unity in our country, led to disillusionment and cynicism, particularly on the part of many young people,
and was a major contributing factor to an era of social unrest and
domestic violence.

Other Fronts in the War in Southeast Asia: Laos and Cambodia. Laos
and Cambodia were sharply affected by the war in Vietnam.

1. *Laos.* In 1961-62, with aid from North Vietnam, communist guerrilla forces (the *Pathet Lao)* overran a large section of the new pro-Western
nation of Laos. Negotiations by the United States, the USSR, and twelve
other nations led to a cease-fire and the establishment of a neutralist coalition government. Despite the truce, Laotian communists continued to
attack government forces and spread their influence.

Laos became deeply involved in the war in Vietnam largely because of
supply trails running from North Vietnam through Laos and into South
Vietnam. U. S. planes used Laos as a base for bombing the Ho Chi Minh
Trail, over which the North Vietnamese were moving men and supplies
from North Vietnam through Laos and into South Vietnam. North Vietnamese troops mounted offensives to reopen the bombed supply routes and
gave active support to the communist-led, anti-government Laotian guerrillas. By the end of 1972, the Pathet Lao controlled 80% of Laos.

A cease-fire agreement was arranged, soon after the truce in Vietnam,
but fighting continued on a lesser scale until 1975. At that time Pathet Lao
forces took over effective control of the country and proclaimed a "People's
Democratic Republic."

2. *Cambodia.* Cambodia was caught up in the military struggle in
Indochina when South Vietnamese and U. S. planes began to attack Viet-
cong forces fleeing into Cambodian territory in the late 1960s. In 1970,
U. S. forces moved into Cambodia to drive communist forces from border

area "sanctuaries" used for attacks on South Vietnam. South Vietnamese forces also moved into Cambodia. Though American ground forces were withdrawn from Cambodia in 1971, air support and other forms of military aid continued. From 1971 to 1973, when the United States withdrew completely from the fighting in Cambodia, communist-led guerrilla and insurgent forces (the *Khmer Rouge),* supported by North Vietnamese troops, continued successful operations against government forces. In 1975, the Cambodian government led by Premier Lon Nol collapsed. In April, the Khmer Rouge marched into Phnom Penh, the capital city, and took over complete control of the country.

Results and Significance of the Communist Victories in Indochina. The communist victories in Indochina have had, and doubtless will continue to have, far-reaching effects on the overall situation in the Far East. **(1)** The Soviet Union and China have moved into the "power vacuum" left by the United States withdrawal. The two giants are competing actively for the friendship and support of Asian nations, both communist and non-communist. **(2)** Most existing defense agreements in the region, notably the Southeast Asia Treaty Organization (SEATO), no longer have relevance. **(3)** The United States is searching for a new political and military strategy in the Far East. We are still a potent economic force in this part of the world, and our naval presence is a major factor in the balance of power. The goal of our diplomacy is to find a way to utilize these assets, both to protect our own interests and to help the people of the region. In pursuing this goal we must take advantage of the leverage given to us by the Soviet-Chinese split.

Part V — THE UNITED STATES AND THE MIDDLE EAST

The Middle East is one of the world's most politically unstable regions. Since 1945, the United States has been forced to take on responsibilities for stability in this area formerly assumed by Great Britain and France.

The Middle East. Several important features of the Middle East will help us understand its role in world affairs.

1. *Land and People.* The Middle East is one of the world's underdeveloped areas. It is made up mainly of Arab nations and peoples. Grinding poverty and widespread illiteracy have given the people of the region one of the lowest standards of living in the world. Most are farmers who eke out a living on lands that are owned by wealthy absentee landlords. It is a region of deserts, mountains, and generally poor soil.

2. *Importance.* The Middle East is of crucial importance in the present-day world situation.

> *(a) Source of Oil.* At present about 40% of the world's oil is produced in the middle East. The region is estimated to have 60% of the world's oil reserves. The leading oil producers are Saudi Arabia, Kuwait, Iran, Iraq, and Abu Dhabi. Most of the capital and facilities

for developing oil production in the Middle East have come from companies in the United States and Western Europe. Local rulers and governments have received huge royalties and profits.

(b) Strategic Location. The Middle East has a strategic location. It is the gateway of three continents — Europe, Asia, and Africa. Vital waterways are located there: the Dardanelles, the Eastern Mediterranean, and the Suez Canal. Great Britain and the United States have naval and air bases in the area. The Western world, particularly Europe, would be seriously handicapped if any hostile nation, such as Russia, controlled the oil reserves of the Middle East.

Arab Nationalism. Since World War II the Middle East has been in a state of acute unrest, brought on by the desire of Arab nations to throw off foreign control, unite the Arab world, and destroy the new Jewish state of Israel. Arab nationalism has taken several forms.

1. *The Arab League.* The Arab League was formed in 1945 to promote Arab solidarity. It now has 18 members, including: Egypt, Syria, Iraq, Jordan, Saudi Arabia, Lebanon, Yemen, Libya, Sudan, Tunisia, Morocco, Algeria, Kuwait, Southern Yemen, Qatar, Bahrein, and the United Arab Emirates. Although the organization has been unable to wipe out the many differences among its members, it has served to unite various Arab factions in their intensification of conflict with Israel.

2. *Opposition to Israel.* The Arab states have been determined to destroy Israel as an independent Jewish state. This sense of "mission" has led to tension, unrest, and four wars between Israel and the Arab states (1947-49, 1956-57, 1967, 1973).

3. *Control of Oil Supplies.* Soon after the Arab-Israeli war of 1973, most of the Arab oil-producing nations demanded a 60% interest in oil operations on their territory. The oil companies were forced to capitulate, and it was understood that this would be only a prelude to complete control of oil production by the various Arab states.

Soon after, the oil-producing states, acting through the *Organization of Petroleum-Exporting Countries* (OPEC), quadrupled the price of their oil exports within a year. This contributed heavily to inflation within the United States and other oil-importing countries. For more than a year, the Arab states used their oil as both a political and an economic weapon. They not only curtailed overall exports to the rest of the world but totally embargoed shipments to the Netherlands and the United States because of their support of Israel in the 1973 war. The guiding aim, partially achieved, was to force anti-Israel, or pro-Arab, policies on customer nations in all parts of the world.

4. *Arab Leaders.* During the 1950s and 1960s, Egypt's popular President, GAMAL ABDEL NASSER, was the most influential Arab leader. Although he failed in his aim of bringing all Arab states into a single federation, he has continued even since his death in 1970 to serve as a symbol of Arab nationalism and unity. More recent leaders include ANWAR SADAT of Egypt, MUAMMAR EL-QADAFFI of Libya, and YASIR ARAFAT of the Palestine Liberation Organization (PLO).

United States Policies in the Mideast. Since World War II, with the rapid decline of British and French influence in the Middle East, the United States has taken a leading role in the affairs of that region.

1. *Anti-Communist Policies.* Knowing that a communist foothold in the Middle East would menace vital oil sources for the United States and Western Europe, our government has been active since World War II in attempting to check the growth of Russian influence. In 1955 the United States helped organize (but did not join) the Central Treaty Organization (CENTO), a short-lived mutual defense alliance against Communist aggression in the Middle East. (Its members were Britain, Turkey, Iran, Iraq, and for a short while, Pakistan).

In 1957, the *Eisenhower Doctrine* promised economic and military aid to nations in the Middle East threatened by aggression. Under this policy, U. S. troops were sent to Lebanon in 1958, at that country's request, to prevent a seizure of power by pro-Nasser, communist-supported nationalists. (Generally speaking, however, the Eisenhower Doctrine has had little effect in preventing internal subversion, and has not been invoked since the late 1950s.)

United States interests in the Middle East conflict with those of the Soviet Union. For some years the USSR has been making strenuous efforts to build its influence in the region. The Russians have a large and growing fleet in the Mediterranean; they give considerable aid to Arab nations; they send armaments and military advisers to Arab lands; and they strongly support the Arab position in the UN. The strategic aims of the Soviet Union include gaining an outlet to the Atlantic Ocean through the Mediterranean Sea, building an economic sphere of influence in the Middle East with its all-important oil resources, and penetrating into the Indian and Pacific oceans by way of the Suez Canal and Persian Gulf.

2. *Aid to Arab Nations.* Starting after World War II, and until the Arab states nationalized their oil properties in the early 1970s, the United States gave or lent substantial sums to the nations of the Middle East. Also, although our government has steadfastly maintained its commitment to the independence of Israel, we have continued to sell arms to the Arabs, as well as Israel. The stated aim of our policy is to avoid "tipping the balance of power" toward either side in the Middle East.

3. *Support of Israel.* Our policies in the Middle East have often reflected a conflict between emotional sympathy for Israel and our immediate economic interests in maintaining good relations with the Arab world. Nonetheless, in recent years the United States has emerged as the world's most steadfast supporter of the security and survival of Israel.

(a) President Truman was one of the first world leaders to extend recognition to Israel. American Jews have sent hundreds of millions of dollars in donations and loans to Israel. The U. S. government has also granted limited economic assistance.

(b) Until the early 1960s, the United States refrained from giving military aid to Israel. This policy was defended on the grounds that such military aid would embitter the Arabs and play into Soviet hands.

(c) After 1962, the flow of Soviet arms to Egypt, and more recently to Syria, seemed to be upsetting the balance of power in the Middle East. Accordingly, the United States has sold limited but increasing quantities of planes and missiles to Israel. The United States has also refused to brand Israel an "aggressor" in UN debates on violations of cease-fires following several of the wars between the Arab states and Israel, and on other occasions. In 1975, the United States joined with other Western nations in voting against and condemning a UN Assembly-adopted resolution criticizing Zionism as "a form of racism and racial discrimination."

Attempts to Promote Stability in the Middle East. The United States has taken a leading role in working to promote peace and stability in the Middle East. Our government has cooperated in peace-keeping operations, has taken the lead in negotiations intended to settle disputes over the Suez Canal, and has helped to arrange cease-fires and truces after the various wars between Israel and the Arab states. The activities of the United States in the more recent crises in this region are described below.

1. *Arab-Israeli Violations of the 1967 Cease-Fire.* From 1967 to 1973, the United States became increasingly concerned over the failure of the cease-fire agreement of 1967 to relieve tensions. An endless cycle of Arab terrorist attacks on Israel, followed by retaliatory Israeli attacks on Arab lands and installations, threatened to explode into a major war that might involve the major powers. The Soviet Union also feared such a war and worked behind the scenes to help defuse threatening situations. On the other hand, the USSR continued to upset the "balance" and to encourage the Arabs by military assistance to Egypt, Syria, and other Arab nations, and by its generally anti-Israel policy.

2. *The U. S. Suez Canal Cease-Fire Proposal of 1970.* Because of escalating violations of the cease-fire in the Suez Canal Zone, the United States in 1970 proposed, and Egypt and Israel (reluctantly) accepted, a "standstill" cease-fire during which intensified peace negotiations would take place. Israel broke off negotiations in 1971, charging that Egypt and the Soviet Union had violated the cease-fire by moving sizable numbers of anti-aircraft missiles inside a 32-mile prohibited zone.

The fundamental difficulty in the situation lay in the fact that the Arab states insisted that Israel withdraw to its pre-1967 boundaries *before* negotiations could begin, while Israel insisted on direct negotiations without such a pre-condition. (As a result of its victory in the Six-Day War of 1967 Israel took—and pending a final settlement, continued to hold—

the Old City of Jerusalem, the Gaza Strip, the Sinai Peninsula, the Arab lands west of the Jordan River, and the Golan Heights bordering Syria.)

3. The October War of 1973. In October 1973, after seven years of Arab bitterness over their stunning defeat in 1967, war broke out again when Egypt and Syria (with some Jordanian support) attacked Israel. Syria took the offensive in the vital Golan Heights region (trying to regain the territory that overlooked Israeli settlements in the valleys below); Egypt threw a major military force across the Suez Canal, capturing Israeli positions on the eastern bank and forcing Israel's forces to retreat into the desert. In 17 days of fighting, Israel's armed forces rolled back the Arab advances and assumed a commanding military position on both fronts. Nonetheless, the initial Arab successes and the heavy Israeli losses were of great strategic and psychological importance.

4. A Limited Agreement between Israel and Egypt. In response to joint Soviet-American diplomatic efforts, a cease-fire was negotiated in 1973. In January 1974, Israel and Egypt agreed to disengage their troops along the Suez Canal, as a first step toward peace negotiations. The disengagement pact included these points: **(a)** Israel agreed to withdraw all troops from the western side of the Canal and to pull back from the eastern side. **(b)** The Egyptians agreed to reduce sharply forces stationed in the area. **(c)** A buffer neutral zone, under the supervision of a *UN Emergency Peace-Keeping Force,* was established between Egyptian and Israeli forces. **(d)** The Suez Canal was to be reopened by Egypt to international navigation (after having been closed for eight years). Both sides surrendered some of their original demands and objectives in return for a cease-fire, a return of all prisoners, and a pullback of enemy forces.

In September 1975, again largely as a result of U.S. Secretary of State Henry Kissinger's "shuttle diplomacy," Egypt and Israeli representatives signed a "disengagement agreement" more far-reaching than that of January 1974. **(a)** Both sides agreed to continue to observe the cease-fire and to renounce the use of force. **(b)** An expanded buffer zone manned by UN troops replaced the former Israeli-occupied area, and Israeli forces were to be withdrawn from this zone. **(c)** American radar technicians were to be stationed in the strategic Giddi and Mitla Passes in the Sinai to monitor the disengagement. **(d)** Israel agreed to hand back to Egypt two oil fields captured during the Six-Day War in 1967.

As a result of this historic agreement, Egypt agreed to allow the passage through the reopened Suez Canal of non-military cargoes destined for Israeli ports. Although most Arab states supported the agreement, President Sadat of Egypt was criticized by Libya, Syria, and the PLO. For Israel, the pact was considered a mixed blessing. Though the presence of American observers was reassuring, the surrender of the two oil fields which had been supplying 55% of Israel's petroleum needs was a major economic loss. As a result of its major role in the negotiations leading to the peace agreement the United States seems to have emerged as the major outside power in the Middle East and to have improved its relations with Egypt.

Part VI — THE UNITED STATES AND AFRICA

In recent years the United States has become increasingly concerned over the development and the problems of the continent of Africa.

Africa's Importance in World Affairs. Africa is of considerable and growing importance in world affairs.

1. *Geography.* Africa is the earth's second largest continent, bigger in area than the United States, China, and India combined. It has one-fifth of the land mass of the world. Africa has been seriously handicapped by its geography, which has long kept it divided into isolated regions. It is a continent of vast plateaus, deserts, dense rain forests, mountains, plains, and dangerous rivers.

2. *Resources.* The African continent contains perhaps the world's largest reservoir of mineral wealth. It has copper, iron, uranium, tin, manganese, diamonds, gold, and oil. Africa produces the major share of the world's uranium, diamonds, gold, and cobalt; it is also an important source of copper and iron ore. At present Africa's agricultural exports exceed its mineral resources in value. It raises and produces for world markets large quantities of rubber, coffee, cocoa, bananas, sugar cane, sisal, and peanuts. The United States, which does over a billion dollars a year in trade with Africa, would be seriously handicapped if it were cut off from Africa's resources.

3. *The Growing African Market.* Africa's population, now estimated at 400 million, is growing rapidly, and will probably exceed 600 million by the year 2000. Its expanding population, plus the needs of new and emerging nations, will make Africa a growing market for industrial products.

4. *Strategic Location.* Because Africa is a source of important raw materials, a growing market, and a center of important world events, it is now considered an area of crucial significance. It is close to Europe, Asia, and the Middle East, and also to vital waterways and trade routes.

5. *Regional Differences.* The vast Sahara Desert, nearly as large as the United States, and stretching across Northern Africa from the Atlantic Ocean to the Red Sea, has created *two* Africas — North Africa, and Africa south of the Sahara. North Africa is much closer in civilization and culture to Europe than it is to "Black Africa" south of the Sahara. This northern region, primarily populated by white Moslems, has always been in contact with Mediterranean countries. Today, it associates itself more closely with the Middle East in its goals and aspirations, than with the rest of Africa. Though Mediterranean Africa is geographically part of the African continent, most discussions of Africa today are concerned with Africa south of the Sahara. This is sometimes called "Black Africa."

6. *Economic Underdevelopment of Africa.* Africa suffers from underdevelopment, like Asia, the Middle East, and Latin America. Fewer than 10% of Africa's population can read and write. Health standards are low.

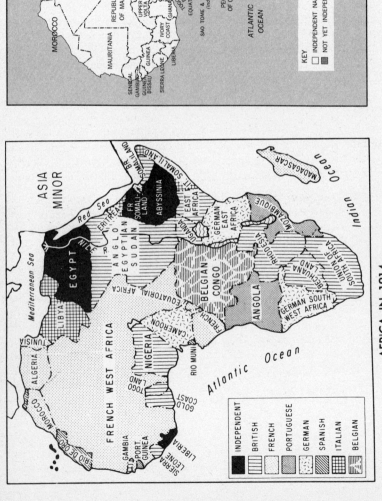

AFRICA TODAY.

Africa, once the main world center of imperialism and colonialism, now consists predominantly of independent countries. The few remaining outposts of colonial rule are expected to be phased out within a relatively few years. The big political issue now facing the continent is "white supremacy" vs. "majority rule" in the south.

AFRICA IN 1914.

Transportation is generally primitive. Living conditions are very poor. Most Africans south of the Sahara live in mud huts with grass roofs, use primitive tools, raise barely enough food to feed themselves from an impoverished soil, and often have to depend on fishing and hunting wild game to keep alive. However, urban population has been growing rapidly, and large cities have become centers of government, industrial and commercial development, and cultural life. (Unfortunately, as large numbers of poor people have fled to the cities to find a better life, there has been a mushrooming of slum "shantytowns" and intensification of such problems as crime and unemployment.)

7. *The New Nations of Africa.* Since World War II, imperialism in Africa has declined rapidly as a result of rising nationalism. Since 1945 the number of independent nations in Africa has grown from 4 to over 40. Today white control has been pushed back to the southern tip of the continent, where it was first established three centuries ago. It is predicted that before long all the peoples of Africa will have gained independence. The new African nations are intensely nationalistic. Their voice is being heard increasingly in UN councils, and they are becoming a growing force in world affairs. In addition to economic underdevelopment, the new nations of Africa face such serious problems as differences in race, language, and religion; tribal differences; and lack of experienced leadership.

A Front for Cold War Rivalry. Africa has in recent years become a major front in the cold war. The Soviet Union and China have been competing with the West for African support. Both sides have given arms, economic aid, and technical assistance to developing African nations, as well as student scholarships for study abroad. The USSR and China, while vying with each other to establish influence in Africa, have also attempted to exploit every condition of disorder and instability (for example, in the Congo). Early fears in the West that communist influence would convert African nations into communist satellites (for example, Mali, Guinea, Ghana) have not been realized. African nations are clearly determined to be their own masters.

United States Policies in Africa. Before World War II, the United States maintained a hands-off policy toward Africa. It did not, in fact, establish a separate State Department Bureau of African Affairs until the mid-1950's. Since that time American policies and programs have tried to join our interests with those of the Africans.

1. *Economic, Technical, and Educational Assistance.* Since World War II, the United States has given African nations over 7 billion dollars in economic and technical assistance of many types.

   (a) Growing Expenditures. Our aid to Africa, while relatively small in dollar volume, has grown more rapidly on a proportionate basis in recent years than aid to any other region.

(b) *Types of Aid.* Africa has received United States development loans and grants from the Agency for International Development. It has received surplus commodities under our Food-for-Peace Program. It has received long-term loans from the Export-Import Bank. Thousands of Americans, many of them in the Peace Corps, have been helping to build roads, dams, schools, and factories. Thousands of African students have received scholarships to study in the colleges .of the United States.

NOTE: Africa is also receiving much aid from sources outside the United States. These sources include the African Development Fund of the Common Market, the World Bank of the UN, and the Organization for Economic Cooperation and Development. In addition, Africa receives aid from the communist bloc. In 1963, African nations established their own African Development Bank to make loans to needy nations.

2. *Support for Self-Determination.* The United States has for the most part favored and supported the movement for African self-determination. This principle is consistent with American values and political ideals. The United States has supported political unification on the premise that strong national governments are the best hope for African stability and economic progress. It has also encouraged movements for African cooperation. Now that most British and French territories have become independent, the United States is less concerned than it was at first with offending its European allies or weakening Western unity in following these policies in Africa.

3. *Opposition to Colonialism.* Closely related to increased United States support for self-determination has been our opposition to continued colonialism. The last major colonial power in Africa, Portugal, gave up its remaining colonies (Angola, Mozambique, Cape Verde Islands, Sao Tome, Principe) in 1975. This was in part a response to American pressure.

4. *Opposition to Racism.* The United States has also supported UN resolutions condemning racism *(apartheid)* in South Africa and calling for an end to arms shipments to that country. To avert racial warfare in Rhodesia and Southern Africa generally, U.S. Secretary of State Henry Kissinger in 1976 worked to develop a political formula that would result in a black majority government in Rhodesia, while at the same time providing acceptable guarantees for the ruling white minority.

Problems of United States Policy Toward Africa. United States policy toward Africa is still evolving. On many issues, we are still "playing it by ear." Basically, however, our policy is one of supporting independence and helping the new nations to develop.

1. *African Suspicion of the United States.* Although African nations generally have recognized the friendly nature of American foreign policies, there has often been suspicion about our actions and motives, for several reasons. The United States has on a number of occasions taken actions that Africans feel are supportive of European colonialism. For example, until Portugal gave up its last African colonies in 1975, Africans were disturbed over continued American aid (economic and military) to that country. African leaders have also criticized the failure of the United States government to halt the purchase of chrome ore from Rhodesia, in disregard of a UN-declared embargo on trade with Rhodesia.

2. *The Communist Challenge.* The United States has been increasingly concerned over communist aid to developing African nations and attempts by the Soviet Union and China to win their support. During the civil war in Angola in 1975 (following the Portuguese withdrawal), Cuba sent troops to help the Russian-backed "Popular Movement for the Liberation of Angola." The United States, denounced Russia's intervention as contrary to the support of détente and called for the withdrawal of Cuban forces. The Popular Movement, however, was successful in gaining control of the country.

3. *Nonalignment.* The leaders of Africa have remained nonaligned in the cold war. As such they feel they have more to gain than to lose, since this policy permits them to develop freely and also gives them a bargaining position between East and West. Though the United States would prefer to have these nations in the Western camp, it no longer criticizes neutrality in the cold war, as it did at first.

4. *Ties With the West.* The communist challenge has not destroyed certain advantages of the United States and the West in their African relations. Many African nations have kept Western legal and parliamentary systems, and French and English have become basic languages throughout most of Africa. Though fully independent, and determined to be their own masters, many African nations have chosen to remain within the British Commonwealth or to retain a special relationship with France. Most governmental systems in Africa today are based on Western models.

5. *Revolts and Military Takeovers.* The United States has been most concerned over the fact that few of the new African regimes have been able as yet to develop stable governments. Parliamentary regimes have repeatedly been overthrown by military coups. Most African nations are today governed by military regimes. Domination of governments by "strong" leaders with military backgrounds is common. Such a climate of political instability makes it difficult to develop consistent policies or enter into long-range planning and commitments.

6. *New U.S. Policy in Africa.* In 1976, the United States announced a major change in its policy toward Africa. Our government is now committed to use its world influence for the following purposes: **(a)** rapid negotiation of a settlement to insure majority rule in Rhodesia; **(b)** independence of Southwest Africa from South Africa; **(c)** the eventual ending of *apartheid* in South Africa. By placing itself squarely behind the thrust for independence and majority rule, and against *apartheid* in South Africa, the United States seems ready to make up for a policy of many years standing that called for cooperation with minority white governments in Africa, while black governments were more or less neglected. Our new program also calls for increased economic aid to needy nations in Africa.

REVIEW TEST (Chapter 30—Part VI)

Select the number preceding the word or expression that best completes each statement or answers each question.

1. The African continent is now an important source of all of the following *except* (1) iron (2) uranium (3) diamonds (4) coal

2. Which of the following bodies of water does *not* touch Africa? (1) Atlantic Ocean (2) Red Sea (3) Mediterranean Sea (4) Persian Gulf

3. All of the following factors help explain the growing recognition by the United States of Africa's importance in world affairs *except* (1) its growth as a market (2) its location (3) its mineral and agricultural wealth (4) its active support of the West in the cold war

4. The government of which of the following African nations differs from the others in its attitude towards race relations? (1) Ethiopia (2) South Africa (3) Nigeria (4) Malawi

5. The United States has warmly supported all of the following for Africa *except* (1) self-determination (2) stability and economic progress (3) technical assistance (4) neutralism

Supply the word or expression that correctly completes each statement.

1. At the present time the United States Assistant Secretary of State for African Affairs is ..?...

2. Thousands of Americans have engaged in the building of roads, schools, dams, and similar activities in Africa as members of the United States ..?...

3. The portion of Africa that has been closely influenced by European civilization is separated geographically from the rest of Africa by the ..?...

Essay Questions

1. Explain three reasons for the growing importance of Africa in world affairs.

2. Discuss two recent changes in Africa that have affected its relationships with the United States.

3. Show how the United States has been attempting to help African nations attain greater economic and political stability.

4. Explain the extent to which Africa has become a "battleground" in the cold war and indicate how this has affected the relationships between the United States and African nations.

5. (a) Assume that you are the United States Secretary of State. Write a brief "position paper" of about 200–250 words outlining present United States policy toward the new nations of Africa and giving reasons in support of this policy. (b) Explain why you as a high school student agree or disagree with this "official" policy.

Part VII — THE UNITED STATES AND LATIN AMERICA SINCE WORLD WAR II

Although the United States has continued its "good-neighbor" policy in the post-World War II era, it has not succeeded in eliminating Latin American hostility and suspicion. Rising social and political tensions in Latin America have called for new programs.

Cooperation between the United States and Latin America Since World War II. The spirit of cooperation that developed among the American states before and during World War II was in a number of important respects continued into the postwar era.

1. *United Nations Membership.* The American states became charter members of the United Nations in 1946, and have frequently voted as a bloc in support of common causes.

2. *Rio Pact.* In 1947, the United States and its Latin American neighbors signed the *Rio Pact* (*Treaty of Rio de Janeiro*), under which they agreed that an armed attack on one would be considered an attack on all.

3. *Organization of American States.* In 1948, the *Organization of American States* (*OAS*) was formed to permit prompt, united action in defense of the Western Hemisphere, and to promote cooperation in economic and cultural affairs. The OAS replaced the Pan-American Union (see page 578).

4. *United States Aid.* Since World War II, the United States has given billions of dollars in loans and grants to Latin American nations under its foreign aid and Point-Four (technical assistance) programs. The *International Cooperation Administration (ICA)* and its successor, the *Agency for International Development (AID),* have provided financial assistance for public health, education and medical programs. From 1961 to 1971, the United States sponsored the *Alliance for Progress,* a program involving expenditures of 20 billion dollars to bring social and economic reform to Latin America. (See page 580.)

5. *Inter-American Development Bank.* In 1961, all the Latin American states, except the United States and Cuba, formed the *Inter-American Development Bank* (*IDB*), an agency for extending loans to Latin American nations for worthwhile development projects. About 45% of the capital of one billion dollars was contributed by the United States. The IDB also administers United States funds provided under the Alliance for Progress.

6. *Cultural Exchanges.* In addition to political and economic cooperation, there has, in recent years, been much cultural interchange between the American states in the form of exchanges of students, athletes, artists, musicians, entertainers, teachers, books, films, and periodicals.

7. *Joint Action Against Communism.* The American States have also taken joint action against the spread of communism in the hemisphere, particularly through the OAS.

Causes for Political and Social Unrest in Latin America. Latin America today is in the midst of growing social and political unrest, brought about by a number of serious problems and challenges.

1. *Low Standard of Living and Lack of Development.* Latin American nations continue to suffer from severe social and economic problems.

(a) Poverty is the rule. According to recent estimates, average incomes in Latin America range from about $80 per person in Haiti to about $750 in Puerto Rico, with an overall average of roughly $300.

(b) Illiteracy is widespread and education virtually non-existent in many regions. This has caused a shortage of doctors, lawyers, scientists, teachers, and engineers.

(c) Most of the economies of Latin countries are predominantly agricultural. There is little industrialization.

(d) Many nations rely on the export of a single crop for income. A single season of bad weather for these one-crop countries can lead to economic disaster. In addition, fluctuations in prices on the world market (for minerals as well as crops) may have a drastic effect on national incomes.

(e) The economic growth of Latin American nations has not kept pace in many cases with their expanding populations, which have the world's fastest growth rate.

(f) Latin Americans are caught up in the worldwide "Revolution of Rising Expectations." There is an increasing desire on the part of the common man for a better way of life. Large numbers of Latin Americans have come to realize that the poverty that exists has resulted from failure to develop stable governments and modern social and economic systems.

2. *Political Instability and Military Dictatorship.* Latin America has, for the most part, continued to be a region of political instability. Military and landholding groups continue to make and unmake governments, while the masses remain helpless and impoverished. In most Latin American nations the military groups exercise great influence upon the government. In many cases the regime depends upon military support to remain in power. Plotting among military rivals leads to instability and frequent military coups. Since the beginning of 1962 alone, there have been about 35 unconstitutional seizures of power. This characteristic of Latin American political life dates back to the days of revolution against Spanish control.

3. *Communism.* Since the successful Castro Revolution in Cuba in 1959, communist influence in Latin America has shown some expansion. Communist promises of land reform, redistribution of wealth, and improved standards of living find fertile ground. The communist strategy often seems to be to incite the military to overthrow stable or democratic governments in the hope that the masses of people will feel that the military regimes are totally unequipped to solve present-day problems, and will then turn to communism. In 1970, Chile elected as President Salvador Allende, who was avowedly committed to Marxism. Allende was assassinated in 1973, during a rightist military coup.

4. *Nationalism.* Latin Americans have always been a proud people. In recent years this nationalistic feeling has taken the form of increased resistance to real or imagined United States interference in Latin American affairs. Latin Americans feel that we have treated them as "second class friends." The United States is also blamed for many of Latin America's economic problems. Communists have found it easy to whip up anti-American feelings, and the issue of "colonialism" is raised whenever the United States takes a step that is disliked.

Suspicion of the United States. There is much good feeling in Latin America for the United States and for the American people in general. There is also a great deal of continuing "anti-North Americanism" and suspicion of our motives and policies.

1. *United States Economic Influence.* Latin Americans resent the obvious domination of some of their industries by the United States and other foreign interests. For example, until 1975, when Venezuela nationalized its oil industry and took over complete control (with compensation to the former owners), several large American oil companies (together with British-controlled enterprises) played the major role in that country's oil prdouction. In Chile, several United States-based companies formerly controlled a large part of the copper industry and thus greatly influenced the national economy. For years, the United Fruit Company dominated economic affairs in Costa Rica, Honduras, and Guatemala. The control exercised by such United States companies is by no means so sweeping as it once was, but the old stereotypes and emotions tend to remain.

2. *Dependence on United States Price Levels.* Latin American nations have been complaining that the United States, which buys about 40% of their exports, unduly influences the price level of their basic exports *(e.g., coffee, cocoa, tropical fruits, copper, iron ore).* They are frustrated over the fact that these prices are usually low in comparison to the prices of American manufactured products which they import.

3. *"Neglect" of Latin America.* For some years Latins have accused the United States of neglecting their interests. They point out that after World War II the United States paid most attention to the problems of Europe and the Far East. From 1945 to 1961, before Alliance for Progress aid began, only 8% of all United States foreign aid went to Latin America.

4. *United States Support of Undemocratic Regimes.* The charge is also frequently made that the United States appeases enemies of democracy in order to "avoid trouble" in Latin America. The United States, it is said, has readily recognized and "played ball with" the regimes of notorious dictators, such as Perez Jimenez of Venezuela (overthrown in 1958) and Fulgencio Batista of Cuba (also overthrown in 1958). Our State Department, critics say, will support any government, no matter how undemocratic, so long as it is sufficiently "anti-communist" and favorable to our economic interests.

5. *United States Control of the Panama Canal Zone.* U. S. control of the Panama Canal Zone has recently been a source of serious friction. In 1964, riots broke out in the Zone when United States high school students raised the American flag in defiance of an agreement that it could only be flown beside the Panamanian flag. This "flag crisis" caused a break in diplomatic relations, but OAS mediation efforts made it possible for the two sides to reach an agreement. Since 1965, the United States and Panama have been trying to work out a new treaty that would increase Panama's role in Canal Zone administration and Canal management, including a larger share of the profits. Our government has agreed that there is to be eventual transfer of sovereignty over the Canal Zone to Panama, with the United States retaining "primary" (rather than *complete)* responsibility for the operation of the waterway. However, there has not yet been complete agreement on such issues as the duration of the new treaty, the economic benefits to be given Panama, the exact degree of responsibility that Panama will have in future Canal management, and the right of the United States to expand Canal facilities. There has recently been sharper criticism of the United States presence in and control over the Canal Zone, not only in Panama itself but also in other Latin American nations, notably Cuba.

6. *United States Intervention in Latin America Affairs.* On several occasions the United States has actively intervened in Latin America to check the spread of communism in this Hemisphere. Most Latin Americans have not been happy over our actions.

(*a*) *Guatemala.* In 1954, we gave aid to insurgents who overthrew a pro-communist regime in Guatemala.

(*b*) *Cuba.* In 1961, we supported an unsuccessful invasion designed to overthrow the Castro government in Cuba. In 1967, the United States forced the Russians to remove atomic missiles in Cuba.

(*c*) *Dominican Republic.* In 1965, U.S. troops were sent into the Dominican Republic by President Lyndon Johnson to protect American lives and to prevent what American diplomats feared might be a communist takeover during a revolt against the existing regime. The United States was severely criticized both at home and abroad for bypassing the OAS by taking military action unilaterally and for exaggerating the danger of a communist uprising.

(*d*) *Chile.* It has been revealed that the U.S. Central Intelligence Agency (CIA) tried as early as 1970 to instigate a coup to bring down the communist-oriented government of President Salvador Allende. Allende was assassinated in a rightist military coup in 1973.

(*e*) *Other CIA Activities in Latin America.* There has been widespread criticism of United States policies following revelations that the CIA actively helped to bring about the military overthrow of governments headed by Joao Goulart in Brazil in 1964 and by Salvador Allende in Chile in the 1970s (see above), and also that it had instigated at least eight separate plots against Prime Minister Fidel Castro of Cuba between 1960 and 1965.

The Castro Revolution in Cuba. The most serious challenge to United States efforts to promote stability in Latin America has been the establishment of a communist dictatorship in Cuba under Fidel Castro.

1. *The Rise of Castro.* In 1958 the harsh Cuban dictatorship of Fulgencio Batista was overthrown by rebel nationalist forces led by Fidel Castro. Instead of establishing a democratic government, as had been expected, Castro imposed a communist-type dictatorship in Cuba, made it a member of the communist bloc, and began a "hate campaign" against the United States.

> *(a)* After seizing power, the Castro government postponed elections, executed opponents and former Batista supporters, expropriated lands and other properties of many Cuban citizens, and nationalized foreign properties without compensation. In addition, the Castro regime signed trade agreements with the Soviet Union and Red China. Thousands of Russian technicians and military advisers were sent to Cuba.

> *(b)* In retaliation for the nationalization of oil, sugar, and other properties owned by United States citizens, the United States cut off imports of Cuban sugar. As Castro moved further into the Soviet orbit, our government broke off diplomatic relations and embargoed all exports to Cuba, except food and medical supplies.

2. *The "Bay of Pigs" Invasion.* In 1961, the United States supported a poorly planned invasion of Cuba by anti-Castro exiles. The ignominious failure of this "Bay of Pigs" invasion was a serious blow to American prestige. Supporters of the anti-Castro rebels accused the United States of not giving sufficient support to the invaders. Opponents of United States policy, including many Latin Americans, condemned our government for intervening in Cuban affairs.

3. *The Cuban Missile Crisis.* Late in 1962, a major crisis occurred, which brought the world to the brink of nuclear war. The United States revealed in the UN that the Soviet Union had placed missiles in Cuba capable of reaching every important city in the Western Hemisphere. President John F. Kennedy issued an ultimatum calling upon the Soviet Union to withdraw its missiles and to dismantle the missile installations. He threatened to take all-out measures, if required, to destroy these installations and to halt Soviet ships bringing supplies to Cuba. Premier Khrushchev's pledge to remove the missiles, and their actual removal shortly thereafter, ended the crisis. Although United States prestige abroad was bolstered by this show of firmness, there was evidence that Soviet troops and other personnel remained on the island.

4. *The Cuban Economy Under Castro.* Although the Cuban standard of living under Castro remains low, it appears to be improving slowly with Russian aid. A national health and medical program has been introduced; more schools and housing have been built; and new industries have been started. Shortages of consumer goods and foodstuffs continue to cause difficulties, and rationing has become a "way of life."

5. *Attempts to Export Castroism.* Only one pro-Marxist government (Chile from 1970 to 1973) has been established in Latin America since Castro came to power in 1958. Nonetheless Americans are disturbed over the fact that Cuban-trained communist agents have been trying to stir up discontent and disorder throughout the Hemisphere. Rebels reportedly armed and trained by Cuba have carried on guerrilla warfare in Bolivia, Colombia, Guatemala, Peru, and Venezuela. Cuban troops were sent to Angola to help a leftist faction take over the government of that African nation after the Portuguese withdrawal. (See page 571.)

6. *Recent Relations with Cuba.* Ever since the Bay of Pigs invasion in 1961, the prevailing mood of U.S.-Cuban relations has been hostility and distrust. But there have also been from time to time some signs of attempts at reconciliation. **(a)** The United States still maintains its own trade embargo against Cuba, but our government voted in 1975 to support the lifting of the 11-year-old ban of the OAS against diplomatic and trade relations with Cuba. This resolution authorized each member to decide individually how it is to deal with Cuba and makes possible normalization of relations. In 1975, the United States lifted its ban on exports to Cuba by foreign subsidiaries of American companies. **(b)** Castro has allowed substantial numbers of Cubans to emigrate to the United States (about 200,000 from 1966 to 1973). **(c)** The United States has decided to end "covert" intelligence operations directed at Cuba. **(d)** There have been in addition a number of "minimal" moves on both sides whose general effect is to lessen strains and hostility. For example, Cuba agreed in 1973 not to allow any further landings of U.S. planes hijacked in flight and forced to fly to Cuba. There has been somewhat less Cuban criticism of the existence of a U.S. naval base at Guantanamo, at the eastern end of the island. Each government has allowed a limited number of officials, businessmen, and other representatives to visit the other country and to attend international conferences together.

Organization of American States. In 1948 the *Organization of American States (OAS)* was established to strengthen the Pan-American Union. It went into operation in 1951. Since that time the OAS has reflected the "ups and downs" of Pan-American relations.

1. *Aims and Structure.* The OAS is a regional organization that seeks to establish means of regional cooperation, peaceful settlement of disputes, and collective self-defense, as authorized in the UN Charter. The OAS charter includes the principle that an attack on one member is an act of aggression against all. The OAS charter provides for regularly scheduled *Inter-American Conferences,* for *Meetings of Foreign Ministers* of member states, for an *Inter-American Defense Board,* and for an *OAS Council.* (The *Pan-American Union* remains as the administrative arm of the OAS.)

2. *Accomplishments of the OAS.* The OAS has proved the value of its existence on a number of occasions.

(a) *Peace-Keeping.* As "keeper of the peace" in the Americas, the OAS has settled a number of disputes among members. In 1964, OAS efforts paved the way for mediation efforts resulting in settlement of the Canal Zone dispute between the United States and Panama. (See page 576.) In 1965, the OAS formulated a plan to settle a turbulent situation in the Dominican Republic (See page 576.) In 1969, in a widely praised action, OAS diplomacy ended a short-lived war between El Salvador and Honduras.

(b) *Policies Adopted by the OAS.* At various meetings, OAS members have considered common problems and have issued joint statements or declarations of principles. At the *Caracas Conference* (Venezuela) of 1954 (10th Inter-American Conference), OAS members pledged united action against communist subversion or intervention in the Western Hemisphere. At the *Santiago Conference* (Chile) of 1959, member states condemned governments that suppressed civil liberties. At the *Punta del Este Conference* (Uruguay) of Foreign Ministers in 1962, OAS members voted to exclude Cuba from participation in the OAS. They also declared that the communist government of Cuba was "incompatible" with the American system. In 1975, at a conference held in Costa Rica, OAS members (including the United States) moved toward a restoration of relations with Cuba by voting to abolish the embargo imposed eleven years earlier on trade and diplomatic relations with Cuba. (During the period of the ban, however, nine nations, including Argentina and Mexico, had continued to maintain more or less normal relations with Cuba.)

(c) *UN Recognition of the OAS.* The UN has recognized the role of the OAS on a number of occasions by referring to it several disputes relating to the Western Hemisphere. In addition, a Latin American nation has always occupied a seat on the Security Council.

3. *Weaknesses and Problems of the OAS.* The successes of the OAS have been matched by equally significant weaknesses.

(a) *Spread of Communism.* The OAS has failed to check the spread of communism in the Western Hemisphere (Guatemala, 1950-54; Cuba, since 1958).

(b) *Bypassing of the OAS.* Some OAS members have brought disputes ("threats against the peace") directly to the UN instead of to the OAS. For example, Castro chose to present his case directly to the UN, rather than to the OAS, when exiles supported by the United States attempted to invade Cuba in 1961.

(c) *Limited Budget.* The OAS has a very inadequate budget. This limits the scope of its activities.

(d) *Lack of a Permanent Military Force.* The OAS has no military force of its own. It has been suggested that a small permanent military force be set up for this purpose.

(e) *Rivalries.* The OAS has not successfully overcome longstanding disagreements and rivalries among the member states. It should be understood that the nations of Latin America are by no means uniform in size, economic interests, national or racial background, cultural developments, or other important respects. Today, as in the past, boundary and other disputes continue to embitter relations between such countries as Argentina and Brazil, Nicaragua and Costa Rica, Bolivia and Paraguay, and El Salvador and Honduras.

4. *Role of the United States in the OAS.* As the most powerful and wealthy member of the OAS, the United States undoubtedly has more influence than any other country belonging to the organization. We pay about two-thirds of the OAS budget, and our representatives are members of all committees. OAS headquarters are located in Washington, D.C. In recent years, however, there has been an increasing tendency for OAS members to assert themselves more strongly and to take independent positions that may be in opposition to the United States. This is true particularly when economic interests are concerned. Moreover, Latin American nations have shown less willingness to accept United States leadership in the UN.

Recent Issues and Policies in Inter-American Affairs. The continuing importance of our relations with the other nations of the Hemisphere is reflected in the issues and policies discussed below.

1. *Economic Development.* Perhaps the most important policy innovations have been in the economic field.

    (a) Alliance for Progress. From 1961 to 1971, the United States and 19 Latin American nations engaged in a joint program for social and economic reform called the *Alliance for Progress.* Under the leadership of President Kennedy, the United States contributed about 10 billion dollars for the program, and the Latin American participants an equal amount. The Alliance showed some positive results, including a sizable rise in gross national product in most of the countries, construction of schools, housing, and health facilities on a fairly large scale, and some limited tax reforms. Overall, however, the program fell far short of achieving its ambitious goals. Among the negative factors contributing to these disappointing results were inflation and continued population growth, which largely nullified gains in agriculture and other areas of production. Critics complained that the overall level of expenditures, in relation to the massiveness of the problems, was "too little and too late." Many observers felt that the Alliance program was weakened by the fact that the governments in some Latin American countries were militaristic, dominated by special interests, and basically hostile to any real social reform.

    (b) As part of a trend toward self-help, several regional groups have become active in Latin American affairs. The *Latin American Free Trade Association* and the *Central American Common Market* have been formed to stimulate trade within the Hemisphere. In 1975, twenty-five nations of the region (not including the United States) set up a new regional body, the *Latin American Economic System* *(SELA),* whose general purpose is to promote economic growth.

Various attempts have been made, with only limited success, to organize Latin American producers of basic commodities into protective associations, somewhat like OPEC (see below). For example, a Union of Banana Exporters was set up in Central America in 1974 in an effort to control the supply of this fruit and to raise prices.

The *Inter-American Development Bank* was set up by 19 Latin American nations and the United States in 1959 to provide financial backing for economic development projects in the Hemisphere. Canada has since become a member.

2. *Nationalization of U.S. Properties.* In recent years, relations between the United States and Latin American states have been somewhat strained by measures taken to nationalize (expropriate) properties owned by United States-based companies in countries such as Chile, Peru, Ecuador, and Venezuela. The companies in question have usually controlled basic resources, notably oil and copper. In some cases, there have been provisions for "compensation," but the terms have rarely been satisfactory to the former owners. The United States has responded by the "Hickenlooper Amendment" (to the Foreign Aid Act of 1962), which requires the President to cut off grants, credits, and other forms of economic aid to any nation that has expropriated American-owned properties "without prompt and reasonable compensation." Such action has been taken for a time against Chile, Peru, and Venezuela.

3. *Oil and Politics.* The *Organization of Petroleum Exporting Countries* (OPEC), discussed on page 563, includes Venezuela, Ecuador, Bolivia, and Mexico in its membership. The policies of OPEC in the 1970s led to a fourfold increase in the price of exported oil. This dealt a severe economic blow not only to the United States but also to various nations, such as Brazil and Chile, which are oil importers.

4. *An Evolving Latin American Policy.* The United States clearly recognizes that the era of unchallenged domination of Hemisphere affairs has come to an end. While we are still by far the largest and strongest nation in the Hemisphere, we must now seek to achieve our aims by cooperation and persuasion, rather than by economic and military power.

While in general we now have more friendly relations with Latin America than at many times in the past, sources of friction remain. Latins still fear domination by the "Colossus of the North." The expropriation of American-owned properties by some Latin American governments has led to "tough" counter-measures in Washington, and this in turn has evoked anxiety and resentment in Latin America. Many critics in Latin America assert that the United States in recent years has been so preoccupied with problems in Europe, Southeast Asia, and Africa, and elsewhere that it has virtually ignored its friends and neighbors in this Hemisphere.

Whatever the validity of such criticisms, there can be no doubt that realistic new policies will have to be developed in the years ahead, not merely to eliminate old grievances but to deal in a postive way with the evolving needs and opportunities of the entire Western Hemisphere.

REVIEW TEST (Chapter 30—Part VII)

Select the number preceding the word or expression that best completes each statement or answers each question.

1. During the past 25 years, in relations with Latin America, the United States has emphasized (1) the Roosevelt Corollary to the Monroe Doctrine (2) the multilateral interpretation of the Monroe Doctrine (3) a revival of the Platt Amendment (4) "dollar diplomacy"

2. The "Bay of Pigs" is in (1) Cuba (2) Panama (3) Nicaragua (4) Argentina

3. The announced purpose of President Kennedy's Alliance for Progress program was to (1) overthrow the Castro regime in Cuba (2) raise the standard of living throughout Latin America (3) eliminate trade barriers between the United States and Latin America (4) unite the democratic governments in Latin America against Latin American dictatorships

4. Most observers in the United States and Latin America would characterize the Alliance for Progress as (1) a complete failure (2) a gain for Latin America but not for the United States (3) a well-meaning program that failed to achieve many of its goals (4) an unqualified success.

5. Most members of the Organization of American States are also members of (1) the UN (2) NATO (3) the Warsaw Pact (4) the Atlantic Community

6. The 1947 Rio Pact provided that (1) American nations outlaw communism in this hemisphere (2) American nations cooperate if any of them is attacked by a nation outside this hemisphere (3) the Pan-American Union be the judge of aggression (4) the American defense zone be limited to the territorial waters within three miles of each country's coast line

7. In order to help in their own development Latin American nations have organized the (1) International Cooperation Administration (2) Agency for International Development (3) Export-Import Bank (4) Inter-American Development Bank

8. Which of the following has been a characteristic of Latin American political life? (1) unconstitutional seizures of power (2) stable governments (3) communist domination of political parties (4) a two-party system

9. Stabilization agreements between Latin American nations and the United States have been negotiated to (1) offset the influence of Castroism (2) make Latin American nations eligible for economic assistance (3) establish higher prices for Latin American goods in United States markets (4) insure the establishment of democratic regimes in Latin America

10. Which of the following is true of Cuba under the Castro dictatorship? (1) It has received little help from the Soviet Union. (2) It has developed an increasingly strong industrial economy. (3) It has been excluded from the United Nations. (4) It has been excluded from the Organization of American States.

Essay Questions

1. Explain three ways in which the United States and its Latin American neighbors have cooperated since World War II.

2. Discuss three present causes of unrest in Latin America.

3. Show how each has been a challenge for the United States in its relationship with Latin America in recent years: (a) suspicion of United States motives and actions (b) communism (c) Castroism.

4. Explain the causes, nature, and results of (a) the "Castro Revolution" in Cuba and (b) the Alliance for Progress.

5. (a) Describe the purposes, organization, and accomplishments of the Organization of American States. (b) Explain two ways in which it resembles the United Nations and one way in which it differs. (c) Do you consider it successful or not? Why?

REVIEWING UNIT EIGHT

Select the number preceding the word or expression that best completes each statement or answers each question.

1. At the turn of the 20th century, United States policy towards China was expressed in the (1) Gentlemen's Agreement (2) "Open-Door" policy (3) Ostend Manifesto (4) Stimson Doctrine

2. The desire to gain territory motivated some of those who urged the entrance of the United States into the (1) Spanish-American War (2) Civil War (3) First World War (4) Second World War

3. The United States has given economic aid to Germany since the end of World War II chiefly to (1) help stop the spread of communism (2) strengthen Germany so that France will not dominate Europe (3) help Germany socialize her industry (4) raise the German standard of living above the prewar level

4. Two nations included in the North Atlantic Treaty Organization are (1) Spain and West Germany (2) Belgium and Sweden (3) the Netherlands and France (4) Ireland and Canada

5. Which of the following groups is a conference paired with a policy endorsed by the meeting? (1) Yalta — international control of atomic energy (2) Vienna — promotion of democracy (3) Potsdam — recognition of Soviet Russia's satellites (4) San Francisco — establishment of the United Nations

6. Presidential action can take the United States into a military conflict without a congressional declaration of war. This fact was illustrated by events involving us with (1) England in 1812 (2) Cuba in 1898 (3) Germany in 1917 (4) Korea in 1950

7. Which of the following factors exerted the *least* influence on overseas expansion of the United States after 1890? (1) growth of industrial production (2) surplus of agricultural products (3) passing of the frontier (4) Spanish-American War

8. An important cause of Latin America's hostility to the United States in the past has been the (1) original statement of the Monroe Doctrine (2) creation of the Pan-American Union (3) establishment of immigration quota for Latin Americans (4) application of the Roosevelt Corollary

9. Which of the following pairs a period in United States history with a phase of foreign policy dominant at that time? (1) 1865–90 — active leadership in world affairs (2) 1890–1903 — rejection of opportunities for imperialism (3) 1904–10 — active role in the Carribean area (4) 1910–18 — isolation from world struggle

10. Which statesman is paired with a policy followed by the United States in the Far East? (1) Cordell Hull — "Alliance for Progress" (2) George C. Marshall — "Point Four" (3) John Hay — "Open Door" (4) Robert Lansing — Containment

*On the time line the letters **A** through **G** represent time intervals as indicated. For **each** event listed below, write the **letter** that indicates the time interval within which the event occurred.*

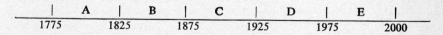

	A		B		C		D		E	
1775		1825		1875		1925		1975		2000

1. The Washington Nine-Power Treaty provided for the continuation of the Open-Door Policy.

2. The Bicentennial of the United States was celebrated at home and abroad.

3. President Franklin D. Roosevelt requested Congress to repeal the "cash-and-carry" principle of the neutrality legislation.

4. The Hawaiian Islands were annexed to the United States by a joint resolution of Congress.

5. A United States warship stopped the British steamer *Trent* and took off two Confederate diplomats.

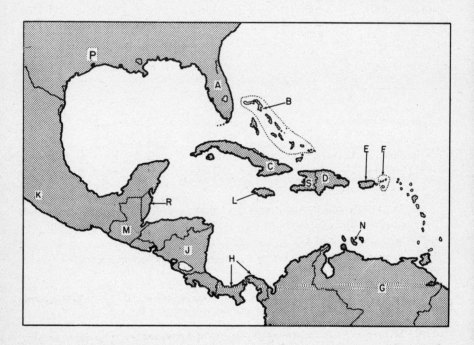

*The statements below identify certain areas of the Caribbean region. For **each** statement, write the **letter** indicating the location of that area on the map.*

1. Acquired by the United States as a result of the Spanish-American War, this island is now a free commonwealth associated with the United States.

2. This area, a protectorate of the United States from 1901 to 1934, experienced a revolution led by Castro in 1959.

3. Conditions in this country, once ruled by Maximilian, caused Wilson to adopt a policy of "watchful waiting" in the 20th century.

4. Originally considered as a possible alternate canal route, this area was occupied as a protectorate by United States troops during the early 20th century.

5. In 1917, the United States extended its naval control over the Caribbean region by purchasing this area from Denmark.

6. The gaining of this area's independence from Colombia was aided by President Theodore Roosevelt in the interest of acquiring United States canal rights.

7. A boundary dispute in this area led to the issuance of the Olney Doctrine in 1895. Today, this country is a major source of petroleum.

8. Site of the main control center for our program of space exploration.

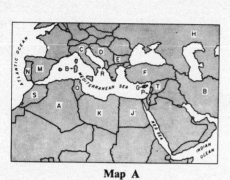

Map A

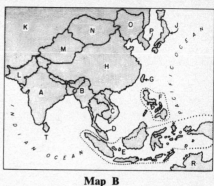

Map B

*For each statement below write the **letter** shown on map **A** above which indicates the location of the country described in the statement.*

1. This NATO country controls the Dardanelles.

2. This Middle Eastern country recently regained control of the Suez Canal as a result of peace negotiations with Israel.

3. This oil-rich country with its capital at Teheran is friendly to the Western world.

4. Although communist, this European nation does not follow Soviet leadership and receives United States aid.

5. In 1964, Nikita Khrushchev was removed from leadership in this country.

*The statements below identify certain areas of the Asiatic world. For **each** statement, write the **letter** indicating the location of that area on map **B** above.*

1. This country, once an enemy of the United States and now considered an ally, is a leading industrial nation of the Far East.

2. This nation, the last stronghold of the Nationalist government of China, was dropped from the UN Security Council to make way for the People's Republic of China.

3. A former protectorate of Japan, the southern part of this country was defended against communist aggression by the United Nations.

4. This anti-communist nation, the world's largest archipelago, lies along the Equator, northwest of Australia.

5. This country, granted its independence by the United States in 1946, has been struggling with formidable internal problems.

6. In this region, the United States became involved in the longest lasting war in its history.

7. This member of the (British) Commonwealth of Nations won its independence as a result of the efforts of Gandhi and Nehru.

8. This country, which became a republic in 1912, is now communist but is bitterly opposed to the policies of the Soviet Union.

Essay Questions

1. The goals of United States foreign policy today, as in the past, are concerned with (a) the security and welfare of our people and (b) the promotion, on the world scene, of American democratic ideals. Show how each of *three* different foreign policies of the United States, each pursued during the 20th century, was based upon either or both of these goals.

2. Increasingly, the Far East has come to play an important part in United States foreign policy. Select China or Japan and for the country selected, give specific information to answer the following: (a) Discuss two reasons why the United States became interested in this country in the 19th century. (b) Discuss two actions taken or policies developed by the United States to meet problems raised by this country during the period 1840–1939. (No credit will be allowed in "b" for repeating information given in answer to part "a.") (c) Discuss two problems which the country selected presents to the United States today.

3. The United States has faced serious foreign relations problems with Latin America during recent years. (a) Describe two changes in the relations between Cuba and the United States in the period between 1898 and the present. (b) Show why two policies of the United States in relation to Latin American nations other than Cuba have been criticized by Latin America. (c) Show how certain other policies of the United States during the 20th century have gained favor in Latin American countries.

4. Select three of the countries below. For each country selected show how the United States has been in agreement or disagreement with that country on an international question or problem during the 20th century: Great Britain, France, Israel, China, Japan. (A different question or problem must be used in each case.)

5. Each of the following was Secretary of State at a time when a major issue of foreign policy was at stake: John Hay, Henry Stimson, Cordell Hull, Dean Acheson, John Foster Dulles, Henry Kissinger. Select five of these Secretaries of State and explain briefly an issue of foreign policy with which each was associated.

6. One of the main aims of United States foreign policy since 1930 has been the containment of fascism and communism. Show briefly, giving specific facts, how each of five of the following has aided in containing either fascism or communism: (a) Stimson Doctrine (b) "Destroyer Deal" (c) Lend-Lease Act (d) Truman Doctrine (e) Marshall Plan (f) Point-Four Program (g) NATO

7. After the end of World War I, the United States was unwilling to accept the responsibilities of world leadership; since World War II, however, the United States has come to accept the role of a world leader. (a) Discuss two reasons why the United States failed to accept the responsibilities of world leadership in the two decades following World War I. (b) Discuss three specific instances that indicate that the United States has accepted the role of world leader since the end of World War II. (c) Explain briefly why the change occurred.

8. Since 1945, the United States government has been increasingly concerned with problems all over the world. (a) Explain how the United States since 1945 has been involved in one foreign problem on each of three different continents. (b) Explain a difficulty in arriving at a solution to each of the problems given in "a."

9. United States foreign policy since 1945 has had three specific goals: (a) defense of the United States against attack, (b) maintenance of world peace, and (c) promotion of economic and social welfare abroad. Discuss two specific means used by the United States in an effort to accomplish each of these goals. (Do not duplicate information.)

The United States In A Changing World

In 1976, the United States moved into its third century as a nation, in a troubled yet hopeful mood. As the 1970s moved to a close and the 1980s began, the nation continued to be confronted with many serious problems at home and with critical issues abroad.

I. DEVELOPMENTS AND PROBLEMS AT HOME

The Carter Administration. Since 1977, the nation has been under the leadership of President Jimmy (James E.) Carter. The Carter administration, like all others, has been marked by both successes and failures. Because we are still in the midst of many of these events and problems, it is difficult to evaluate the overall record of the administration.

Before becoming President, Jimmy Carter had been a naval officer, a successful farmer and businessman, and a popular Governor of Georgia. Although a relative "unknown" in national politics, Carter campaigned vigorously to win the Democratic nomination for President in 1976. Then, in a close election, he defeated the Republican nominee, the incumbent President, Gerald R. Ford. Carter's success was made possible by the support of labor, blacks, and liberals, and by the return of many white Southerners to the Democratic fold.

The Carter administration, it is generally agreed, has had a number of notable achievements to its credit. Nevertheless, as the President's term approached its end, his popularity appeared to be declining. This was attributed primarily to the failure to control the inflationary rise in prices and to cope with the energy crisis. The President was also criticized for being unable to get Congress to enact a number of his promised programs, such as welfare reform, measures to bring about full employment, national health insurance, and an effective strategy for helping the nation's big cities.

A Conservative Trend. A noteworthy trend in American political life during the late 1970s was the growing strength of a movement generally labeled as *conservative,* although some observers preferred to call it *moderate.* This was marked by a broad-based "revolt" against higher taxes, by a national mood that questioned the limits of governmental power, and by a demand for less participation by government in the economy.

The "tax revolt" was symbolized by the phrase *Proposition 13.* This proposition was an amendment to the California Constitution approved by the voters of that state in 1978. It placed a drastic limit on taxation of real property (real estate). In addition, it required a two-thirds vote of the State Legislature (rather than a simple majority) for any future increase in state taxes. By mid-1979, voters in some 25 other states had used the ballot initiative to approve state constitutional amendments modeled on the California proposition, although some were not nearly so drastic. In addition, many states reduced personal income taxes; a number reduced sales and other taxes.

There was strong criticism of tax-cutting measures of the Proposition 13 variety. It was argued that lower governmental revenues would inevitably mean a cut in governmental services, including education and aid to the needy and to senior citizens. In a number of states, measures calling for tax cuts or limitations were turned down.

Another symptom of the "neo-conservatism" of the 1970s was a demand to lessen the role of government in general—and especially the Federal government—in American economic life. A significant move in this direction was taken when the Civil Aeronautics Board was deprived of its power to set the rates charged by domestic airlines. A proposal was also made to "deregulate" the trucking industry. This was vigorously opposed both by most trucking companies and by the Teamsters Union.

Political Developments. President Carter was pledged to reorganize the complex "bureaucratic" structure of the Executive branch of the Federal government. The aims were to cut unnecessary jobs, lower costs, and improve efficiency.

A *Civil Service Reform* Act in 1978 aimed at restructuring and modernizing the entire Federal civil service. Some agencies which seemed to have outlived their usefulness were phased out. Among these was the *Civil Aeronautics Board,* which previously had controlled rates and fares charged by American airlines.

In 1977, at Carter's urging, Congress created a new Cabinet-level *Department of Energy*. Proposals for a new *Department of Education* have not been approved as yet.

The mid-term Congressional elections of 1978 preserved Democratic control of both houses of Congress. The Republicans made some gains, but they were small in relation to the usual pattern of "off-year" elections.

The Economy and Inflation. In general, the 1960s and 1970s were a period of economic prosperity and growth, although it was clear that the ups and downs of the business cycle were still in effect.

From 1973 to 1975, the nation experienced its worst recession since World War II. There was a marked business slowdown and relatively high unemployment. At the same time, *inflation* continued (see below).

After 1975, the economy recovered. For 1978, the gross national product or GNP (the total value of all the goods and services produced annually) stood at about 1.4 trillion dollars, as compared with 1.2 trillion dollars for 1973. (Both these figures are expressed in "constant dollars" of 1972 purchasing power, so as to allow for the effects of inflation.)

More than 96 million individuals had jobs in 1979, by far the highest figure in our history. Also, people were earning more than ever. Earnings reached an all-time high, with an average of about $250 per week in manufacturing industries. In general, business showed good sales and profits.

There were, however, some serious dark spots in the economy in the late 1970s. Although more people were employed than ever before, *unemployment* remained a problem. In 1979, about 6 million Americans who wanted to work were without jobs—about 6% of the total work force. The growth rate of American industry showed strong signs of slowing down, thus providing fewer new jobs, especially for young people entering the work force.

Another strongly negative factor was the continuing rapid rise in the price level—*inflation*. The dollar that brought 100 cents worth of goods in 1967 was down to 49 cents by mid-1979, with the prospect that it would fall to 44 cents within a year. Many workers, although taking home more money in wages than ever before (after taxes), found that they actually had less buying power than a few years previously. There had been a decrease in their *real wages*. People with fixed or semi-fixed incomes—such as retirees depending mainly on Social Security payments and other pensions—found themselves especially hard hit.

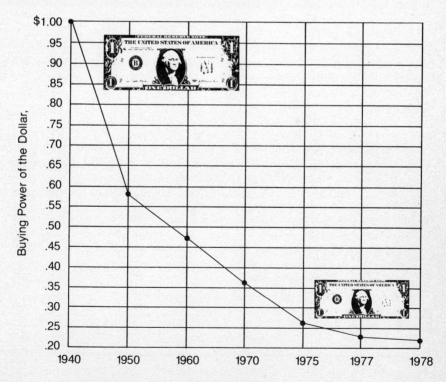

This graph shows how much the buying power of the dollar has shrunk since 1940.

Source: Bureau of Labor Statistics

Economists were not in full agreement on the causes of the inflation. Among the factors usually mentioned were: (1) a sharp increase (more than six times over) in the cost of the oil we were buying from OPEC nations; the continued huge deficits in the budget of the Federal government, leading to borrowing and to the release of more money into the economy; constantly increased consumer spending and the proportionate rise of consumer debt; effective pressure by labor unions for higher wages and other benefits; maintenance of artificially high prices by powerful corporations, many of them operating on an international basis; the nation's big deficit year after year in its trade with the rest of the world; and a marked slowing down in the rate of productivity increase of American industry.

The Carter administration took a number of different steps in its efforts to curb the inflation. One of these was a campaign to cut governmental spending and to narrow the budgetary deficit. The Federal Reserve system sought to tighten credit by raising interest rates and also to curb the growth of the monetary supply by various methods. A campaign was launched by the administration to persuade business, labor and the general public to accept voluntary *guidelines,* limiting pay increases to 7% and price increase to 5.75%.

By the close of 1979, there was general agreement that the administration's inflation-control program was not being effective. In some quarters there was a demand for *direct governmental controls* to stabilize prices and wages, but such a program was generally opposed by business, labor unions, and the administration itself. There was considerable fear that the uncontrolled inflation would lead to a major depression. If this occurred, the price rise would presumably be halted, but at a terrible price.

Foreign Trade. The United States in recent years has been running an *unfavorable balance* in its trade with the rest of the world. This means that we have been buying more from foreign nations than we have been selling to them. (The overall trade balance is made up of both physical merchandise sold by one nation to another, and of *invisible items,* such as tourist expenditures, loans, and banking services.)

The unfavorable trade balance has been caused in large part by our increased imports of oil and by higher prices charged by the OPEC nations. (The increase was more than 600% from 1973 to the end of the 1970s.) However, other factors also played a part, such as relatively low production and higher costs by some American industries and aggressive competition by nations such as Japan and West Germany.

As a result of the nation's weak foreign trade position, the value of the U.S. dollar plunged in international markets. In other words, the dollar was worth less in terms of "hard" currencies such as the West German mark and the Japanese yen, and also in terms of gold. The plunging value of the dollar had an upsetting value on all international financial dealings. Also, it contributed to the severe inflation in the United States. The Carter administration, in cooperation with foreign governments, took various steps to "defend the dollar," and this campaign met with some success, although the value of gold continued to rise.

Efforts were also made to increase world trade by reducing barriers such as tariffs and by creating more efficient and orderly conditions for carrying on such trade. In April 1979, after more than five years of negotiations, representatives of 99 nations, including the United States, agreed upon a program of revisions in the international *General Agreement on Tariffs and Trade* or GATT. (See page 390.) Although this 1979 pact still had to be ratified by the governments of the signatory nations, it seemed to have a strong potential for increasing the flow of international trade. The United States agreed to make important tariff concessions on about 87% of the industrial products we now import, but trade experts asserted that we would show far greater increases in exports, providing a net gain of from one to 10 billion dollars annually in our international trade balance. Some American industries, already hard hit by imports from countries such as Japan, were wary of this new program. In many cases, they were strongly supported by the labor unions in those industries.

The Bakke Case. This is widely regarded as the most important civil rights court case since the desegregation decision of 1954.

Alan Bakke, a white man, sought admission to the medical school of the University of California at Davis. He was rejected. Bakke then sued the university on the grounds that 16 places in the entering medical school class (out of a total of 100) had been reserved for minority group students. Bakke claimed that some of those admitted under this program had qualifications inferior to his. Thus, he claimed, he was being deprived of the "equal protection of the laws" guaranteed by the 14th Amendment. He said that he was the victim of *"reverse (anti-white) discrimination."*

The case reached the Supreme Court, which ruled in 1978 that the university's "quota system" for minority-group students was unconstitutional, and that Bakke would have to be admitted to the medical school. On the other hand, the Court gave its approval to programs of *affirmative action,* designed to give special help and consideration to members of underprivileged minority groups. But the court indicated that such programs would have to be designed so as to avoid infringing on the rights of other groups.

The head of the U.S. Civil Rights Commission claimed to be heartened by the decision and recommended an all-out program of affirmative action in various areas of the nation's economic life. Strong encouragement for such an approach came with the Supreme Court's decision in the *Weber Case* (1979). The Court ruled that a private employer had the legal right to give preference to members of minority groups in selecting employees to receive the benefits of special training programs for better jobs. This held true even though the employer (the Kaiser Steel Company) had not been accused of prior discrimination. The compensatory preference could be continued until the proportion of minority group people in the more desirable job categories was roughly equal to their proportion in the general community population.

Poverty and Unemployment. Poverty continues to be a major challenge for American society. At the close of the 1970s, about 25 million Americans were still living below the "poverty line." This "line" was defined by the United States government as an annual income of less than $6700 per year for a family of four ($5700 for farm families).

The "war on poverty" continues to be fought in many ways by both public and private agencies. It has been estimated that the nation is now spending about 150 billion dollars per year for this purpose. The following sections summarize the main aspects of this program.

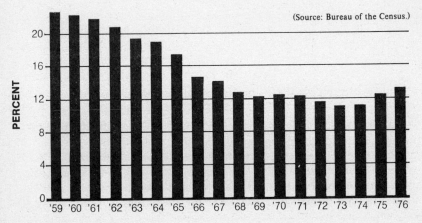

(Source: Bureau of the Census.)

This graph shows the proportion of Americans living below the poverty level from 1959 through 1976. Although, there has been some progress since 1959, there are still about 25 million Americans stuck in the "poverty" category.

1. *Attempts to Promote Employment.* The Johnson, Nixon, Ford and Carter administrations have tried to reduce "hard core unemployment" by giving special training and counseling to unemployed people, and also by providing public service jobs.

    (*a*) The *Comprehensive Employment and Training Act* of 1973 (CETA) provided funds for public service jobs and job training in areas with high unemployment. In 1978, CETA was extended by the Carter administration, with changes to improve administration. In 1978, about 360,000 jobs were CETA-funded.

    (*b*) The *Humphrey-Hawkins Act* of 1978 (officially the *Full Employment and Balanced Growth Act*) requires the President to set annual goals for employment, production, and inflation for five years. The aim is to reduce the national jobless rate to 4% and inflation to 3% by 1983. As originally written, this bill was designed to make the Federal government the "employer of last resort" by providing public service jobs whenever unemployment exceeded 4% of the work force. The bill, according to critics, was "watered down" to such an extent that it has become of little importance.

(c) The Carter program also set up special job training for groups with higher-than-average unemployment rates, including blacks, Hispanic-Americans, young people, migrant farmworkers, the handicapped, Vietnam veterans, and American Indians.

(d) The proposed Federal budget for 1980, however, projected cuts in public-service jobs. This reflected the administration's determination to cut public spending as a means of fighting inflation.

2. Direct Help to the Needy. In recent years, the Federal, state, and local governments have spent many billions of dollars on "welfare" programs to help needy Americans. About 75% of all funds spent have been Federal. The disbursements have been in the form of cash payments, unemployment compensation, food stamps, medical care, job training, and public housing projects. In 1979 about 30 million Americans were receiving such aid.

The so-called "relief" or "welfare" program of direct financial aid to needy individuals and families has been widely criticized as being costly, wasteful, and bogged down in bureaucratic red tape. Also, the charge is made that the program encourages people to continue on relief rather than look for jobs, and that it tends to break up families. A welfare reform program presented by the Carter administration in 1977 was turned down by Congress. A more modest program was recommended to Congress in 1979. This was designed to raise benefit payments where needed, to ease the financial burden on state and local governments, and to create more than 400,000 new jobs for people now on relief.

3. Increased Social Security Benefits. Social Security benefits have continued to move upward, according to a predetermined schedule geared to the cost of living. The maximum monthly retirement benefit for a worker retiring at the age of 65 was $553 per month, as of 1979. The figure for a retired couple was $804 per month. Nearly 35 million Americans were receiving retirement and other Social Security benefits in 1979.

At the same time, the Social Security taxes paid by workers and their employers have also been rising sharply. Some critics believe that the burden of Social Security taxes is already so high that further increases would be unfair and dangerous to the health of the economy. There is some demand for financing the system in part from general revenues, rather than depending entirely on the present special taxes.

4. Increased Minimum Wages. The minimum wage, applying to most workers in the United States, increased from $2.30 per hour in 1977, to $2.65 in 1978, and to $2.90 in 1979. The minimum rate was scheduled to go to $3.00 in 1980, and to $3.35 in 1981.

It is argued in some quarters that the minimum wage rates have become so high that they actually discourage employment of unskilled or "marginal" workers, particularly young people without experience or specialized training.

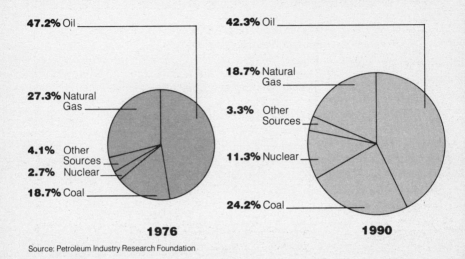

47.2% Oil

27.3% Natural Gas

4.1% Other Sources
2.7% Nuclear
18.7% Coal

1976

42.3% Oil

18.7% Natural Gas

3.3% Other Sources

11.3% Nuclear

24.2% Coal

1990

Source: Petroleum Industry Research Foundation

Sources of energy in the United States in 1976, and projected for 1990.

Energy Policy. The energy crisis has emerged as one of the most pressing problems facing the United States today. It has been caused by constantly increasing consumption of petroleum and other fuels; by the decline of domestic production of petroleum; by the policies of the petroleum-exporting countries (OPEC), designed both to raise prices of petroleum and to limit sales; and for a time by the interruption of oil production in Iran during the 1979 revolution in that country.

President Carter has presented programs to deal with the energy crisis. Congress has enacted some of these proposals into law. Others have gone into effect as a result of Presidential initiative.

(*a*) Consolidation of a number of energy agencies and activities into a new *Department of Energy.*

(*b*) Measures to place a priority on increased coal production and use.

(*c*) Gradual decontrol of the price of natural gas, and also phasing out of Congressionally mandated controls on the price of domestic crude oil. The purpose of this is to discourage consumption (through higher prices) and to stimulate production.

(*d*) Improvement of public transportation as means of cutting down on use of private automobiles.

(*e*) Research to develop new sources of energy, such as solar energy and production of synthetic fuels.

(*f*) Special tax incentives to encourage owners of homes and other buildings to conserve energy by means of improved insulation and by conversion to coal and solar heating.

(*g*) A special "gas-guzzler" tax to encourage production of more fuel-efficient automobiles.

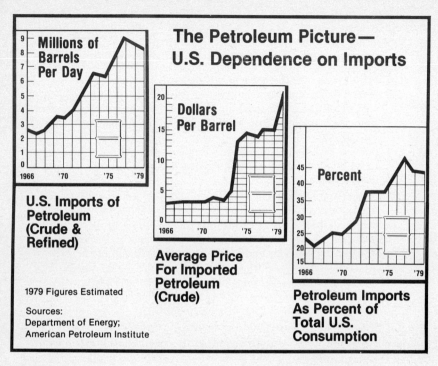

The Petroleum Picture—
U.S. Dependence on Imports

Millions of Barrels Per Day

U.S. Imports of Petroleum (Crude & Refined)

1979 Figures Estimated

Sources:
Department of Energy;
American Petroleum Institute

Dollars Per Barrel

Average Price For Imported Petroleum (Crude)

Percent

Petroleum Imports As Percent of Total U.S. Consumption

Until recently, it was widely hope that increased production of nuclear energy would help materially to meet our energy needs. (By 1979, about 13% of all electrical power in the country was coming from nuclear plants.) However, the nuclear program has met increasing resistance. Opponents stress the possibility of accidents that may cause widespread destruction, as well as the formidable problem of disposal of nuclear wastes. A major setback to the nuclear energy program occurred in 1979 as a result of a serious malfunction in the Three Mile Island installation near Harrisburg, Pennsylvania. Although a disaster was avoided, popular confidence in nuclear energy was badly shaken. It seemed clear after this incident that for the time being at least there would be no major expansion of nuclear energy facilities.

Gasoline shortages in 1979 gave strong evidence that the energy problems of the United States were far from being solved. There was general agreement that the programs adopted thus far were not adequate to deal with the situation. Blame was assigned freely—to the Carter administration, to Congress, to the greedy and hostile OPEC nations, to the wasteful American consumer, and to the major oil companies, which, it was alleged were exploiting the situation to make huge profits. Whatever the validity of the criticisms, it seemed clear that the energy crisis would not be easily overcome, and that it would call for far-reaching social and economic changes, and possibly for some painful sacrifices by the American people in the years ahead.

Environmental Protection and Conservation. The late 1970s have been marked by strong emphasis on the need to control environmental pollution and to conserve and develop the nation's natural resources. Steps taken for this purpose under the Carter administration include the following:

(*a*) Setting up a new *Department of Energy*.

(*b*) Setting aside additional millions of acres in Alaska and elsewhere as wilderness areas, protected against future sale or commercial exploitation. Also adding large areas to existing National Parks, National Forests, etc.

(*c*) Passage of a *Strip Mining Act*, requiring mining operators to restore to its original contours any land that has been "stripped" for mineral sources, such as coal.

(*d*) Support of Department of Interior efforts to enforce the *Endangered Species Act* of 1973. This applies to both animal and plant wild life.

(*e*) Proposals by President Carter to Congress for a stronger, more comprehensive water conservation policy, particularly designed to combat droughts in the West and severe water shortages in many urban areas.

(*f*) Amending the *Clean Air Act* of 1970, to set higher standards of air quality. At the same time, the amendment permitted the Environmental Protection Agency (EPA) to make certain exceptions in special situations of particular importance to industry.

(*g*) Banning of some dangerous pesticides by the EPA.

(*h*) An order by the U.S. Food and Drug Administration to publicize the dangers that may result from aerosol cans using fluorocarbons.

At the same time, there has been growing resistance to the programs and demands of the environmentalists. It has been argued that the emphasis on environmental protection has become unbalanced and unreasonable, thus adding to the costs of doing business and hampering normal economic development. This, it is said, has been an important inflationary influence. The environmentalists answer that they oppose only those business activities that threaten a healthful and attractive environment. They deny that the programs they advocate would involve excessive costs.

The struggle between the environmentalists and their opponents has become most acute in relation to national energy policy. Two important questions are: To what extent should we increase the use of coal, as a substitute for unavailable oil and natural gas? (Many types of coal release pollutants into the air.) Is it safe and desirable to continue vigorous development of nuclear energy? (See the preceding section.)

The Urban Crisis. By the late 1970s, the deterioration of American cities, particularly the larger and older cities, has become a major national concern. The *urban crisis* was marked by widespread unemployment and poverty, high crime rates, physical decay, declining services, pressing financial problems, and in general a lowered "quality of life." Older cities in the Northeast and Middle West continued to lose population both to their own suburbs and to other regions such as the South (the "Sunbelt").

Some of our largest cities, such as New York, Boston, and Philadelphia, found themselves hard pressed to meet their basic financial needs. New York narrowly averted bankruptcy by means of special state and Federal aid. Cleveland became the first large city in the nation since the depression to default on its obligations. Many cities reduced the school year and even faced possible closing of their public schools.

In the "inner cities" (the older downtown areas), there were many signs of decay, such as stretches of gutted buildings, rubble-strewn empty lots, and boarded-up stores that attract vandals and arsonists.

Aid to the cities has taken various forms. The Federal government has helped with loans and grants for mass transit and construction of various public works. The cities have also been helped by Federal money for housing, welfare, education, and other purposes. In 1979, more than 16 billion dollars in Federal funds was earmarked for urban programs.

The Carter administration has committed itself to a new, more comprehensive urban policy under the *Housing and Community Development Act* of 1977. This program stresses the rehabilitation of entire neighborhoods in an effort to "turn around" physical and economic decline. The largest grants are to go to the neediest cities, and to the most deprived neighborhoods within those cities.

The picture is far from being entirely bleak. Many cities are moving vigorously to help themselves, with state and Federal aid. In some cities, such as Philadelphia, Chicago, and San Francisco, old neighborhoods have been rehabilitated and have attracted new businesses, as well as many residents who otherwise might have settled in the suburbs.

The Women's Movement. One of the most notable aspects of the civil rights movement in recent years has been the drive of women for full equality in all areas of our society. The *Women's Liberation (feminist)* movement charges that American women historically have been the victims of systematic discrimination, and that they have been forced to accept an inferior status in employment, in the professions, in government, in education, and in social, political, and economic affairs generally.

Women have made important gains since the 1950s. They are now far better represented than formerly in private employment, particularly in executive and professional jobs. They hold many more important governmental posts, both elective and appointive. They play a significant part in all fields of education, as both students and teachers. Some of these gains have been the result of legislation, such as the Equal Employment Opportunity Act of 1972 and the Equal Credit Opportunity Act of 1974. But even more the progress has been due to changes in public attitudes and standards. Effective educational and public-relations campaigns by organizations such as the National Organization of Women have played a big part in this.

Many women, however, feel that the change has not gone far enough and that a constitutional amendment is needed to eliminate injustices that remain. In 1971, an *"Equal Rights Amendment"* was drafted and was quickly approved by both houses of Congress. This proposed amendment (which would be the 27th) states simply: "Equality of rights under the law

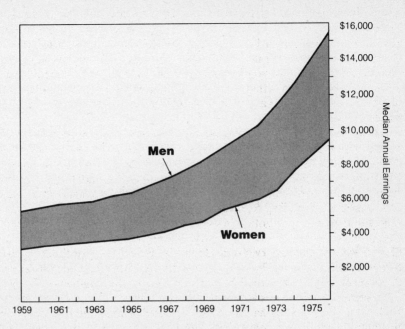

Average earnings for women in the United States continue to lag behind those of men. (U.S. Labor Department)

shall not be denied or abridged by the United States or by any state on account of sex."

The approval of 38 states was needed to ratify the ERA. At first state ratifications came quickly. Then strong opposition developed. Opponents charged that such an amendment was unnecessary; that it would lead to endless litigation; and that it would deprive women of various forms of protective treatment (*e.g.,* exemption from the military draft) that they have traditionally enjoyed. Supporters of ERA answered that the objections were far-fetched, and that opponents were ignoring the need for a broad statement of national policy.

By 1979, 35 of the required 38 states had ratified. The original seven-year period set for ratification expired in 1979, but Congress extended the deadline by another 39 months.

II. CURRENT ISSUES IN AMERICAN FOREIGN AFFAIRS

United States-Soviet Relations. Although *détente* remains a key policy in American foreign relations, it has not yet produced a dramatic improvement in our dealings with the Soviet Union.

There have been some positive or encouraging signs, including the following: **(1)** the *Helsinki Agreements* of 1975 (pages 534-535); **(2)** the easing of restrictions on persons who want to emigrate from the Soviet Union, especially Jews, eager to resettle in the United States or Israel; **(3)** release by the Soviet Union of citizens who had been sent to prison for disagreement with government policies (in response to criticisms by President Carter, 1979); **(4)** some increase in Soviet-American trade during the 1970s. (Many believe that Soviet concessions on emigration and other matters are a result of a desire to gain trade privileges from the United States.)

There were many other developments, however, that suggested "cracks" in the policy of détente, and perhaps a new period of strains and rivalry. These included: **(1)** the rapid strengthening of the Soviet military machine, particularly the fleet build-up in the Mediterranean and the use of naval base facilities provided by Libya in the Mediterranean and South Yemen at the mouth of the Red Sea; **(2)** Soviet support of the Arab states in their opposition to peace negotiations between Egypt and Israel, sponsored by the United States; **(3)** Soviet military intervention in Africa. Using mainly Cuban troops, this intervention led to a victory for pro-Soviet guerrilla forces in the former Portuguese colonies of Angola and Mozambique (1975), and to victory for Ethiopia in its war with Somalia (1977-78).

In spite of such provocations, the official position of the Carter administration continues to be that the policy of détente holds the best possibilities for building a secure peace. This applies particularly to agreements for limitations of nuclear arms.

Support of Human Rights. The Carter administration forthrightly championed human rights in other countries. In large part, this was done by insisting that our trade and other dealings with these countries be linked to their demonstrated respect for such rights. This policy was an important factor in inducing the Soviet Union to ease up on restrictions which prevented Jews in that country from emigrating to Israel and the United States.

Congress passed legislation barring security (military) aid to any country that persistently violated human rights. As a result, the United States cut off or limited military aid to a number of countries in Africa, Latin America, and Asia (*e.g.,* Rhodesia, Nicaragua, Chile). (The President is permitted to make exceptions in this policy when he feels that the national security interests of the United States may be endangered. This applied, for example, to the government of the Shah in Iran, before his fall early in 1979; and also to the Philippine Republic, where the United States has important military bases.)

SALT II. In 1979, after almost seven years of negotiation, representatives of the United States and the Soviet Union agreed on a new treaty for limitation of strategic (nuclear) arms. This agreement is know as *SALT II*. It is a successor to the SALT I agreement of 1972 (see pages 530-531). The key provisions of SALT II are:

(*a*) The treaty is to run until December 31, 1985.

(*b*) Each of the two powers agrees to accept a limitation of 2250 "delivery vehicles" for nuclear weapons. (This includes ICBM's, submarine-launched missiles, and long-range bombers.)

(c) Limitations are set on sub-categories of nuclear weapons. Such limitations apply to MIRVs (multiple independently targeted re-entry vehicles), American cruise missiles, and Soviet "Backfire" bombers. All of these are highly sophisticated weapons with advanced capabilities of speed and accuracy.

(d) While existing missile types may be modernized to increase capabilities, only one new type of land-based missile may be introduced by either of the powers during the treaty period.

SALT II was signed in Vienna in June, 1979 by President Carter and President Brezhnev. The treaty was not to go into effect, however, until approved by the U.S. Senate. A long and bitter debate was expected.

Supporters of SALT II argued that the agreement would limit the Soviet challenge and buildup. It would leave the United States in a strong and secure position, while rendering unnecessary the expenditure of many billions of dollars on developing new weapons.

Critics of SALT II maintained that it involved a serious danger of "freezing" the United States into a position of inferiority in strategic weapons. Thus, the Soviet Union might be in a position within a few years to threaten a knockout blow at this country. Some critics, such as former Secretary of State Henry Kissinger, called for further negotiations to remedy the treaty's alleged weaknesses.

NATO. The United States remains committed to NATO as a means of providing security against any possible Soviet aggression. To meet the challenge of growing Soviet military power, NATO member nations agreed in 1978 to increase their military budgets by 3% a year.

The European NATO nations have some reservations regarding details of SALT II, but in general they endorse the idea of an arms limitation agreement with the Soviet Union.

They have also welcomed the normalizing of relations between the United States and China as a deterrent to Soviet global activity and "adventurism." (About a quarter of all Soviet military forces today are deployed to face Communist China in Asia.)

A weakening factor in NATO has been the hostility between Greece and Turkey as a result of their dispute over Cyprus. Both of these nations have reduced their military contributions to NATO.

The United States and the Common Market. In the late 1970s, there were serious disagreements between the United States and the European Economic Community (Common Market). Each party accused the other of excessive protectionism. It appeared, however, that the multilateral GATT agreements, reached in 1979 after five years of negotiation, would settle some of these complaints (page 590). The agreements gave the United States greater access to European markets, especially for farm products. In return the United States agreed to lower tariff rates on many industrial imports from Common Market members.

The United States endorsed the admission of Greece and Spain into the Common Market in 1979, as well as the pending admission of Portugal and Turkey. These admissions are regarded as a step toward European unity.

The United States and China. One of the most far-reaching developments in United States foreign affairs in recent years has been the recognition of the People's Republic of China. This is the Communist regime that controls the mainland, with a population of about 900 million people. The capital is at Peking.

This major change in our foreign policy came about after almost 30 years of hostility to the Peking regime. Relations began to improve in the early 1970s. In 1971, the United States supported the admission of the People's Republic to the UN. The People's Republic took over the permanent seat on the Security Council that had formerly been held by the Nationalist Chinese government headed by Chiang Kai-shek. Nationalist China was then expelled from the UN. In 1972, at the invitation of Premier Mao Tse-tung, President Nixon visited Communist China. This was followed by the beginning of cultural and educational exchanges, by steps to increase trade, and by other forms of cooperation.

President Carter continued the Nixon policy of building better relations with the People's Republic of China. Negotiations were held on various levels to deal with the complex problems that had accumulated over the years of non-recognition. The climax came on January 1, 1979, when the two powers resumed full diplomatic relations. Shortly after, Vice Premier Teng Hsiao-ping of China visited the United States. His talks in Washington resulted in agreements for the United States technological assistance to China, for additional cultural exchanges, for the opening of consulate offices in both countries, and for eventual exchange of ambassadors. The two powers are *not* allies, but they have agreed to cooperate as much as possible to promote their mutual interests, and to work out conflicts without use of force.

What caused this "diplomatic revolution"? One of the most important factors undoubtedly was the desire of both the United States and the People's Republic to check the power and influence of the Soviet Union. Since the late 1950s, the People's Republic and the Soviet Union, once close friends, have become bitter enemies.

The economic motive is also a compelling factor. Americans hope to tap the vast potential market represented by 900 million Chinese. (Japan and European nations have already moved to build trade relations with the People's Republic.) The Chinese, for their part, are extremely eager to benefit from American achievements in industrial and agricultural technology. Both parties apparently feel that the ideological differences that once separated them are no longer a compelling reason for acting as though the other side did not exist.

Under the agreement with Communist China, the United States ended its mutual defense treaty with Nationalist China, located on the island of Taiwan. However, we will continue to sell weapons to Nationalist China, and we have stated that we will oppose a forceful takeover of Taiwan by Communist China.

There has been strong criticism of this policy. It is charged that we "sold out" a loyal ally (Nationalist China), and that we have compromised our opposition to Communism as a world force. Supporters of the new policy answer that we must accept the world the way it is. The Soviet Union is now the greatest threat to world peace, and we can do much to counter-balance Soviet power by "playing off" the two Communist giants against each other. We do not approve of the Marxist philosophy of the Peking regime, but the fact remains that this regime does control 900 million people, and there is nothing to be gained by pretending that it is not a major factor in world affairs.

The United States and Japan. Japan remains the chief ally of the United States in the Far East. In recent years, however, relations between the two powers have been somewhat strained because of disputes over trade. The trouble is that Japan has been selling more to us than she buys from us. In 1978, this trade imbalance reached almost 12 billion dollars. This huge deficit was a major reason for the unfavorable balance of payments that hampered the United States in its economic dealings with the other nations of the world. The weakness of the dollar was one result of this.

The Japanese claimed that their trade surplus was the result of natural economic forces, particularly their ability to produce quality goods at lower prices than other developed nations. But Americans pointed to high Japanese tariffs, quotas, and other barriers to importation of goods from the United States and Europe. In response to severe pressure, Japan has modified some of these barriers and also limited exports of some goods such as textiles. But many observers feel that unless far more is done to admit American products to the Japanese market, there may be an all-out trade war between Japan and the United States, with possible effects on political relations.

In addition, there has been an increasing demand that Japan shoulder a larger part of the financial burden of providing adequate security forces, and also do more to extend economic aid to underdeveloped nations, such as Egypt and Turkey.

The United States and the Middle East. The United States considers the Middle East one of the most important regions in the world from the standpoint of maintaining global peace and stability. Our policy in this region in recent years has had three main components.

1. The United States has been following a line of "even-handedness" as between Israel and the Arab states. We are committed to the existence of Israel, and have been providing military aid as means of maintaining a military balance. But we have also agreed to sell armaments, especially planes, to Saudi Arabia, Egypt, and other nations in this region.

2. The United States has taken steps whenever and wherever possible to counter growing Soviet influence in the region.

3. The United States has become an active partner and mediator in negotiations for a peace between Israel and the Arab nations, especially between Israel and Egypt.

Following an historic visit by President Anwar Sadat of Egypt to Israel in 1977. President Carter became the chief "architect" in the process of building peace after more than thirty years of bitter hostility. President Carter and President Sadat met with Premier Menahem Begin of Israel at Camp David, Maryland, in September, 1978. Six months later (March, 1979) Israel and Egypt signed a peace treaty based directly on the Camp David accords. The main features of the treaty were (1) The Sinai Peninsula, occupied by Israel since the 1967 war, was to be returned to Egypt over a three-year period. (2) Normalized diplomatic relations were to be established gradually between the two nations. (3) Israeli ships were to have the same rights of free passage through the Suez Canal as the ships of any other nation. (4) Within a month after ratification of the treaty, Israel and Egypt were to begin negotiations for extending self-rule to Palestinians living in the West Bank and Gaza Strip regions. (Both areas were occupied by Israel after the 1967 war.) (5) Other Arab nations were invited to join in establishing Palestinian autonomy and arranging peace treaties with Israel.

Many difficult issues remained to be solved before the peace became a functioning reality. One of the most important was to define exactly the nature of Palestinian "self-rule" or "autonomy" in the Gaza Strip and West Bank. The Palestine Liberation Organization (PLO), devoted to the destruction of Israel, hoped to undermine the talks between Israel and Egypt on this and other subjects and to impose itself as the sole representative of the Palestinian people. Another issue was the right of Israel to continue to establish settlements in the West Bank (opposed by both Egypt and the United States). Still another issue was the status of Jerusalem. The city has been entirely controlled by Israel since the Six-Day War of 1967, but the Arabs, led by Jordan, assert their legal and historic right to hold the "Old City" area.

The United States cannot "solve" these and other problems, but it continues to encourage Israel and Egypt to continue to negotiate in a fair and open-minded spirit and to arrive at reasonable agreements. Another aim of our diplomacy is to convince the more "moderate" Arab states, such as Saudi Arabia and Jordan, that they have more to gain from taking part in the peace process than from opposing and denouncing it.

The United States and Iran. The United States for many years maintained friendly relations with the Iranian government headed by Shah Mohammed Riza Pahlevi. Iran, a leading power in the Middle East, was one of our main suppliers of oil. American technology and armaments played a major part in strengthening the Shah's regime.

The Shah's government, however, was bitterly opposed by many elements within Iran as being corrupt and repressive. After a year of bloody riots, the Shah fled from Iran in January, 1979.

This overturn led to the establishment of an "Islamic Republic" under the Muslim religious leader Ayatollah Ruholla Khomeini. (Iran is a non-

Arab Muslim state.) There was a parliamentary structure of government headed by Premier Mehdi Barzargan, but this has been largely bypassed. The country has actually been ruled by a secret Islamic Revolutionary Council and local revolutionary committees. Hundreds of "enemies of the revolution" have been executed. Before many months had passed, growing opposition to the new regime by leftists, liberals, and other secular (non-religious) groups threatened to plunge the country into civil war.

The United States government during the early stages of the revolution expressed its confidence in the Shah but took no direct action to bolster his regime. Since then, we have followed a generally "hands-off" policy in Iran. Although the Khomeini regime encouraged anti-American sentiments, the Carter administration felt that nothing was to be gained by taking sides, or by seeking to pressure the Iranian rulers. Iranian oil production for a time was cut off almost completely. Later it was resumed, and sizable quantities flowed to the United States, although still well below "normal" levels.

The United States and Africa. The major concerns of the United States in recent years have been the growth of Communist influence, and the problem of minority white rule in Rhodesia and South Africa.

1. *Communist Influence in Africa.* The Soviet Union and Cuba have moved aggressively to increase their influence in various parts of Africa.

(*a*) After *Angola* in southwest Africa gained its independence from Portugal in 1975, a civil war broke out. With the help of troops from Communist Cuba, Agostino Neto, a Marxist, took over control of the government.

(*b*) In 1975, a Communist state was set up in *Mozambique* in southeast Africa, following a ten-year struggle for independence from Portugal. Soviet influence, in the form of technicians and military advisers, was a major factor in the situation.

(*c*) In 1977, *Somalia* and *Ethiopia* went to war over a disputed area called the *Ogaden,* located in the "Horn" of east Africa. The Soviet Union and Cuba, which had previously favored Somalia, switched their support to Ethiopia, making possible an Ethiopian victory.

The United States has made it clear that it favors the anti-Communist groups in these African struggles and has denounced the intervention of the Soviet Union and Cuba. However, we have not intervened actively because our policy is to avoid "meddling" in internal African affairs. Critics have charged that our policy is too passive and is playing directly into the hands of the Communists.

2. *The United States and Rhodesia.* In Rhodesia, in southern Africa, a tiny white minority (about 250,000) has ruled over a black population of 6 million for many years. This has led to an explosive situation that is the cause of great concern to the United States and Great Britain.

In 1970, Rhodesia, until then a self-governing British colony, declared itself independent. It has since managed to survive in spite of diplomatic isolation, a total British trade embargo, and United States economic sanctions, including a ban on purchase of Rhodesian chrome ore.

In the late 1970s, black Rhodesians organized political and guerrilla groups to oppose the regime of Prime Minister Ian Smith, a staunch supporter of "white supremacy." In 1978, moderate black nationalist leaders of the *Popular Front* signed an agreement with the Smith government providing for black majority rule under a new constitution. The plan called for elections in which blacks could vote freely and would be able to elect a black majority government. The agreement also provided many guarantees for the white minority, including (according to critics) a degree of political power not justified by their numbers.

This agreement was denounced as a "sell-out" by leaders of the more radical black factions, particularly the *Patriotic Front,* which continued to carry on guerrilla war. Britain and the United States felt that these groups commanded much popular support and therefore should be brought into the negotiations. The UN Security Council and the five so-called "front line" African states dedicated to ending white minority rule in Rhodesia—Angola, Botswana, Mozambique, Tanzania, and Zambia—also criticized the settlement because it excluded left-wing groups, such as the Patriotic Front.

As a result of elections held in 1979 under the new constitution, a new multi-racial parliament was elected, and Bishop Abel Muzorewa, a black man, became Prime Minister. The country was renamed *Zimbabwe-Rhodesia.*

Foreign observers on the scene felt that the election had been fairly conducted. The U.S. Senate accordingly called for an end to our trade ban with Rhodesia. But President Carter refused to go along with this. He pointed out that the new government had been set up under a constitution drafted and approved by only the white minority—4% of the total population. The President also emphasized that refusal to lift the trade ban would protect American interests by preventing a dangerous split with the states of black Africa.

3. *The United States and South Africa.* Until the late 1970s, there was a close bond between the United States and South Africa, in spite of the latter's policy of *apartheid.* Apartheid calls for enforced separation of the white and black races, with the whites in a position of total dominance, politically, economically, and socially. The Nixon and Ford administrations maintained generally good relations with South Africa and received some promises that the apartheid policies would be liberalized.

The Carter administration has taken a much more critical attitude toward South Africa. U.S. Ambassador to the UN Andrew Young voted in favor of a UN arms embargo against South Africa; the U.S. State Department denounced the assassination of Stephen Biko, a noted young black leader.

South Africa's white leaders, in turn have criticized the United States for "meddling" in South African affairs. They have accused the United States of reneging on an agreed-upon plan to give independence to Southwest Africa (Namibia), and they charge that the United States has sided with the South-West Africa People's Organization, an allegedly communist-backed group.

South Africa, with a population of almost 27 million (about 17% white) is by far the richest and most industrially advanced nation in Africa. Since it is a neighbor of Rhodesia, it is considered the key to a peaceful solution in that country. Thus, the growing feeling among white South Africans that they will have to "go it alone" has, in the opinion of many, reduced the ability of the United States to influence events in Africa, and especially in the southern part of the continent. But supporters of our policies maintain that we must continue to indicate our opposition to a regime based on ideas of racial superiority, and should go even further in that direction.

The United States and Latin America. The United States in recent year has had to cope with many serious problems involving our neighbors in the Western Hemisphere. We shall consider here the situation in **Panama, Mexico, and Nicaragua.**

1. *The Panama Canal Treaties.* In 1964, there were bloody riots in Panama and in the Panama Canal Zone protesting United States policies in regard to the Panama Canal. After thirteen years of on-and-off negotiations, the United States Senate in 1978 approved two treaties with Panama that radically changed the situation.

(*a*) Under the treaties, Panama will gain full control of the Canal by the year 2000. It will then have sovereign authority to operate the Canal and regulate shipping. Until that time a Panama Canal Commission, consisting of five Americans and four Panamanians, will operate the waterway.

(*b*) Until assuming full control in 2000, Panama will receive a greatly increased share of Canal tolls, totaling at least 10 million dollars a year. (Previously, Panama received 2.3 million dollars annually.)

(*c*) Within 2½ years of ratification of the treaties, Panama will gain full control over the Canal Zone.

(*d*) The United States will continue to protect the Canal until its turnover to Panama in the year 2000. Thereafter, the United States will have the right to intervene militarily to insure the neutrality of the Canal.

The United States Senate ratified the treaties after bitter debate. Critics charged that the new arrangements would weaken our security, open the possibility of strong Soviet and Cuban influence, and give in unnecessarily to unreasonable Panamanian nationalist demands. Supporters of the treaties argued that it was important to demonstrate that the United States could change its policies and treat its small neighbors with respect and generosity. This would greatly improve our "image" and relations throughout Latin America. It was emphasized that under the treaties, the United States still had the right to take action to defend the Canal in a genuine emergency. Also, it was pointed out that it would be extremely difficult to defend the Canal against sabotage if it remained an American property.

2. *Mexico.* The relations of the United States with Mexico have been greatly affected by our urgent need to gain increased access to Mexico's vast, newly discovered deposits of oil and natural gas.

When President Carter visited Mexico in 1979, President Jose Lopez Portillo of Mexico emphasized that if the United States wished to share in Mexico's oil and gas wealth, it would have to deal with Mexico as a full equal. He called for an end to decades of "neglect, arrogance, and misunderstanding" in United States relations with Mexico. Although American spokesmen did not necessarily agree that these criticisms were fully justified, it was clear that a new era in Mexican-United States affairs had begun.

The two nations also agreed to cooperate more closely on the control of migrant workers. Some migrant farm laborers move from Mexico to the United States under legal arrangements sanctioned by the two governments. But for many years, there has also been an illegal movement of masses of poor, jobless Mexicans across the border into the United States. Mexico has been struggling with an extremely high unemployment rate, in some cases as high as 40%. Thus, there has been little incentive for the Mexican government to try to control the illegal immigration of "wetbacks" (so called because they enter the United States by wading across shallow parts of the Rio Grande).

Efforts by the United States to stop the flow of migrants and to return persons illegally resident in the United States to Mexico have sometimes been denounced by Mexican representatives as inhumane and arrogant. The only real solution to this problem is economic development and better job opportunities in Mexico. Meanwhile, there is hope that the two governments, working cooperatively can help to bring the situation under better control.

3. *Nicaragua.* Growing instability in Central America and South America has created additional headaches for the United States. In Nicaragua, Honduras, Guatemala, El Salvador, and other countries, there has been a pattern of political unrest, guerrilla violence, terrorism and in some cases open warfare. The background of this situation is the grinding poverty of most people and a demand for land reform, higher wages, and other social and economic reforms.

The worst upheaval in recent years has been in Nicaragua. For many years, the United States has maintained friendly relations with the repressive Nicaraguan regime headed by members of the Somoza family. The relationship changed when the Carter administration criticized the government headed by President Anastasio Somoza for its violations of human rights. This led to a cutback in military aid to Nicaragua.

The Somoza regime faced a formidable rebellion by forces known as the *Sandinistas.* This uprising had the support of a wide spectrum of the Nicaraguan people, including workers and peasants, many professional and business people, and Catholic priests and laymen. These various groups disagreed on many issues, but they shared a common purpose of overthrowing the Somoza dictatorship.

The United States at first tried to maintain a position of strict non-intervention in the conflict. In June 1979, however, at the urging of U.S. Secretary of State Cyrus Vance, the Organization of American States passed a resolution calling for the resignation of Somoza. This was to be followed by the organization of a new government that would have the support of the people and would be able to restore representative government. Faced with this internal and external opposition to his regime, Somoza resigned and left for exile in the United States (July, 1979).

INDEX

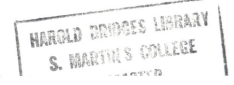
This book is due for return on or before the last date shown below.

79

Don Gresswell Ltd., London, N21   Cat. No. 1208   DG 02242/71

1855212455